THIRD EDITION

DIVERSITY& INCLUSION

IN SPORT ORGANIZATIONS

George B. Cunningham

TEXAS A&M UNIVERSITY

Consulting Editor, Sport Management Series

Packianathan Chelladurai

Holcomb Hathaway, Publishers

Scottsdale, Arizona

Library of Congress Control Number: 2015940813

Photo Credits:
Cover, clockwise from top: Patrick Chai/123RF, Dean Drobot/123RF, Supannee Hickman/123RF, Igor Mojzes/123RF, rido/123RF, Hongqi Zhang/123RF, Antonio Diaz/123RF. *Spine:* natursports/123RF. *Back cover, top to bottom:* Songquan Deng/123RF, Cathy Yeulet/123RF. *Page i,* Supannee Hickman/123RF; *page vi,* Pavle Marjanovic/123RF, Wavebreak Media Ltd/123RF; *page vii,* Visions of America LLC/123RF, Wavebreak Media Ltd/123RF; *page xix,* liorpt/123RF, Wavebreak Media Ltd/123RF; *page xxi,* zimmytws/123RF, szefei/123RF; *page xxiii,* Andres Rodriguez/123RF, Alessandro Guerriero/123RF; *page 2,* Stephen Coburn/123RF, tammykayphoto/123RF, Cathy Yeulet/123RF; *page 28,* Carlos Caetano/123RF, Cathy Yeulet/123RF, Ruth Peterkin/123RF; *page 48,* Mike Flippo/123RF, Pavel Shchegolev/123RF, Cathy Yeulet/123RF; *page 66,* Alex Grichenko/123RF, Tyler Olson/123RF, Herbert Kratky/123RF; *page 96,* smith- esmith/123RF, Alexander Mitrofanov/123RF, Dmitriy Shironosov/123RF; *page 126,* Chiya Li/123RF, kzenon/123RF, marcovarro/123RF; *page 148,* Corbis, Anna Martynova/123RF, Sam D'Cruz/123RF; *page 168,* Syda Productions/123RF, Andriy Popov/123RF, Cathy Yeulet/123RF; *page 192,* Mike Flippo/123RF, Herbert Kratky/123RF, Leung Cho Pan/123RF; *page 212,* gemenacom/123RF, Igor Mojzes/ 123RF, Chris Van Lennep/123RF; *page 240,* alandi/123RF, Cathy Yeulet/123RF, Mark Herreid/123RF; *page 268,* Joyce Vincent/Dreams- time, Jamie Roach/123RF, Cathy Yeulet/123RF; *page 286,* Visions of America LLC/123RF, Walt Adams/123RF, Dmitriy Shironosov/123RF; *page 310,* Visions of America LLC/123RF, Cyntia Estrada/123RF, Cathy Yeulet/123RF; *page 334,* Sura Nualpradid/123RF, Susan Leggett/ 123RF, mjanic/123RF; *page 355,* nedjenn/123RF, Wavebreak Media Ltd/ 123RF; *page 361,* Danny Hooks/123RF, Wavebreak Media Ltd/123RF.

Consulting Editor, Sport Management Series
Packianathan Chelladurai

Please note: The author and publisher have made every effort to provide current website addresses in this book. However, because web addresses change constantly, it is inevitable that some of the URLs listed here will change following publication of this book.

Holcomb Hathaway, Publishers, Inc.
8700 E. Via de Ventura Blvd., Suite 265
Scottsdale, Arizona 85258
480-991-7881
www.hh-pub.com

10 9 8 7 6 5 4 3 2 1

Print ISBN: 978-1-62159-040-8
Ebook ISBN: 978-1-62159-041-5

Printed in the United States of America.

dedication

For Melissa, Harper, and Maggie

BRIEF CONTENTS

Preface   *xix*

Acknowledgments   *xxi*

About the Author   *xxiii*

PART I   FOUNDATIONS OF DIVERSITY AND INCLUSION   1

1   Overview of Diversity and Inclusion   3

2   Theoretical Tenets of Diversity and Inclusion   29

3   Stereotypes, Prejudice, and Discrimination   49

PART II   FORMS OF DIVERSITY   65

4   Race   67

5   Sex and Gender   97

6   Age   127

7   Mental and Physical Ability   149

8   Appearance   169

9   Religious Beliefs   193

10   Sexual Orientation, Gender Identity, and Gender Expression   213

11   Social Class   241

PART III   CREATING AND SUSTAINING
INCLUSIVE SPORT ORGANIZATIONS   267

12 **Organizational Inclusiveness**   269

13 **Interpersonal Inclusiveness**   287

14 **Diversity Training**   311

15 **Change and Inclusion Through Sport**   335

Author Index   355
Subject Index   361

CONTENTS

Preface   xix

Acknowledgments   xxi

About the Author   xxiii

PART I   FOUNDATIONS OF DIVERSITY AND INCLUSION   1

1 Overview of Diversity and Inclusion   3

Learning Objectives   3

Diversity Challenge   3

DEFINITIONS   5

Diversity   5

Inclusion   6

DIVERSITY IN THE FIELD: *The United Nations' Efforts on Social Inclusion and Diversity   8*

FORMS OF DIVERSITY   8

ALTERNATIVE PERSPECTIVES: *Listing the Various Diversity Dimensions   9*

Surface-Level Diversity   10

Deep-Level Diversity   10

Relationship Between Surface- and Deep-Level Diversity   11

UNDERSTANDING THE EMPHASIS ON DIVERSITY AND INCLUSION   11

Changing Demographics   12

Changing Attitudes Toward Work   17

Changes in the Nature of Work   17

Legal Mandates   20

Social Pressures   20

Negative Effects of Exclusion   21

Benefits of Diversity and Inclusion   21

PROFESSIONAL PERSPECTIVES: The Importance of Diversity and Inclusion   22

PUTTING IT ALL TOGETHER   22

Chapter Summary   23

Questions for Discussion   24

Learning Activities   24

Web Resources   24

Reading Resources   25

REFERENCES   25

Theoretical Tenets of Diversity and Inclusion   29

Learning Objectives   29

Diversity Challenge   29

DEFINING THEORY   30

PROFESSIONAL PERSPECTIVES: The Importance of Theory   32

THEORIES USED TO UNDERSTAND DIVERSITY   32

Managerial Theories   32

Sociological Theories   35

ALTERNATIVE PERSPECTIVES: *Intersectionality   39*

Social Psychological Theories   39

ALTERNATIVE PERSPECTIVES: *Ways of Studying Diversity   42*

DIVERSITY IN THE FIELD: *Stigma of Being Lesbian, Gay, Bisexual, or Transgender   43*

Chapter Summary   44

Questions for Discussion   44

Learning Activities   45

Web Resources   45

Reading Resources   45

REFERENCES   46

Stereotypes, Prejudice, and Discrimination   49

Learning Objectives   49

Diversity Challenge   49

STEREOTYPES   51

ALTERNATIVE PERSPECTIVES: *Race, Gender, and Stereotypes   53*

PREJUDICE   53

Directionality of Prejudicial Attitudes   53

DIVERSITY IN THE FIELD: *Prejudice as Negative Attitudes Toward Others   54*

Explicit and Implicit Prejudice 54

DISCRIMINATION 56

Access Discrimination 57

Treatment Discrimination 57

OUTCOMES OF BIAS 58

Physiological Effects 58

Psychological Effects 58

ALTERNATIVE PERSPECTIVES: *Prejudice against LGBT Individuals and All-Cause Mortality* 59

Vocational and Sport Participation Outcomes 60

PROFESSIONAL PERSPECTIVES: Discrimination in the Hiring Process 60

Chapter Summary 61

Questions for Discussion 62

Learning Activities 62

Web Resources 62

Reading Resources 62

REFERENCES 63

PART II FORMS OF DIVERSITY 65

Race 67

Learning Objectives 67

Diversity Challenge 67

KEY TERMS 69

RACE IN THE WORK ENVIRONMENT 69

DIVERSITY IN THE FIELD: *Multirace Population in the United States Grows* 70

BOX: *The law, employment, and race* 71

Salary 71

Leadership Positions 72

Occupational Segregation 75

POSSIBLE EXPLANATIONS FOR LEADERSHIP UNDERREPRESENTATION OF RACIAL MINORITIES 76

Macro-Level Factors 77

Meso-Level Factors 80

DIVERSITY IN THE FIELD: *Glass Cliffs and Coaching* 83

Micro-Level Factors 84

RACE AND PARTICIPATION IN PHYSICAL ACTIVITY AND SPORT 86

Physical Activity Participation 86

Sport Participation 87

DIVERSITY IN THE FIELD: *Stacking and Tasking*   *88*

Chapter Summary   90

Questions for Discussion   90

Learning Activities   91

Web Resources   91

Reading Resources   91

REFERENCES   92

Sex and Gender   97

Learning Objectives   97

Diversity Challenge   97

SEX AND GENDER   98

PROFESSIONAL PERSPECTIVES: Using Sexist Language   99

Performing Gender   100

ALTERNATIVE PERSPECTIVES: *Sport Performance Along a Continuum   103*

GENDER IN THE WORK ENVIRONMENT   103

Participation in the Workforce   103

BOX: *Laws affecting women and men in the work environment   104*

Earnings   105

Leadership Roles   106

BOX: *Title IX   107*

POSSIBLE EXPLANATIONS FOR LEADERSHIP UNDERREPRESENTATION OF WOMEN   109

Macro-Level Factors   109

DIVERSITY IN THE FIELD: *Elite Athletes as Mothers   111*

Meso-Level Factors   112

ALTERNATIVE PERSPECTIVES: *Men Breaking Gender Roles   113*

Micro-Level Factors   115

GENDER AND PARTICIPATION IN PHYSICAL ACTIVITY AND SPORT   116

Physical Activity Participation   116

Sport Participation   116

BOX: *Subtle forms of mistreatment of athletes   120*

Chapter Summary   121

Questions for Discussion   121

Learning Activities   122

Web Resources   122

Reading Resources   122

REFERENCES   123

Age   127

Learning Objectives   *127*

Diversity Challenge   *127*

BACKGROUND AND KEY TERMS   **129**

   BOX: *Age and employment laws*   *130*

   DIVERSITY IN THE FIELD: *Bridge Employment in College Athletics*   *131*

AGE BIAS AND THE WORKPLACE   **131**

   Age Sterotypes   131

   Age and Prejudice   134

   Age Discrimination   135

   DIVERSITY IN THE FIELD: *Young Coaches in the NCAA*   *136*

   PROFESSIONAL PERSPECTIVES: Training Employees Over Age 50   137

   ALTERNATIVE PERSPECTIVES: *Caring for the Elderly*   *138*

      Additional Considerations   138

   BOX: *Relative age effects and sport performance*   *139*

AGE AND PARTICIPATION IN SPORT, PHYSICAL ACTIVITY, AND LEISURE   **140**

   DIVERSITY IN THE FIELD: *Influence of Age on Sport Consumption*   *143*

Chapter Summary   *143*

Questions for Discussion   *144*

Learning Activities   *144*

Web Resources   *145*

Reading Resources   *145*

REFERENCES   **145**

Mental and Physical Ability   149

Learning Objectives   *149*

Diversity Challenge   *149*

DEFINITION, INCIDENCE, AND BACKGROUND   **150**

   BOX: *Legal mandates related to disability*   *151*

   DIVERSITY IN THE FIELD: *Trying to Get Around ADA Guidelines*   *151*

BIAS AGAINST PERSONS WITH DISABILITIES   **153**

   Stereotypes   154

   Prejudice   154

   BOX: *Language and disability*   *155*

   Discrimination   156

   ALTERNATIVE PERSPECTIVES: *Requests for Accommodations Are Made by All Employees*   *159*

BOX: *Developing human resource systems to counter discrimination*   160

ABILITY AND PHYSICAL ACTIVITY AND SPORT PARTICIPATION   160

Physical Activity Participation   160

Disability Sport   161

PROFESSIONAL PERSPECTIVES: Trends and Issues in Disability Sport   162

Chapter Summary   164

Questions for Discussion   165

Learning Activities   165

Web Resources   165

Reading Resources   165

REFERENCES   166

8 Appearance   169

Learning Objectives   169

Diversity Challenge   169

WEIGHT   170

Background   171

ALTERNATIVE PERSPECTIVES: *Is the BMI the Best Measure of Body Fat?   171*

Incidence of Obesity   172

Anti-Fat Bias in the Workplace   172

BOX: *Lack of legal protections for persons considered overweight or obese   173*

BOX: *Weight-based prejudice, race, and culture   174*

DIVERSITY IN THE FIELD: *Weighing the Coaching Options   176*

DIVERSITY IN THE FIELD: *Anti-Fat Attitudes Toward Customers   176*

Weight and Physical Activity Participation   177

ALTERNATIVE PERSPECTIVES: *Negative Effects of Viewing Thin Models   179*

HEIGHT   179

Key Terms   179

Effects of Height in the Workplace   179

ATTRACTIVENESS   182

Background Information   182

BOX: *What makes faces beautiful?   183*

Attractiveness in the Workplace   183

BOX: *Perceived attractiveness and support for inequality   184*

Attractiveness and Sport Participation   184

DIVERSITY IN THE FIELD: *Women's Head Scarves and Sport Participation   185*

Chapter Summary   186

Questions for Discussion   187

Learning Activities   187

Web Resources   187

Reading Resources   188

REFERENCES   188

Religious Beliefs   193

Learning Objectives   193

Diversity Challenge   193

BACKGROUND AND KEY TERMS   194

    The Emphasis on Religion   195

RELIGION IN THE WORKPLACE   197

    BOX: *Legal mandates related to religion in the workplace   198*

    Strategic Decisions   198

    Ethical Behavior   199

    BOX: *Religious influence on teaching ethics   201*

    Leadership   201

    Stress   202

    Religion as a Basis for Categorization   202

    BOX: *Religious fundamentalism and bias   203*

    DIVERSITY IN THE FIELD: *Religion and Soccer   204*

RELIGION AND SPORT PARTICIPATION   205

    Influence on Sport Participation   205

    ALTERNATIVE PERSPECTIVES: *Some Sports Are Tolerated   205*

    DIVERSITY IN THE FIELD: *Church-Organized Sport Leagues   206*

    ALTERNATIVE PERSPECTIVES: *Sport as Religion   206*

    Athletes' Use of Religion   207

Chapter Summary   208

Questions for Discussion   208

Learning Activities   209

Web Resources   209

Reading Resources   209

REFERENCES   210

Sexual Orientation, Gender Identity, and Gender Expression   213

Learning Objectives   213

Diversity Challenge   213

BACKGROUND   214

Key Terms   215

ALTERNATIVE PERSPECTIVES: *Determining Sexual Orientation Through Implicit Tests*   *216*

Demographics   217

Historical Context   219

SEXUAL PREJUDICE AND GENDER PREJUDICE   220

Background and Key Terms   220

DIVERSITY IN THE FIELD: *Sexual Prejudice Toward Coaches*   *221*

Gender and Sexual Stigma   221

BOX: *Employment protections for LGBT individuals*   *223*

ALTERNATIVE PERSPECTIVES: *Prejudice Is Bad for Your Health*   *225*

SEXUAL ORIENTATION, GENDER IDENTITY, AND WORK   225

Work Experiences   225

Sexual Orientation Disclosure   229

ALTERNATIVE PERSPECTIVES: *Negative Outcomes of Revealing at Work?*   *232*

LGBT Diversity as a Source of Advantage   232

SEXUAL ORIENTATION AND SPORT AND PHYSICAL ACTIVITY PARTICIPATION   233

Chapter Summary   234

Questions for Discussion   235

Learning Activities   235

Web Resources   235

Reading Resources   236

REFERENCES   236

Social Class   241

Learning Objectives   241

Diversity Challenge   241

BASIC CONCEPTS   243

Socioeconomic Status (Materialistic) Approach   243

Social Class Approach   246

ALTERNATIVE PERSPECTIVES: *Class as a Reflection of Capital*   *247*

CLASSISM   248

Cognitive Distancing   248

Interpersonal Distancing   250

Institutional Distancing   250

DIVERSITY IN THE FIELD: *Inequitable Wage Distributions in College Athletics*   *252*

DIVERSITY IN THE FIELD: *Housing and the Olympics*   *255*

ALTERNATIVE PERSPECTIVES: *Are There Benefits to Displacement?*   *255*

BOX: *Health outcomes of classism* 256

PROFESSIONAL PERSPECTIVES: Alternate Conceptions of Social Class   258

SPORT AND SOCIAL MOBILITY   260

Chapter Summary 261

Questions for Discussion 262

Learning Activities 262

Web Resources 263

Reading Resources 263

REFERENCES 263

PART III   CREATING AND SUSTAINING INCLUSIVE SPORT ORGANIZATIONS   267

12 **Organizational Inclusiveness** 269

Learning Objectives 269

Diversity Challenge 269

EFFECTIVENESS OF DIVERSITY AND INCLUSION PROGRAMS   271

Pressures for Greater Inclusion   271

Engaging in the Change Process   273

MULTILEVEL MODEL OF DIVERSITY AND INCLUSION   273

BOX: *Diversity management models* 274

Individual Level   276

PROFESSIONAL PERSPECTIVES: Importance of Difficult Dialogues in the Workplace   277

Leader Level   277

Organizational Level   277

Macro Level   279

ALTERNATIVE PERSPECTIVES: *Inclusion Despite the Community* 279

ALLIES AND COMMITMENT TO DIVERSITY   280

Allies   280

DIVERSITY IN THE FIELD: *Athlete Ally* 280

Commitment   281

Chapter Summary 282

Questions for Discussion 282

Learning Activities 283

Web Resources 283

Reading Resources 283

REFERENCES 284

13 Interpersonal Inclusiveness 287

Learning Objectives 287

Diversity Challenge 287

THE CONTACT HYPOTHESIS 288

   Conditions of Contact 288

   Intergroup Anxiety 291

   Influence of Status 292

   Contact Hypothesis Limitations 292

   BOX: *Generalizing the effects of contact* 293

   Indirect Contact 293

   DIVERSITY IN THE FIELD: *Quidditch, Bias, and Inclusion* 294

SOCIAL CATEGORIZATION STRATEGIES FOR REDUCING BIAS 295

   Decategorization 296

   ALTERNATIVE PERSPECTIVES: *Cross-Categorization Strategies for Managing Diverse Groups* 297

   Recategorization 299

   PROFESSIONAL PERSPECTIVES: Recategorization on a Soccer Team 300

   Intergroup Contact 302

   Integrated Model 303

Chapter Summary 305

Questions for Discussion 306

Learning Activities 307

Web Resources 307

Reading Resources 307

REFERENCES 307

14 Diversity Training 311

Learning Objectives 311

Diversity Challenge 311

PREVALENCE OF DIVERSITY TRAINING 312

EFFECTS OF DIVERSITY TRAINING 314

   Positive Effects 314

   Negative Effects 315

   Making Sense of the Effects 315

DESIGNING AND DELIVERING EFFECTIVE DIVERSITY TRAINING PROGRAMS 316

   Needs Analysis 317

   DIVERSITY IN THE FIELD: *How a Needs Analysis Shows the Need for Diversity Training* 318

Pre-Training Conditions   319

Training Methods   321

Post-Training Conditions   323

ALTERNATIVE PERSPECTIVES: *Evaluating Diversity Training Effectiveness*   *326*

GENERAL PRINCIPLES   327

PROFESSIONAL PERSPECTIVES: Diversity Behind the Face   328

Chapter Summary   329

Questions for Discussion   330

Learning Activities   330

Web Resources   331

Reading Resources   331

REFERENCES   331

Change and Inclusion Through Sport   335

Learning Objectives   335

Diversity Challenge   335

PROFESSIONAL PERSPECTIVES: The Importance of Sport-for-Development and Peace Programs   338

SPORT AND SOCIAL CHANGE   338

Key Terms   338

Historical Context   340

SDP OUTCOMES   341

Benefits of SDP   341

ALTERNATIVE PERSPECTIVES: *Effects of SDP Programs on Volunteers and Spectators*   *343*

Shortcomings of SDP   345

EFFECTIVE DELIVERY OF SDP PROGRAMS   347

Needs Assessment   348

DIVERSITY IN THE FIELD: *Evidence-Based Programming*   *349*

Inclusive Spaces   350

Sport, Educational, and Enrichment Components   350

Chapter Summary   351

Questions for Discussion   352

Learning Activities   352

Web Resources   352

Reading Resources   352

REFERENCES   353

Author Index   355
Subject Index   361

PREFACE

Diversity and inclusion are, and will continue to be, among the most important issues managers encounter, and this is particularly true in the sport industry. The United States and most other countries are growing more diverse, in terms of both demographics and attitudes, and today's sport organizations reflect this diversity. Organizational strategies to promote, create, and sustain inclusiveness can influence employees' attitudes, group processes, and the organization's overall effectiveness. Following diversity-related legal requirements, or failing to do so, can also have meaningful implications for an organization. Consequently, it is of paramount importance that managers understand the effects of diversity and inclusion and the strategies to manage differences effectively. The purpose of the third edition of *Diversity and Inclusion in Sport Organizations* is to provide students with such an understanding.

As the book's new title suggests, the third edition now includes the important concept of inclusion, which is discussed parallel to diversity. I present evidence to support the notion that both must be present for people, groups, and organizations to thrive.

I have divided the book into three parts. Part I provides an overview of diversity and inclusion. Chapter 1 defines diversity and inclusion and then analyzes why diversity warrants attention by students and managers. The focus of Chapter 2 is on the theoretical tenets of diversity and inclusion, with a focus on the three primary theoretical approaches—managerial, sociological, and social psychological—as well as the practical implications associated with each. Chapter 3 addresses stereotypes, prejudice, and discrimination, the theoretical tenets undergirding those constructs, and their associated outcomes.

Part II is devoted to the various forms of diversity and inclusion. Specifically, I focus on race (Chapter 4), sex and gender (Chapter 5), age (Chapter 6), mental and physical ability (Chapter 7), appearance (Chapter 8), religious beliefs (Chapter 9), sexual orientation, gender identity, and gender expression (Chapter 10), and social class (Chapter 11). New to this edition, in each chapter I include a brief discussion of legal issues associated with the topic, thereby allowing the reader to consider the laws that influence employment decisions and sport and physical activity opportunities while studying the particular diversity dimension.

Part III focuses on creating and sustaining inclusive sport organizations. In Chapters 12 and 13, I highlight several strategies that can be used to effectively manage diverse work environments and promote inclusion. The emphasis in the former chapter is on organization-wide strategies, while the focus in the latter is on smaller groups. Chapter 14 is devoted to diversity training. Here, I underscore the importance of this training and provide the steps to design, implement, and evaluate effective diversity training programs. Finally, this edition discusses change and inclusion through sport (Chapter 15). In this new chapter, I offer an overview of sport for development and peace programs, potential outcomes, and guiding principles for those who are using sport to promote social change.

The book is intended for upper-level undergraduate and graduate students. Teachers, coaches, managers, marketers, and administrators also will benefit from the text's information. Because the sport industry is composed of many segments, examples are drawn from a bevy of sources—professional sports, university athletics, fitness organizations, physical education, recreation and leisure settings, and nonprofit entities such as the Y.

The Book's Special Features

- **Diversity Challenge.** Each chapter opens with a Diversity Challenge, a real-life scenario introducing the chapter's topic. It is followed by a series of questions to prompt readers to think about the issues raised.

- **Diversity in the Field.** These sidebars present real-life examples to help readers comprehend chapter concepts.

- **Professional Perspectives.** These recurring boxes reflect interviews of leading professionals with responsibilities in sport (e.g., a sport industry employment recruiter, professors, an athletic director, a high school coach) and provide students with practical, informed opinions on the chapter content.

- **Alternative Perspectives.** Because many topics and issues stimulate a wide range of opinions, I have included Alternative Perspectives boxes to provide readers with additional sides of a discussion.

- **Questions for Discussion, Learning Activities, Reading Resources, and Web Resources.** Each chapter concludes with discussion questions, student activities, and sources of additional information. Many of the Learning Activities are designed for students to explore in small groups. The annotated Web Resources augment chapter material by providing links to online resources such as professional associations, electronic methods of testing prejudicial attitudes, resources for diversity training, and others. Finally, the annotated Reading Resources recommend additional informative books related to the chapter's discussions.

- **Ancillaries.** An Instructor's Manual, a PowerPoint presentation, and a test-bank are available for instructors who adopt this text for course use.

I am excited about diversity and inclusion and what they mean for sport, sport organizations, and people associated with the sport industry. I hope I have reflected my enthusiasm in the text and that it will be passed on to instructors and readers. I welcome your comments and look forward to any and all feedback. Please contact me in care of Holcomb Hathaway, Publishers, at feedback@hh-pub.com.

ACKNOWLEDGMENTS

I would like to thank the wonderful colleagues and students with whom I have worked. In particular, I enjoyed my collaborative efforts with Dr. Michael Sagas, Dr. Janet Fink, and Dr. John Singer. A large debt of gratitude is owed to all of my students, past and present, especially Melanie L. Sartore-Baldwin, Jacqueline McDowell, Claudia Benavides-Espinoza, Woojun Lee, and E. Nicole Melton. They were a joy to work with, and they also reviewed the book and provided helpful and constructive feedback along the way. I am grateful to my doctoral advisor, Packianathan Chelladurai, for his guidance in my professional preparation and for encouraging me to write this book.

I also offer my sincere thanks to the reviewers of this and past editions, at various stages of completion: Thomas J. Aicher, University of Cincinnati; Roxanne Allen, McNeese State University; Debra Blair, Temple University; Elaine Blinde, Southern Illinois University Carbondale; Glenna Bower, University of Southern Indiana; Willie Burden, Georgia Southern University; Eddie Comeaux, University of California, Riverside; Alison Doherty, The University of Western Ontario; Courtney Flowers, University of West Georgia; JoAnne Graf, Florida State University; Christy Greenleaf, University of North Texas; C. Keith Harrison, University of Central Florida; Louis Harrison, University of Texas at Austin; Lori Head, Idaho State University; Nancy Lough, University of Nevada, Las Vegas; Fritz Polite, University of Tennessee; Brenda A. Riemer, Eastern Michigan University; Cecile Reynaud, Florida State University; Karen Rickel, Gonzaga University; Claudia Santin, Concordia University Chicago; Melanie Sartore-Baldwin, East Carolina University; Brian Sather, Eastern Oregon University; Jennifer Spry-Knutson, Des Moines Area Community College; Ellen Staurowsky, Drexel University; and Eli Wolff, Brown University. Their input during the writing process was very helpful.

I also thank Colette Kelly, Gay Pauley, and others at Holcomb Hathaway, Publishers. I enjoyed working with them and will forever be indebted to them for the opportunity they have provided.

Finally, I am also thankful for my family: my wife, Melissa, and our two girls Harper and Maggie. They are my everything.

ABOUT THE AUTHOR

George B. Cunningham (Ph.D., The Ohio State University) is a Professor and Associate Dean for Academic Affairs and Research in the College of Education and Human Development at Texas A&M University. He is the Marilyn Kent Byrne Chair for Student Success and also serves as the Director for the Laboratory for Diversity in Sport, which is dedicated to producing and disseminating research related to all forms of diversity in the sport context. Author of more than 180 articles and book chapters, Cunningham focuses his research in the areas of diversity, group processes, and employee attitudes. Within the diversity domain, he investigates the underrepresentation of various groups in leadership positions, the impact of dissimilarity on subsequent outcomes and behaviors, and strategies for capitalizing on the benefits of diversity and inclusion. His research has been published in various journals, including those in the sport domain (e.g., *Journal of Sport Management, Sport Management Review,* and *Sociology of Sport Journal*), the area of social psychology (e.g., *The Journal of Social Psychology, Journal of Applied Social Psychology, Sex Roles,* and *Group Dynamics*), and in various management journals (e.g., *Organizational Analysis, Journal of Business and Psychology*), among others. Cunningham is a Research Fellow of the North American Society for Sport Management and also served as President of that organization.

Cunningham and his wife, Melissa, have two daughters, Harper and Maggie. His free time is spent with his family, cycling, or coaching soccer.

PART

FOUNDATIONS OF DIVERSITY AND INCLUSION

chapter 1
Overview of Diversity and Inclusion 3

chapter 2
Theoretical Tenets of Diversity and Inclusion 29

chapter 3
Stereotypes, Prejudice, and Discrimination 49

Overview of Diversity and Inclusion

LEARNING objectives

After studying this chapter, you should be able to:

- Define the concepts of diversity and inclusion.
- List and explain the various forms of diversity.
- Discuss the various factors that have contributed to increased interest in diversity and inclusion.

DIVERSITY CHALLENGE

Sport offers the potential to impact people's lives in many positive ways. According to Sport England, physically active people are less likely to be ill, are at a reduced risk of heart disease and various cancers, and have lower healthcare costs than their less active counterparts. School-aged children who participate in sport are absent less frequently, have enhanced self-esteem, and are less likely to engage in criminal behaviors than are their peers. Sport managers have long heralded these benefits of sport, and their effects are seen around the world.

Unfortunately, opportunities to participate in sport are frequently reserved for people in positions of privilege. Research suggests that only 3 in 10 children regularly participate in sport. The numbers drop precipitously among low-income children, racial minorities, and children in rural communities, as well as for many girls. As one example, people with household incomes of $100,000 or greater are much more likely than others to participate in sport, and the proportion of these individuals (33 percent) outpaces their representation in the general U.S. population (20 percent). The built environment contributes to this trend, as the number of parks and public facilities supporting recreation is limited, particularly in low income areas; thus, opportunities for free play are constrained.

This is what makes the Aspen Institute's Project Play initiative so important. Project Play is designed to reverse this trend and engage more children in sport. Its efforts are multipronged, with a focus on:

- *People:* training coaches and administrators to lead youth sport teams and programs effectively;
- *Places:* ensuring the built environment is designed to encourage children to engage in formal and informal forms of play; and
- *Programs:* recognizing diversity in age, gender, culture, skill, and income to build and design effective programs.

Project Play brought together leaders from various domains, including sport, medicine, media, business, government, and philanthropy, to tackle the issues. The organization recognized that a multidisciplinary approach that drew on the expertise of leaders from various fields was needed to address a problem so large and complex. As a result of these efforts, the initiative has spurred action from a number of sport partners. For example, the U.S. Olympic Committee (USOC) developed a guide for athlete development and sport research, and that entity also developed a vision statement for youth sport development. Diversity and inclusion are central elements in both of these efforts.

Sources: www.sportengland.org; www.aspenprojectplay.org / Sagas, M., & Cunningham, G. B. (2014). *Sport participation rates among underserved American youth.* Gainesville, FL: University of Florida Sport Policy & Research Collaborative.

CHALLENGE REFLECTION

Suppose the Project Play organizers asked you to contribute to the initiative. How would you respond to the following questions?

1. What are the major issues facing youth sport and youth sport development today?

2. Beyond what was briefly presented here, how do people's characteristics, such as age, race, income, physical and mental ability, and gender, affect their opportunities to be physically active?

3. What are steps you would take to make sport inclusive for all people, irrespective of their individual differences?

Diversity and inclusion are vital topics in sport and physical activity today. As the opening scenario illustrates, differences do make a difference. People's demographics, attitudes, beliefs, and psychological characteristics influence the access they have to physical activity services and various opportunities, as well as how they are treated when participating in sport or working in sport organizations. Substantial evidence also indicates that differences among teammates or work group members are associated with a number of desired outcomes, such as creativity and productivity. A confluence of trends and events—including changing national and workplace demographics, shifts in societal expectations, and various diversity-related laws, among others—has brought these points to the forefront for sport managers. The effective management of sport organizations means marketing and reaching out to consumers from a variety of backgrounds, it means ensuring that workplace cultures and systems are designed to create and maintain inclusive places where all people can thrive, and it means knowing the various regulatory issues pertaining to diversity and inclusion in organizational environments. Because diversity and inclusion are now central issues for sport managers, coaches, and other physical activity professionals, it is crucial they understand the effects of diversity and inclusion in the workplace, as well as the underlying reasons for these dynamics. This understanding will allow for effective teams and workplaces, inclusive of all persons.

This chapter provides an overview of diversity and inclusion. In the first section, I draw from various authors' work to develop definitions of key terms. This is followed by a discussion of the various forms of diversity and how people differ. The third section includes identification and analysis of the seven factors contributing to the current interest in and importance of diversity and inclusion. Finally, I offer an overview of the remainder of the text.

DEFINITIONS

This section includes several definitions of diversity and inclusion.

Diversity

To begin developing a working definition of diversity, consider the following definitions used by others in this field:

> Diversity represents "a characteristic of social grouping that reflects the degree to which objective or subjective differences exist between group members." (van Knippenberg & Schippers, 2007, p. 516)

> Diversity is reflected by "heterogeneity and the demographic composition of groups or organizations." (Roberson, 2006, p. 228)

> "Workforce diversity refers to the composition of work units in terms of the cultural or demographic characteristics that are salient and symbolically meaningful in the relationships among group members." (DiTomaso, Post, & Parks-Yancy, 2007, p. 473)

> Diversity describes "the distribution of differences among the members of a unit with respect to a common attribute." (Harrison & Klein, 2007, p. 1200)

> Diversity "refers to the variations of traits, both visible and not, of groups of two or more people." (Lambert & Bell, 2013, p. 13)

We can draw several points from these definitions. First, diversity is concerned with groups and dyads, the latter of which refers to two people working together, such as a supervisor and her subordinate. People must be able to compare their attributes to the characteristics of others. Without a comparison point, people do not know if they are similar to or different from others within a particular context. Consequently, we can say that diversity is principally a dyadic or group-related topic.

Second, diversity is concerned with differences among people. How, for example, do marketers working together on a project differ from one another on various attributes? The focus on differences means that diversity is concerned with variations among group members. Let's further consider the group of marketers to illustrate this point. Suppose the group comprises eight women working for a professional baseball team. Given that women are underrepresented in professional sports, such an occurrence would certainly be unusual, but as the group comprises all women, it would not be diverse along the lines of gender. On the other hand, the group would be maximally diverse on gender lines if it included four women and four men.

Third, diversity is concerned with both objective and subjective ways in which people differ. By objective differences, we are referring to readily observable or quantifiable differences. These might include demographic characteristics, such as age, or psychological differences, such as political preference. In either of these categories, we can objectively note group heterogeneity. Subjective differences, on the other hand, depend on people's perceptions of being different. In many ways, subjective evaluations are just as influential as objective ones in their impact on group processes and outcomes. In studies of physical activity participants (Cunningham, 2006) and coaches (Cunningham, 2007), I have observed that perceptions of being different from others are better indicators of subsequent outcomes, such as satisfaction or turnover intentions, than are objective measures of diversity. The two are related, of course, as people are most likely to believe they are different from others when they actually are. There are also other factors that could potentially influence the relationship between objective and subjective assessments of diversity, such as how important that diversity dimension is to the evaluator, organizational support for diversity, and the manner in which the diversity dimension affects group processes, among others.

Finally, diversity is concerned with differences that are socially meaningful. Konrad (2003) noted that "focusing on any individual difference, rather than differences having strong meaning and stemming from or coinciding with significant power differences among groups, would make all groups diverse, and would therefore make the entire concept of workplace diversity meaningless" (p. 7). Some characteristics are socially relevant because of historical, cultural, or systemic phenomena that have served to privilege some people over others. When people vary along these domains, the differences mean something to those individuals and can influence how they interact with one another. On the other hand, other forms of difference do not have social meaning attached to them and as a result have no bearing on people's experiences or opportunities. To illustrate this point, let us consider an under-10 (U10) girls soccer team that I coach. Of the 12 players on the team, 3 kicked naturally with their left foot, while 9 kicked naturally with their right. At more advanced levels of competition, these differences might mean something, but these players, who are largely novices to the game, did not notice these variations. (In fact, we were in good shape if the players kicked the ball at all.) Other differences, though, could have (and perhaps did) influence the interactions among the players. The team was racially diverse, with five Latinas, five Whites, one African American, and one Asian American. It was also marked by language diversity, as two of the girls came from homes in which Spanish was the primary language spoken (as an aside, this allowed us to sing "Happy Birthday" to the players in both Spanish and English). Finally, the team was also diverse based on social class, with some girls coming from families that were affluent and others coming from families that were poor. These differences—those based on race, language, and social class—are meaningful to people and are associated with how people interact with one another, the opportunities they have in life, and the incidences of discrimination they might experience.

Drawing from this discussion, we can define diversity as *the presence of socially meaningful differences among members of a dyad or group*. This definition highlights several important elements: (a) the presence of objective and subjective differences, (b) that are socially relevant, (c) for members of a particular social unit.

Inclusion

In addition to defining diversity, defining *inclusion* is also important. Though the two terms are frequently used in tandem (e.g., by the United Nations; see the Diversity in the Field box on p. 8), they are operationally and theoretically distinct. Consider first how other authors have defined this construct.

> Inclusion is "the degree to which an employee perceives that he or she is an esteemed member of the work group through experiencing treatment that satisfies his or her needs for belongingness and uniqueness." (Shore, et al., 2011, p. 1265)

> Inclusion "involves how well organizations and their members fully connect with, engage, and utilize people across all types of differences." (Ferdman, 2014, p. 4)

> An organization is inclusive "to the extent that its policies, practices, and leadership demonstrate that all individuals in the organization have valuable experiences, skills, and ideas to contribute and can integrate their uniqueness without pressure to assimilate in order to be accepted." (Nishii & Rich, 2014, p. 331)

> Inclusion means "being fully part of the whole while retaining a sense of authenticity and uniqueness." (Ferdman, 2010, p. 37)

These definitions bring to light several important points. First, inclusion is experienced by individuals but takes on a shared property (see also Kozlowski & Klein, 2000). Let us consider a fitness club to illustrate this point. The individual fitness club participants develop their evaluations of whether they feel included. To the degree that members of the organization collectively share the belief in feelings of inclusion, then we could say the fitness club has an inclusive exercise environment.

The next two points are intertwined and presented together. From an optimal distinctiveness standpoint (Brewer, 1991), inclusion at its core satisfies two basic human needs: (1) the need to feel valued, accepted, and part of a larger group; and (2) the need to be recognized for and able to express fully one's individuality and the personal identities that one considers important. Let's first look at the need for belongingness. The need to feel loved, connected, accepted, and part of something larger is well documented. It is the reason why universities across the nation spend so much time and energy holding orientation camps for their new-entry students; they want those students to feel an intense connection to the university. Sport marketers also recognize this, as they spend considerable time developing strategies to get consumers to identify closely with their respective sport teams. Uniqueness and individuality are also important, though. As much as people want to feel they are a part of something, they do not want to feel as though they are just some nameless cog in the machine—a dynamic Orwell (1949) recognized long ago in his provocative book *1984*. Instead, people have a desire to express and have others recognize their uniqueness and the multifaceted identities they possess.

Inclusive organizations recognize and embrace these dual, potentially countervailing tensions. In these organizations, inclusion means respecting, celebrating, and embracing the various ways in which people differ; establishing structures and processes that allow people to express their multiple identities at work; and, because differences are valued and seen as a source of learning and enrichment, engaging people such that they have a sense of belonging and connection with the workplace. Thus, from the organizational level of analysis, inclusion represents *the degree to which employees are free to express their individuated self and have a sense of workplace connectedness and belonging.*

DIVERSITY   IN THE FIELD

The United Nations' Efforts on Social Inclusion and Diversity.
As part of its Sport for Development and Peace initiative, the United Nations (UN) articulated ways in which sport can serve to promote social inclusion and diversity. This international governing body holds that, at its best, sport can enable individuals to develop values and communication skills necessary to manage conflict effectively. Sport can also be used for capacity building at the community level. The UN believes these benefits are most likely to materialize among traditionally marginalized populations, including First Nations peoples, people experiencing homelessness, girls and women, and asylum seekers, among others. The UN recommends policy makers "include sport as a tool in government strategies, to address the challenges confronting excluded populations and to prevent conflict arising from these challenges." It articulated the following programmatic steps:

1. Consider the role gender can play in access to sport and ensure that girls and women are fully included in the peace-building process.

2. Involve key stakeholders and larger populations in sport for peace activities.

3. Remain mindful of the potential vulnerabilities among underrepresented groups.

4. Guarantee that people with disabilities are included in sport for peace activities.

5. Remain cognizant of cultural and societal influences when choosing the appropriate sport activities to build peace.

6. Involve the beneficiaries of the sport for peace activities in the process.

7. Engage key partners to ensure that a positive ethical message is conveyed to impacted communities.

8. Apply the "do not harm" principle in all activities.

9. Use existing social spaces where people naturally congregate as a way of leveraging the attractiveness of the sport for peace activities.

Source: www.un.org/wcm/content/site/sport/home/unplayers/memberstates/pid/16005

My perspective is that organizations have a moral imperative to develop and maintain inclusive workplace environments. Growing evidence also suggests that inclusion is associated with desired work outcomes. Roberson (2006) interviewed diversity officers at large publicly traded organizations and found the participants not only differentiated between diversity and inclusion but also offered a business case for inclusive practices. One participant in the interviews noted that inclusion meant "recognizing, understanding, and respecting all the ways we differ, and leveraging those differences for competitive business advantage" (p. 220). Similarly, Shore and her colleagues (2011) argued that inclusive work groups were likely to have high-quality employee relations and enhanced creativity; their organizational members were likely to be committed and satisfied and to perform well on their tasks. We explore the relationships among diversity, inclusion, and organizational effectiveness later in this chapter and throughout the text.

Because people differ in so many ways, it is useful to classify the types of differences. I discuss such a typology in the following section.

FORMS OF DIVERSITY

O ften discussions related to diversity center on race, gender, and age. Reflecting this focus, some early research and theoretical paradigms adopted a demographic approach, such as organizational demography (Pfeffer, 1983) or relational

ALTERNATIVE perspectives

Listing the Various Diversity Dimensions. This chapter offers a classification scheme for parsimoniously conceptualizing the various ways in which people differ. However, sport organizations frequently develop diversity statements that include a long list of ways in which people differ. Consider the example from USA Rugby (n.d.):

> USA Rugby is proud to serve a diverse membership of players, coaches, officials and fans and is committed to creating and promoting a culture of inclusion and mutual respect, regardless of race, color, creed, national origin, religious beliefs, sex, age, gender identity, disability or sexual orientation.

As another example, the athletics department at the University of Vermont (n.d.) developed the following:

The Department of Athletics strives to create a diverse, inclusive community in which all students and staff members feel safe, respected and valued—regardless of any aspect of one's identity, including but not limited to race, ethnicity, national origin, sex, gender identity, sexual orientation, religion, socioeconomic status, ability or age.

In many respects, listing the various diversity dimensions has value, as the sport organization specifically articulates those forms of difference that are meaningful within that context. A potential problem occurs, however, when a diversity dimension is not included. For example, social class is not included in USA Rugby's statement; thus, people who are poor and might have been traditionally excluded from formal sport opportunities might not feel that USA Rugby is concerned with attracting them to the sport.

---

demography (Tsui & Gutek, 1999). As the scholarship developed, researchers began to include additional and varied forms of difference: culture, language, physical and mental ability, education, attitudes, beliefs, and so on. While some sport organizations choose to write exhaustive lists of the ways in which people differ (see the Alternative Perspectives box), another approach is to classify the various diversity dimensions into a smaller, more parsimonious number of categories. Harrison, Price, and Bell (1998) offer a useful way of doing so, suggesting that the various diversity dimensions can be subsumed under two broad categories: surface-level and deep-level.

Forms of diversity. EXHIBIT **1.1**

Surface-level diversity: differences among individuals based on readily observable characteristics such as age, sex, race, and physical ability.

Deep-level diversity: differences among individuals based on psychological characteristics.

■ *Information diversity:* those differences based on knowledge and information, oftentimes resulting from variations in education, functional background, training, and organizational tenure.

■ *Value diversity:* those differences in values, attitudes, and beliefs.

Source: Adapted from Harrison, Price, & Bell (1998) and Jehn, Northcraft, & Neale (1999).

Surface-Level Diversity

Surface-level diversity refers to those diversity dimensions that are readily observed, including gender, race, age, and, in some cases, ability and language. Because of how easily they are observed, people make quick judgments about themselves and others based on surface-level characteristics. This process occurs almost instantaneously. As an illustrative example, researchers have shown that people use facial cues to categorize others as White or African American in a matter of milliseconds (Miller, Maner, & Becker, 2010). As we will discuss in Chapter 2, these categorizations can then result in biases and negative evaluations of the target. They can also influence how members of underrepresented groups react. An exerciser who is elderly, for example, knows quickly how similar she is to others in the exercise class and, as a result, forms opinions about the degree to which she might "fit in" with others in the class.

Deep-Level Diversity

Deep-level diversity refers to those differences that are not readily observed. Examples include attitudes, beliefs, values, and culture. They are usually invisible and not known by the observer unless the target discloses the information. Let us illustrate the point by continuing with the example of the exerciser who is elderly. She may observe that she is older than others in the exercise class; however, after talking to and getting to know the other participants, she might come to learn that she shares with them many deep-level similarities, such as congruent religious or political beliefs. Thus, people can be similar in some characteristics but different in others.

Jehn, Northcraft, and Neale (1999) further break down deep-level diversity by considering *information diversity* and *value diversity*.

Information diversity. Information diversity refers to differences based on knowledge or information that members bring to an organization or group. Members may vary in their functional background, level of education, amount of training, or tenure in the organization. For example, sport organization executive boards are frequently composed of members from various business sectors in the community, including banking, coaching, and marketing. Thus, the board members bring a variety of experiences and sources of information to the board, thereby increasing the level of information diversity.

Value diversity. The second category of deep-level diversity is value diversity. A group has high value diversity when there are variations in members' attitudes toward work, personal preferences, or beliefs. These differences may be based on personality attributes, such as conscientiousness, or personal traits, such as the value one attaches to sport and physical activity. Suppose some members of an athletic department place top priority on education and moral citizenship, while others value individual and team performance. In this case, the employees' attitudes toward athletics differ; thus, that athletic department is characterized by value diversity.

Relationship Between Surface- and Deep-Level Diversity

Although I have presented surface-level and deep-level diversity as distinct constructs, the two are likely intertwined. On the one hand, people might form assumptions about the relationships between the two constructs—e.g., "Berta is from a Latin American country (surface level), so she probably likes soccer more than I do (deep level)" or "We would enhance the creativity (deep level) if we had more women in our group (surface level)." In many cases, these associations are based on stereotypes, but there is evidence that the two diversity forms are related in some instances. In one study, I collected data from track and field coaching staffs to determine if objective measures of diversity were associated with subjective assessments (Cunningham, 2007). I found this was the case for both age and racial diversity, though the latter relationship was significantly stronger than the former. In the second study, again with track and field coaches, I examined the effects of perceived diversity on subsequent outcomes. I found that as the perceived surface-level diversity increased, so too did the belief that the coaching staff had deep-level diversity. These perceptions were then reliably associated with coworker satisfaction and plans to leave the coaching staff; that is, the greater the perceived deep-level diversity of the coaching unit, the more likely the coaches were to express dissatisfaction with others on the staff and to indicate they intended to leave. I have observed a similar pattern of results among people participating in physical activity classes (Cunningham, 2006).

Surface- and deep-level diversity forms might also work together to form *faultlines* (Lau & Murnighan, 1998; Thatcher, 2013). Faultlines represent dividing lines that split groups into two or more subgroups based on a combination of various diversity dimensions. A minor league baseball team's grounds crew would have a faultline, for example, if half of the crew consisted of three women who were young and had a college education, while the other three persons were older men with only a high school education. In this case, we are considering two surface-level attributes—gender and age—and one deep-level attribute—educational attainment. The dimensions cross such that, within this particular group, individuals who possess one characteristic (i.e., being a woman) have the other distinguishing characteristics, too (i.e., being young and college educated). As I mentioned previously, people use various cues to classify themselves and others into social groups, and this categorization process can result in bias and stereotyping. The theory of faultlines suggests this process is made easier when multiple categories align, as age, gender, and education did in the example. When this occurs, people will engage in behaviors that promulgate similarities in their own subgroup and distinguish it from other subgroups. As a result, effective group functioning becomes difficult.

UNDERSTANDING THE EMPHASIS ON DIVERSITY AND INCLUSION

In the next section, we consider why the topics of diversity and inclusion are so important and have received such interest. There are seven specific factors: changing demographics, changing attitudes toward work, changes in the nature of work, legal mandates, social pressures, negative effects of exclusion, and the benefits of diversity and inclusion (see Exhibit 1.2). Each of these is discussed in greater detail next.

EXHIBIT   1.2   Factors contributing to interest in, and importance of, diversity and inclusion.

Changing demographics: Increases in the median age, proportion of racial minorities, women in the workforce, and inequity of income distribution in the United States.

Changing attitudes toward work: Changes in the commitment and loyalty toward employers and decreasing connection with the workplace among employees.

Changes in the nature of work: Increases in the number of organizations that structure work around teams, the impact of globalization, and the frequency of mergers and acquisitions.

Legal mandates: Federal and state laws that require equal employment opportunities for all persons, irrespective of demographic characteristics or background.

Social pressures: The notion that organizations have a moral and ethical obligation to have a diverse, inclusive workplace.

Negative effects of exclusion: Exclusive organizational practices and cultures can lead to negative outcomes such as low satisfaction, conflict, and poor team performance.

Value-in-diversity/inclusion hypothesis: Diversity/inclusion can positively influence desired individual, group, and organizational outcomes.

Changing Demographics

One of the primary factors spurring interest in diversity and inclusion is simple numbers: there is greater heterogeneity in many countries than ever before. This is certainly the case in the United States, where significant changes in the racial, sex, socioeconomic status, and age composition of the country took place during the 20th century. These shifts have continued into the 21st century and will do so in the foreseeable future. Changes in the population correspond to changes in organizational environments, thus making diversity and inclusion organizational realities. I examine specific demographic shifts below.

Racial minority representation

From 1980 to 2000, the Hispanic population in the United States doubled. Significant growth occurred for other racial groups, as well, as evidenced in Exhibit 1.3. By 2050, the minority population is expected to be 235.7 million of a total U.S. population of 429 million; thus, racial minorities will represent roughly 55 percent of the population. Whites are expected to comprise 46.3 percent of the population in 2050, down from 64.7 percent in 2010. The Hispanic population is projected to increase significantly, representing about one of three Americans by 2050. The proportion of African Americans is expected to decrease slightly (from 12.2 to 11.8 percent), while Asian Americans' share of the population is expected to increase from 4.5 to 7.6 percent. These changes have been reflected in the workforce, and as a result, the employees of sport and physical activity organizations have grown, and will grow, more racially diverse. Consequently, people are likely to be working with, working for, or supervising someone who is racially different. Furthermore, potential customers will also become more racially diverse; therefore, managers will have

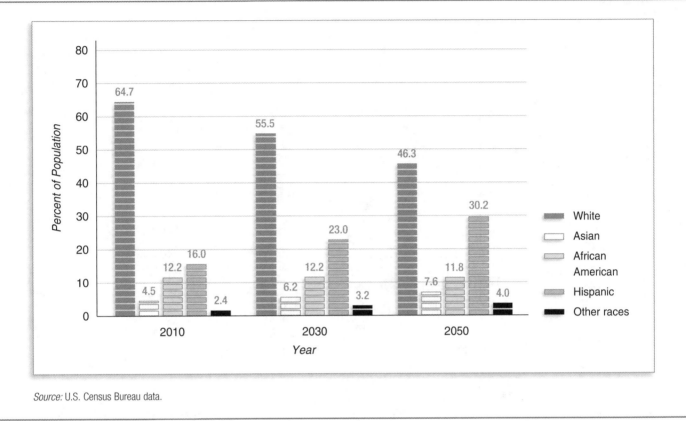

Source: U.S. Census Bureau data.

to devise strategies aimed at attracting those customers to their goods and services. A more detailed discussion of race and racial diversity is provided in Chapter 4.

Median age

Changes in the median age of the U.S. population have also been dramatic. According to the U.S. Census Bureau, at the beginning of the 20th century, the median age was 22.9 years. This figure increased such that by the year 2000, more than half of the U.S. population was over 35.3 years of age. Much of that change is a result of the large number of babies born in the 1940s and 1950s—the baby boom generation. As the baby boomers have grown older, so too has the overall population. The population of persons age 65 and older grew tenfold in the 20th century; furthermore, projections indicate that the U.S. population will continue to grow older into the 21st century, so that by 2050, one in five people will be over age 65 (see Exhibit 1.4). Not only is the nation growing older, but people are also working to a later age, resulting in greater age diversity within all organizations, including those for sport and physical activity, and an older potential consumer base. Just as strategies are needed to attract persons from different racial groups to purchase an organization's goods and services, so too is there a need to devise plans to draw older customers to the organization. A more in-depth treatment of age and age diversity is offered in Chapter 6.

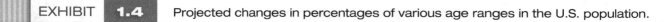

EXHIBIT 1.4   Projected changes in percentages of various age ranges in the U.S. population.

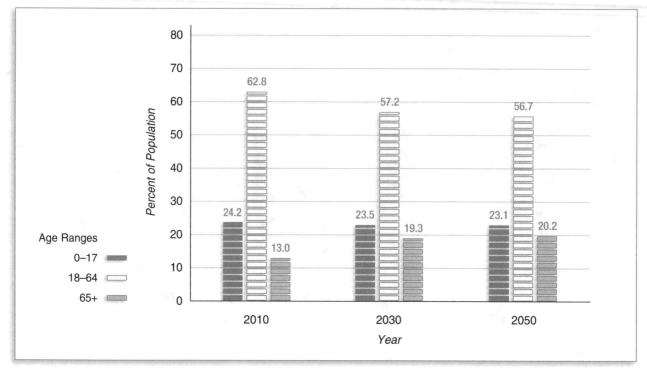

Source: U.S. Census Bureau data.

Sex composition

The sex composition of the United States has also changed, though this shift is not as dramatic as those in age and race. The U.S. Census Bureau reports that the U.S. population shifted from majority male at the beginning of the 20th century to majority female by the century's midpoint. At the end of the 20th century, women still outnumbered men. Although women continue to enter the workforce in increasing numbers, they are still less likely to be members of the workforce than men; see Exhibit 1.5. It should be noted, however, that the magnitude of the difference in the proportion of men and women in the workforce has decreased over time. As with the other forms of diversity, the increase in the proportion of working women means that sex diversity in all types of organizations has increased, as well. Sex, gender, and sex diversity are discussed in greater detail in Chapter 5.

Socioeconomic status

Changes also have occurred with respect to socioeconomic status. Data from the U.S. Census Bureau indicate that in 1967 the median household income in 2012 dollars was $42,934, a figure that increased to $51,017 by 2012. In isolation, these figures tell us only that in today's dollars, people make more money now than they did 45 years ago. However, other data indicate that the share of aggregate income is increasingly un-

Number of women and men working full time, 1967 to 2009. | EXHIBIT | 1.5

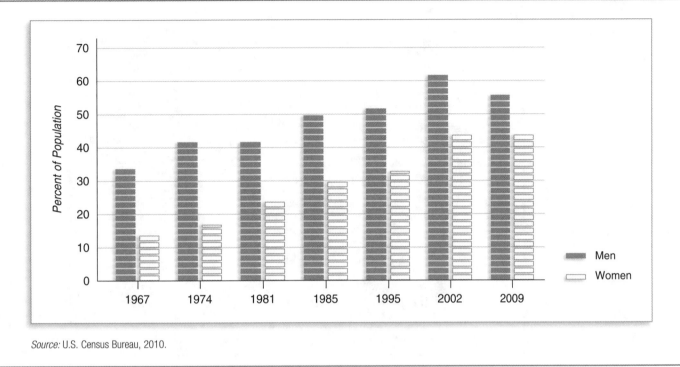

Source: U.S. Census Bureau, 2010.

evenly dispersed. In 1967, the top 5 percent of all households possessed a 17.2 percent share of aggregate income. By 1980, the share had dropped to 16.5 percent. However, since 1980, the share of aggregate income held by the top 5 percent has increased. By 2012, the top 5 percent of all households possessed 22.3 percent of the aggregate income. The Gini Index, a measure that summarizes the dispersion of income over the entire income distribution, also increased during that time. This increase means that income is increasingly being received by one group of people (see Exhibit 1.6). As the exhibit indicates, the socioeconomic status of the U.S. population has changed over time, with the distribution of wealth growing increasingly inequitable. In Chapter 11, we spend more time discussing socioeconomic status and social class, the latter of which combines socioeconomic status and issues of power and privilege.

Global changes

Demographic changes are evident in other areas of the world, as well. Let us consider examples from three countries: Canada, China, and Egypt.

In Canada, Statistics Canada (2014) predicts an aging of the population: the median age was 27.2 years in 1956 and is projected to be 46.9 years in 2056. Canada is also expected to become more racially and ethnically diverse; for instance, Aboriginal persons represented 3.9 percent of the population in 2006, a figure that could grow to 5.3 percent by 2031.

China has also witnessed demographic shifts. According to World Population Review (2014), in 2014, 1.39 billion people lived in China, making it the most

EXHIBIT   1.6   Income inequality over time.

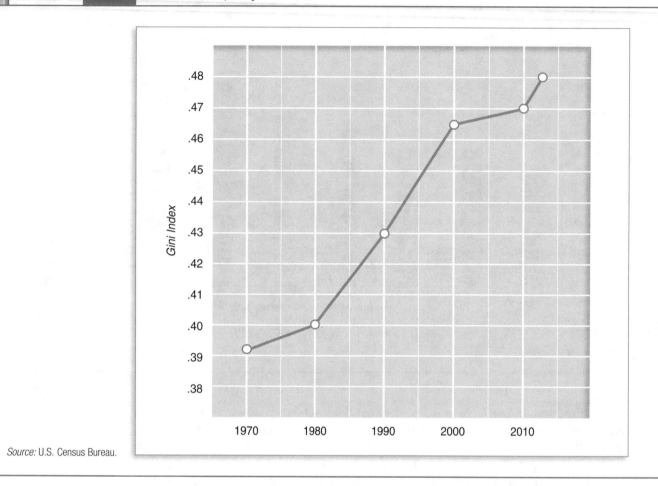

Source: U.S. Census Bureau.

populous country in the world, with 19 percent of the world's overall population. Like other countries, China has an aging population, which means that after years of steady growth, its overall population will begin to decline in coming years. The country also has 56 officially recognized ethnic groups. Rapid economic growth has influenced Chinese citizens: in the 1980s, 64 percent of the population lived on $1 USD per day; in 2014, only 10 percent did so.

According to data from the United Nations, Egypt's population has increased substantially and will continue to do so. The population was 44.9 million in 1980, increased to 78.1 million in 2010, and is expected to reach 121.8 million by 2050. As in other countries, though, the population is expected to increase in age: in 2010, 5.5 percent of the population was age 65 or older; this percentage is expected to increase to 12.3 percent by 2050. Many Egyptians (57.2 percent in 2000) currently live in rural settings, but this is expected to shift in coming years, such that by 2050, 60 percent will live in urban areas.

These three examples show that demographic changes are occurring around the world. While there are some similarities across countries, such as the aging of the populace, other changes are particular to specific countries. It is important for sport managers, coaches, and other physical activity professionals to remain cognizant of these transitions and the ways they may influence characteristics of the organizational environment.

Changing Attitudes Toward Work

Although people frequently point to demographic shifts as the primary reason for an interest in diversity and inclusion, a host of other factors influence this interest. Changes in employees' attitudes toward work represent one such factor, and this manifests itself in several ways. First, traditional employment patterns called for people to spend their entire career in one organization, moving up the ranks as they progressed in tenure and skills. This certainly still happens in some instances, but a more common pattern is for people to move from one organization to another—and in some cases, one occupation to another—during their career. Professional development and skill acquisition are now important, helping organizations increase productivity in the workplace and individual employees further their knowledge, skills, abilities, and employability. The end results are a workforce that is more transient than in the past, greater variance of tenure among work group members, and decreased connection with the workplace among employees.

All of these points are relevant, but let us devote more attention to the decreased sense of connection with the workplace. Considerable evidence indicates that people seek meaning in their lives and want to feel connected to something, and this is frequently expressed through a strong personal identity (Ramarajan, 2014). Historically, the organization in which one worked might have served as a source of identity, an identity that a person could readily express at work—e.g., "I am a Barcelona FC employee." However, as workplace–employee commitments have weakened, so has the degree to which people express this identity. Consequently, people increasingly bring other identities important to them into the workplace. These identities might be based on their religious beliefs, their sexual orientation, their political leanings, and so on. They might seek to incorporate these identities into their work, again as a way of seeking and realizing meaning in their lives. This means two things: (1) as people bring their various identities to the workplace (a form of deep-level diversity), the ways in which they differ increase; and (2) the importance of inclusion is heightened, as employees bring their individuated self to work while also seeking connection to the workplace.

Changes in the Nature of Work

Another reason diversity and inclusion have become such important topics for managers, particularly in sport organizations, is that the nature of work has changed. Most sport organizations offer services rather than tangible goods (Chelladurai, 2014), and operations are increasingly structured around work teams (Ilgen, Hollenbeck, Johnson, & Jundt, 2005). Both of these factors substantially influence the role of differences in the workplace, as we will discuss next. The impact of two other factors, globalization and mergers and acquisitions, will also be discussed.

Service-based organizations

A key element of service-based organizations is the interaction with the client. In sport, this interaction might occur between a personal trainer and an exerciser, a ticket salesperson and a customer, and so on. Just as in other contexts where people interact with one another on a personal basis, differences can affect the relationship. For example, Sagas and I found that when customers believed they were different from their service providers, their satisfaction with the exchange decreased (Cunningham & Sagas, 2006). Amount of interaction influenced these effects such that dissatisfaction increased as the customer and service provider spent more time together. There is also evidence that women working in service-based organizations sometimes experience customer-based sexual harassment, which has the potential to affect their psychological, physical, and workplace well-being negatively (Morganson & Major, 2014).

Team-based work

The team-based nature of the work structure in many sport organizations also influences diversity's effects in the workplace. To illustrate this point, let us compare your hypothetical experience as an employee at a minor league Hockey Club B to the experience of your friend who works at Hockey Club A. In Hockey Club A, people work in silos, completing their tasks by themselves and coming together only to discuss what they have accomplished (or, potentially, to collaborate, though the latter rarely occurs). In Hockey Club B, employees from various functional areas work in teams to complete their tasks. In this way, they can draw on expertise, perspectives, and experiences from a broad array of people, increasing decision-making capacity. Clearly, the number and nature of interactions differ in the two workplaces, as employees in the latter accomplish work together, in a reciprocal fashion. Differences among employees are also more likely to manifest in Hockey Club B. At Club B you interact with group members on a regular basis and depend on them to accomplish your work. The differences between you and your coworkers are likely to influence your ability to accomplish your tasks. On the other hand, your friend at Club A rarely interacts with others in the workplace, and dissimilarities among coworkers are unlikely to affect the outcomes of your friend's work one way or the other. Thus, task interdependence serves to influence the relationship between group differences and work outcomes (van Knippenberg, De Drue, & Homan, 2004).

Globalization

Globalization has also affected the nature of work and influenced the emphasis on diversity and inclusion. Sport is a global phenomenon, and as such, sport organizations routinely seek to (a) expand their reach into various markets around the world, and (b) attract and retain the most talented athletes, irrespective of the country in which they were born. At the league level, major sport leagues, such as the National Basketball Association (NBA) and Major League Baseball (MLB), play games in other countries in order to generate interest in the sports and expand their fan base. At the team level, the globalization of players is aptly illustrated by the San Antonio Spurs, who won the 2014 NBA title. Their roster included athletes

MLB players from around the world.   EXHIBIT   **1.7**

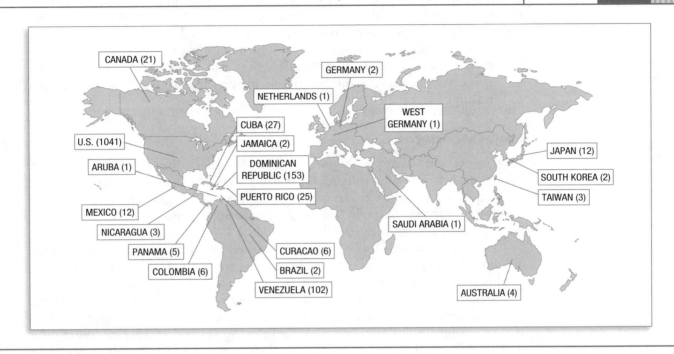

MLB players from around the world.   EXHIBIT   **1.7**

Source: Data from Baseball Almanac. Major league baseball players by birthplace during the 2014 season. www. baseball-almanac.com/players/birthplace.php

from seven nations, as well as a U.S. territory, the Virgin Islands (Walters, 2014). As teammates from varied backgrounds join a team, they bring with them histories, playing styles, and backgrounds, all of which can add richness to the team's pursuit of a championship. The globalization of sport is also observed in Major League Baseball, as illustrated in Exhibit 1.7.

Mergers and acquisitions

Mergers and acquisitions also influence diversity and inclusion in organizational environments. On an international scale, Nike acquired Converse for $200 million in 2003, and Adidas purchased Reebok for $3.8 billion in 2005 (Rovell, 2005). Perhaps more common are mergers at the local or community level, as will sometimes take place between sport clubs. For example, in 2013, Sports Club United and Schaumburg Athletic Association—two youth club sport entities in Illinois—merged to form a single entity. The leaders of the clubs explained, "The principle of this merger is founded on 'One Community, One Club.' We have two similar programs in the same community competing for the same resources and striving to attain the same goals. Embracing this collaboration will create a positive environment that fosters unity and the opportunity for our families and players to achieve their goals" (Schaumburg Athletic Association, n.d.). Such mergers and acquisitions have the potential to impact how people interact with one another. When organizations join together, so do members of formerly distinct entities.

In the case of club sports, decisions about coaching, access and inclusion, player selection, cost of participation, and motivation for competition all might vary between the two original organizations. Ideally, the different perspectives, which represent forms of deep-level diversity, can be leveraged to help the organization approach tasks in novel ways, thereby improving decision-making capabilities. However, it is also possible that the differences will make coordination, merging the various talents, and creating a common identity daunting tasks (Van Leeuwen & van Knippenberg, 2014).

Legal Mandates

Legal issues, particularly personnel matters, also affect diversity and inclusion in sport organizations. Who is hired, the benefits they are offered, how they are treated on the job, and their termination are all affected by laws and regulations at local, state, and federal levels. Within the United States, these matters are governed primarily by civil rights legislation passed in the 1960s and later in the 1990s.

Laws are also culturally bound: the norms and values of a particular geographic area frequently influence which groups receive workplace protection. For example, in the United States as of this writing, federal employment protections are in place that prohibit discrimination based on race, age, sex, and religion. Similar protections are lacking in the areas of sexual orientation, gender identity, and weight. Some states or municipalities, however, do forbid discrimination based on these aspects of diversity. Such increased protection typically occurs in politically progressive areas, where the population more readily embraces inclusive principles.

Within the context of sport, recreation, and physical education, Title IX represents one of the most noteworthy laws passed in the 20th century. It holds that all persons, irrespective of their sex, be afforded equal opportunities to participate in federally funded educational activities. While the law does not specifically mention sport or physical activity, its connection with federally funded educational activities means it touches many areas of sport. Chapter 5 provides a fuller discussion of its impact.

Social Pressures

Social pressures represent another reason for the heightened interest in diversity and inclusion. From this perspective, there is a moral or ethical responsibility to ensure that organizations have a diverse workforce and an inclusive environment. In some cases, this moral obligation will come from within the workplace. Doherty and Chelladurai (1999) argued that a sport organization's valuing of diversity will stem from the leaders' view that diversity is a moral imperative. Singer and I also observed this (Cunningham & Singer, 2009). In an effort to understand diversity and inclusion best practices within the National Collegiate Athletic Association (NCAA), we interviewed campus administrators and athletic department personnel, and also analyzed various forms of archival data, such as strategic plans, newspaper articles, and other reports. We found that in the top athletic departments, diversity and inclusion started with employees' valuing diversity. They sensed a moral obligation to treat people equitably, they saw difference as a source of learning, and they developed an ethos of inclusion within the organizational environment.

In other cases, the moral obligation for diversity and inclusion can come from external stakeholders, such as customers, potential players, or possible employees. Considerable evidence shows that sport organizations are rewarded for demonstrating their commitment to diversity and inclusion. For example, companies' stock prices increase relative to their competitors' when the company wins diversity awards (Johnston & Malina, 2008) or has a history of inclusive workplace practices (Wang & Schwarz, 2010), suggesting stockholders care about inclusiveness. Consumers express similar interest, as they are more likely to purchase products from companies demonstrating diversity and inclusion than they are from other entities (Tuten, 2005). Finally, prospective employees (Lee & Cunningham, in press) and people considering joining fitness clubs (Cunningham & Melton, 2014) favor and express more positive attitudes toward sport organizations they believe are diverse and that have a strong culture of inclusiveness. Together, this research evidence suggests people have an expectation for sport organizations to be inclusive; they reward the organizations when such expectations are met and penalize them when this is not the case.

Negative Effects of Exclusion

Evidence seems to suggest that dissimilarity among group members can result in strained processes and poor outcomes, leading some observers to suggest that managers should attend to diversity because of the potential negative effects. There is growing evidence, though, that such sentiments represent a case of misplaced attributions: it is not diversity that results in negative effects, but a lack of inclusive policies, or more simply, the presence of exclusive organizational practices. When sport organizations have exclusive organizational practices and differences are seen as deficits, there is a lack of respect, and people do not feel connected to the larger entity. However, in inclusive workplaces, people's differences are recognized, appreciated, and seen as a source of learning. Here, differences become a source of competitive advantage (Roberson, 2006). Note that in both cases diversity is present, but what varies is the level of exclusion or inclusion.

Let's consider Nishii's (2013) recent study of biomedical firms to illustrate this point. She found that as a climate of exclusion increased, the levels of conflict within the groups increased, and the members' overall satisfaction with the group decreased. We would expect as much based on the previous discussion of inclusive work environments. Importantly, Nishii also found that exclusion interacted with the gender diversity of the group to influence various outcomes. When exclusion was high, gender diversity was negatively associated with satisfaction and positively correlated with conflict. Although her work is set within the context of biomedical fields, the findings are still instructive for our understanding of sport organizations: the level of exclusion hurts important group outcomes.

Benefits of Diversity and Inclusion

The evidence that diversity and inclusion add value to the workplace represents the final factor that has led to an increased interest in the topic. Coaches and administrators are always keen on improving performance, so if they are offered evidence that

professional
PERSPECTIVES

The Importance of Diversity and Inclusion. Peter Roby served as director of the Center for Sport in Society, an entity that was created based on the idea that "sport can play an important role in helping to create social change," and is currently the athletic director at Northeastern University. According to Roby, there are several reasons why diversity has become such a major issue in sport and physical activity. Primarily, he suggests that sport highlights differences among people—differences based on sex, age, race, religion, life experiences, and learning style. Roby explains that "there is a lot that people can benefit from as a result of being exposed to difference." In addition, "with regard to sport in particular, one of the values that we see in sport is how much it acts as a great common denominator—how it brings people from different backgrounds together under the common umbrella of sport." Sport serves as an educational tool—what people learn about diversity in the context of sport can be applied to their everyday lives.

diverse, inclusive workplaces contribute to this desired end, they are likely to listen.

A number of experimental and cross-sectional studies show that diversity can bring value to the workplace through enhanced decision making, greater creativity, learning from others, and the like. In drawing from this work, I sought to understand these dynamics from the administrator's point of view. To do so, I collected qualitative data from 245 NCAA Division I athletic administrators, asking them what value diversity had in their workplace. They identified a number of areas, as depicted in Exhibit 1.8. Their responses showed that most administrators believed employee diversity was associated with improved internal processes, such as idea generation, inclusion, learning, and role modeling. They also thought diversity helped them to reflect the communities in which they lived and to provide a better role model to students. Finally, some pointed to enhanced workplace productivity (Cunningham, 2008).

Peter Roby, a longtime sport manager, also identified a number of benefits associated with organizational diversity and inclusion. These sentiments are captured in the Professional Perspectives box.

PUTTING IT ALL TOGETHER

A s the preceding discussions illustrate, diversity and inclusion are important topics for coaches and sport administrators. Because sport organizations have become more diverse over time—along both surface-level and deep-level dimensions—the emphasis on these topics is in some respects reactionary in nature. That just tells part of the story, though. As discussed throughout the chapter, real benefits can be associated with having inclusive workplaces in which people of various backgrounds and beliefs can thrive. Creating and sustaining a diverse and inclusive workplace also has proactive qualities, as doing so gives a sport organization its best chance to succeed moving forward.

The purpose of this text is to provide readers with an overview, understanding, and analysis of diversity and inclusion in sport organizations. Part I offers an overview of the theories undergirding these topics (Chapter 2) and of prejudice and discrimination (Chapter 3). I provide definitions and key points, introduce and explain relevant theories, and outline the effects of prejudice and discrimination on persons in the workplace.

Part II is devoted to various forms of diversity. I examine the ways in which people differ and how these differences influence people's lives and experiences, as well as organizational initiatives and functioning. In doing so, I focus on race

Benefits of diversity in intercollegiate athletics.   EXHIBIT 1.8

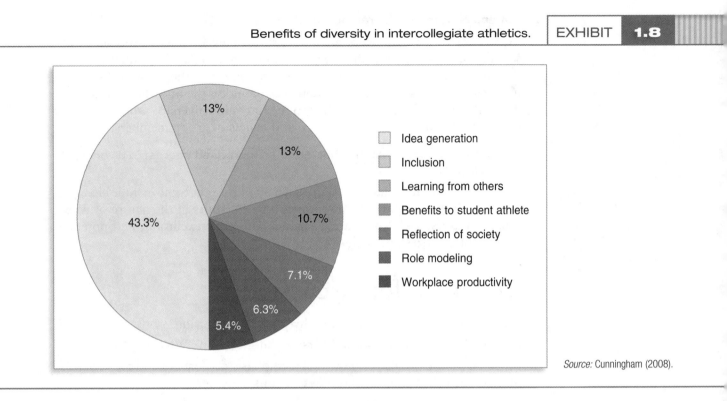

Source: Cunningham (2008).

(Chapter 4), sex and gender (Chapter 5), age (Chapter 6), mental and physical ability (Chapter 7), appearance (Chapter 8), religious beliefs (Chapter 9), sexual orientation and gender identity (Chapter 10), and social class (Chapter 11).

Part III is devoted to strategies that can be used to make sport inclusive. In this section, I examine strategies for developing inclusive groups (Chapter 12) and organizations (Chapter 13). Diversity training is a key element of these activities, so Chapter 14 is devoted to this topic. Finally, in Chapter 15, I offer an analysis of how sport can be used to create social change in communities around the world. Thus, the focus shifts from the effects on sport organizations to how sport organizations can positively affect inclusion and social justice in their communities.

chapter SUMMARY

This chapter provided an opening glimpse of diversity and inclusion in sport organizations. As the Diversity Challenge illustrated, these topics are important issues for persons involved in sport and physical activity, and they will be for years to come. After reading this chapter, you should be able to do the following:

1. **Define diversity and inclusion.**

    Diversity is the presence of socially meaningful differences among members of a dyad or group. Inclusion refers to the degree to which employees are free to express their individuated self and have a sense of workplace connectedness and belongingness.

2. **List and explain the different forms of diversity.**

Two forms of diversity were identified: surface-level, which is related to observable characteristics, and deep-level, which is related to differences in psychological characteristics. Deep-level diversity is further broken down into information diversity, or those differences based on the knowledge and information that members bring to the group, and value diversity, which is related to differences in the values, attitudes, and beliefs of group members.

3. **Discuss the different factors that led to an increased interest in diversity and inclusion.**

The factors that have made diversity such an important topic include changing demographics, changing attitudes toward work, shifts in the nature of work, legal mandates, social pressures, negative effects of exclusion, and potential benefits of diversity and inclusion.

QUESTIONS for discussion

1. Why is it important to understand diversity and inclusion?
2. Do you differentiate between diversity and inclusion? Why or why not?
3. Based on your experiences, how much emphasis do coaches and managers place on diversity and inclusion? Why is this the case?
4. Consider the ways in which people differ. Are some differences more meaningful than others within sport organizational settings? Why is this the case?
5. What is the most compelling reason to focus on diversity and inclusion? Provide the rationale for your response.

learning ACTIVITIES

1. Several demographic trends were noted in this chapter. Visit the U.S. Census Bureau website (www.census.gov) and gather data concerning other demographic and population trends. Also search for similar websites offering information about other countries. How are the major trends in the United States similar to and different from those in other countries?
2. Some people oppose an emphasis on diversity and inclusion within the workplace or educational settings. Why do you think this is the case, and are there counterarguments? Divide into small groups, with each adopting a particular position. Be prepared to present your position to the class.

WEB resources

■ **Laboratory for Diversity in Sport,** www.diversityinsport.com
Research center focusing on diversity and inclusion in sport and physical activity; includes various resources.

■ **Center for the Study of Sport in Society,** www.sportinsociety.org

Organization devoted to the study of sport in society; focuses on issues concerning race and disability, among others.

■ **Diversity, Inc.,** www.diversityinc.com

Site devoted to diversity in the general organizational context.

reading RESOURCES

Bell, M. P. (2011). *Diversity in organizations* (2nd ed.). Mason, OH: Thomson South-Western.

A diversity textbook with a business management focus; the author devotes considerable attention to race and ethnicity, as well as addressing other topics.

Brooks, D., & Althouse, R. (2007). *Diversity and social justice in college sports: Sport management and the student athlete.* Morgantown, WV: Fitness Information Technology.

An edited text that focuses on a host of diversity-related issues in college sports, with a particular focus on race.

Roberson, Q. M. (Ed.) (2013). *The Oxford handbook of diversity and work.* New York: Oxford University Press.

A collection of chapters from many of the leading diversity and inclusion scholars around the world.

REFERENCES

Brewer, M. B. (1991). The social self: On being the same and different at the same time. *Personality and Social Psychology Bulletin, 17,* 475–482.

Chelladurai, P. (2014). *Managing organizations for sport and physical activity: A systems perspective* (4th ed.). Scottsdale, AZ: Holcomb Hathaway.

Cunningham, G. B. (2006). The influence of demographic dissimilarity on affective reactions to physical activity classes. *Journal of Sport and Exercise Psychology, 28,* 127–142.

Cunningham, G. B. (2007). Perceptions as reality: The influence of actual and perceived demographic dissimilarity. *Journal of Business and Psychology, 22,* 79–89.

Cunningham, G. B. (2008). Understanding diversity in intercollegiate athletics. *Journal for the Study of Sports and Athletes in Education, 2,* 321–338.

Cunningham, G. B., & Melton, E. N. (2014). Signals and cues: LGBT inclusive advertising and consumer attraction. *Sport Marketing Quarterly, 23,* 37–46.

Cunningham, G. B., & Sagas, M. (2006). The role of perceived demographic dissimilarity and interaction in customer service satisfaction. *Journal of Applied Social Psychology, 36,* 1654–1673.

Cunningham, G. B., & Singer, J. N. (2009). *Diversity in athletics: An assessment of exemplars and institutional best practices.* Indianapolis, IN: National Collegiate Athletic Association.

DiTomaso, N., Post, C., & Parks-Yancy, R. (2007). Workforce diversity and inequality: Power, status, and numbers. *Annual Review of Sociology, 33,* 473–501.

Doherty, A. J., & Chelladurai, P. (1999). Managing cultural diversity in sport organizations: A theoretical perspective. *Journal of Sport Management, 13,* 280–297.

Ferdman, B. M. (2010). Teaching inclusion by example and experience: Creating an inclusive learning environment. In K. M. Hannun, L. Booysen, & B. B. McFeeters (Eds.), *Leading across differences: Cases and perspectives—Facilitator's guide* (pp. 37–50). San Francisco: Pfeiffer.

Ferdman, B. M. (2014). The practice of inclusion in diverse organizations. In B. M. Ferdman & B. R. Deane (Eds.), *Diversity at work: The practice of inclusion* (pp. 3–54). San Francisco: Jossey-Bass.

Harrison, D. A., & Klein, K. J. (2007). What's the difference? Diversity constructs as separation, variety, or disparity in organizations. *Academy of Management Review, 32,* 1199–1228.

Harrison, D. A., Price, K. H., & Bell, M. P. (1998). Beyond relational demography: Time and the effects of surface- and deep-level diversity on work group cohesion. *Academy of Management Journal, 41,* 96–107.

Ilgen, D. R., Hollenbeck, J. R., Johnson, M., & Jundt, D. (2005). Teams in organizations: From input-process-output models to IMOI models. *Annual Review of Psychology, 56,* 517–543.

Jehn, K. A., Northcraft, G. B., & Neale, M. A. (1999). Why differences make a difference: A field study of diversity, conflict, and performance in workgroups. *Administrative Science Quarterly, 44,* 741–763.

Johnston, D., & Malina, M. A. (2008). Managing sexual orientation diversity: The impact on firm value. *Group and Organization Management, 33,* 602–625.

Konrad, A. M. (2003). Defining the domain of workplace diversity scholarship. *Group & Organization Management, 28,* 4–17.

Kozlowski, S. W. J., & Klein, K. J. (2000). A multilevel approach to theory and research in organizations: Contextual, temporal, and emergent processes. In K. J. Klein & S. W. J. Kozlowski (Eds.), *Multilevel theory, research, and methods in organizations: Foundations, extensions, and new directions* (pp. 3–90). San Francisco: Jossey-Bass.

Lambert, J. R., & Bell, M. P. (2013). Diverse forms of difference. In Q. M. Roberson (Ed.), *The Oxford handbook of diversity at work* (pp. 13–31). New York: Oxford University Press.

Lau, D. C., & Murnighan, J. K. (1998). Demographic diversity and faultiness: The compositional dynamics of organizational groups. *Academy of Management Review, 23,* 325–340.

Lee, W., & Cunningham, G. B. (in press). A picture is worth a thousand words: The influence of signaling, organizational reputation, and applicant race on attraction to sport organizations. *International Journal of Sport Management.*

Miller, S. L., Maner, J. K., & Becker, D. V. (2010). Self-protective biases in group categorization: Threat cues shape the psychological boundary between "us" and "them." *Journal of Personality and Social Psychology, 99,* 62–77.

Morganson, V. J., & Major, D. A. (2014). Exploring retaliation as a coping strategy in response to customer sexual harassment. *Sex Roles, 71,* 83–94.

Nishii, L. H. (2013). The benefits of climate for inclusion for gender-diverse groups. *Academy of Management Journal, 56,* 1754–1774.

Nishii, L. H., & Rich, R. E. (2014). Creating inclusive climates in diverse organizations. In B. M. Ferdman & B. R. Deane (Eds.), *Diversity at work: The practice of inclusion* (pp. 330–363). San Francisco: Jossey-Bass.

Orwell, G. (1949). *1984.* New York: Harcourt.

Pfeffer, J. (1983). Organizational demography. *Research in Organizational Behavior, 5,* 299–357.

Ramarajan, L. (2014). Past, present, and future research on multiple identities: Toward an interpersonal network approach. *The Academy of Management Annals, 8,* 589–659.

Roberson, Q. M. (2006). Disentangling the meanings of diversity and inclusion in organizations. *Group & Organization Management, 31,* 212–236.

Rovell, D. (2005, August 3). Reebok, Adidas have plenty of issues to solve. *ESPN.* Retrieved from http://sports.espn.go.com/espn/columns/story?columnist=rovell_darren&id=2123332.

Schaumburg Athletic Association (n.d.). Retrieved from https://saa.light.sportspilot.com/HOME.aspx

Shore, L. M., Randel, A. E., Chung, B. G., Dean, M. A., Ehrhart, K. H., & Singh, G. (2011). Inclusion and diversity in work groups: A review and model for future research. *Journal of Management, 37,* 1262–1289.

Statistics Canada (2014). Demographic change. Retrieved from http://www.statcan.gc.ca/pub/82-229-x/2009001/demo/int1-eng.htm

Thatcher, S. M. B. (2013). Moving beyond a categorical approach to diversity: The role of demographic faultiness. In Q. M. Roberson (Ed.), *The Oxford handbook of diversity at work* (pp. 52–70). New York: Oxford University Press.

Tuten, T. L. (2005). The effect of gay-friendly and non-gay-friendly cues on brand attitudes: A comparison of heterosexual and gay/lesbian reactions. *Journal of Marketing Management, 21,* 441–461.

Tsui, A. S., & Gutek, B. A. (1999). *Demographic differences in organizations: Current research and future directions.* New York: Lexington Books.

University of Vermont (n.d.). Retrieved from http://www.uvmathletics.com/sports/2014/7/8/SAD_0708145750.aspx?path=sad

USA Rugby (n.d.). *Diversity statement.* Retrieved from http://usarugby.org/about-usarugby/diversity-statement.

van Knippenberg, D., De Drue, C. K. W., & Homan, A. C. (2004). Work group diversity and group performance: An integrative model and research agenda. *Journal of Applied Psychology, 89,* 1008–1022.

van Knippenberg, D., & Schippers, M. C. (2007). Work group diversity. *Annual Review of Psychology, 58,* 515–541.

Van Leeuwen, E., & van Knippenberg, D. (2014). Organizational identification following a merger: The importance of agreeing to differ. In S. A. Haslam, D. van Knippenberg, M. J. Platow, & N. Ellemers (Eds.), *Social identity at work: Developing theory for organizational practice* (pp. 205–222). New York: Psychology Press.

Wang, P., & Schwarz, J. L. (2010). Stock price reactions to GLBT nondiscrimination policies. *Human Resource Management, 49,* 195–216.

Walters, J. (2014, June 6). The international conspiracy behind the success of the San Antonio Spurs. *Newsweek*. Retrieved from www.newsweek.com

World Population Review (2014). China population 2014. Retrieved from http://worldpopulationreview.com/countries/china-population/

Theoretical Tenets of Diversity and Inclusion

DIVERSITY CHALLENGE

The word *theory* may suggest somewhat negative connotations—the qualities of being abstract, esoteric, or lacking practical relevance. All of these are labels I have heard applied to theory. But in reality, people theorize all of the time, just not formally. They develop explanations for why different phenomena occur. They seek to explain how and why various activities take place. They may even discuss when and where the events will likely occur. All of these are examples of theorizing.

Police detectives, for instance, will develop theories for why suspects commit crimes. Students create explanations for their performance on exams. Sport fans, though, are perhaps the most prolific theorists of them all. Amber Lee explains:

There are only a few segments of life and society more ripe for conspiracy theories than sports. All of the critical elements needed to fuel skepticism and suspicion of the official narrative are present—secretive institutions and power-brokers, vast amounts of money changing hands, heated rivalries and seemingly improbable events.

Some conspiracy theories on Lee's list include the ideas (a) that David Stern fixed the 1985 NBA draft to ensure the New York Knicks could select Patrick Ewing with the first pick; (b) that University of Nevada–Las Vegas threw the 1991 men's basketball championship game against Duke University as part of a point-shaving scam; and (c) that famed teamster Jimmy Hoffa was buried under Giants Stadium. Although she rebuffs the top conspiracy theories, Lee acknowledges that others have ultimately been supported. For example, various people developed arguments that cyclist Lance Armstrong's success was attributable to drug usage—an allegation that turned out to be true.

These examples confirm that people do theorize on a regular basis. The process helps them to understand various organizational practices and offer explanations for unusual occurrences. Theorizing also takes place in discussions of diversity and inclusion. Renowned trainers and consultants, such as Taylor Cox, Jr. and Roosevelt Thomas, ground their educational exercises in theory. In fact, Thomas argues that without theory, the "quick fix" approaches managers frequently seek are doomed to fail. He notes, "We have to be careful about giving people skills and tactics without the conceptual underpinning." Thus, while educational efforts should include a host of elements (e.g., role playing, practical examples, and case studies), leaders in the field suggest that theory should provide the *foundation* for these efforts. Luckily, as mentioned, those involved in sport are savvy veterans when it comes to theorizing.

Sources: Johnson, C. D. (2008). It's more than the five to do's: Insights on diversity education and training from Roosevelt Thomas, a pioneer and thought leader in the field. *Academy of Management Learning & Education, 7,* 406–417. / Lee, A. (2013, February 1). The dumbest conspiracy theories in sports. *Bleacher Report.* Retrieved from http://bleacherreport.com/articles/1510093-the-dumbest-conspiracies-in-sports-history.

CHALLENGE REFLECTION

1. In your experience, what are common attitudes toward theory and the process of theorizing?

2. Thomas noted that managers often want a "quick fix" without understanding the underlying principles of the issue. Why do you think this is the case?

3. What steps can be taken to make people more aware of how they can increase understanding of diversity and inclusion?

A s the Diversity Challenge illustrates, even though people use and develop theories on a regular basis, they are frequently averse to the idea of studying theory. This antipathy is not limited to students; organizational leaders often seek to have their questions answered without first seeking to understand the underlying concepts or principles. Despite this tendency to avoid theory, it *is* important to appreciate and examine the theoretical foundations of diversity and inclusion. Doing so allows coaches and managers to engage in better decision making and to be proactive in managing their teams and organizations. Indeed, the best theories not only inform research but also assist in teaching, engagement, and practice (Cunningham, 2013; Doherty, 2013).

Given this perspective, the purpose of this chapter is to provide an overview of the theories undergirding the discussion of diversity and inclusion. To do so, I begin by defining the term *theory* and elaborating on why theory is important in the study of diversity and inclusion. Next, I discuss the major categories of theory related to these topics, briefly outlining the specific theories in each category and their major tenets. I also describe the application of the theories in sport organizations.

DEFINING THEORY

T *heory* refers to "a statement of constructs and their relationships to one another that explain[s] how, when, why, and under what conditions phenomena take place" (Cunningham, 2013, p. 1). For our purposes here, we can consider a construct to be a variable of interest. Surface-level diversity and creativity are two example constructs. Propositions refer to relationships among constructs. For example, one might propose that as the surface-level diversity of a group increases, so too does the creative environment within that entity.

Theory also offers ideas about *when* the relationships are likely to take place. These are often called boundary conditions (Bacharach, 1989), and we can think of them as "if–then" conditions or conditional statements. Let us extend the previous example further. We might argue that surface-level diversity results in more creativity when the organizational culture is inclusive. However, when the culture is one that is exclusive or discriminatory in nature, then individual differences might only take away from the effectiveness and creativity of the group. These relationships are illustrated in Exhibit 2.1.

Finally, and perhaps most importantly, theory organizes, explains, and predicts (Bacharach, 1989; Cunningham, Fink, & Doherty, in press; Kerlinger & Lee, 2000). Thus, theory moves beyond describing what is occurring—diversity is associated with greater creativity when the environment is inclusive—to explain *why* it is happening. Not only does this enhance understanding of the issue at hand, but it also makes it possible to predict subsequent phenomena. To continue with our working example, we might think that surface-level diversity is associated with creativity when the culture is inclusive because in inclusive workplaces, differences are seen as a source of growth and learning (Ferdman, 2014). When this attitude prevails, differences based on race, for example, allow for more ideas to be expressed and for information to be discussed in an open and constructive manner. The end result is better, more creative decisions (see also van Knippenberg, De Drue, & Homan, 2004). On the other hand, in exclusive workplace cultures, certain groups are privileged over others and differences are seen as deficits. In this case, surface-level diversity should actually hurt the group processes that allow for creative decisions. Both of these relationships are depicted in Exhibit 2.1.

Relationships among surface-level diversity, creativity, and inclusion. EXHIBIT 2.1

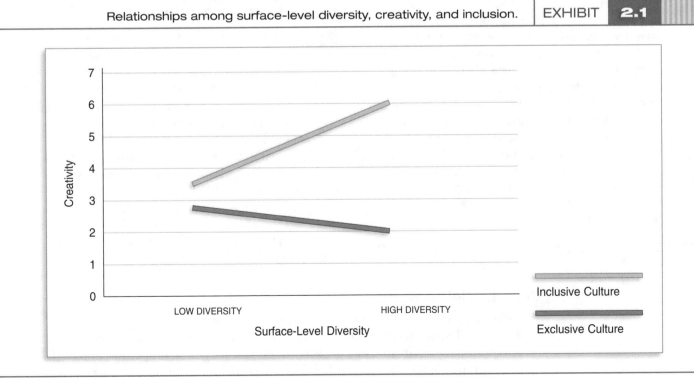

The best theories have practicality and utility. This is perhaps most frequently illustrated in the research process. Theory has been described as the cornerstone of good scholarship (Cunningham, 2013), the foundation for new knowledge generation (Doherty, 2013), and the primary aim of science (Kerlinger & Lee, 2000). Thus, theory is clearly important in scholarly endeavors and in research related to diversity and inclusion.

In addition to guiding research, theory is also an important element in learning, teaching, engagement, and practice (Doherty, 2013; Fink, 2013; Irwin & Ryan, 2013). Admittedly, these connections are not always made. Irwin and Ryan illustrated as much by pointing to a famous quote from former MLB player Yogi Berra: "In theory, there is no difference between theory and practice. In practice, there is" (as cited in Irwin & Ryan, 2013, p. 12). However, the presence of a theory–teaching or theory–practice gap does not render theory useless; instead, it points to the need to strengthen such ties. For learning, teaching, engagement, and practice, theory helps people to move beyond "quick fix" solutions to a deeper understanding of the issue at hand. Theory allows students and sport managers to explain phenomena and ultimately make educated predictions of future occurrences.

professional
PERSPECTIVES

The importance of theory. Melanie Sartore-Baldwin is an associate professor at East Carolina University. Her research focuses on diversity, broadly defined, and in particular issues related to women, sexual orientation, and gender identity. According to Sartore-Baldwin, theory "helps us understand the world in which we live. It represents an interwoven system of concepts, questions, ideas, beliefs, and relationships that provides the ability to better understand phenomena and guides our inquiries into why and how things happen the way they do." She points to several reasons why theory is important in the study of diversity and inclusion, including its importance in research, inquiry, and change efforts in teams and sport organizations. She notes, "Without theory, interventions could not be implemented and progress could not be made." As one who is interested in stigma and group relationships, Sartore-Baldwin has drawn from various social psychological theories in a number of her studies. In her teaching and research, Sartore-Baldwin seeks to create social change. She suggests that "theoretical models seeking to break down deeply imbedded hierarchical structures that result in vast disparities between and injustices among social groups have great utility in understanding the effects of diversity within the sport context."

THEORIES USED TO UNDERSTAND DIVERSITY

Given the primacy of theory in understanding diversity and inclusion, in the next section I offer an overview of the relevant theories in this area. In doing so, I classify them into three groups: managerial, sociological, and social psychological (see Exhibit 2.2). Before continuing, I would like to point out two caveats: First, I highlight the *main* theories used in diversity research and education; thus, there will necessarily be some that are excluded. Second, you will likely notice that the theories interrelate in some ways. This is increasingly common, as scholars are likely to draw from multiple disciplines to develop their frameworks (Chelladurai, 2013; Fink, 2013).

Managerial Theories

Managerial theories focus on how diversity and inclusion affect an organization's operations. Theoreticians might explore the relationships among employee diversity, inclusive environments, group processes (e.g., conflict, decision making), organizational outcomes (e.g., effectiveness, employee retention), and external

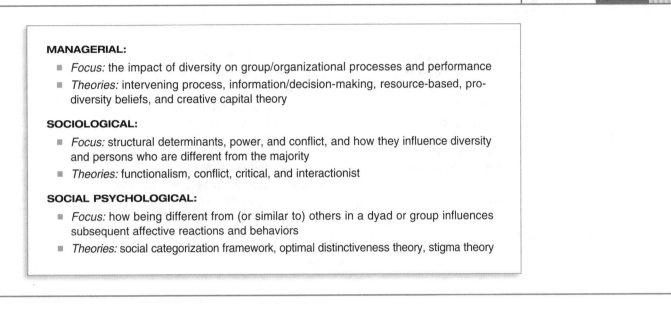

Theories of diversity. EXHIBIT 2.2

MANAGERIAL:

- *Focus:* the impact of diversity on group/organizational processes and performance
- *Theories:* intervening process, information/decision-making, resource-based, pro-diversity beliefs, and creative capital theory

SOCIOLOGICAL:

- *Focus:* structural determinants, power, and conflict, and how they influence diversity and persons who are different from the majority
- *Theories:* functionalism, conflict, critical, and interactionist

SOCIAL PSYCHOLOGICAL:

- *Focus:* how being different from (or similar to) others in a dyad or group influences subsequent affective reactions and behaviors
- *Theories:* social categorization framework, optimal distinctiveness theory, stigma theory

stakeholder evaluations (e.g., attraction to the workplace, perceptions of social responsibility).

Intervening process and information/decision-making theories

Although exceptions exist, most of the early managerial theories seemed to cast some diversity forms as beneficial to workplace functioning and others as not. Pelled's (1996) intervening process theory offers one example. She focused on diversity, conflict, and group effectiveness. In drawing from various examples, Pelled suggested that highly visible, "low job-related" differences—such as age, gender, and race—are associated with power differences and history-based frictions. When group members differ along these dimensions, there is likely to be emotional fighting, discord, and distrust, all of which will hurt group effectiveness. Other kinds of difference have less social relevance but are potentially associated with the idea generation and the varied perspectives that people bring to the group. Thus, educational diversity, functional background diversity, and tenure diversity are all expected to result in better decisions and improved group functioning. Exhibit 2.3 offers a summary.

Information/decision-making theory (Gruenfeld, Mannix, Williams, & Neale, 1996) draws from some of the same principles. As with intervening process theory, group member differences in education, tenure, and functional background are expected to result in improved group processes and effectiveness. Benefits manifest from the connections people have with others, and, hence, their access to information. For example, in a cross-departmental group examining effective hiring practices, marketing people can speak with their marketing colleagues across the country, just as communications people can access information from their colleagues. They then bring these unique inputs back to the group, resulting in better, more informed decisions.

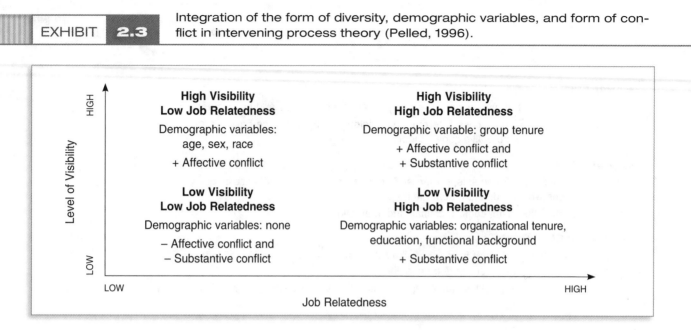

An underlying notion in both of these theories is the idea that some diversity forms (e.g., educational or functional diversity) can be good because they are associated with new sources of knowledge and understanding; on the other hand, other diversity forms (e.g., differences based on race, age, and gender) presumably result in negative outcomes because these differences have historically been sources of strife and conflict among different groups.

A sport manager could conceivably use these perspectives to argue for surface-level homogeneity while striving for informational diversity. Such a perspective is problematic on multiple fronts. First, it is socially and legally irresponsible to seek surface-level similarity in the workforce. Second, other managerial theoretical perspectives show the fallacy of such beliefs. Let's take a look at three examples.

Resource-based theory

First, Barney (1991) developed what he called the resource-based view of the firm. This theory holds that an organization has a competitive advantage over its counterparts when it possesses resources that are considered valuable, rare, and difficult to imitate. Drawing from this idea, various scholars have argued that diversity represents one such resource. As Richard, Murthi, and Ismail (2007) note, "The most valuable natural resource in the world is not oil, diamonds, or even gold; it is the diverse knowledge, abilities, and skills immediately available from cultural diversity" (p. 1213). Implicit in this argument is the notion that the organizational culture is one where divergent thoughts and perspectives are effectively leveraged—that is, the work environment is inclusive. We have drawn from these ideas to show that racial diversity in coaching staffs (a diversity dimension that is not considered "job related" in intervening process theory) is associated with greater success of college athletic teams (Cunningham & Sagas, 2004).

Pro-diversity theory

The second example comes from van Knippenberg and Schippers (2007), who suggested that people's diversity beliefs would influence the relationship between diversity and subsequent outcomes (see also van Knippenberg, Haslam, & Platow, 2007). When people hold pro-diversity beliefs, which is akin to holding inclusive attitudes, diversity will likely result in improved organizational outcomes. Absent such a mindset, the positive effects of diversity will probably be muted. I have observed this pattern across multiple studies set in the college athletics context. When athletic departments are marked by inclusiveness and pro-diversity attitudes, diversity is associated with improved group processes (Cunningham, 2008), creativity in the workplace (Cunningham, 2011a), and improved organizational effectiveness (Cunningham, 2009, 2011b). These patterns are consistent with the relationships depicted in Exhibit 2.1. Anderson (2011) has observed similar findings in his analysis of men's sport teams; specifically, in teams with inclusive cultures, the presence of gay athletes served to bring a team closer together and increase cohesion.

Creative capital theory

The final example comes from the field of geography and Florida's (2002, 2003, 2012) creative capital theory. Florida proposed that creative people are the drivers of regional economic development, such as the growth that has occurred in Austin, Texas, and Seattle, Washington. Creative people desire to live in communities where technological innovation is high, there is a concentration of highly educated people, and inclusion is the norm. One indicator of inclusiveness is the number of lesbian, gay, bisexual, and transgender (LGBT) individuals in the community. Florida reasons that prejudice against LGBT persons is commonplace in some areas, and that communities that embrace and celebrate sexual orientation and gender identity diversity are likely to be accepting of most other differences, too. We applied these principles in our own work and found support for this theory. Specifically, Melton and I (Cunningham & Melton, 2014) found that people were attracted to fitness clubs that advertised LGBT inclusiveness, and they believed such clubs were diverse across a number of dimensions. This perceived diversity was then associated with an increased desire to join the club.

Together, these theories offer a meaningful departure from the traditional managerial theory approach to diversity. Rather than seeing some diversity forms as helpful and others as not, recent theoretical advancements suggest that *all* diversity forms can be sources of learning, improved decision making, creativity, and overall effectiveness. The key to realizing these benefits is ensuring that the workplace culture is inclusive—one where people can freely express their various differences, allowing those around them to benefit from their perspectives. We will discuss strategies to create and sustain an inclusive work environment in the third section of the book.

Sociological Theories

In addition to considering diversity's effects on organizational operations, it is also useful to consider how issues such as power and conflict relate to diversity in society, the sport industry, and sport organizations. Therein lies the importance of sociological theories and their focus on macro issues, such as societal norms, institutional practices, and organizational policies. There are numerous theories under the sociological umbrella, and Eitzen and Sage (2009) suggest they can be grouped into four categories: functionalism, conflict theory, critical theories, and interactionist theory.

Functionalism

Functionalism focuses on how sport contributes to the positive attributes of society, such as persistence, cohesion, community, and cooperation, to name a few (Eitzen & Sage, 2009). From this perspective, sport can serve to reinforce desired values and norms in society. It does so by bringing people together, socializing youth, or serving as a model for how people can strive for and achieve success.

Street Soccer, a sport played around the world by people experiencing homelessness, provides a useful example. Street Soccer is a sport-for-development initiative, where the focus is on using sport and physical activity to generate meaningful social change (Lyras & Welty Peachey, 2011). This has occurred in many of its programs. For example, participants in the Australian Street Soccer program developed social bonding and strong connections with others and experienced increased self-esteem (Sherry & Strybosch, 2012). Other benefits of this program included increased community support for housing, vocational improvement, and education among people experiencing homelessness. In other cases, participants in the Street Soccer program developed strong community ties and increased their level of volunteerism (Welty Peachey, Borland, Lyras, & Cohen, 2013). We spend more time discussing ways of using sport to create positive social change in Chapter 15.

Conflict theory

Conflict theory offers a very different lens for viewing diversity and sport, as the focus is on issues related to disharmony, social unrest, and conflict (Eitzen & Sage, 2009). Political power, social structures, and wealth distribution are key issues. Drawing heavily from Karl Marx, this theory holds that people tend toward competition, not cooperation, resulting in discord among social groups. Those with political or economic capital use their privilege and status to subjugate others and maintain their own standing in society. Sometimes they do so explicitly, such as through a show of force. In other cases, the elite maintain their privilege through the use of more subtle avenues, such as through the media, schools, religious organizations, or other social institutions.

Let us examine the structure of professional sport as an example. Conflict theorists might argue that professional sport is arranged to privilege the rich and powerful at the expense of others. According to the Team Marketing Report's (n.d.) Fan Cost Index for the 2013–2014 season, it cost a family of four $326.60 to attend an NBA game and $459.65 to attend a National Football League (NFL) game. These costs must be juxtaposed against household incomes in the United States. According to the U.S. Census Bureau, the median household income in 2012 was $51,017, and earners in the top 5 percent had household incomes of $191,157 or more. As illustrated in Exhibit 2.4, purchasing season tickets is a much more feasible option for high-income individuals than it is for others. In fact, the average American household would have to spend 7 percent of its annual income to have NFL season tickets and 26 percent of its income for NBA season tickets. Thus, even though professional sport facilities are

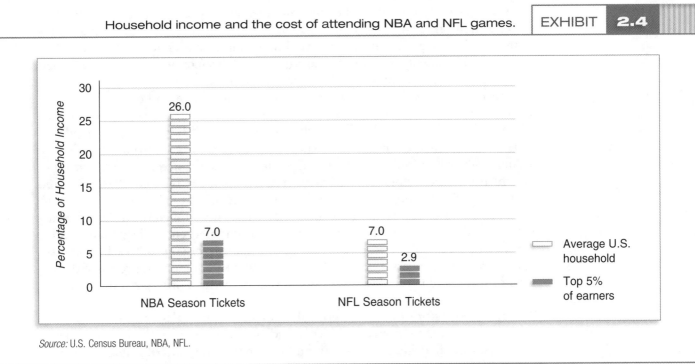

Source: U.S. Census Bureau, NBA, NFL.

routinely funded with public monies (Crompton & Howard, 2013), attending such events is usually only an option for the wealthy.

Critical theories

Critical theories focus on power and how it operates in organizations (Eitzen & Sage, 2009). These theories also incorporate concepts related to human agency, which refers to the way people make choices concerning their actions and behaviors. We highlight three critical theories here: hegemony theory, feminist theory, and critical race theory.

Hegemony theory. This theory focuses on the political, economic, and cultural patterns of power and dominance within society. Sage (1998) explains: "Hegemony theory sensitizes us to the role dominant groups play in American government, economic systems, mass media, education, and sport in maintaining and promoting their interests" (p. 10). Their cultural and social privilege offers opportunities and power to some groups at the expense of others, such as heterosexuals over LGBT individuals, men over women, rich over poor, and Whites over racial minorities. Researchers applying this perspective focus on how issues related to race, gender, sexual orientation, and class, as some examples, operate within sport and reproduce social norms and patterns. For instance, Cooky, Wachs, Messner, and Dworkin (2010) examined the media's responses to radio host Don Imus's pejorative comments directed toward the Rutgers University women's basketball team. The authors concluded that the media portrayals of the incident helped reinforce common narratives related to gender, race, and sexuality in America.

Feminist theory. Much of the scholarship in the area of gender, sport, and physical activity has adopted a critical feminist approach. Feminist theory makes two assumptions. First, people are gendered beings, and their experiences within sport and sport organizations are gendered in nature. This means that the cultural arrangements within society are such that men and traditional masculinities are valued more than women and femininity. Thus, girls and women have been oppressed within these settings, and the activities in which they thrive are seen as inferior.

Second, because girls and women have been oppressed and devalued in many contexts, there is a need to develop strategies to change those conditions (Eitzen & Sage, 2009). As a result of such change, women will become empowered and able to change their environments. Many scholars have drawn from these ideas to examine women in leadership positions, their access to those roles, and the manner in which their behaviors are evaluated (for a review, see Burton, 2015). Ely and Padavic (2007) also drew from a feminist theory perspective to review and critique the organizational research on sex differences. They questioned the utility of focusing on sex differences and instead correctly argued that attention be paid to gender, identities people hold, and power within and outside organizations. In doing so, they shifted the conversation from sex differences to the more appropriate discussion of social and psychological processes that perpetuate differentiation.

Critical race theory. The final critical theory we examine is critical race theory. This perspective grew from critical legal studies and has been applied in a number of contexts, including education, sport, and leisure (Hylton, 2009). Primacy is placed on race and racism and the role they play in people's experiences, organizational activities, and cultural arrangements. The theory rests on five key assumptions (see Singer, 2005; Tate, 1997):

1. Racism is endemic in society, deeply embedded in cultural norms, institutions, and laws.
2. There is value in drawing from several ways of knowing, including ideas from liberalism, feminism, and critical legal studies.
3. Civil rights legislation, while beneficial in many respects, is frequently undermined and implemented too slowly to make meaningful change.
4. Popular values embraced in society, such as meritocracy, color-blindness, and objectivity, are frequently perpetuated as a way of protecting the self-interests of society's elite.
5. Storytelling, context specificity, and relative truths allow for more complete ways of knowing and allow for the voices of the oppressed to be heard.

Scholars have increasingly drawn from this perspective within sport and leisure studies (e.g., Bimper, Harrison, & Clark, 2013; Erueti & Palmer, 2014). For example, Carter-Francique, Hart, and Steward (2013) used critical race theory to examine the experiences of African Americans participating in college sports, finding that the athletes experienced social isolation and alienation.

Thus far, we have discussed theories about the ways in which gender, race, social class, and sexual orientation influence sport and physical activity. Of course, people hold several identities at once, making ideas related to intersectionality all the more important. See the Alternatives Perspectives box for a deeper discussion of these issues.

Interactionist theory

Interactionist theory represents a departure from the sociological theories focusing on structural forces and instead seeks to understand how people give meaning to their lives. There is no single reality or truth, but people define these beliefs based on their lived experiences and interactions with others. Sociologists refer to this as the social construction of reality (Eitzen & Sage, 2009). The meanings we give to various diversity dimensions are socially constructed and mean different things to different people. As one example, some consider men who sleep with other men to be gay or bisexual; however, Anderson (2008), in a study of male cheerleaders, observed that men who identified as heterosexual would sleep with other men as a form of sexual recreation. Thus, what is considered gay, bisexual, or heterosexual depends on how the individuals making the determination socially construct their reality.

Social Psychological Theories

Social psychological theories, forming the final class of theories, focus on the individual in relation to others. In some cases, this might mean examining how being different from or similar to others in a particular context affects an individual's well-being. In other cases, scholars might attend to ways that individuals can express identities important to them in the workplace. Still others involve a focus on how different characteristics are devalued in society and, as a result, have a stigma attached to them. Each of these subjects falls under the broad umbrella of social psychology, and the underlying theoretical rationales for each are discussed here.

Social categorization framework

Much of the research examining how people experience work in groups draws from the social categorization framework. Two theories, social identity theory (Tajfel & Turner, 1979) and self-categorization theory (Turner, Hogg, Oakes, et al., 1987), contribute to this framework. According to these theories, people classify the self and others into groups. This is not necessarily a bad thing, as it helps us make sense of and quickly

ALTERNATIVE perspectives

Intersectionality. In many cases, people think about diversity along singular diversity dimensions. For example, we might consider how race, gender, or sexual orientation affects people's opportunities to be physically active. Although such an approach might be appropriate in some settings, people do not have just a single identity that influences their opportunities and experiences. Instead, they have multiple identities (i.e., multiple diversity dimensions) that operate simultaneously.

Crenshaw (1991) recognized as much when she developed the term *intersectionality*. Her original works focused on race and gender, as she noted various inequalities Black women experienced. Intersectionality brings to light the multiple forms of exclusion women of color experience due to various structural and systemic pressures. More recent iterations of the theory also bring to the forefront issues related to gender expression, sexual orientation, social class, and ability. Importantly, intersectionality scholars do not adhere to additive effects of various identities, but instead focus on the qualitative effects of multiple differences. As Watson and Scraton (2013) explain, "It moves beyond an additive approach that deals with fixed, static concepts of gender, race, class and looks at inequalities at the intersections and at how they are routed through each other with no single cause" (p. 37).

Pavlidis and Fullagar (2013) adopted an intersectionality perspective in their study of roller derby. This is a full-contact sport in which women roller skate around a circular track, with the aim of having a particular player on each team lap the opposing players. The other players on the team seek to hinder the opposing players' progress. Pavlidis and Fullagar observed that women were able to express various identities important to them while participating in the sport. This served to empower them in some instances, but, because of social pressures, it also resulted in negative affect. The authors concluded: "Roller derby exists as a fluid leisure space where passion and frustration, pride and shame, disgust and pleasure, anger and love, play out amidst everyday negotiations about women's sameness or difference" (p. 433).

categorize a very complex world. The classifications can be based on a number of attributes—such as baseball team fandom (e.g., Texas Rangers or New York Yankees), sexual orientation (e.g., lesbian or heterosexual), and many others. People use this process to define themselves in terms of a social identity. Once the categorizations are made, people engage in social comparisons, and they do so automatically. Thus, they create "us" and "them" distinctions, with the "us" representing similar others and the "them" representing those who are different.

These two processes—social categorization and social comparison—result in intergroup bias (Ferguson & Porter, 2013). In this case, in-group members (the "us") are viewed positively, afforded more trust, and given more help than are out-group members (the "them"). The end result is stereotyping and intergroup bias or prejudice. This sequencing is important because categorization is not negative itself; again, it is a natural process that helps us navigate our social worlds. It is when the categorization results in stereotyping and bias that the negative effects of being different come to light.

The social categorization framework has been instrumental in understanding how groups work and the effects of diversity within these settings. For example, Sartore (2006) drew from the social categorization framework to develop her arguments related to discrimination in the performance evaluation process. She suggested that demographic dissimilarity between (for example) an athletic director and a coach would likely result in categorization and stereotyping, which would, in turn, negatively affect the coach's performance evaluation. Over time, this pattern could result in decreased motivation and performance by the coach. Exhibit 2.5 provides an illustrative summary of this relationship.

EXHIBIT **2.5**   The effects of performance appraisal bias.

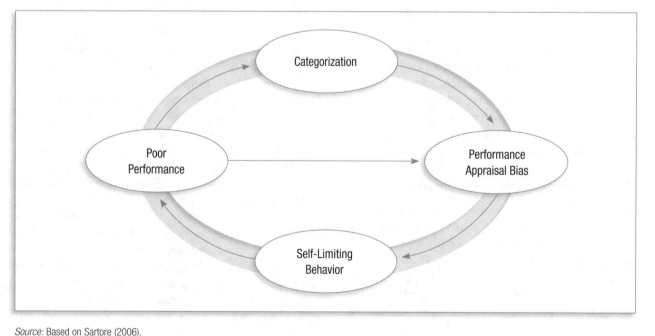

Source: Based on Sartore (2006).

Optimal distinctiveness theory

Brewer (1991) expanded on the original social categorization framework to develop her optimal distinctiveness theory. As discussed in Chapter 1, this theory holds that people have two potentially contradictory needs: (a) to express their individuated self and have their identities recognized by others, and (b) to feel a sense of belonging in a larger group. When both of these needs are met, optimal distinctiveness is achieved.

This theory has two primary implications for our understanding of diversity and inclusion. The first comes in our discussions of intergroup bias and stereotyping. From an optimal distinctiveness perspective, if the needs are not met at desired levels, then intergroup bias is likely to occur (Brewer, 2007). For example, when people perceive a threat to their distinctiveness, they are likely to engage in activities that highlight the differences between in-groups and out-groups.

The second implication comes in the area of inclusion. Recall from Chapter 1 that inclusion refers to the degree to which employees are free to express their individuated self and have a sense of workplace connectedness and belonging. Clearly, optimal distinctiveness informed this perspective, as it highlights the two needs people have. From a managerial standpoint, this means that teams and organizations should be designed in ways that allow for personal expression while also engendering a sense of attachment.

Stigma theory

Stigma refers to "an attribute that produces a social identity that is devalued or derogated by persons within a particular culture at a particular point in time" (Paetzold, Dipboye, & Elsbach, 2008, p. 186). Goffman (1963) penned what is widely considered to be the foundational book in this area. He suggested that people would experience stigma if they had a moral shortcoming, possessed some sort of physical abnormality or imperfection, or had been born with characteristics that were devalued. Jones, Farina, Hastorf, and their colleagues (1984) later expanded on Goffman's work to classify stigmas related to disability along six dimensions (see Exhibit 2.6). It is important to note that stigmas are socially constructed and context specific. What

Dimensions of stigma. | EXHIBIT 2.6

Stigmas can be classified along six dimensions:

1. *Disruptiveness,* or the degree to which the disability influences social interactions or communications among people.
2. *Origin,* or the degree to which one is seen as responsible for her or his disability.
3. *Aesthetic qualities,* or the extent to which the disability negatively influences one's attractiveness.
4. *Course,* or the extent to which the disability is transient or permanent.
5. *Concealability,* or the degree to which the disability can be plainly observed by others.
6. *Peril,* or the degree to which one's disability could cause others harm.

Source: Jones et al. (1984).

ALTERNATIVE perspectives

Ways of Studying Diversity. In addition to examining the theories used to understand diversity and inclusion, we can also explore ways in which scholars study these topics. Researchers generally employ either the categorical, compositional, relational, or managerial approach (Cunningham & Fink, 2006; Tsui & Gutek, 1999).

- **Categorical approach.** Scholars who adopt a categorical approach compare the experiences and behaviors of one demographic group to those of another. For example, there is some evidence that working-class people who are poor spend less time engaging in physical activity than do their more affluent counterparts. Activity levels and motivation to lead a healthier life were associated with lower body mass index (BMI) scores (Peterson, Dubowitz, Stoddard, et al., 2007). Persons adopting a categorical perspective generally view demographic characteristics as important cues about how people will behave, their attitudes toward others, and how they will be treated in sport organizations. This approach is popular among scholars interested in studying issues related to race, gender, age, social class, and sexual orientation, and they will frequently draw from sociological theories to develop their arguments. While prevalent, the categorical approach does have limitations. Most notably, this research approach presumes that people from one group (e.g., women) generally have the same attitudes or experiences and can, therefore, be compared to members of another group (e.g., men). While this assumption might hold in some cases, there are many others where considerable variance exists in group members' attitudes. In fact, in some instances variance within a group is greater than that between groups.

- **Compositional approach.** When adopting a compositional perspective, scholars focus on social units, such as work groups, athletic teams, or physical education classes. The interest here is in the characteristics of the group and how they influence subsequent processes and outcomes. For example, Waltemyer and I (2009) collected data from National Hockey League (NHL) teams and found that as nationality diversity increased, assists decreased. We reasoned this was due to communication patterns among players, such that language and cultural differences might impede coordination among teammates. The compositional approach has value because it allows scholars to focus on how characteristics of a group or team,

as a whole, affect important processes and outcomes. Scholars will frequently draw from managerial theories to develop their research questions and design their studies. This approach also has limitations. First, by focusing solely on the group, this approach disregards the influence of individuals. Second, it assumes that differences affect all groups similarly, and this might not be the case. For instance, in our study, it was possible that some of the diverse hockey teams had overcome their language differences by playing together for a number of years. We did not examine this possibility.

- **Relational approach.** The relational approach to the study of diversity and inclusion serves to combine the categorical and compositional approaches. Here, the focus is on the individual in relation to others or the group. Scholars draw from social psychological theories to develop their hypotheses. The underlying premise is that being different from others will affect an individual's experiences, attitudes, and behaviors. As one research example, Jackson, Harwood, and Grove (2010) collected data from athlete dyads (i.e., people who teamed with another person to compete against other dyads, such as in doubles tennis) and found that when members of a dyad differed in their goals for the competition, their level of relationship commitment and relationship satisfaction suffered. As with the other perspectives, the relational approach is not without its limitations. The main drawback is that it focuses solely on individual characteristics without considering contextual factors.

- **Managerial approach.** Finally, researchers adopting the managerial approach seek to understand how administrators and coaches can create inclusive units and capitalize on the benefits of diversity. Scholars draw from any of the three classes of theories to develop their arguments. To illustrate, Spaaj, Farquharson, Magee, and their colleagues (2014) conducted interviews with coaches, administrators, and staff at Australian sport clubs to examine how those clubs managed diversity. The authors observed a discrepancy between stated policies and practice. Also, the clubs focused on the business case for diversity rather than a social obligation, which resulted in exclusionary practices. As this example demonstrates, a managerial approach allows scholars to understand how diversity and inclusion affect both opportunities for individuals and the functioning of the workplace. There are limitations to this theory, as well. One is that researchers taking this approach tend to focus on describing diversity in organizations rather than developing strategies managers, educators, and coaches can use to better the organization. When strategies are suggested, they usually have not been empirically tested. A key component of a strategy's validity evidence is testability. If a strategy cannot be tested, its ultimate utility is questionable.

DIVERSITY IN THE FIELD

Stigma of being lesbian, gay, bisexual, or transgender.
In July 2014, Ian Thorpe announced he was gay. The news was noteworthy on several fronts. First, Thorpe is a highly decorated Australian swimming star, having won five Olympic gold medals. He had denied that he was gay for over a decade. Doing so, he said, resulted in depression, alcoholism, and attempted suicide. Over time, he came to see the benefits of disclosing his true sexual orientation. In an interview with Sir Michael Parkinson, Thorpe noted, "The lie became so big that I didn't want people to question my integrity."

Thorpe's long-standing denial of his sexual orientation caused some observers, such as Matt Peacock, to question whether identifying as lesbian, gay, bisexual, or transgender was a stigmatizing characteristic within the sport context. For instance, Thorpe indicated that, by denying his gay identity, he "was trying to be what I thought was the right athlete by other people's standards. . . . Part of me didn't know if Australia wanted its champion to be gay." Recent data support Thorpe's hesitation. In a 2014 study sponsored by the Australian Sports Commission, 84 percent of LGBT Australian athletes surveyed indicated they had heard anti-LGBT language, 28 percent had witnessed bullying, 28 percent had observed social exclusion, and 13 percent had seen physical abuse toward LGBT individuals.

These data, when coupled with Thorpe's commentary, suggest LGBT status might be a stigmatizing condition in the Australian sport context. Work from Eric Anderson and others shows that attitudes toward LGBT individuals have improved considerably over time, but there is still much work to be done.

Sources: Anderson, E. (2011). *Inclusive masculinity: The changing nature of masculinities.* London: Routledge. / Buzinski, J. (2014, July 13). Ian Thorpe: "I'm comfortable saying I'm a gay man." *Outsports.com.* Retrieved from www.outsports.com/2014/7/13/5895025/ian-thorpe-im-comfortable-saying-im-a-gay-man. / Buzinski, J. (2014, July 15). Gay Australian athletes report widespread homophobia. *Outsports.com.* Retrieved from www.outsports.com/2014/7/15/5902705/gay-australia-athletes-report-widespread-homophobia-bingham-cup. / Peacock, M. (2014, July 14). Ian Thorpe's coming out raises questions about homosexuality and stigma in sport. *ABC.* Retrieved from www.abc.net.au/news/2014-07-14/thorpes-coming-out-sheds-light-on-gay-stigma-in-sport/5596482.

is stigmatizing in one setting will likely not be in another. As one example, being a sexual minority might be stigmatizing in some areas of the United States (e.g., the South) but not in others (e.g., the Northwest). The Diversity in the Field box above offers a broader discussion of the potential stigma associated with being LGBT.

People who possess a stigmatized characteristic frequently have poor work experiences (Hebl & King, 2013). They are likely to underperform on tests when they are mindful of their stigmatizing condition. They also experience discrimination: relative to their peers, people with a stigmatized characteristic are likely to have poorer letters of recommendation written for them, experience more bias in the selection process, lack opportunities for training and development, and receive less pay. They also face subtle forms of discrimination, as people smile at them less, use fewer words when conversing, and are generally less friendly. As we will discuss throughout the text, these patterns are observed across a number of diversity dimensions, including race, ability, weight, sexual orientation, gender identity, and religious beliefs, among others.

chapter SUMMARY

This chapter focused on various theories and how they can be used to understand diversity and inclusion in sport organizations. As the Diversity Challenge illustrated, knowledge of the basic theories that undergird diversity is crucial in fully understanding this complex topic. The theories we use to study diversity influence the questions we ask, the focus of our examination, and the way we see the world in general.

After reading the chapter, you should be able to do the following:

1. **Explain what a theory is and why theory is important in understanding diversity and inclusion.**

   Theory provides "a statement of constructs and their relationships to one another that explain[s] how, when, why, and under what conditions phenomena take place" (Cunningham, 2013, p. 1). Theory is important because of its practicality and its utility in helping managers understand their complex social surroundings.

2. **Discuss the different classes of theory used to understand diversity and inclusion.**

   Three classes of theory are used to study diversity: managerial, sociological, and social psychological. Managerial theories focus on the impact of diversity on organizational outcomes. Sociological theories focus on structural issues, power, and conflict, and how these factors influence diversity and persons who differ from the majority. Finally, social psychological theories focus on how being dissimilar from others in social settings influences an individual's affect and behavior.

3. **Discuss how the different theories can be applied to diversity issues within organizations for sport and physical activity.**

   Managerial theories illustrate the need to recognize how the various types of diversity influence work- and team-related outcomes. The sociological theories require managers to ask questions about how organizational factors, such as power structure, influence the experiences of persons who differ from the majority. Finally, social psychological theories suggest that managers should pay attention to the composition of work groups and employee–customer relationships, as surface- and deep-level differences within these relationships can lead to negative outcomes.

QUESTIONS for discussion

1. Some readers may express an aversion to a discussion of theory. Prior to studying this chapter, what were your attitudes toward theory? Identify several benefits of studying theory that you learned from the chapter.
2. One definition of theory is presented in the chapter, but there are many ways to think about it. How would you define theory in your own words?
3. How do issues of power in organizations influence people who differ from the majority?
4. Social psychological theories suggest that being different from others in a dyad or group will negatively influence subsequent affective reactions and behaviors. How might a manager reduce these negative effects?

5. Four approaches to the study of diversity were identified. Which approach makes the most sense to you? Why?

learning ACTIVITIES

1. Some people believe that students should not be taught theory, because it has limited applicability to workplace settings. Divide into groups and argue the pros and cons of understanding theory and theoretical principles as they apply to diversity in sport organizations.

2. Visit a local sport organization and ask the manager, employees, and athletes how diversity and inclusion impact the workplace, group dynamics, and overall outcomes for the organization. Then, compare their responses with the theoretical tenets outlined in this chapter.

3. Visit your school's athletic department and ask administrators and student-athletes how diversity and inclusion impact the department, group dynamics, and outcomes. Compare their responses with the theoretical tenets outlined in this chapter.

WEB resources

■ **Gender and Diversity in Organizations,** http://division.aomonline.org/gdo/

A division of the Academy of Management; provides diversity resources related to research and teaching.

■ **Laboratory for Diversity in Sport,** www.diversityinsport.com

Provides overviews of research initiatives, as well as other diversity-related online sources.

■ **North American Society for the Sociology of Sport,** www.nasss.com

Provides a resource center and directory of experts in several diversity-related areas.

reading RESOURCES

Giulianotti, R. (2004). *Sport and modern social theorists*. Basingstoke, UK: Palgrave MacMillan.

Examines the contributions of major social theorists to our critical understanding of modern sport; includes contributions from Marx, Weber, Durkheim, Adorno, Gramsci, Habermas, Merton, C. Wright Mills, Goffman, Giddens, Elias, Bourdieu, and Foucault.

Sport Management Review, Volume 16, Issue 1.

Contains an exchange among various scholars about the utility of theory in the field, how it is developed, and how it can be applied in different settings.

Van Lange, P. A., Krulanski, A. W., & Higgins, E. T. (Eds.) (2011). *The handbook of theories of social psychology* (Vol. 2). Thousand Oaks, CA: Sage.

Contains chapters of direct relevance to diversity and inclusion, including chapters focusing on implicit theories, social identity theory, optimal distinctiveness theory, and others.

REFERENCES

Anderson, E. (2008). Being masculine is not about who you sleep with...: Heterosexual athletes contesting masculinity and the one-time rule of homosexuality. *Sex Roles, 58,* 104–115.

Anderson, E. (2011). Updating the outcome: Gay athletes, straight teams, and coming out at the end of the decade. *Gender & Society, 25,* 250–268.

Bacharach, S. B. (1989). Organizational theories: Some criteria for evaluation. *Academy of Management Review, 14,* 496–515.

Barney, J. (1991). Firm resources and sustained competitive advantage. *Journal of Management, 17,* 99–120.

Bimper, A. Y., Jr., Harrison, L., Jr., & Clark, L. (2013). Diamonds in the rough: Examining the case of successful black male athletes in college sport. *Journal of Black Psychology, 39,* 107–130.

Brewer, M. B. (1991). The social self: On being the same and different at the same time. *Personality and Social Psychology Bulletin, 17,* 475–482.

Brewer, M. B. (2007). The importance of being *we*: Human nature and intergroup relations. *American Psychologist, 62,* 728–738.

Burton, L. J. (2015). Underrepresentation of women in sport leadership: A review of research. *Sport Management Review, 18,* 155–165.

Carter-Francique, A., Hart, A., & Steward, A. (2013). Black college athletes' perceptions of academic success and the role of social support. *Journal of Intercollegiate Sport, 6,* 231–246.

Chelladurai, P. (2013). A personal journey in theorizing in sport management. *Sport Management Review, 16,* 22–28.

Cooky, C., Wachs, F. L., Messner, M., & Dworkin, S. L. (2010). It's not about the game: Don Imus, race, class, gender, and sexuality in contemporary media. *Sociology of Sport Journal, 27,* 139–159.

Crenshaw, K. (1991). Mapping the margins: Intersectionality, identity politics, and violence against women of color. *Stanford Law Review, 43,* 1241–1299.

Crompton, J. L., & Howard, D. R. (2013). Costs: The rest of the economic impact story. *Journal of Sport Management, 27,* 379–392.

Cunningham, G. B. (2008). Commitment to diversity and its influence on athletic department outcomes. *Journal of Intercollegiate Sport, 1,* 176–201.

Cunningham, G. B. (2009). The moderating effect of diversity strategy on the relationship between racial diversity and organizational performance. *Journal of Applied Social Psychology, 36,* 1445–1460.

Cunningham, G. B. (2011a). Creative work environments in sport organizations: The influence of sexual orientation diversity and commitment to diversity. *Journal of Homosexuality, 58,* 1041–1045.

Cunningham, G. B. (2011b). The LGBT advantage: Examining the relationship among sexual orientation diversity, diversity strategy, and performance. *Sport Management Review, 14,* 453–461.

Cunningham, G. B. (2013). Theory and theory development in sport management. *Sport Management Review, 16,* 1–4.

Cunningham, G. B., & Fink, J. S. (2006). Diversity issues in sport and leisure: Introduction to a special issue. *Journal of Sport Management, 20,* 455–465.

Cunningham, G. B., & Melton, E. N. (2014). Signals and cues: LGBT inclusive advertising and consumer attraction. *Sport Marketing Quarterly, 23,* 37–46.

Cunningham, G. B., & Sagas, M. (2004). People make the difference: The influence of human capital and diversity on team performance. *European Sport Management Quarterly, 4,* 3–22.

Cunningham, G. B., Fink, J. S., & Doherty, A. J. (in press). Developing theory in sport management. In G. B. Cunningham, J. S. Fink, & A. J. Doherty (Eds.), *Routledge handbook of theory in sport management.* London, UK: Routledge.

Doherty, A. (2013). Investing in sport management: The value of good theory. *Sport Management Review, 16,* 5–11.

Eitzen, D. S., & Sage, G. H. (2009). *Sociology of North American sport* (8th ed.). Boulder, CO: Paradigm Publishers.

Ely, R., & Padavic, I. (2007). A feminist analysis of organizational research on sex differences. *Academy of Management Review, 32,* 1121–1143.

Erueti, B., & Palmer, F. R. (2014). Te Whariki Tuakiri (the identity mat): Maori elite athletes and the expression of ethno-cultural identity in global sport. *Sport in Society, 17,* 1061–1075.

Ferdman, B. M. (2014). The practice of inclusion in diverse organizations. In B. M. Ferdman & B. R. Deane (Eds.), *Diversity at work: The practice of inclusion* (pp. 3–54). San Francisco: Jossey-Bass.

Ferguson, M., & Porter, S. C. (2013). An examination of categorization processes in organizations: The root of intergroup bias and a route to prejudice reduction. In Q. M. Roberson (Ed.), *The Oxford handbook of diversity and work* (pp. 98–114). New York: Oxford.

Fink, J. S. (2013). Theory development in sport management: My experience and other considerations. *Sport Management Review, 16,* 17–21.

Florida, R. (2002). The economic geography of talent. *Annals of the Association of American Geographers, 92,* 743–755.

Florida, R. (2003). Cities and the creative class. *City & Community, 2,* 3–19.

Florida, R. (2012). *The rise of the creative class, revisited.* New York: Basic Books.

Goffman, E. (1963). *Stigma: Notes on the management of spoiled identity.* New York: Simon & Schuster.

Gruenfeld, D. H., Mannix, E. A., Williams, K. Y., & Neale, M. A. (1996). Group composition and decision making: How member familiarity and information distribution affect process and performance. *Organizational Behavior and Human Decision Processes, 67,* 1–15.

Hebl, M. R., & King, E. B. (2013). The social and psychological experience of stigma. In Q. M. Roberson (Ed.), *The Oxford handbook of diversity and work* (pp. 115–131). New York: Oxford University Press.

Hylton, K. (2009). *"Race" and sport: Critical race theory.* New York: Routledge.

Irwin, R. L., & Ryan, T. D. (2013). Get real: Using engagement with practice to advance theory transfer and production. *Sport Management Review, 16,* 12–16.

Jackson, B., Harwood, C. G., & Grove, J. R. (2010). On the same page in sporting dyads: Does dissimilarity on 2 x 2 achievement goal constructs impair relationship functioning? *Journal of Sport & Exercise Psychology, 32,* 805–827.

Jones, E., Farina, A., Hastorf, A., Markus, H., Miller, D., Scott, R., & de Sales-French, R. (1984). *Social stigma: The psychology of marked relationships.* San Francisco: W. H. Freeman.

Kerlinger, F. N., & Lee, H. B. (2000). *Foundations of behavioral research* (4th ed.). Fort Worth, TX: Harcourt College Publishers.

Lyras, A., & Welty Peachey, J. (2011). Integrating sport-for-development theory and praxis. *Sport Management Review, 14,* 311–326.

Paetzold, R. L., Dipboye, R. L., & Elsbach, K. D. (2008). A new look at stigmatization in and of organizations. *Academy of Management Review, 33,* 186–193.

Pavlidis, A., & Fullagar, S. (2013). Narrating the multiplicity of 'Derby Grrrl': Exploring intersectionality and the dynamics of affect in Roller Derby. *Leisure Sciences, 35,* 422–437.

Pelled, L. H. (1996). Demographic diversity, conflict, and work group outcomes: An intervening process theory. *Organization Science, 7,* 615–631.

Peterson, K. E., Dubowitz, T., Stoddard, A. M., Troped, P. J., Sorensen, G., & Emmons, K. M. (2007). Social context of physical activity and weight status in working class populations. *Journal of Physical Activity and Health, 4,* 381–396.

Richard, O. C., Murthi, B. P. S., & Ismail, K. (2007). The impact of racial diversity on intermediate and long-term performance: The moderating role of environmental context. *Strategic Management Journal, 28,* 1213–1233.

Sage, G. H. (1998). *Power and ideology in American sport: A critical perspective* (2nd ed.). Champaign, IL: Human Kinetics.

Sartore, M. L. (2006). Categorization, performance appraisals, and self-limiting behavior: The impact on current and future performance. *Journal of Sport Management, 20,* 535–553.

Sherry, E., & Strybosch, V. (2012). A kick in the right direction: Longitudinal outcomes of the Australian Community Street Soccer Program. *Soccer & Society, 13,* 495–509.

Singer, J. N. (2005). Addressing epistemological racism in sport management research. *Journal of Sport Management, 19,* 464–479.

Spaaj, R., Farquharson, K., Magee, J., Jeanes, R., Lusher, D., & Gorman, S. (2014). A fair game for all? How community sports clubs in Australia deal with diversity. *Journal of Sport & Social Issues, 38,* 346–365.

Tajfel, H., & Turner, J. C. (1979). An integrative theory of intergroup conflict. In W. G. Austin & S. Worchel (Eds.), *The social psychology of intergroup relations* (pp. 33–47). Monterey, CA: Brooks/Cole.

Tate, W. F. (1997). Critical race theory and education: History, theory, and implications. In M. Apple (Ed.), *Review in research education 2* (pp. 191–243). Washington, DC: American Educational Research Association.

Team Marketing Report (n.d.). Fan cost index. Retrieved from https://www.teammarketing.com/btSubscriptions/fancostcontroller/index

Tsui, A. S., & Gutek, B. A. (1999). *Demographic differences in organizations: Current research and future directions.* New York: Lexington Books.

Turner, J., Hogg, M. A., Oakes, P. J., Reicher, S. D., & Wetherell, M. S. (1987). *Rediscovering the social group: A self-categorization theory.* Oxford, UK: B. Blackwell.

van Knippenberg, D., De Drue, C. K. W., & Homan, A. C. (2004). Work group diversity and group performance: An integrative model and research agenda. *Journal of Applied Psychology, 89,* 1008–1022.

van Knippenberg, D., Haslam, S. A., & Platow, M. J. (2007). Unity through diversity: Value-in-diversity beliefs, work group diversity, and group identification. *Group Dynamics: Theory, Research, and Practice, 11,* 207–222.

van Knippenberg, D., & Schippers, M. C. (2007). Work group diversity. *Annual Review of Psychology, 58,* 515–541.

Waltemyer, D. S., & Cunningham, G. B. (2009). The influence of team diversity on assists and team performance among National Hockey League teams. *International Journal of Sport Management, 10,* 391–409.

Watson, B., & Scraton, S. J. (2013). Leisure studies and intersectionality. *Leisure Studies, 32,* 35–47.

Welty Peachey, J., Borland, J., Lyras, A., & Cohen, A. (2013). Sport for social change: Investigating the impact of the SSUSA Cup. *ICHPER-SD Journal of Research, 8,* 3–11.

Stereotypes, Prejudice, and Discrimination

LEARNING objectives

After studying this chapter, you should be able to:

- Define and discuss the different forms of bias, including stereotyping, prejudice, and discrimination.
- Discuss the theoretical underpinnings used to explain bias in sport.
- Discuss the effects of bias on subsequent outcomes.

DIVERSITY CHALLENGE

In February of 2014, Ray Rice, a player on the Baltimore Ravens of the NFL, struck his fiancée until she was unconscious. Video footage showed Rice dragging the semiconscious woman from a hotel elevator, her feet dragging as he pulled her across the floor. As a result of the incident, Rice pleaded not guilty to third-degree aggravated assault. He avoided a criminal trial by participating in an intervention process later in 2014.

In response to the event, the NFL suspended Rice for two games to start the season. He was also fined over $500,000. Rice was still able to participate in the team's training camp and preseason activities.

While a half-million-dollar fine is substantial, many observers felt the penalty was too lenient. This could be seen, for example, in people's reactions on social media. Sports writer Alicia Jessop compared the fines for beating one's wife (two games) and smoking marijuana (four games). The website Awful Announcing tweeted: "The NFL suspends Ray Rice 2 games for assaulting his fiancée. The NFL sus-

pends Terrelle Pryor 5 games over free tattoos." Former NFL star Jim Trotter tweeted: "I wonder if @nflcommish would've been as lenient if it had been his daughter or sister laying unconscious outside the elevator."

As these comments illustrate, various stakeholders saw Ray Rice's punishment as insufficient. Television host Keith Olbermann took this perspective further, arguing that the punishment reflected discrimination toward women in sport. In a segment on his ESPN2 program, Olbermann offered a long list of language, behaviors, and organizational practices that all signal a devaluing of women in sport. He then argued, "By some tiny amount each one of those things lowers the level of basic human respect for women in sports. And sooner or later, there are so many tiny amounts that the level of basic human respect is gone altogether. . . . Eventually after all the b-words and ho comments and penis remarks and nudity demands and waitress jokes, the most powerful national sports league in the world can then get away with suspending a wife-beater for just two games."

Rice's actions and the subsequent penalty are both deplorable. And, as Olbermann notes, this is just one of many examples where women have faced prejudice, discrimination, and a general devaluing within the sport context.

Sources: Matthews, C. (2014, July 25). Keith Olbermann's powerful speech about lack of respect for women in sports is a must watch. *Huffington Post.* Retrieved from: http://www.huffingtonpost.com/2014/07/25/keith-oblermann-nfl-sexism-ray-rice_n_5621973.html. / Ray Rice suspended 2 games. (July 25, 2014). *ESPN.* Retrieved from: http://espn.go.com/nfl/story/_/id/11257692/ray-rice-baltimore-ravens-suspended-2-games.

CHALLENGE   REFLECTION

1. In your estimation, was Rice justly penalized?

2. Does the Rice penalty reflect a devaluing of women in sport that operates at a broader, deeper level?

3. How prevalent are prejudice and discrimination, of any kind, in sport and physical activity?

E ven 50 years after major civil rights legislation (e.g., Civil Rights Act of 1964) and gender equity mandates (Title IX of the Education Amendments of 1972) were passed, gender bias persists. The Diversity Challenge focuses on gender bias in the NFL, but the problem is rampant throughout sport. The same charge can be placed for other prejudices, such as those against lesbian, gay, bisexual, and transgender individuals; racial minorities; religious minorities; persons with disabilities; and all others who are different from the typical majority member. These patterns not only leave a dark stain on the sport industry but also hurt individuals, diminish the experiences they have in sport, and reduce the likelihood of future participation.

The purpose of this chapter is to explore the issue of differential treatment in the sport industry. In doing so, I highlight what Cuddy, Fiske, and Glick (2008) refer to as the three components of bias: *stereotypes*, which exist in the cognitive domain; *prejudice*, which operates in the affective area; and *discrimination*, which is a behavioral dimension. See Exhibit 3.1.

EXHIBIT   3.1   The three components of bias.

1. **Stereotypes:** Within the cognitive domain; represent the beliefs about the attributes, skills, and attitudes members of a certain group possess.

2. **Prejudice:** Within the affective domain; the differential evaluation of a group or an individual based on her or his group membership.

3. **Discrimination:** Within the behavioral domain; negative treatment of individuals due to their group membership.

STEREOTYPES

Stereotypes are "the traits that we view as characteristic of social groups, or of individual members of those groups, and particularly those that differentiate groups from each other" (Stangor, 2009, p. 2). They include beliefs we have about different people, their attributes, and their skills. Stereotypes are a key cause of bias and poor treatment of people who differ from the self. They are also temporally and socially bound; the notions people have of others can and do shift over time, varying from one context to another.

Stereotypes represent a collection of beliefs we have about others. Stereotypes become operationalized in various ways. The stereotype content model suggests that stereotypes exist along two domains: warmth and competence (Cuddy et al., 2008; Fiske & Tablante, 2015). Warmth includes several evaluations, such as how moral, trustworthy, friendly, and sincere an individual or group is. Competence captures judgments related to people's confidence, intelligence, ability to execute tasks, and creativity. People develop ideas about how well others embody these characteristics, and they form judgments and display behavioral tendencies based on these assessments. These dual domains of stereotyping allow for what Cuddy and colleagues (2008) refer to as ambivalent stereotypes: a person might consider members of a group to be strong in one domain but weak in another. The warmth dimension generally is more prominent than the competence dimension in how people perceive others (Fiske & Tablante, 2015).

In Exhibit 3.2, I draw from Fiske's work (Cuddy et al., 2008; Fiske & Tablante, 2015) to offer an illustrative summary of these dynamics. The first quadrant includes people who are believed to be warm but lacking in competence. Researchers have found that adults in the United States consider persons with disabilities and the elderly, among others, to belong in this category. These evaluations are likely to elicit feelings of pity. The second quadrant includes people who have low ratings in both warmth and competence, and adults in the United States generally place the poor, people from the Middle East, and people on welfare, among others, in this quadrant. Disapproval is usually expressed toward these individuals. The third quadrant includes people who are rated as low in warmth but high in competence—a combination usually prompting feelings of envy. Adults in the United States generally place Asians, Jews, and the rich, among others, in this category. Finally, the fourth quadrant includes people who are regarded as both competent and warm. This category usually includes in-group members, persons with privilege in society, and those held in high esteem, and adults in the United States tend to place Christians, middle-class individuals, and housewives in this quadrant. These stereotypes usually elicit feelings of admiration. While much of the research has been conducted in the United States, evidence suggests that these evaluations develop across the world; of course, the individuals placed within each quadrant differ, given the social construction of stereotypes (Cuddy et al., 2008).

The influences of stereotypes are seen throughout sport in a variety of ways, one of which is in feelings about who is suitable for leadership positions. There is some evidence that mismatches between stereotypical roles for members of certain groups and the context in which we find those individuals can trigger negative reactions toward the individual. This is particularly the case when it comes to women in leadership roles (Burton, Grappendorf, & Henderson, 2011; Rudman & Phelan,

EXHIBIT 3.2   Stereotypes based on warmth and competence.

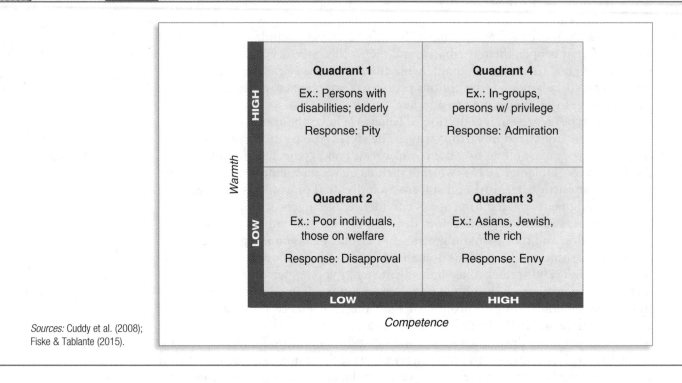

Quadrant 1

Ex.: Persons with
disabilities; elderly

Response: Pity

Quadrant 4

Ex.: In-groups,
persons w/ privilege

Response: Admiration

Quadrant 2

Ex.: Poor individuals,
those on welfare

Response: Disapproval

Quadrant 3

Ex.: Asians, Jewish,
the rich

Response: Envy

HIGH   LOW   Warmth

LOW   HIGH

Competence

Sources: Cuddy et al. (2008);
Fiske & Tablante (2015).

2008). People might hold positive attitudes toward women leading rugby clubs, but these attitudes would not be as positive as those held toward men in the same role—the differences result from who would stereotypically be expected to serve in that role. This example shows that (1) prejudice can result even absent negative attitudes, and (2) prejudice is contextual in nature and, therefore, more subtle than commonly thought (Eagly & Diekman, 2005).

Of equal importance, evidence also indicates that most people take steps to overcome preconceptions they might harbor, if social norms dictate that they do so. As Duguid and Thomas-Hunt (2015) note, this information is particularly relevant when discussing strategies to reduce stereotyping and prejudice. People will generally adhere to social norms and expectations of others (see also Goldstein, Cialdini, & Griskevicius, 2008), and this is also the case with stereotyping. As Duguid and Thomas-Hunt observed across a number of experimental studies, participants were more likely to stereotype when told of its prevalence, relative to when they were told that stereotyping was rare. However, when participants were told that many people sought to overcome their stereotype preconceptions, they did so as well. This pattern held for both explicit and subtler forms of stereotyping.

Stereotypes can also influence sport performance and physical activity levels. The stereotype threat model (Steele, 1997) speaks to the link between stereotypes and performance. Within sport, common stereotypes include that African Americans are better athletes than Whites and that men outperform women. Sport performance suffers when people are mindful of these stereotypes, relative to when they are not (e.g., Hively & El-Alayli, 2014). Similarly, the degree to which people endorse stereotypes toward themselves can affect their own physical activity levels. A study of retired persons living in France showed that physical activity levels were (1) positively associated with endorsement of stereotypes about the benefits of exercise and aging, and (2) negatively associated with internalization of stereotypes about the risks of elderly adults being physically active (Emile, Chalabaev, Stephan, et al., 2014).

Thus far, we have discussed examples of stereotypes based on single dimensions of diversity. As noted in Chapter 2, though, people will frequently respond to multiple diversity dimensions in tandem. The Alternative Perspectives box highlights these dynamics and their influence on stereotype content.

PREJUDICE

Prejudice is a psychological construct representing an evaluation of or attitude toward another group or individual. Usually, we consider prejudice to be a negative attitude that a person consciously expresses. As we will see, however, neither of these assumptions is necessarily correct.

Directionality of Prejudicial Attitudes

Let's consider the first element first: the nature of the attitude. Many sociologists and social psychologists consider prejudice to reflect a negative evaluation of another entity (e.g., person, group, organization). Allport (1954), for instance, wrote that prejudice reflected "*antipathy* based on faulty and inflexible generalization" (p. 9, emphasis added), while Crandall, Eshleman, and O'Brien (2002) defined prejudice as "a *negative evaluation* of a group or of an individual on the basis of group membership" (p. 359, emphasis added). Prejudice expressed as a negative attitude is certainly evident in the sport context, as illustrated in the Diversity in the Field box.

Evidence also exists showing that people can have prejudice without negative attitudes toward others. From a social psychological perspective,

ALTERNATIVE perspectives

Race, Gender, and Stereotypes. Many people think about stereotypes along certain domains in isolation, such as gender stereotypes, racial stereotypes, and the like. It is possible, however, that stereotypes interact, such that the beliefs we have about a group along one domain combine with beliefs about that group along another domain. Galinsky, Hall, and Cuddy (2013) conducted six studies, some of which were experimental and some of which involved analyzing archival data, to examine this possibility. They focused specifically on the potential overlap of racial and gender stereotypes; that is, the extent to which racial stereotypes differed in their gender content. In their first study, they observed that African Americans were considered to be most masculine, Asians were considered least masculine, and Whites were in the middle. They then examined whether these patterns held across different situations, two of which were directly relevant for our discussion of diversity and inclusion in sport organizations. In one of their studies, they asked participants to select applicants for a stereotypically feminine leadership role (i.e., one requiring collaboration and relationship building) or a stereotypically masculine leadership role (i.e., one requiring fierceness and competitiveness). Consistent with their initial findings, for the "masculine" jobs, participants selected African Americans most frequently and Asians least frequently; Whites fell in the middle. Finally, the authors analyzed archival data from the NCAA to examine the racial composition of 30 different sports. They first had participants rate the sports from 1 (extremely feminine) to 10 (extremely masculine). They then assessed the relationship between these ratings and the proportions of African Americans and Asians participating in the sports. Results showed that as the masculinity ratings increased, African Americans were more likely to be student-athletes in the sport, relative to Asians. In discussing these findings, Galinsky, Hall, and Cuddy correctly noted that "the gender content of racial stereotypes has important real-world consequences" (p. 498).

DIVERSITY | IN THE FIELD

Prejudice as Negative Attitudes Toward Others. Prejudice will frequently manifest in negative attitudes or expressions toward people different from the self. For example, Donald Sterling, the longtime owner of the NBA's Los Angeles Clippers, was fined $2.5 million and banned from the league for life after making racist comments during a recorded conversation. During the conversation, Sterling told his girlfriend not to bring African Americans to Clippers games and admonished her for posting pictures of herself with African Americans (including NBA Hall of Famer Magic Johnson) on her social media account.

Negative attitudes in sport are not a problem only in the United States. In Spain, 18,000 fans posted anti-Semitic comments on Twitter following Real Madrid's loss to Maccabi Tel Aviv in a major European men's basketball tournament. Also in Spain, a fan threw a banana at Barcelona's Brazilian-born Dani Alves as part of a racist taunt. Alves responded by eating the banana, which brought a wave of support from politicians and other athletes. These are just two examples where prejudice was manifested toward members of underrepresented groups.

Sources: Glover, B. (2014, April 29). Adam Silver issues lifetime ban, $2.5M fine to Clippers owner Donald Sterling. SportsIllustrated.com. Retrieved from www.si.com/nba/point-forward/2014/04/29/adam-silver-issues-lifetime-ban-2-5m-fine-clippers-owner-donald-sterling. / Minder, R. (2014, May 22). Fans in Spain revel in their prejudices, and social media fuels hostilities. *New York Times.* Retrieved from www.nytimes.com/2014/05/23/world/europe/fans-in-spain-reveal-their-prejudices-and-social-media-fuels-the-hostilities.html?_r=0.

it is possible for individuals to have *positive* attitudes toward both people who are like them (the in-group) and those who are not (the out-group). Bias or prejudice would be present, even when attitudes toward both groups are positive, if an individual has a more positive attitude toward the in-group than the out-group. This is what Brewer (2007) calls *relative positivity.*

Let's consider an example to illustrate this point. National polling has shown that Whites in the United States have increasingly positive attitudes toward racial minorities, and, thus, we might expect the outcomes of prejudice to be decreasing. However, there is persistent evidence of discrimination in housing, hiring, and other contexts. Some of this discrimination is systemic, meaning that the social systems in place perpetuate the current conditions, but the differences are also attributable to the fact that Whites hold more positive attitudes toward other Whites than toward racial minorities. Hence, prejudice remains (Rudman, 2004).

Explicit and Implicit Prejudice

Let's now consider whether people are necessarily aware that they express prejudice. This question brings to light the distinction between explicit and implicit forms of prejudice.

Explicit forms of prejudice are what most people consider when they think about prejudice. Explicit forms are attitudes toward dissimilar others that people consciously and deliberately maintain (Dovidio, Kawakami, & Beach, 2001). With these forms, people can articulate their prejudice, or lack thereof, and act accordingly. For example, polling organizations such as the Pew Research Center and Gallup regularly report on trends in Americans' attitudes toward different groups. These polls deal with explicit forms of prejudice, as the respondents indicate to pollsters whether they have positive, negative, or ambivalent attitudes toward the targets in question.

Explicit forms of prejudice are socially constructed. In particular societies and times, it might be appropriate and normative to express prejudice against certain groups (Crandall et al., 2002). This speaks to the social construction of prejudice. For example, Crandall and colleagues have shown that, within American culture, the confluence of various values and norms makes it socially acceptable to express prejudice against some groups, such as people who have committed child abuse or rape, but not others, such as persons with disabilities. The social acceptability of prejudice will correspond with subsequent behaviors. As a result, housing choices, voting rights, and employment opportunities all vary depending on the socially constructed acceptability of prejudice.

Experimental work I completed with Ferreira and Fink helps to demonstrate how this manifests in the sport setting (Cunningham, Ferreira, & Fink, 2009). Consistent with what was presented in the Diversity Challenge, we thought that sexism would be more commonly accepted in sport contexts than other forms of prejudice, such as racism; as a result, sexist comments (e.g., "Of course we lost. We played like a bunch of girls.") might be viewed as more palatable than racist ones (e.g., "Of course we lost. The other team had more Black players than we do."). We conducted an experiment where college students responded to these comments, and we found support for our expectations. We also found that the reactions were affected by the demographics of the commenter: racist comments made by a White person and sexist comments made by a man elicited the strongest aversion. We also asked people to write an explanation of why they responded as they did. Indicative of the deeply engrained belittlement of women in American culture, one participant wrote: "I think that saying that playing like a bunch of girls is not very offensive because girls' basketball is not even close to the level that men's basketball is, even though it is sexist I do not find it offensive" (p. 68).

Not all prejudice is deliberately expressed. Therein lies the importance of *implicit* attitudes, which determine our automatic responses to stimuli. Implicit attitudes are elicited when there is a match between an external stimulus and the individual's association set that links the stimulus with various attributions (Blair, Dasgupta, & Glaser, 2015). These reactions are automatic and do not require deliberate thought on the part of the actor. Implicit attitudes also operate independently of what Blair and colleagues call "perceived truth value" (p. 666); that is, the associations can be triggered even when the individual does not believe them to be accurate. People hold implicit attitudes toward a variety of stimuli, such as different sodas or political candidates, but for our purposes we focus on attitudes toward social groups. In this case, we refer to the attitudes as *implicit prejudice.*

Explicit and implicit prejudice are conceptually distinct from one another, and while they are empirically related, there is not necessarily a one-to-one association (Blair et al., 2015). Thus, an individual can express a lack of explicit prejudice yet still harbor implicit prejudicial attitudes. This accounts for the fact that, although most people believe they are fair-minded and maintain egalitarian values, at the same time they hold implicit prejudicial attitudes toward various groups. These automated responses are most likely to manifest when social forces are weak, such as when individuals are presented with ambiguous information (Son Hing, Chung-Yan, Hamilton, & Zanna, 2008). Personnel selection, assessment of athletic performance, and evaluation of one's job performance represent possible examples.

Because people might be unaware of their implicit prejudices, they are likely to discriminate in subtle ways, such as standing far away from someone who is different or not making frequent eye contact with the person.

To illustrate these dynamics, consider a study we completed examining parents' attitudes toward LGBT coaches (Cunningham & Melton, 2014). Melton and I had previously surveyed parents on the topic, and for this work we interviewed persons who had already expressed (via questionnaire) positive attitudes toward, including support for, sexual minority coaches. Thus, the respondents' explicit attitudes were positive. We asked them to elaborate on these sentiments and to discuss what that support looked like and how it was developed. For some parents, support for LGBT coaches was unequivocal in nature: they clearly had positive attitudes and were able to articulate these beliefs effectively. In other cases, the parents described what we called qualified support. They expressed support yet did so in ways that reinforced stereotypes about LGBT individuals. For example, one participant commented: "My attitude is that people can live the way they want to *as long as* they don't promote it" (p. 392). Another said, "Sure, I actually don't have a problem with any gender issues. *The only issue I would have is if* the person that was coaching was a sexual predator" (p. 392). While these parents expressed support, they did so in ways that were qualified and that perpetuated myths about LGBT individuals (e.g., as sexual predators). These attitudes served dual purposes, allowing the parents to express positive attitudes toward LGBT coaches (and thus not identify as prejudiced) but still discriminate in subtle ways. We argued that such sentiments epitomized the implicit biases people hold toward LGBT coaches.

DISCRIMINATION

Discrimination represents the final element of bias. Allport (1954) considered discrimination to be a behavior that "comes about only when we deny to individuals or groups of people equality of treatment" (p. 51). More recently, Dovidio, Brigham, Johnson, and Gaertner (1996) defined discrimination as "inappropriate treatment of individuals due to their group membership" (p. 279). These definitions highlight two important points. First, unlike stereotypes and prejudice, which are psychological processes, discrimination is a behavioral construct. Second, discrimination is concerned with the unfair or inappropriate treatment of individuals or groups.

We can draw from the theoretical explanations outlined in Chapter 2 to understand why discrimination might occur. From a critical theory perspective, the denial of opportunities would result from efforts among those in power seeking to maintain their privilege while also subjugating others. Systemic issues also contribute to discrimination, as biases embedded into schools, legal systems, religious institutions, and so on advantage some groups over others. Alternatively, from a social psychological perspective, people might afford more liking to and preference for people who are like them; as a result, opportunities for people who differ from them would be limited. From a social psychological perspective, this in-group favoritism should be observed among all groups—that is, a heterosexual might demonstrate the same amount of in-group favoritism as a sexual minority would.

The differential treatment can take several forms, so it is useful to differentiate further between two types of discrimination: access and treatment (Greenhaus, Parasuraman, & Wormley, 1990).

Access Discrimination

Access discrimination prevents members of a particular social group from obtaining a job or entering a profession (Greenhaus et al., 1990). There is considerable evidence of access discrimination in sport and physical activity. As one example, Acosta and Carpenter (2014) conducted a 37-year longitudinal study of women in sport. They examined girls' and women's access to sport participation, as well as their representation as coaches. Results from their analyses show that women are continually underrepresented in head coaching positions. Women represent just 43.4 percent of the head coaches of women's teams and less than 4 percent of the head coaches of men's teams. In another study, among men's college teams, a colleague and I showed that access discrimination also affects African Americans in the coaching ranks (Cunningham & Sagas, 2005).

This form of discrimination is not limited to employment, as access discrimination can limit participation opportunities for various groups. For instance, women and racial minorities face both economic and access discrimination when they pursue participation opportunities in outdoor programs (Schwartz & Corkery, 2011). Among Latinos, immigrants and persons from low-income families face various barriers to being physically active, including access to facilities, safety, and the availability of others with whom they can exercise (Harrolle, Floyd, Casper, et al., 2013). Finally, Australian adults living in rural communities face some of the same barriers as persons living in urban areas (e.g., family commitments); however, they also experience constraints unique to the rural setting, such as geographic climate and systemic norms that do not value exercise (Eley, Bush, & Brown, 2014).

Treatment Discrimination

Whereas access discrimination denies people the opportunity to join a sport organization or be physically active, treatment discrimination occurs within an organization or in the course of an activity. In this case, individuals or members of a particular group have differential access to resources, experience negative behaviors directed toward them, or are afforded fewer chances for growth than they deserve (Greenhaus et al., 1990). For instance, power differences among women and men serve to reinforce gendered practices and policies in sport that are frequently taken for granted (Velija, Ratna, & Flintoff, 2014). As a result, cultural practices that privilege men and masculine qualities, such as gendered language, remain uncontested.

As with access discrimination, treatment discrimination can affect people who are participating in sport and physical activity. If people do not feel welcome in a sport environment, they are unlikely to continue in that activity, or their sport experience will not be fully optimized. As one example, Shimmell, Gorter, Jackson, and their colleagues (2013) conducted a study in which they interviewed youth with cerebral palsy and their parents. The authors asked the participants about their physical activity levels, as well as factors that encouraged or disallowed greater activity. One of the more salient barriers to emerge from these interviews was the attitude of others. Service providers sometimes conveyed the notion that the youths were not welcome or were a nuisance in the facility—perspectives that ultimately served to discourage the youths from being physically active.

OUTCOMES OF BIAS

Stereotypes, prejudice, and discrimination negatively affect people in a number of ways. We can classify these outcomes into three categories: physiological, psychological, and vocational and sport participation effects.

Physiological Effects

The physiological effects of bias affect people's physical health and well-being. Considerable evidence shows that, relative to their peers, minorities have higher rates of obesity, certain cancers, and cardiovascular disease; have less access to healthy food; have poor healthcare options; and experience higher mortality rates. The differences in physical health remain even after we take into account other factors that could influence the findings, such as family income and age. Prejudice, interpersonal discrimination, and systemic forms of subjugation all contribute to these effects. These differences reflect what health officials and scholars call *health disparities*. According to the Centers for Disease Control and Prevention (CDC, 2008), health disparities "are preventable differences in the burden of disease, injury, violence, or opportunities to achieve optimal health that are experienced by socially disadvantaged groups."

Policy makers and public health officials undertake considerable efforts to identify ways to combat health disparities. Results from a study I conducted with Walker suggest that one possible solution might be ensuring opportunities to be physically active (Walker & Cunningham, 2014). We drew from survey data collected from African Americans in rural communities in Texas. About one in five of the participants lived in "food deserts": communities where healthy food options were scarce, and when the food was available, financial barriers prevented these individuals from obtaining it. We examined the relationships among food deserts, physical activity, and self-reported health status. When activity levels were low, people who lived in a food desert had poor health, as we would expect. However, when physical activity levels were high, people in a food desert were as healthy as those who were not. This research underscores the importance of ensuring safe, affordable, and accessible spaces for recreation and physical activity (see also Gordon-Larson, Nelson, Page, & Popkin, 2006).

Interestingly, the effect of bias on physical health is also observed among those who *express* prejudice. See the Alternative Perspectives box on the facing page.

Psychological Effects

Bias also negatively affects people psychologically. The minority stress model helps explain the possible underlying dynamics (Meyer, 2003). From this perspective, all people have general stressors in their lives, but minorities have stressors in addition to those that others experience. These stressors are continuous in nature because they are recurrent in the systems within a given society. Finally, the stressors are not caused by the individual—that is, there is not something wrong with the individual; instead, the stressors result from the social systems and structures that produce and reproduce the biases minorities experience.

Schmitt, Branscombe, Postmes, and Garcia (2014) conducted a meta-analysis to examine the effects of experiencing prejudice on people's psychological well-being. In a meta-analysis, the researchers collect and analyze data from numerous studies to identify patterns and relationships among variables, using statistical methods to account for differences in sample size, measurement errors, and so on. These researchers collected data from 328 studies, which included a total of 144,246 participants. They observed that the more discrimination people experienced, the more likely they were to have negative psychological outcomes. The pattern varied across some factors. Following are some of the results of the meta-analysis:

- The relationship between prejudice and psychological outcomes was stronger for some types of discrimination, such as physical or mental ability, HIV+ status, and sexual orientation, than it was for other forms, such as those based on gender or race.

- Prejudice is likely to have a positive association with some outcomes, such as depression or anxiety, and a negative relationship with others, such as life satisfaction. The strength of associations differs, though, as prejudice is more likely to reinforce the negative outcomes than it is to dampen the effects of the positive outcomes.

- The effect of discrimination on psychological outcomes was stronger for children than for other sample groups.

- The effects varied based on the type of stigmatizing characteristic. The researchers suggested this could be due to the degree to which discrimination is socially legitimized (see also Crandall et al., 2002). In their analyses, the weakest effects were observed for racism and sexism, while the effects were strongest for discrimination based on sexual orientation, mental or physical ability, HIV+ status, and being overweight. It is more socially legitimate to discriminate based on the latter characteristics than the former.

ALTERNATIVE perspectives

Prejudice Against LGBT Individuals and All-Cause Mortality. Much of the attention on bias and physical health focuses on those who experience stereotypes, prejudice, and discrimination, and rightly so. There is also evidence, though, that bias negatively affects *those who express it.* Hatzenbuehler, Bellatorre, and Muennig (2014) collected data from various large-scale, national surveys so that they were able to link the responses to the survey with mortality data by cause of death. For example, if a person completed the questionnaire in 1980, the researchers examined the person's responses and linked them with other data that showed whether the person was alive or dead by 2008. They also collected other data that could account for death rates, such as age, race, marital status, nationality, gender, income, education, and self-reported health. The researchers found that, even after statistically controlling for the other variables, LGBT prejudice impacted all-cause mortality (i.e., whether a person died or not). People who expressed high levels of prejudice lived 2.5 years less than those who expressed low levels of prejudice. These findings are consistent with earlier research showing that Whites with high levels of racial prejudice died sooner than their less prejudiced counterparts (Lee, Muening, & Kawachi, 2012). The authors concluded: "The deleterious health consequences of prejudice are not merely confined to minority group members, but may also result in increased mortality risk for majority group members" (p. 335).

The overall results show that perceived discrimination negatively affects the psychological well-being of the target.

Vocational and Sport Participation Outcomes

Bias can also affect the careers people pursue, their opportunities for promotion, their experiences in the work environment, and their physical activity/sport participation.

Access discrimination clearly limits a person's opportunities to be active or to enter a given line of work. The effects reach beyond individuals who are explicitly denied access to certain opportunities. Let's consider the career choices people make. An individual pursues a career based on a number of factors, including the person's confidence in executing the tasks, the positive outcomes associated with the line of work, and the barriers the person anticipates encountering (Lent, Brown, & Hackett, 1994). When people believe that others like them experience negative stereotypes, prejudice, and discrimination in a certain occupation, they are unlikely to pursue that line of work. Instead, they are more likely to pursue a career in an area where they anticipate opportunities and have seen others like them excel (Cunningham, Bruening, Sartore, et al., 2005). These same patterns are likely to manifest in the promotions people seek, such as an assistant's intention of becoming a head coach or athletic director. The Professional Perspectives box offers other examples.

As is the case in other industries, bias also affects people's experiences working in sport organizations. Bias can come from coworkers, supervisors, or customers. Variations in pay, promotion rates, development opportunities, mentoring, and overall quality of work can all be affected by bias. The effects are harmful for sport organization employees. For example, even small differences in pay rates can, over time, amount to meaningful differences. According to the National Women's Law Center (2014), women experience a wage gap as soon as they enter the workforce, as women younger than 25 working full time earn about 88 percent of what men do. Over time, these differences compound, such that by the time women reach retirement age, they will have lost an average of $464,320 due to wage gaps (assuming a 40-year career of year-round, full-time employment). Similar patterns occur for promotional rates, as slight preferences shown to majority members at lower levels of the organizational hierarchy result, over time, in substantial gaps in top leadership positions as they move up the ranks.

Similar dynamics occur among people participating in sport and physical activity. These involve the choices people make about the sport and physical activity

professional PERSPECTIVES

Discrimination in the Hiring Process. Becky Heidesch is the founder and CEO of Women's Sports Services (WSS), an organization specializing in job placement for women, minorities, and professional athletes. According to Heidesch, the sports industry, like many others, has traditionally been dominated by White males. Recently, however, progress has been made in diversifying the workforce. This progress grew from an awareness that a diverse staff can help a firm identify with and relate to people from different backgrounds. Although a push for greater diversity is evident, there are still many instances of discrimination, particularly among women and racial minorities. These are not the only persons facing such barriers, however. As Heidesch notes, "Certainly we see age discrimination across the board." Such discrimination often arises from perceptions among sport organization decision makers that older employees might not fit into the organization's culture. Discrimination can also take place based on an applicant's attractiveness.

forms in which they participate, as well as their experiences while doing so. Burdsey (2011) offered a good example. He interviewed British Asian players who participated at high levels of cricket. The players reported hearing verbal abuse from various people, including referees, players, and fans. Some players noted the psychological toll it took on them, while others adopted various coping mechanisms, such as treating the verbal abuse as a joke or competitive banter. Burdsey correctly notes that "jokes can underpin divisive and exclusionary aspects of sporting subcultures, and they represent a powerful and symbolic means by which minorities are marginalized from dominant player collectives" (p. 273).

chapter SUMMARY

The focus of this chapter was on bias and its three components: stereotypes, prejudice, and discrimination. As illustrated in the Diversity Challenge, bias is still prevalent in the context of sport and physical activity. It influences the opportunities people have, how others think about them, their experiences in sport and physical activity, and the choices they make about their future. After reading this chapter, you should be able to:

1. **Define and discuss the different forms of bias, including stereotyping, prejudice, and discrimination.**

    Bias is reflected in three ways. The first is stereotyping, which is in the cognitive domain. Stereotypes represent beliefs about the attributes, skills, and attitudes members of a particular group possess. Prejudice is an affective component of bias and represents the differential evaluation of a group or an individual based on group membership. Finally, discrimination exists in the behavioral domain and represents the negative treatment of individuals because of their group membership.

2. **Discuss theoretical underpinnings used to explain bias in sport.**

    Various theories help explain bias in sport. The stereotype content model holds that beliefs about other people vary along two domains: warmth and competence. Social psychological theories help to explain prejudice, in terms of both the content (whether based on negative evaluations or relative positivity) and the nature (explicit or implicit) of the prejudice. Finally, critical theories and social psychological theories help explain why people are denied access to sport and sport organizations, as well as why they are treated differently in those contexts.

3. **Discuss the effect of bias on subsequent outcomes.**

    Bias affects people in three areas. The first is physiological and includes physical health and well-being. The second is psychological and includes outcomes such as depression, anxiety, and life satisfaction. Finally, bias can affect people's sport and vocational outcomes, such as their access to sport, physical activity, and certain types of employment; their experiences in those settings; and their economic status.

QUESTIONS for discussion

1. How do stereotypes affect people's participation in sport and physical activity?

2. Think about different groups and how they might map on the stereotype content model. How would you go about deflecting or rebutting some of these stereotypical perceptions?

3. What are the major differences between explicit and implicit forms of prejudice? What are examples of each?

4. Which form of prejudicial attitude is most prevalent in sport today? Are some sectors of sport and physical activity more likely to see certain types of prejudice than others? Why do you think this is the case?

5. With federal, state, and local statutes mandating equal employment opportunities, is discrimination still a problem? Why or why not?

6. What are the major distinctions between access and treatment discrimination?

learning ACTIVITIES

1. Visit the Project Implicit website (https://implicit.harvard.edu/implicit/) and test your implicit attitudes toward various targets (e.g., age, race, disability).

2. Look online for recent examples of discrimination and prejudice in the context of sport and physical activity. Based on your discoveries, which group or groups are most likely to face discrimination?

WEB resources

Australian Human Rights Commission, www.humanrights.gov.au

Australian agency aimed at eliminating discrimination in various contexts, including sport.

Institute for Diversity and Ethics in Sport, www.tidesport.org

Provides reports concerning diversity and discrimination in university athletics and professional sport settings.

Project Implicit, https://implicit.harvard.edu/implicit/

Provides an electronic demonstration of how to test for implicit attitudes.

reading RESOURCES

Dovidio, J. F., Glick, P., & Budman, L. A. (Eds.). (2005). *On the nature of prejudice: Fifty years after Allport*. Malden, MA: Blackwell.

An edited collection of essays from the leading social psychologists in the field; focuses on the contributions of Allport's original work related to prejudice; provides updates to the theory and directions for future inquiry.

Mikulincer, M., & Shaver, P. R. (Eds.) (2015). *APA handbook of personality and social psychology*. Washington, DC: American Psychological Association.
> Edited collection of essays related to intergroup processes; contains specific sections on prejudice and changing intergroup processes.

Nelson, T. D. (Ed.) (2009). *Handbook of prejudice, stereotyping, and discrimination*. New York: Psychology Press.
> Edited volume with a focus on the three main areas of bias: stereotyping, prejudice, and discrimination.

REFERENCES

Acosta, R. V., & Carpenter, L. J. (2014). *Women in intercollegiate sport: A longitudinal study—thirty-seven year update—1977–2014*. Unpublished manuscript, Brooklyn College, Brooklyn, NY.

Allport, G. W. (1954). *The nature of prejudice*. Cambridge, MA: Addison-Wesley.

Blair, I. V., Dasgupta, N., & Glaser, J. (2015). Implicit attitudes. In M. Mikulincer & P. R. Shaver (Eds.), *APA handbook of personality and social psychology* (vol. 1, pp. 665–691). Washington, DC: American Psychological Association.

Brewer, M. B. (2007). The importance of being we: Human nature and intergroup relations. *The American Psychologist, 62*(8), 726–738.

Burdsey, D. (2011). That joke isn't funny anymore: Racial microaggressions, color-blind ideology and the mitigation of racism in English men's first-class cricket. *Sociology of Sport Journal, 28*, 261–283.

Burton, L. J., Grappendorf, H., & Henderson, A. (2011). Perceptions of gender in athletic administration: Utilizing role congruity to examine (potential) prejudice against women. *Journal of Sport Management, 25*, 36–45.

Centers for Disease Control and Prevention. (2008). *Community Health and Program Services (CHAPS): Health disparities among racial/ethnic populations*. Atlanta: U.S. Department of Health and Human Services.

Crandall, C. S., Eshleman, A., & O'Brien, L. (2002). Social norms and the expression and suppression of prejudice: The struggle for internalization. *Journal of Personality and Social Psychology, 82*, 359–378.

Cuddy, A. J. C., Fiske, S. T., & Glick, P. (2008). Warmth and competence as universal dimensions of social perception: The stereotype content model and the BIAS map. *Advances in Experimental Social Psychology, 40*, 61–149.

Cunningham, G. B., Bruening, J., Sartore, M. L., Sagas, M., & Fink, J. S. (2005). The application of social cognitive career theory to sport and leisure career choices. *Journal of Career Development, 32*, 122–138.

Cunningham, G. B., Ferreira, M., & Fink, J. S. (2009). Reactions to prejudicial statements: The influence of statement content and characteristics of the commenter. *Group Dynamics: Theory, Research, & Practice, 13*, 59–73.

Cunningham, G. B., & Melton, E. N. (2014). Varying degrees of support: Understanding parents' positive attitudes toward LGBT coaches. *Journal of Sport Management, 28*, 387–398.

Cunningham, G. B., & Sagas, M. (2005). Access discrimination in intercollegiate athletics. *Journal of Sport and Social Issues, 29*, 148–163.

Dovidio, J., Kawakami, K., & Beach, K. (2001). Implicit and explicit attitudes: Examination of the relationship between measures of inter-group bias. In R. Brown & S. L. Gaertner (Eds.), *Blackwell handbook of social psychology: Intergroup processes* (pp. 175–197). Oxford, England: Blackwell.

Dovidio, J. F., Brigham, J. C., Johnson, B. T., & Gaertner, S. L. (1996). Stereotyping, prejudice, and discrimination: Another look. In C. N. Macrae, C. Stangor, & M. Hewstone (Eds.), *Stereotypes and stereotyping* (pp. 85–102). New York: Springer.

Duguid, M. M., & Thomas-Hunt, M. C. (2015). Condoning stereotyping? How awareness of stereotyping prevalence impacts expression of stereotypes. *Journal of Applied Psychology, 100*, 343–359.

Eagly, A. H., & Diekman, A. B. (2005). What is the problem? Prejudice as an attitude-in-context. In J. F. Dovidio, P. Glick, & L. A. Rudman (Eds.), *On the nature of prejudice: Fifty years after Allport* (pp. 19–35). Malden, MA: Blackwell.

Eley, R., Bush, R., & Brown, W. (2014). Opportunities, barriers, and constraints to physical activity in rural Queensland, Australia. *Journal of Physical Activity and Health, 11*, 68–75.

Emile, M., Chalabaev, A., Stephan, Y., Corrion, K., & d'Arripe-Longueville, F. (2014). Aging stereotypes and active lifestyle: Personal correlates of stereotype internalization and relationships with level of physical activity among older adults. *Psychology of Sport and Exercise, 15*, 198–204.

Fiske, S. T., & Tablante, C. B. (2015). Stereotyping: Processes and content. In M. Mikuliner & P. R. Shaver (Eds.), *APA handbook of personality and social psychology* (pp. 457–507). Washington, DC: American Psychological Association.

Galinsky, A. D., Hall, E. V., & Cuddy, A. J. C. (2013). Gendered races: Implications for interracial marriage, leadership selection, and athletic participation. *Psychological Science, 24*, 498–506.

Goldstein, N. J., Cialdini, R. B., & Griskevicius, V. (2008). A room with a viewpoint: Using social norms to motivate environmental conservation in hotels. *Journal of Consumer Research, 35*, 472–482.

Gordon-Larson, P., Nelson, M. C., Page, P., & Popkin, B. M. (2006). Inequality in the built environment underlies key health disparities in physical activity and obesity. *Pediatrics, 117*, 417–424.

Greenhaus, J. H., Parasuraman, S., & Wormley, W. M. (1990). Effects of race on organizational experiences, job performance, evaluations, and career outcomes. *Academy of Management Journal, 33*, 64–86.

Harrolle, M. G., Floyd, M. F., Casper, J. M., Kelley, K. E., & Bruton, C. M. (2013). Physical activity constraints among Latinos. *Journal of Leisure Research, 45*, 74–90.

Hatzenbuehler, M. L., Bellatorre, A., & Muennig, P. (2014). Anti-gay prejudice and all-cause mortality among heterosexuals in the United States. *American Journal of Public Health, 104*, 332–337.

Hively, K., & El-Alayli, A. (2014). "You throw like a girl": The effects of stereotype threat on women's athletic performance and gender stereotypes. *Psychology of Sport and Exercise, 15*, 48–55.

Lee, Y. J., Mueening, P., & Kawachi, I. (2012, May). *Do racist attitudes harm community health including both Blacks and Whites?* Paper presented at the annual meeting of the Population Association of America, San Francisco.

Lent, R. W., Brown, S. D., & Hackett, G. (1994). Toward a unifying social cognitive theory of career and academic interest, choice, and performance [Monograph]. *Journal of Vocational Behavior, 45*, 79–122.

Meyer, I. H. (2003). Prejudice, social stress, and mental health in lesbian, gay, and bisexual populations: Conceptual issues and research evidence. *Psychological Bulletin, 129*, 674–697.

National Women's Law Center (2014, April 25). How the wage gap hurts women and families. Retrieved from http://www.nwlc.org/resource/how-wage-gap-hurts-women-and-families.

Rudman, L. A. (2004). Social justice in our minds, homes, and society: The nature, causes, and consequences of implicit bias. *Social Justice Research, 17*, 129–142.

Rudman, L. A., & Phelan, J. E. (2008). Backlash effects for disconfirming gender stereotypes in organizations. *Research in Organizational Behavior, 28*, 61–79.

Schmitt, M. T., Branscombe, N. R., Postmes, T., & Garcia, A. (2014). The consequences of perceived discrimination for psychological well-being: A meta-analytic review. *Psychological Bulletin, 140*, 921–948.

Schwartz, A., & Corkery, M. R. (2011). Barriers to participation among underrepresented populations in outdoor programs. *Recreational Sports Journal, 35*, 130–144.

Shimmell, L. J., Gorter, J. W., Jackson, D., Wright, M., & Galuppi, B. (2013). "It's the participation that motivates him": Physical activity experiences of youth with cerebral palsy and their parents. *Physical & Occupational Therapy in Pediatrics, 33*, 405–420.

Son Hing, L. S., Chung-Yan, G. A., Hamilton, L. K., & Zanna, M. P. (2008). A two-dimensional model that employs explicit and implicit attitudes to characterize prejudice. *Journal of Personality and Social Psychology, 94*, 971–987.

Stangor, C. (2009). The study of stereotyping, prejudice, and discrimination within social psychology: A quick history of theory and research. In T. D. Nelson (Ed.), *Handbook of prejudice, stereotyping, and discrimination* (pp. 1–23). New York: Psychology Press.

Steele, C. M. (1997). A threat in the air: How stereotypes shape intellectual identity and performance. *American Psychologist, 52*, 613–629.

Velija, P., Ratna, A., & Flintoff, A. (2014). Exclusionary power in sports organizations: The merger between the Women's Cricket Association and the England Wales Cricket Board. *International Review for the Sociology of Sport, 49*, 211–226.

Walker, J. E. O. Y., & Cunningham, G. B. (2014). The influence of perceived access to healthy food and physical activity on the subjective health of African Americans in rural communities. *American Journal of Health Studies, 29*, 165–171.

II
PART

FORMS OF DIVERSITY

chapter 4
Race   67

chapter 5
Sex and Gender   97

chapter 6
Age   127

chapter 7
Mental and Physical Ability   149

chapter 8
Appearance   169

chapter 9
Religious Beliefs   193

chapter 10
Sexual Orientation and Gender Identity   213

chapter 11
Social Class   241

Race

LEARNING objectives

After studying this chapter, you should be able to:

- Define *race, ethnicity,* and *minority,* and describe the differences among these concepts.
- Discuss the underrepresentation of racial minorities in sport and identify factors contributing to this state.
- Articulate the influence of race on the experiences of sport and physical activity participants.

DIVERSITY CHALLENGE

During the 1980s, Dexter Manley played professional football for the NFL's Washington Redskins. He was selected for the Pro Bowl based on his accomplishments as a defensive end and won two Super Bowl rings while playing with the Redskins. Despite these achievements, and despite having received a college degree from Oklahoma State University, Manley was illiterate until age 30. Manley's situation was not an isolated incident. Another player, Kevin Ross, was functionally illiterate but played four seasons at Creighton University. He was admitted to the university even though he scored only 9, with a possible high score of 36, on the ACT entrance exam. While Ross attended the university, other students took his exams for him, and the athletic department hired a secretary to complete his homework assignments.

Some might be tempted to suggest this is a problem of yesteryear, but there is evidence to the contrary. A survey conducted by the news agency CNN revealed that 7 to 18 percent of college athletes in revenues sports (i.e., football, men's basketball, women's basketball) read at or below the fourth-grade level. African Americans make up the majority of the athletes in these sports. The CNN analysis included data collected from several of the top universities in the United States, so it is not necessarily only sub-par institutions that are engaging in this practice, either. For example, the University of North Carolina at Chapel Hill is regularly listed as one of the top public universities in the United States; however, an athletic advisor at that university commented that 1 in 12 of the athletes with whom she interacted read at or below the third-grade level.

Anecdotes pertaining to Dexter Manley and Kevin Ross, as well as the CNN data, all suggest that racial minority players are used for their athletic talents so a university may benefit. The players were streamlined into "easy" classes and had their assignments completed for them. After their eligibility was exhausted, the benefits stopped. Even though the NCAA and the U.S. Department of Education passed new rules concerning the academic progress of student-athletes, the abuses have continued.

Sources: Moore, K. (2004, July 1). Tackling illiteracy: Former Washington Redskin Pro Bowl defensive end Dexter Manley keynote speaker. *The Connection Newspapers.* Retrieved from www.connectionnewspapers.com/article.asp?archive=true&article=34303&paper=62&cat=109. / Outside the lines: Unable to read. (2002, March 17). ESPN.com. Page 2. Retrieved from http://sports.espn.go.com/page2/tvlistings/show103transcript.html. / Richardson: "I'm supposed to make a difference." (2002, February 28). ESPN.com. Retrieved from http://a.espncdn.com/ncb/s/2002/0228/1342915.html. / Ganin, S. (2014, January 8). CNN analysis: Some college athletes play like adults, read like 5th graders. Retrieved from http://edition.cnn.com/2014/01/07/us/ncaa-athletes-reading-scores/.

CHALLENGE   REFLECTION

1. In your estimation, how commonplace are cases like Dexter Manley or Kevin Ross today?

2. Is a university exploiting a student-athlete if the school provides a scholarship in exchange for athletic services?

3. What can be done to address this issue?

As the Diversity Challenge illustrates, race has the potential to influence people's experiences in the sport context, including their educational attainment while participating in sport. Racism and racial ideologies have historically limited opportunities for racial minorities—a pattern observed around the world (Adair, 2011). Although explicit forms of racism might have decreased, implicit racism persists, and racist principles and practices remain deeply embedded within cultures, systems, and institutions. The end result is differences in physical activity participation opportunities and experiences, evidence of access and treatment discrimination in sport organizations, and racist ideals engrained into the sport and physical activity industry.

The purpose of this chapter is to examine the categorical effects of race in greater detail. In doing so, I largely compare the experiences of racial minorities to those of Whites. This decision is based on the history of oppression and subjugation of racial minorities and the privileging of Whites in the United States and other countries around the world (Feagin, 2006; Zinn, 2003). This legacy has resulted in institutionalized forms of racism and the fact that Whites' experiences in sport are qualitatively different from those of their peers. In addition, much of the discussion in this chapter focuses on African Americans. I based this decision on the prominent presence of African Americans in sports today and the resultant scholarly emphasis on this population of athletes. I offer this rationale in hopes that readers recognize the focus is a reflection of historical context and available research, and not intended as a dismissal of the experiences among other racial minorities.

The chapter is organized as follows: I begin with a discussion of the terms *race, ethnicity,* and *minority,* differentiating among these important and commonly used terms. The focus then shifts to the influence of race in the work environment, including the impact of race on access, wages, and work experiences. Finally, the chapter turns to the role of race in sport and physical activity participation.

KEY TERMS

I n this section, we define *race, ethnicity,* and *minority*—terms that are sometimes used interchangeably but that actually have very different meanings (Eitzen & Sage, 2009). A focus on race means classifying people based on supposed genetic similarities and differences. Ethnicity, on the other hand, does not refer to aspects of biology but instead focuses on cultural patterns among groups of people. People from a particular ethnic group share a cultural heritage, language, customs, and so on. They might also have common norms, beliefs, and values.

Some people suggest the concept of race lacks validity evidence and so avoid use of this word, preferring the term *ethnicity* (Abercrombie, Hill, & Turner, 2000). They point to the fact that there are many more similarities than differences between people who are supposedly of different races. Others combine the terms, seeking to capture both the genetic variations and the cultural underpinnings; the use of *racio-ethnic* is one example (Richard & Miller, 2013; see also the Diversity in the Field box on the following page). Recognizing these critiques, I suggest there are many good reasons to continue to use the term *race*. First, even though there might be few genetic differences among people from different races, the word *race* does have historically engrained social meanings associated with it (Booth, 2011; Coakley, 2015). Race is a social construction, and people within a particular culture do attach social meanings to supposed biological differences. The social construction of race has an impact on all persons: consistent with critical race theory (Hylton, 2009), it has an impact on peoples' opportunities and experiences, and it is often at the forefront of social, political, educational, and religious issues. As such, it is important to consider race, the meanings people attach to their own race and the race of others, and the theories that can help us understand how race affects people in sport and physical activity.

The term *minority* refers to a collection of individuals who share a common characteristic and face discrimination in society because of their membership in that group (Coakley, 2015). Minorities face systemic forms of discrimination and will sometimes have a sense of social togetherness because of their shared lived experiences (Bell, McLaughlin, & Sequeira, 2004). This perspective de-emphasizes numbers, as a numerical minority can still be the social majority. Within the context of sport and physical activity, all persons who are not White, including African Americans, Asians, Hispanics, and so forth, are considered racial minorities.

RACE IN THE WORK ENVIRONMENT

A s outlined in Chapter 1, racial minorities represent a large segment of the U.S. population, and their proportion is only expected to increase. U.S. Census Bureau estimates suggest Whites, who constituted 64.7 percent of the population in 2010, will comprise 46.3 percent by 2050. Already, in four states racial minorities represent the majority of all residents (California, Hawaii, New Mexico, and Texas). Other nations, such as Canada and New Zealand, are also witnessing an increasingly diverse racial and ethnic populace.

Despite forming a substantial proportion of the population, racial minorities have historically faced personal and systemic forms of bias, and this pattern continues today. Racial minorities are more likely than Whites to face housing discrimination and to be subjected to hate crimes. They also experience poorer health outcomes,

DIVERSITY   IN THE FIELD

Multirace Population in the United States Grows. In 2000, the U.S. Census Bureau allowed people to self-identify with more than one race, and the agency continued this practice in the 2010 Census. The two data collection points allow us to examine how the population of multirace individuals has changed. Both the number and proportion of people who identify as multiracial increased. In fact, the proportion of people who reported more than one race increased by about one-third. The most common combination was two races (92 percent), and four groupings far outnumbered other combinations: White and Black (20 percent),

White and some other race (19 percent), White and Asian (18 percent), and White and American Indian or Alaskan Native (16 percent). The Census Bureau also identified other trends. For example, persons living in the western United States were most likely to report more than one race, while people living in the Midwest were least likely to do so. At the state level, residents of California and Texas were most likely to report more than one race. These data show that people increasingly conceptualize race in complex ways, and the area in which a person lives is associated with these dynamics.

Source: Two or more races population: 2010. (2012, September). U.S. Census Bureau. Available at: http://www.census.gov/prod/cen2010/briefs/c2010br-13.pdf.

including shorter life spans, higher infant mortality rates, lower self-reported health assessments, and higher incidences of various illnesses, such as AIDS, diabetes, and certain forms of cancer (Adler & Rehkopf, 2008; Schnittker & McLeod, 2005).

This pattern of prejudice and discrimination carries over into the work environment. Despite a number of federal, state, and local laws forbidding racial discrimination in the employment context, racial minorities face discrimination in wages earned (see Exhibit 4.1), their representation in leadership positions, and their access to various occupations.

EXHIBIT 4.1   Median household incomes by race of householder, 2013.

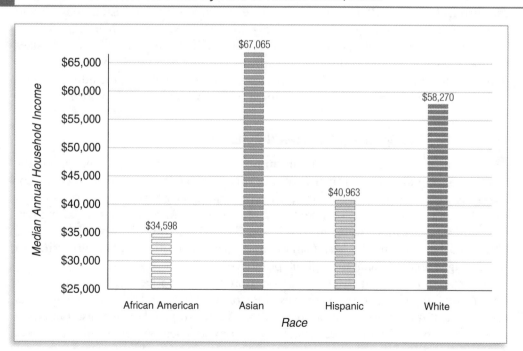

Source: U.S. Census
Bureau data, 2013.

The law, employment, and race

A number of laws forbid employment decisions based on the race of the applicant or employee. At the federal level, most of these prohibitions exist as part of Title VII of the Civil Rights Act of 1964. This law applies to (a) all organizations with at least 15 employees, including state and local governments, (b) labor unions, (c) employment agencies, and (d) the federal government.

Title VII protects people from discrimination based on their race or skin color in hiring and firing decisions, promotions, compensation, and training opportunities. This law also prohibits employment decisions based on the stereotypes associated with people from a particular race—assumptions about people's work ethic, personal traits, or their overall abilities. The law also forbids employers from making employment decisions based on membership in or affiliation with race- or ethnic-based organizations (e.g., the Black Coaches and Administrators), attendance at schools or places of worship that might be associated with a particular racial group (e.g., having attended a historically Black college or university, such as Grambling State University), or a spouse's race.

Title VII prohibitions also include the following:

■ **Race-related characteristics and conditions.** Discrimination based on a characteristic often associated with a particular race (e.g., specific hair texture, skin color) is unlawful. Organizations cannot make employment decisions based on conditions that predominantly affect members of one race more than they do members of other races unless it can be conclusively demonstrated that such practices are job-related and are a business necessity. For example, a fitness club that has a policy of not hiring people with sickle cell anemia discriminates against African Americans because that condition is predominantly found among members of that race and is not job related.

■ **Harassment.** Harassment takes many forms, including racial slurs, racial jokes, comments that could be deemed offensive, and other verbal or physical contact that is based on one's race.

■ **Segregation or classification of employees.** An organization may not physically isolate members of a racial minority group from other employees or from customers. This prohibition also applies to the assignments people receive. It is unlawful, for example, to assign Hispanics to a mostly Hispanic division or geographic region. Finally, it is also illegal to group people from a protected class into certain positions. Suppose an athletic department always assigns African American employees to life skills coordinator or academic advisor positions, as opposed to positions dealing with development or finances, based on the assumption that people in the coordinator and advisor positions have the most contact with the athletes, many of whom are also African American. Classifying employees in this manner is unlawful. Based on NCAA data (2014; www.ncaa.org), this practice actually does occur frequently.

■ **Preemployment inquiries.** With a few exceptions, it is always unlawful to ask job applicants what their race is. Employers that use affirmative action in the hiring process or track applicant flow may ask for information on race. Under these circumstances, it is best that the employer use a separate form to keep this information separate from the application. This ensures that the information will not be used in the remainder of the selection process.

According to the Equal Employment Opportunity Commission (EEOC), 33,068 complaints of racial discrimination were reported in 2013. In that same year, the Commission recovered $112.7 million in damages for the charging parties and other aggrieved persons. This figure does not include additional monies obtained through litigation. In addition to race discrimination, color discrimination charges are prevalent.

Salary

One example where discrimination is evident is in the area of earnings. According to the Bureau of Labor Statistics (BLS), in 2014, Asians earned the highest salaries, followed by Whites, African Americans, and Hispanics (see Exhibit 4.2). Gender influenced these patterns, as the disparity between Hispanic and African American

 EXHIBIT **4.2**   Weekly earnings based on race and gender.

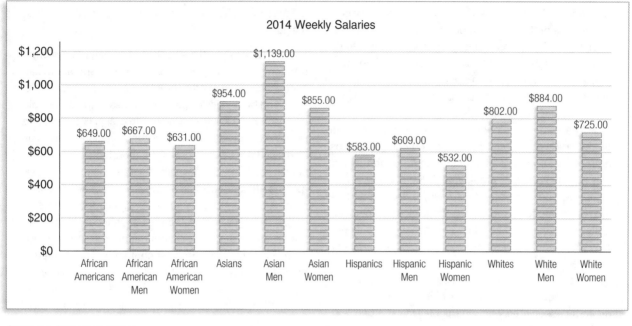

2014 Weekly Salaries

African Americans $649.00, African American Men $667.00, African American Women $631.00, Asians $954.00, Asian Men $1,139.00, Asian Women $855.00, Hispanics $583.00, Hispanic Men $609.00, Hispanic Women $532.00, Whites $802.00, White Men $884.00, White Women $725.00

Source: U.S. Department of Labor.

men's salaries and the salaries of their Asian and White counterparts is greater than the disparity for the same groups of women. For instance, Hispanic men earned 69 percent of what White men earned, whereas Hispanic women earned 73 percent of what White women earned. This pattern holds for each racial group.

There is evidence of salary discrimination against racial minorities participating at the highest level of sport. Perhaps not surprisingly, this discrimination manifests in nuanced ways. Among NBA players, there is no evidence of salary discrimination when all players and all salary ranges are considered. However, a more nuanced analysis shows that among the upper-echelon players, Whites earned 18 percent more than African Americans (Hamilton, 1997). Subtle forms of salary discrimination are also present among NFL quarterbacks. When all quarterbacks from 1971 to 2006 are considered, there are no differences in salary between Whites and African Americans. However, further analyses show that Whites are differentially rewarded for their performance relative to African Americans: at the upper end of the salary range (i.e., among the elite quarterbacks), Whites receive greater salary returns for their passing performance than do African Americans (Berri & Simmons, 2009).

Leadership Positions

Racial minorities also face discrimination when it comes to their access to key leadership positions. There are a number of ways to examine this issue. One method is to compare the portion of racial minorities in leadership roles to their representation in the general population. For instance, if Whites represent 64.7 percent of the U.S. population, then we would expect to see a similar proportion of Whites serving as head coaches, general managers, and so on. This is a good metric for considering the representation of people in business roles, such as general manager or development officer. In these roles, business acumen is a more important requirement than previous playing experience. Jon Daniels, the general manager of MLB's Texas Rangers, who started his career in professional baseball as an intern rather than a player, is an example.

Using this method of comparison, we see that Whites are overrepresented in key administrative positions across college and professional sport in the United States. As shown in Exhibit 4.3, Whites are substantially more likely to hold upper-level managerial roles (approximately 80 percent) than would be expected based on their proportion in the general U.S. population (64.7 percent).

While it is appropriate to compare the proportion of upper-level administrators by race to that of the U.S. population, this is not necessarily the case when we wish to determine whether racial discrimination takes place in the coaching ranks.

Overrepresentation of Whites among senior administrators.   EXHIBIT   **4.3**

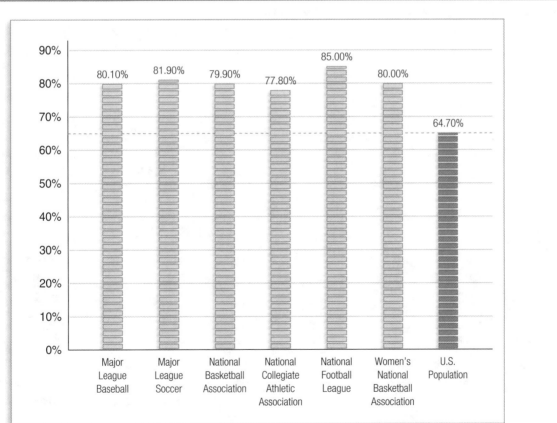

Note: Data from NCAA, MLB, NBA, and WNBA based on 2013 year. Data from MLS and NFL based on 2012 year.

Source: Data collected from the Institute for Diversity and Ethics in Sport, www.tidesport.org.

From a practical standpoint, not all people in the general population have an equal chance to coach at the professional or collegiate level; instead, former players are the most viable applicants for these roles (Cunningham & Sagas, 2002; Everhart & Chelladurai, 1998). Since this is the case, we should compare the proportions in coaching to the proportions of players in each particular setting—not to the proportions in the broader population.

Exhibit 4.4 summarizes the proportions of players, assistant coaches, and head coaches by race across different sport contexts. In just one case, the NBA, the proportion of racial minority head coaches (46.7 percent) outpaces the proportion of minorities in the U.S. population (33 percent). Assistant coaches fare better: in MLB, the NBA, men's college basketball, women's college basketball, and the WNBA, the proportion of racial minority assistant coaches is greater than the proportion of minorities in the U.S. population. This might lead one to conclude that these sport leagues are places of opportunity and diversity. However, when we compare the

| EXHIBIT | 4.4 | Representation of racial minorities as players, assistant coaches, and head coaches (2013). |

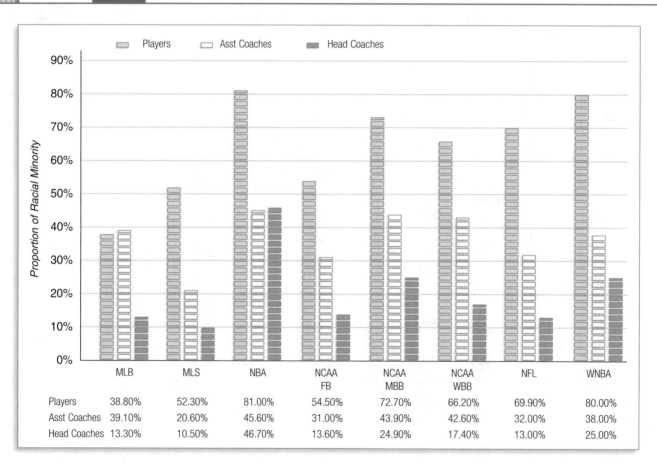

	MLB	MLS	NBA	NCAA FB	NCAA MBB	NCAA WBB	NFL	WNBA
Players	38.80%	52.30%	81.00%	54.50%	72.70%	66.20%	69.90%	80.00%
Asst Coaches	39.10%	20.60%	45.60%	31.00%	43.90%	42.60%	32.00%	38.00%
Head Coaches	13.30%	10.50%	46.70%	13.60%	24.90%	17.40%	13.00%	25.00%

Note: For comparison purposes, note that in 2010, racial minorities comprised 33 percent of the general U.S. population.

Source: www.tidesport.org; www.ncaa.org. NCAA data are based on Division I schools and exclude historically Black colleges and universities.

proportions of coaches to the more appropriate standard—the proportion of athletes in each sport—we arrive at a different conclusion. In this case, we see that with the exception of MLB, every sporting context examined has a substantially greater proportion of racial minority players than coaches of color.

The contrasts are striking. For example, in the Women's National Basketball Association, 80 percent of the players are racial minorities, more than *three times* the proportion of head coaches. The disparities are even greater in the NFL, where players are *5.4 times* as likely to be racial minorities as the head coaches. These two leagues are representative of the broader sport landscape. Collectively, these data suggest that sport is a place where racial minority athletes have substantial opportunities, but where leadership positions are largely reserved for Whites (see also Hawkins, 2013).

Occupational Segregation

Occupational segregation refers to the clustering of people into particular occupational roles based on their demographic characteristics. For employees and prospective employees, occupational segregation can limit career choices and opportunities and create wage disparities (Brynin & Guveli, 2012). Among employers, occupational segregation can influence stereotypes and ideas about who is suitable for a particular position.

To illustrate these dynamics, let's look at how the U.S. Bureau of Labor Statistics classifies various occupations, and racial differences in these groupings. This agency groups occupations in five broad categories: (1) management and professional; (2) sales and office; (3) natural resources, construction, and maintenance; (4) production, transportation, and material moving; and (5) service. The BLS then offers the racial breakdown of workers who occupy those roles, with a particular focus on African Americans, Asians, Hispanics, and Whites (see Exhibit 4.5). These data from 2010 show that management and professional positions are the most popular occupations for Asians and Whites. Given the high pay associated with being a manager or holding some sort of professional degree, it might not be surprising that these two racial groups are also the highest earners (refer back to Exhibit 4.2). On the other hand, many service jobs are generally low paying, and these are common occupations for African Americans and Hispanics. Thus, while there can certainly be wage discrimination within occupations, these data support the idea that one negative outcome of occupational segregation is wage differences among different racial groups (Brynin & Guveli, 2012).

Occupational segregation is also present in sport and physical activity. Let's consider the NCAA, which offers a robust data set spanning a number of years, to examine this issue (see www.ncaa.org). In 2013, there were 3,845 people working in the role of athletic director, associate athletic director, academic advisor, or life skills coordinator at the Division I level. Whites held 81 percent of these positions, African Americans occupied 14 percent, and people from other racial backgrounds held the remaining 6 percent. Based on these data, we might conclude that Whites are overrepresented in these roles, while the proportion of African Americans closely mirrors their representation in the U.S. population. But there is more to the story: the White administrators are much more likely to hold the athletic director or associate athletic director roles (57 percent), whereas the African American administrators are more

| EXHIBIT | 4.5 | Racial representation across six occupations in the United States (2010). |

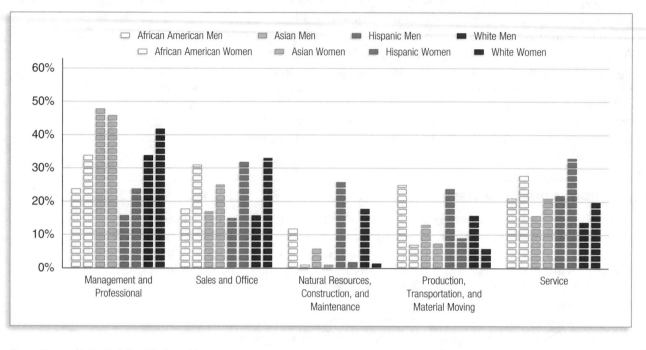

Source: Bureau of Labor Statistics, http://www.bls.gov.

likely to hold the academic advisor or life skills coordinator roles (69 percent). Similar patterns occur in coaching, as well: Whites are more likely to hold head coaching or coordinator roles than are their racial minority peers.

These data suggest that people of color are pigeonholed into certain types of jobs, in both the coaching and administrative areas. There is also evidence that African American administrators are aware of occupational segregation's prevalence, and they point to discrimination, dubious hiring practices, a lack of career role models, and limited social networks as explanations (McDowell & Cunningham, 2007; McDowell, Cunningham, & Singer, 2009).

POSSIBLE EXPLANATIONS FOR LEADERSHIP UNDERREPRESENTATION OF RACIAL MINORITIES

A number of factors are associated with the underrepresentation of racial minorities in leadership positions in sport organizations, which can best be understood from a multilevel perspective (Cunningham, 2010a, 2010b). This perspective takes into account societal and industry (i.e., macro-level) factors, organizational characteristics and practices (i.e., meso-level factors), and individual-level determinants (i.e., micro-level factors). Multilevel theorizing is consistent with a systems view of organizations (Chelladurai, 2014), which recognizes that factors at various levels of analysis are affected by and affect those at other levels. For example, a person's attitudes toward African Americans (a micro-level factor) are potentially shaped by previous experiences with African American leaders (a micro-level factor), organizational policies related to diversity and inclusion (a meso-level factor), and the norms and practices of the surrounding community (a macro-level factor). In the following sections, I present the factors that underlie underrepresentation of minority members in organizational leadership. Exhibit 4.6 offers a summary.

Macro-Level Factors

Macro-level factors operate at the industry or societal level. They are external to the athletic department yet still exert considerable influence. These factors include institutionalized practices, the political climate, and stakeholder expectations.

Institutionalized practices

Practices within a given context become institutionalized when, because of habit, history, and tradition, they become taken for granted, standardized, and assumed to be "the way things are done." Environmental pressures result in organizations' coming to resemble one another, both in terms of how they operate and in the type of employees they attract. Over time, these factors become further embedded, solidified, and, therefore, highly resistant to change. New members of an organization or profession are socialized to learn that these practices are legitimate, further perpetuating the practices (for a review, see Washington & Patterson, 2011).

As you will recall from Chapter 2, critical theory holds that racism is institutionalized, or endemic, in American society (Hylton, 2009; Tate, 1997). This means that racist elements underpin the foundations of the major institutions,

Multilevel explanation for bias toward racial minority leaders. **EXHIBIT 4.6**

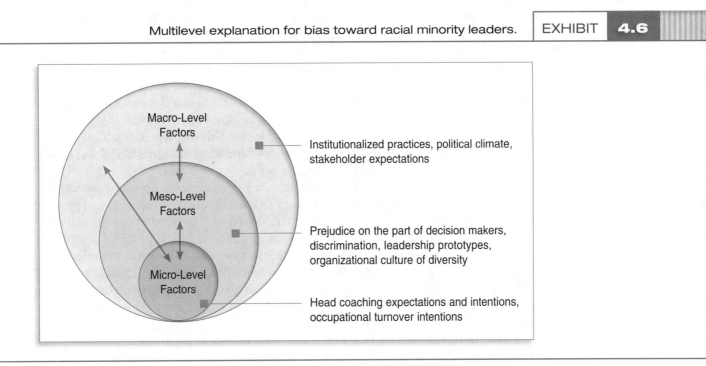

such as religion, education, and the legal system, to name a few, and that racism is embedded into their practices and systems. In fact, evidence suggests that the United States is the only Western country whose origins are directly linked with racial prejudice and oppression (Feagin, 2006). Racism has been solidified into the country's cultural fabric and value systems. As one example, the notion of meritocracy (i.e., that hard work and skillfulness allow people to rise to the top) necessarily privileges Whites over racial minorities (Schultz & Maddox, 2013), as discussed in Chapter 11.

Sport is not exempt from institutionalized racism (Hylton, 2009; Long, Robinson, & Spracklen, 2005). Racist ideologies are such that Whites are cast as the standard to which others are compared. Consistent with the stereotype content model discussed in Chapter 3 (Cuddy, Fiske, & Glick, 2008), racial minorities are perceived as lacking both intellectual competence and warmth, and this results in their negative evaluation. These perspectives are reinforced through media portrayals (Buffington, 2005; Cunningham & Bopp, 2010) and expressed through language and socialization tactics (Coakley, 2015). The end result is an "othering" of racial minorities, a privileging of Whites, and institutionalized, legitimated forms of racism in the hiring process and in work environments.

Political climate

The political climate is another macro-level factor influencing the underrepresentation of racial minorities in leadership positions. The prevailing political climate during an administration or era, coupled with the accompanying social dynamics, influence sport in a number of ways, including the public funding of sport facilities (Davis-Delano & Crosset, 2008), attitudes toward labor rights (Simmons & Harding, 2009), educational opportunities (West & Currie, 2008), and social justice initiatives (Dean, 2013). As legislative examples, consider the Civil Rights Act of 1964, which, among other achievements, guaranteed employment protection for women and racial minorities in the United States, and the Voting Rights Act of 1965, which ensured the voting privileges of racial minorities. These represent more progressive legislation at the federal level and were both signed into law under President Lyndon Johnson. On the other hand, some conservative administrations have been marked by attempts to reduce equal opportunities; for example, federal administrators sought to limit the scope of Title IX, which mandates equal opportunities for girls and women in federally funded educational activities, under the presidencies of both Ronald Reagan and George W. Bush.

The political environment also affects equal employment opportunities and the enforcement of laws governing employment (Marshall, 2005). Enforcement of equal employment legislation and fair labor practices is more stringent when the political climate is more progressive than when it is more conservative. A project I completed with Benavides-Espinoza (2008) offers an illustrative example, as we observed that sexual harassment claims filed with federal agencies mirrored the political environment in the United States at the time. This led us to conclude that "the actions and social policies of the President of the United States may set the tone for the political environment, and in a related way, the emphasis on civil rights" (p. 781).

The political climate in a particular area is also likely to affect bias toward racial minorities. In more progressive areas, opportunities for persons of color should increase, while the same is not necessarily the case in conservative political environments. Anecdotal evidence supports this contention: at Ivy League schools, which are located in the more progressive East Coast of the United States, nearly 50 percent (7 of 16) of the football and men's basketball coaches were African American in 2009—a percentage far greater than in any other athletic conference (Robinson, 2009).

Stakeholder expectations

Stakeholder expectations represent a third macro-level factor influencing the underrepresentation of racial minorities in leadership positions. Stakeholders are key constituents to an organization and can be either internal or external to the workplace. In college sports, stakeholders might include coaches, administrators, faculty, athletes, alumni, boosters, community members, and so on. From a strategic management perspective, gaining insights into and addressing the perceptions, needs, and wants of key strategic stakeholder groups can result in optimal organization–environment fit, thereby increasing the success the organization enjoys.

Alumni and boosters are two stakeholder groups that exert particular influence on athletic department operations, including personnel decisions. As one key indicator of how influential these stakeholders are, consider that during the decade beginning in 2004, one of every seven dollars (14 percent) generated by NCAA Football Bowl Subdivision athletic departments came from alumni and booster donations (Fulks, 2014). This amounts to roughly $8.7 million in annual monies. Given their tremendous financial influence, the persuasive power of alumni and boosters is undeniable.

Economic reliance on alumni and boosters influences employment decisions because there is a perceived need to hire employees with whom these stakeholders can identify. This perceived need is most heightened when the organization is hiring coaches, particularly those who coach football—a sport that has been referred to as the "front porch" of an institution (Beyer & Hannah, 2000). As Michael Rosenberg of the *Detroit Free Press* (2004) noted:

> It is largely about money. It is about a face to show the alumni, especially the ones with big wallets. College coaches don't just coach; they are, in many ways, the public faces of their schools. And if the big donors don't like a coach because of his weight/accent/skin color, schools will stay away.

Richard Lapchick drew similar conclusions:

> I have had discussions with people in searches for coaches and athletic directors that the final decision was made to hire a White male because they were afraid their alumni, who also happen to be strong boosters of the football program, would not contribute nearly as much or as readily to an African American athletic director or football coach. (as cited in Wong, 2002, p. 1)

These quotations illustrate (1) the perception that boosters want to identify with football coaches, (2) the perceived role of demographic similarity in this match, and (3) the resultant considerable influence of boosters in a coach's selection. These factors may result in a preference for White coaches over coaches of color.

Meso-Level Factors

Meso-level factors are those operating at the organizational and group level. In the model presented here, I have identified two factors influencing the underrepresentation of racial minority leaders: organizational culture and bias in personnel decisions.

Organizational culture

According to Schein (1990), the term *organizational culture* refers to the basic assumptions and beliefs in the workplace that are passed down over time and considered valid by most of the employees. It is manifested through observable artifacts, values, and basic assumptions. In short, the culture represents the underlying values of a workplace.

One aspect of workplace culture is an organization's inclusiveness. As discussed in Chapter 1, the inclusiveness of a work environment can substantially affect diversity-related outcomes. Inclusive sport organizations have policies, organizational activities, and leader behaviors that reinforce the belief that all people have the potential to contribute uniquely to the workplace. Employees are able to express their unique identities freely while still feeling a sense of connectedness and belonging (Ferdman, 2014; Nishii & Rich, 2014). When the workforce is diverse, inclusive sport organizations thrive in terms of organizational performance, the recruitment and retention of talented employees, and employee attachment to the organization (Cunningham, 2008, 2009).

Research I conducted with Singer sheds further light on how inclusive organizational cultures might affect the representation of racial minorities. We conducted interviews with university administrators, athletic directors, and coaches in a number of high-performing athletic departments. Our research indicated that athletic departments characterized by a culture of diversity and inclusion were likely to have diversity enmeshed in all organizational activities, to create mentoring and development opportunities, and to have proactive top management leadership who engage in bold recruitment and attraction strategies (Cunningham & Singer, 2009). Such workplaces stand in stark contrast to those with a culture of similarity (e.g., Doherty & Chelladurai, 1999; Fink & Pastore, 1999)—those with closed membership, homogeneous leadership teams, unstructured hiring and promotion standards, and a view of diversity as a liability rather than an asset. These findings suggest the organizational culture is key in increasing the representation of racial minorities in leadership positions.

Bias in personnel decisions

Bias in personnel decisions is also likely to influence the underrepresentation of racial minorities in leadership positions. As you will recall from Chapter 3, bias is manifested in three ways: through stereotypes, prejudice, and discrimination. In the following sections we discuss how each can affect personnel decisions to result in underrepresentation of minorities in leadership.

Stereotypes. Evidence suggests that people develop stereotypes about who they think is a typical leader and then, based on these ideas, develop notions about who would be the ideal (prototypical) leader (Lord & Maher, 1991). This cognitive process is important because people use it when they evaluate candidates for a position. Those who possess the "typical" characteristics are considered a good fit, and those who do not have these characteristics receive negative evaluations.

In many cases, leadership stereotypes are also racialized, meaning our ideas about who should and should not be a leader are influenced by stereotypes about different racial groups (Rosette, Leonardelli, & Phillips, 2008). In many Western countries, this means that Whites are perceived as more suitable for leadership roles than are members of racial minorities. There is some evidence to support as much. People consistently see Whites in leadership positions within business and the public sector. This pattern has been consistently observed throughout U.S. history, where political (44 of the 45 presidents) and business leaders (e.g., John D. Rockefeller, Steve Jobs, Warren Buffett) have predominantly been White. This historical conditioning shapes how people perceive potential leaders and who they think should hold leadership roles. Indeed, Rosette and colleagues found that Whiteness was seen as a prototype for business leaders—though not necessarily for everyday employees—and White leaders were considered to be more effective than leaders of color, especially when an organization's success was attributed to the leader.

We have also observed that personal factors can influence ideas about who is suitable for leadership roles. One such factor is the applicant's perceived racial identity (Steward & Cunningham, in press). When members of racial minorities have a strong racial identity, they are believed to challenge existing norms and conventions—something that is potentially threatening to Whites. We conducted an experiment to examine these ideas and how they might affect hiring recommendations for people applying for an athletic director position. Participants reviewed job application packets, which included information signaling a strong racial identity (e.g., through organizational membership) or lacking such information. These manipulations were successful, as perceptions of the applicant's racial identity varied based on the information included on the resume. Pointing to the importance of perceived racial identity, Whites rated strongly identified members of racial minorities as being a poorer fit for the job than their more weakly identified counterparts. Thus, Whites penalize members of racial minorities they believe strongly identify with their race (see also Kaiser & Pratt-Hyatt, 2009).

Prejudice. In addition to stereotypes, prejudice results in biased decision making that affects the underrepresentation of racial minority leaders. In Chapter 3, we noted that explicit forms of prejudice are largely seen as socially unacceptable, so implicit prejudicial attitudes are more common. With regard to race, this form of prejudice takes the form of aversive racism (Dovidio & Gaertner, 2004; Gaertner & Dovidio, 2000; Son Hing, Chung-Yan, Hamilton, & Zanna, 2008). With aversive racism, individuals consciously and sincerely support egalitarian ideals and do not believe they personally harbor prejudiced feelings toward racial minorities; nonetheless, these persons unconsciously have feelings of unease with members of these groups and, therefore, seek to avoid interracial interactions. When such intergroup contact is unavoidable, a person with aversive racism will experience anxiety and discomfort and will try to end the interaction as quickly as possible.

Finally, the behaviors of persons with aversive racism differ from those of "old fashioned" racism, which is associated with open discrimination. Unlike "old fashioned" racism, aversive racism will not lead a person to discriminate in situations where social norms are strong or when discriminatory acts could be attributed to the self. Rather, a person with aversive racism will tend to discriminate when the normative structure is weak, when there are vague guidelines for the appropriate course of action, and when a negative response can be attributed to a factor other than race—this is called the attributional-ambiguity effect.

Aversive racism is likely to affect members of racial minorities in leadership roles in a number of areas, including helping behaviors and employment decisions (Pearson, Dovidio, & Gaertner, 2009). Let's first consider helping: persons with aversive racism are unlikely to offer help to racial minorities when social norms do not dictate doing so. Within the employment context, we know that all people need and receive help in their careers. Everyone has associates who alert them to opportunities, offer guidance on tough decisions, advocate on their behalf, and so on. A person with aversive racism is less likely to offer help to members of racial minorities unless there are specific instructions or norms to do so—for example, if the person was appointed as a mentor as part of an organizational mentoring system.

Aversive racism might also affect the way a decision maker reviews applications. Prejudice is most likely to manifest when situations are ambiguous—a characteristic of many candidate searches. All applicants have strengths, just as they do weaknesses, so when decision makers choose to attend to some weaknesses and not others, this can influence the final selection. With aversive racism, decision makers are more likely to highlight the weaknesses of racial minorities than they are similar shortcomings among Whites (Dovidio & Gaertner, 2000). As these two examples show, the prevailing norms, processes, and structures for making personnel decisions create situations ripe for aversive racism to prevail and for African Americans to continue to be underrepresented in those employment roles.

Discrimination. Finally, evidence suggests that discrimination hinders racial minorities' advancement to leadership positions. Recall from Chapter 3 that two forms of discrimination exist: access discrimination, which prevents members of a particular group from entering a particular job, organization, or profession, and treatment discrimination, which "occurs when subgroup members receive fewer rewards, resources, or opportunities on the job than they legitimately deserve on the basis of job-related criteria" (Greenhaus, Parasuraman, & Wormley, 1990, pp. 64–65).

Let's first take a look at access discrimination. We know from Exhibits 4.3 and 4.4 that racial minorities are underrepresented in leadership positions relative to what we would expect given the available applicant pool. There is also evidence that their underrepresentation in leadership positions is at least partially attributable to the race of the person making the personnel decisions. Specifically, we conducted a study of college men's basketball coaching staffs (Cunningham & Sagas, 2005). Drawing from the notion, presented earlier in the chapter, that former players represent the best pool of potential coaches, we compared the proportion of assistant coaches of color on the staff to the corresponding percentage

DIVERSITY IN THE FIELD

Glass Cliffs and Coaching. As research has shown, members of racial minorities face access discrimination when seeking coaching opportunities. There is also evidence that when they do earn head coaching roles, they work for teams that have historically been poor performers. Cook and Glass (2013) analyzed 30 years of data for NCAA men's basketball coaches. They found that racial minorities were more likely than were Whites to take over for losing squads. They referred to this phenomenon as the "glass cliff" (see also Ryan & Haslam, 2007), as racial minorities tended to receive opportunities in situations where history suggests the coach would fail. Cook and Glass also observed that coaches of color had shorter tenures than did White coaches (4.8 vs. 5.8 years) and were likely to be replaced by a White coach. This is what the authors called the "savior effect." They concluded: "Decision makers blame organizational struggles on individual leaders who were placed in precarious positions at the point of hire. This lessens minority leaders' ability to demonstrate their leadership capability and reproduces biases regarding minorities' ability to lead effectively" (p. 182).

of all former men's basketball players who had graduated (48 percent). The results were telling. Overall, African Americans represented only 33 percent of all assistant coaches—a proportion significantly less than 48 percent. The results varied considerably, however, when the race of the head coach was taken into account. African Americans comprised just 30 percent of the coaches on staffs headed by a White head coach but represented 45 percent of the coaches on staffs headed by an African American. This pattern suggests that the underrepresentation of African Americans was due to their lack of access to coaching positions when the head coach was White. Equally striking, among the staffs guided by a White head coach, *one in six* (or 16.2 percent) did not have any assistant coaches of color. (See the Diversity in the Field box above for additional information about the types of leadership roles members of racial minorities receive.)

There is reason to suspect findings like these would also be observed among administrators in the college athletics context. Given that 87.2 percent of athletic directors are White (NCAA, 2014) and the evidence that people are likely to hire others who are racially similar to themselves, we should not be surprised by the underrepresentation of racial minorities as head coaches and athletic administrators. Powell (2008) advanced similar arguments, albeit from a different perspective: "As long as blacks are unable to hold true power in sports, the issue of hiring will remain" (p. 213).

From the above discussion, one should not conclude that this is just a college sports problem: there is evidence of access discrimination in other sport settings, too. Volz (2013), for example, analyzed data for Major League Baseball from 1975 to 2008. He observed that African American and Hispanic former players are both significantly less likely than their White counterparts to manage teams in the major leagues. These effects remained even after statistically taking into account other variables, such as playing performance, education, coaching experience, and so on, that could affect a player's ascension to the leadership role.

Treatment discrimination also negatively affects coaches of color. The available research suggests that racial minority coaches face open hostility from Whites (Lawrence,

2004). Within coaching, they are often valued more for their ability to recruit and associate with athletes (most of whom are African American) than for their coaching talents (Cunningham & Bopp, 2010), and they may not receive just returns for the networks they have developed or the experience and education they have accumulated (Sagas & Cunningham, 2005; Sartore & Cunningham, 2006). Similar patterns occur among professors in sport fields (Burden, Harrison, & Hodge, 2005; Hodge, 2014).

Finally, the failures of racial minority leaders are often presumed to represent the capabilities of all racial minority members—a dynamic not observed among Whites. The end result is that racial minorities receive a single chance to be successful, while Whites often have multiple opportunities. This is aptly demonstrated among college football coaches, where only one African American coach (Tyrone Willingham) has been fired from one job but still coached elsewhere (Demirel, 2014). In addition, as failures of an individual are attributed to other members of a particular race, all racial minorities may face an uphill battle in acquiring coveted positions. Fritz Hill, a former coach at San Jose State University, noted: "Race will no longer be an issue when the day comes that an African American football coach is unsuccessful, but you still go and replace him with another African American coach" (as cited in Demirel, 2014).

Micro-Level Factors

Finally, we explore how micro-level factors affect the underrepresentation of racial minority leaders. Micro-level factors are influences specific to an individual. Even though the focus in this section is on the individual, keep in mind the influence of societal and organizational factors on individuals. Differences between racial minorities and Whites in (for example) occupational turnover are not genetically determined; instead, they are shaped by people's lived experiences, their encounters with racism and discrimination (or lack thereof), and their observations of others in the sport industry.

In considering the impact of micro-level factors, it is important to note that researchers have continually *failed* to observe support for one possible explanation: human capital. This term refers to the investments people make in their own education, skills, abilities, and experience. Studies of athletes (Sack, Singh, & Thiel, 2005), coaches (Sagas & Cunningham, 2005), and administrators (McDowell & Cunningham, 2007) have shown consistently that human capital does not explain discrimination toward racial minorities. Noting that the human capital explanation lacks empirical support, we consider three other possibilities: differences in social capital, vocational interests, and occupational turnover.

Social capital

Social capital is concerned with the social networks and connections people maintain. In general, having strong social networks—such as knowing many people in the professions and having high-status contacts who can advocate for you—will assist one's career advancement. The effects are not uniform across races, though (Day & McDonald, 2010). Same-race networks benefit Whites' promotion rates, but mixed-race social contacts benefit racial minority members' promotion rates.

This finding might be explained by the overrepresentation of Whites in hiring positions; thus, if racial minorities want to advance in their career, having social networks that include Whites might be beneficial. In addition, strong professional relationships with network members benefit Whites, while more informal relationships benefit racial minorities. This is likely a function of racial minorities' need to have multiple contacts across a broad range of areas as a way of accessing as much information as possible. Finally, African Americans benefit from having a large number of high-status contacts, but this effect is not observed among Whites. Day and McDonald suggest this pattern likely emerged because racial minorities lack power and privilege in sport, so having high-status individuals in their social networks likely helps buffer these effects.

Vocational interests

Vocational interests refers to the degree to which an individual seeks leadership roles, such as senior administrator, athletic director, or head coach. These interests are largely a function of the beliefs that one could complete the necessary tasks, would not encounter insurmountable barriers, and would have pleasant experiences in the potential role (Lent, Brown, & Hackett, 1994).

There is some evidence that, among racial minorities, current athletes, assistant coaches, and mid-level administrators who are exploring the possibility of entering coaching or moving up in the athletics ranks anticipate barriers, believe their race will hinder their advancement, and see few professional role models (Cunningham, Bruening, & Straub, 2006; Kamphoff & Gill, 2008). Even though they hold these beliefs, they still believe sport will offer them a satisfying career and have strong intentions to pursue that path (see also Cunningham & Singer, 2010). The latter is a particularly important point. Although some differences exist in the anticipated career outcomes among racial minorities and Whites, we have not observed, across all of our research, differences in the desire to pursue a career in sport organizations or intentions to apply for higher-level positions. Thus, commonly held sentiments among some administrators, such as "we would love to hire more racial minorities, but they are simply not applying," ring false. Commenting on why he keeps applying for jobs despite the racial discrimination he has experienced in his career, one coach noted, "After a while, it makes you think, 'Why go through with it?' because you've seen the track record. But at the same time, you have to make yourself go through with it because you don't want to allow the excuse, 'Well, they're not applying'" (as cited in Wixon, 2006).

Occupational turnover

Finally, although limited advancement opportunities and repeated experiences of discrimination do not quell minority coaches' aspirations to be a head coach, some evidence indicates that these factors do contribute to career longevity. Across a number of studies in different contexts, we have observed that racial minorities plan on leaving coaching earlier than Whites (Cunningham et al., 2006; Cunningham & Sagas, 2004, 2007; Cunningham, Sagas, & Ashley, 2001). A number of factors contribute to this trend, including health concerns, a lack of time with family, a lack of advancement opportunities, low career satisfaction, and treatment discrimination.

Racial differences in occupational turnover can have serious repercussions, not the least of which is a potential supply-side shortage of African Americans to fill head coaching positions. As Tsui and Gutek (1999) articulated, "Small effects could accumulate and lead to non-trivial consequences. For example, a small tendency for the most different groups to leave can, over time, result in increasingly more homogeneous groups as one moves up the organizational hierarchy" (p. 40). The data presented in Exhibit 4.4 support this contention: in most coaching contexts, the proportion of African Americans trends negatively as they move up the organizational hierarchy (i.e., from player to assistant coach to head coach). When the differential turnover rate is coupled with the macro- and meso-level factors already working against their advancement, a more complete picture explaining the underrepresentation of African Americans in coaching positions becomes crystallized.

RACE AND PARTICIPATION IN PHYSICAL ACTIVITY AND SPORT

W e now shift to a focus on how race affects people's engagement in sport and physical activity, as well as their experiences in those activities.

Physical Activity Participation

There is considerable evidence of racial differences in how frequently people participate in physical activity, or exercise. Exhibit 4.7 offers an overview of the percentage of adult Americans who meet the recommended guidelines for participation in aerobic exercise and muscle-strengthening activities.

Across the board, only one in five adults (20.6 percent) met such guidelines in 2012, though this is an improvement since 2008 (18.2 percent). Germane to our discussion is the evidence of racial differences in these trends. Whites are significantly more likely to meet these guidelines than are each of the other comparison groups, with the exception of Native Americans in 2012. Given that health habits among adults are formed during adolescence, not surprisingly White youth are found to be more active than their racial minority counterparts (Ianotta & Wang, 2013). These participation patterns are also evident outside the United States, as, for example, just a fraction of First Nations youth in Canada (7.4 percent) meets the recommended physical activity levels (Lemstra, Rogers, Thompson, & Moraros, 2013).

Several factors contribute to these trends. Historically, various forms of oppression, racism, and segregation limited the participation of racial minorities in sport, and in many respects, vestiges of these practices continue today. For example, Jewish Israeli college students are 2.7 times as likely to meet physical activity recommendations as their Arab Israeli counterparts (Shuval, Weissblueth, Brezism, et al., 2009). These findings are attributable to a number of factors, including the oppressed, ethnic minority status of Arab Israelis and the limited environmental structures they have to support an active lifestyle. More recently, race has influenced sport participation primarily through two dynamics: cultural norms and social class. Prevailing cultural norms influence sport participation by sending signals about what is popular and appropriate (Eitzen & Sage, 2009). These norms

Race and meeting recommended physical activity guidelines. | EXHIBIT | **4.7**

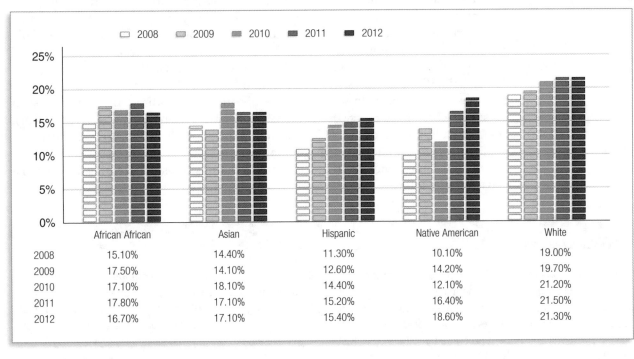

	African African	Asian	Hispanic	Native American	White
2008	15.10%	14.40%	11.30%	10.10%	19.00%
2009	17.50%	14.10%	12.60%	14.20%	19.70%
2010	17.10%	18.10%	14.40%	12.10%	21.20%
2011	17.80%	17.10%	15.20%	16.40%	21.50%
2012	16.70%	17.10%	15.40%	18.60%	21.30%

Source: www.healthypeople.gov.

explain why some activities (e.g., snow skiing) are more popular among some groups (i.e., Whites) than others. Social class also influences the amount of time people spend working or engaged in other activities, including sport and exercise (Marshall, Jones, Ainsworth, et al., 2007). As previously noted, many racial minorities have less discretionary income than Whites, on average, and this difference corresponds to the differing participation levels among the groups.

Sport Participation

Racial differences also exist in how frequently people participate on formal sport teams, as well as the positions they play. Relative to their population, racial minorities are less likely to participate in formal sport than are Whites (Coakley, 2015). There are exceptions: African Americans are highly represented in basketball and football, while Latinos are well-represented in soccer, softball, and baseball. There are also some sports, though, where few if any racial minorities participate; these include skiing, yachting, and stock car racing.

A number of factors affect racial minorities' participation in sport, such as support from others, the threat of deportation, and the number of generations the family has resided in the country (Coakley, 2015). Evidence also shows that the delivery of sport can influence participation. Kanters, Bocarro, Edwards, and colleagues (2013) conducted a study of how the delivery of sport in junior high schools (grades 6 through 8) affected students' participation. Half of the schools had interscholastic sport programs, while the other half had only intramural sports programs, the latter of which are generally considered more inclusive. They found that African Americans and children from low-income families had substantially greater sport involvement when the school had intramural sports. This pattern held true not only across sports in which African Americans usually participate, such as basketball (30.3 percent vs. 8.1 percent) and football (25.9 percent vs. 4.7 percent), but also in those sports in which their involvement has traditionally been low, such as soccer (14.7 percent vs. 0.8 percent), volleyball (12.4 percent vs. 1.1 percent), and softball (4.4 percent vs. 0.3 percent). Thus, the inclusiveness of the sport program affects racial minorities' participation.

There is also evidence that race affects the positions people play, a topic discussed in the following box.

DIVERSITY IN THE FIELD

Stacking and Tasking. Race influences the positions employees hold in organizations, and it influences the positions athletes play on teams. This phenomenon, called *stacking,* occurs when "minority athletes are overrepresented in some playing positions and underrepresented in others" (Sack et al., 2005, pp. 300–301). Stacking exists across a variety of contexts, including baseball (Gonzales, 1996), rugby (Hallinan, 1991), and hockey (Lavoie, 1989).

Why stacking occurs, however, is less clear. From one perspective, social closure theory, decision makers intentionally discriminate against athletes of color, ensuring that high-status jobs are reserved for Whites. Social closure theory holds that organizational decision makers intentionally discriminate against women and persons of color, and as a result the high-status, high-paying jobs are reserved for White men (Bonacich, 1972; Weeden, 2002). Applied to the sport context, this means that central, important positions would be set aside for Whites, while more peripheral positions would be occupied by members of racial minorities. From the human capital perspective, on the other hand, positions are assigned based on the skills and abilities athletes possess. Sack and colleagues (2005) tested these two theories in the MLB context. As expected, most (71 percent) of the African Americans played in the outfield, compared to relatively few Whites (25 percent) and Hispanics (36 percent). After variations in speed and power were accounted for, the effects of race on playing position still existed, albeit in a reduced fashion. These findings support the social closure theory, suggesting that baseball managers might be "assigning disproportionate numbers of African Americans to the outfield because of racial prejudice or for other reasons that have little to do with the skills the players bring to the league" (p. 313).

Some researchers have questioned the prevalence of stacking, citing concerns with its theoretical merits (Chelladurai, 2014) or suggesting that discrimination occurs in different, subtler ways (Bopp & Sagas, 2014). To the latter point, Bopp and Sagas suggested racial tasking is now more likely to occur, whereby, within a given athletic position, Whites and members of racial minorities are asked to perform different tasks, and these tasks privilege Whites over their counterparts. To illustrate this thesis, the authors collected data regarding the rushing and passing attempts of college quarterbacks. Within American football, skilled passers are likely to be more valued than are skilled rushing quarterbacks, and subsequent playing (in the NFL) and coaching careers both favor strong passers. These dynamics are important because, relative to African Americans, White quarterbacks are asked to pass more and run the ball less. In fact, African Americans are asked to run the ball twice as often as Whites. Bopp and Sagas suggest these differences are attributable to antiquated stereotypes about African Americans' mental and physical abilities.

Finally, there is some evidence that racial minorities have poor experiences while participating in sport. This comes in the form of stereotyping, prejudice, and discrimination.

Just as racial stereotypes influence attitudes about who should and should not be a leader, race also affects perceptions about athletes' physical and mental abilities. Prevailing stereotypes cast African Americans, for example, as superior athletes but lacking in intellectual capabilities. This results in people's associating African Americans' athletic accomplishments with natural abilities rather than hard work (Kobach & Potter, 2013). These stereotypes also affect how people view African American college athletes: these individuals are frequently assumed to be on campus solely for athletic pursuits and not for academic endeavors (Harrison, Sailes, Rotich, & Bimper, 2011). These stereotypes exist for both women and men participating in sport (Withycombe, 2011) and are frequently gendered in nature (Galinsky, Hall, & Cuddy, 2013).

In addition, although some observers suggest sport is a space where prejudice is either minimized or completely eliminated (Brown, Jackson, Brown, et al., 2003), there is persistent evidence that racial minorities confront prejudice during their sport participation. For example, racism and xenophobia are prevalent across many professional soccer settings, including in Spain, where slogans, symbols, and other cultural artifacts reinforce racist ideologies (Llopis-Goig, 2013). Evidence of racism also exists in American college athletics, where athletes report feelings of social isolation and alienation (Carter-Francique, Hart, & Steward, 2013).

Finally, members of racial minorities also experience discrimination in sport. This is seen in college athletics, where athletes report differential treatment from coaches and support staff (Singer, 2005, 2008), and NCAA academic reform policies often do more harm than good to athletes of color (Cunningham, 2012). There is also some evidence that felt discrimination from coaches is a function of racial dissimilarity, particularly among African Americans playing for White head coaches (Cunningham, Miner, & McDonald, 2013). Robidoux's research (2004) on race relations in southern Alberta, Canada, further exemplifies these points, albeit in a different context. Robidoux found that native persons frequently faced antagonistic environments while participating in sport, and Euro-Canadians sometimes viewed them in a negative light. Youth hockey participants in Robidoux's study told of being called a variety of racial slurs, such as "wagon burners" and "prairie niggers," by both the opposing players and those players' parents. On the other hand, Euro-Canadian hockey participants and their parents objected to the highly physical style of the teams made up of native persons and often advocated segregation. As one parent of a Euro-Canadian player noted, "Sportsmanship on the part of the Kaini team was non-existent. . . . Perhaps these teams should make up their own league with their own 'rules' and be forced to travel long distances for competition" (p. 29). These studies illustrate the sometimes unique experiences of racial minorities participating in sport and the need for administrators and coaches to make sport accessible to *all* persons, irrespective of their race.

chapter SUMMARY

This chapter focused on the categorical effects of race in sport and physical activity organizations. As illustrated in the Diversity Challenge, race has a substantial impact on the way people are treated while participating in sport and physical activities. The same is true for employees because race influences the way people are treated, people's behaviors in relation to their work and to others, and the aspirations people possess. After reading this chapter, you should be able to:

1. **Define race, ethnicity, and minority, and describe the differences among these concepts.**

   Though sometimes used interchangeably, the concepts of race and ethnicity have distinct meanings. Race refers to a social category used to differentiate people based on supposed genetic differences. Ethnicity, on the other hand, refers to the cultural heritage of a particular group of people, with an emphasis on the common culture certain groups of people share. Finally, a minority group is a collection of persons who share common characteristics and face discrimination in society because of their membership in that group.

2. **Discuss the experiences of racial minorities in sport, and identify the factors contributing to this state.**

   Racial minorities are underrepresented in both coaching and administrative positions. Macro-level factors (i.e., institutionalized practices, political climate, stakeholder expectations), meso-level factors (i.e., organizational cultures, biased decision making), and micro-level factors (i.e., social capital, vocational interests, occupational turnover intentions) all contribute to this phenomenon.

3. **Articulate the influence of race on the experiences of sport and physical activity participants.**

   Race is associated with participation in both physical activity and formal sports, with racial minorities having fewer opportunities than Whites. Race is also associated with negative experiences in sport and exercise, resulting from racial stereotypes, prejudice, and discrimination.

QUESTIONS for discussion

1. What are the primary distinctions between race and ethnicity? Do you think that the distinction between the two terms is meaningful? Why or why not?
2. Though the proportion of racial minorities in various countries is increasing, they continue to be disadvantaged in several areas. What are some of the reasons for this differential treatment?
3. Various factors were identified to help explain the underrepresentation of racial minorities in the coaching profession. Which of these factors is most important? Why?
4. Discuss the various ways that race influences sport and physical activity participation.

5. What is the difference between stacking and racial tasking? Which do you believe is more prevalent today? Why?

6. Race influences the treatment of sport participants in several ways. Which of the factors identified in the chapter has the largest impact on sport participants? Why?

learning ACTIVITIES

1. What is the best comparison point to use when discussing the representation of racial minorities in coaching positions? What are the pros and cons of the different benchmarks discussed in the chapter (e.g., the composition of the general population versus the composition of the pool of former athletes)? Divide into two groups, with each group adopting one perspective, and discuss.

2. Using online resources, identify mandates in different countries that address either racial equality in general or racial equality in the sport and physical activity context.

WEB resources

■ **Black Athlete,** www.blackathlete.net

Site devoted to issues and controversies concerning African American athletes of all ages and skill levels.

■ **Black Coaches and Administrators,** www.bcasports.org

Provides several resources, including the annual Hiring Report Card for college football teams.

■ **Commission for Racial Equality,** www.cre.gov.uk

British association aimed at achieving racial equality in several contexts, including sport and physical activity.

reading RESOURCES

Adair, D. (2011). *Sport, race, and ethnicity: Narratives of differences and diversity.* Morgantown, WV: Fitness Information Technology.

Offers a historical overview of race and racism in sport from various contexts around the world.

Feagin, J. R. (2006). *Systemic racism: A theory of oppression.* New York: Routledge.

Provides a historical overview of race and racism in the United States; focuses on the racial realities held by members of different racial groups.

Long, J., & Spracklen, K. (Eds.). (2011). *Sport and challenges to racism.* Hampshire, UK: Palgrave Macmillan.

Provides essays about racism, racial discrimination, and ways to end these practices in sport.

REFERENCES

Abercrombie, N., Hill, S., & Turner, B. S. (2000). *The Penguin dictionary of sociology* (4th ed.). New York: Penguin Books.

Adair, D. (2011). *Sport, race, and ethnicity: Narratives of differences and diversity*. Morgantown, WV: Fitness Information Technology.

Adler, N. E., & Rehkopf, D. H. (2008). U.S. disparities in health: Descriptions, causes, and mechanisms. *Annual Review of Public Health, 29*, 235–252.

Bell, M. P., McLaughlin, M. E., & Sequeira, J. M. (2004). Age, disability, and obesity: Similarities, differences, and common threads. In M. S. Stockdale & F. J. Crosby (Eds.), *The psychology and management of workplace diversity* (pp. 191–205). Malden, MA: Blackwell.

Berri, D. J., & Simmons, R. (2009). Race and the evaluation of signal callers in the National Football League. *Journal of Sports Economics, 10*, 23–43.

Beyer, J. M., & Hannah, D. R. (2000). The cultural significance of athletics in U.S. higher education. *Journal of Sport Management, 14*, 105–132.

Bonacich, E. (1972). A theory of ethnic antagonism: The split labor market. *American Sociological Review, 37*, 547–559.

Booth, D. (2011). History, race, sport: From objective knowledge to socially-responsible narratives. In D. Adair (Ed.), *Sport, race, and ethnicity: Narratives of differences and diversity* (pp. 13–39). Morgantown, WV: Fitness Information Technology.

Bopp, T., & Sagas, M. (2014). Racial tasking and the college quarterback: Redefining the stacking phenomena. *Journal of Sport Management, 26*, 136–142.

Brown, T. N., Jackson, J. S., Brown, K. T., Sellers, R. M., Keiper, S., & Manuel, W. J. (2003). "There's no race on the playing field": Perceptions of racial discrimination among White and Black athletes. *Journal of Sport & Social Issues, 27*, 162–183.

Brynin, M., & Guveli, A. (2012). Understanding the ethnic pay gap in Britain. *Work, Employment and Society, 26*, 574–587.

Buffington, D. (2005). Contesting race on Sundays: Making meaning out of the rise in the number of Black quarterbacks. *Sociology of Sport Journal, 21*, 19–37.

Burden, J. W., Jr., Harrison, L., Jr., & Hodge, S. R. (2005). Perceptions of African American faculty in kinesiology-based programs at predominantly White American institutions of higher education. *Research Quarterly for Exercise and Sport, 76*, 224–237.

Carter-Francique, A., Hart, A., & Steward, A. (2013). Black college athletes' perceptions of academic success and the role of social support. *Journal of Intercollegiate Sport, 6*, 231–246.

Chelladurai, P. (2014). *Managing organizations for sport and physical activity: A systems perspective* (4th ed.). Scottsdale, AZ: Holcomb Hathaway.

Coakley, J. (2015). *Sports in society: Issues and controversies* (11th ed.). New York: McGraw-Hill.

Cook, A., & Glass, C. (2013). Glass cliffs and organizational saviors: Barriers to minority leadership in work organizations? *Social Problems, 60*, 168–187.

Cuddy, A. J. C., Fiske, S. T., & Glick, P. (2008). Warmth and competence as universal dimensions of social perception: The stereotype content model and the BIAS map. *Advances in Experimental Social Psychology, 40*, 61–149.

Cunningham, G. B. (2008). Commitment to diversity and its influence on athletic department outcomes. *Journal of Intercollegiate Sport, 1*, 176–201.

Cunningham, G. B. (2009). The moderating effect of diversity strategy on the relationship between racial diversity and organizational performance. *Journal of Applied Social Psychology, 36*, 1445–1460.

Cunningham, G. B. (2010a). Occupational segregation of African Americans in intercollegiate athletics administration. *Wake Forest Journal of Law & Policy, 2*, 165–178.

Cunningham, G. B. (2010b). Understanding the under-representation of African American coaches: A multi-level perspective. *Sport Management Review, 13*, 395–406.

Cunningham, G. B. (2012). Diversity and academic reform. *Journal of Intercollegiate Sport, 5*, 54–59.

Cunningham, G. B., & Benavides-Espinoza, C. (2008). A trend analysis of sexual harassment claims: 1992–2006. *Psychological Reports, 103*, 779–782.

Cunningham, G. B., & Bopp, T. D. (2010). Race ideology perpetuated: Media representations of newly hired football coaches. *Journal of Sports Media, 5*(1), 1–19.

Cunningham, G. B., Bruening, J. E., & Straub, T. (2006). Examining the under-representation of African Americans in NCAA Division I head-coaching positions. *Journal of Sport Management, 20*, 387–417.

Cunningham, G. B., Miner, K., & McDonald, J. (2013). Being different and suffering the consequences: The influence of head coach-player racial dissimilarity on experienced incivility. *International Review for the Sociology of Sport, 48*, 689–705.

Cunningham, G. B., & Sagas, M. (2002). The differential effects of human capital for male and female Division I basketball coaches. *Research Quarterly for Exercise and Sport, 73*, 489–495.

Cunningham, G. B., & Sagas, M. (2004). Racial differences in occupational turnover intent among NCAA Division IA assistant football coaches. *Sociology of Sport Journal, 21,* 84–92.

Cunningham, G. B., & Sagas, M. (2005). Access discrimination in intercollegiate athletics. *Journal of Sport and Social Issues, 29,* 148–163.

Cunningham, G. B., & Sagas, M. (2007). Perceived treatment discrimination among coaches: The influence of race and sport coached. *International Journal of Sport Management, 8,* 1–20.

Cunningham, G. B., Sagas, M., & Ashley, F. B. (2001). Occupational commitment and intent to leave the coaching profession: Differences according to race. *International Review for the Sociology of Sport, 16,* 131–148.

Cunningham, G. B., & Singer, J. N. (2009). *Diversity in athletics: An assessment of exemplars and institutional best practices.* Indianapolis, IN: National Collegiate Athletic Association.

Cunningham, G. B., & Singer, J. N. (2010). "You'll face discrimination wherever you go": Student athletes' intentions to enter the coaching profession. *Journal of Applied Social Psychology, 40,* 1708–1727.

Davis-Delano, L. R., & Crosset, T. (2008). Using social movement theory to study outcomes in sport-related social movement. *International Review for the Sociology of Sport, 43,* 115–134.

Day, J. C., & McDonald, S. (2010). Not so fast, my friend: Social capital and the race disparity in promotions among college football coaches. *Sociological Spectrum, 30,* 138–158.

Dean, D. (2013). Museums as sites for historical understanding, peace, and social justice: Views from Canada. *Peace and Conflict: Journal of Peace Psychology, 19,* 325–337.

Demirel, E. (2014, January 10). Black college football coaches don't get second chances. *The Daily Beast.* Retrieved from http://www.thedailybeast.com/articles/2014/01/10/black-college-football-coaches-don-t-get-second-chances.html.

Doherty, A. J., & Chelladurai, P. (1999). Managing cultural diversity in sport organizations: A theoretical perspective. *Journal of Sport Management, 13,* 280–297.

Dovidio, J. F., & Gaertner, S. L. (2000). Aversive racism and selection decisions: 1989 and 1999. *Psychological Science, 11,* 319–323.

Dovidio, J. F., & Gaertner, S. L. (2004). Aversive racism. *Advances in Experimental Social Psychology, 36,* 1–52.

Eitzen, D. S., & Sage, G. H. (2009). *Sociology of North American sport* (8th ed.). Boulder, CO: Paradigm Publishers.

Everhart, B. C., & Chelladurai, P. (1998). Gender differences in preferences for coaching as an occupation: The role of self-efficacy, valence, and perceived barriers. *Research Quarterly for Exercise and Sport, 68,* 188–200.

Feagin, J. R. (2006). *Systemic racism: A theory of oppression.* New York: Routledge.

Ferdman, B. M. (2014). The practice of inclusion in diverse organizations. In B. M. Ferdman & B. R. Deane (Eds.), *Diversity at work: The practice of inclusion* (pp. 3–54). San Francisco: Jossey-Bass.

Fink, J. S., & Pastore, D. L. (1999). Diversity in sport? Utilizing the business literature to devise a comprehensive framework of diversity initiatives. *Quest, 51,* 310–327.

Fulks, D. L. (2014). *Revenues/expenses: 2004–13 NCAA Division I intercollegiate athletics programs report.* Indianapolis: National Collegiate Athletic Association.

Gaertner, S. L., & Dovidio, J. F. (2000). *Reducing intergroup bias: The Common Ingroup Identity Model.* Philadelphia: Psychology Press.

Galinsky, A. D., Hall, E. V., & Cuddy, A. J. C. (2013). Gendered races: Implications for interracial marriage, leadership selection, and athletic participation. *Psychological Science, 24,* 498–506.

Gonzales, G. L. (1996). The stacking of Latinos in Major League Baseball: A forgotten minority? *Journal of Sport and Social Issues, 20,* 134–160.

Greenhaus, J. H., Parasuraman, S., & Wormley, W. M. (1990). Effects of race on organizational experiences, job performance, evaluations, and career outcomes. *Academy of Management Journal, 33,* 64–86.

Hallinan, C. (1991). Aborigines and positional segregation in the Australian Rugby League. *International Review for the Sociology of Sport, 26,* 69–81.

Hamilton, B. H. (1997). Racial discrimination and professional basketball salaries in the 1990s. *Applied Economics, 29,* 287–296.

Harrison, L., Jr., Sailes, G., Rotich, W. K., & Bimper, A. Y., Jr. (2011). Living the dream or awakening from the nightmare: Race and athletic identity. *Race, Ethnicity and Education, 14,* 91–103.

Hawkins, B. (2013). *The new plantation: Black athletes, college sports, and predominantly White NCAA institutions.* New York: Palgrave Macmillan.

Hodge, S. R. (2014). Ideological repositioning: Race, social justice, and promise. *Quest, 66,* 169–180.

Hylton, K. (2009). *"Race" and sport: Critical race theory.* New York: Routledge.

Ianotta, R. J., & Wang, J. (2013). Trends in physical activity, sedentary behavior, diet, and BMI among US adolescents, 2001–2009. *Pediatrics, 132,* 606–614.

Kaiser, C. R., & Pratt-Hyatt, J. S. (2009). Distributing prejudice unequally: Do Whites direct their prejudice toward strongly identified minorities? *Journal of Personality and Social Psychology, 96,* 432–445.

Kamphoff, C., & Gill, D. (2008). Collegiate athletes' perceptions of the coaching profession. *International Journal of Sports Science & Coaching, 3,* 55–71.

Kanters, M. A., Bocarro, J. N., Edwards, M. B., Casper, J. M., & Floyd, M. F. (2013). School sport participation under two sport policies: Comparisons by race/ethnicity, gender, and socioeconomic status. *Annals of Behavioral Medicine, 45* (Suppl 1), S113–S121.

Kobach, M. J., & Potter, R. F. (2013). The role of mediating sports programming on implicit racial stereotypes. *Sport in Society, 16,* 1414–1428.

Lavoie, M. (1989). Stacking, performance differentials, and salary discrimination in professional hockey. *Sociology of Sport Journal, 6,* 17–35.

Lawrence, S. M. (2004). African American athletes' experiences of race in sport. *International Review for the Sociology of Sport, 40,* 99–110.

Lemstra, M., Rogers, M., Thompson, A., & Moraros, J. (2013). Prevalence and correlates of physical activity within on-reserve First Nations youth. *Journal of Physical Activity and Health, 10,* 430–436.

Lent, R. W., Brown, S. D., & Hackett, G. (1994). Toward a unifying social cognitive theory of career and academic interest, choice, and performance. *Journal of Vocational Behavior, 45,* 79–122.

Llopis-Goig, R. (2013). Racism, xenophobia and intolerance in Spanish football: Evolution and responses from the government and civil society. *Soccer & Society, 14,* 262–276.

Long, J., Robinson, P., & Spracklen, K. (2005). Promoting racial equality within sports organizations. *Journal of Sport & Social Issues, 29,* 41–59.

Lord, R., & Maher, K. (1991). *Leadership and information processing.* New York: Unwin Hyman.

Marshall, A. M. (2005). *Confronting sexual harassment: The law and politics of everyday life.* Burlington, VT: Ashgate.

Marshall, S. J., Jones, D. A., Ainsworth, B. E., Reis, J. P., Levy, S. S., & Macera, C. A. (2007). Race/ethnicity, social class, and leisure-time physical inactivity. *Medicine & Science in Sports & Exercise, 39,* 44–51.

McDowell, J., & Cunningham, G. B. (2007). The prevalence of occupational segregation in athletic administrative positions. *International Journal of Sport Management, 8,* 245–262.

McDowell, J., Cunningham, G. B., & Singer, J. N. (2009). The supply and demand side of occupational segregation: The case of an intercollegiate athletic department. *Journal of African American Studies, 13,* 431–454.

NCAA (2014). Race and gender demographics search. Available: http://web1.ncaa.org/rgdSearch/exec/main

Nishii, L. H., & Rich, R. E. (2014). Creating inclusive climates in diverse organizations. In B. M. Ferdman & B. R. Deane (Eds.), *Diversity at work: The practice of inclusion* (pp. 330–363). San Francisco: Jossey-Bass.

Pearson, A. R., Dovidio, J. F., & Gaertner, S. L. (2009). The nature of contemporary racism: Insights from aversive racism. *Social and Personality Psychology Compass, 3,* 314–338.

Powell, S. (2008). *Souled out? How Blacks are winning and losing in sports.* Champaign, IL: Human Kinetics.

Richard, O. C., & Miller, C. D. (2013). Considering diversity as a source of competitive advantage in organizations. In Q. M. Roberson (Ed.), *The Oxford handbook of diversity and work* (pp. 239–250). New York: Oxford University Press.

Robidoux, M. A. (2004). Narratives of race relations in Southern Alberta: An examination of conflicting sporting practices. *Sociology of Sport Journal, 21,* 287–301.

Robinson, J. (2009, January 8). Yale hires new coach and racial issue fades for the Ivys. *New York Times.* Retrieved from http://www.nytimes.com.

Rosenberg, M. (2004). Two few: Of 117 football coaches, two are black; it's called institutional racism. *Detroit Free Press.* Accessed from http://www.freep.com.

Rosette, A. S., Leonardelli, G. J., & Phillips, K. W. (2008). The White standard: Racial bias in leader categorization. *Journal of Applied Psychology, 93,* 758–777.

Ryan, M. K., & Haslam, S. A. (2007). The glass cliff: Exploring the dynamics surrounding the appointment of women into precarious leadership positions. *Academy of Management Review, 32,* 549–572.

Sack, A. L., Singh, P., & Thiel, R. (2005). Occupational segregation on the playing field: The case of Major League Baseball. *Journal of Sport Management, 19,* 300–318.

Sagas, M., & Cunningham, G. B. (2005). Racial differences in the career success of assistant football coaches: The role of discrimination, human capital, and social capital. *Journal of Applied Social Psychology, 35,* 773–797.

Sartore, M. L., & Cunningham, G. B. (2006). Stereotypes, race, and coaching. *Journal of African American Studies, 10*(2), 69–83.

Schein, E. (1990). Organizational culture. *American Psychologist, 45,* 109–119.

Schnittker, J., & McLeod, J. D. (2005). The social psychology of health disparities. *Annual Review of Sociology, 31,* 75–103.

Schultz, J. R., & Maddox, K. B. (2013). Shooting the messenger to spite the message: Exploring reactions to claims of racism. *Personality and Social Psychology Bulletin, 39,* 346–358.

Shuval, K., Weissblueth, E., Brezism, M., Araida, A., & DiPietro, L. (2009). Individual and socioecological correlates of physical activity among Arab and Jewish college students living in Israel. *Journal of Physical Activity and Health, 6,* 306–314.

Simmons, L., & Harding, S. (2009). Community-labor coalitions for progressive change. *Journal of Workplace Behavioral Health, 24,* 99–112.

Singer, J. N. (2005). Understanding racism through the eyes of African American male student-athletes. *Race Ethnicity and Education, 8,* 365–386.

Singer, J. N. (2008). Benefits and detriments of African American male athletes' participation in a big-time college football program. *International Review for the Sociology of Sport, 43,* 399–408.

Son Hing, L. S., Chung-Yan, G. A., Hamilton, L. K., & Zanna, M. P. (2008). A two-dimensional model that employs explicit and implicit attitudes to characterize prejudice. *Journal of Personality and Social Psychology, 94,* 971–987.

Steward, A. D., & Cunningham, G. B. (in press). Racial identity and its impact on job applicants. *Journal of Sport Management.*

Tate, W. F. (1997). Critical race theory and education: History, theory, and implications. In M. Apple (Ed.), *Review in research education 2* (pp. 191–243). Washington, DC: American Educational Research Association.

Tsui, A. S., & Gutek, B. A. (1999). *Demographic differences in organizations: Current research and future directions.* New York: Lexington Books.

Volz, B. D. (2013). Race and the likelihood of managing in Major League Baseball. *Journal of Labor Research, 34,* 30–51.

Washington, M., & Patterson, K. D. W. (2011). Hostile takeover or joint venture: Connections between institutional theory and sport management research. *Sport Management Review, 14,* 1–12.

Weeden, K. A. (2002). Why do some occupations pay more than others? Social closure and earnings inequality in the United States. *American Journal of Sociology, 108,* 55–101.

West, A., & Currie, P. (2008). School diversity and social justice: Policy and politics. *Educational Studies, 34,* 241–250.

Withycombe, J. L. (2011). Intersecting selves: African American female athletes' experiences in sport. *Sociology of Sport Journal, 28,* 478–493.

Wixon, M. (2006, May 17). Black coaches see dearth of opportunity in suburbs: High schools diverse, but few land top football jobs. *Dallas Morning News.* Retrieved May 17, 2006, from www.dallasnews.com.

Wong, E. (2002). The mystery of the missing minority coaches. *New York Times Online.* Retrieved from http://www.nytimes.com/2002/01/06/weekinreview/ideas-trends-getting-with-program-mystery-missing-minority-coaches.html.

Zinn, H. (2003). *A people's history of the United States: 1492–present.* New York: HarperCollins.

Sex and Gender

LEARNING objectives

After studying this chapter, you should be able to:

- Explain the meaning of *sex* and *gender* and the differences between the two concepts.
- Discuss the ways men's and women's experiences differ in the workplace.
- Describe gender differences in participation in physical activity and sport.

DIVERSITY CHALLENGE

Historically, sport was created by men, for men. As a result, it often seems as though all things male and masculine are privileged in sport. Despite advances over the years, an imbalance toward men can still be seen in participation rates, the monies and resources devoted to sport teams on university campuses, the media coverage of women's and men's sporting events, prize monies at major sport events, and leadership opportunities. Furthermore, the activities in which girls and boys compete, as well as their accomplishments in them, are differentially valued. Forms of physical activity in which young girls might engage are often seen as frivolous (e.g., jumping rope, ballet, cheer), leading to girls' discarding such activities by the time they reach adolescence; on the other hand, physical activities in which boys typically engage (e.g., running, football) are valued by society and have become the foundation of institutionalized sport.

These imbalances make the accomplishments of Nancy Lieberman all the more impressive. Lieberman dominated

women's basketball for years. She was a 1976 Olympian, contributed to two national championships while attending Old Dominion University, was the 1984 MVP of the Women's American Basketball Association, and at age 50 was the oldest person ever to play in the Women's National Basketball Association (WNBA). After her playing career, Lieberman served as head coach and general manager of the WNBA's Detroit Shock and also served as president of the Women's Sports Foundation.

Lieberman's accomplishments reach beyond women's basketball. She is recognized as the only woman ever to play in an all-male league, the United States Basketball League (1986–87). In 2009, Lieberman was named head coach of an NBA Development League team in Frisco, Texas. In that capacity, she became the first woman to serve as head coach of a men's professional basketball team, a feat described by the Women's Sports Foundation as her "most historic achievement." She also led the team to a playoff birth—its first. Commenting on the achievement,

Lieberman noted, "I can't look at anything as daunting because then it becomes overwhelming. I look at it as an unbelievable opportunity to do something positive for the sport I love. I've been on every level of this. I'm certainly used to being the first female or the only female to do something. It's second nature to me."

CHALLENGE REFLECTION

1. Some suggest that men are privileged in sport and women are disadvantaged. Do you agree with this perspective? Why or why not?

2. Nancy Lieberman was the first female coach of a men's professional basketball team. Do you think this accomplishment will open opportunities for women in basketball or other sports? Why or why not?

As the Diversity Challenge illustrates, gender is an important topic within the context of sport and physical activity. Women and men have historically had different access to sport and physical activity participation, as well as to leadership positions within those settings. Leaders, teammates, and work colleagues routinely treat women differently from men. Although there are exceptions, such as Nancy Lieberman's ascension to various leadership roles, the presence of a few women in top leadership roles does not nullify the gendered dynamics in sport. Instead, their presence in the roles makes them unusual—it is, after all, what makes them exceptions. This suggests that many other women do not have the same opportunities.

In this chapter, I continue with an examination of the categorical effects of diversity with a focus on sex and gender. In the first section, I present the concepts of sex, gender, and gender role identities. This is followed by a discussion of the experiences of men and women in the workplace, and I present an integrated framework to help understand these patterns. Finally, I explore the experiences of sport participants and whether such experiences differ between women and men.

Before proceeding, it is important to note that many of the topics discussed in this chapter intersect with those in Chapter 10 (on sexual orientation and gender identity). For instance, considerable evidence indicates that women face discrimination in the workplace and that this limits their career progression—a topic discussed in subsequent sections. Evidence also indicates that women face discrimination when others perceive them to be lesbian. For instance, rival coaches will try to "use" a coach's lesbian status against her when recruiting potential athletes. So as not to create redundancy, I limit the latter discussion and related topics to Chapter 10.

SEX AND GENDER

Although the terms are sometimes used interchangeably, there are differences between *sex* and *gender* (see Exhibit 5.1). As Powell (2011) notes, sex is a biological classification based on physiological properties and reproductive organs. Doctors assign a sex to a child at birth based on their assessment of these characteristics. *Gender,* on the other hand, is related to the social role expectations

Defining *sex* and *gender*.   EXHIBIT   **5.1**

Though often used interchangeably, *sex* and *gender* are distinct terms.

- **Sex:** a biological classification of individuals based on their physiological properties and reproductive apparatus.

- **Gender:** the social roles expected of men and women, including expectations related to attitudes, behaviors, and interests perceived to be appropriate for, or typical of, men and women. (The gender roles people adopt are influenced by at least four factors: parents, peers, schools, and the media.)

for women and men. Discussions of gender focus on the roles, attitudes, behaviors, and interests believed to be appropriate for, or typical of, members of one sex relative to the other. As one of my friends explains, "Sex is concerned with what is between your legs, while gender is what is in your head."

Let's consider some examples to illustrate the point. Sex differences represent variations that have biological foundations. Exercise physiologists who find that male and female mice respond differently to various exercise regimens are finding sex differences. Physiological responses are independent of social constructions about what it means to be a woman or man. On the other hand, gender differences arise from the social conditions placed on women and men, and are not rooted in the biology of the individual. For example, social constructions about the appropriate roles for mothers who work mean that for these mothers work–life balance can be a continual struggle. This potential strain makes the role of organizational support all the more important for women's retention in sport, as well as in other industries (Bruening & Dixon, 2008). We can also consider girls' interest in sport. Contrary to the view that girls and women are simply "made differently" from boys and men and, therefore, do not have an innate interest in sport, gender socialization and opportunities to participate in such endeavors actually account for many—if not most—perceived differences (for an overview, see Messner & Solomon, 2007).

professional PERSPECTIVES

Using Sexist Language. An important topic associated with gender issues concerns the use of sexist language— for example, the use of a false generic such as *mankind*, or the use of *girl* to refer to an adult woman. Sexist language implies that the masculine is the norm, and it perpetuates male privilege in society. It also serves to ostracize women and encourages them to disengage from professional opportunities (Stout & Dasgupta, 2011).

Parks and Roberton have extensively investigated sexist language among sport management students (Parks & Roberton, 2002, 2004). Their research shows that men are more likely than women to endorse sexist language and to offer biased rationales for doing so. For example, one person in their research commented: "A woman . . . will never be one hundred percent equal to a man. It is a concept that needs to be faced" and "If women want to be men, have them get a sex change." They have also found that attitudes toward women help explain why people endorse sexist language, concluding that sexist language may be important, from a symbolic standpoint, to people who either consciously or unconsciously believe that men are superior to women. The question, then, is how is the use of sexist language to be reduced or eliminated? Their research suggests that when people become aware of how sexist language negatively affects others, they make efforts to be more inclusive in their dialogue.

Although sex might be assumed to be a binary construct consisting of females and males, such is not always the case. Instead, there are people whose sex assigned at birth does not match their identities or expressions. We cover this topic more fully in Chapter 10. Additionally, some individuals seek to reinforce a gender binary such that females should express feminine characteristics (e.g., dependence, gentleness) while males should express masculine characteristics (e.g., aggressiveness, independence). However, as we will discuss in the following sections, this dichotomy does not exist, either. To borrow from Cahn (2011), despite the fact that many people like nice, clean categories, nature is disorderly and generally does not abide our preferences.

Performing Gender

Bem (1974, 1977) offered a foundational perspective of gender, suggesting that masculinity and femininity are distinct: a person could conceivably rank high on both attributes, low on both, or somewhere in between. Using this reasoning, Bem developed the Bem Sex-Role Inventory (BSRI). Based on their responses, individuals can be classified into one of four categories:

- *Masculine:* high masculinity, low femininity
- *Feminine:* low masculinity, high femininity
- *Androgynous:* high masculinity, high femininity
- *Undifferentiated:* low masculinity, low femininity

Bem's notion of androgyny—a word that comes from the Greek *andr* (meaning man) and *gyne* (meaning woman)—is unique to the gender identity literature. People with androgynous characteristics are thought to possess more desirable outcomes, such as high self-esteem and greater confidence, than people in other categories.

These relationships are nicely captured in a study of Brazilian adults (Carver, Vafaei, Guerra, et al., 2013). In this study, the authors asked the participants to complete a version of the BSRI and then classified them into the aforementioned categories. The authors observed that women and men were equally likely to be classified as masculine, just as they were equally likely to be classified as androgynous. The authors concluded that biological sex and gender are indeed different constructs.

In seeking to expand on Bem's work, Woodhill and Samuels (2003) suggested that gender roles can be both positive and negative. Consider the following: An elite-level swim coach with high levels of independence, ambition, compassion, and tolerance would fit desirable masculine (the first two characteristics) and feminine (the latter two characteristics) gender roles and be considered *positively* androgynous. Another swim coach might have high levels of both selfishness and submissiveness, characteristics that are negative attributes of masculinity and femininity, respectively. The latter coach would be considered *negatively* androgynous. The same distinctions can be made for people with only feminine, or only masculine, characteristics. The demarcation of gender roles in this manner is useful when we examine various outcomes, such as overall well-being. Woodhill and Samuels, for example, found that positively androgynous people scored higher on indicators of mental health and well-being than persons who were negatively androgynous, negatively masculine, negatively feminine, or undifferentiated androgynous. Thus, the gender roles that one adopts can have a meaningful impact on a variety of outcomes and overall well-being.

Gender socialization

How and what to think about gender is something that we learn, and this learning occurs throughout our lifetimes. The communities in which we live, music to which we listen, movies we watch, friends with whom we interact, and many other factors all socialize us. They teach us what is appropriate or not within a given time or setting.

Martin and Ruble (2009) focused on the developmental aspect of gender socialization—that is, how people learn about gender from birth through adolescence. They observed that children develop ideas about gender at a very young age. Consider, for instance, that children begin using gender labels in their speech at around 18 months. They begin to stereotype about behaviors and relational capacities among other boys and girls by age 4. Children as young as 6 are able to differentiate among the status associated with various jobs, and by the time they reach 11, they are able to attach the gender associations with those positions. For example, children at this age view "jobs for men" as more prestigious than "jobs for women." Finally, there is evidence that preschoolers react negatively to their peers who violate gender norms.

Given that these are all learned behaviors, it is useful to consider the various gender socialization agents. Drawing from a number of sources (Kane, 1995; Martin & Ruble, 2009; Powell, 2011; Valian, 1999), we consider five primary influences: parents, peers, schools, the media, and sport.

Parents. Parents play an influential part in children's gender role identity development (Powell, 2011; Valian, 1999). Parents transfer ideas to children about the appropriate roles for women and men in the world. Parents' views toward gender—conveyed both explicitly and implicitly to their children—and their behaviors influence how children think about and perform gender roles. For instance, in heterosexual households, when both parents work, children are likely to hold egalitarian views toward gender roles. In households where women are not physically active, children learn the message that sport and exercise are not activities for women (see also Johnson & Allen, 2013). Parents also encourage various behaviors among their children. This is done, for example, by giving boys and girls different toys, dressing them in different-colored clothes, and encouraging different kinds of physical activity.

Peers. Children's peers also influence their ideas about gender (Valian, 1999). This occurs partly through the ways in which the children respond to one another. Interestingly, girls respond favorably to other girls, irrespective of whether the peer behaviors are feminine, masculine, or neutral. Boys, on the other hand, play favorably with other boys who display masculine behaviors, but not necessarily with those who do not. This behavior is modeled by children as young as age two, leading Valian to conclude, "In this respect, two-year-olds are already like adults" (p. 54). The influence of their peers continues as children mature, such that through their interactions, the children learn what gender roles are appropriate, normative, or deviant within a given context.

Schools. Schools also influence the development of gender roles (Powell, 2011; Valian, 1999). Girls generally perform better academically than boys in school—a trend that exists in all academic areas, including math and science, across all ages, and through all levels of education. The differences in grades are not necessarily the result of varying cognitive ability; rather, they are usually the result of the girls' better work habits and study skills. Ironically, though, boys often receive more attention, both positive and negative, in the classroom than do girls. They are called on more often, praised more, criticized more, and express more ideas that are both rejected and accepted. Though girls volunteer to answer questions more often than boys do, they are called on less frequently and are afforded less time to provide answers. The cumulative effects potentially result in lower self-esteem among girls, relative to boys. This, in turn, negatively influences girls' choice of academic course work, the degrees they seek, and the career paths they pursue.

Mass media. Media—television, movies, print, radio, and the Internet—have a significant influence on individuals and on the culture, prompting some observers to suggest that they "have become one of the most powerful institutional forces for shaping values and attitudes in modern culture" (Kane, 1988, pp. 88–89). The media affect how we think, influence our attitudes toward various topics, and shape our perceptions of the roles men and women should play in society. Fink (in press) highlights as much in her analysis of how women and women's teams are portrayed by the media. Not only do women receive less coverage than men, but they also are depicted in qualitatively different ways. There is continued evidence that women frequently are portrayed in hypersexualized ways, their accomplishments are minimized, and photographs show them in passive poses rather than in athletic ones. The end result is a devaluing of women and their achievements, including in sport.

Sport. Finally, the structure and delivery of sport serve to socialize people related to gender and gender roles (Kane, 1995). Sport is usually designed in such a way that it magnifies differentiation between women and men. The differences are perpetuated and rigorously maintained so as to promote the ideas that (1) men are superior athletically to women, and (2) the differences are biologically based and, therefore, inherent.

Let's consider an example to illustrate this point: the structure of sport differs based on the sex of the participant. At early ages, boys and girls are separated and play with similarly sexed others. As they age, the differences between boys and girls are maintained and accentuated. Greater value is placed on skills predominantly observed among men (e.g., dunking a basketball), while the importance of skills accentuated in women's games (e.g., passing, team-based offensive schemes) is minimized. There are also different standards, such as the number of sets played in professional tennis (best of three for women, best of five for men) that privilege men and perpetuate the notion they are physically superior.

Kane (1995) suggests that conceptualizing sport performance along a continuum could break down these barriers, a point discussed in the Alternative Perspectives box.

ALTERNATIVE perspectives

Sport Performance Along a Continuum. Sport performance is frequently cast in such a way that it positions men as naturally superior to women—something based in biology. Proponents of such an idea will point to record holders: the fastest man is faster than the fastest woman, the long-jump record is held by a man, the strongest people on earth are men, and so on.

Mary Jo Kane, a professor at the University of Minnesota—where she also serves as director of the Tucker Center for Research on Girls & Women in Sport—suggests such thinking masks the accomplishments of women and perpetuates the notion that men are naturally better athletes. As an alternative, she suggests considering sport performance along a continuum. At one end is exceptional performance, and at the other is poor performance. Examination of the data will show that both women and men fall all along the continuum. Thus, some women will outperform some men, just as some men will outperform some women. Note that if men were inherently better athletes than women, such a dispersion would not occur.

Let's consider the Rock 'n' Roll San Antonio Marathon. In 2013, with 1,504 men running the full marathon, the top performer (Michael Wardian) completed the 26.2-mile race with a time of 2:31:19. That same year, 1,178 women completed the race, with the top performer (Jena Kincaid) doing so in 3:05:11. Alone, these data would support the notion of men's superiority. But what the data do not show is that Kincaid ran her marathon quicker than 1,491 of the men who ran the same race. Thus, the notion that all men are naturally superior to all women—when it comes to completing a marathon or participating in any other sport—is simply not correct.

GENDER IN THE WORK ENVIRONMENT

We now turn our attention to women and men in the workplace, examining the differences and similarities between women and men in workforce participation, earnings, and representation in management and leadership positions. Across these domains, men generally fare better than do women, despite a host of laws mandating gender equality in the workplace (see the box on the next page).

Participation in the Workforce

Men are more likely to enter the workforce than are women, though the gap has narrowed over the decades. According to the U.S. Census Bureau, in 1961, there were 61 women for every 100 men in the workforce. By 2009, this gap had narrowed to 77 women for every 100 men. The year 2009 was also the peak year for women's participation in the workforce.

The U.S. Bureau of Labor Statistics offers additional data to consider. In 2012, most women (57.7 percent) who could work chose to do so. A number of factors are associated with rates of employment among women. One of these is race, as African American and Hispanic women are more likely than Whites and Asians to experience unemployment. Divorced women are more likely to be employed than are married women. Among mothers, women with children age five or younger are less likely to work than their peers with older children.

Laws affecting women and men in the work environment

Many of the legal protections for women in the workplace are provided by Title VII of the Civil Rights Act of 1964, which was later amended by the Civil Rights Act of 1991. As discussed in Chapter 4, this law protects individuals against employment discrimination on the basis of race, color, religion, sex, or national origin. It applies to employers who are involved in interstate commerce and have 15 or more employees, including federal, state, and local government; educational institutions; labor unions; and players associations.

Title VII prohibits discrimination based on a person's sex. It is unlawful to make employment decisions related to hiring, firing, compensation, the availability or type of training, or any other term, condition, or privilege of employment based on an employee's sex. Employment decisions that are based on gender stereotypes concerning traits, abilities, or performance are also forbidden. This law prohibits employers from intentionally or unintentionally creating policies that disproportionately exclude people on the basis of sex for reasons that are not related to the job.

Title VII prohibitions include the following:

- **Sexual harassment.** The term *sexual harassment* covers a variety of behaviors, including requesting sexual favors and creating a hostile work environment. A hostile work environment exists "when an employee is subjected to repeated unwelcome behaviors that do not constitute sexual bribery but are sufficiently severe and pervasive that they create a work environment so hostile that it substantially interferes with the harassed employee's ability to perform his or her job" (Sharp, Moorman, & Claussen, 2014, p. 142). People of either sex can be sexually harassed. This prohibition also covers same-sex harassment.

- **Pregnancy-based discrimination.** Title VII was amended by the Pregnancy Discrimination Act of 1978. Pregnancy-related protections include hiring, pregnancy and maternity leave, health insurance, and fringe benefits.

Another issue related to sex discrimination is inequality of compensation for women and men. The Equal Pay Act of 1963 requires that women and men in the same organization receive equal pay for equal work. The jobs do not have to be identical; rather, the jobs have to be substantially equal. For example, if a kinesiology department hires two professors, a woman and a man, who have the same rank, possess roughly the same experience, and perform the same duties, both professors must be paid the same salary, even though they may teach different courses.

Five factors are considered to determine violations of the Equal Pay Act:

1. **Skill.** The pay may differ between women and men if the two people have dissimilar job-related skills. For example, a coach with 500 career wins is considered to have more skill than a coach with only 42 career wins, because the number of games won is a job-related skill. However, two ticket-clerk jobs at a professional sport franchise are considered equal even if one of the clerks has a master's degree, because the advanced degree is not required for the job.

2. **Effort.** Compensation can vary if there are differences in the physical or mental efforts needed to complete a certain task or hold a particular job. For example, an employee at a fitness club who is charged with moving the weight machines around the facility exerts considerably more physical effort than the employee who checks the membership status of patrons when they enter the facility. Thus, the former employee may be paid more than the latter, regardless of the employees' sex.

3. **Responsibility.** People who hold more meaningful responsibilities may be paid more than their counterparts. A regional salesperson who also coordinates the efforts and responsibilities of other salespeople earns a greater salary because of the extra responsibilities. It should be noted, however, that the increased responsibilities must be meaningful.

4. **Working conditions.** Two factors are considered with respect to working conditions: the physical surroundings and hazards. People with more challenging or difficult work conditions may be paid more than others.

5. **Establishment (place of employment).** The Equal Pay Act applies only to differences in compensation among employees of the same organization.

Based on the number of complaints filed with the EEOC (27,687 in 2013), it appears that incidents of sex discrimination are common. Companies that discriminate based on sex can receive severe financial punishments. In 2013 alone, over $126.8 million in damages were collected for persons who made complaints. (This figure does not include damages recovered through litigation.) In addition, EEOC data indicate that an additional 7,256 sexual harassment complaints were filed in 2013. During that year, $44.6 million in damages were collected.

Earnings

Despite their increased presence in the workforce and laws mandating equal pay among women and men (see Exhibit 5.2), men are paid more, on average, than women. Wage differences between men and women have been found since the beginning of data collection on the topic. According to the U.S. Census Bureau, women earned 78 percent of what men, on average, did in 2013. This figure has improved considerably since 1960, when women earned 60 cents to the dollar of what men earned; yet, the earnings gap persists.

Differences in earnings are present throughout sport. Wage differences between women and men are seen among administrators, coaches, and athletes. As one illustrative case, let's consider professional tennis. Although major tournaments, such as Wimbledon, pay the same amount to the winners of the women's and men's draws (£1.76 million in 2014), a gender gap remains among the lesser-known tournaments. As a result, women earn about 23 percent less than men (Flake, Dufur, & Moore, 2012). Some might argue that the pay gap exists because men play a best of five, while women play a best of three—differences that, as we previously noted, are based on notions of physical superiority among men. However, spectators and

Women-to-men earnings ratio in the United States, 1960 to 2013. | EXHIBIT | 5.2

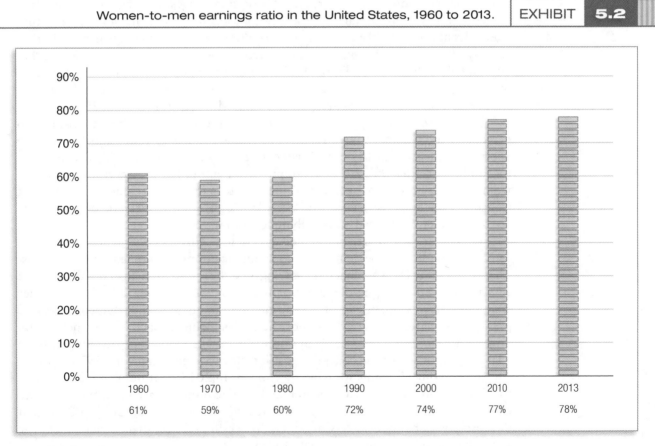

Source: U. S. Census Bureau.

other constituents pay for the entertainment of the match, irrespective of its length (Flake et al., 2012). A male tennis player who dominates his competition in straight sets throughout the tournament is not paid less than one who wins the tournament by playing the maximum five sets in each match. Why, then, should women be paid less for playing two or three sets per match? Contrary to the view that men are paid more because consumer demand is higher for men's tennis, Flake and colleagues note that tournament tickets routinely allow access to both women's and men's events, and there is no consistent evidence that men's tennis has higher television ratings than women's. Thus, alternate explanations for the differences in earnings are not plausible.

Leadership Roles

Women have historically been underrepresented in organizational management and leadership positions. As recently as 1972, women filled only 17 percent of all management positions. Times changed, however, and by 1995 women filled 42.7 percent of all management positions (Stroh, Langlands, & Simpson, 2004). In 2012, according to the Catalyst Institute, women comprised 51.5 percent of the persons working in management and professional positions within the United States. The numbers in Canada were lower (35.4 percent). These data suggest that women are making strides within organizational settings. A closer look at the data, however, reveals that women continue to be considerably underrepresented in top management positions. A study of Fortune 500 companies conducted by the Catalyst Institute indicated that women held only 14.3 percent of all corporate officer positions and only 8.1 percent of the top-earning positions in these companies. Over one in four companies had *no* women corporate officers (Soares, Bartkiewicz, Mulligan-Ferry, et al., 2013).

Similar trends are apparent in sport organizations. Women represent only 36 percent of the commissioners for the Australian Sports Commission (Australian Sports Commission, 2014) and 36 percent of the executive board members in Sport England (Sport England, 2014). Examples from within North America include that women represent only 27 percent of the directors of the Coaching Association of Canada (Coaching Association of Canada, 2014) and 43 percent of the USOC board of directors (United States Olympic Committee, 2014).

Women are also underrepresented as coaches. This was not always the case. In 1972, women held 90 percent of the coaching positions for women's college teams. That year, Title IX was enacted, barring sex discrimination in federally funded educational activities (see the accompanying box). As a result, additional monies were directed to women's sports, resulting in an increase in the compensation and prestige associated with coaching those activities. Being a coach of a women's team now became an attractive, viable option for many men, and they steadily occupied a larger proportion of the coaching positions for women's teams. By 1978, only 58 percent of women's teams were led by women. In 2014, that number had dropped to 43.4 percent (Acosta & Carpenter, 2014). The numbers are far worse when we consider the head coaches among men's teams, where women hold just 3 percent of those positions (Acosta & Carpenter, 2014). In practice, then, coaching college sports has largely become an activity for men.

The underrepresentation of women in management and leadership positions is referred to as the "glass ceiling" (Valian, 1999). This concept describes the in-

Title IX

A law that significantly influences sport organizations is Title IX, which states:

> No person in the United States shall, on the basis of sex, be excluded from participation in, be denied the benefits of, or be subjected to discrimination under any educational program or activity receiving Federal financial assistance. (Title IX of the Education Amendments of 1972, P.L. 92-318, 20 U.S.C. § 1681)

Note that the words *sport, athletics, physical education,* and *recreation* do not appear in the law. Nevertheless, this legislation affects sport perhaps more than any other educational program or activity. In essence, it requires that equal opportunities be provided to women and men participating in activities that receive federal financial assistance. Because almost every high school and institution of higher education in the United States receives some federal financial assistance, either directly or indirectly, the law influences almost all aspects of amateur athletics. The following brief history of and overview of compliance with the law draws from Carpenter and Acosta's (2005) comprehensive and authoritative text, *Title IX*.

HISTORY OF TITLE IX

Title IX was passed in 1972 as part of the Education Amendments. The law provided little direction to administrators about how to provide equal opportunities for men and women in educational settings. Thus, the Office of Civil Rights (OCR) developed regulations that "would breathe an enforceable life into Title IX" (Carpenter & Acosta, 2005, p. 6). Congress approved these regulations in 1975, giving them the force of law. The regulations are used by organizations and the courts to interpret, measure, and enforce Title IX.

Of particular application to athletics are the following regulations:

▪ **Section 106.37:** When athletic scholarships are offered, they must be offered to both women and men in proportion to the number of women and men participating in athletics overall.

▪ **Section 106.41(a):** No person shall, on the basis of sex, be excluded from, denied the benefits of, or be discriminated against in any form of athletics (e.g., interscholastic, intercollegiate, club, or intramural).

▪ **Section 106.41(b):** Separate athletic teams can be formed for women and men. If a school supports a men's team but does not offer a similar sport for women, then women must be allowed to try out for the men's team. The exceptions to this are contact sports such as rugby, ice hockey, football, and basketball.

▪ **Section 106.41(c):** Schools that support athletic teams should provide equal opportunities to both women and men. To do so, the athletic director should consider 10 factors:

1. whether the teams are congruent with the interests and abilities of members of both sexes;
2. the provision of equipment and supplies;
3. the manner in which games and practices are scheduled;
4. travel and per diem;
5. coaching and academic counseling;
6. compensation of the coaches and academic tutors;
7. the provision and quality of locker rooms and facilities (both practice and game);
8. the provision of medical and training staff and their facilities;
9. the provision of housing, dining facilities, and dining services; and
10. overall publicity.

Later policy interpretations identified two additional factors: recruitment and support services. Thus, the financial aid regulations identified in Section 106.37, the 10 regulations in Section 106.41(c), and the two factors identified in the policy interpretations established 13 areas to consider in the enforcement of Title IX.

Institutions had until 1978 to comply with the law, but few met the deadline. In 1984, a meaningful blow was dealt to Title IX by the U.S. Supreme Court's decision in *Grove City College v. Bell,* 465 U.S. 555. The Court addressed two issues:

1. Does the word *program* refer to the institution as a whole or to individual programs within that entity?
2. Does an institution have to receive direct federal funding in order for it to be subject to Title IX guidelines?

(continued)

Title IX, *continued*

With respect to the first issue, the Court found that only those units receiving federal monies were included in the term *program*. Therefore, if an athletic department did not receive federal funds, it was not bound by Title IX regulations. However, with respect to the second issue, the Court ruled that an institution did not have to receive direct federal funds to be subject to the Title IX regulations.

The effects of the *Grove City* decision were severe. Because many (if not most) university athletic departments did not receive federal monies, they were now not subject to Title IX. As a result, many schools immediately cut women's scholarships and selected women's teams to be cut at the end of the academic year. In addition, all complaints that had been filed with the OCR were closed, and many Title IX lawsuits were dismissed.

According to Carpenter and Acosta (2005), Congress considered the Supreme Court's interpretation of *program* to be incorrect. To remedy this situation, the Civil Rights Restoration Act of 1987 was passed over President Reagan's veto in 1988. This Act clarified issues surrounding the word *program*. According to the Civil Rights Restoration Act, the term *program* refers to the entire institution, not just individual programs within that entity. Most physical education departments and athletic departments do not receive federal funds; however, the universities in which they are housed *do* receive such funds. Thus, every entity within a university now fell under Title IX guidelines.

Two other cases of particular relevance to the history of Title IX are *Franklin v. Gwinnett County Public Schools,* 503 U.S. 60 (1992) and *Jackson v. Birmingham Board of Education,* 544 U.S. 167 (2005). The key issue in *Franklin* was whether or not monetary damages could be awarded to persons who successfully sued under Title IX. In this case, a student who had been sexually harassed filed a Title IX lawsuit, but neither the statute nor the regulations contained any language related to monetary damages. The Supreme Court unanimously ruled that monetary damages could be awarded under Title IX. As a result of this ruling, Title IX enforcement changed dramatically. It is now in the best financial interest of institutions to comply with Title IX mandates. Failing to do so means losing potentially large sums of money—money the institutions can ill afford to relinquish. The *Jackson* case is also relevant. Roderick Jackson, a male coach of a girls' high school basketball team,

alleged that the girls on the team were discriminated against. He complained to the Board of Education about this discrimination and was subsequently fired. He sued the board, claiming that his termination was in retaliation for complaining about the discrimination. The Supreme Court ruled that Title IX whistle-blowers who were subjected to retaliation for filing a Title IX claim could recover damages.

TITLE IX COMPLIANCE

The 1979 policy interpretations, together with a 2003 letter of clarification, established a three-prong test for evaluating Title IX compliance by universities and colleges (Carpenter & Acosta, 2005). According to this framework, often referred to as *the three-prong test,* a school must select one of the following in order to be compliant with the law:

1. Provide participation opportunities for female and male athletes that are in proportion to their respective enrollments at the university (referred to as substantial proportionality). [Note that the numbers need not be equal; they need only be in proportion. Consider the following examples, which are based on U.S. Department of Education data (n.d.). In 2013, women represented 47 to 48 percent of the athletes at both Rutgers University and Virginia Commonwealth University. During that same year, women constituted 48 percent of the undergraduates at Rutgers and 56 percent of the undergraduates at Virginia Commonwealth. Using these data, we can conclude that Rutgers was in compliance with Title IX, while Virginia Commonwealth University was not. The two schools had different compliance outcomes, even though they provided the same opportunities for female athletes.]

2. Demonstrate a history and continued practice of program expansion for athletes of the underrepresented sex. [Under this condition, the school need not be compliant at the time of its evaluation; rather, it only has to demonstrate that it has continually strived to be more equitable and provide opportunities for persons of the underrepresented sex to develop their skills and compete in athletic events.]

3. Effectively demonstrate that the programs and opportunities offered are congruent with the interests and abilities of the underrepresented sex (referred to as the accommodation of interest and ability test). [Critics from both sides have weighed in on this test. One might ask, if

---

Title IX, *continued*

women are the underrepresented sex and do not have an interest in playing varsity sports, why should the athletic department spend the time and money to field a team? On the other hand, interest in sports may wane if opportunities are not provided. How can an athletic department claim in good faith that women are not interested in participating in sports if few women's sports are offered? If sports are offered, perhaps they would attract women to the campus who might not otherwise have come.]

In its 2003 letter of clarification, the OCR notes that, traditionally, schools have viewed substantial proportionality (the first prong) as a "safe harbor" for Title IX compliance. That is, they primarily sought to satisfy this requirement to the neglect of the other prongs. This is a misinterpretation. According to the OCR, each of the three tests is a viable option for determining Title IX compliance, and no single test is preferred over the others.

---

visible, but certainly real, barrier that limits the upward progression of women in the organizational context. In addition to the glass ceiling, women also encounter "glass walls" (akin to the occupational segregation discussed in Chapter 4; Stroh et al., 2004). Glass walls prevent people from moving laterally within an organization or profession. For example, women are often employed in the administrative ranks of university athletic departments in positions called Senior Woman Administrator. They are rarely seen in management positions in fund raising or those that oversee men's sports, even though men are routinely charged with overseeing women's sports (NCAA, 2014). Rather, these positions, which have high prestige and may be considered requisite stepping-stones to becoming a head athletic director, are generally reserved for men. These ideas are consistent with the notion of male hegemony—one of the critical theories discussed in Chapter 2.

POSSIBLE EXPLANATIONS FOR LEADERSHIP UNDERREPRESENTATION OF WOMEN

In the following section, I offer possible explanations for the underrepresentation of women in leadership positions. Given the usefulness of multilevel thinking in such an endeavor (see Chapter 4; see also Burton, 2015), I focus the explanations at the macro-, meso-, and micro-levels of analysis. See Exhibit 5.3 for a summary.

Macro-Level Factors

Macro-level factors are those activities and influences that operate at the industry and societal levels of analysis. These include the nature of sport, stakeholder expectations, and gender norms, among others.

Nature of sport

Sport is a field that routinely calls for people to log 12- to 15-hour days. Whether it is the coach who spends countless hours in practices, games, recruiting, and the like, or the administrator who oversees the budgets, operations, and promotions of the

EXHIBIT   5.3 Multilevel model explaining the underrepresentation of women in leadership positions.

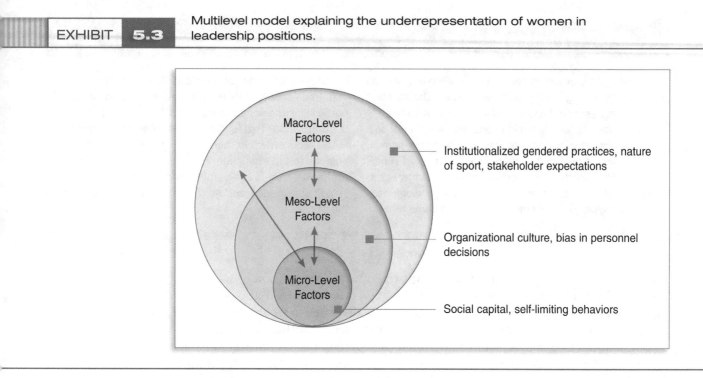

sport organization, people in sport work long hours. Time for other life activities, such as those related to friends and family, must be reduced or given half-heartedly, or these activities must be put on hold for another time. Women are more likely than men to experience stress resulting from conflicts between time spent at work and time spent with family, a phenomenon known as *work–family conflict* (Dixon & Bruening, 2005). Gender stereotypes call for the woman to spend more time than the man on family and domestic duties. Thus, women are more likely than men to have to choose between coaching and family or find a compromise between the two (but see also Shein & Chen, 2011, for a discussion of work–family enrichment, where work–life interface positively contributes to one or both domains). These factors affect women's overall well-being and desire to remain in coaching (Allen & Shaw, 2009). See the Diversity in the Field box for additional information about how work–family conflict influences elite athletes.

Stakeholder expectations

External stakeholders are people who have an interest in a sport organization's operations and success. They can be internal (e.g., players, coaches) or external (e.g., community members, boosters), and they wield influence through their voice, money, and power. In many cases, their expectations for the sport organization serve to reinforce gendered norms and stereotypes. These dynamics can help to perpetuate the underrepresentation of women in leadership, especially when the individuals doing the hiring rely on these stakeholders or give preference to their requests.

Schull, Shaw, and Kihl (2013) captured these dynamics in their study of a change in leadership at an NCAA member athletic department. One group of

DIVERSITY   IN THE FIELD

Elite Athletes as Mothers.   Many elite athletes are also parents. A well-known example is that of Ken Griffey, who played Major League Baseball with his son, Ken Griffey, Jr. However, just as we find in coaching, the potential strain created by balancing the time needed to be a parent with the time needed to be an elite athlete is often greater for women than it is for men. For instance, Lorena Ochoa, the number-one-ranked female golfer in the world, retired from golf at age 28 in 2010, citing the desire to spend more time raising her children. Other elite athletes, such as tennis's Lindsay Davenport, have retired or taken extended leaves of absence in order to spend time with their children. Elite male athletes do not often make similar career choices, however, and this may be due, in part, to the variations in gender stereotypes for women and men.

Palmer and Leberman (2009), in noting this trend, interviewed elite female athletes to understand how they balance family and sport obligations. The authors found that the athletes in their study managed the multiple roles and potential constraints (e.g., guilt, lack of time) by emphasizing the centrality of sport to their sense of self. The women also pointed to the importance of strong social networks, as well as concerted efforts to integrate the two roles. Based on their study, Palmer and Leberman discussed the importance of developing practices and policies that allow mothers to achieve and sustain elite status. Possible examples include flextime schedules and alternate work locations, among others.

stakeholders for this department consisted of men who had given generously to the university and athletic department in the past. These individuals used their collective influence to shape media messages concerning who should (a man) and should not (a woman) be the next athletic director. They used politically savvy techniques to promote men for the position and cast women as ill suited for the role. In doing so, they helped construct the narrative of an ideal man who would, they felt, best serve the interests of the department. Their influence was effective and helped determine who was hired for the role.

Institutionalized gendered practices

Institutionalized gendered practices represent a third macro-level factor influencing the underrepresentation of women in leadership positions. Through such practices, ideas about gender and appropriate roles and behaviors of women and men become entrenched within a given culture. These norms and values become embedded into everyday systems and institutions, influencing the way people think and act, as well as what they take for granted. For example, many Western religious teachings hold that men should lead women—a mindset that has resulted in men's serving as the head of the family, women's being forbidden to hold certain roles in places of worship, and different role expectations for women and men. As noted, these ideals are largely culturally bound; some Eastern religious traditions, in fact, feature a feminine deity (Simmer-Brown, 2001).

Institutionalized sexism can also privilege men over women in the employment arena. This occurs, for example, through occupational segregation, where women are overrepresented in some roles (e.g., nursing, clerical work, elementary school teaching) and underrepresented in others (e.g., manufacturing, truck driving). Similar patterns occur in sport, where men hesitate to fill certain positions because they feel these are "women's work" (Shaw & Slack, 2002, p. 93). Coaching is frequently portrayed as best suited for men, even though many coaching activities, such as nurturing athletes, facilitating their play, and providing them with individualized consideration, are more associated with the feminine nature than the masculine (Knoppers, 1992; Walker & Sartore-Baldwin, 2013).

Perhaps not surprisingly, the roles associated with men are often the highest-paid professions and the places where the largest wage gaps exist. However, even in jobs thought to be suited for women, women are routinely paid less than their male counterparts. In fact, Glynn and Wu (2013) analyzed data from the Bureau of Labor Statistics and found that of the 538 job titles listed, women were paid more (on average) in *only* 7. These seven professions (respiratory therapist, computer support specialist, operations research analyst, stock clerk, medical scientist, accounting, packer) collectively represent 3 percent of all women workers; thus, for the remaining 97 percent, men are paid more, on average. The sexism that reproduces these wage differences operates in a similar manner to privilege men over women when it comes to holding leadership positions in sport.

Meso-Level Factors

Meso-level factors are those operating at the organizational level. These include bias in personnel decisions and organizational culture, among others.

Bias in personnel decisions

As you will recall from Chapter 3, bias is expressed at the cognitive level through stereotypes, at the affective level through prejudice, and at the behavioral level through discrimination. Each of these types of bias can occur in the making of personnel decisions and negatively affect women's representation as leaders in sport organizations.

Stereotypes. In her classic work, Schein (1973, 1975) asked middle managers to rate how well a list of descriptors matched a woman in general, a man in general, and an effective middle manager. She observed that the characteristics believed to embody the successful middle manager were closely aligned with those thought to describe a man in general. This was true for both male and female respondent managers in her sample. Thus, to think of a successful manager was to think of a man, not a woman. Although her work was conducted 40 years ago, Schein's findings are still applicable today (Koenig, Eagley, Mitchell, & Ristikari, 2011). The strength of these associations has decreased over time, but they remain salient and are likely to be reinforced among men.

These stereotypes persist in sport, as people are likely to associate leadership with men and masculine characteristics (Burton, Barr, Fink, & Bruening, 2009; Hovden, 2010). Furthermore, people are more likely to use masculine, rather than feminine, pronouns when they describe an ideal manager (Knoppers & Anthonissen, 2008). Employees are likely to make different, gender-based attributions for leader behaviors, such that "a strong man is direct and a direct woman is a bitch" (Shaw & Hoeber, 2003, p. 347). If organizational decision makers associate "being a manager" with "being a man," then women are at a distinct disadvantage in the hiring and promotion processes.

Prejudice. Prejudice also affects the underrepresentation of women in leadership roles. In some cases, the prejudice is associated with gendered stereotypes of leaders. Women are penalized when they violate leadership expectations—for instance, when a woman acts in ways perceived to be masculine, such as being aggressive or dominant (Rudman & Phelan, 2008). This penalty is manifested through prejudice and lower evaluations of the counter-stereotypical woman relative to her peers and to men. This linkage occurs for several reasons (Rudman, Moss-Racusin, Phelan, & Nauts, 2012). In some cases, people want to take steps to justify and maintain the status quo, while in other cases, non-stereotypical women might be viewed as a threat. For still others, they express prejudice as a way of supporting dominant gendered systems and beliefs. Irrespective of the reason, women face prejudice and, as a result, are deemed to be ill suited for leadership roles. Similar penalties exist for men who violate normative gender roles, as discussed in the Alternative Perspectives box.

Discrimination. Finally, discrimination limits women's opportunities for leadership roles. This discrimination takes several forms. Consistent with access discrimination, organizational decision makers could prefer men over women when filling coaching vacancies. In the athletics context, this means that athletic directors, most of whom are men, prefer other men to serve as coaches. Regan and I (2012) conducted a study whereby we collected data from 611 community colleges in the United States and examined the demographics of the athletic director and head coaches of three women's sports: basketball, volleyball, and softball. Most (82.7 percent) of the athletic directors were men, and as we expected, men were likely to hire other men to lead the women's basketball and softball teams. In addition, the gender of the athletic director was associated with the homogeneity of the head coaches: a male athletic director was more likely to have an all-male staff, just as a female athletic director was more likely to have an all-female staff. Thus, both women and men are likely to hire persons similar to themselves, and, as men are overrepresented in hiring positions, this pattern results in an underrepresentation of women.

In many respects, power is at the heart of discrimination (Sartore & Cunningham, 2007). Tucker Center's Mary Jo Kane commented on the status of women coaching women's teams: "I think it can be summed up in one word: power. The stakes have gotten higher—there's money, scholarships, TV contracts. It's a new career for men,

ALTERNATIVE perspectives

Men Breaking Gender Roles. People routinely develop stereotypes about the qualifications of leaders, and these include notions of assertiveness, dominance, and decisiveness—characteristics people stereotypically associate with men rather than with women. These stereotypes serve to disadvantage women because women are not believed to embody the characteristics needed to be a leader; when they do, they are judged harshly for displaying counter-stereotypical traits.

Because of these dynamics and women's underrepresentation in leadership roles, women have been the focus of most scientific inquiries into stereotypes surrounding leadership. There is also evidence, though, that men face backlash when they do not follow gender roles. In an experimental study testing these topics, Moss-Racusin, Phelan, and Rudman (2010) examined reactions to modest men who were applying for a lab manager position. Participants believed the modest man violated gender stereotypes for men, and they also believed him to be weak and uncertain. The authors concluded that men who do not adhere to gendered norms face backlash. The authors suggested that, being cognizant of this, men are likely to take steps to avoid these negative reactions, such as conforming to masculine norms, even though these norms might not be consistent with their beliefs.

and men have taken it over" (as cited in Anderson, 2001, p. 88). Consistent with the previous discussion of gender stereotypes, Kane also suggests, "I think there is still some deep-seated cultural assumption that if you want to take your program big time, you want to get a *real* coach, so you should get a male coach" (as cited in Anderson, 2001, p. 88). Thus, gender stereotypes about power may lead organizational decision makers to decide consciously to hire men over women (discrimination), thinking that men are more likely have "what it takes" to be a successful coach.

Treatment discrimination also influences the underrepresentation of women in coaching positions. Female middle managers (e.g., assistant coaches) are afforded fewer opportunities to engage in meaningful work activities, such as budget oversight or leading men's sports, a pattern that results in less varied work experiences for women relative to men (Hoffman, 2010; Tiell, Dixon, & Lin, 2012). Because current women coaches are treated differently, variations appear in the career outcomes achieved by men and women. A study I conducted with Sagas (Cunningham & Sagas, 2002) offers evidence of this. We surveyed male and female assistant coaches of men's and women's university athletics teams and found that the women had more valued human capital investments (e.g., investments made in playing experience, winning playing honors) than the men. In fact, 25 percent of all the men in the sample had never played university athletics, compared with only 3.3 percent of women without such experience. Nevertheless, the men had longer coaching tenures and more of the desired attitudes toward coaching (e.g., head coaching intentions) than the women. Although women had greater human capital, they did not receive the return on such investments that men did. Kirchmeyer notes, "Low returns for female managers can be explained by perceptual distortions and cognitive biases among employers that lead to discriminatory practices" (1998, p. 675).

Organizational culture

Organizational culture is the final meso-level factor. Recall from Chapter 4 that culture refers to the basic assumptions and beliefs in the workplace that are passed down over time and considered valid by most of the employees (Schein, 1990). Values, processes, organizational artifacts (e.g., banners, trophies), and practices all represent elements of culture. In many respects organizational cultures in which women are marginalized and subjugated are commonplace in sport (Cunningham, 2008). These cultures have been established and maintained over time such that they now are taken for granted. When this occurs, people do not think about or critically examine structures, values, and processes that privilege men over women. When questioned about it, employees will frequently note that the practices are commonplace and routine. Thus, change becomes challenging.

That many sport organizations have organizational cultures that privilege men is disappointing. Such work environments limit women's contributions to sport and the prospects of inclusive workplaces where all can thrive. There is evidence, for instance, that inclusiveness not only enhances women's commitment to the workplace and their intentions to remain there, but produces the same effects among men (Spoor & Hoye, 2013). Organizational cultures that privilege men also reinforce the notion that men are best suited for leadership positions (Knoppers & McDonald, 2010), thereby ensuring women's underrepresentation in those roles.

Micro-Level Factors

Finally, micro-level factors also affect the underrepresentation of women in leadership positions. These are elements operating at the individual level of analysis and include social capital and self-limiting behaviors, among others.

It is important to note that micro-level factors do not operate in a vacuum. Men are not, for example, predisposed to remain in coaching any more than women are. Instead, any gender differences in vocational interests, turnover, or social networks are a function of other factors operating at the meso and macro levels (Cunningham, Bergman, & Miner, 2014). Failure to recognize these influences results in blaming the victim: women are faulted for their attitudes and behaviors related to sport. Such attributions are false.

Social capital

As noted in Chapter 4, *social capital* refers to the social networks people maintain. This capital includes the number of contacts people have, how close their relationships are with these individuals, and the influence members of the network have in the workplace and sport industry. The social network members provide important information about opportunities, and they also advocate on behalf of the individual (Seibert, Kraimer, & Liden, 2001).

The "old boy's network" is alive and well within sport. It serves to privilege men, ensuring their maintenance as the power holders in sport (Kilty, 2006). Social capital differences affect the presence of women across the sport industry, including whether they serve as coaches of men's teams (Walker & Bopp, 2010). Women and men working in sport not only have different amounts of social capital, but they enjoy different returns on their social capital investments. Sagas and I observed these effects in a study of collegiate athletics administrators (Sagas & Cunningham, 2004). We examined the role of both human capital investments and social capital investments in the promotions women and men received. Consistent with the idea of differential returns, men's social capital investments resulted in increased promotions, while similar returns were not apparent for women.

Self-limiting behaviors

Societal pressures to maintain certain gender roles, influential stakeholders advocating for men to be leaders, a work structure that allows for little attention to one's personal life, bias among leaders, an organizational culture privileging men, and differential returns for social capital investments—all of these are messages that women routinely receive, and they say that men are best suited for leadership roles in sport. Over time, this feedback can become internalized, and when it does, women might stop seeking advancement or even decide to leave sport altogether. These actions are referred to as self-limiting behaviors. They are the result of continuous negative feedback—at the macro, meso, and micro levels—pertaining to women's ability and their effectiveness (Norman, 2010; Sartore & Cunningham, 2007).

Self-limiting behaviors take several forms. In some cases, it might be limited attraction to leadership roles and other forms of advancement. We have observed as much in studies of assistant coaches of college sports teams in both the United States (Sagas, Cunningham, & Pastore, 2006) and Canada (Cunningham, Doherty, &

Gregg, 2007). In these studies, women, relative to men, expressed fewer intentions to become a head coach and were less likely to have applied for a head coaching position in the past. In other cases, self-limiting behaviors mean that women leave sport sooner than men. In a study I conducted with Sagas and Ashley, 68 percent of the women in the sample reported that they planned to leave the profession before age 45, whereas only 15 percent of men expressed similar plans (Sagas, Cunningham, & Ashley, 2000). A similar pattern exists among sport officials (Tingle, Warner, & Sartore-Baldwin, 2014). Collectively, the self-limiting behaviors—again, behaviors resulting from the various macro-, meso-, and micro-level factors—limit the number of women in leadership roles.

GENDER AND PARTICIPATION IN PHYSICAL ACTIVITY AND SPORT

We now shift to a focus on how gender affects people's engagement in sport and physical activity, as well as their experiences in those activities. In each domain examined, men and boys participate at higher levels than do women and girls. These differences are a reflection of the gendered nature of sport—a context that privileges men and activities associated with them, all the while trivializing and objectifying women and their activities.

Physical Activity Participation

In Exhibit 5.4, drawing from information on the HealthyPeople.gov website, I offer an overview of the physical activity patterns among women and men. Overall, only one in five adults in the United States meets recommended guidelines for engaging in aerobic activity and muscle-strengthening activity. Men are significantly more likely to meet these guidelines than are women. This difference occurs in all five years considered. The data also show that women are significantly more likely than men to engage in no physical activity. Fortunately, the rates of sedentary behaviors have decreased over time. In 2007, over 40 percent of women engaged in no physical activity; this proportion dropped to 30.8 percent by 2012. Similar patterns have occurred among men, though the decrease is not as substantial (38.3 percent to 36.7 percent).

Finally, the gender differences observed among adolescents are even greater than those among adults. Again drawing from the HealthyPeople.gov data, 18.4 percent of youth in grades 9–12 meet physical activity guidelines. Boys are more than twice as likely as girls to meet these guidelines: 24.8 percent versus 11.4 percent, respectively. Only *1 in 11 girls* meets the federal guidelines.

Sport Participation

Gender differences also exist in participation on formal sport teams. One place this pattern is seen is in high school athletics within the United States. Exhibit 5.5 offers a summary of data collected from the 2013–14 High School Athletic Survey, conducted by the National Federation of State High School Associations. This graph yields a historical overview of girls' involvement in athletics, as shown through their percentage of total participants. Two points are particularly relevant. First, substan-

Percentages of men and women meeting physical activity guidelines.

EXHIBIT **5.4**

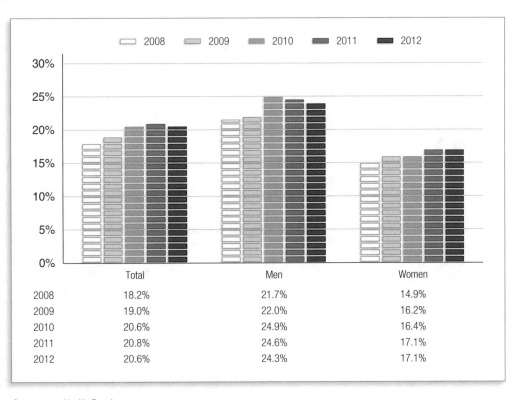

	Total	Men	Women
2008	18.2%	21.7%	14.9%
2009	19.0%	22.0%	16.2%
2010	20.6%	24.9%	16.4%
2011	20.8%	24.6%	17.1%
2012	20.6%	24.3%	17.1%

Source: www.HealthyPeople.gov.

tial changes have occurred over time. In the 1971–72 academic year (the year prior to Title IX's enactment), girls represented just 7 percent of all high school athletes. In the years following Title IX, the participation began to narrow, dropping from an 85 percent difference in 1971–72 to a 17 percent difference in 2001–02. That gap has remained relatively constant since 2001–02. This brings us to the second point: girls continue to be underrepresented as high school athletics participants. Girls constituted 42 percent of all participants during the 2013–14 academic year. This figure is lower than what we would expect based on their proportion of all high school students: 48 percent, according to the U.S. Census Bureau.

Similar patterns are apparent within college sports. According to the NCAA (2014), women represented 42 percent of all athletes (*n* = 150,016) during the 1999–2000 academic year despite the fact that women outnumber men among college undergraduates. This participation gap continues today, as 43 percent of all NCAA college athletes during the 2012–13 year were women (*n* = 203,571).

Finally, evidence suggests that gender differences exist in how people experience sport. That is, participation rates vary between men and women, but so too does the quality of their experiences while participating. We will examine three ways these differences are manifested: the marginalization of women and women's sports, sexual abuse of women, and the objectification of women.

EXHIBIT   **5.5**   Boys' versus girls' participation in high school athletics.

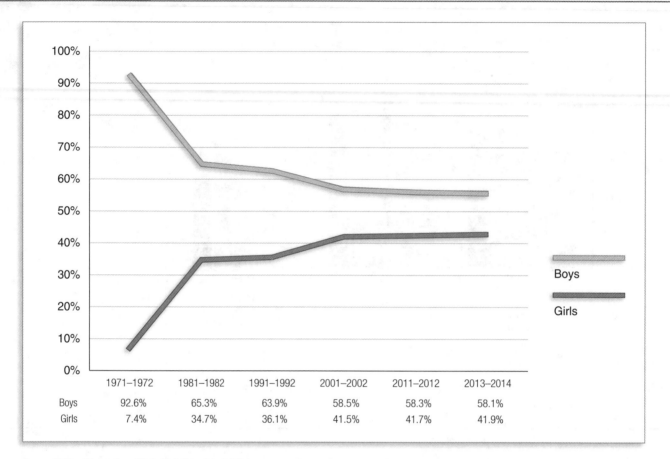

	1971–1972	1981–1982	1991–1992	2001–2002	2011–2012	2013–2014
Boys	92.6%	65.3%	63.9%	58.5%	58.3%	58.1%
Girls	7.4%	34.7%	36.1%	41.5%	41.7%	41.9%

Source: National Federation of State High School Associations.

Marginalization

Women and women's sport are frequently marginalized. We see this, for example, in the difference in attention paid to men's sports and to women's sports. Sport activities associated with boys and men receive more coverage in newspapers, in online sites, in radio broadcasts, and on television (Fink, in press). In fact, so much attention is devoted to men's sports that sport and men are automatically associated with one another. Illustrative of this point, the sports-focused website ESPN does give some attention to women's sports, but most of the site is devoted to men, their sports, and their accomplishments. Why else would ESPN create a separate site, ESPNW—a site devoted to female athletes and women's sports? The absence of the corresponding ESPNM, which might include content focusing on male athletes and their sports, suggests that the primary focus of ESPN is men and men's sports.

The marginalization of women's sports is also seen in the delivery of sport. In many interscholastic athletics events, the girls' teams regularly play prior to the boys' teams, as a sort of opening act, so to speak. At the collegiate level, comparatively less money is devoted to women's sports, to their coaches, and to their operations (Fulks, 2014). Finally, as Coakley (2015) has noted, programs for boys and men are unlikely to be cut when budget cuts occur because they are considered to be more legitimate—again, a phenomenon that illustrates the gendered nature of sport.

Sexual abuse

It is possible for any athlete to experience sexual abuse from teammates, coaches, or sport administrators; however, evidence suggests that girls and women are at a heightened risk of this behavior. Research from the International Olympic Committee suggests that sexual abuse and harassment of female athletes take place at all age levels, across all levels of competition. These behaviors include sexual jokes, threatening and intimidating language and behavior, and actions that are sexual in nature. Such abuse has a negative effect on the athletes' psychological well-being, their physical health, and their performance (see www.olympic.org/sha). Mistreatment also negatively affects individuals who observe the abuse, as well as the group as a whole (Cunningham et al., 2014).

Rodríguez and Gill (2011) examined this topic in a study of former female athletes from Puerto Rico. Some of the athletes told of feeling "like a piece of meat" (p. 329) when they were harassed. The women reported that verbal abuse, such as crude verbal abuse or sexual remarks, was more common and socially sanctioned than were physical forms of harassment. The mistreatment took a negative psychological and physical toll on the athletes, including feelings of disgust, guilt, shame, and fear. The athletes also reported negative consequences associated with reporting the harassment; not only were their careers hurt, but they were blamed for the occurrences and cast in a disparaging light. Women in the study told of using several coping techniques, including avoidance, seeking social support from others, resistance, confronting the harasser, and seeking advocacy.

For a discussion of subtle forms of mistreatment of athletes, see the box on the following page.

Objectification

Girls and women participating in sport are frequently objectified, with a focus placed on their femininity, attractiveness, and body over their athletic prowess (Sartore-Baldwin, 2012). This is observed in fans' treatment of women, media portrayals, and the marketing of women's sports.

Fans represent one source of objectification. Rodríguez and Gill's (2011) study spoke of this, noting that fans engaged in sexually explicit taunts and chants directed toward the players. In their sport consumption behavior, fans also reinforce gender stereotypes and the preference for femininity among female athletes. Sports considered feminine in nature are routinely the most viewed women's sports at the Olympic Games (e.g., gymnastics, ice skating). In some cases, the gender of fans affects their consumption of women's sports. In an experimental study, Jones and Greer (2011) observed that men were more interested in reading about the results from a volleyball match (a stereotypically feminine sport) when a feminine-looking (rather than masculine-looking) female athlete was photographed. For women, the type of sport did not affect their interest, but they did prefer to read stories when a masculine-looking female athlete was depicted.

Subtle forms of mistreatment of athletes

In addition to overt forms of harassment, women are subjected to subtle kinds of mistreatment. These come in many forms, including microaggressions and incivility. *Microaggressions* refer to "the everyday verbal, nonverbal, and environmental slights, snubs, or insults, whether intentional or unintentional, that communicate hostile, derogatory, or negative messages to target persons based solely on their marginalized group membership" (Sue, 2010, p. 3). The use of gendered language or differential access to fields for boys' and girls' teams represent possible examples. *Incivility,* on the other hand, refers to "low intensity deviant behavior with ambiguous intent to harm the target, in violation of workplace norms for mutual respect" (Andersson & Pearson, 1999, p. 457). Examples include supervisors ignoring or speaking over women in their work environment, among others. In both cases, the mistreatment is subtle in nature, yet nonetheless harmful.

Subtle forms of mistreatment gradually affect an individual, one small slight at a time. Some of my colleagues have referred to this as "death by a thousand cuts."

Others have used another analogy to illustrate the point: If you place a frog in a pot of boiling water, it will recognize the danger and jump out immediately. This is akin to overt forms of mistreatment, such as quid pro quo sexual harassment. In this case, because the behavior is so overt, the psychological and behavioral reaction is strong and immediate. On the other hand, if you place a frog in a pot of water that is room temperature and slowly bring it to a boil, the frog will remain in the water until it dies. This is analogous to subtle forms of mistreatment. A woman might dismiss one seemingly innocuous joke or a single case where someone spoke over her. Over time, when this kind of abuse continues, the effects accumulate, negatively affecting the woman's psychological, health, and behavioral outcomes. However, because the mistreatment was subtle in nature, it is difficult to pinpoint any particular case that "broke the camel's back." Instead, the cumulative effects of slights, jokes, and general mistreatment over time resulted in the harmful outcomes (see also Cunningham, Miner, & McDonald, 2013).

The media portray women in hypersexualized ways, reinforcing gender stereotypes (Cooky, Messner, & Hextrum, 2013; Kane, 2013). Whereas male athletes are routinely depicted in active poses—such as throwing a pitch during a baseball game—the same is not true for women. Instead, they are frequently shown in supportive poses, such as cheering on a teammate, or outside of the sport context altogether, such as in a dinner gown. The media is likely to focus on a woman's appearance, femininity, and heterosexuality, reinforcing gendered norms. These patterns are observed across media types, including print, radio, and major online news sites. There is some evidence, though, that new media, such as blogs and Twitter, might offer more balanced, equitable coverage of women and women's sports (Eagleman, Burch, & Vooris, 2014).

Finally, women are routinely objectified in sport marketing efforts. Female athletes who are hired as product endorsers are frequently depicted in hypersexualized poses—a tendency not observed among men. Some evidence suggests that when people are asked to evaluate the effectiveness of a female athlete as a product or event endorser, her attractiveness is one of the primary factors they consider (Cunningham, Fink, & Kenix, 2008; Fink, Parker, Cunningham, & Cuneen, 2012). It is possible that marketers might use these results to justify a "sex sells" mentality, even though the practice has damaging effects on various sport stakeholders.

The objectification of women in sport has several negative outcomes. First, it trivializes sport participants, casting them as sex objects rather than serious athletes. This is contrary to how elite athletes prefer to be depicted (Kane, LaVoi, & Fink, 2013). Second, as a testament to people's interconnectedness with one another (Cunningham,

2014), the effects reach beyond the specific consumer or athletes involved in the portrayal. In a series of experiments, Daniels (Daniels, 2009, 2012; Daniels & Wartena, 2011) shows that girls and women who view images of hypersexualized athletes have negative body images themselves and express feelings of anger. Boys viewing such images see women as sex objects. However, the effects can be reversed. When they view women in athletic poses, girls and women have positive body images and believe female athletes are role models, while boys value women for their accomplishments.

chapter SUMMARY

This chapter focused on the experiences of men and women in regard to their gender in the sport context. The Diversity Challenge demonstrated the substantial influence of sex and gender on who participates in sport, the allocation of resources, and attitudes toward sport. In the workplace, work experiences, compensation, access to managerial and leadership positions, and attitudes toward their careers differ between women and men. After reading this chapter, you should be able to:

1. **Explain the meaning of *sex* and *gender* and the differences between the two concepts.**

   Sex refers to the biological characteristics, such as reproductive organs, that distinguish women and men. *Gender,* on the other hand, refers to the social roles expected of women and men, with an emphasis on the concepts of masculinity and femininity. Though the two terms are sometimes used interchangeably, they have different meanings and connotations.

2. **Discuss the ways men's and women's experiences differ in the workplace.**

   Across a variety of contexts, research shows that, relative to men, women are less likely to be members of the workforce, they receive less compensation for their work, and they are less likely to hold upper-echelon management positions. These trends are present in the sport and physical activity context. Factors at the macro level (institutionalized gendered practices, nature of sport, stakeholder expectations), meso level (bias in personnel decisions, organizational culture), and micro level (social capital, self-limiting behaviors) all influence the underrepresentation of women in leadership positions.

3. **Describe gender differences in participation in physical activity and sport.**

   Girls and women, relative to boys and men, are more likely to be sedentary and less likely to engage in physical activity or in formal sport. They are also likely to have poorer experiences than boys and men while participating in those activities. These differences are manifested through marginalization, sexual abuse, and objectification.

QUESTIONS for discussion

1. What are the primary gender stereotypes associated with women and men? Are those stereotypes observable today?
2. What are the primary factors that influence the formation of gender stereotypes? Which is likely to have the strongest impact?

3. What is the influence of gender stereotypes on participation in sport and physical activity?

4. Why are gender differences in earnings still present today? Are they more likely to be seen in one context than in another?

5. What are the basic tenets of Title IX, and what are the steps an athletic department can take to comply with the law?

6. Several potential explanations for the underrepresentation of women in management and leadership positions were discussed in the chapter. Which is the most important in explaining this phenomenon? Why?

7. Why does the participation of women in sport and physical activity lag behind that of men? What steps can sport managers take to reverse this trend?

learning ACTIVITIES

1. Suppose you are involved in searching for a coach for a women's team at your university. What emphasis would you put on the gender of the coach in the hiring process? What about the assistant coaches? Divide into two groups and discuss.

2. Search online for the presence of female administrators in national sport organizations such as USA Basketball.

WEB resources

▪ **National Association of Collegiate Women Athletic Administrators,** www.nacwaa.org

Provides information for administrators who are women.

▪ **Title IX,** www.titleix.info

Provides an overview of Title IX across various domains of higher education, including sport.

▪ **Women's Sports Foundation,** www.womenssportsfoundation.org

Provides a wide range of resources related to girls' and women's participation in sport.

reading RESOURCES

Messner, M. A. (2010). *Out of play: Critical essays on gender and sport.* Albany, NY: SUNY Press.

Offers an overview of the key topics related to gender and sport, including the gendered nature of sport, intersectionality, violence, and gendered imagery.

Powell, G. N. (2011). *Women and men in management* (4th ed.). Thousand Oaks, CA: Sage.

Comprehensive overview of the issues surrounding women in the workplace; examines historical aspects, sex and gender, and the influence of sex and gender on employment decisions, leadership, and career aspirations.

Roper, E. A. (Ed.) (2013). *Gender relations in sport*. Boston: Sense Publishers.

An edited volume for introductory students; focuses on several key issues, including Title IX, sexual harassment, gender and media, and intersectionality, among others.

REFERENCES

Acosta, R. V., & Carpenter, L. J. (2014). *Women in intercollegiate sport: A longitudinal study—thirty-seven year update—1977–2014.* Unpublished manuscript, Brooklyn College, Brooklyn, NY.

Allen, J. B., & Shaw, S. (2009). Women coaches' perceptions of their sport organization's social environment: Supporting coaches' psychological needs? *The Sport Psychologist, 23,* 346–366.

Anderson, K. (2001, January/February). Where are all the women coaches? *Sports Illustrated for Women, 3*(1), 86–91.

Andersson, L. M., & Pearson, C. M. (1999). Tit for tat? The spiraling effect of incivility in the workplace. *Academy of Management Review, 24,* 452–471.

Australian Sports Commission (2014). *The Board.* Retrieved from www.ausport.gov.au.

Bem, S. L. (1974). The measurement of psychological androgyny. *Journal of Consulting and Clinical Psychology, 42,* 155–162.

Bem, S. L. (1977). On the utility of alternative procedures for assessing psychological androgyny. *Journal of Consulting and Clinical Psychology, 45,* 196–205.

Bruening, J. E., & Dixon, M. A. (2008). Situating work-family negotiations within a life-course perspective: Insights on the gendered experiences of NCAA Division I head coaching mothers. *Sex Roles, 58,* 10–23.

Burton, L. J. (2015). Underrepresentation of women in sport leadership: A review of research. *Sport Management Review, 18,* 155–165.

Burton, L. J., Barr, C. A., Fink, J. S., & Bruening, J. E. (2009). "Think athletic director, think masculine?": Examination of the gender typing of managerial subroles within athletic administration positions. *Sex Roles, 61,* 416–426.

Cahn, S. (2011). Testing sex, attributing gender: What Caster Semenya means to women's sports. *Journal of Intercollegiate Sport, 4,* 38–48.

Carpenter, L. J., & Acosta, R. V. (2005). *Title IX.* Champaign, IL: Human Kinetics.

Carver, L. F., Vafaei, A., Guerra, R., Freire, A., & Phillips, S. P. (2013). Gender differences: Examination of the 12-item Bem Sex Roles Inventory (BSRI-12) in an older Brazilian population. *PLOS ONE, 8* (10), 1–7.

Coaching Association of Canada. (2014). *Board of directors.* Retrieved from www.coach.ca.

Coakley, J. (2015). *Sports in society: Issues and controversies* (11th ed.). New York: McGraw-Hill.

Cooky, C., Messner, M. A., & Hextrum, R. H. (2013). Women play sport, but not on TV: A longitudinal study of televised news media. *Communication & Sport, 1,* 203–230.

Cunningham, G. B. (2008). Creating and sustaining gender diversity in sport organizations. *Sex Roles, 58,* 136–145.

Cunningham, G. B. (2014). Interdependence, mutuality, and collective action in sport. *Journal of Sport Management, 28,* 1–7.

Cunningham, G. B., Bergman, M. E., & Miner, K. N. (2014). Interpersonal mistreatment of women in the workplace. *Sex Roles, 71,* 1–6.

Cunningham, G. B., Doherty, A. J., & Gregg, M. J. (2007). Using social cognitive career theory to understand head coaching intentions among assistant coaches of women's teams. *Sex Roles, 56,* 365–372.

Cunningham, G. B., Fink, J. S., & Kenix, L. J. (2008). Choosing an endorser for a women's sporting event: The interaction of attractiveness and expertise. *Sex Roles, 58,* 371–378.

Cunningham, G. B., Miner, K., & McDonald, J. (2013). Being different and suffering the consequences: The influence of head coach-player racial dissimilarity on experienced incivility. *International Review for the Sociology of Sport, 48,* 689–705.

Cunningham, G. B., & Sagas, M. (2002). The differential effects of human capital for male and female Division I basketball coaches. *Research Quarterly for Exercise and Sport, 73,* 489–495.

Daniels, E. A. (2009). Sex objects, athletes, and sexy athletes: How media representations of women athletes can impact adolescent girls and college women. *Journal of Adolescent Research, 24,* 399–422.

Daniels, E. A. (2012). Sexy versus strong: What girls and women think of female athletes. *Journal of Applied Developmental Psychology, 33*(2), 79–90.

Daniels, E. A., & Wartena, H. (2011). Athlete or sex symbol: What boys think of media representations of female athletes. *Sex Roles, 65,* 566–579.

Dixon, M. A., & Bruening, J. E. (2005). Perspectives on work–family conflict in sport: An integrated approach. *Sport Management Review, 8,* 227–253.

Eagleman, A., Burch, L. M., & Vooris, R. (2014). A unified version of London 2012: New-media coverage of gender, nationality, and sport for Olympics consumers in six countries. *Journal of Sport Management, 28,* 457–470.

Fink, J. S. (in press). Female athletes, women's sport, and the sport media commercial complex: Have we really "come a long way, baby"? *Sport Management Review.*

Fink, J. S., Parker, H. M., Cunningham, G. B., & Cuneen, J. (2012). Female athlete endorsers: Determinants of effectiveness. *Sport Management Review, 15,* 13–22.

Flake, C. R., Dufur, M. J., & Moore, E. L. (2012). Advantage men: The sex pay gap in professional tennis. *International Review for the Sociology of Sport, 48,* 366–376.

Fulks, D. L. (2014). *Revenues & expenses: 2004–2013 NCAA Division I intercollegiate athletics programs report.* Indianapolis, IN: National Collegiate Athletic Association.

Glynn, S. J., & Wu, N. (2013, April). The gender wage gap differs by occupation. *Center for American Progress.* Retrieved from www.americanprogress.org.

Hoffman, J. (2010). The dilemma of the senior woman administrator role in intercollegiate athletics. *Journal of Issues in Intercollegiate Athletics, 3,* 53–75.

Hovden, J. (2010). Female top leaders—prisoners of gender? The gendering of leadership discourses in Norwegian sports organizations. *International Journal of Sport Policy, 2,* 189–203.

Johnson, R. C., & Allen, T. D. (2013). Examining the links between mothers' work experiences, physical activity, and child health. *Journal of Applied Psychology, 98,* 148–157.

Jones, A., & Greer, J. (2011). You don't look like an athlete: The effects of feminine appearance on audience perceptions of female athletes and women's sports. *Journal of Sport Behavior, 34,* 358–377.

Kane, M. J. (1988). Media coverage of the female athlete before, during, and after Title IX: *Sports Illustrated* revisited. *Journal of Sport Management, 2,* 87–99.

Kane, M. J. (1995). Resistance/transformation of the oppositional binary: Exposing sport as a continuum. *Journal of Sport & Social Issues, 19,* 191–218.

Kane, M. J. (2013). The better sportswomen get, the more the media ignore them. *Communication & Sport, 1,* 231–236.

Kane, M. J., LaVoi, N. M., & Fink, J. S. (2013). Exploring elite female athletes' interpretations of sport media images: A window into the construction of social identity and "selling sex" in women's sports. *Communication & Sport, 1*(3), 269–298.

Kilty, K. (2006). Women in coaching. *The Sport Psychologist, 20,* 222–234.

Kirchmeyer, C. (1998). Determinants of managerial career success: Evidence and explanation of male/female differences. *Journal of Management, 24,* 673–692.

Knoppers, A. (1992). Explaining male dominance and sex segregation in coaching: Three approaches. *Quest, 44,* 210–227.

Knoppers, A., & Anthonissen, A. (2008). Gendered managerial discourses in sport organizations: Multiplicity and complexity. *Sex Roles, 58,* 93–103.

Knoppers, A., & McDonald, M. (2010). Scholarship on gender and sport in *Sex Roles* and beyond. *Sex Roles, 63,* 311–323.

Koenig, A. M., Eagley, A. H., Mitchell, A. A., & Ristikari, T. (2011). Are leadership stereotypes masculine? A meta-analysis of three research paradigms. *Psychological Bulletin, 137,* 616–642.

Martin, C. L., & Ruble, D. N. (2009). Patterns of gender development. *Annual Review of Psychology, 61,* 353–381.

Messner, M. A., & Solomon, N. M. (2007). Social justice and men's interests: The case of Title IX. *Journal of Sport and Social Issues, 31,* 162–178.

Moss-Racusin, C. A., Phelan, J. E., & Rudman, L. A. (2010). When men break the gender roles: Status incongruity and backlash against modest men. *Psychology of Men & Masculinity, 11,* 140–151.

NCAA (2014). Race and gender demographics search. Available: http://web1.ncaa.org/rgdSearch/exec/main

Norman, L. (2010). Bearing the burden of doubt: Female coaches' experiences of gender relations. *Research Quarterly for Exercise and Sport, 81,* 506–517.

Palmer, F. R., & Leberman, S. I. (2009). Elite athletes as mothers: Managing multiple identities. *Sport Management Review, 12,* 241–254.

Parks, J. B., & Roberton, M. A. (2002). The gender gap in student attitudes toward sexist/nonsexist language: Implications for sport management education. *Journal of Sport Management, 16,* 190–208.

Parks, J. B., & Roberton, M. A. (2004). Attitudes toward women mediate the gender effect on attitudes toward sexist language. *Psychology of Women Quarterly, 28,* 233–239.

Powell, G. N. (2011). *Women & men in management* (4th ed.). Thousand Oaks, CA: Sage.

Regan, M. R., & Cunningham, G. B. (2012). Analysis of homologous reproduction in community college athletics. *Journal for the Study of Sports and Athletes in Education, 6*(2), 159–170.

Rodríguez, E. A., & Gill, D. L. (2011). Sexual harassment perceptions among Puerto Rican female former athletes. *International Journal of Sport and Exercise Psychology, 9,* 323–337.

Rudman, L. A., Moss-Racusin, C. A., Phelan, J. E., & Nauts, S. (2012). Status incongruity and backlash effects: Defending the gender hierarchy motivates prejudice against female leaders. *Journal of Experimental Social Psychology, 48,* 165–179.

Rudman, L. A., & Phelan, J. E. (2008). Backlash effects for disconfirming gender stereotypes in organizations. In P. A. Brief & B. M. Staw (Eds.), *Research in organization behavior* (vol. 4, pp. 61–79). New York: Elsevier.

Sagas, M., & Cunningham, G. B. (2004). Does having the "right stuff" matter? Gender differences in the determinants of career success among intercollegiate athletic administrators. *Sex Roles, 50,* 411–421.

Sagas, M., Cunningham, G. B., & Ashley, F. B. (2000). Examining the women's coaching deficit through the perspective of assistant coaches. *International Journal of Sport Management, 1,* 267–282.

Sagas, M., Cunningham, G. B., & Pastore, D. (2006). Predicting head coaching intentions of male and female assistant coaches: An application of the theory of planned behavior. *Sex Roles, 54,* 695–705.

Sartore, M. L., & Cunningham, G. B. (2007). Ideological gender beliefs, identity control and self-limiting behavior within sport organizations. *Quest, 59,* 244–265.

Sartore-Baldwin, M. L. (2012). Gender issues in sport & physical activity. In G. B. Cunningham & J. N. Singer (Eds.), *Sociology of sport and physical activity* (pp. 329–351). College Station, TX: Center for Sport Management Research and Education.

Schein, E. (1990). Organizational culture. *American Psychologist, 45,* 109–119.

Schein, V. E. (1973). The relationship between sex role stereotypes and requisite management characteristics. *Journal of Applied Psychology, 57,* 95–100.

Schein, V. E. (1975). Relationships between sex role stereotypes and requisite management characteristics among female managers. *Journal of Applied Psychology, 60,* 340–344.

Schull, V., Shaw, S., & Kihl, L. A. (2013). "If a woman came in … she would have been eaten alive": Analyzing gendered political processes in the search for an athletic director. *Gender & Society, 27,* 56–81.

Seibert, S. E., Kraimer, M. L., & Liden, R. C. (2001). A social capital theory of career success. *Academy of Management Journal, 44,* 219–237.

Sharp, L. A., Moorman, A. M., & Claussen, C. L. (2014). *Sport law: A managerial approach* (3rd ed.). Scottsdale, AZ: Holcomb Hathaway.

Shaw, S., & Hoeber, L. (2003). "A strong man is direct and a direct woman is a bitch": Gendered discourses and their influence on employment roles in sport organizations. *Journal of Sport Management, 17,* 347–375.

Shaw, S., & Slack, T. (2002). "It's been like that for donkey's years": The construction of gender relations and the cultures of sports organizations. *Culture, Sport, Society, 5,* 86–106.

Shein, J., & Chen, C. P. (2011). *Work–family enrichment: A research of positive transfer.* Rotterdam: Sense Publishers.

Simmer-Brown, J. (2001). *Dakini's warm breath: The feminine principle in Tibetan Buddhism.* Boston: Shambhala Publications.

Soares, R., Bartkiewicz, M. J., Mulligan-Ferry, L., Fendler, E., & Kun, E. W. C. (2013). *2013 Catalyst Census: Fortune 500 women executive officers and top earners.* New York: Catalyst.

Spoor, J. R., & Hoye, R. (2013). Perceived support and women's intentions to stay at a sport organization. *British Journal of Management, 25,* 407–424.

Sport England (2014). *Board and executive team.* Retrieved from www.sportengland.org.

Stout, J. G., & Dasgupta, N. (2011). When *he* doesn't mean *you*: Gender-exclusive language as ostracism. *Personality and Social Psychology Bulletin, 37,* 757–769.

Stroh, L. K., Langlands, C. L., & Simpson, P. A. (2004). Shattering the glass ceiling in the new millennium. In M. S. Stockdale & F. J. Crosby (Eds.), *The psychology and management of workplace diversity* (pp. 147–167). Malden, MA: Blackwell.

Sue, D. W. (2010). Microaggressions, marginality, and oppression: An introduction. In D. M. Sue (Ed.), *Microaggression and marginality: Manifestation, dynamics, and impact* (pp. 3–24). Hoboken, NJ: John Wiley & Sons.

Tiell, B. S., Dixon, M. A., & Lin, Y. (2012). Roles and tasks of the senior woman administrator in role congruity theory perspective: A longitudinal progress report. *Journal of Issues in Intercollegiate Athletics, 5,* 247–268.

Tingle, J. K., Warner, S., & Sartore-Baldwin, M. L. (2014). The experience of former women officials and the impact on the sporting community. *Sex Roles, 71,* 7–20.

United States Department of Education (n.d.). The equity in athletics data analysis cutting tool. Retrieved from http://ope.ed.gov/athletics/.

United States Olympic Committee (2014). *Board of directors.* Retrieved from www.teamusa.org.

Valian, V. (1999). *Why so slow? The advancement of women.* Cambridge, MA: MIT Press.

Walker, N. A., & Bopp. T. (2010). The under-representation of women in the male-dominated workplace: Perspectives of female coaches. *Journal of Workplace Rights, 15,* 47–64.

Walker, N. A., & Sartore-Baldwin, M. L. (2013). Hegemonic masculinity and the institutionalized bias toward women in men's collegiate basketball: What do men think? *Journal of Sport Management, 27,* 303–315.

Woodhill, B. M., & Samuels, C. A. (2003). Positive and negative androgyny and their relationship with psychological health and well-being. *Sex Roles, 48,* 555–565.

Age

LEARNING objectives

After studying this chapter, you should be able to:

- Discuss the various ways in which age and age diversity are conceptualized.
- Provide an overview of how age is related to stereotypes, prejudice, and discrimination in the work environment.
- Analyze the intersection of age and sport, physical activity, and leisure participation.

DIVERSITY CHALLENGE

Physical inactivity rates in the United States have steadily risen over time, to the detriment of the country and its citizens. In fact, the World Health Organization estimates that over 60 percent of the population does not achieve the minimum recommendations for daily physical activity. According to the American Heart Association, a lack of physical activity is associated with a host of health problems, including heart disease, high blood pressure, diabetes, obesity, and low levels of "good" cholesterol. Conversely, participating in regular physical activity provides multiple benefits. According to the American Heart Association, it can

- help prevent bone loss (reducing the risk of fractures) and reduce the risk of many diseases associated with aging.
- increase muscle strength and improve balance and coordination, which can reduce the likelihood of falling and help maintain functionality and independence.

- reduce the incidence of coronary heart disease, hypertension, non-insulin-dependent (type 2) diabetes, colon cancer, depression, and anxiety.

Most people do not engage in the recommended levels of physical activity, and participation levels continually decrease with age. This is particularly noteworthy in Western countries, where the average age continues to increase. Thus, if trends continue, the current physical activity patterns will only be exacerbated over time.

Of course, physical inactivity is not characteristic of all persons, even all seniors. Rather, many persons age 50 and over are very active. The Senior Games prove that it is possible to remain active later in life, and that many people do. This is an event, held every two years, that affords persons age 50 to 100+ the opportunity to participate competitively in 18 medal sport events (e.g., archery, race walking) and 7 exhibitions (e.g., fencing, sailing). The 2013 Games were held in the Cleveland, Ohio, area. The Games are a major undertaking: the 2013 event saw 10,088 athletes competing at 19 different cites, and an additional 18,000 visitors came to watch the Games take place. The economic impact was estimated to be $36.1 million. David Gilbert, President and CEO of the Greater Cleveland Sports Commission, remarked, "The 2013 National Senior Games was a success on every level."

Sources: In the news (2009). 2013 National Senior Games impact study reveals higher than expected economic activity. Retrieved from www.clevelandsports.org. / American Heart Association (2014, April). The price of inactivity. Retrieved from www.americanheart.org. / American Heart Association (2015, January). Physical activity in older Americans. Retrieved from www.americanheart.org.

CHALLENGE REFLECTION

1. Despite the many benefits of regular physical activity, participation rates decrease with age. Why is this the case?

2. Organizations such as the Senior Games not only address the problem of physical inactivity but also have the potential to affect other outcomes. What are some of these outcomes, and why are these effects observed?

3. What can sport managers do to increase the physical activity levels of seniors?

A s the Diversity Challenge illustrates, one's age plays a meaningful role in sport and physical activity participation. Age also affects a person's experience within sport organizations: it influences the opportunities people have, their interactions with their coworkers and supervisors, and how they relate to others in groups. Indeed, there are at least three reasons for interest in the analysis of age in the workplace (Posthuma & Campion, 2009). First, as outlined in Chapter 1, the average age of populations around the world is increasing, meaning that in many places, people are likely to work with others who differ from them in age. This can trigger age-related effects, such as stereotyping. Second, people are likely to work longer than they have in the past. This is in part attributable to the needs of employees, as longer life spans mean employment must be continued longer than in the past or more funds will be needed for the retirement years. Longer employment not only will result in larger contributions to retirement systems but also will reduce the strain on such programs. With older individuals remaining in the workforce, ageism (i.e., age-based prejudice), age stereotypes, and age discrimination have become more prevalent than they have ever been (Nelson, 2009; North & Fiske, 2012).

Interestingly, despite these factors, scholars and sport managers have devoted comparatively little attention to age-based biases. To illustrate, I conducted a search on the academic database PsycINFO for three keywords: *ageism*, *sexism*, and *racism*. Results indicate that *sexism* appears 2.9 times as frequently as *ageism*, and *racism* appears 8.9 times as often. This disparity is all the more curious when we consider that old age is a category into which virtually all people are likely to enter. The purpose of this chapter, therefore, is to attempt to remedy this situation. To do so, I first provide an overview of key terms and statistics related to age. The discussion then moves to an analysis of the intersection of age and employment. Subsumed in this section is an overview of age-related stereotypes, the impact of these stereotypes on subsequent work-related outcomes, and important factors that might affect the relationship between age and work outcomes. In the final section, I examine how age influences sport, physical activity, and leisure participation.

BACKGROUND AND KEY TERMS

What is "old"? The players on the U10 (under 10) girls' soccer team I coach consider me old (at 39 years), and yet I am hopeful that I have yet to reach the midpoint of my life. (As an aside, I am not as ambitious about my age as a colleague of mine, who upon turning 40 commented that he looked forward to the next two-thirds of his life.) Thus, in some respects, what qualifies as old is in the eye of the beholder.

From an employment standpoint, there are more concrete definitions of "old," in terms of age-related cutoff points (at least within the United States). The Age Discrimination in Employment Act of 1967 (ADEA) sets 40 as the age when people become protected from various organizational practices. For instance, when an organization is searching for a new sport marketing director, not to hire a candidate solely because she is over age 40 is illegal, just as it would be impermissible to terminate her employment in the organization for the same reason. The box on the following page offers additional information about age and employment legislation.

In the sport context, age affects when people can participate in different sport events. In youth soccer, leagues will frequently separate athletes based on two-year increments, such as U6, U8, and so on. In U6, players younger than age 6 compete against one another, while in U8 soccer, players age 6 and 7 participate. The Champions Golf Tour is a professional golf association for players who are at least age 50. Another example is the NBA: as of 2014, a player has to be at least 19 to participate in the NBA.

U.S. Census Bureau estimates suggest that the average age of U.S. residents will continue to increase during this century. In 2012, 43.1 million persons were age 65 or older, which represented 13.7 percent of the population. As the Baby Boomers continue to age, this proportion will grow. In 2030, all Baby Boomers will be at least age 65, which will mean that roughly one in five people (20.3 percent) in the United States will be expected to fall into this age group. By 2050, nearly 21 percent of all U.S. residents are expected to be age 65 or older. Of course, as one age group increases its proportion in the total population, others must decrease. This pattern is observed among persons age 18 to 64 years (i.e., the years in which people have traditionally worked): the proportion of persons in this age group is expected to decrease from 62.8 percent of the population in 2012 to 57.6 percent in 2050.

The aging of the U.S. population coincides with an increasing proportion of employees who choose to work past the traditional retirement age (i.e., 65 years). Several factors influence this trend (Mehrotra & Wagner, 2009). First, in an effort to encourage longer employment tenures, Social Security was altered so that those who work past the typical retirement age will receive increased monthly Social Security benefits. Second, the fact that most working employees receive health insurance

Age and employment laws

People over age 40 are protected from discrimination by the Age Discrimination in Employment Act. This law protects both current employees and job applicants. Employers cannot legally discriminate against people because of their age with respect to any aspect of employment, including hiring, firing, promotion, compensation, benefits, and the quality of job assignments. The Act also protects people from retaliation if they file a complaint. The ADEA applies to all organizations with at least 20 employees, including state and local governments, employment agencies, labor unions, and the federal government. Protections under the law also include the following:

- **Apprenticeship programs.** Under most circumstances, it is unlawful for apprenticeship programs to set age limits.

- **Job notices and advertisements.** When advertising for a position, it is unlawful to include age preferences or limitations. The only exception is when age is a bona fide occupational qualification.

- **Preemployment inquiries.** Although it is *not* unlawful to ask prospective employees for their age or date of birth, the EEOC has indicated that such requests will be closely scrutinized to ensure that they are made for lawful purposes.

- **Benefits.** Some older employees may need more medical care than their younger counterparts. Because of the cost of such care, this may serve as a disincentive to hire older employees or provide

them with benefits. The Older Workers Benefit Protection Act of 1990 amended the ADEA to guarantee benefits to older workers.

- **Waivers of ADEA rights.** Some organizations offer special early retirement packages to their older employees for a variety of cost-saving and human resource reasons. The ADEA and the Older Workers Benefit Protection Act allow for early retirement if the employee willingly chooses to waive his or her rights. A valid waiver must

  - be written and understandable by all parties;
  - explicitly refer to ADEA rights and claims;
  - not surrender future rights or claims;
  - be in exchange for something that is valuable (e.g., a retirement package worth more than a standard retirement);
  - recommend that the employee seek legal advice before signing; and
  - provide the employee with at least three weeks to consider the agreement and one week to revoke the agreement, even after the document is signed.

Although not as commonplace as sex or racial discrimination, age discrimination is prevalent in the workplace. In 2013, the EEOC received 21,396 claims of age discrimination. Not including other money awards from litigation, the EEOC recovered $97.9 million from organizations that were found to have discriminated on the basis of age.

coverage through the workplace means they are incentivized to remain employed until at least age 65, when they become eligible for Medicare. Third, many workers express concerns about having adequate funds after retirement. Only 52 percent of retirees receive some form of pension income; thus, nearly half of the retired workforce lives off personal savings and Social Security benefits. These dynamics make working longer, thereby accruing more Social Security benefits and greater savings, an appealing option.

A fourth factor influencing the trend to later retirement is that many older workers continue to work as a way to stay active and engaged in meaningful activities (see the Diversity in the Field box for a discussion of bridge employment). Fifth, compared to generations past, older workers today are healthier and can, therefore,

DIVERSITY IN THE FIELD

Bridge Employment in College Athletics. Bridge employment takes place when a person retires from a full-time job and takes on employment on a part-time basis (Bell, 2007). This practice has many benefits to both employees and employers, including increased flexibility and the ability to draw on the employee's considerable expertise and knowledge accrued from a lifetime of employment.

Bridge employees serve in many roles within sport, including as ushers or security, as guest services personnel, or in other capacities. A colleague of mine and I conducted a study with bridge employees in a university athletics de-partment to examine their attitudes toward the workplace (Cunningham & Mahoney, 2004). We observed that bridge employees in this context are particularly loyal and committed to the workplace. The average person in our sample had worked for the university for over 7 years, and some for up to 30 years. They also demonstrated high levels of commitment to the athletic department and were eager to engage in training exercises that they thought would benefit the delivery of the sport product. Thus, consistent with Bell's (2007) contention, bridge employees in this context added considerable value to the workplace.

remain engaged in the workforce for longer periods of time. Sixth, the United States is now primarily a service economy, which means that only a small number of jobs require strenuous physical labor. Instead, most work now requires only light physical exertion, which means that the physical demands of most lines of work do not limit older persons from participating. Finally, many of the Baby Boomers are more educated than older employees were in the past, and this is particularly the case for women. This education is important because labor force participation rates increase threefold for persons over age 50 who have a college degree, relative to those who dropped out of high school. Collectively, all these factors tend to result in older persons staying in the workforce for longer periods of time. As a consequence, age diversity is increasing, including within sport organizations.

AGE BIAS AND THE WORKPLACE

Recall that bias includes stereotypes, prejudice, and discrimination (Cuddy, Fiske, & Glick, 2008). Each of these operates in regard to age within the work environment.

Age Stereotypes

In their comprehensive review of the literature, Posthuma and Campion (2009) identified several age-related stereotypes, which are outlined in Exhibit 6.1 and below (see also Shore & Goldberg, 2005).

Poor-performance stereotype

Perhaps the most common stereotype of older employees is that their job performance is expected to lag behind that of their younger counterparts (Posthuma & Campion, 2009). This stereotype might be based on a number of factors, including the belief that older employees have low mental ability, cannot handle stress, or are less competent.

EXHIBIT **6.1** Age-related stereotypes in the workplace.

Age-related stereotypes represent beliefs or expectations about employees based on their age or presumed age. **Common stereotypes include**:

1. **Poor performance:** the belief that older employees perform at lower levels than their counterparts.

2. **Resistance to change:** the belief that older employees are averse to change and set in their ways.

3. **Ability to learn:** the belief that older employees are less able to learn new materials or techniques.

4. **Shorter tenure:** the belief that older employees will remain in the organization for a shorter time than younger employees.

5. **More costly:** the belief that older employees cost more to the organization because of salaries, healthcare, and retirement costs.

6. **More dependable:** the belief that older employees are more responsible and trustworthy than their younger counterparts.

Though performance stereotypes do exist, the evidence actually suggests otherwise; in fact, there are many cases where performance actually improves with age (Waldman & Avolio, 1986). The stereotype might appear to be true because of the time needed to complete tasks, as younger employees generally complete work more quickly. However, they do so with more mistakes. When both time and quality of the work are taken into account, older and younger workers are equally productive (Prenda & Stahl, 2001). For instance, young sales representatives might make more calls, but older representatives might be more thorough when making the calls.

Ng and Feldman (2008) examined this very issue by combining the results across 380 research studies in a meta-analysis. Their study yielded interesting findings. In some cases, older and younger adults did not vary in their performance, such as when they completed their primary job tasks or when performance was measured by the creativity of the product. In other cases, though, age did have an effect. Older employees were found to engage in more helping behaviors at work, be safer on the job, engage in less substance abuse, be absent less frequently, and exhibit less aggression. The one area where they lagged was in training performance. Taken as a whole, Ng and Feldman's research suggests that, if anything, older workers are more productive than younger ones. These findings have led some to suggest that there is greater variability in performance *within* age groups than *between* them (Posthuma & Campion, 2009).

Resistance-to-change stereotype

People also hold the stereotype that older workers are more resistant to change than are younger ones (Posthuma & Campion, 2009). The idea that older people have an aversion to change could reflect a belief that older people are set in their ways or hesitant to engage in training to learn new skills. In a classic study illustrating this point, Rosen and Jerdee (1976) found that students thought older workers would be unreceptive to changing their negative job behaviors and would lack motivation to adapt to new technologies in the workplace. Not surprisingly, students were likely to favor young employees in promotions, training, and job transfers. A follow-up study (Rosen & Jerdee, 1977) that used a sample of working professionals confirmed this pattern of findings, thereby eliminating concerns that the findings were observed only among college students.

These stereotypes have persisted: students still believe older workers are unwilling to change their negative work habits (Weiss & Maurer, 2004). As with many of the other stereotypes, there is little empirical evidence to support this belief. In fact, evidence suggests the opposite is actually the case—that younger employees exhibit a stronger aversion to change than their older counterparts (Kunze, Boehm, & Bruch, 2013).

Lower-ability-to-learn stereotype

Another stereotype negatively affecting senior employees is the belief that they have low capacities to learn to use new tools, procedures, or materials (Posthuma & Campion, 2009). Ng and Feldman (2012) examined this point in a subsequent meta-analysis. Across all of the studies, there was a small negative association between age and willingness to engage in new learning and development opportunities. That said, the magnitude of the association was small, explaining less than 1 percent of the variance, which suggests that the stereotype tends to exaggerate the truth.

Shore and Goldberg (2005) provide a detailed description of the different types of learning and how they are affected by age. Specifically, as a person ages, there are corresponding performance decrements in information processing speed, working memory, and attentional abilities. However, intellectual abilities that involve verbal skills are not affected by age, and other forms of intelligence do not regress until late in life, past one's working age. Based on this evidence, Shore and Goldberg concluded that "these results do not suggest that older workers are less able to learn; rather, they underscore the need for organizations to consider different training and development approaches as people age in order to optimize learning" (p. 214). See the Professional Perspectives box titled "Training Employees Over Age 50," later in the chapter.

Shorter-tenure stereotype

A fourth stereotype negatively affecting older workers is the belief that they will leave the organization sooner than their younger counterparts (Posthuma & Campion, 2009). If this does occur, then the organization will have to recruit, attract, retain, and train a new employee, all of which can cost thousands of dollars. Further, current training efforts, which also require considerable resources, are thought to be a risky investment in older employees, because the employer might not reap a return on the investment.

Despite these sentiments, the empirical evidence does not support this stereotype (Hedge, Borman, & Lammlein, 2006). As noted in Chapter 1, the notion that an employee will remain with a sport organization for an entire career has increasingly become outdated. Instead, an employee is likely to move from one organization to another several times throughout a career. Thus, the notion that younger employees will remain with the organization longer than older employees is unfounded. Furthermore, the benefits of training are often realized in the short term, so concerns related to older employees' tenure are misplaced.

Some evidence indicates that workplace culture can play a role in the retention of older employees. Specifically, older employees express intentions to remain in an organization when there are practices in place that tend to their needs, when supervisors fairly implement these practices, and when the employees feel their contributions are valued (Armstrong-Stassen & Schlosser, 2011).

More-costly stereotype

Another stereotype negatively affecting the opportunities and experiences of older workers is that they are overly expensive to the organization (Posthuma & Campion, 2009). Older workers, relative to younger ones, are generally paid higher wages and are closer to retirement. According to the stereotype, older workers also become ill more frequently and, therefore, use more benefits. People might use this evidence to support a belief that older employees are costly, a drain on resources, and a bad investment for the organization.

Despite the prevalence of this stereotype, there is little empirical evidence to support the notion that younger employees are the better economic alternative for an organization. Let's return to Ng and Feldman's (2012) meta-analysis to examine part of the stereotype: the belief that an older worker's level of health results in higher costs to the organization than a younger employee would require. The researchers found that older employees tended to have higher blood pressure and cholesterol. However, age was not related to a host of other outcomes, such as subjective health and poor physical health symptoms.

Dependability stereotype

The final age-related stereotype, dependability, actually serves to benefit older workers to the detriment of their younger counterparts (Posthuma & Campion, 2009). Specifically, older workers are considered to be loyal, trustworthy, stable, and committed to the workforce. They are also less likely to steal from their employer or to be absent from work than their younger counterparts (Hedge et al., 2006). Younger employees, on the other hand, are sometimes seen as irresponsible, unreliable, and not loyal to the workplace (Bell, 2007).

Age and Prejudice

Ageism refers to negative attitudes people hold toward others who vary from them in age. Ageism is most frequently reflected in prejudice against older employees. Ageism goes largely unchecked because it is institutionalized in nature (Nelson, 2009). We see disparaging comments about elderly people made on television, and it is common to express pity for people who have reached a certain age. Cosmetic lines are marketed to help consumers reduce the effects of aging. As Nelson concludes, "We are told innumerable ways throughout our life, that aging is bad. Young is good, and old is not" (p. 432).

There are a number of potential explanations for these negative sentiments about aging. One possibility comes from what is called terror management theory (Becker, 1973). This theory holds that, when confronted with their own mortality, people will engage in a variety of behaviors aimed at distancing themselves from death, thereby lessening their anxiety. One such behavior involves developing negative attitudes toward older individuals and stronger affective ties with younger individuals (see also Popham, Kennison, & Bradley, 2011).

Generational differences and resource scarcity might also help explain prejudice toward older adults (North & Fiske, 2012). From this perspective, ageism is likely to manifest because (1) younger people seek to limit older persons' control over and access to limited resources, such as wealth, prestige, and employment opportunities; (2) older individuals are believed to consume more than their share of limited resources, such as government services or, in the context of work, salary; and (3) younger people are seeking to maintain generational identity boundaries, a desire likely rooted in terror management ideations. Together, these three domains—succession, consumption, and identity—are likely to engender animosity toward older adults.

Age Discrimination

Discrimination represents the final form of age bias. It is likely influenced by the stereotypes people have developed and the negative attitudes they hold toward older employees. Drawing from Shore and Goldberg's (2005) work, we can consider discrimination along several domains. These are outlined in Exhibit 6.2.

Job search and unemployment

Older adults spend considerably more time searching for jobs and remaining unemployed than do their younger counterparts. In 2013, the Department of Labor

The influence of age on work opportunities and experiences. | EXHIBIT 6.2

A person's age has the potential to influence various opportunities and experiences encountered in the workplace, including:

1. Job search and unemployment
2. Selection
3. Training and development
4. Mentoring
5. Performance and promotion potential
6. Exiting the organization

estimated that older adults remained unemployed for an average of 53 weeks, compared to just 19 weeks for teenagers. These effects are particularly damaging for adults who experience unemployment in their 50s, even resulting in decreased life expectancy compared to individuals who do not experience such critical life shifts (Coile, Levine, & McKnight, 2014; Noelke & Beckfield, 2014).

Selection

Older employees are routinely disadvantaged in the selection process (Perry & Parlamis, 2007). Age has a direct effect, such that younger applicants are preferred over older ones. Certain factors affect the relationship between age and selection. One of these is the type of transition that is taking place. Older employees who are switching careers (as opposed to staying within a particular line of work but transitioning between organizations) are typically viewed most negatively by personnel decision makers (Fritzsche & Marcus, 2013).

Another factor that influences the occurrence of age discrimination is the type of job for which the candidate is applying. In some cases, a pattern called prototype matching takes place: a job applicant's age is compared with the age of the general or prototypical person currently in the position (Shore & Goldberg, 2005). Note that these prototypes are linked with the prevalent stereotypes associated with age. "Old" jobs are those in which experience and tenure are valued, physical labor is kept to a minimum, and people oversee "big picture" operations. These might include the position of head coach or coordinator or manager of a sporting goods store. "Young" jobs are those in which high energy is needed, people must be able to handle a number of tasks simultaneously, and familiarity with new technologies is valued. These might include jobs in marketing and promotions or the position of sports information director. Given that there are many more "younger" jobs than "older" ones, this limits the opportunities for older job seekers. See the Diversity in the Field box for additional discussion of prototype matching.

DIVERSITY   IN THE FIELD

Young Coaches in the NCAA. In many cases, a person must serve many years as an assistant or associate head coach before having the opportunity to take the reins as a head coach. Increasingly within the NCAA, however, athletic directors have turned to young coaches to guide their men's basketball teams, and sometimes the coach is only a few years older than the players on the team. Consider these coaches' ages when they were hired at their respective schools: Andy Toole (29, Robert Morris), Chris Collins (39, Northwestern), Richard Pitino (31, Minnesota), Josh Pastner (31, Memphis), and Brandon Miller (34, Butler).

ESPN columnist Myron Medcalf (2014) notes that although hiring younger coaches is less common among well-established programs, it is a trend in the mid-major conferences. The hiring trend is attributable, at least in part, to player preferences. At Northwestern, players told the athletic director, Jim Phillips, that they wanted someone who was both personable and relatable. This, according to Phillips, is what set the younger Collins apart from older candidates, even though the older coaches had more experience. In line with this sentiment, Medcalf commented, "Young coaches might have an edge when it's necessary to relate to their players. In most cases, they're more connected to players culturally and socially than veteran coaches."

Training and development

Training and development represent a third area in which older employees face discrimination. With rapidly changing technologies and workplace dynamics, employers must provide effective training and development for employees to ensure workplace competitiveness. The same is true for individual employees, as failing to update one's skills can have serious negative career consequences. Despite the advantages of training, older employees are frequently not afforded opportunities for training and professional development (Van Rooij, 2012). This could be due to stereotypes about their ability to learn and their motivation to adapt to new techniques and strategies, discussed earlier. These stereotypes probably influence sport organizations' willingness to provide development opportunities for older workers.

Of course, when people are not afforded training opportunities, their professional skills do not develop. This can result in stagnation in their work and squelching of their intellectual curiosity. Thus, the failure to offer training and development for older employees will end up hurting both the employee and the effectiveness of the organization. See the Professional Perspectives box for a discussion of best practices in training employees over age 50.

Mentoring

The age of a person influences the mentoring he or she receives. This could be an effect of the perceived career stage of the employee, as organizations are likely to devote time and energy to develop the skills of younger employees, hoping for a long-term payoff (Kulik, Ryan, Harper, & George, 2014). The same pattern appears in mentoring, where mentors tend to seek out and invest more time with younger employees, perhaps believing they are in greater need of professional development and career coaching. Such beliefs affect the type of mentoring older employees receive; in particular, there is some evidence that older employees tend to receive informal mentoring, are unlikely to receive guidance about their career progression, and have short relationships with their mentors (Finkelstein, Allen, & Rhoton, 2007).

Performance and promotion potential

As previously noted, one of the most prevalent age-related stereotypes is that performance declines with age. If this were the case, all else equal, a 50-year-old should perform more poorly than a 30-year-old. However, the empirical evidence sim-

professional
PERSPECTIVES

Training Employees Over Age 50. According to a 2008 AARP study (2008a), most employees age 50 or older enjoy the training and development opportunities afforded them, and when such programs are offered, these employees participate in large numbers. The study also indicated that education influenced participation: persons with a four-year college degree were 70 percent more likely to have taken employee-based training over the previous two years than employees with a high school degree or less. In response to these findings, Deborah Russell, AARP's Director of Workforce Issues, said, "For employers to be successful in recruiting and retaining 50-plus workers, they will need to consider ongoing training as a key strategy. Ongoing training and development is what mature workers view as a top attraction in an ideal workplace" (AARP, 2008b).

Furthermore, the type of training offered has been found to make a meaningful difference in its effectiveness. Callahan, Kiker, and Cross (2003) found that a combination of training approaches, such as using lectures, modeling, and active participation, improved the training performance of older workers. Additionally, training that occurred in small groups and that allowed for self-pacing was also linked with training effectiveness. Thus, it is important for sport organizations not only to offer training and development opportunities but also to consider the method and structure of the training in order to maximize the benefits of such programs.

ply does not support this contention. In fact, when performance is considered as a multidimensional construct, the data suggest that age is positively associated with a number of performance indicators (Ng & Feldman, 2008).

Despite these findings, the negative stereotypes persist, and they affect the promotion potential of older workers. That is, older workers are seen as having little promise or potential for advancement. The effects are especially pronounced when there is a mismatch between the employee and the supervisor. Shore, Cleveland, and Goldberg (2003) report that "employees who are older than their managers suffer negative consequences when examining data most relevant to their careers—promotability, managerial potential, and development" (p. 535). This could be a result of supervisor–subordinate dissimilarity or career timetable effects. As an example, a 55-year-old employee of Foot Locker who works for a 35-year-old manager might be seen as "lagging behind" in her career, and the manager's ratings of her career potential and promotion potential are likely to reflect such a perception.

Exiting the organization

Employees can exit the organization in one of three ways: voluntary turnover, involuntary turnover (i.e., layoffs, downsizing, firing), or retirement. Interestingly, there is no relationship between age and voluntary turnover, meaning older and younger employees are equally likely to leave the organization on their own volition (Healy, Lehman, & McDaniel, 1995). There are differences, however, in layoffs because older employees are frequently targeted. This is attributable to the fact that older workers are more likely than younger ones to occupy mid-level managerial positions, which are so often the target of corporate layoffs, as well as to negative age-related stereotypes (Perry & Parlamis, 2007). Being targeted in corporate downsizing is particularly troubling for employees over age 50 because it substantially reduces their future employment opportunities (Chan & Stevens, 2001; see also Perry & Parlamis, 2007).

ALTERNATIVE perspectives

Caring for the Elderly. The word *dependent* most often brings to mind the situation of a child living in the home, but increasingly working-age people are tasked with caring for their elderly relatives, and this can affect their work (Kossek, Colquitt, & Noe, 2001). In many cultures, children are separated from their parents in order for the children to form a personal identity independent of their parents. When these children are later required to care for their elderly parents, the situation can be stressful, and the clear separation of identity can become muddled or even lost completely. This can have a negative effect on the employee both at home and in the workplace. In one study, employees who cared for elderly dependents tended to perform poorly at work and reported lower well-being, relative to those who did not have such responsibilities (Kossek et al., 2001). Home and family care decisions are more likely to have a negative impact on the employee when the organizational climate (or atmosphere) discourages the sharing of family concerns. These findings provide another perspective on the effects of age in the workplace, showing that the age of an employee's dependents can influence the manner in which work is experienced.

Additional Considerations

Thus far, I have focused on age-related bias and the degree to which age affects work experiences and outcomes. Although age independently and directly influences these outcomes, a number of factors also may modify this influence either positively or negatively. These factors include an employee's age relative to coworkers', the organizational climate, and human resource practices. See the Alternative Perspectives box at left for a discussion of another age-related factor that might influence employee well-being—in this case, the effect of taking care of an elderly family member on a younger person's employee well-being.

An employee's age relative to her or his coworkers and supervisor can modify the influence of age on work experiences and outcomes. Recall from Chapter 2's discussion of relational diversity that people generally prefer to be around others who are similar to themselves; thus, people who differ from the other(s) in a dyad or group are likely to be negatively affected. In some organizations, the social norms and historical precedents question the appropriateness of a manager who is "too young," creating tensions and unease (Perry, Kulik, & Zhou, 1999). This might occur, for instance, when a head coach is younger than some of the players on her team, or when an athletic director is similar in age to some coaches' children. In such situations, the older employees might engage in withdrawal behaviors, such as being absent from or not fully engaged in their work (Perry et al., 1999).

Relative age also affects sport performance, albeit through a different mechanism. The box below offers an overview of these effects.

Second, organizational climate might influence the relationship between age and work outcomes. Here, we focus on the age diversity of the sport organization, including the mix of younger and older employees. When the workforce is diverse in terms of age and such diversity is not supported by the organization, age-related incidents are likely to occur, such as the violation of age norms and behaviors, stereotype activation, and in-group/out-group distinctions. All of these can affect people's attitudes toward age diversity and their belief that there is a climate of age discrimination in the workplace. When such beliefs take hold, employees'

Relative age effects and sport performance

Youth sports are structured such that athletes of particular ages compete against one another. Leagues frequently achieve this by establishing cutoff dates, such that children born between (for example) September 1, 2005, and August 31, 2006, all play against one another. Such classification schemes are logical, but they create an advantage for children born early in the age band, something referred to as the relative age effect (RAE). This effect—which can last into adulthood—occurs in a variety of settings within sport, such as hockey, track, and soccer, as well as outside of it, such as in the classroom (see Wattie, Schorer, & Baker, in press). Although physiological explanations might be significant early on, the enduring nature of RAE suggests that sociocultural factors might be at play, too (Hancock, Adler, & Côté, 2013). Performance differences between younger and older players might correspond with feelings of confidence and interest in the sport among the players. Coaches and parents are likely to reinforce these sentiments. For their part, coaches might be more likely to select and nurture the athletic advancement of the more physically mature older players. Parental expectations and reinforcement are also influential, as they might encourage the older-grouped children to pursue the tasks in which they excel relative to their peers. Thus, children born earlier in the age band, relative to their younger counterparts, may develop greater confidence and more positive attitudes toward sport, enjoy initial performance advantages, and receive greater reinforcement from parents and coaches. Over time, these forces advantage older children and adolescents, creating relative age effects.

attachment to the workplace is likely to decrease, as is overall organizational performance (Kunze, Boehm, & Bruch, 2011). On the other hand, organizational climates supportive of age diversity are associated with performance gains and overall effectiveness (Boehm, Kunze, & Bruch, 2014).

Finally, human resource practices might influence the effects of age-related stereotypes on work outcomes. Posthuma and Campion (2009) outlined several approaches that can reduce negative effects of age-related bias:

1. Using job-specific information in making decisions concerning selection and promotions can help eliminate age bias and stereotyping. Skill is much more important than age in predicting job performance; thus, focusing on applicants' skill sets, rather than their age, should result in fair and effective selection processes.

2. Training and development efforts that target ageism help managers avoid stereotyping workers by (a) highlighting the prevalence of stereotyping and the ways in which it is manifested and (b) elucidating the many benefits that workers of all ages bring to the organization.

3. Viewing older workers as a source of competitive advantage reduces negative work experiences. Consider, for instance, that older workers bring a wealth of institutional knowledge and expertise to the workplace—an understanding of situations that arises only from experience. Thus, older employees potentially bring benefits to the organization that their younger counterparts cannot.

4. Adding complexity, rather than reducing it, improves employees' cognitive functioning and, as a result, their job performance. Managers should not be tempted to simplify an older employee's job when they are concerned that the person is losing cognitive abilities.

AGE AND PARTICIPATION IN SPORT, PHYSICAL ACTIVITY, AND LEISURE

Age is negatively associated with physical activity, meaning that as people age, they become less active. Research coordinated by the U.S. Office of Disease Prevention and Health Promotion in its *Healthy People* initiative illustrates as much. As Exhibit 6.3 shows, people over age 65 are substantially more likely to lead sedentary lives than are younger people, and this trend has persisted over time. In 2012, people age 65 and over were 1.7 times as likely as their younger counterparts to be sedentary. Similar trends emerge when we consider the proportion of adults who obtain recommended levels of moderate physical activity each week. As Exhibit 6.4 shows, younger adults are 1.5 times more likely to reach this goal as persons age 65 and over. There is a silver lining in both cases: over the five years of data analyzed, the proportion of people leading sedentary lives has decreased, while the proportion of those reaching recommended physical activity levels has increased. This trend holds across all age groups.

A number of factors are associated with decreased sport and physical activity participation across the lifespan. First, there is a positive relationship between age

Percentages of adults who lead sedentary lives, by age group.   EXHIBIT   **6.3**

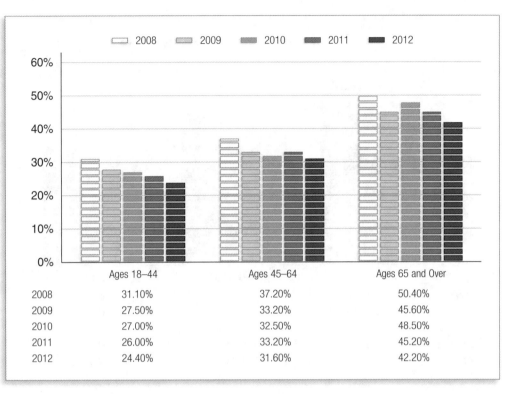

	Ages 18–44	Ages 45–64	Ages 65 and Over
2008	31.10%	37.20%	50.40%
2009	27.50%	33.20%	45.60%
2010	27.00%	32.50%	48.50%
2011	26.00%	33.20%	45.20%
2012	24.40%	31.60%	42.20%

Source: Data from HealthyPeople.gov.

and disability status: as people grow older, they are more likely to experience physical and psychological disabilities. And, although physical activity opportunities for people with disabilities have improved, they are still limited, relatively speaking. Another reason has to do with sport programming. Many sport leagues are geared toward children and adolescents—an important time to encourage physical activity, as behaviors formed during this stage in life typically carry over into adulthood. However, as people age, formal programming and social support for physical activity engagement usually wane. We need only observe community soccer fields during soccer season or a list of offerings from a city's parks and recreation department to observe as much. Noting this decline in community support and the benefits of being active, some retirement communities offer organized sport and physical activities for their residents.

Researchers have shown that age is also associated with the sports people prefer to watch. The Diversity in the Field box on page 143 explores this research.

Age also influences participation in leisure-time activities. Leisure is different from sport in that the former refers to "an inherently satisfying activity that is characterized by the absence of obligation. Free time alone is not necessarily leisure. Instead, the key variable is how a person defines tasks and situations to

EXHIBIT   6.4   Percentages of adults who meet guidelines for moderate physical activity, by age group.

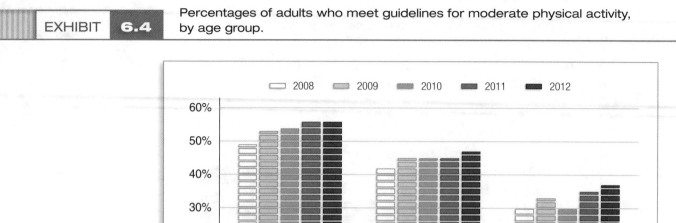

	Ages 18–44	Ages 45–64	Ages 65 and Over
2008	48.80%	41.60%	30.40%
2009	53.40%	44.80%	32.80%
2010	53.80%	45.20%	30.50%
2011	55.80%	44.90%	34.90%
2012	56.10%	46.90%	37.50%

Source: Data from HealthyPeople.gov.

create intrinsic meaning. Thus, leisure implies feeling free and satisfied" (Mehrotra & Wagner, 2009, p. 295). Retirees engage in a number of leisure activities, including reading or writing, exercising, traveling, listening to music, and participating in religious and spiritual activities (James & Wink, 2007). Thus, contrary to the belief that retirees tend to become disengaged, research indicates that many lead busy, active lives.

One of the most popular leisure activities for retirees is volunteering. This is particularly the case for persons over age 65, who spend twice as much time volunteering as persons under age 50. They participate in these activities for a host of reasons, including the need to keep active, to meet others, to achieve a sense of satisfaction, and to become identified with the entity for which they are volunteering. In fact, people who volunteer are generally happier and healthier than their counterparts who do not (Mehrotra & Wagner, 2009).

Retirees' level and type of volunteerism varies by race. Mehrotra and Wagner (2009) note that "volunteering as a way to help others through informal social networks is common in minority communities" (p. 298). Among African Americans, service to one's church provides a way to incorporate hard work into leisure

Influence of Age on Sport Consumption. Discussions of the influence of age on sport consumption often center on Generation Y consumers, those born between 1977 and 1994 (Bennett, Henson, & Zhang, 2003; Stevens, Lathrop, & Bradish, 2005). These persons are highly sought after by sport marketers because of the size of the generation (78 million in the United States) and their spending habits. The spending potential of this generation is expected to reach $300 billion.

Because of these characteristics, many efforts have been made to examine the preferences, attitudes, and behaviors of Generation Y. Persons in this demographic favor purchasing sports apparel and athletic shoes, and the same-sex parent plays an influential role in purchase deci-

sions (Stevens et al., 2005). Generation Y consumers are Internet savvy and are likely to watch at least 2 hours of television daily (Bennett et al., 2003). In terms of their sport preferences, Generation Y consumers most prefer to watch football, soccer, and track and field. Interestingly, these persons also prefer action sports, such as those found at the X Games, over more traditional sport forms, such as baseball, basketball, and hockey. They are more likely to watch the X Games or Gravity Games on television than they are to watch the World Series or the World Cup (Bennett et al., 2003). These findings suggest that the popularity of extreme or action sports may continue to grow, especially when we consider the size and spending potential of Generation Y sport consumers.

experiences and service to the community. Asians have been found to volunteer more often in Asian organizations that reinforce their cultural value systems. Native Americans volunteer in ways that provide mutual assistance to others, such as by providing food and shelter to elderly individuals. Finally, Hispanic communities tend to concentrate their volunteer efforts on services that provide neighborhood assistance, care for those who are elderly, and mutual aid.

chapter SUMMARY

The purpose of this chapter was to examine the effects of age on people's work and their sport, physical activity, and leisure activities. Age has a meaningful impact on the stereotypes people encounter, the way in which they experience work, and the opportunities they have in the workplace. As the Diversity Challenge illustrated, age is usually associated with a decrease in physical activity levels, but it does not have to be; rather, many seniors actively participate in sport and physical activity, as well as leisure-time activities.

After reading this chapter, you should be able to:

1. **Discuss the various ways in which age and age diversity are conceptualized.**

    Age and age diversity can be discussed in many ways. According to antidiscrimination laws, people are protected from various organizational practices at age 40. Sport organizations, such as the Senior Games and the Champions Tour, set age 50 as the minimum for participation. Finally, age can be understood further in terms of generational differences.

2. **Provide an overview of how age is related to stereotypes, prejudice, and discrimination in the work environment.**

   Age is associated with stereotypes about older employees and their work (e.g., poor performance, resistance to change, limited ability to learn, short tenure, higher costs, and more dependability). Ageism refers to negative attitudes people hold against persons who differ from them in age, and it is largely institutionalized within Western cultures. Both stereotypes and prejudice underlie age-based discrimination at work, negatively affecting older employees. There are also factors affecting the relationship between age and discrimination: effects are modified by the employee's age relative to coworkers and her or his supervisor, the organizational climate with regard to age discrimination, and the organization's human resource practices.

3. **Analyze the intersection of age and sport, physical activity, and leisure participation.**

   Participation in sport and exercise generally decreases with age. Leisure participation, especially volunteering, increases with age, particularly after age 65.

QUESTIONS for discussion

1. What are the reasons why people choose to work past retirement age? Which of these do you think is the most important? Why?

2. What are the common age-related stereotypes, and which of these is most prevalent? Why?

3. Most of the research related to age diversity focuses on older employees. Do younger employees also face age-related stereotypes? If so, what are they?

4. Research suggests that older employees learn differently from their younger counterparts. Knowing this, what are steps managers can take to facilitate older employees' learning in the workplace?

5. How might a sport manager design a volunteer program that would attract older adults of various races?

learning ACTIVITIES

1. Sport organizations can engage in certain human resource practices that help mitigate incidents of age discrimination. In groups, develop a list of such practices as they relate to selection and promotion.

2. Using the Internet, identify sport organizations and sport events that target senior athletes. Based on your search, how would you characterize the available sport and physical activity opportunities for seniors?

3. Research either local or national sport organizations to determine if they attempt to attract or use the services of older volunteers.

WEB resources

- **Administration on Aging,** www.aoa.gov

  Part of the Department of Health and Human Services; provides up-to-date statistics on older Americans across a number of subject areas.

- **National Senior Games Association,** www.nsga.com

  Offers information about the National Senior Games, competitive sport events for persons age 50 or older.

- **Sport and Development,** www.sportanddev.org/en/learnmore/ sport_education_and_child_youth_development2

  Offers an overview of how sport and education can be used for child and youth development efforts.

reading RESOURCES

Beatty, P. T., & Visser, R. M. S. (Eds.) (2005). *Thriving in an aging workforce: Strategies for organizational and systemic change.* Malabar, FL: Krieger.

This edited text focuses on the way in which age intersects with seven organizational issues: selection, training, career development, employee relations, health, pensions, and retirement.

Field, J., Burke, R. J., & Cooper, C. L. (Eds.) (2013). *The SAGE handbook of aging, work, and society.* Thousand Oaks, CA: Sage.

An edited text examining the role of age and age diversity in the workplace.

Mehrotra, C. M., & Wagner, L. S. (2009). *Aging and diversity: An active learning experience* (2nd ed.). New York: Routledge.

Offers a comprehensive overview of how age influences a number of life activities, including work, leisure participation, and retirement.

REFERENCES

AARP (2008a). Investing in training 50+ workers: A talent management strategy. Retrieved from http://assets.aarp.org/rgcenter/econ/invest_training.pdf

AARP (2008b). AARP Study: Employer training programs productive for workers 50 and over. Retrieved from http://www.aarp.org/about-aarp/press-center/info-06-2008/employee_training_study.html

Armstrong-Stassen, M., & Schlosser, F. (2011). Perceived organizational membership and the retention of older workers. *Journal of Organizational Behavior, 32,* 319–344.

Becker, E. (1973). *The denial of death.* New York: Free Press.

Bell, M. P. (2007). *Diversity in organizations.* Mason, OH: Thomson South-Western.

Bennett, G., Henson, R. K., & Zhang, J. (2003). Generation Y's perceptions of the action sports industry segment. *Journal of Sport Management, 17,* 95–115.

Boehm, S. A., Kunze, F., & Bruch, H. (2014). Spotlight on age-diversity climate: The impact of age-inclusive HR practices on firm-level outcomes. *Personnel Psychology, 67,* 667–704.

Callahan, J. S., Kiker, D. S., & Cross, T. (2003). Does method matter? A meta-analysis of the effects of training method on older learner training performance. *Journal of Management, 29,* 663–680.

Chan, S., & Stevens, A. H. (2001). Job loss and employment patterns of older workers. *Journal of Labor Economics, 19,* 484–521.

Coile, C. C., Levine, P. B., & McKnight, R. (2014). Recessions, older workers, and longevity: How long are recessions good for your health? *American Economic Journal: Economic Policy, 6*(3), 92–119.

Cuddy, A. J. C., Fiske, S. T., & Glick, P. (2008). Warmth and competence as universal dimensions of social perception: The stereotype content model and the BIAS map. *Advances in Experimental Social Psychology, 40,* 61–149.

Cunningham, G. B., & Mahoney, K. L. (2004). Self-efficacy of part-time employees in university athletics: The influence of organizational commitment, valence of training, and training motivation. *Journal of Sport Management, 18,* 59–73.

Finkelstein, L. M., Allen, T. D., & Rhoton, L. A. (2007). An examination of the role of age in mentoring relationships. *Group & Organization Management, 28,* 249–281.

Fritzsche, B., & Marcus, J. (2013). The senior discount: Biases against older career changers. *Journal of Applied Social Psychology, 43,* 350–362.

Hancock, D. J., Adler, A. L., & Côté, J. (2013). A proposed theoretical model to explain relative age effects in sports. *European Journal of Sport Science, 13,* 630–637.

Healy, M. C., Lehman, M., & McDaniel, M. (1995). Age and voluntary turnover: A quantitative review. *Personnel Psychology, 48,* 335–344.

Hedge, J. W., Borman, W. C., & Lammlein, S. E. (2006). *The aging workforce: Realities, myths, and implications for organizations.* Washington, DC: American Psychological Association.

James, J. B., & Wink, P. (Eds.). (2007). *The crown of life: Dynamics of the early postretirement period.* New York: Springer.

Kossek, E. E., Colquitt, J. A., & Noe, R. A. (2001). Caregiving decisions, well-being, and performance: The effects of place and provider as a function of dependent type and work–family climates. *Academy of Management Journal, 44,* 29–44.

Kulik, C. T., Ryan, S., Harper, S., & George, G. (2014). Aging populations and management. *Academy of Management Journal, 57,* 929–935.

Kunze, F., Boehm, S. A., & Bruch, H. (2011). Age diversity, age discrimination climate and performance consequences—a cross organizational study. *Journal of Organizational Behavior, 32,* 264–290.

Kunze, F., Boehm, S., & Bruch, H. (2013). Age, resistance to change, and job performance. *Journal of Managerial Psychology, 28,* 741–760.

Medcalf, M. (2014, October). Coaches not defined by age: Athletic directors handing the keys to younger and younger coaches—with success. *ESPN.com.* Retrieved from www.espn.com.

Mehrotra, C. M., & Wagner, L. S. (2009). *Aging and diversity: An active learning experience* (2nd ed.). New York: Routledge.

Nelson, T. D. (2009). Ageism. In T. D. Nelson (Ed.), *Handbook of prejudice, stereotyping, and discrimination* (pp. 431–440). New York: Psychology Press.

Ng, T. W., & Feldman, D. C. (2012). Evaluating six common stereotypes about older workers with meta-analytical data. *Personnel Psychology, 65,* 821–858.

Ng, T. W. H., & Feldman, D. C. (2008). The relationship of age to ten dimensions of job performance. *Journal of Applied Psychology, 93,* 392–423.

Noelke, C., & Beckfield, J. (2014). Recessions, job loss, and mortality among older US adults. *American Journal of Public Health, 104*(11), e126–e134.

North, M. S., & Fiske, S. T. (2012). An inconvenienced youth? Ageism and its potential intergenerational roots. *Psychological Bulletin, 138,* 982–997.

Perry, E. A., & Parlamis, J. D. (2007). Age and ageism in organizations: A review and consideration of national culture. In A. M. Konrad, P. Prasad, & J. K. Pringle (Eds.), *Handbook of workplace diversity* (pp. 345–370). Thousand Oaks, CA: Sage.

Perry, E. L., Kulik, C. T., & Zhou, J. (1999). A closer look at the effects of subordinate–supervisor age differences. *Journal of Organizational Behavior, 20,* 341–357.

Popham, L. E., Kennison, S. M., & Bradley, K. I. (2011). Ageism, sensation-seeking, and risk-taking behavior in young adults. *Current Psychology, 30,* 184–193.

Posthuma, R. A., & Campion, M. A. (2009). Age stereotypes in the workplace: Common stereotypes, moderators, and future research directions. *Journal of Management, 35,* 158–188.

Prenda, K. M., & Stahl, S. M. (2001). The truth about older workers. *Business and Health, 19,* 30–35.

Rosen, B., & Jerdee, T. H. (1976). The influence of age stereotypes on managerial decisions. *Journal of Applied Psychology, 61,* 428–432.

Rosen, B., & Jerdee, T. H. (1977). Too old or not too old? *Harvard Business Review, 55,* 97–106.

Shore, L. M., Cleveland, J. N., & Goldberg, C. B. (2003). Work attitudes and decisions as a function of manager age and employee age. *Journal of Applied Psychology, 88,* 529–537.

Shore, L. M., & Goldberg, C. B. (2005). Age discrimination in the workplace. In R. L. Dipboye & A. Collela (Eds.), *Discrimination at work: The psychological and organizational bases* (pp. 203–225). Mahwah, NJ: Lawrence Erlbaum.

Stevens, J., Lathrop, A., & Bradish, C. (2005). Tracking Generation Y: A contemporary sport consumer profile. *Journal of Sport Management, 19,* 254–277.

Van Rooij, S. W. (2012). Training older workers: Lessons learned, unlearned, and relearned from the field of instructional design. *Human Resource Management, 51,* 281–298.

Waldman, D. A., & Avolio, B. J. (1986). A meta-analysis of age differences in job performance. *Journal of Applied Psychology, 71,* 33–38.

Wattie, N., Schorer, J., & Baker, J. (in press). The relative age effect in sport: A developmental systems model. *Sports Medicine.*

Weiss, E. M., & Maurer, T. J. (2004). Age discrimination in personnel decisions: A reexamination. *Journal of Applied Social Psychology, 34,* 1551–1562.

Mental and Physical Ability

LEARNING objectives

After studying this chapter, you should be able to:

- Provide a definition of *disability* and an overview of the historical background related to mental and physical ability.
- Discuss the work experiences of, and educational and work opportunities for, persons with disabilities.
- Describe the sport and physical activity opportunities for and experiences of people with disabilities.

DIVERSITY CHALLENGE

Erik Weihenmayer is an accomplished mountain climber who has scaled what is referred to as the Seven Summits—the highest mountains on each of the Earth's seven continents. Unlike others who have accomplished this rare feat, Weihenmayer is blind. In fact, he is the only person who is blind ever to climb Mount Everest. Interestingly, this fact alters how people view his achievements. As Weihenmayer described, "When I was learning how to climb mountains as a blind person, I had a lot of encouragement from experts. But after I summited Mount Everest, these people weren't ready to accept what I had done at face value. Some said I must have cheated; one even claimed I had an unfair advantage: 'I'd climb Mount Everest too if I couldn't see how far I had to fall.'"

Weihenmayer is not the only athlete with a disability who has encountered skepticism about his accomplishments. When athletes such as Markus Rehm (the German long jumper, who has one leg amputated) compete and beat their able-bodied peers, some observers express doubts about how they did so. In the case of track and field events, they express concerns about the benefits of prostheses.

While the criticisms may be rooted in concerns for fairness and justice, elements of stereotypes and prejudice may also be involved. Persons with disabilities are often stereotyped as being less skilled and less capable than others. These stereotypes subsequently influence the opportunities and experiences persons with disabilities have, whether in sport or other work organizations. Weihenmayer correctly notes that it is important to remain cognizant of the training, effort, and determination that allow all athletes to succeed, including those with disabilities. He says, "We mustn't lose sight of what makes an athlete great. It's too easy to credit . . . [athletes'] success to technology. Through birth or circumstance, some are given certain gifts, but it's what one does with those gifts, the hours devoted to training, the desire to be the best, that is at the true heart of a champion."

Sources: Samuel, E. (2008, June 1). Oscar Pistorius' Olympic quest opens ethical debate over use of prosthetics. *New York Daily News.* Retrieved from http://nydailynews.com. / Southern Methodist University (2009, August 4). Federation deems prostheses unfair (2014, July 30). ESPN.com. Retrieved from http://espn.go.com/olympics/trackandfield/story/_/id/11285062/german-federation-drops-amputee-long-jumper-markus-rehm-team. / Weihenmayer, E. (2008, April 25). Oscar Pistorius. *Time.* Retrieved from www.time.com.

CHALLENGE   REFLECTION

1. Does the use of prosthetics provide an unfair advantage for sprinters? How does the use of prosthetics differ from other medical treatment, such as a golfer having Lasik eye surgery or a pitcher getting Tommy John surgery (i.e., ulnar collateral ligament reconstruction)?

2. Is it conceivable that, if there were an advantage, an athlete might choose to amputate a leg in order to wear a prosthesis?

3. What are other cases in sport where a person's disability could be seen as an advantage?

A s the Diversity Challenge illustrates, perceptions of an athlete's performance are often shaped, at least in part, by the person's physical and mental ability. When people doubt the accomplishments of athletes with disabilities, they discount the hours upon hours of training, as well as the athletes' accomplishments in various sport venues. What's more, it is unlikely that these same individuals would question the work ethic of able-bodied runners. Comments such as those quoted in the Diversity Challenge are not uncommon; instead, as noted above, persons with disabilities are often stereotyped as being less skilled and less capable than others. These stereotypes subsequently influence the opportunities and experiences persons with disabilities have in work organizations and in physical activity and sport participation.

The purpose of this chapter is to examine these issues in further depth. Specifically, I first provide a definition of *disability* and offer a brief historical overview of issues related to mental and physical disabilities. This is followed by a discussion of the educational and work opportunities available for persons with disabilities, and then by an overview of their participation in physical activity and sport, the state of disability sport, and the primary issues affecting athletes in that context.

DEFINITION, INCIDENCE, AND BACKGROUND

T he term *disability* is sometimes difficult to define. For some impairments, such as a complete absence of sight or hearing, the existence of a disability is evident. For others, such as partial hearing loss or some psychological disorders, it may be less evident whether and to what extent the disability impairs an individual's life. The Americans with Disabilities Act of 1990 (ADA) defines what constitutes a disability within the employment context. From a legal perspective, a disability exists when a person has a mental or physical impairment that largely restricts one or more major life activities, when there is a recorded history of such, or when the person is considered to have such impairment.

Legal mandates related to disability

The Americans with Disabilities Act prohibits private organizations; local, state, and federal government entities; employment agencies; and labor unions from discriminating against persons with disabilities (either mental or physical). A person is considered to have a disability when she or he possesses an impairment (whether physical or mental) that significantly restricts one or more major life activities. A major life activity, as defined in the ADA, is an activity that is fundamental to human life—"caring for oneself, performing manual tasks, walking, seeing, hearing, speaking, breathing, learning, and working" (Americans with Disabilities Act, 1985).

Within sport, as well as other business contexts, a qualified person with a disability is one who can perform the basic elements of a job with reasonable accommodations. Reasonable accommodations are those that the employer can make without undue hardship, and they may include restructuring the nature of the job (e.g., modifying the work schedule), making existing facilities readily accessible by persons with a disability, or modifying equipment.

Employers are not required to lower the job standards. If a person with a disability cannot perform the basic job functions with reasonable accommodations, then the person need not be hired. The employer is not required to provide employees with items such as glasses or hearing aids.

The ADA covers medical examinations and inquiries, as well as drug and alcohol abuse. Employers cannot ask job applicants if they have preexisting medical conditions, but they can ask if the applicants are able to perform the basic duties related to the job. Medical examinations are permissible when they are required of *all* job applicants. The examinations must be job related and consistent with the employer's overall business needs. With respect to drugs and alcohol, the ADA does not apply to people who take illegal drugs. Mandatory drug testing is legal, and employers can hold substance abusers who have disabilities to the same performance standards as other employees.

In 2013, the EEOC received 25,957 claims of disability discrimination and recovered over $109.2 million in damages.

See the box above for a discussion of the legal mandates related to disability, and the Diversity in the Field box for information about compliance with ADA in sport facilities.

DIVERSITY IN THE FIELD

Trying to Get Around ADA Guidelines. In 2014, the University of Massachusetts completed its three-year renovation of McGuirk Stadium. This project, which cost $34.5 million, was undertaken as part of the university's move to a higher level of competition. The facelift included a new training facility, locker room, coaching suites, and film rooms. New field turf was also included in the project.

Interestingly, the renovations did not include making the press box compliant with ADA guidelines. In most cases, when an existing structure is renovated, it must be brought up to current standards. If a facility undergoes major renovations, then all elements need to be improved to meet standards; absent such makeovers, older facilities can remain out of compliance for years. The McGuirk Stadium renovation normally would have meant the university would have to bring the 50-year-old facility up to current standards. However, as the press box does not actually touch the stadium, there was no legal requirement to comply with ADA rules for the press box.

University spokesperson Edward Blaguszewski indicated the decision was a financial one, suggesting the university had to make trade-offs during difficult financial times. However, Christine Griffin, executive director of the Disability Law Center, saw things differently, suggesting the university is "responsible for ensuring that people have full access in their communities." Griffin noted that, rather than trying to find loopholes in the law, the university "should be looking at how to make it more accessible" (Redington, 2014).

According to the World Health Organization, approximately 15 percent of the world's population has a disability—over 1 billion people. According to the U.S. Census Bureau, the proportion within the United States is slightly higher, as 18.7 percent of all persons (303.9 million) had a disability in 2010. This proportion is consistent with 2005 figures. About 12.6 percent have a severe disability. The U.S. Census Bureau groups disability status into three categories: communicative, mental, or physical (see Exhibit 7.1 for a definitional overview). For adults with a disability, most disabilities are in the physical domain, followed by mental disabilities, and then communicative disabilities. Of course, it is possible for a person to have more than one disability.

The incidence of disability status is not evenly distributed across the population. Exhibit 7.2 shows the relationship between disability status and age. The differences are striking, as people age 80 or older are eight times as likely to have a disability as people younger than age 15. This relationship is largely explained by the general deterioration of health as people age, including higher probabilities of heart disease, certain types of cancer, and diabetes. As noted in Chapters 1 and 6, most industrialized countries are experiencing an increase in the age of their populations, so the relationship between age and disability status is particularly meaningful.

The census data show that other demographics are also associated with disability status. Women are more likely to have a disability than are men (19.8 percent and 17.4 percent, respectively). When considering the effects of race, it is useful to look at age-adjusted estimates because of the large differences in the median age among groups. With this adjustment, African Americans are most likely to have a disability (22.2 percent), followed by Latinos (17.8 percent), non-Hispanic Whites (17.6 percent), and Asians (14.5 percent).

These patterns illuminate what Bell, McLaughlin, and Sequeira (2004) refer to as the "permeable boundaries" of disability. Many diversity forms cannot be changed (e.g., race), but in some instances one's disability status can change: an individual can become ill or have an accident and then be considered a person with a disability. An

---

EXHIBIT 7.1   Disability categories, as defined by the U.S. Census Bureau.

The U.S. Census Bureau describes disabilities along three domains:

1. **Communicative domain:** people with a communicative disability are blind or have difficulty seeing; are deaf or have difficulty hearing; and/or express speech in a way that others find difficult to understand.

2. **Mental domain:** people with a mental disability have a disability in the area of learning, intellectual ability, or development, and/or have dementia, Alzheimer's disease, or senility.

3. **Physical domain:** people with a physical disability require an aid to move (e.g., a wheelchair, a walker); have trouble moving short distances (e.g., a quarter of a mile), climbing stairs, or grasping objects; and/or have other conditions that limit their mobility.

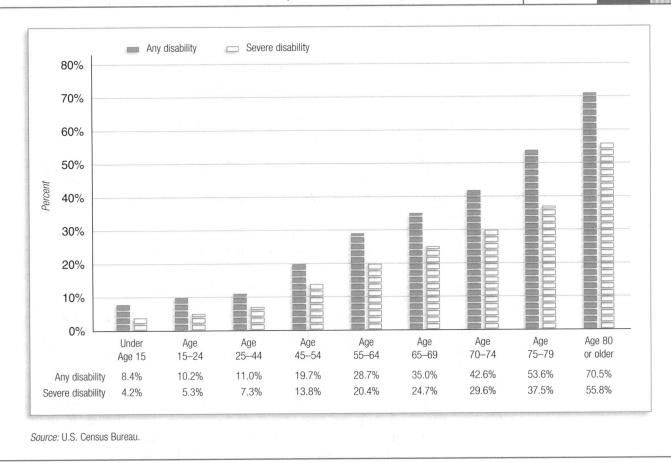

	Under Age 15	Age 15–24	Age 25–44	Age 45–54	Age 55–64	Age 65–69	Age 70–74	Age 75–79	Age 80 or older
Any disability	8.4%	10.2%	11.0%	19.7%	28.7%	35.0%	42.6%	53.6%	70.5%
Severe disability	4.2%	5.3%	7.3%	13.8%	20.4%	24.7%	29.6%	37.5%	55.8%

Source: U.S. Census Bureau.

example of the changeable nature of this type of physical diversity is illustrated by the career of Michael Teuber of Germany. Teuber was an avid, able-bodied windsurfer and snowboarder. After an automobile accident, however, he had limited use of his legs—about 65 percent of their previous capacity. He began mountain biking for re-habilitation and soon became an avid cyclist. This love of cycling led him to compete, and he has done quite well. In fact, Teuber is a Paralympic world champion, a Eu-ropean cycling champion, and a winner of other medals in various forms of cycling, including road racing, trail racing, and pursuit racing (DePauw & Gavron, 2005). It is important to note, however, that while some disabilities are permeable, others are not. For people born with disabilities, those disabilities are likely to be permanent and, thus, socially constructed, much like race and gender.

BIAS AGAINST PERSONS WITH DISABILITIES

A s with other forms of diversity, bias toward persons with disabilities is re-flected in stereotypes, prejudice, and discrimination (see, e.g., Cuddy, Fiske, & Glick, 2008).

Stereotypes

People hold a number of negative stereotypes about persons with disabilities, including the belief that they

- do not have the requisite skills to perform their work effectively;
- increase the time demands placed on their supervisors;
- increase healthcare costs for the rest of the workplace; and
- have poor emotional adjustment, including being overly bitter, nervous, and depressed (for an overview, see Kulkarni & Lengnick-Hall, 2014; Stone-Romero, Stone, & Lukaszewski, 2007).

Ren, Paetzold, and Colella (2008) examined disability stereotyping by aggregating the results from 51 experimental studies. Consistent with a contention put forward by Stone-Romero and colleagues, they found that people routinely expected poorer performance from persons with disabilities than from able-bodied persons, leading them to conclude, "These results may stem from perceptions of the individual with a disability as unsuitable for employment because of stigmatized views of the disability itself or because of negative perceptions regarding the ability of a person with a disability to perform a job" (p. 199).

We can better understand the nature of these stereotypes by returning to the stereotype content model discussed in Chapter 3 (Fiske, Cuddy, Glick, & Xu, 2002). As you will recall, according to this model, stereotypes exist along two dimensions: warmth and competence. People who have traditionally held privileged status in the United States are highly rated along both domains, but this is not the case for people with disabilities. Instead, evidence indicates that people regard persons with mental and physical disabilities as being warm but lacking in competence. This results in people expressing both pity and compassion for persons with disabilities (Colella & Stone, 2005). Compared to compassion, pity is more condescending and is often accompanied by the view that the person with a disability is inferior (Colella & Stone, 2005).

Clearly, pity toward persons with disabilities can have negative effects. Fiske et al. (2002) argue that pity was an inherently mixed emotion because it combined sympathy and superiority. Thus, while people who feel pity might express compassion for persons with disabilities (i.e., awareness that they do have a disability and the potential distress that it might cause), they also view such people as inferior and subordinate. In the workplace, such prejudice might result in low leader-member exchange relationships or low performance expectations, both of which were outlined previously.

Prejudice

The work experiences of persons with disabilities are also affected by prejudice. From a historical perspective, negative perceptions of persons with disabilities have persisted over time. As Bell (2007) explains, these perceptions are manifested in attitudes, distancing, and language (see the box on the facing page). In former times, as well as in some cultures today, persons with disabilities were considered undesirable, defective, and unwanted. These attitudes led to efforts to alienate or remove persons with disabilities. In ancient Greece, babies with club feet were abandoned to die. In the United States in the past, schools would separate children with sensory impairments from their peers, similar to the way people were segregated based on their race. Sometimes individuals with disabilities found it necessary to hide their disabilities; one famous politician had an agreement with the press that they would not photograph him using a cane. Language, such as use of the terms *cripple, deaf and dumb,* or *crazy,* reflects commonly held negative perceptions of persons with disabilities. Another example is the more recent use of the term *retarded* to refer to persons who are perceived as unusual, silly, or out of the ordinary.

> ## Language and disability
>
> As with any discussion of diversity, the language we use is of considerable importance. Some scholars, such as Thomas and Smith (2009), use the term *disabled people,* while others, such as Misener and Darcy (2014), prefer the term *persons with disability.* In this book, I opt for the latter—a people-first approach. As DePauw and Gavron (2005) correctly note, doing so recognizes persons as individuals first rather than placing the focus on their disability.

We discussed stigma in Chapter 2, and it is worth returning to the topic here in order to understand better why prejudice takes place. According to Paetzold, Dipboye, and Elsbach (2008), stigma "represents an attribute that produces a social identity that is devalued or derogated by persons within a particular culture at a particular point in time" (p. 186). Stigmas are socially constructed and specific to a particular context. A characteristic that is stigmatizing in one context might not be viewed as such in another. Within the work environment, disability might be considered stigmatizing because it runs counter to cultural norms and expectations of healthiness and is different from what is "normal" (Saal, Martinez, & Smith, 2014). As a result, a person who has visible disabilities might experience uneasy social interactions, heightened anxiety in her or his counterparts, and even behavioral distancing on their part (Dovidio, Pagotto, & Hebl, 2011).

Of course, not all disabilities elicit the same reactions, and neither are they stigmatized in the same fashion. Jones, Farina, Hastorf, and colleagues (1984) propose six factors influencing how people react to persons with disabilities:

1. *Disruptiveness,* or the degree to which the disability influences social interactions or communications among people;
2. *Origin,* or the degree to which a person is seen as responsible for her or his disability;
3. *Aesthetic qualities,* or the extent to which the disability negatively influences the person's attractiveness;
4. *Course,* or the extent to which the disability is transient or permanent;
5. *Concealability,* or the degree to which the disability can be plainly observed by others; and
6. *Peril,* or the degree to which a disability is believed to cause others harm.

In drawing from this framework and discussions of how it applies to the work environment (McLaughlin, Bell, & Stringer, 2004), several points become clear. First, the concept of stigma helps explain why some disabilities are met with greater resistance than others. Consider, for instance, the factors listed above as they pertain to HIV/AIDS status. Persons with HIV/AIDS might be seen as responsible for contracting the illness (high in origin), might have their physical appearance negatively affected by the disease (high in aesthetics), will be affected by the illness for the remainder of their life (high in course), and might be seen as a risk to others (high in peril). These perceptions differ from perceptions of a person who has suffered a stroke: the person did not cause the illness (low in origin), and the person's physical appearance may or may not be affected (moderate level of aesthetics). Negative physical effects might be overcome through rehabilitation, and the person might not be affected for the rest of his or her life (low in course). Finally, others cannot "catch" a stroke from the person (low in peril). Thus, a person with HIV/AIDS is likely to be more stigmatized than one who recently suffered a stroke, and the bias and discrimination affecting those two individuals would vary accordingly.

Second, the definition of stigma also helps explain why prejudice varies by context. For instance, a person with a mental disability might be viewed less warmly in the youth sport context, where the disability might impede the person's performance relative to others, than in the Special Olympics setting, where mental disabilities are a normal part of participation. Note here that the mental disability remains constant while the stigma attached to it, as well as subsequent bias and discrimination, varies in each context.

Discrimination

Both stereotypes and prejudice influence the discrimination that people with disabilities face in the work environment. Persons with disabilities face discrimination when they are searching for employment, on the job, and in their career advancement efforts.

Preemployment discrimination

According to the U.S. Census Bureau, 41.1 percent of persons who were aged 21 to 64 and had a disability were employed in 2010. This is considerably lower than the corresponding percentage among able-bodied persons (79.1 percent; see Exhibit 7.3). Lower still is the percentage of persons with a severe disability employed at this time—roughly a quarter (27.5 percent). People with disabilities only in the communicative domain were the most likely to be employed (73.4 percent)—a proportion substantially higher than that of persons with disabilities only in the mental domain (51.9 percent) or only in the physical domain (40.8 percent).

Some might suggest that differences in educational attainment account for these lower percentages of employment. According to data from the Bureau of Labor Statistics, in 2013, compared to their able-bodied peers, persons with disabilities were more likely to have earned less than a high school diploma (21.9 percent vs. 10.3 percent) and less likely to have a college degree or higher (16.2 percent vs. 34.0 percent). However, these differences do not account for all of the variance in workforce participation. Again drawing from the Bureau of Labor Statistics data, even with equal educational attainment, persons with disabilities are less likely than their able-bodied counterparts to be employed. The most telling data are for those individuals with a bachelor's degree or greater: among this group, able-bodied persons are 2.6 times as likely to be employed as are persons with disabilities.

These data suggest that various discriminatory practices limit workforce participation among persons with disabilities. As one example, there is evidence that people's verbal and nonverbal behaviors vary based on whether they are interacting with a person with a disability or with an able-bodied individual (Dovidio et al.,

Employment status among people with disabilities.   EXHIBIT   **7.3**

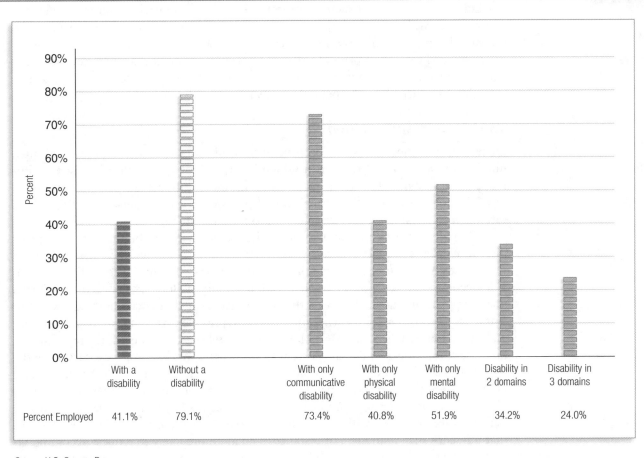

	With a disability	Without a disability		With only communicative disability	With only physical disability	With only mental disability	Disability in 2 domains	Disability in 3 domains
Percent Employed	41.1%	79.1%		73.4%	40.8%	51.9%	34.2%	24.0%

Source: U.S. Census Bureau.

2011). Even though people generally express positive attitudes (e.g., warmth) toward persons with disabilities and feel positively toward disability-inclusive organizations (Macdougall, Nguyen, & Karg, 2014), they discriminate in subtle ways. The discrimination manifests verbally in that, when compared to other conversations they have, exchanges with people with disabilities are usually shorter and more terse. There is also evidence of physical distancing: people will sit farther away from and make fewer movements toward a person with a disability. These subtle cues have the potential to make for awkward exchanges and a heightened sense of anxiety in interactions, neither of which benefits the person with a disability (Dovidio et al., 2011).

Evidence also suggests that persons with disabilities are rated differently from their able-bodied peers in the selection process. A study Hooks and I completed offers an illustrative example (Hooks & Cunningham, 2013). In our experiment, participants rated applicants with a disability as a poor fit for a personal trainer position, even when the applicant was highly qualified. Fit perceptions were important, as they were strongly associated with hiring recommendations. Another experiment offers additional insights into selection bias against persons with disabilities. Hebl and Skorinko (2005) considered the timing of applicants' disclosure of their disability status. Applicants who disclosed such information early in the interview were viewed more favorably, considered to be happier, and believed to be more capable than those who did not. People who disclosed early were also considered to be better psychologically adjusted than their peers. Hebl and Skorinko reasoned that interviewers might believe someone who openly discusses the disability is well-adjusted and comfortable with the disability; thus, the person is viewed favorably.

Workplace discrimination

Once they join the workforce, persons with disabilities face discrimination along a number of fronts, the foremost of which is pay. According to the U.S. Census Bureau, these individuals earn a median annual income of $23,532. This represents just 72 percent of what their able-bodied peers earn on average ($32,688). These differences persist across levels of educational attainment.

One of the most common ways in which people with disabilities face workplace discrimination is in reactions to requests for accommodations. The Americans with Disabilities Act requires that organizations with at least 15 employees make "reasonable accommodation" for a person with a disability, as long as the accommodation does not place undue hardship on the organization. Such an accommodation for an employee who is hard of hearing might be a requirement that her manager face her and speak loudly when addressing her. A person who uses a wheelchair might need a taller desk (or blocks under the current desk) because his knees hit the current desk.

The ADA places the responsibility for requesting an accommodation on the employee. Interestingly, approximately 4 out of 10 employees with disabilities do not make any requests for accommodations (Schur, Nishii, Adya, et al., 2014). A number of factors are associated with the decision not to make a request, including social norms that influence such requests. For instance, men are more likely to request accommodations as the severity of their disability increases, though no such relationship exists for women (Baldridge & Swift, 2013). This pattern might result from socially constructed norms related to help-seeking behavior and its interplay with gender norms. In other cases, not making accommodation requests is linked to the anticipated imposition the accommodation might cause. People with disabilities will withhold accommodation requests when they believe (1) there would be substantial financial costs, (2) doing so would negatively influence others, and (3) negative social consequences could follow the request (Baldridge & Veiga, 2006). Although the anticipation of financial cost inhibits requests, the evidence suggests that, in fact, most accommodations either do not cost anything or have minimal monetary costs (less than $500; Schur et al., 2014).

There is also evidence to support the notion that managers do not view all requests the same. For instance, managers respond negatively when they receive a request from a person whom they perceive to be responsible for his or her own disability (Florey & Harrison, 2000). They respond favorably, however, to requests from persons whose previous performance has been high. Stigma also affects managers' reactions. Requests from people who are highly stigmatized (e.g., those with AIDS) are met with negative attitudes and perceived as unfair, particularly when compared with requests from people with less-stigmatized disabilities, such as cerebral palsy (McLaughlin et al., 2004). Of course, persons with disabilities are not the only ones who make requests for accommodations, as outlined in the Alternative Perspectives box.

When a person with a disability makes a request for accommodation, failure to grant the request is not only illegal in most cases, but is also bad business. When requests are denied, employees' satisfaction in the workplace is likely to decrease, while their perceptions of discrimination increase (Moore, Konrad, Yang, Ng, & Doherty, 2011). On the other hand, managers believe granting requests results in improved productivity, improvements in the worker's morale, and a decrease in stress (Schur et al., 2014). Coworkers also take note of these benefits, indicating that granting requests for employees with disabilities also improves interactions with other coworkers (Schur et al., 2014).

Career advancement

Finally, Kulkarni and Lengnick-Hall (2014) note that persons with disabilities face discrimination in their personal development and career advancement opportunities. One area of discrimination is in the leadership positions they are afforded. Few people with disabilities obtain leadership roles in the workplace, and when they do, they are often placed in precarious situations, where the units have a history of failure and there is little opportunity for success. These are referred to as *glass cliffs,* as the positions are risky (Ryan & Haslam, 2007). When persons with disabilities take on such leadership roles, they have few opportunities to be successful, receive little support from others, and work with limited organizational resources (Wilson-Kovacs, Ryan, Haslam, & Rabinovich, 2008). All of these factors serve to limit their potential effectiveness.

In other cases, norms and expectations about who should or should not be a manager affect the career advancement of persons with disabilities. When a person envisions a successful manager, an able-bodied person likely comes to mind—one, by the way, who is also a White male. On the other hand, thoughts of a person with a disability within the sport organization are likely linked with peripheral job roles. This disconnect is meaningful, as persons with disabilities are unlikely to have opportunities for career advancement or to take on leadership roles if people do not consider them as leadership material (Roulstone & Williams, 2014). As a result, people with disabilities report feeling the need to engage in advocacy efforts on their own behalf in order to overcome negative performance and leadership stereotypes (Kulkarni & Gopakumar, 2014).

Leaders can structure the human resource system in ways that serve to decrease the incidence of discrimination against persons with disabilities. These are highlighted in the following box.

ALTERNATIVE perspectives

Requests for Accommodations Are Made by All Employees. We frequently think of requests for accommodations as being made by persons with disabilities, but in actuality able-bodied persons make requests, too. A study conducted by Schur and colleagues (2014) of more than 5,000 employees from multiple companies demonstrated as much. The researchers observed that 28.1 percent of able-bodied persons had made requests for accommodations. Some of the requests were made for health reasons, but most were for other purposes. The requests included flexible work schedules, the ability to complete some or all of the work from home, restructuring of job duties, and the like. Most of the participants in the study reported that their requests were fully granted, but the percentage was higher for able-bodied persons (79.3 percent) than it was for persons with disabilities (72.6 percent). The accommodations positively affected the able-bodied employees' work, resulting in greater productivity and satisfaction, as well as an increased likelihood of remaining with the organization (see also Lauzun, Morganson, Major, & Green, 2010).

Developing human resource systems to counter discrimination

The human resource system in the workplace might influence whether or not persons with disabilities face prejudice and discrimination (Bell, 2007). This influence can be seen in the selection process, compensation and benefits, training, and performance evaluations.

- *Selection.* Organizations should use the job description in selecting persons who are able to perform the job effectively, with or without reasonable accommodations. Indeed, "having and using a job description can help organizations in selecting appropriately in all situations (not just with applicants with disabilities)" (Bell, 2007, p. 361).

- *Compensation.* Persons with disabilities should be paid based on the worth of the job, coupled with their education, experience, and skills. Disability status *should not* be considered in the compensation process.

- *Training and development.* Persons with disabilities should be provided all of the opportunities other employees are afforded. Not doing so is illegal and thwarts the career advancement opportunities of persons with disabilities.

- *Performance evaluation.* All employees should be evaluated on a regular basis, irrespective of their disability status. Job performance standards should be explicitly outlined and used as the criteria for evaluations. Failure to evaluate performance fairly and accurately not only hurts the employee's development but also is deleterious to the organization.

ABILITY AND PHYSICAL ACTIVITY AND SPORT PARTICIPATION

In addition to considering the effects of ability in the workplace, it is also instructive to examine persons with disabilities' participation in sport and physical activity. In doing so, we consider participation rates and people's experiences during activity.

Physical Activity Participation

The data portal of the Healthy People initiative (found at www.healthypeople.gov) allows for analysis of physical activity with a focus on persons with activity limitations. Relative to their able-bodied peers, persons with activity limitations are 1.9 times as likely to lead sedentary lives (48.3 percent vs. 25.7 percent, respectively), and this trend has persisted over time. Persons with disabilities are also less likely than are able-bodied individuals to engage in the recommended levels of moderate or vigorous physical activity (see Exhibit 7.4).

The low participation rates for individuals with a disability result from a number of factors. Fay (2011) notes that sport is viewed as a luxury for persons with disabilities, not as an inalienable right. This perspective is reinforced through stereotypes, prejudice, and discrimination that have been maintained throughout history, reinforced in public law, and advanced in sport policy. Participation opportunities for youth with disabilities are similarly limited. This is attributable to a lack of resources, coaches, informal sport experiences, and playing space; as a result, the chance for young people with disabilities to develop skills and confidence in the sport domain are thwarted (see also Hodge & Runswick-Cole, 2013). The socially constructed and legitimated bias toward physically active persons with disabilities also gives rise to the potential for internalized ableism (Fay, 2011): persons

Participation in recommended levels of physical activity.   EXHIBIT   **7.4**

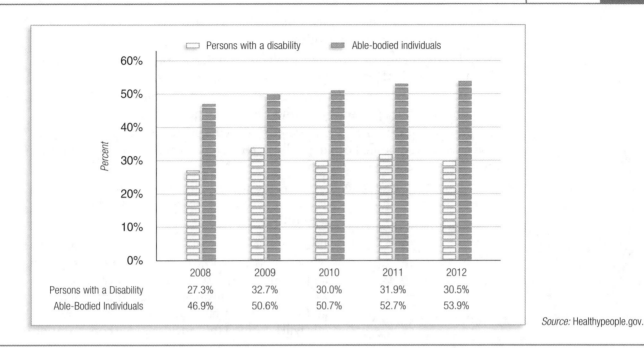

	2008	2009	2010	2011	2012
Persons with a Disability	27.3%	32.7%	30.0%	31.9%	30.5%
Able-Bodied Individuals	46.9%	50.6%	50.7%	52.7%	53.9%

Source: Healthypeople.gov.

with disabilities come to accept the prejudices and stereotypes others hold, and in so doing potentially limit what they believe they can accomplish.

Some researchers have drawn from a leisure constraints perspective to examine factors influencing participation among persons with disabilities (Sotiriadou & Wicker, 2014). In this perspective, individual, interpersonal, and structural factors all have the potential to shape one's leisure activities, including physical activity. Consistent with this view, evidence suggests that as the restrictive nature of the disability increases, physical activity levels decrease (an individual constraint), people who are not partnered are more active (interpersonal constraint), and work obligations interfere more with an individual's physical activity levels (structural constraint; Sotiriadou & Wicker, 2014). Thus, various factors in people's lives, operating at different levels, affect their opportunities to be active.

Disability Sport

Although physical activity levels among persons with disabilities remain low, the popularity and availability of formal sport opportunities have increased over the past decade. *Disability sport* refers to "sport that has been designed for or is specifically practiced by athletes with disabilities" (DePauw & Gavron, 2005, p. 80). This definition includes sports designed specifically for persons with disabilities, such as goal ball for athletes who are blind; sports that able-bodied persons practice that are altered or modified to include athletes with disabilities, such as wheelchair basketball; and sports that require little or no modification, such as swimming.

Interactive (see interactive.uk.net), an organization devoted to ensuring that persons with disabilities have opportunities to be physically active, offers another lens for classifying disability sport. This organization considers inclusion as the key to delivering sport opportunities and defines those opportunities as follows:

- *Fully inclusive activities:* Athletes of all abilities participate without modification or adaptation of the activity.
- *Modified or integrated activities:* Athletes with disabilities participate alongside able-bodied athletes, with some changes to the rules, area, or equipment.
- *Parallel activities:* Athletes are grouped based on their ability, competing at the same time but against others who share their impairment.
- *Adapted activities, or reverse integration:* All athletes participate in sports that have been modified or adapted specifically for persons with disabilities; thus, all use a common adaptation.
- *Discrete, or segregated, activities:* Athletes with disabilities compete against other athletes with disabilities in an activity; able-bodied athletes are purposefully separated.

professional
PERSPECTIVES

Trends and Issues in Disability Sport. Eli Wolff is a two-time Olympic soccer athlete, a graduate of Brown University, and current director of the Inclusive Sports Initiative at the Institute for Human Centered Design; he also directs the Sport and Development Project at Brown University. According to Wolff, one of the major issues in the area of disability sport today is the inclusion and integration of persons with disabilities within the fabric of mainstream sport. To what degree do mainstream sport organizations at every level of sport actually embrace disability sport opportunities? The answer, according to Wolff, is that full integration and inclusion are still a distant goal.

Wolff points to two primary barriers for persons with disabilities who wish to participate in sport: attitudes toward such participation and the portrayal of disability sport in the media. Wolff notes that there is a misconception about "what it means to be a person with a disability in sport." Too often, people pity disability sport athletes rather than recognizing their efforts as athletes. The same trend occurs in the media, where athletes with disabilities are often portrayed as sources of inspiration for others. This stands in contrast to focusing on the athletes' accomplishments and athletic prowess. Wolff argues that in order to overcome such barriers, awareness of these issues needs to be raised. People in the media, athletes, coaches, and supporters all need to know that the status quo is not how disability sport "has to be."

Interactive suggests that sport organizations can work across the spectrum to ensure inclusion for all persons, irrespective of their ability. An organization can work through the classification scheme, adding one impairment at a time, so that it gradually will become a fully inclusive sport organization for persons of all abilities.

The Eastern Collegiate Athletic Conference (ECAC, www.ecacsports.com) provides an example of how sport organizations can embrace these principles. In January 2015, the ECAC became the first NCAA-sanctioned conference to offer varsity sport opportunities for athletes with disabilities. The conference developed a multilayered strategy: in some events, reasonable accommodations will be provided, while in others, ECAC will add adapted activities. The conference plans to add various sports, such as sled hockey, sitting volleyball, and wheelchair basketball, among others. In speaking of this historic and inclusive decision, ECAC president Kevin McGinniss noted, "This historic action systemically includes student-athletes with disabilities in intercollegiate sports for the first time in any NCAA division. I believe this action will allow many more athletes, including wounded veterans returning to college, to experience the benefits of competitive intercollegiate sports" (Eastern Collegiate Athletic Conference, 2015).

As Legg, Fay, Hums, and Wolff (2009; see also Hums & MacLean, 2013) note, many of the advancements in disability sport can be traced to the efforts of neurosurgeon Sir Ludwig Guttman. During and after World War II, sport and exercise were used in rehabilitation efforts for wounded soldiers. Guttman recognized the effectiveness of this approach, particularly in reducing boredom during the rehabilitation process. Thus, in 1944 he opened the Spinal Injuries Center at Stoke Mandeville Hospital in England, with a particular emphasis on sport. Within four years, sport as a form of rehabilitation had grown into a competitive venture, with patients in different wards competing against one another. This soon blossomed into an international competition when a team from the Netherlands competed in 1952. The official title of the competition was the Stoke Mandeville Games. The event grew in magnitude, and in 1960 the competition was staged as the Paralympic Games in Rome at the same time as the Olympics. Since that time, the Paralympic Games have been staged in tandem with the Olympic Games every four years. To illustrate the growth of the Paralympic Games, 400 athletes from 23 countries competed in 1960; in 2004, nearly 3,700 athletes representing 136 different countries competed in the Athens Games.

Of course, the Paralympics represent just one of many forms of disability sport (see Exhibit 7.5 for discussion).

Athletes with disabilities report mixed experiences competing in sport. Just as in broader society, athletes with disabilities can face marginalization, stigmatization, and exclusion (Dane-Staples, Lieberman, Ratcliff, & Rounds, 2013; Kitchin & Howe, 2014; Purdue & Howe, 2012). This is observed among athletes and reproduced through the media. Persons with disabilities are underrepresented in print and television media. As an example, the BBC broadcast more than 500 hours of the 2000 Olympic Games but devoted only 10 hours to the Paralympic Games that same year (Brittain, 2004). Athletes describe the limited coverage they do receive as fleeting, and the Paralympics and its participants receive no attention after the two or three weeks following the closing ceremonies. The lack of coverage by the BBC is particularly perplexing when we consider that it is a federally funded broadcast; thus, commercial viability (which is sometimes claimed as the reason for a lack of coverage) is not applicable.

Not only do persons with disabilities receive little media attention, but the coverage they do receive is often condescending and trivializing. Thomas and Smith (2009) note that the media frequently depict persons with disabilities as passive objects of charity. The stereotypical representations serve to evoke fear and pity. The media are also more likely to focus on athletes' disabilities than their athletic

Large-scale disability sport events. EXHIBIT **7.5**

Paralympic Games: A showcase of elite athletes with disabilities, including visual impairments, cerebral palsy, amputations, spinal cord injuries, and (on a limited basis) athletes with mental impairments; includes both winter and summer contests.

Deaflympics: Elite competition for athletes who are deaf. The first summer Deaflympics were held in 1924 in Paris, with the winter Deaflympics added in 1949.

Special Olympics: Sport opportunities for persons with cognitive and developmental disabilities; focus on development and social interaction of the athletes and not elite competition.

prowess. Stories often concentrate on how the athlete overcame obstacles (i.e., disabilities) and demonstrated courage. These patronizing portrayals, which serve to perpetuate stereotypes of these athletes as objects of pity, are notably absent in media coverage of able-bodied athletes, where the focus is instead on their athletic ability and performance on the field.

Despite these negative experiences, many athletes with disabilities report that disability sport serves as a site for them to challenge stereotypes and develop physically, psychologically, and socially. For instance, athletes in adapted (i.e., reverse integration) activities develop a positive athlete identity through their participation, coming to see themselves as athletes, not disabled athletes (Spencer-Cavaliere & Peers, 2011). Identity formation is important, as it allows people to combat prejudices, develop effective social networks, experience success, and feel fully enmeshed into the sport experience (Lundberg, Taniguchi, McCormick, & Tibbs, 2011). For combat veterans, sport and physical activity allow those with psychological disorders to improve their psychological and social well-being (Caddick & Smith, 2014). Positive outcomes include symptom reduction of post-traumatic stress disorder, active coping, improved self-concept, enhanced sense of achievement, and improved overall social well-being. The benefits are not limited to athletes, as disability sport spectators also report improved attitudes toward the sport and better behavioral tendencies toward athletes with disabilities (de Haan, Faull, & Kohe, 2014).

chapter SUMMARY

The purpose of this chapter was to outline the effects of mental and physical ability in the workplace and sport. As the case of Marcus Rehm in the opening Diversity Challenge illustrates, ability influences people's opportunities and experiences. After reading this chapter, you should be able to:

1. **Provide a definition of *disability* and an overview of the historical background related to mental and physical ability.**

   People are considered to have a disability if they have a mental or physical impairment that limits one or more major life activities. Historically, people with disabilities have faced discrimination and been ostracized by others.

2. **Discuss the work experiences of, and educational and work opportunities for, persons with disabilities.**

   Persons with disabilities experience bias in the work environment. There is evidence of negative stereotypes concerning their abilities and aptitude; prejudice that is historically rooted and, today, manifested through stigma; and discrimination that occurs prior to employment, on the job, and in people's career development opportunities.

3. **Describe the sport and physical activity opportunities for and experiences of people with disabilities.**

   People with disabilities are less physically active than are able-bodied individuals. Opportunities to participate in disability sport have grown substantially. Nevertheless, a number of issues affect its delivery, including negative attitudes toward athletes with disabilities, barriers to inclusion, and lack of accessibility.

QUESTIONS for discussion

1. The chapter provided a brief historical overview of issues related to mental and physical disabilities. Are some of the ways that persons with disabilities historically faced discrimination still present today? What are examples?

2. Identify some of the factors that may influence requests for accommodation by persons with disabilities in the workplace. What might be done to overcome some of the potential barriers?

3. Why are the athletic accomplishments of persons with disabilities brought into question by able-bodied athletes?

4. Disabilities are stigmatized in several ways. Which of the dimensions of stigma, as identified by Jones and colleagues (1984), is most influential?

5. What might be some ways sport managers could market directly to individuals with disabilities?

learning ACTIVITIES

1. Using the Internet, identify sport organizations and sport events that target athletes with disabilities. Based on your search, how would you characterize the sport and physical activity opportunities available for persons with disabilities?

2. Using the Internet, identify common requests for accommodations within sport organizations and the price incurred to the organization for making such accommodations. Are the prices more or less than you would have anticipated? What impacts would the accommodations have on the organization?

WEB resources

National Disability Sports Alliance, www.ndsaonline.org

Organization that serves as the governing body for competitive sport for persons with disabilities.

International Paralympic Committee, www.paralympic.org

Serves as the official website of the Paralympic movement.

Global Disability Research in Sport and Health Network, www.disability researchinsportandhealth.ca

An organization of researchers focusing on disability issues in the sport and physical activity context.

reading RESOURCES

DePauw, K. P., & Gavron, S. J. (2005). *Disability sport* (2nd ed.). Champaign, IL: Human Kinetics.

Provides a historical account of disability sport and athletes with disabilities; also addresses the current challenges and controversies surrounding disability and sport.

Hums, M. A., & MacLean, J. C. (2013). *Governance and policy in sport organizations* (3rd ed.). Scottsdale, AZ: Holcomb Hathaway.

Provides an overview of governance and policy issues in sport, with one of the most comprehensive treatments of the Paralympics in the literature.

Thomas, N., & Smith, A. (2009). *Disability, sport and society: An introduction.* New York: Routledge.

Provides an overview of the theories and policies related to disability and sport, with a particular emphasis on sport in the United Kingdom.

REFERENCES

Americans with Disabilities Act, 45 C.F.R. 843(j)(2)(i) (1985).

Baldridge, D. C., & Swift, M. L. (2013). Withholding requests for disability accommodation: The role of individual differences and disability attributes. *Journal of Management, 39,* 743–762.

Baldridge, D. C., & Veiga, J. F. (2006). The impact of anticipated social consequences on recurring disability accommodation requests. *Journal of Management, 32,* 158–179.

Bell, M. P. (2007). *Diversity in organizations.* Mason, OH: Thomson South-Western.

Bell, M. P., McLaughlin, M. E., & Sequeira, J. M. (2004). Age, disability, and obesity: Similarities, differences, and common threads. In M. S. Stockdale & F. J. Crosby (Eds.), *The psychology and management of workplace diversity* (pp. 191–205). Malden, MA: Blackwell.

Brittain, I. (2004). Perceptions of disability and their impact upon involvement in sport for people with disabilities at all levels. *Journal of Sport and Social Issues, 28,* 429–452.

Caddick, N., & Smith, B. (2014). The impact of sport and physical activity on the well-being of combat veterans: A systematic review. *Psychology of Sport and Exercise, 15,* 9–18.

Colella, A., & Stone, D. L. (2005). Workplace discrimination toward persons with disabilities: A call for some new research directions. In R. L. Dipboye & A. Colella (Eds.), *Discrimination at work: The psychological and organizational bases* (pp. 227–253). Mahwah, NJ: Lawrence Erlbaum.

Cuddy, A. J. C., Fiske, S. T., & Glick, P. (2008). Warmth and competence as universal dimensions of social perception: The stereotype content model and the BIAS map. *Advances in Experimental Social Psychology, 40,* 61–149.

Dane-Staples, E., Lieberman, L., Ratcliff, J., & Rounds, K. (2013). Bullying experiences of individuals with visual impairment: The mitigating role of sport participation. *Journal of Sport Behavior, 36*(4), 365–386.

de Haan, D., Faull, A., & Kohe, G. Z. (2014). Celebrating the social in soccer: Spectators' experiences of the forgotten (Blind) Football World Cup. *Soccer & Society, 15,* 578–595.

DePauw, K. P., & Gavron, S. J. (2005). *Disability sport* (2nd ed.). Champaign, IL: Human Kinetics.

Dovidio, J. F., Pagotto, L., & Hebl, M. R. (2011). Implicit attitudes and discrimination against people with disabilities. In R. L. Wiener & S. L. Willborn (Eds.), *Disability and ageing discrimination* (pp. 157–183). New York: Springer.

Eastern Collegiate Athletic Conference (2015). ECAC board of directors cast historic vote to add varsity sports opportunities for student-athletes with disabilities in ECAC leagues and championships. Retrieved from http://www.ecacsports.com/news/2014-15/sports_opportunities_for_student-athletes_with_disabilities_in_ECAC_leagues_and_championships.

Fay, T. (2011). Disability in sport—it's our time: From the sidelines to the frontlines (Title IX—B). *Journal of Intercollegiate Sport, 4,* 63–94.

Fiske, S. T., Cuddy, A. J. C., Glick, P., & Xu, J. (2002). A model of (often mixed) stereotype content: Competence and warmth respectively follow from perceived status and competition. *Journal of Personality and Social Psychology, 82,* 878–902.

Florey, A. T., & Harrison, D. A. (2000). Responses to informal accommodation requests from employees with disabilities: Multistudy evidence on willingness to comply. *Academy of Management Journal, 43,* 224–233.

Hebl, M. R., & Skorinko, J. L. (2005). Acknowledging one's physical disability in the interview: Does "when" make a difference? *Journal of Applied Social Psychology, 35,* 2477–2492.

Hodge, N., & Runswick-Cole, K. (2013). "They never pass me the ball": Exposing ableism through the leisure experiences of disabled children, young people and their families. *Children's Geographies, 11,* 311–325.

Hooks, T., & Cunningham, G. B. (2013, May). *Prejudice against persons with disabilities in the fitness context.* Paper presented at the annual conference for the North American Society for Sport Management, Austin, TX.

Hums, M. A., & MacLean, J. C. (2013). *Governance and policy in sport organizations* (3rd ed.). Scottsdale, AZ: Holcomb Hathaway.

Jones, E., Farina, A., Hastorf, A., Markus, H., Miller, D., Scott, R., & de Sales-French, R. (1984). *Social stigma: The psychology of marked relationships.* San Francisco: W. H. Freeman.

Kitchin, P. J., & Howe, P. D. (2014). The mainstreaming of disability cricket in England and Wales: Integration "One Game" at a time. *Sport Management Review, 17,* 65–77.

Kulkarni, M., & Gopakumar, K. V. (2014). Career management strategies of people with disabilities. *Human Resource Management, 53,* 445–466.

Kulkarni, M., & Lengnick-Hall, M. L. (2014). Obstacles to success in the workplace for people with disabilities: A review and research agenda. *Human Resource Development Review, 13,* 158–180.

Lauzun, H. M., Morganson, V. J., Major, D. A., & Green, A. P. (2010). Seeking work-life balance: Employees' requests, supervisors' responses, and organizational barriers. *The Psychologist-Manager Journal, 13*(3), 184–205.

Legg, D., Fay, T., Hums, M. A., & Wolff, E. (2009). Examining the inclusion of wheelchair events within the Olympic Games 1984–2004. *European Sport Management Quarterly, 9,* 243–258.

Lundberg, N. R., Taniguchi, S., McCormick, B. P., & Tibbs, C. (2011). Identity negotiating: Redefining stigmatized identities through adaptive sports and recreation participation among individuals with a disability. *Journal of Leisure Research, 43*(2), 205–225.

Macdougall, H. K., Nguyen, S. N., & Karg, A. J. (2014). 'Game, Set, Match': An exploration of congruence in Australian disability sport sponsorship. *Sport Management Review, 17,* 78–89.

McLaughlin, M. E., Bell, M. P., & Stringer, D. Y. (2004). Stigma and acceptance of persons with disabilities. Understanding aspects of workforce diversity. *Group & Organization Management, 29,* 302–333.

Misener, L., & Darcy, S. (2014). Managing disability sport: From athletes with disabilities to inclusive organisational perspectives. *Sport Management Review, 17,* 1–7.

Moore, M. E., Konrad, A. M., Yang, Y., Ng, E. S., & Doherty, A. J. (2011). The vocational well-being of workers with childhood onset of disability: Life satisfaction and perceived workplace discrimination. *Journal of Vocational Behavior, 79,* 681–698.

Paetzold, R. L., Dipboye, R. L., & Elsbach, K. D. (2008). A new look at stigmatization in and of organizations. *Academy of Management Review, 33,* 186–193.

Purdue, D. E. J., & Howe, P. D. (2012). See the sport, not the disability: Exploring the Paralympic paradox. *Qualitative Research in Sport, Exercise and Health, 4,* 189–205.

Redington, P. (2014, September). UMass avoids ADA compliance with McGuirk upgrade. *Daily New Hampshire Gazette.* Retrieved from http://www.gazettenet.com/sports/umasssports/13725560-95/umass-avoids-ada-compliance-with-mcguirk-upgrade.

Ren, L. R., Paetzold, R. L., & Colella, A. (2008). A meta-analysis of experimental studies on the effects of disability on human resource judgments. *Human Resource Management Review, 18,* 191–203.

Roulstone, A., & Williams, J. (2014). Being disabled, being a manager: "Glass partitions" and conditional identities in the contemporary workplace. *Disability & Society, 29,* 16–29.

Ryan, M. K., & Haslam, S. A. (2007). The glass cliff: Exploring the dynamics surrounding the appointment of women to precarious leadership positions. *Academy of Management Review, 32,* 549–572.

Saal, K., Martinez, L. R., & Smith, N. A. (2014). Visible disabilities: Acknowledging the utility of acknowledgment. *Industrial and Organizational Psychology, 7,* 242–248.

Schur, L., Nishii, L., Adya, M., Kruse, D., Bruyére, S. M., & Blank, P. (2014). Accommodating employees with and without disabilities. *Human Resource Management, 53,* 593–621.

Sotiriadou, P., & Wicker, P. (2014). Examining the participation patterns of an ageing population with disabilities in Australia. *Sport Management Review, 17,* 35–48.

Spencer-Cavaliere, N., & Peers, D. (2011). "What's the difference?" women's wheelchair basketball, reverse integration, and the question (ing) of disability. *Adapted Physical Activity Quarterly, 28,* 291–309.

Stone-Romero, E. F., Stone, D. L., & Lukaszewski, K. (2007). The influence of disability on role-taking in organizations. In A. M. Konrad, P. Prasad, & J. K. Pringle (Eds.), *Handbook of workplace diversity* (pp. 401–430). Thousand Oaks, CA: Sage.

Thomas, N., & Smith, A. (2009). *Disability, sport and society: An introduction.* New York: Routledge.

Wilson-Kovacs, D., Ryan, M. K., Haslam, S. A., & Rabinovich, A. (2008). "Just because you can get a wheelchair in the building doesn't necessarily mean that you can still participate": Barriers to the career advancement of disabled professionals. *Disability & Society, 23,* 705–717.

Appearance

LEARNING objectives

After studying this chapter, you should be able to:

- Understand key terms and different standards related to appearance.
- Discuss the influence of weight, height, and attractiveness on how people are viewed by others.
- Outline the influence of some aspects of appearance on physical activity and sport participation and promotion.

DIVERSITY CHALLENGE

The fitness industry is a multibillion-dollar segment of the U.S. economy, and it makes substantial economic contributions in countries worldwide. For example, Gold's Gym, founded in Venice Beach, California, in 1965, now has more than 600 gyms in 25 countries around the world. Bally Total Fitness has more than 400 gyms located in such countries as the United States, Canada, South Korea, China, and the Bahamas. The focus of these organizations, and others like them, is to help people reach their fitness goals. For many people, the goal is losing weight or increasing overall health and fitness levels. Therefore, these gyms are open to all types of customers, young and old, fit and unfit.

Although many fitness organizations are open to a diverse membership, they may not always be so open to diversity among their employees. There may be a bias in favor of hiring individuals who appear fit over those who do not appear fit, suggesting the presence of anti-fat attitudes. Jennifer Portnick's situation indicates that this is so. Portnick, who stands 5'8" and weighs 240 pounds, participated

in high-impact aerobics for 15 years. Given her stamina and demonstrated excellence in the activity, her instructor, Kristi Howard, encouraged her to seek an aerobics certification with Jazzercise. Howard noted, "She has everything it takes. Jennifer is very healthy. She is not pooped out and sucking for air in class."

However, Ann Rieke, district manager for Jazzercise, saw things differently and denied Portnick's request for certification. Rieke wrote that although she believed Portnick "will be a fabulous instructor someday," she did not currently have the "fit appearance" needed to be a Jazzercise instructor. She further suggested that Portnick, who is primarily a vegetarian, change her diet and try body sculpting. Portnick protested. After receiving her protest, Maureen Brown, the director for programs and services for Jazzercise, agreed with Rieke's initial conclusion. She indicated to Portnick that "a Jazzercise applicant must have a higher muscle-to-fat ratio and look leaner than the public. People must believe Jazzercise will help them improve, not just maintain their level of fitness. Instructors must set the example and be the role models for Jazzercise enthusiasts."

After Brown's decision, Portnick obtained certification through the Aerobics and Fitness Association of America and currently teaches six high-energy, low-impact classes each week. She filed a discrimination suit against Jazzercise, arguing that she did not receive certification because the company's decision was based on her physical characteristics, not on her qualifications as a potential aerobics instructor. The suit was dismissed when Jazzercise agreed to eliminate fit appearance as a prerequisite for the company's instructors and franchisees.

Sources: Fernandez, E. (2002, February). *Teacher says fat/fitness can mix: S.F. mediates complaint Jazzercise showed bias.* SFGate.com. Retrieved from www.sfgate.com/cgi-bin/article.cgi?file=/chronicle/archive/2002/02/24/MN187100.DTL. / Portnick's Complaint (2002, May 20). *People, 57,* 139 / www.ballyfitness.com / www.goldsgym.com.

CHALLENGE REFLECTION

1. How much should a fitness instructor's appearance influence customers' perceptions of the instructor's capabilities and ability to train them?

2. Should a fitness organization such as Jazzercise be able to select its employees and trainers based, at least in part, on the applicant's physical characteristics? Why or why not?

3. If you believe fitness organizations should be able to choose to hire only those people who appear physically fit, should this same standard apply to all organizations? Why or why not?

4. What are other situations where a physical characteristic might be considered a prerequisite to holding a particular position?

D iscussions of diversity often focus on race, gender, or age, with some discussions also centering on social class or more deep-level characteristics. Appearance is rarely considered. However, as the Diversity Challenge illustrates, the way people look has the potential to influence a host of outcomes, including their opportunities to lead fitness classes. Indeed, one's appearance can affect a constellation of outcomes, including career aspirations, work experiences, and interactions with others. The influence of appearance is evident in advertisements and promotions, where slim and often athletically built persons are chosen to endorse fitness organizations and related products.

The purpose of this chapter is to explore the influence of appearance in greater depth. I begin with a discussion of issues related to a person's weight, and then I turn the attention to height. In the final section, I highlight the influence of physical attractiveness on people's experiences in society, the workplace, and sport.

WEIGHT

I n this section, I provide an overview of the diversity research related to weight. I introduce key terms, discuss the effects of weight in the workplace, and offer an analysis of the effects of weight on fitness promotion and physical activity participation.

Background

Scholars and practitioners use various terms related to weight, and in some cases the meanings differ. According to the Centers for Disease Control and Prevention (n.d.), people who are overweight or obese have a body weight that exceeds what is considered healthy for their height. The CDC uses the body mass index (BMI) to make such determinations, with the following formula:

weight / (height in inches)^2 x 703

To illustrate, let us consider two people who weigh 200 pounds, but who vary in height. A person who is 5'7" would have a BMI of 31.3 and fall into the obese range. On the other hand, a person who is 6'4" would have a BMI of 24.3 and fall into the normal or healthy weight category.

Some, however, have questioned the validity of the BMI, particularly for persons with high levels of muscle mass. Consider San Francisco 49er tight end Vernon Davis. At 6'3" and 258 pounds, Davis has a BMI of 32.2, which is considered obese. However, the football player has 4 percent body fat, which is considered very lean (Wuebben, n.d.). Thus, for Davis and other athletes like him, the BMI does not offer an accurate estimate of healthy weight. See the Alternative Perspectives box for further discussion of assessments of healthy weight.

Although biomedical terms are frequently used to describe healthy weight, some observers criticize their usage. Activists argue that use of terms such as *obese* and *overweight* belies an assumption that there is such a thing as a "normal" weight—a point they dispute (Solovay, 2000). Many such standards were based on data obtained from insurance companies, whose measurements came from middle-class Whites (Bell, 2007). Obviously, what is "normal" or the standard for middle-class Whites might be very different from what is "normal" for other groups. It can also be argued that people who are clinically categorized as overweight might be healthier than persons who are thin as a result of unhealthy practices (e.g., anorexia). Given these concerns, activists propose use of terms such as *fat, fatness,* and *corpulent* (Duncan, 2008).

This debate highlights the difficulties and ambiguity surrounding issues related to weight. Nevertheless, there is general consensus among national and international agencies, such as the National Institutes of Health (NIH), the World Health Organization (WHO), and the Centers for Disease Control and Prevention, that a continuum exists from normal to overweight, obese, and morbidly obese, and that health outcomes grow progressively worse toward the high end of that continuum. Furthermore, determining precisely where a person falls on a medical continuum

ALTERNATIVE perspectives

Is the BMI the Best Measure of Body Fat? Scholars and practitioners regularly use the BMI as an indicator of whether a person has a healthy weight (e.g., Kegler, Swan, Alcantara, et al., 2014; Zook, Saksvig, Wu, & Young, 2014). For the average adult, this measure corresponds to the level of body fat, but for others, such as athletes and others who are muscular, the BMI is not accurate. In this case, other measures might offer better reflections of body fat. Alternatives include measuring waist circumference or skinfold thickness (e.g., Durnin & Womersley, 1974). For example, men with waists of 40 inches or greater and women with waists of 35 inches or greater are considered unhealthy. More advanced methods include use of ultrasound, computed tomography, and magnetic resonance imaging (MRI; Centers for Disease Control and Prevention, n.d.). The latter techniques might offer more precise body fat estimates, but they are also more expensive and time intensive.

of fatness misses the larger point that fatness has negative associations. This affects people in their lives, their relationships, and their work (Bell, 2007).

Incidence of Obesity

According to the WHO (2015), the incidence of obesity is increasing globally and has doubled since 1980. More than 1.4 billion people worldwide are overweight, and 500 million of them are considered clinically obese. Although there is considerable consternation about the obesity rates in Western countries such as the United States, obesity is also regularly observed in developing countries. Rates vary widely among populations: although some countries, such as China and Japan, have low obesity rates (around 5 percent), other countries have much higher rates. In Samoa, for instance, three of every four people are considered obese.

The WHO points to several factors that contribute to obesity, including diet, activity level, and genetics. People have largely moved away from consuming fresh foods, fruits, and vegetables and, instead, now consume processed foods that lack complex carbohydrates but are high in saturated fats and sugars. Technology and urbanization have also had an impact on physical activity levels. Where people might have performed manual labor in the past, in today's service-and-information economy, jobs require comparatively minimal levels of energy expenditure. City infrastructures often encourage people to take cars or public transportation rather than walk or ride a bicycle. Finally, genetics influence people's weight. Studies of adopted children who were separated from their biological parents early in life suggest that the adoptees' weight is closely associated with that of their biological parents.

Anti-fat Bias in the Workplace

As the Diversity Challenge illustrated, people who are considered overweight or obese encounter stereotypes, prejudice, and discrimination. These anti-fat biases have the potential to affect their well-being negatively, both inside and outside the work environment.

Stereotypes

Many negative stereotypes exist about people who are considered overweight or obese, leading Roehling (1999) to conclude that these individuals are considered "fat but not 'jolly'" (p. 983). Common stereotypes of job applicants and employees who are considered overweight or obese include the belief that they lack self-control and self-discipline; are lazy; lack conscientiousness; are incompetent; are sloppy and unkempt, and maintain poor hygiene; are likely to be absent frequently; and are generally unhealthy (Roehling, 1999). Returning to Fiske, Cuddy, Glick, and Xu's (2002) stereotype content model (discussed in Chapter 3), it is likely these stereotypes emanate from notions that those who are overweight or obese are low in both competence and warmth. Individuals who are poor, homeless, or on public assistance—persons who experience considerable prejudice and discrimination—are also believed to be low in competence and warmth (Fiske et al., 2002).

Persons who work in the sport industry also maintain these stereotypes, as evidenced through a study Sartore and I conducted (Sartore & Cunningham, 2007). We conducted three experiments where participants reviewed applications for a personal trainer position. Each application contained a picture of the applicant along with the applicant's qualifications, experience, and education. Across all of the studies, participants ascribed more negative attributions to the job applicants believed to be overweight or obese than they did to the thinner applicants. In some cases, unqualified thin applicants received more favorable ratings than more qualified heavier applicants.

Recognizing that some people do actively maintain these weight-based stereotypes, it is useful to consider whether there is any validity to these beliefs. Roehling, Roehling, and Odland (2008) provided a direct analysis of this issue. They collected data from two samples—one from an archival data set of U.S. residents ages 25 to 74 and the other of college students in the midwestern United States—to examine the relationship between BMI and personality factors associated with stereotypes. These personality factors included extraversion, conscientiousness, agreeableness, and stability. Their results showed there was no empirical evidence to support the stereotypes. If anything, people with a higher BMI were more agreeable than their counterparts.

Prejudice

Evidence also indicates that persons who are considered overweight or obese are stigmatized and face prejudice (Brochu, Gawronski, & Esses, 2011; Puhl & Heuer, 2009). In some cases, the prejudice is explicit: people outwardly and openly express anti-fat attitudes. In fact, such perspectives have been described as one of the last forms of acceptable prejudice (Brochu et al., 2011). The social acceptability of this form of prejudice is evidenced by the lack of legal protections for persons who

Lack of legal protections for persons considered overweight or obese

As of 2014, no laws are in place that specifically address the issue of obesity discrimination. This does not mean, however, that people have not successfully sued on the basis of such differential treatment. These suits are usually brought under the Rehabilitation Act of 1973, which prohibits discrimination on the basis of disability alone (Bell, McLaughlin, & Sequeira, 2004). In *Cook v. Rhode Island,* 10 F.3d 17 (1st Cir. 1993), Cook was denied employment at a state facility because it was believed her obesity would limit her job performance, even though Cook had performed at high levels in her previous job. The employer also believed that Cook would miss more time from work compared to other candidates and that the state would face more compensation claims because of her condition. The court, in finding in Cook's favor, ruled that obesity was a disability because it resulted from a metabolic dysfunction.

Because most suits similar to Cook's are not successful, various groups advocate the adoption of laws and ordinances to prohibit weight discrimination (Bell et al., 2004). Local ordinances in San Francisco and Santa Cruz, California, and the District of Columbia prohibit discrimination on the basis of weight. These laws and ordinances can help people such as Jennifer Portnick fight discrimination and overcome the barriers they encounter because of their weight.

are considered overweight or obese (see the box on the previous page), as well as the lack of attention given to weight discrimination among scholars (Ruggs, Law, Cox, et al., 2013).

In addition, evidence suggests that physical educators hold moderate anti-fat attitudes and tend to consider weight to be largely a function of personal control (Greenleaf & Weiller, 2005). Students aspiring to work in the sport and fitness industry also endorse anti-fat beliefs (Chambliss, Finley, & Blair, 2004; Duncan, 2008). One student in Duncan's analysis, when asked to respond to the notion that people who are fat are abused by society, wrote, "In a way it makes me feel bad for people that are fat. But then again I don't feel bad because most of the fat people aren't trying to do anything about it. But honestly, it's hard to hear people actually say that . . . [they] can't help being fat, it runs in their family. They should do something about their body, stop eating so much and exercise three to four times a week" (p. 2).

The box at left offers additional discussion of explicit forms of weight-based prejudice and indicates that its expression varies by race and culture.

As with other forms of prejudice, people can and do maintain implicit prejudices toward persons they believe to be overweight or obese. For instance, some health professionals *who specialize in obesity* express high levels of implicit anti-fat bias and endorse implicit stereotypes of people who are fat as being stupid, indolent, and worthless (Schwartz, Chambliss, Brownell, et al., 2003). In studies, not all health professionals expressed such viewpoints; rather, younger persons, women, fit individuals, and persons with few obese friends all expressed more prejudice than their counterparts. Implicit biases have been found among fitness professionals in multiple countries (Dimmock, Hallett, & Grove, 2009; Robertson & Vohora, 2008).

Weight prejudice has a detrimental effect on people's well-being. As BMI increases, so too do a person's concerns about being stigmatized and about what others think. This stigma concern is negatively associated with psychological well-being (Hunger & Major, in press). Prejudice also has the potential to affect people's health-related behaviors, as people who experience weight bias are less likely to exercise, particularly when they do not believe the world is a just or fair place (Pearl & Dovidio, in press).

Weight-based prejudice, race, and culture

Generally speaking, people in Western cultures express prejudice toward persons they believe to be overweight or obese. Several factors affect these attitudes (Crandall, Nierman, & Hebl, 2009). One factor is race. Whites are more likely to express weight-based prejudice than are either African Americans or Hispanics. For Hispanics, acculturation matters, as Hispanics who adopt dominant cultural views and values are more likely to express prejudice than are their peers who are less acculturated. Culture also affects the expression of prejudice. People who live in individualist countries, such as Australia or Poland, are more likely to express weight-based prejudice than are those in collectivist countries, such as India or Turkey.

Discrimination

People believed to be overweight experience discrimination inside and outside the workplace. As a testament to the quick socialization process with regard to attitudes about weight, children as young as three years reject people considered overweight or obese (Cramer & Steinwert, 1998). Large-scale surveys show that overweight adolescents and teens are subjected to discrimination; 20 to 50 percent indicated they had been teased or bullied about their weight (Crandall et al., 2009). The effects of such abuse are dramatic. Youth who are overweight believe that their weight will negatively affect their lives, limit their opportunities, and thwart their chances to be healthy (Economos, Bakun, Herzog, et al., 2014). Overweight youth are more likely to engage in risky healthy behaviors, such as purging—behaviors influenced by their depressive symptoms (Armstrong, Westen, & Janicke, 2014). They are also at increased risk of suicidal tendencies (Crandall et al., 2009).

Among adults, weight discrimination negatively affects a person's psychological well-being (Crandall et al., 2009) and overall health. With respect to the latter, Sutin and Terracciano's (2013) work is particularly enlightening. They collected data on more than 6,000 participants age 50 and older. Among those who were overweight, but not obese, participants who experienced weight discrimination were 2.5 times as likely to be obese four years later, compared to those who did not experience such mistreatment. The effects were even more damaging for persons who were already obese, as they were over 3 times as likely to remain obese as their obese peers who did not experience weight discrimination. The authors reasoned that these patterns were likely attributable to (1) the psychological distress associated with discrimination—which might result in more eating, (2) decreased confidence in physical activity, and (3) avoidance of physical activity.

Discrimination toward persons who are overweight or obese is also observed in the work environment, a fact attributable to the lower status and stigmatized nature of being overweight or obese (Vartanian & Silverstein, 2013). As previously noted, overweight and obese job applicants are considered a poor fit for the job and are unlikely to be recommended, relative to their peers (Sartore & Cunningham, 2007). Employees' weight affects how much they are paid (Judge & Cable, 2011), and the differences are meaningful. *Ceteris paribus*, women who are 25 pounds heavier than average-weight women will earn $389,300 less over a 25-year career. There is a different pattern for men, as they are penalized for being *underweight*. This is because society generally favors larger, muscular men. All else equal, men who weigh 25 pounds less than the average man will earn $210,925 less over a 25-year career.

Anti-fat attitudes have a damaging effect on people's work experiences, particularly in industries where a premium is placed on appearance, as in sport (see the next Diversity in the Field box). In this context, the ideal body type is lean and muscular (Vogel, 1999), and people who deviate from that standard are viewed negatively. As we saw in the Diversity Challenge in the case of the fitness industry, job applicants who are considered to be overweight might be viewed as a bad fit for the organization and as ill-equipped to instruct others on how to lead a healthy lifestyle. Of course, people can be unhealthy and have low BMI scores, just as they can be healthy and have higher BMI scores; nevertheless, anti-fat attitudes and stereotypical norms both serve to disadvantage people who do not fit the ideal body type. As a result, persons considered to be overweight suffer discrimination in the selection process, in promotions received, and in performance evaluations (Rudolf, Wells, Weller, & Baltes, 2009). Key stakeholders also negatively evaluate people with larger waistlines, and this is true even when we take into account other factors that might influence their evaluations (King, Rogelberg, Hebl, et al., in press). In fact, the findings are observed even among top-level executives, suggesting the effects of weight-based discrimination span across hierarchical levels.

Weighing the Coaching Options. There are several requisite qualifications for a person to become a head coach in the NFL, including success as an assistant coach or administrator, leadership qualities, and quality coaching contacts. In addition to these qualities, Charlie Weis believed that most owners seek coaches with a certain body type. Therefore, Weis, who was overweight, opted for gastric bypass surgery, a risky procedure designed to reduce the size of the stomach to allow for weight loss. Unfortunately for Weis, the surgery almost killed him. In fact, a Catholic priest gave last rites two days after the surgery. Weis ultimately recovered and went on to help the New England Patriots win a Super Bowl as their offensive coordinator. He then served as head coach of the Notre Dame Fighting Irish from 2005 to 2009. That he went to such lengths to obtain a head coaching position demonstrates two points: (1) there is a very strong perception that people who are overweight or obese do not have access to head coaching positions, and (2) people will go to great lengths to realize their dream of becoming a head coach (Mortensen, 2002).

Just as employees who are perceived to be overweight experience discrimination, the same is true for customers, as evidenced in the Diversity in the Field box titled "Anti-fat Attitudes Toward Customers."

Moderators

As with most issues, the aforementioned effects are not uniform across all situations. Instead, demographic factors, the type of job, and an applicant's qualifications all potentially influence the relationship between weight status and work outcomes.

Demographics of the discrimination target can influence the incidence of weight discrimination. For example, some evidence suggests that race affects discrimination, in that overweight Whites might be more heavily penalized than their overweight peers of other races (Finkelstein, Frautschy Demuth, & Sweeney, 2007). This is likely attributable to differences across cultures in the acceptability of larger body types. Similarly, women are routinely penalized more for being overweight than are men (Judge & Cable, 2011). Some evidence suggests that race and sex interact to predict discrimination. Vanhove and Gordon (2014) aggregated data from across field studies (i.e., those not performed in a laboratory setting) and found that sex

Anti-fat Attitudes Toward Customers. Researchers at Rice University showed that the general treatment of consumers who are obese is substantially poorer than the treatment of those whose weight is normal (King, Shapiro, Hebl, et al., 2006). They designed a study in which 10 young women donned "fat suits" to make them appear heavier than they really were. The women shopped at various stores in the Houston area and noted the responses they received from the salespersons. In general, salespeople spent little time with the women who were overweight and, in some cases, even wondered aloud why shoppers who are overweight would bother patronizing a particular store. The researchers also found that the treatment the women received was better if they were drinking a diet cola or discussing weight loss. The research shows that when people believe justification for prejudice exists, they will discriminate against overweight people in subtle, covert ways.

and race interacted to predict discrimination. Specifically, White women experienced significantly more discrimination than their male peers of any race.

The type of job for which a person is applying might also affect whether the individual faces discrimination. People who are obese are more likely to be hired for jobs that do not require face-to-face interaction, such as inside telephone sales, than jobs that require such interaction (Bellizzi & Hasty, 1998). These findings are consistent with meta-analysis findings showing that weight bias has more impact in sales positions than in managerial positions (Rudolf, Wells, Weller, & Baltes, 2009). Although the effects appear to be lesser for executives than for managers, it is important to remember that even persons in executive positions face discrimination based on their weight (King et al., in press).

Finally, the qualifications of applicants might influence the occurrence of discrimination, and, conversely, applicants' weight status can affect how their qualifications are viewed. In general, when a job applicant is thin, better qualifications give rise to more favorable ratings, but the same is not the case for applicants who are perceived to be overweight. In the latter case, both highly qualified and unqualified applicants face barriers to employment. This is particularly the case in the sport context, where a premium is placed on appearance (Sartore & Cunningham, 2007). In other settings, the effects are more nuanced, and weight bias is likely to appear only when applicants are marginally qualified for the job (Finkelstein et al., 2007). In such a case, decision makers can justify their discrimination by pointing to other factors (e.g., the applicant did not have enough experience), whereas such excuses are not available when an applicant is highly qualified.

Weight and Physical Activity Participation

Weight also affects people's physical activity levels. Persons who, based on their BMI, are considered of healthy weight are significantly more likely to meet recommended physical activity levels than are their overweight or obese peers (Spees, Scott, & Tucker, 2012; Tucker, Welk, & Beyler, 2011). This is true for both self-reported data and objective measures of physical activity (i.e., use of an accelerometer). Further investigation into the intensity of the activity reveals that those who engage in moderate levels of physical activity do not vary considerably by weight status; instead, the differences become apparent in those participating in vigorous levels of physical activity (see Exhibit 8.1).

Persons thought to be overweight may choose not to exercise because they are self-conscious about others seeing them participate, especially when the activities are difficult for them to complete (Carron, Hausenblas, & Estabrooks, 2003). This is understandable, especially if many of the other participants have lean or muscular body types. Some people experience social physique anxiety, which occurs when they believe others are evaluating their body type (Carron et al., 2003). Those who experience such anxiety are likely to exercise in private (e.g., in their home) or to wear loose-fitting clothes. Social physique anxiety also influences a person's choice of activities. For example, women with social physique anxiety are likely to have a positive attitude toward aerobics classes that emphasize health rather than appearance (Raedeke, Focht, & Scales, 2007).

EXHIBIT 8.1

Moderate and vigorous physical activity among healthy weight, overweight, and obese individuals.

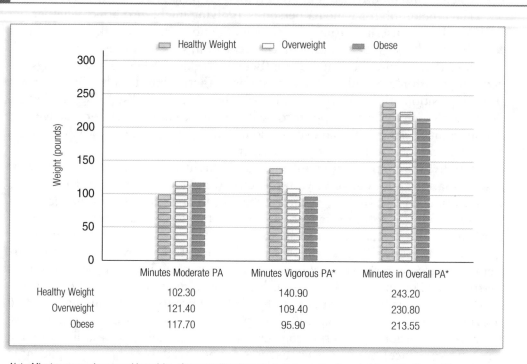

	Minutes Moderate PA	Minutes Vigorous PA*	Minutes in Overall PA*
Healthy Weight	102.30	140.90	243.20
Overweight	121.40	109.40	230.80
Obese	117.70	95.90	213.55

Note: Minutes per week engaged in activity, after controlling for various demographic characteristics. *Significant differences based on weight status.

Source: Data from Spees et al. (2012).

Health and fitness clubs play a potentially key role in this area. The way these clubs position themselves and promote the benefits of physical activity influences people's subsequent exercise intentions. Woods and I conducted an experimental study in which participants viewed an advertisement for a new fitness club and then reported their reactions to the club and their interest in joining (Cunningham & Woods, 2011). The advertisements varied by their focus (appearance: "Look better instantly and get your best body ever," or wellness: "Learn fitness and nutrition strategies; acquire lifelong wellness") and the sex of the model. Results showed that people agreed more with the fitness club's culture when the advertisement focused on wellness rather than appearance, irrespective of the model's gender in the advertisement. Participants' agreement with the club's culture was reliably associated with their interest in joining the club.

These findings suggest that the dominant marketing theme among most fitness clubs—that is, "if you exercise then you will lose weight"—might be misguided. A different, perhaps more effective, approach would be to focus on how membership in a club can result in being healthy, irrespective of one's weight. Use of fit, athletic models—the type who appear predominantly in fitness club advertisements—might be similarly misguided. What is interesting is that clubs' marketing efforts may not effectively reach the primary target audience or the people who need sport and exercise the most—those who are overweight or obese. Recall from Chapter 2 that the social categorization framework for understanding diversity holds that people will have positive attitudes toward and trust those people who are similar to them (in-group members). If that is true, then use of models who are thin and have well-defined muscles will be most effective in attracting people who already embody those characteristics. Persons who are overweight or obese may view those product endorsers as out-group members; hence, the positive attitudes toward, and the trust afforded to, such endorsers are likely to be low. Based on these arguments, for more effective ads, sport and fitness organizations should use models who represent all body types. Of course, drawing from the matchup hypothesis literature, the product endorsers should demonstrate some level of physical fitness. See the box at right for further discussion of this issue.

HEIGHT

T he purpose of this section is to offer an overview of height with regard to issues of diversity and inclusion. Specifically, I first define key terms and then highlight the effects of height in the workplace.

Key Terms

The average height for women and men varies depending on time (people have grown taller over time) and location. According to Fryar, Gu, and Ogden (2012), the average height for adult women in the United States is 5'3", and the average height for adult men is 5'9" (see Exhibit 8.2). Only 5 percent of women are taller than 5'8", while the corresponding height for men is 6'2". Among women and men, Whites and African Americans are about 2 inches taller, on average, than Hispanics. Given these figures, discussions of "taller" people refer to people whose height is above the national average.

Effects of Height in the Workplace

Height influences a number of social interactions among people, including their choice of partner—and this is particularly prevalent among women (Yancey & Emerson, in press). Interestingly, though, organizational scientists have devoted relatively little attention to the influence of height in the work environment. Much of the research that has focused on height was conducted in the early to mid-1900s, when researchers investigated the links between height and a number of attributes,

---

ALTERNATIVE perspectives

Negative Effects of Viewing Thin Models. Companies often use ultra-thin models in advertisements for skin care or beauty products to entice consumers to purchase their products. In 2004, Dove began a new ad campaign, called *Campaign for Real Beauty,* for its hand and body lotions. The women in the advertisements were of varying ages, races, heights, and body types. Some were pregnant, some were curvaceous, and others were thin. By incorporating "real women with real bodies and real curves," Dove broadened the definition of beauty.

In contrast to exceptions such as the Dove campaign, most advertisers use thin models to promote their products. This is presumably done because it is assumed that people viewing the advertisements will have more positive attitudes toward a product when it is presented in conjunction with images of thin people. However, evidence suggests that viewing thin models can have negative effects (Boothroyd, Tovée, & Pollet, 2012). Specifically, continually seeing images of overly thin women in the media contributes to negative body image among the girls and women who view them. Thus, seeing more average or overweight models in advertisements could potentially benefit viewers and their perceptions of themselves.

EXHIBIT **8.2**   Height by race and sex.

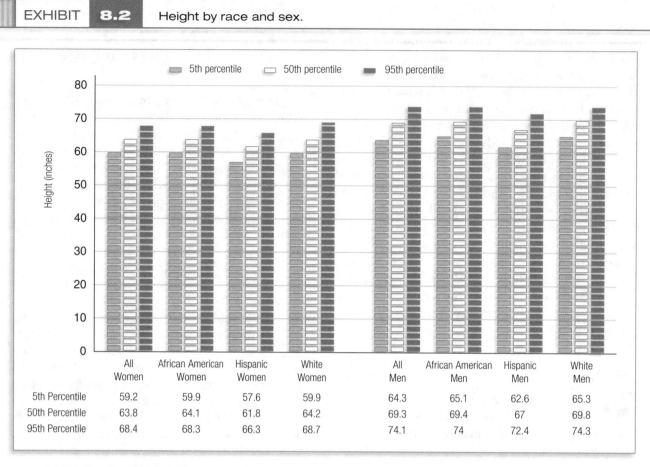

	All Women	African American Women	Hispanic Women	White Women	All Men	African American Men	Hispanic Men	White Men
5th Percentile	59.2	59.9	57.6	59.9	64.3	65.1	62.6	65.3
50th Percentile	63.8	64.1	61.8	64.2	69.3	69.4	67	69.8
95th Percentile	68.4	68.3	66.3	68.7	74.1	74	72.4	74.3

Source: Data from Fryar, Gu, & Ogden (2012).

particularly leadership and performance (Garrison, 1933; Kitson, 1922). The link between height and leadership does have some anecdotal support: consider, for instance, that for over 100 years, there has not been a single U.S. president whose height was below the national average. That said, leadership theories generally have moved from the study of immutable individual characteristics to a more behavioral and contingency focus (Robbins & Judge, 2007).

Despite the lack of work in the area, some compelling evidence indicates that height does make a difference in social status, a finding that appears to be true across species of animals (Blaker & van Vugt, 2014). Judge and Cable (2004) provide evidence of this phenomenon in the work environment, with a particular focus on leadership, status, and career success. These authors suggest that physical height is positively associated with social esteem and self-esteem—that is, people have higher regard for taller people, and taller people are also likely to have greater self-confidence and perceptions of self-worth than their peers. Both of these factors are thought to influence various measures of performance: people who are confident and who are well thought of by others generally perform well. Finally, those who perform well in their tasks are more likely than their peers to ascend into leadership positions and be well compensated.

Judge and Cable (2004) conducted a number of studies to test their theoretical model. In the first study, they aggregated findings from past studies to examine the overall relationships among the variables. As expected, they found that height is positively associated with social esteem, ascension into leadership positions, and performance. In the next set of analyses, the authors analyzed longitudinal data collected from more than 4,000 people to examine the effects of height on earnings. After controlling for the possible confounding effects of gender, weight, and age, they found that taller people earn appreciably more than their shorter counterparts. For instance, a person who stands 72 inches tall is expected to earn *$5,525 more per year* than a person who is 65 inches tall. Over a 30-year career, this amounts to $165,750 in earnings—without even accounting for interest. Subsequent analyses confirmed this effect of height on income and it remained constant over time; thus, women and men who are taller than their counterparts earn more, and they continue to do so over time.

Gladwell (2007) addressed this issue in his book titled *Blink*. Specifically, he collected data from about half of the Fortune 500 companies, asking each about the characteristics of its CEO. He found that the average male CEO was just under 6 feet tall, nearly 3 inches taller than the national average. He also observed that 58 percent of the male CEOs were over 6 feet tall—a proportion substantially higher than the U.S. average of 14.5 percent. Even more remarkable, although only 3.9 percent of all American men stand 6'2" or taller, nearly a third of the Fortune 500 CEOs reached this mark. Finally, although millions of American men have a height under 5'6", only 10 male CEOs in Gladwell's sample were of this height.

In explaining his findings, Gladwell (2007) points to implicit biases that favor taller people. Consider, for instance, that the average height for entry-level employees is likely to mirror that of the U.S. population, which is 5'9". As employees progress up the managerial ranks, however, the average height increases, and, as noted, male CEOs average 3 inches taller than the national average. This is not because people explicitly think taller people are better; rather, people subconsciously associate height and stature with power and leadership—a relationship observed throughout nature. Gladwell explains, "Most of us, in ways that we are not entirely aware of, automatically associate leadership ability with imposing physical stature. We have a sense of what a leader is supposed to look like, and that stereotype is so powerful that when someone fits it, we simply become blind to other considerations" (p. 88).

These findings have potential consequences for other diversity dimensions. Few would suggest that managers are explicitly biased against short people. After all, it would be preposterous to promote people merely because they are tall. However, although explicit attitudes might not be at work, the evidence suggests that implicit attitudes are. Similarly, some might argue that stereotypes and biases against women, racial minorities, and sexual minorities are a thing of the past. However, if implicit biases contribute to people ascending to leadership positions based on something as innocuous as height, then how much more likely is it that other implicit biases favor historically dominant groups, such as men, heterosexuals, or Whites?

Just as people express implicit favoritism toward and bestow esteem upon those who are tall, there is evidence that influences might work in the other direction, such that people in powerful positions perceive subordinates' height differently than do others. Yap, Mason, and Ames (2013) conducted two experimental studies in which they manipulated the perceived power that people held. They then asked the participants to view photographs of people and estimate their height. The researchers subtracted the estimated height from the actual height to assess the degree to which those in power underestimated others' height. Across both studies, persons who believed they were in powerful positions *underestimated* others' height, while those who did not believe they were in powerful positions *overestimated* the targets' height. It is not just that the powerful underestimate others' height; they overestimate their own height, as well (Duguid & Goncalo, 2012). These findings indicate that power has a way of distorting people's perceptions of themselves and others—estimations that reinforce socially constructed ideas of who is powerful.

ATTRACTIVENESS

In the final section, I provide an overview of the research related to attractiveness. As with the other sections, I first introduce key concepts. The discussion then moves to an analysis of how attractiveness influences both people's work experiences and their sport participation.

Background Information

People's attractiveness can influence how others treat them and the career success they enjoy (see the box on the facing page for an overview of the factors influencing perceptions of facial attractiveness). Langlois, Kalakanis, Rubenstein, and colleagues' (2000) impressive study aptly demonstrates these effects. They aggregated the results from more than 1,800 studies that covered a 67-year time frame (1932–1999) and observed the following:

- Contrary to the notion that various cultures have distinct ideas about what is attractive, there is some agreement both within and between cultures about who is attractive and who is not. This effect holds for both children and adults. Similarly, uniformity was found in attractiveness ratings across ethnicities. These findings led Langlois's group (2000) to conclude "that beauty is not simply in the eye of the beholder" (p. 399).

- Attractive and unattractive people are judged differently. Relative to their unattractive counterparts, attractive children are perceived to be more positively adjusted and to display greater interpersonal competence, while attractive adults are thought to have more social appeal, be better adjusted, and be more interpersonally competent.

- Attractive children and adults are treated better than their less attractive counterparts on a constellation of outcomes, including positive interactions, allocation of rewards, attention, and provision of help and cooperation.

- Behavioral differences are also present. Attractive children have been shown to be better adjusted emotionally, to display greater intelligence, and to be more popular than their unattractive counterparts. Differences in adults were observed for occupational success, physical health, social skills, mental health, and intelligence.

What makes faces beautiful?

Are there characteristics that make a person's face beautiful? According to psychologists, several factors are involved, including averageness, symmetry, and sexual dimorphism (Little, Jones, & DeBruine, 2011; Rhodes, 2006). With respect to the first characteristic, contrary to what people might expect, the evidence suggests that the more average a face is—that is, it has few distinctive features—the more beautiful it is perceived. Thus, typical faces, which more closely resemble the population average, have consistently rated higher in attractiveness than have very distinct faces. With respect to the second characteristic, symmetrical faces are preferred over asymmetrical ones. These effects remain irrespective of the person's sex or race, or the sex of the rater. Finally, sexual dimorphism, which refers to the characteristics generally observed among men and women that differentiate the sexes, affects perceptions of beauty. For instance, after puberty, testosterone in men stimulates growth of the jaw bone, cheek bones, brow ridge, facial hair, and the center of the face. Growth in these areas is inhibited in women because of an increase in estrogen. The presence of estrogen also increases the lip size of women relative to men. These dynamics potentially result in a typically masculine look in some men and a typically feminine look in some women. Femininity among women is associated with attractiveness, as is masculinity among men—though to a lesser extent. These effects are particularly robust in developed, urban environments (Scott, Clark, Josephson, et al., 2014).

Attractiveness in the Workplace

As in other parts of life, attractive people are advantaged in the work environment. Attractiveness is positively associated with a number of work outcomes, including perceived fit with the organization, selection, performance appraisals, perceived leadership effectiveness, promotions, and terminations (Commisso & Finkelstein, 2012; Hosoda, Stone-Romero, & Coates, 2003; Jawahar & Mattsson, 2007). Evidence also suggests that male leaders' facial characteristics are associated with organizational performance (Wong, Ormiston, & Haselhuhn, 2011). Men whose faces have a high width-to-height ratio are perceived to be more aggressive, willing to take risks, and able to develop a stronger sense of power than their peers (Carré, McCormick, & Mondloch, 2009; Haselhuhn & Wong, 2012). Drawing from this work, Wong and colleagues thought certain facial characteristics among men would result in better performance, especially when the management structure deferred considerable power to the chief executive. Their analysis of Fortune 500 firms confirmed these expectations. Physical characteristics are associated with other diversity-related behaviors, as illustrated in the box on page 184.

Attractiveness also affects the credibility of sports reporting. Some observers have suggested that sports reporters' appearance affects their notoriety, particularly among women (Clavio & Eagleman, 2011). Noting this pattern, Hahn and Cummins (2014) examined how women reporters' attractiveness affected their perceived credibility among both female and male readers. They found that credibility ratings depended on the sex of the reporter and the athlete covered. Participants considered attractive men to be more credible than their less attractive counterparts; however, attractive women were not believed to be credible when they were reporting on male athletes. These findings suggest that ideas of attractiveness are gender-based and promote many of the gendered ideologies discussed in Chapter 5.

Perceived attractiveness and support for inequality

People generally evaluate attractive people positively. There is also evidence that the more people believe they are attractive, the less likely they are to support equality and social justice. In five studies, Belmi and Neale (2014) observed that as perceived attractiveness increased, so too did a person's perceived social class. This linkage is important because perceived social class was negatively related to both support for hierarchical equality and monetary donations to social justice causes. These patterns remained even after the researchers took into account power, status, and self-esteem. Based on these results, the authors concluded: "If what we see in the mirror after we wake up in the morning can affect our attitudes and beliefs about how the world should be, then society's cultural preoccupation with physical appearance may have more far-reaching consequences than were previously imagined" (p. 147).

Attractiveness and Sport Participation

Research related to physical activity rates among attractive and unattractive people is scarce. There is, however, emerging research pertaining to the association of attractiveness with athleticism or physical prowess. Throughout evolutionary history, individuals with desirable traits have advertised these characteristics to attract mates. For instance, peahens are attracted to peacocks with large, colorful trains, because these feathers indicate underlying desirable traits (i.e., a large amount of caloric energy and resistance to environmental stressors), and it is beneficial for the female to pass along these traits to her offspring (Williams, Park, & Wieling, 2010).

Just as large and colorful feathers are desired among peacocks, in humans, physical superiority and athleticism have always been important in selecting and competing for mates, especially among males (Williams et al., 2010). In many respects, the world of sport is a stage designed to advertise these characteristics (Miller, 2000), and research suggests that athletic traits are highly heritable (Missitzi, Geladas, & Klissouras, 2004). Furthermore, testosterone is an important hormone directly influencing athleticism, and it is also associated with desirable facial features in men, such as a strong jaw line and prominent brow ridge (see also Rhodes, 2006). Considering that athleticism and facial attractiveness (as a result of high testosterone) are linked to heritable fitness, researchers have begun to explore the possibility of an association between facial attractiveness and athleticism.

As far-fetched as this association might seem, there is actually evidence to support it (De Block & Dewitte, 2009). In one study, Park, Buunk, and Wieling (2007) examined the attractiveness ratings of professional soccer and hockey players. In both sports, the authors argued that goal-keepers/goalies and strikers/forwards are likely to be the most athletic members of the team because of the skills needed to compete effectively in those positions. Defenders, on the other hand, require considerable endurance but comparatively less athleticism. Thus, if attractiveness is associated with athleticism, then the former group (i.e., goal-keepers/goalies and strikers/forwards) should be rated as more attractive than the latter (i.e., defenders). Ratings of facial attractiveness from female students largely

DIVERSITY IN THE FIELD

Women's Head Scarves and Sport Participation. The garments people wear can influence their sport participation opportunities. For instance, many Muslim women wear a traditional hijab, or head scarf, and they desire to do so while participating in sport, as well. However, until 2007, they were unable to do this and participate in international taekwondo competitions. Recognizing that this prohibition limited women's participation in the sport, the World Tae-kwondo Federation (WTF) changed the rule to allow women to wear a hijab under their protective head gear. Dae Won Moon, chair of the WTF technical committee, commented that "this measure means that taekwondo is one of the few sports that treats women and men equally in the Muslim world." He went on to comment that "we believe that our respect for others' cultures and beliefs will allow taekwondo to enhance its status as an Olympic sport."

Source: http://english.aljazeera.net/sport/2009/09/200991621752992657.html.

confirmed these expectations. In a later study, Williams and colleagues (2010) examined the linkage between facial attractiveness and performance among professional football quarterbacks. Using the NFL's quarterback rating system as the measure of performance, the authors found a positive association between attractiveness and quarterback performance.

Appearance also influences people's sport participation in other ways, as illustrated in the Diversity in the Field box above.

Attractiveness also affects female athletes and their participation in the marketing of their sports. Women often feel as though they have to emphasize their attractiveness and femininity by wearing makeup and dressing fashionably. These behaviors are particularly important for women participating in sports associated with masculinity, such as basketball, in order to combat lesbian labels (Hargreaves, 2000). Ross and Shinew (2008), in their compelling qualitative study, found that women athletes practiced "selective femininity" (p. 51). In this case, the athletes were cognizant of and tried to reinforce their femininity in select contexts, such as gymnastic competitions, but not in other contexts, such as classrooms or practice. Thus, the athletes practiced femininity only on occasions that they chose.

With respect to attractiveness and marketing efforts, a number of researchers have examined factors that influence the commercial effectiveness of female athlete endorsers. The match-up hypothesis regularly serves as the theoretical lens in these investigations. From this perspective, endorsers are most effective when there is a match, or "fit," between the endorser and the product being endorsed (Kamins, 1990). The skill of the athlete endorser should influence perceptions of fit, especially when a sport-related product (e.g., a sports drink) is being promoted. Attractiveness also affects perceived fit of women endorsers, particularly when women athletes promote sport events (e.g., Fink, in press; Liu & Brock, 2011). As my colleagues and I have noted, "It is possible that people have come to associate some sports with the attractive athletes who participate in them (e.g., tennis and Maria Sharapova)" (Cunningham, Fink, & Kenix, 2008, p. 373).

We experimentally examined how expertise and attractiveness contributed to the perceived fit of a female athlete who endorsed the NCAA Tennis National

Championship. We found that attractiveness and expertise were both positively associated with perceived fit, but that these effects were qualified by a significant expertise-by-attractiveness interaction. Specifically, among highly qualified athletes, attractive and unattractive endorsers were viewed as equally appropriate endorsers. This was not the case for unqualified endorsers, however; attractive athletes were greatly preferred over unattractive ones. The latter findings lend support to the growing literature that suggests women athletes are rewarded more for their appearance than for their physical prowess.

chapter SUMMARY

The purpose of this chapter was to examine the influence of appearance on how people experience work, sport, and physical activity, as well as on sport participation and promotion. As illustrated in the case of Jennifer Portnick and Jazzercise in the Diversity Challenge, appearance has the potential to shape a person's opportunities. People who do not fit the norm, by being perceived as overweight, as too short, or as unattractive, are faced with a number of challenges. After reading this chapter, you should be able to:

1. **Understand key terms and different standards related to appearance.**

   Three elements of appearance were highlighted in this chapter: weight, height, and attractiveness. With respect to weight, some agencies and scientists classify people based on their BMI or their percentage of body fat relative to lean muscle. Activists argue against this approach and suggest that such standards ignore variations in people's bodies. In terms of height, the average height for adult women in the United States is 5'3", and the average height for adult men is 5'9". Individuals who deviate from this mean are considered short or tall. Finally, attractiveness is based on averageness, symmetry, and sexual dimorphism; assessments of what is considered attractive are fairly consistent across cultures, sexes, and ethnicities.

2. **Discuss the influence of weight, height, and attractiveness on how people are viewed by others.**

   Weight, height, and attractiveness have been shown to influence a bevy of work outcomes, including access to positions, performance appraisals, opportunities for promotion, and earnings. Persons who are considered to be overweight experience work in a negative manner, while persons who are tall and attractive are generally thought to experience work well and to be privileged in their prospects for promotion.

3. **Outline the influence of appearance on exercise participation and physical activity.**

   The available literature suggests that adults who are considered to be overweight are less likely to exercise than their counterparts, though no differences exist among children. Research related to physical activity levels and the other two diversity dimensions, height and attractiveness, is not available. Attractiveness, however, does influence the experiences people have while participating in sport.

QUESTIONS for discussion

1. Some consider weight to be a function of individual choices, while others point to environmental and genetic influences. What is your position, and why do you hold it?

2. Why are persons who are considered overweight ascribed negative attributes? Do you think similar ascriptions occur for persons who are underweight?

3. Research suggests that people implicitly prefer leaders who are tall. Why is this the case? Has this been your experience?

4. People have been shown to interact in a positive manner with attractive people, while the same cannot be said of their interactions with unattractive people. Why do you think these differences exist?

5. Are there times when being attractive would hurt a person in a job hunt? If so, when is this likely to occur?

6. Choose one of the aspects of attractiveness discussed in this chapter and reflect upon your personal concerns and considerations of this factor. Why is this issue important to you, and what are its implications?

learning ACTIVITIES

1. Using online resources, identify job postings for fitness clubs. Does the advertisement include language designed to attract persons who might be considered fit or athletic looking?

2. One could argue that attractiveness *should* be considered in personnel decisions since clients might respond more favorably to attractive than to unattractive persons. An alternative point of view is that such an approach is unreasonable and could be used to justify preferential hiring based on other diversity dimensions (e.g., race). As a class, divide into two teams and debate these positions.

WEB resources

The Obesity Society, www.naaso.org

National society dedicated to the scientific study of obesity and obesity-related issues, including discrimination.

Rudd Center, www.yaleruddcenter.org

An academic research center that seeks to improve the world's diet, reduce obesity, and ameliorate weight stigma.

World Health Organization, www.who.int

An international agency responsible for providing leadership on health matters worldwide, shaping the research agenda, setting health standards, and providing health-related support to countries.

reading RESOURCES

Brownwell, K. D., Schwartz, M. B., Pugh, R. M., & Rudd, L. (2005). *Weight bias: Nature, consequences and remedies.* New York: Guilford Press.

Edited text from leading scholars in the field; explores the nature and causes of weight discrimination, as well as ways to combat the discrimination.

Rothblum, E., & Solovay, S. (Eds.) (2009). *The fat studies reader.* New York: New York University Press.

A collection of essays addressing anti-fat bias and weight discrimination; also introduces the field of fat studies.

Health Psychology

A journal published by the American Psychological Association that regularly includes articles focusing on the psychological effects of anti-fat attitudes.

REFERENCES

Armstrong, B., Westen, S. C., & Janicke, D. M. (2014). The role of overweight perception and depressive symptoms in child and adolescent unhealthy weight control behaviors: A mediation model. *Journal of Pediatric Psychology, 39,* 340–348.

Bell, M. P. (2007). *Diversity in organizations.* Mason, OH: Thomson South-Western.

Bell, M. P., McLaughlin, M. E., & Sequeira, J. M. (2004). Age, disability, and obesity: Similarities, differences, and common threads. In M. S. Stockdale & F. J. Crosby (Eds.), *The psychology and management of workplace diversity* (pp. 191–205). Malden, MA: Blackwell.

Bellizzi, J. A., & Hasty, R. W. (1998). Territory assignment decisions and supervising unethical selling behavior: The effects of obesity and gender as moderated by job-related factors. *Journal of Personal Selling & Sales Management, 18*(2), 35–49.

Belmi, P., & Neale, M. (2014). Mirror, mirror on the wall, who's the fairest of them all? Thinking that one is attractive increases the tendency to support inequality. *Organizational Behavior and Human Decision Processes, 124,* 133–149.

Blaker, N. M., & van Vugt, M. (2014). The status-size hypothesis: How cues of physical size and social status influence each other. In J. T. Cheng, J. L. Tracey, & C. Anderson (Eds.), *The psychology of social status* (pp. 119–137). New York: Springer.

Boothroyd, L. G., Tovée, M. J., & Pollet, T. V. (2012). Visual diet versus associative learning as mechanisms of change in body size preferences. *PLOS One, 7*(11), e48691.

Brochu, P. M., Gawronski, B., & Esses, V. M. (2011). The integrative prejudice framework and different forms of weight prejudice: An analysis and expansion. *Group Processes & Intergroup Relations, 14,* 429–444.

Carré, J. M., McCormick, C. M., & Mondloch, C. J. (2009). Facial structure is a reliable cue of aggressive behavior. *Psychological Science, 20,* 1194–1198.

Carron, A. V., Hausenblas, H. A., & Estabrooks, P. A. (2003). *The psychology of physical activity.* New York: McGraw-Hill.

Centers for Disease Control and Prevention (n.d.). Defining overweight and obesity. Retrieved from http://www.cdc.gov/obesity/adult/defining.html

Chambliss, H. O., Finley, C. E., & Blair, S. N. (2004). Attitudes toward obese individuals among exercise science students. *Medicine and Science in Sports and Exercise, 36,* 468–474.

Clavio, G., & Eagleman, A. N. (2011). Gender and sexually suggestive images in sports blogs. *Journal of Sport Management, 25,* 295–304.

Commisso, M., & Finkelstein, L. (2012). Physical attractiveness bias in employee termination. *Journal of Applied Social Psychology, 42,* 2968–2987.

Cramer, P., & Steinwert, T. (1998). Thin is good, fat is bad: How early does it begin? *Journal of Applied Developmental Psychology, 19,* 429–451.

Crandall, C. S., Nierman, A., & Hebl, M. (2009). Anti-fat prejudice. In T. D. Nelson (Ed.), *Handbook of prejudice, stereotyping, and discrimination* (pp. 469–487). New York: Psychology Press.

Cunningham, G. B., Fink, J. S., & Kenix, L. J. (2008). Choosing an endorser for a women's sporting event: The interaction of attractiveness and expertise. *Sex Roles, 58,* 371–378.

Cunningham, G. B., & Woods, J. (2011). For the health of it: Advertisement message and attraction to fitness clubs. *American Journal of Health Studies, 26,* 4–9.

De Block, A., & Dewitte, S. (2009). Darwinism and the cultural evolution of sports. *Perspectives in Biology and Medicine, 52,* 1–16.

Dimmock, J. A., Hallett, B. E., & Grove, J. R. (2009). Attitudes toward overweight individuals among fitness center employees: An examination of contextual factors. *Research Quarterly for Exercise and Sport, 80,* 641–647.

Duguid, M. M., & Goncalo, J. A. (2012). Living large: The powerful overestimate their own height. *Psychological Science, 23,* 36–40.

Duncan, M. C. (2008). The personal is political. *Sociology of Sport Journal, 25,* 1–6.

Durnin, J. V., & Womersley, J. (1974). Body fat assessed from total body density and its estimation from skinfold thickness: Measurements on 481 men and women aged from 16 to 72 years. *British Journal of Nutrition, 32*(1), 77–97.

Economos, C. D., Bakun, P. J., Herzog, J. B., Dolan, P. R., Lynskey, V. M., Markow, D., ... & Nelson, M. E. (2014). Children's perceptions of weight, obesity, nutrition, physical activity and related health and socio-behavioural factors. *Public Health Nutrition, 17,* 170–178.

Fink, J. S. (in press). Female athletes, women's sport, and the sport media commercial complex: Have we really "come a long way, baby"? *Sport Management Review.*

Finkelstein, L. M., Frautschy Demuth, R. L., & Sweeney, D. L. (2007). Bias against overweight job applicants: Further explorations of when and why. *Human Resource Management, 46,* 203–222.

Fiske, S. T., Cuddy, A. J., Glick, P., & Xu, J. (2002). A model of (often mixed) stereotype content: Competence and warmth respectively follow from perceived status and competition. *Journal of Personality and Social Psychology, 82,* 878–902.

Fryar, C. D., Gu, Q., & Ogden, C. L. (2012). Anthropometric reference data for children and adults: United States, 2007–2010. *National Center for Health Statistics Vital and Health Statistics, Series 11,* 1–48.

Garrison, K. C. (1933, July). A study of some factors related to leadership in high school. *Peabody Journal of Education,* 11–17.

Gladwell, M. (2007). *Blink: The power of thinking without thinking.* New York: Back Bay Books.

Greenleaf, C., & Weiller, K. (2005). Perceptions of youth obesity among physical educators. *Social Psychology of Education, 8,* 407–423.

Hahn, D. A., & Cummins, R. G. (2014). Effects of attractiveness, gender, and athlete–reporter congruence on perceived credibility of sport reporters. *International Journal of Sport Communication, 7,* 34–47.

Hargreaves, J. (2000). *Heroines of sport: The politics of difference and identity.* London: Routledge.

Haselhuhn, M. P., & Wong, E. M. (2012). Bad to the bone: Facial structure predicts unethical behaviour. *Proceedings of the Royal Society B: Biological Sciences, 279*(1728), 571–576.

Hosoda, M., Stone-Romero, E., & Coates, G. (2003). The effects of physical attractiveness on job-related outcomes: A meta-analysis of experimental studies. *Personnel Psychology, 56,* 431–462.

Hunger, J. M., & Major, B. (in press). Weight stigma mediates the association between BMI and self-reported health. *Health Psychology.*

Jawahar, I. M., & Mattsson, J. (2007). Sexism and beautyism effects in selection as a function of self-monitoring level of decision maker. *Journal of Applied Psychology, 90,* 563–573.

Judge, T. A., & Cable, D. M. (2004). The effect of physical height on workplace success and income: Preliminary test of a theoretical model. *Journal of Applied Psychology, 89,* 428–441.

Judge, T. A., & Cable, D. M. (2011). When it comes to pay, do the thin win? The effect of weight on pay for men and women. *Journal of Applied Psychology, 96,* 95–112.

Kamins, M. A. (1990). An investigation into the match-up hypothesis in celebrity advertising: When beauty may only be skin deep. *Journal of Advertising, 19*(1), 4–13.

Kegler, M. C., Swan, D. W., Alcantara, I., Feldman, L., & Glanz, K. (2014). The influence of rural home and neighborhood environments on healthy eating, physical activity, and weight. *Prevention Science, 15,* 1–11.

King, E. B., Rogelberg, S. G., Hebl, M. R., Braddy, P. W., Shanock, L. R., Doerer, S. C., & McDowell?Larsen, S. (in press). Waistlines and ratings of executives: Does executive status overcome obesity stigma? *Human Resource Management.*

King, E. B., Shapiro, J. R., Hebl, M. R., Singletary, S. L., & Turner, S. (2006). The stigma of obesity in customer service: A mechanism for remediation and bottom-line consequences of interpersonal discrimination. *Journal of Applied Psychology, 91,* 579–593.

Kitson, H. D. (1922). Height and weight as factors in salesmanship. *Journal of Personnel Research, 1,* 289–294.

Langlois, J. H., Kalakanis, L., Rubenstein, A. J., Larson, A., Hallam, M., & Smoot, M. (2000). Maxims or myths of beauty? A meta-analytic and theoretical review. *Psychological Bulletin, 126,* 390–423.

Little, A. C., Jones, B. C., & DeBruine, L. M. (2011). Facial attractiveness: Evolutionary based research. *Philosophical Transactions of the Royal Society B: Biological Sciences, 366*(1571), 1638–1659.

Liu, M. T., & Brock, J. L. (2011). Selecting a female athlete endorser in China: The effect of attractiveness, match-up, and consumer gender difference. *European Journal of Marketing, 45,* 1214–1235.

Miller, G. (2000). *The mating mind: How sexual choice shaped the evolution of human nature.* New York: Random House.

Missitzi, J., Geladas, N., & Klissouras, V. (2004). Heritability in neuromuscular coordination: Implications for motor control strategies. *Medicine and Science in Sport and Exercise, 36,* 233–240.

Mortensen, C. (2002, July). *Seeking new image, Patriots' Weis almost loses life.* ESPN.com. Retrieved from http://espn.go.com/chrismortensen/s/2002/0724/1409 547.html.

Park, J. H., Buunk, A. P., & Wieling, M. B. (2007). Does the face reveal athletic flair? Positions in team sports and facial attractiveness. *Personality and Individual Differences, 43,* 1960–1965.

Pearl, R. L., & Dovidio, J. F. (in press). Experiencing weight bias in an unjust world: Impact on exercise and internalization. *Health Psychology.*

Puhl, R. M., & Heuer, C. A. (2009). The stigma of obesity: A review and update. *Obesity, 17,* 941–964.

Raedeke, T. D., Focht, B. C., & Scales, D. (2007). Social environmental factors and psychological responses to acute exercise for socially physique anxious females. *Psychology of Sport and Exercise, 8,* 463–476.

Rhodes, G. (2006). The evolutionary psychology of facial beauty. *Annual Review of Psychology, 57,* 199–226.

Robbins, S. P., & Judge, T. A. (2007). *Organizational behavior* (12th ed.). Upper Saddle River, NJ: Prentice Hall.

Robertson, N., & Vohora, R. (2008). Fitness vs. fatness: Implicit bias towards obesity among fitness professionals and regular exercisers. *Psychology of Sport and Exercise, 9*(4), 547–557.

Roehling, M. V. (1999). Weight-based discrimination in employment: Psychological and legal aspects. *Personnel Psychology, 52,* 969–1016.

Roehling, M. V., Roehling, P. V., & Odland, L. M. (2008). Investigating the validity of stereotypes about overweight employees: The relationship between body weight and normal personality traits. *Group & Organization Management, 33,* 392–424.

Ross, S. R., & Shinew, K. J. (2008). Perspectives of women college athletes on sport and gender. *Sex Roles, 58,* 40–57.

Rudolf, C. W., Wells, C. L., Weller, M. D., & Baltes, B. B. (2009). A meta-analysis of empirical studies of weight-based bias in the workplace. *Journal of Vocational Behavior, 74,* 1–10.

Ruggs, E. N., Law, C., Cox, C. B., Roehling, M. V., Wiener, R. L., Hebl, M. R., & Barron, L. (2013). Gone fishing: I–O psychologists' missed opportunities to understand marginalized employees' experiences with discrimination. *Industrial and Organizational Psychology, 6,* 39–60.

Sartore, M. L., & Cunningham, G. B. (2007). Weight discrimination, hiring recommendations, person-job fit and attributions: Implications for the fitness industry. *Journal of Sport Management, 21,* 172–193.

Schwartz, M. B., Chambliss, H. O., Brownell, K. D., Blair, S. N., & Billington, C. (2003). Weight bias among health professionals specializing in obesity. *Obesity Research, 11,* 1033–1039.

Scott, I. M., Clark, A. P., Josephson, S. C., Boyette, A. H., Cuthill, I. C., Fried, R. L., ... & Penton-Voak, I. S. (2014). Human preferences for sexually dimorphic faces may be evolutionarily novel. *Proceedings of the National Academy of Sciences, 111*(40), 14388–14393.

Solovay, S. (2000). *Tipping the scales of injustice: Fighting weight-based discrimination.* Amherst, NY: Prometheus Books.

Spees, C. K., Scott, J. M., & Tucker, C. A. (2012). Differences in amounts and types of physical activity by obesity status in US adults. *American Journal of Health Behavior, 36,* 56–65.

Sutin, A. R., & Terracciano, A. (2013). Perceived weight discrimination and obesity. *PLOS One, 8*(7), e70048.

Tucker, J. M., Welk, G. J., & Beyler, N. K. (2011). Physical activity in US adults: Compliance with the physical activity guidelines for Americans. *American Journal of Preventive Medicine, 40,* 454–461.

Vanhove, A., & Gordon, R. A. (2014). Weight discrimination in the workplace: A meta-analytic examination of the relationship between weight and work-related outcomes. *Journal of Applied Social Psychology, 44,* 12–22.

Vartanian, L. R., & Silverstein, K. M. (2013). Obesity as a status cue: Perceived social status and the stereotypes of obese individuals. *Journal of Applied Social Psychology, 43*(S2), E319–E328.

Vogel, A. (1999). Female fit-body stereotype. *Fitness Management, 25,* 38–41.

Williams, K. M., Park, J. H., & Wieling, M. B. (2010). The face reveals athletic flair: Better National Football League quarterbacks are better looking. *Personality and Individual Differences, 48,* 112–116.

Wong, E. M., Ormiston, M. E., & Haselhuhn, M. P. (2011). A face only an investor could love: CEOs' facial structure predicts their firms' financial performance. *Psychological Science, 22,* 1478–1483.

World Health Organization (2015). Obesity and overweight. Retrieved from http://www.who.int/mediacentre/factsheets/fs311/en/

Wuebben, J. (n.d.). Freak of nature: Is Vernon Davis the NFL's best-ever athlete? Check the numbers. *Muscle and Fitness*. Retrieved from www.muscleandfitness.com.

Yancey, G., & Emerson, M. O. (in press). Does height matter? An examination of height preferences in romantic coupling. *Journal of Family Issues*.

Yap, A. J., Mason, M. F., & Ames, D. R. (2013). The powerful size others down: The link between power and estimates of others' size. *Journal of Experimental Social Psychology, 49,* 591–594.

Zook, K. R., Saksvig, B. I., Wu, T. T., & Young, D. R. (2014). Physical activity trajectories and multilevel factors among adolescent girls. *Journal of Adolescent Health, 54,* 74–80.

Religious Beliefs

DIVERSITY CHALLENGE

Some people are fond of saying that sport is their religion, or similar phrases. Likening his trips to watch the Pittsburgh Steelers to others' pilgrimages to holy cities, fan Brent Osborn wrote on a banner, "Some people go to Jerusalem. I go to Pittsburgh." His signage, coupled with his devotion to the team, allowed Osborn to win the NFL's "Fan Flag Challenge." He is not the only fan, athlete, or team to mix sport and religion. Consider the following examples:

- MLB player Andrew McCutchen wore a cross on his arm band during the 2014 season.
- Mike Rossman, a former boxer, wore the Star of David on his boxing trunks.
- Bilqis Abdul-Qaadir, a collegiate basketball player who is Muslim, wore the hijab (the traditional head covering) during her playing days in 2010. (It is perhaps fortunate

she played basketball rather than soccer, as FIFA, soccer's international governing body, does not allow head covers to be worn during competition.)

- Members of the Gates City Christian boys' basketball team wear pants instead of shorts since the latter expose too much of their skin, violating their religious tenets.

Other sport leagues and their teams have religious ties. The first line of the Little League pledge, which is recited by teams prior to each competition, is "I trust in God." The NHL's Columbus Blue Jackets had a "Faith and Family Night" at one of their 2014 contests against the San Jose Sharks. After the game, spectators stayed to listen to a concert with Unspoken, a Christian pop-rock band, performing. As these examples illustrate, religious beliefs often are incorporated into sport and the entertainment associated with the events.

Sources: Benson, C., & Remillard, A. (2014, January). Is religion losing ground on sports? *Washington Post.* Retrieved from www.washingtonpost.com / Columbus Blue Jackets (n.d.). Faith & Family Night with the Blue Jackets! Retrieved from http://bluejackets.nhl.com/club/page.htm?id=101269 / Lukas, P. (2014, September). Uni Watch: Faith and attire. *ESPN.* Retrieved from www.espn.com.

CHALLENGE **REFLECTION**

1. Are you aware of any other sport teams that use religious themes to attract people to the event?

2. What are the advantages and disadvantages of sport organizations' use of such marketing techniques?

3. How might employees' religious beliefs influence their attitudes and behaviors in the workplace?

As the Diversity Challenge demonstrates, sport and religion are often intertwined. For a host of reasons, now more than ever before, people are likely to integrate their religious beliefs into their everyday work activities, athletes are likely to turn to their religious beliefs to make sense of their sport participation, and sport organizations may incorporate religion and faith into their efforts to attract fans to their events. These dynamics are important because people's religious beliefs have the potential to influence their attitudes, the decisions they make at work, and how well they integrate with others in the workplace or on an athletic team. Interestingly, despite the importance of religion to many people, this topic has received little interest in the diversity literature. In fact, Hicks (2003) has commented, "If the respective fields of leadership and management studies have avoided religion, the academic discipline of religious studies has overlooked the workplace" (p. 3). Consequently, sport managers must remain cognizant of how this form of deep-level diversity influences the workplace's culture, processes, and outcomes.

The purpose of this chapter is to examine the influence of religion in sport organizations. The chapter begins with a discussion of religion and spirituality and the distinctions between those two constructs. I then highlight the influence of religion in the workplace. In the final section of the chapter, I provide an overview of how athletes incorporate religion into their sport participation.

BACKGROUND AND KEY TERMS

To understand the effects of religious beliefs in the workplace, it is first necessary to define basic terms. Koenig, King, and Carson (2012) define *religion* as "beliefs, practices, and rituals related to the *transcendent,* where the transcendent is God, Allah, HaShem, or a Higher Power in Western religious traditions, or to Brahman, manifestations of Brahman, Buddha, Dao, or ultimate truth/reality in Eastern traditions" (p. 45, emphasis in original). Religion serves multiple functions (Bruce, 2011; Durkheim, 1965; Koenig et al., 2012). At the individual level, it brings people closer to the divine, provides emotional support, and serves as a source of meaning. Religion is also interpersonal in nature, creating social bonds and shared values among people who have similar beliefs. At the institutional level, religion provides a form of social control by prescribing certain behaviors that are consistent with the values, norms, and beliefs of that faith and of society. Finally, religion provides a form of social integration, uniting people of a common belief system. Religion brings together people of diverse backgrounds, reaffirms the basic customs and values of a society, and unites people in ways that transcend the individual self.

Some authors contrast religion with the concept of *spirituality,* with the latter term conceptualized as "the basic feeling of being connected with one's complete self, others, and the entire universe" (Mitroff & Denton, 1999, p. 83). Each person is spiritual on account of being human (Del Rio & White, 2012). Terms associated with spirituality include *self-actualization, wholeness, meaning, purpose, life force, virtue,* and *interconnectedness,* among others (Hicks, 2002). Authors who distinguish between the two concepts often view religion as being structured and organized, as providing external controls, and as being divisive. On the other hand, spirituality is viewed as being broad and inclusive, providing inner peace, and being the ultimate end in itself (Mitroff & Denton, 1999). For example, one CEO in Mitroff and Denton's study explained, "Not only do you not have to be religious in order to be spiritual, but it probably helps if you are not religious, especially if you want your spirituality to grow and be a basic part of your life" (p. 87).

While some, such as the aforementioned CEO, clearly distinguish between religion and spirituality, others note the connectedness between the two constructs (Koenig et al., 2012), particularly when it comes to the work environment (Chan-Serafin, Brief, & George, 2013). In fact, Bailey (2001) asserts that "a meaningful conversation about spirituality sans religion is dubious" (p. 367). I adopt a similar position here. Consider, for example, that many of the terms associated with spirituality, such as *passion, self-actualization,* or *virtue* (Hicks, 2002), are also associated with many people's religious beliefs. Furthermore, Mitroff and Denton (1999) suggest that spirituality is (1) the basic belief that there is a supreme being that governs the universe; (2) the notion that the higher power affects all things; and (3) the ultimate source of meaning in one's life. Christians, Jews, and Muslims would, for the most part, make similar statements about God and their religious beliefs. Given the similarities between and overlap of the two concepts, in the following discussion I use the terms *religion* and *religious beliefs.*

The Emphasis on Religion

Interest in the interactions among religion, work, and sport has increased over the past several decades, and this is attributable to a number of factors. First, a large majority of the world's population—84 percent, to be exact—follows some religious belief system (PEW Research Center, 2012). Exhibit 9.1 offers an overview of the major religious groups and the percentages of persons affiliated with them. Most people who identify as religious are Christian, followed by Muslims, Hindus, and Buddhists. In interpreting the data, it is important to note that roughly one in six persons express no religious affiliation, which makes them the third largest group, more populous than Catholics. Finally, as a testament to the influence of culture and similarly minded others, most people (73 percent) live in a region where their religious group makes up the majority of the population. This is particularly the case for Hindus, as 97 percent of all Hindus live in the three countries where Hindus are the majority: India, Nepal, and Mauritius. Most Christians (87 percent), Muslims (73 percent), and persons who express no affiliation (71 percent) also live in countries where the majority of residents share their religious beliefs.

EXHIBIT 9.1   Religious affiliations of people around the world.

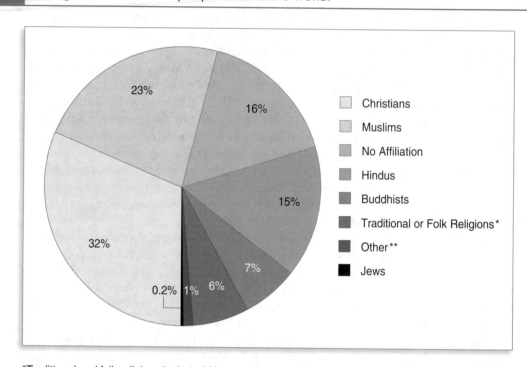

*Traditional and folk religions include African traditional religions, Chinese folk religions, and religious traditions of native persons in the U.S. and Australia.

**Religions classified as "other" include Baha'i, Jainism, Shintoism, and Taoism, among others.

Source: Data from PEW Research Center (2012).

These statistics are important because religion can influence people's values, attitudes, and behaviors—effects observed at the individual, interpersonal, and group levels (Durkheim, 1965; Spilka, Hood, Hunsberger, & Gorsuch, 2003). Religious ceremonies are held for major life events, such as birth, death, marriage, and certain birthdays. Religious tenets influence what is permissible within particular cultures, as well as the laws and policies regulating these practices. Examples include same-sex marriage, divorce, the sale of alcohol on Sundays, holidays observed, and the hours during which some businesses are open. People have used their religious beliefs to justify everything from engaging in violence to pursuing equal rights to engaging in efforts to disassemble social stratification (Edwards, Christerson, & Emerson, 2013; Hinojosa, 2014). Collectively, these factors suggest that (1) people in leadership positions are likely to subscribe to a particular religious belief system and (2) religion has the potential to influence a person's life meaningfully; thus, these leaders' attitudes and behaviors are probably shaped, at least in part, by religious tenets.

The changing nature of work has affected the emphasis on religion in the work environment (Benefiel, Fry, & Geigle, 2014). As noted in Chapter 1, sport organizations have undergone meaningful changes. Corporate scandals have eroded employees' trust in upper management. Changing technologies and organizational restructuring have resulted in downsizing and variations in the nature of work. The loyalty previously offered by organizations to employees is perceived to be weaker than it once was, making work life uncertain. Despite these negative changes, people are spending more time at work now than they ever have before. Time spent away from home in other activities, such as attending social gatherings, has decreased, while the hours spent at work have increased. This dynamic causes people to seek greater meaning in their lives, a quest that often leads to greater integration of religious and work identities (Osman-Gani, Hashim, & Ismail, 2013). As they seek greater meaning, employees are likely to merge their religious beliefs, values, and identities into their work (Lynn, Naughton, & Vander Veen, 2010). Thus, for many employees, the two identities are no longer separate, and religion is no longer viewed as something to be kept out of the workplace. For example, the Christian Faculty Network is found on many college campuses and serves as a social network for university faculty and staff of the Christian faith.

Finally, external pressures might influence the infusion of religious principles into the workplace. Some customers prefer to patronize organizations that profess to conduct their business practices in line with a specific set of religious principles. This can incentivize business owners not only to develop structures and missions consistent with such belief systems but also to advertise and promote these links. As an example, the goal of the website Christian Owned & Operated (www. christianownedandoperated.com) is to allow businesses in Houston, Texas, and the surrounding area to promote their Christian ties. Organizations listed in the directory agree to the following: "We are a *Christian Owned and Operated Business* who believes Jesus Christ came into this world as God's one and only son, to forgive us of our sins and give everlasting life to those who accept him as their Lord and Savior. We operate our business under the same guiding principles taught by Jesus Christ" (emphasis in original). Several sport organizations are listed, including Trinity Wellness, New Life Fitness, and Texas Spirit Cheer Company, to name a few. Promotional networks are not limited to Christian-based organizations—other websites support or promote organizations following Buddhist principles (such as Buddhist Business Network, www.buddhistbusiness.com) and Jewish businesses (such as the Jewish Business Network of Southern New Jersey, www.jbnsnj.org), among others.

RELIGION IN THE WORKPLACE

Because religious beliefs can be important to people in their work life, it is useful to consider possible effects in the workplace. Religious beliefs can influence a variety of work-related outcomes, including strategic decisions, ethical behavior, leadership, and stress. In addition, religion serves as a basis for categorization and, as a result, can influence how well people integrate into a group. Each of these topics is discussed in turn below.

As religion increasingly infuses work, it is important that managers remain mindful of the legal ramifications. I provide an overview in the following box.

Legal mandates related to religion in the workplace

Discrimination on the basis of religion is prohibited by Title VII. Under Title VII:

- Employers cannot treat people more or less favorably because of their religious affiliation.

- Employees cannot be forced to participate in religious ceremonies or prayers as a condition of employment. This issue often arises in the context of team prayers.

- Employers must accommodate their employees' sincerely held religious beliefs unless doing so would cause undue hardship to the employer. Reasonable accommodations include flexible work hours and the ability to exchange working assignments with other employees. Unreasonable accommodations are those that impose hardships on other employees, jeopardize workplace safety, or decrease efficiency.

- Employers cannot restrict an employee's religious expression any more than other forms of expression that might have a comparable effect. For example, an employer may not restrict personal, silent prayers when they do not negatively impact performance.

- Employers must take all reasonable steps to prevent religious harassment in the workplace.

Charges of religious discrimination are not as prevalent as other forms. In 2013, the EEOC received 3,721 complaints of religious discrimination. This is only a fraction of the number of complaints/claims filed in other categories: racial (29,732), sex (25,162), age (19,241), and disability (23,364). In 2013, the EEOC recovered $11.2 million in damages for individuals claiming religious discrimination.

Strategic Decisions

Leaders might draw from their religious beliefs to inform their organizational decision making (Phipps, 2012). Conceptually, it is reasonable to assume that people's religious beliefs can influence their decisions across life contexts—for example, the partner they seek in life; the social organizations in which they are involved; and, in the workplace, the strategic decision making in which they engage. A number of factors are likely to influence whether this occurs. Religious identity is one such factor, as the influence of religious beliefs on decision making is likely to be stronger when religious beliefs are central to the person's identity. Organizational context is another influential factor, as it is possible for a leader to have strong religious beliefs but, because of the organizational culture in place, not be at liberty to express those beliefs at work or turn to them in the decision-making process. Similarly, stakeholder expectations can influence the role of religious beliefs in strategic decision making.

A number of examples from sport illustrate how religion can influence strategic decision making. Brigham Young University is an institution affiliated with the Church of Jesus Christ of Latter-Day Saints; in fact, it is named after the second president of the church. The university follows Mormon principles, which require that university athletic teams not participate in events on Sundays. This requirement certainly impacts the university's athletic scheduling practices and has influenced other entities, as well. When the university's basketball teams play in the NCAA national tournament, they are always placed in those team brackets that play on Thursdays and Saturdays, rather than the men's alternative Friday and Sunday brackets.

As another example, prayer is a common occurrence at high school football games, particularly those held in the southern United States. These prayers are unconstitutional, but they are nonetheless led by coaches and athletic administrators and are broadcast over the public address system at events (Beck, Goldfine, Marley, et al., 2009; Gillentine, Goldfine, Phillips, et al., 2004). Certainly there are cultural influences, as the South is generally considered the most religious part of the United States; however, there is also evidence that athletic directors' religious beliefs factor into these decisions. Miller, Lee, and Martin (2013) found that nearly all athletic directors (90 percent) indicated that their religious beliefs influenced their decision making at work, a high proportion indicated that their athletic teams had team-only prayers prior to the games, and few (30 percent) considered the legal ramifications of their actions.

Dunn and Stevenson (1998), in their study of a church hockey league, found additional evidence of how religious beliefs influence strategic decisions. This hockey league was designed to promote the values and norms of evangelical Christians—a design reflected in many of the league rules. For example, body contact was prohibited—a rarity in hockey. Community prayers were said prior to the games, and swearing was prohibited, as was beer in the locker rooms prior to and after the games. Finally, official team standings were not maintained—all teams made the playoffs. The league's cooperative nature, as evidenced by its rules, differs markedly from other recreational hockey leagues.

As a final example, some health promotion specialists have started to use faith-based initiatives to encourage physical activity participation. Bopp, Wilcox, Laken, and colleagues (2009) examined the efficacy of this approach among a sample of African Americans. They believed that faith-based initiatives would be particularly helpful among this population, because "African Americans have high levels of religiosity, are more likely to attend church and use religion as a coping strategy, and indicate that religion or prayer contributes to their physical health" (p. 569). Among a sample of persons attending African Methodist Episcopal churches in South Carolina, the researchers implemented a program that incorporated elements of both the Health-e-AME Physical-e-Fit program and the 8 Steps to Fitness program. Their program was designed to increase people's awareness of the importance of regular physical activity, their participation in physical activity programs, and the emphasis placed by church leaders on the promotion of regular exercise. In their study, Bopp and colleagues compared a group of people who went through the program with a control group of people who did not. They found that, compared with persons in the control group, persons who went through the program showed greater losses in their BMI, decreased blood pressure, decreased depression, and more physical activity enjoyment. These findings are encouraging and suggest that faith-based interventions can serve as tools to encourage physical activity and decrease obesity levels.

Ethical Behavior

Because certain forms of moral behavior (e.g., "love your neighbor as yourself") are common across the five major religions (Kriger & Seng, 2005), it might be expected that people with strong religious beliefs, irrespective of their particular religion, will behave differently from those who do not have strong religious beliefs, particularly with regard to ethics. In some instances, this reasoning holds true. For example, people with strong religious beliefs are unlikely to use illicit or illegal substances (DeWall, Pond, Carter, et al., 2014). However, when it comes to business ethics, the picture is mixed, with some studies showing no relationship and others showing a strong relationship between religiosity and ethical behavior or other desired behaviors at work (see Weaver & Agle, 2002; Weaver & Stansbury, 2014).

One potential way to understand these equivocal findings is to apply the social identity theory portion of the social categorization framework (see Chapter 2) to the issue (see Weaver & Agle, 2002). We know that people maintain various identities—student, woman, golfer, Episcopalian, and the like. The salience of these identities is likely to change depending on the context. In some situations, being a fan of your favorite team is most important, and that identity shapes your attitudes and behaviors (e.g., giving a high-five to another fan at a game). For most people, however, being a fan is not the primary identity in all situations. At home the role of partner or mother might be the most salient, just as at church being an Episcopalian might be the most salient. Having a certain social identity that remains the most salient in a particular context influences the attitudes, preferences, and behaviors that a person exhibits in that context.

Social identity salience is particularly important in the discussion of religious beliefs and ethical behavior. If a person's religious identity remains salient across most social contexts, including work, then that individual's attitudes, preferences, and behaviors are likely to be shaped by her or his religious beliefs. On the other hand, if the religious identity of a person is primed on Sundays, but the work identity is primed at work, then it is less likely that the attitudes and behaviors of that individual at work will be guided by religious beliefs. According to Weaver and Agle (2002), "The more salient religion is for a person—that is, the larger role it plays in one's self-identity—the more difficult it will be for other factors to push aside or thwart the influence of religious expectations" (p. 85).

Of course, certain factors could influence the expected positive relationship between religious identity and ethical behavior. These include organizational commitment and the presence of others in the workplace who share the same religion (Weaver & Agle, 2002; Weaver & Stansbury, 2014). If an employee is highly committed to the organization, this commitment will tend to counteract the salience of the person's religious identity while at work. One cannot serve two masters; employees will either be committed and highly identified with their work or committed and highly identified with their religion, but not both. A strong commitment to the workplace may negate (or at least reduce) the effects of an individual's religious beliefs on ethical behavior.

The presence in the workplace of others who share a person's religious beliefs is likely to increase the power of those beliefs to guide actions in the workplace. For example, if a Christian has many coworkers who also identify themselves as Christians, the identity of being a Christian is likely to be reinforced at work. Furthermore, there is likely to be greater accountability for one's actions among the Christian coworkers. Because the religious salience is likely to be high in that work environment, the link between religious beliefs and ethical behavior is likely to be positive. For additional discussion of the influence of religion on ethics, see the following box.

Religious influence on teaching ethics

Joel Evans, Linda Trevino, and Gary Weaver are professors who specialize in the study of organizational ethics. In one of their studies, they were interested in discovering the factors that influence whether or not MBA programs include ethics in their curricula. The best predictor of that outcome was whether or not the university had a religious affiliation, with religious-based schools being more likely to require ethics training than their counterparts. They looked to professors who taught at those universities to help them understand their findings. One professor, who taught at a Roman Catholic–affiliated institution, commented, "Our commitment to ethics . . . comes from the founding fathers . . . and the tradition found in their order, which is primarily that of missionary work with a clear emphasis on social justice" (Evans, Trevino, & Weaver, 2006, p. 281). Thus, the religious institutions emphasized ethics, morality, and social justice, and, as a result, the MBA curricula reflected those forms of social control.

Leadership

As previously noted, a person's religious beliefs have the potential to influence work-related attitudes and behaviors, and this is certainly the case with leadership. A number of scholars have developed frameworks showing the relationship between religious or spiritual beliefs and leader behaviors (Kriger & Seng, 2005; Whittington, Pitts, Kageler, & Goodwin, 2005). Most of this work, however, has adopted a Western approach to religion, focusing on Christian or Jewish principles. Missing from this dialogue is attention to Eastern religious beliefs. Eisenbeiss (2012) addressed this shortcoming by drawing from the religious and ethical teachings of the world's major religions to develop an integrative framework. She suggested that ethical leaders have four central orientations: human, justice, responsibility and sustainability, and moderation (see Exhibit 9.2 for definitions of

Orientations of ethical leaders.   EXHIBIT **9.2**

Human orientation: refers to the belief that all people should be treated with dignity and respect, rather than as a means to an end. This orientation is expressed in the full recognition of people's rights and concern with their well-being.

Justice orientation: refers to the mindset of making fair, consistent decisions that do not privilege one group over another. This orientation is expressed through a concern for fairness and diversity, and an opposition to discrimination.

Responsibility and sustainability: refers to the leader's focus on long-term success, as well as the concern for society and the environment. This orientation is expressed in a sense of obligation to the company and community, the long-term viability of the organization, and recognition that her or his actions have the potential to impact the environment and future generations.

Moderation orientation: refers to the leader's humility, restraint, and self-control. This orientation is reflected in the leader's temperance, humbleness, and ability to balance organizational objectives with stakeholder interests.

Source: Eisenbeiss (2012).

each). Leaders who express these orientations are likely to engender trust among followers and customers, which should, ultimately, result in improved organizational success.

Another leadership style with religious overtones is that of servant leadership (van Dierendonck, 2011). Servant leaders recognize their moral responsibility not only to their organization but also to their followers, customers, and others with a stake in the organization. The moral compass that servant leaders use is what separates them from other leaders. Servant leaders focus on empowering others, are humble, demonstrate authenticity, create an environment where people feel safe, clearly demonstrate to followers what is expected of them, and act as both role models and caretakers (van Dierendonck, 2011). Recognizing the value of such characteristics, Burton and Welty Peachey (2013) argued that more servant leaders are needed in sport organizations, as they would have the potential to transform the sport setting. Specifically, servant leaders would develop organizational cultures of trust and helping behaviors; their followers would work collaboratively with one another; and, as a result, the sport organization would thrive (see also Parris & Welty Peachey, 2013). The authors also suspected that external pressures for ethical decision making would result in more leaders adopting a servant leadership mindset.

Stress

A person's religious beliefs can produce stress in the workplace (Exline & Bright, 2011; Gebert, Boerner, Kearney, et al., 2014). Leaders might wrestle with the best way to accommodate or encourage spirituality in the workplace. Religious differences among coworkers might result in interpersonal disagreements, heightening felt discrimination and stress. Finally, as people integrate their religious and work identities, they might develop personal conflicts or crises of faith, both of which can negatively affect their work experiences. These dynamics are particularly relevant in sport, where competition, superiority, and dominating others are emphasized—characteristics that might contrast with the values of many religions, such as cooperativeness, humility, and helpfulness (Bennett, Sagas, Fleming, & Von Roenn, 2005).

Several outcomes can result from this stress. In some situations, people might refrain from integrating their religious and workplace identities. In others, they might develop coping mechanisms to help them manage the stress. For instance, people might turn to their religious beliefs as a source of comfort and guidance (Bennett et al., 2005). Third, inclusive sport organizations are likely to develop systems and processes that allow these differences to serve as a source of learning and growth. For example, organizations might offer mediation or prayer rooms, while others might intentionally engage in dialogue focusing on religious differences and how they can contribute to perspective taking, empathy, and growth. These are consistent with strategies outlined in Chapter 13.

Religion as a Basis for Categorization

People's religious beliefs can shape how they see themselves and others. Recall from Chapter 2 and our discussion of the social categorization framework that people categorize themselves and others into social groups. This process is based on characteristics that are important to the individual or that are salient in a particular context. Thus, if a person's religious beliefs are particularly important, she will refer to religion to identify who is similar and who is different from herself. For a person to whom religion is not particularly important, religion might become salient when he is surrounded by like-minded others, such as while attending a Fellowship of Christian Athletes meeting. In this situation, religion would be used to differentiate the self from others, even though the individual does not generally prioritize religion. Finally, a person who believes she is threatened might seek to identify with a social group that offers a clearly defined and distinctive identity (Hogg, 2014). Religious groups offer one such identity.

Though researchers have not often considered religion as a basis for categorization, there is evidence to suggest that it does serve this purpose. Burris and Jackson (2000), for instance, suggested that "religion has been numbered—along with gender, ethnicity and nationality—among the core social categories around which an individual's social identity is organized" (p. 257). Later, Weeks and Vincent (2007) showed empirically that people spontaneously categorize the self and others with a religious dimension. As these authors note, "An individual's religious beliefs serve as a dominant schema, acting as a filter and organizer as they view the world" (p. 318). The categorization process is especially salient among religious fundamentalists (Schaafsma & Williams, 2012), irrespective of their religion (Kunst, Thomsen, & Sam, 2014). For further discussion of religious fundamentalism and bias, see the accompanying box.

Religious fundamentalism and bias

Although the positive effects of incorporating religious and spiritual beliefs in the workplace are frequently noted, the potential exists for negative effects, as well. A number of authors have observed that religious leaders are less likely than their non-religious counterparts to promote diversity or strive for fully inclusive work environments (Lips-Wiersma, Dean, & Fornaciari, 2009; Mazereeuw-van der Duijn Schouten, Graafland, & Kaptein, 2014). This is perhaps most evident when we consider religious fundamentalists—individuals who hold a steadfast set of beliefs that there is one set of inerrant teaching (truths) about people and their relationship with a deity (Altemeyer & Hunsberger, 1992). Religious fundamentalists believe there is one true path to the deity and one correct set of teachings. Deviations from these beliefs are rejected, as are the people who profess them. Evidence suggests that it is religious fundamentalism, not religion *per se,* that is associated with categorization and prejudice toward others (Johnson, Rowatt, Barnard-Brak, et al., 2011).

Melton and I have observed the effects of religious fundamentalism on bias toward sexual minorities. In our first study, we found that as parents' religious fundamentalism increased, so too did their prejudice toward lesbian, gay, and bisexual coaches (Cunningham & Melton, 2012). These effects were particularly strong for Whites, Asians, and Latinos. In our next study, we observed a strong relationship between fundamentalism and sexual prejudice (Cunningham & Melton, 2013). Importantly, though, we also found that contact with lesbian and gay persons affected this relationship: when the participants had lesbian and gay friends, the relationship between fundamentalism and sexual prejudice was negated. These findings show that, while religious fundamentalism is generally associated with bias, its effects can be offset.

Categorization of the self and others based on religion may have a number of potential outcomes. First, consistent with the relational diversity perspective outlined in Chapter 2, people who differ religiously from the majority might have poor work experiences. Indeed, in a study of NCAA athletic administrators, I observed as much, as people who differed religiously from others in the department perceived that their values differed—that is, they had different ideas about what is right, good, or valuable (Cunningham, 2010). These effects were particularly pronounced when religion was important to the individual (i.e., when the religious personal identity was strong). Persons who perceived that they differed from others based on their religion and values were also less satisfied with their jobs than were their coworkers. These outcomes were observed even after we took into account other factors, such as the person's age, gender, and race.

Another outcome of religious categorization is integration into a group. Ragins (2008) recounts the story of a Jewish professor at a Catholic university:

My mother told me not to take a job at a Catholic university. She told me they'd fire me once they found out I'm Jewish. I thought she was so old school, until my first day on the job. The ex-Dean told me that he moved from a neighborhood because "there were too many Jews there." I decided not to tell anyone I was Jewish. But then my colleagues became my friends, and one day I found myself putting up Christmas ornaments before they came over. I was denying who I was in my very own home. So I decided to come out of the "Jewish closet" at work. I found out later that the Provost kept a list of the Jewish faculty. He added me to the list. (p. 194)

As this story illustrates, people's religious beliefs can influence how others see them, the manner in which they interact with others, and how well they integrate into a social group. Bias also affects how willing people are to work with others who are religiously different, particularly when the perceiver is highly religious (King, McKay, & Stewart, 2014).

Religious categorization can influence fan behavior, as illustrated in the Diversity in the Field box.

DIVERSITY   IN THE FIELD

Religion and Soccer. Soccer is the most popular sport in the world, and its supporters are the most fanatical. This is especially the case in Ireland with the rivalry between Glasgow's premier soccer clubs, Rangers F.C. and Celtic F.C. *Sports Illustrated* columnist Grant Wahl described the rivalry as "a purity of hatred that involved politics, class, and above all, religion." Most Rangers supporters are Protestant, whereas Celtic supporters are largely Catholic. For years, the players on the teams reflected these religious divisions, and for years, violence has erupted between the rival teams' fans.

In fact, stabbings and bar fights in Glasgow are routinely investigated for Celtic-Rangers links. The players embody disdain for the other team's religious links. Rangers forward Paul Gascoigne once celebrated a goal against Celtic by mimicking a flute player—his way of commemorating William of Orange's victory over the Catholics at the Battle of the Boyne in 1690. Similarly, Celtic players find special meaning in crossing themselves when they score against their rivals. As this case illustrates, religious affiliation and categorization influence the dynamics among soccer fans and players.

Source: Adapted from Wahl (1999).

RELIGION AND SPORT PARTICIPATION

R eligious beliefs affect sport participants in two ways. First, religion influences who participates in sport and their reasons for doing so. Second, some athletes rely on their religious beliefs while participating.

Influence on Sport Participation

People's religious beliefs can influence their degree of sport participation and their reasons for participation. Eitzen and Sage (2009) provide a historical account of the issue. According to them, primitive societies used sport and physical activity to defeat their foes, influence supernatural forces, or increase crop and livestock fertility. The ancient Greeks employed sport in a religious context. In fact, the early Olympics were a religious performance intended to please Zeus. In contrast to these cultures' use of sport in various religious capacities, according to Eitzen and Sage, early 17th-century Puritans viewed sport as antithetical to Christian ideals. Eitzen and Sage note that no Christian group opposed sport and sport participation more than the Puritans. See the box at right for a different understanding of how the Puritans viewed sport. Opposition to sport was largely maintained by Christian churches in North America until the 20th century. Subsequently, however, changes in the United States—industrialization, urbanization, and an awareness of the health benefits of sport and physical activity—resulted in a more positive relationship between sport and religion. Eitzen and Sage note that church leaders "gradually began to reconcile play and religion in response to pressure from medical, educational, and political leaders for games and sport. Increasingly, churches broadened their commitment to play and sport endeavors as a means of drawing people together" (p. 170). Consequently, some churches now include sport in their social programs, and attendees are often actively involved in sport and physical activity (see also Hoffman, 1999). See the Diversity in the Field box (p. 206) for one such example.

Other religions also influence decisions about who participates in sport and their reasons for participating. For example, Walseth and Fasting (2003) found that Egyptian women's participation in sport and physical activity was largely shaped by their Islamic beliefs (for further discussion, see Benn, Pfister, & Jawad, 2010). The women in their study believed that Islam called for people to be physically active for various reasons, including to care for their overall health and to be ready in case of war. Because Islam says that women may participate in sport as long as the sport movements are not "exciting" for men who might watch them, the extent to which the women participated in sport

ALTERNATIVE perspectives

Some Sports Are Tolerated. Some authors suggest that the Puritans were adamantly opposed to all sport and recreation (Eitzen & Sage, 2009). Rader (1999), however, feels differently. True, the Puritans prohibited sport and recreational activities held on the Sabbath or that resulted in undesirable outcomes such as drunkenness. Under other circumstances, however, they viewed sport as beneficial and rejuvenating. To be "acceptable," they felt, a sport should refresh people so they could better execute their worldly and spiritual callings. Rader notes, "Believing that all time was sacred (and therefore one's use of it was accountable to God), conscientious Puritans approached all forms of play with excruciating caution" (p. 7). Their rigid rules did not apply to children, who played with toys and were allowed to swim and skate as long as they were orderly while doing so. Evidently, the rules also did not apply to military training. All men aged 16 to 60 met regularly for required military training and engaged in jumping, foot races, horse racing, and shooting at marks (Rader, 1999). These exceptions suggest that the Puritans have often been mislabeled as "anti-sport."

DIVERSITY   IN THE FIELD

Church-Organized Sport Leagues. A number of churches use sport as a way to extend their outreach efforts. As Eitzen and Sage (2009) note, "Social service is a major purpose of the religious leaders who provide play and recreation under the auspices of their churches" (p. 173). These outreach programs are seen as another avenue through which the churches can "promote 'the Lord's work'" (p. 173).

One example of a sport-based outreach program is the basketball league organized by Central Baptist Church in Bryan, Texas. According to the church website (www.central bcs.org/sports/), the league is based on the following values:

Upward Sports

- *Expectation of God moments:* We believe that God is at work all around us.
- *The life of integrity:* We believe that how we live is more important than what we say.
- *The opportunity to serve:* We believe that it is a privilege to serve others.
- *The discipline of excellence:* We believe in exceeding expectations.
- *The priority of children:* We believe that every child is a winner.

and physical activity depended on whether they adopted a more modern or more traditional view of Islam. Women who adopted a more modern view of Islam considered most activities (not including gymnastics, dancing, and aerobics) appropriate and not likely to excite men. Women with a more traditional view felt that all sport forms were inappropriate unless the sport was conducted in sex-segregated venues. Because such venues were limited in Egypt, so was their sport participation.

An alternative view of the relationship between sport and religion is the suggestion that sport has become a form of religion for some participants and fans. The following Alternative Perspectives box highlights this perspective.

ALTERNATIVE perspectives

Sport as Religion. Many observers focus on the relationship between sport and religion. From a different perspective, some, such as Eitzen and Sage (2009) or Shilling and Mellor (2014), have argued that sport can be considered a form of religion or a sacred phenomenon (see also the Diversity Challenge that opened this chapter). Consider the following parallels:

- Each religion has its revered deity or deities. Similarly, sports superstars are "worshipped" by adoring fans.
- Religion has priests and clergy. The equivalent persons in sport are the team coaches, who direct the destinies of their players and often play to the emotions of the fans.

- Religion has holy places, such as mosques or churches, while sport also has revered places, such as Wrigley Field.
- Religious shrines are commonplace, and they preserve sacred symbols that followers can see and admire. Similarly, sports have halls of fame where the notable achievements of teams, players, and coaches are celebrated.
- Religions sponsor a number of holidays and festivals that call for communal involvement. Within sport, the Super Bowl and the Olympics both serve similar functions, bringing people together to celebrate the pageantry.

Athletes' Use of Religion

Many athletes turn to religious beliefs or employ prayers or rituals while participating in sport. Though research in this area is generally scarce, Coakley (2015) suggests that there are seven reasons why athletes use religion (see Exhibit 9.3).

Athletes use religion as a way of coping with the anxiety-producing uncertainty that is a fact of life in many sports, whether the uncertainty pertains to the risk of bodily harm, pressure to perform well, or not knowing whether they will be traded or cut from a team. Some athletes use prayer, scriptures, meditation, or other religious rituals to reduce this anxiety. Athletes may also use religion as a way of keeping out of trouble. As previously discussed, individuals who hold strong religious beliefs may behave differently from those who do not. Their beliefs also provide focus in their lives. Thus, even in environments that offer temptations to behave in ways contrary to their beliefs, some athletes return to their religious traditions for inspiration and guidance.

Coakley (2015) notes that athletes also use religion to give personal meaning to their sport participation. Athletes spend countless hours training and practicing. Even in team sports, the focus is primarily on the self and improving individual performance. How do people rationalize spending so much time focusing on the self or, from another perspective, so much time focusing on sport in general? Athletes of faith often consider sport participation an act of worship, bringing glory to God. In addition, some athletes use religion to keep their sport participation in perspective. If an athlete perceives that her participation is part of God's calling, then facing challenges in sport becomes easier. The athlete does not become so consumed by sports that she is overwhelmed by its challenges and the failures that regularly occur in that context.

Religion is also used to increase team unity. Former NFL coach George Allen commented that religion and prayer united teammates like no other factor he witnessed as a coach (Coakley, 2015). In a related way, some coaches use religion as a way of motivating and controlling their athletes. Given that most religious traditions emphasize following commands and being obedient to those in control, coaches might use religious tenets to persuade athletes to obey team rules.

Finally, some athletes use religious beliefs as a means to improve performance. While this might take the form of praying for specific wins, many athletes will pray

Athletes' use of religion.   **EXHIBIT 9.3**

Athletes use religion for one or more of the following reasons:

- Reduce anxiety
- Keep away from trouble
- Give meaning to sport participation
- Gain perspective
- Increase team unity
- Maintain social control
- Achieve personal success

Source: Coakley (2015).

that they perform to the best of their ability, and if success comes as a result, then so be it. Other athletes pray as a way of showing their gratitude for their athletic abilities. The latter kind of prayer expresses gratitude for performance rather than petitioning for success.

chapter SUMMARY

This chapter focused on the intersection of religion and sport. Unlike other, more visible diversity dimensions, an individual's religious beliefs are generally not known to others unless they are disclosed. Nevertheless, as the Diversity Challenge illustrates, religious beliefs have the potential to affect people's actions, preferences, and beliefs substantially. Religious beliefs also influence strategic decision making, organizational practices, and marketing efforts. After reading this chapter, you should be able to:

1. **Define** *religion* **and** *spirituality* **and discuss the differences between the two.**

   Religion is defined as a set of beliefs and practices related to sacred things that unites all those who adhere to them (Durkheim, 1965). The influence of religion is seen at the individual, interpersonal, institutional, and social integration levels. *Spirituality* is the feeling of connectedness and unity with others and the universe (Mitroff & Denton, 1999).

2. **Provide an overview of how religious beliefs influence people's work behaviors.**

   Religion has been shown to influence people's strategic decisions, ethical behavior, leadership, and ways of managing stress in the workplace. In addition, religion can serve as a basis for categorization, in which case people who are religiously different from the majority are likely to have negative work experiences.

3. **Discuss the influence of religion among sport participants.**

   Religious beliefs influence how and why people participate in sport. Sport participants use religion to (a) reduce anxiety, (b) avoid trouble, (c) give meaning to sport participation, (d) gain perspective, (e) increase team unity, (f) serve as a source of control, and (g) achieve personal success.

QUESTIONS for discussion

1. Some people distinguish between religion and spirituality. Do you? If so, what do you feel are the major differences between religion and spirituality? If not, how are the two concepts similar?

2. Is the influence of religion on organizational practices stronger or weaker in sport than it is in other contexts? Why or why not?

3. How much should a person's religious beliefs influence the decisions one makes on behalf of an organization, such as its strategic path? Why?

4. It has been suggested that sport has become a religion for some participants. What are the pros and cons of this argument? Do you agree with this perspective?

5. In your experience, how much do athletes rely on their religious beliefs while participating in sport? What is the primary reason for this reliance?

learning ACTIVITIES

1. The courts have consistently ruled that public school coaches cannot lead their teams in prayer. Divide the class into two groups and debate the issue. Would the arguments be the same if the person leading the prayer was the instructor of this class?

2. As an outside assignment, interview current and former athletes about the degree to which they incorporated religion into their playing careers. If they did, in what ways was it incorporated, and what were the outcomes of doing so?

WEB resources

Fellowship of Christian Athletes, www.fca.org

An organization that challenges coaches and players to use sport to spread their Christian faith.

Jewish Community Centers Association of North America, www.jcca.org

An organization that helps its affiliates offer education, Jewish identity-building, and cultural and recreational programs for persons of all ages and backgrounds.

Athletes in Action, www.athletesinaction.org

An international organization that uses sport competition as a way for athletes to spread their Christian faith.

reading RESOURCES

Benn, T., Pfister, G., & Jawad, H. (Eds.) (2010). *Muslim women and sport*. London: Routledge.

An edited book that offers a conceptual framework for understanding the sport and physical activity experiences of Muslim women; contains contributions from women and men, as well as Muslins and non-Muslims.

Hicks, D. A. (2003). *Religion and the workplace: Pluralism, spirituality, leadership*. New York: Cambridge University Press.

Offers one of the most comprehensive treatments of religion in the workplace.

Koenig, H., King, D., & Carson, V. B. (2012). *Handbook of religion and health*. Oxford, UK: Oxford University Press.

A comprehensive collection of chapters offering an overview of religion and spirituality, and their effects on people's health and well-being.

REFERENCES

Altemeyer, B., & Hunsberger, B. E. (1992). Authoritarianism, religious fundamentalism, quest, and prejudice. *International Journal for the Psychology of Religion, 2*, 113–133.

Bailey, J. R. (2001). Book review of J. A. Conger and associates: Spirit at work: Discovering the spirituality in leadership. *The Leadership Quarterly, 12*, 367–368.

Beck, J., Goldfine, B., Marley, S., Seidler, T., & Gillentine, A. (2009, June). *Prayer at interscholastic athletic events in the United States: A regional analysis.* Paper presented at the annual conference of the North American Society for Sport Management, Columbia, SC.

Benefiel, M., Fry, L. W., & Geigle, D. (2014). Spirituality and religion in the workplace: History, theory, and research. *Psychology of Religion and Spirituality, 6*, 175–187.

Benn, T., Pfister, G., & Jawad, H. (Eds.) (2010). *Muslim women and sport.* London: Routledge.

Bennett, G., Sagas, M., Fleming, D., & Von Roenn, S. (2005). On being a living contradiction: The struggle of an elite intercollegiate coach. *Journal of Beliefs & Values, 26*, 289–300.

Bopp, M., Wilcox, S., Laken, M., Hooker, S. P., Parra-Medina, D., Saunders, R., ... & McClorin, L. (2009). 8 Steps to Fitness: A faith-based, behavioral change physical activity intervention for African Americans. *Journal of Physical Activity and Health, 6*, 568–577.

Bruce, S. (2011). Defining religion: A practical response. *International Review of Sociology, 21*, 107–120.

Burris, C. T., & Jackson, L. M. (2000). Social identity and the true believer: Responses to threatened self-stereotypes among the intrinsically religious. *British Journal of Social Psychology, 39*, 257–278.

Burton, L., & Welty Peachey, J. (2013). The call for servant leadership in intercollegiate athletics. *Quest, 65*, 354–371.

Chan-Serafin, S., Brief, A. P., & George, J. M. (2013). How does religion matter and why? Religiosity and the organizational sciences. *Organization Science, 24*, 1585–1600.

Coakley, J. (2015). *Sports in society: Issues and controversies* (11th ed.). New York: McGraw-Hill.

Cunningham, G. B. (2010). The influence of religious personal identity on the relationships among religious dissimilarity, value dissimilarity, and job satisfaction. *Social Justice Research, 23*, 60–76.

Cunningham, G. B., & Melton, N. (2012). Prejudice against lesbian, gay, and bisexual coaches: The influence of race, religious fundamentalism, modern sexism, and contact with sexual minorities. *Sociology of Sport Journal, 29*, 283–305.

Cunningham, G. B., & Melton, E. N. (2013). The moderating effects of contact with lesbian and gay friends on the relationships among religious fundamentalism, sexism, and sexual prejudice. *Journal of Sex Research, 50*, 401–408.

De Wall, C. N., Pond, R. S., Jr., Carter, E. C., McCullough, M. E., Lambert, N. M., Finchman, F. D., & Nezlek, J. B. (2014). Explaining the relationship between religiousness and substance use: Self-control matters. *Journal of Personality and Social Psychology, 107*, 339–351.

Del Rio, C. M., & White, L. J. (2012). Separating spirituality from religiosity: A hylomorphic attitudinal perspective. *Psychology of Religion and Spirituality, 4*, 123–142.

Dunn, R., & Stevenson, C. (1998). The paradox of the church hockey league. *International Review for the Sociology of Sport, 32*, 131–141.

Durkheim, E. (1965). *The elementary forms of religious life.* New York: Free Press.

Edwards, K. L., Christerson, B., & Emerson, M. O. (2013). Race, religious organizations, and integration. *Annual Review of Sociology, 39*, 211–228.

Eisenbeiss, S. A. (2012). Re-thinking ethical leadership: An interdisciplinary integrative approach. *The Leadership Quarterly, 23*(5), 791–808.

Eitzen, D. S., & Sage, G. H. (2009). *Sociology of North American sport* (8th ed.). Boulder, CO: Paradigm Publishers.

Evans, J. M., Trevino, L. K., & Weaver, G. R. (2006). Who's in the ethics driver's seat? Factors influencing ethics in MBA curriculum. *Academy of Management Learning & Education, 5*, 278–293.

Exline, J., & Bright, D. S. (2011). Spiritual and religious struggles in the workplace. *Journal of Management, Spirituality and Religion, 8*, 123–142.

Gebert, D., Boerner, S., Kearney, E., King, J. E., Jr., Zhang, K., & Song, L. J. (2014). Expressing religious identities in the workplace: Analyzing a neglected diversity dimension. *Human Relations, 67*, 543–563.

Gillentine, A., Goldfine, B., Phillips, D., Seidler, T., & Scott, D. (2004). Prayer at athletic events. *Strategies, 18*(1), 13–15.

Hicks, D. A. (2002). Spiritual and religious diversity in the workplace: Implications for leadership. *The Leadership Quarterly, 13*, 379–396.

Hicks, D. A. (2003). *Religion and the workplace: Pluralism, spirituality, leadership.* New York: Cambridge University Press.

Hinojosa, F. (2014). *Latino Mennonites: Civil rights, faith, and evangelical culture.* Baltimore, MD: Johns Hopkins University Press.

Hoffman, S. (1999). The decline of civility and the rise of religion in American sport. *Quest, 51,* 69–84.

Hogg, M. A. (2014). From uncertainty to extremism: Social categorization and identity processes. *Current Directions in Psychological Science, 23,* 338–342.

Johnson, M. K., Rowatt, W. C., Barnard-Brak, L. M., Patock-Peckham, J. A., LaBouff, J. P., & Carlisle, R. D. (2011). A mediational analysis of the role of right-wing authoritarianism and religious fundamentalism in the religiosity–prejudice link. *Personality and Individual Differences, 50,* 851–856.

King, J. E., Jr., McKay, P. F., & Stewart, M. M. (2014). Religious bias and stigma: Attitudes toward working with a Muslim co-worker. *Journal of Management, Spirituality & Religion, 11,* 98–122.

Koenig, H., King, D., & Carson, V. B. (2012). *Handbook of religion and health.* Oxford, UK: Oxford University Press.

Kriger, M., & Seng, Y. (2005). Leadership with inner meaning: A contingency theory of leadership based on the worldviews of five religions. *The Leadership Quarterly, 16,* 771–806.

Kunst, J. R., Thomsen, L., & Sam, D. L. (2014). Late Abrahamic reunion? Religious fundamentalism negatively predicts dual Abrahamic group categorization among Muslims and Christians. *European Journal of Social Psychology, 44,* 337–348.

Lips-Wiersma, M., Dean, K. L., & Fornaciari, C. J. (2009). Theorizing the dark side of the workplace spirituality movement. *Journal of Management Inquiry, 18,* 288–300.

Lynn, M. L., Naughton, M. J., & Vander Veen, S. (2010). Connecting religion and work: Patterns and influences of work-faith integration. *Human Relations, 64,* 675–701.

Mazereeuw-van der Duijn Schouten, C., Graafland, J., & Kaptein, M. (2014). Religiosity, CSR attitudes, and CSR behavior: An empirical study of executives' religiosity and CSR. *Journal of Business Ethics, 123,* 437–459.

Miller, J. F., Lee, K., & Martin, C. L. L. (2013). An analysis of interscholastic athletic directors' religious values and practices on pregame prayer in Southeastern United States: A case study. *Journal of Legal Aspects of Sport, 23,* 91–106.

Mitroff, I. I., & Denton, E. A. (1999). A study of spirituality in the workplace. *Sloan Management Review, 40,* 83–92.

Osman-Gani, A. M., Hashim, J., & Ismail, Y. (2013). Establishing linkages between religiosity and spirituality on employee performance. *Employee Relations, 35,* 360–376.

Parris, D. L., & Welty Peachey, J. (2013). Encouraging servant leadership: A qualitative study of how a cause-related sporting event inspires participants to serve. *Leadership, 9,* 486–512.

PEW Research Center (2012, December). *The global religious landscape.* Retrieved from http://www.pewforum.org/2012/12/18/global-religious-landscape-exec/.

Phipps, K. (2012). Spirituality and strategic leadership: The influence of spiritual beliefs on strategic decision making. *Journal of Business Ethics, 106,* 177–189.

Rader, B. G. (1999). *American sports: From the age of folk games to the age of televised sport* (4th ed.). Upper Saddle River, NJ: Prentice Hall.

Ragins, B. R. (2008). Disclosure disconnects: Antecedents and consequences of disclosing invisible stigmas across life domains. *Academy of Management Review, 33,* 194–215.

Schaafsma, J. & Williams, K. D. (2012). Exclusion, intergroup hostility, and religious fundamentalism. *Journal of Experimental Social Psychology, 48,* 829–837.

Shilling, C., & Mellor, P. A. (2014). Re-conceptualizing sport as a sacred phenomenon. *Sociology of Sport Journal, 31,* 349–376.

Spilka, B., Hood, R. W., Jr., Hunsberger, B., & Gorsuch, R. (2003). *The psychology of religion: An empirical approach* (2nd ed.). New York: Guilford.

van Dierendonck, D. (2011). Servant leadership: A review and synthesis. *Journal of Management, 27,* 1228–1261.

Wahl, G. (1999, May). Holy war. *Sports Illustrated.* Retrieved from http://www.si.com.

Walseth, K., & Fasting, K. (2003). Islam's view on physical activity and sport: Egyptian women interpreting Islam. *International Review for the Sociology of Sport, 38,* 45–60.

Weaver, G. R., & Agle, B. R. (2002). Religiosity and ethical behavior in organizations: A symbolic interactionist perspective. *Academy of Management Review, 27,* 77–97.

Weaver, G. R., & Stansbury, J. M. (2014). Religion in organizations: Cognition and behavior. In M. Lounsbury, P. Tracey, & N. Phillips (Eds.), *Research in the sociology of organizations* (vol. 41, pp. 65–110). Bingley, UK: Emerald.

Weeks, M., & Vincent, M. A. (2007). Using religious affiliation to spontaneously categorize others. *The International Journal for the Psychology of Religion, 17,* 317–331.

Whittington, J. L., Pitts, T. M., Kageler, W. V., & Goodwin, V. L. (2005). Legacy leadership: The leadership wisdom of the Apostle Paul. *The Leadership Quarterly, 16,* 749–770.

Sexual Orientation, Gender Identity, and Gender Expression

LEARNING objectives

After studying this chapter, you should be able to:

- Define *sexual orientation, gender identity,* and *gender expression,* and discuss the major historical issues associated with these terms.

- Discuss the experiences of lesbian, gay, bisexual, and transgender persons working in sport organizations and other environments.

- Identify sport participation and physical activity opportunities for lesbian, gay, bisexual, and transgender individuals.

DIVERSITY CHALLENGE

For lesbian, gay, and bisexual athletes, disclosing their sexual orientation to others on the team is a fearful experience. In many cases, the athletes have spent their lives participating in sport and hanging around fields, gyms, and locker rooms where prejudicial language can be heard. They also face many cultural constraints, with some members of society expressing the belief that same-sex attractions are wrong and immoral. Finally, there are relatively few major athletes who have disclosed they are lesbian, gay, or bisexual; thus, role models to guide the disclosure are few in number. Collectively, these factors make the disclosure process a complicated one and contribute to the high number of lesbian, gay, and bisexual athletes who withhold such personal information from their teammates, coaches, and administrators.

Despite the pressures to conceal one's sexual orientation when it is not heterosexual, growing evidence indicates that those who do come out are often met with open arms. Consider, for instance, the case of rugby player Gareth Thomas, now retired. He was captain of the 2005 Wales team, which captured the Grand Slam victory. That same year, he served as captain for the British Lions squad that toured New Zealand. He has more than 100 caps to his name, which makes him the most accomplished Welsh player in history and places him sixth among all Rugby Union players ever, as of 2009. For nearly 20 years, he kept his sexual orientation a secret until, in 2006, he told his coach and two of his teammates. He expected the worst: there were no openly gay rugby players at that time, and a culture of hypermasculinity and heteronormativity permeated the sport. Despite Thomas's trepidation, his teammates and coach reacted to the news with support, acceptance, and comfort.

According to Cyd Zeigler, a manager of Outsports.com, Thomas's story is consistent with the nearly 200 stories he has heard since 1999. Although athletes hear negative language in the locker room prior to their coming out, once they do, their teammates are usually supportive, and the harsh language stops. This was the case, for instance, with Derrick Gordon, who in 2014 became the first NCAA Division I men's basketball player to come out as gay. This is not to suggest that all stories are positive; for example, Brittney Griner encountered a hostile culture of prejudice and discrimination while playing basketball at Baylor. What it does show, though, is that there are many cases where athletes who once hid their sexual orientation are now open about it, and the response has been a welcoming one.

Sources: Brady, E. (2014, April). Athletes who come out as gay find similar reaction. *USA Today.* Retrieved from www.usatoday.com/story/sports/2014/04/10/derrick-gordon-michael-sam-out-gay-athlete-cyd-ziegler/7564657 / Griner, B. (2014). *In my skin: My life on and off the basketball court.* New York: HarperCollins. / Weathers, H. (2009, December). British Lions rugby legend Gareth Thomas: "It's ended my marriage and nearly driven me to suicide. Now it's time to tell the world the truth—I'm gay." *Mail Online.* Retrieved from www.dailymail.co.uk. / Zeigler, C. (2014, July). Lesbian basketball couple alleges homophobia at Univ. of Richmond, inspired to create change in sports. *Outsports.com.* Retrieved from www.outsports.com/2014/7/27/5943145/leah-johnson-miah-register-lesbian-richmond.

CHALLENGE   REFLECTION

1. Unlike Thomas or Gordon, many male athletes who reveal that they are gay do so after their playing careers are over. Why do you think this is the case? Why is it the case for men and not necessarily for women?

2. How would the presence of a gay teammate influence the dynamics on a team, if at all?

3. Why do you think relatively few athletes, as compared with the general population, disclose they are lesbian, gay, or bisexual?

A s a deep-level characteristic and possible source of stigma (Ragins, 2008), the sexual orientation of individuals who are lesbian, gay, or bisexual (LGB) is often not known to others; while not directly observable by others, sexual orientation is nevertheless very important in sport. Sport has been described as a context where heterosexuality is the norm (Sartore & Cunningham, 2009a) and people who deviate from this norm are cast as "others." The Diversity Challenge illustrates this point, noting that Gareth Thomas hid his sexual identity from his coaches and teammates for nearly half his life for fear of negative reactions. Although the cases of Thomas and Gordon show that LGB athletes are increasingly welcomed by their teammates, there is considerable evidence in both the popular and academic press that lesbian, gay, bisexual, and transgender (LGBT) individuals face prejudice; are subjected to discrimination in the workplace and on the playing field; and, in some cases, experience physical abuse.

The purpose of this chapter is to examine the intersection of sexual orientation, gender identity, gender expression, and sport. In doing so, I first define key constructs and then offer a historical overview of the topic. The discussion then turns to sexual prejudice and gender prejudice, including a definition of each term and an overview of antecedents and outcomes of these attitudes. I then focus on the workplace experiences of LGBT individuals and close the chapter by discussing LGBT participation in sport and physical activity.

BACKGROUND

T he purpose of this section is to offer an overview of key terms and their definitions, as well as related demographics and historical background related to the constructs of interest.

Key Terms

Sexual orientation, gender identity, and gender expression are separate constructs, with different meanings. *Sexual orientation* refers to "an enduring pattern of emotional, romantic, and/or sexual attractions to men, women, or both sexes," as well as "a person's sense of identity based on those attractions, related behaviors, and membership in a community of others who share those attractions" (American Psychological Association, 2008, p. 1). Depending on how sexual orientation is measured, LGB individuals comprise between 1 and 21 percent of the population (Savin-Williams, 2006), with most estimates near 10 percent. To put this in perspective, consider that the U.S. population in 2015 was roughly 320 million people; thus, there were about 3.2 million lesbian, gay, or bisexual individuals living in the country at the time. This is more than the proportion of Asians, but less than the proportion of Hispanics. Thus, sexual minorities constitute a sizeable segment of the U.S. population.

Lesbian, gay, and bisexual

What do we mean when we say someone is lesbian, gay, or bisexual? Historically, people viewed sexual orientation as a binary construct: a person was either heterosexual or homosexual. More recently, researchers have categorized people as heterosexual, bisexual, or homosexual (Sell, 1997). Kinsey and his colleagues challenged this assumption decades ago (Kinsey, Pomeroy, & Martin, 1948; Kinsey, Pomeroy, Martin, & Gebhard, 1953). They considered sexual orientation as existing on a continuum from completely heterosexual to completely homosexual, with various gradations between, including bisexuality. In line with this perspective, Savin-Williams and Vrangalova (2013) demonstrated that a small but meaningful proportion of people (between 7.6 and 9.5 percent of women, and 3.6 to 4.1 percent of men) consider themselves mostly heterosexual, expressing a slight amount of same-sex attraction but not enough to consider themselves bisexual. This attraction increases during the teenage years, peaks in a person's early 20s, and then remains stable over time.

Sexual orientation is complex, with dimensions beyond simply the sex of a person's sexual partners, and includes self-image, fantasies, attractions, and behaviors (Ragins & Wiethoff, 2005). These elements can interact in seemingly contradictory ways (Savin-Williams, 2014). A person can, for example, be attracted to and have fantasies about both women and men, yet exhibit exclusively heterosexual behavior. Contradictions such as this make it difficult to obtain precise estimates of the number of persons who are LGB. The malleability of one's sexuality also makes it difficult to gauge the number of persons who are LGB. Some people do not recognize their LGB identity until late in their lives. Others form relationships with members of the opposite sex after years of having a same-sex partner.

An interesting study from Korchmaros, Powell, and Stevens (2013) illustrates this complexity. They collected data from members of LGBT groups, asking them about their self-identified sexual orientation, their preference of sex partners, and the type of sexual partners they had had recently. They found that for many of the participants (23 percent for men, 41 percent for women), their stated sexual orientation did not match their preference in sexual partners. For example, a woman might identify as bisexual but prefer only women as sexual partners. In other cases,

ALTERNATIVE perspectives

Determining Sexual Orientation Through Implicit Tests.
Most assessments of a person's sexual orientation are accomplished through direct measures. For instance, researchers will often employ a paper-and-pencil questionnaire that requests the study participants to indicate their sexual orientation. However, there are other ways of assessing people's sexual orientation—or at least the degree to which they prefer same-sex partners. One tool is the Implicit Association Task (IAT). In this technique, a computer times how quickly people associate pictures with various terms. For instance, compared to a heterosexual man, a gay man might more quickly associate the word *attractive* with a picture of an attractive man. The opposite would also hold, so that a heterosexual man would more quickly identify an attractive woman as "desirable" than would a gay man. Through several iterations of this process, researchers can determine a person's preference for men or women. Snowden, Wichter, and Gray (2008) did precisely this in their study of 50 heterosexual men and 25 gay men. In fact, the IAT scores correctly predicted the participants' self-identified sexual orientation 96 percent of the time.

the predominant classification schemes proved to be inadequate: some people identified as other than heterosexual, lesbian, gay, or bisexual (e.g., they preferred the term *queer*), while some did not have a preference in sexual partners because they did not have sex.

Anderson's (2008) study of collegiate cheerleaders highlights these complexities. Despite the fact that all of the men in this study self-identified as heterosexual and indicated that they were attracted to women, many of the men (40 percent) also engaged in sexual encounters with other men. They challenged the "one-time rule," which holds that a one-time same-sex experience is enough to categorize a person as gay; instead, the cheerleaders in this study constructed the same-sex encounters as either (1) means to an end (i.e., the encounter led to further intimate contact with women) or (2) a form of sexual recreation. In neither case did the same-sex interactions serve to challenge the respondents' self-identity as heterosexual or to reduce their attraction to women. Thus, consistent with critiques of a concept of sexual orientation that depends solely on sexual experiences, Anderson observed that sexual orientation is a complex, multidimensional, and sometimes seemingly contradictory construct. For additional discussion of determining sexual orientation, see the Alternative Perspectives box.

Transgender

It is also important to consider constructs and definitions pertaining to transgender persons. Beemyn and Rankin (2011) define *gender identity* as "an individual's sense of hir own gender, which may be different from one's birth gender or how others perceive one's gender" (p. 20). (Note the authors' use of *hir* as a gender-neutral pronoun that can be used in place of *her* or *him*. The words *ze* and *sie* have both been suggested as gender-neutral replacements for *she* and *he*.)

Gender identity refers to the gender with which an individual identifies. In some cases, a person's gender identity might be congruent with the sex assigned at birth (i.e., the decision that a doctor makes at a baby's birth, based on the external genitalia); in other cases, the gender identity and sex might differ. Related to gender identity is *gender expression,* a construct Beemyn and Rankin (2011) define as "how one chooses to indicate one's gender identity to others through behavior and appearance, which includes clothing, hairstyle, makeup, voice, and body characteristics" (p. 21). The way people express their gender can change over time and can vary based on context. For example, a cross-dresser might present as a woman in most situations but not in others.

These terms inform the discussion of transgender, intersex, and cisgender individuals. According to Carroll (2014), *transgender* "describes an individual whose gender identity (one's psychological identification as a boy/man or girl/woman) does not match the person's sex at birth" (p. 368). For instance, Kye Allums, who played on the women's basketball team at George Washington University, was born with a female body. In 2010, Allums announced that his gender identity was that of a man and he preferred to be known as a male player, thus becoming the first transgender athlete to compete at NCAA athletics (Steinmetz, 2014). Allums' sex assigned at birth was that of a female, but his gender identity and gender expression were both that of a man. Gates (2011) estimates there are about 700,000 transgender persons in the United States.

Transgender individuals should not be confused with people who have intersex conditions. People with intersex conditions have "atypical combinations of chromosomes, hormones, genitalia, and other physical features" (Buzuvis, 2011, p. 11). Most people with intersex conditions identify as either male or female and do not experience ambiguity about their gender identity. In fact, most people who have an intersex condition are not aware of it unless they learn about it during a medical procedure (Carroll, 2014).

Cisgender refers to persons "whose gender assigned at birth has always coincided with their identity/expression" (Beemyn & Rankin, 2011, pp. 197–198). The term *cis* has a Latin origin, meaning "the same side as." Thus, a person who is assigned a female sex at birth, who identifies as a woman, and whose gender expression is also that of a woman would be considered cisgender.

Though I will use the terms *transgender* and *cisgender* throughout the chapter, it is important to note that this terminology is not universally accepted. In Beemyn and Rankin's (2011) comprehensive study, 1,211 persons identified as transgender. These persons also offered *479 unique descriptors* they believed better captured their gender identity and expression. Examples include "genderqueer," "cross-dresser," "bigender," and "two-spirited," among others. Despite these variations, the term *transgender* is commonly used in the popular press, among academic societies, and in academic writing; hence, I follow this practice here.

Demographics

The PEW Research Center conducted a large study of LGBT individuals in the United States (Taylor, 2013). Comparing these data to other sources allows for an analysis of the demographics among LGBT individuals relative to the U.S. population as a whole. In terms of race, the demographics of LGBT individuals in the PEW study generally mirrored those of the larger U.S. population, though slight variations were present. Relative to the U.S. population, there were fewer African Americans who identified as LGBT and more Hispanics who did so (see Exhibit 10.1). Results also indicate that LGBT individuals who took part in the PEW survey were well educated (see Exhibit 10.2). They were more likely than the U.S. population to have completed some college or earned at least a bachelor's degree. Finally, the PEW study identified differences in annual family income (see Exhibit 10.3). LGBT respondents in the study had lower family incomes than the U.S. population. This could be a result of LGBT individuals' being more likely than heterosexuals to live in single-person households.

EXHIBIT **10.1**   Racial demographic characteristics of LGBT Americans.

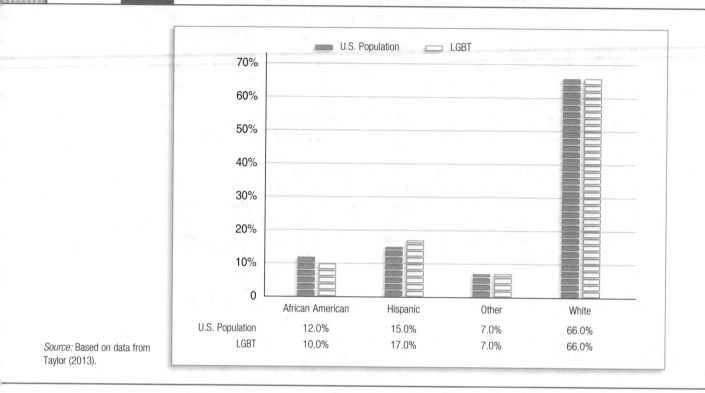

Source: Based on data from Taylor (2013).

EXHIBIT **10.2**   Education demographics of LGBT Americans.

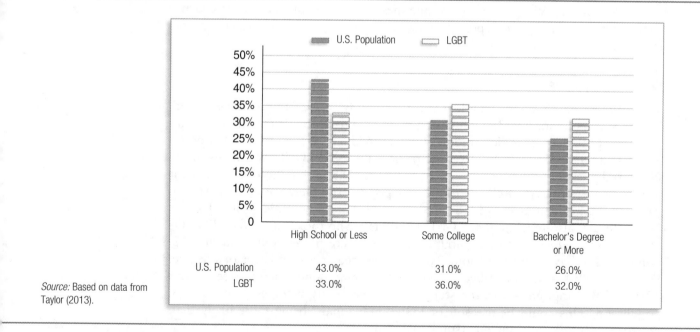

Source: Based on data from Taylor (2013).

Income demographics of LGBT Americans.   EXHIBIT **10.3**

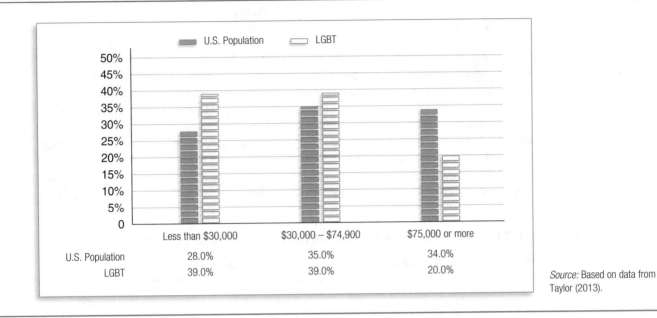

	Less than $30,000	$30,000 – $74,900	$75,000 or more
U.S. Population	28.0%	35.0%	34.0%
LGBT	39.0%	39.0%	20.0%

Source: Based on data from Taylor (2013).

Historical Context

Scientific thinking about sexual orientation has changed over the years, and so too have people's attitudes toward individuals who are LGBT. As recently as 1973, the American Psychiatric Association classified individuals who are LGBT as suffering from a mental illness. That classification has since changed, and subsequent to that time, attitudes toward gender and sexual minorities have improved, as well. Herek (2009) illustrates this point:

■ Since the early 1970s, the General Social Survey has asked whether same-sex sexual relations are "always wrong, almost always wrong, wrong only sometimes, or not wrong at all." From 1973 to 1993, two of three people considered such relations to be "always wrong." Since 1993, that figure has dropped. In 1995, 54 percent of those surveyed considered same-sex sexual relations as "always wrong," and the figures have remained steady since that time.

■ Since 1982, Gallup polls have asked whether homosexuality should be considered an acceptable alternative lifestyle. In 1982, homosexuality was considered unacceptable by 51 percent of respondents, compared with 34 percent who considered it acceptable, and the gap increased to 19 points in 1993 (57 percent to 38 percent). During the 1990s, the trend reversed, and in 2003, 54 percent of those surveyed considered homosexuality as an acceptable lifestyle (43 percent did not). In 2007, the acceptability ratings increased to 57 percent.

■ As a final indicator, the ongoing American National Election Studies have asked people about their feelings toward gay men and lesbians for several decades. They use the Feeling Thermometer, where people's feelings toward a particular group can range from 0 (very cold or unfavorable feelings) to 100 (very warm or favorable feelings). In 1984, the mean rating for feelings toward gays and lesbians (as a collective group) was 30. Feelings have improved since that time, from 39 in 1996 to 49 in 2004. Despite this positive trend, it is worth noting that there was still a sizable proportion of people (15 percent) who gave gays and lesbians a zero.

These figures suggest that attitudes toward homosexuality, persons who are LGBT, and the rights of people who are LGBT have become more positive over time. While this might be the case, gender and sexual minorities do not necessarily believe they experience substantial social acceptance. In a national study of LGBT Americans (Taylor, 2013), fewer than one in five indicated there was considerable social acceptance of LGBT individuals. More common was the belief that there was some support (59 percent of the respondents) or that there was little to no acceptance (21 percent). Also, some professionals in the sport industry question whether attitudes toward LGBT individuals have improved. See the box on the next page.

SEXUAL PREJUDICE AND GENDER PREJUDICE

T he purpose of this section is to review sexual prejudice and gender, its antecedents, and the manner in which it affects the lives and opportunities of LGBT individuals.

Background and Key Terms

Though attitudes related to persons who are LGBT have become more positive, these individuals still experience considerable prejudice and discrimination. Researchers have used various terms to describe this process, including *homophobia, heterosexism, sexual prejudice,* and *gender prejudice. Homophobia* was coined in the 1960s by psychologist George Weinberg to describe the dread that heterosexuals felt toward sexual minorities and the self-loathing that individuals who were LGBT felt toward themselves (Weinberg, 1972). This term focuses on the individual and the irrational fears (hence, the use of "phobia" in the word) she or he has of sexual minorities and their lifestyles.

Heterosexism is different from homophobia in that it focuses more on macro elements of prejudice (Herek, 2000). Specifically, *heterosexism* refers to the cultural system of arrangements that privileges heterosexuality and casts a negative light on individuals who are LGBT and their behaviors, relationships, and communities. Like other "isms," such as racism or sexism, heterosexism is socially constructed over time, specific to a particular society or context, and ingrained into the institutions (e.g., laws, religion, education) within that society.

The third term, *sexual prejudice,* refers to the negative attitudes held toward an individual because of that person's sexual orientation (Herek, 2000). Like other prejudices, sexual prejudice is an attitude, directed toward people who belong (or are perceived to belong) to a social group, and it is negative, such that it encompasses hostility or dislike. Herek notes that this construct is preferred over that of homophobia for several reasons: (1) unlike homophobia, sexual prejudice conveys no *a priori* assumptions about the genesis of the negative attitudes; (2) the construct allows researchers to incorporate the study of anti-gay attitudes into a rich social psychological tradition that studies prejudice; and (3) using the term does not suggest

DIVERSITY   IN THE FIELD

Sexual Prejudice Toward Coaches. Though attitudes toward LGBT individuals have improved over the years, in many ways, sport remains a context where sexual prejudice and heterosexism are very much alive. This is particularly the case for coaches of women's teams (Griffin, 2012; for a discussion of trans prejudice, see Love, 2014). As of 2014, there was only one NCAA Division I women's basketball coach who was publicly out as a lesbian: Portland State's Sherri Murrell. This does not mean that Murrell is the only coach who is lesbian. She indicated that she knows many coaches who have concealed their sexual orientation—so many, in fact, that she thought that was the expected culture in the sport. Reflecting on this trend, Murrell noted, "The world around us is changing, but our profession is still in the Dark Ages."

Cindy Russo, head coach at Florida International, echoed these sentiments, suggesting not much has improved in her 40 years as a head coach. She commented, "There is a fear among parents that if their son or daughter is around a gay person, it is going to make them gay, like it's a contagious disease. . . . There is still so much prejudice and ignorance out there. Male coaches, and some women, will say to parents, 'Do you know so-and-so's gay?' It just takes that to put a little doubt in their minds. And it works." She also indicated that parents and recruits ask her about the presence of gay athletes and coaches: "I've had the question asked many times, how I feel about gay players on the team, or if I have any gay players on my team. I tell them, 'Honestly, it's not something I talk about. I can tell you if there are gay people on my team, they are respectable and have high integrity, and to me, that's all that matters.' I'm to an age where you just get tired of it."

The lack of out coaches negatively affects others. Murrell notes that other coaches in the profession will call her, expressing the desire to disclose their lesbian identity but remaining fearful for their careers. It also affects women's retention in the field; the culture for players and athletes who are lesbian, as well as for others who support LGBT equality; and the psychological well-being of current coaches. In addition, the culture of heterosexism affects the coaches who do get fired because of their sexual orientation, whether at the high school or college level.

Sources: Colloff (2005); Kaufman (2014).

that anti-gay attitudes are irrational or evil, as the term *homophobia* does. Consistent with this perspective, throughout the chapter I use the term *sexual prejudice* to refer to a negative attitude toward individuals who are LGBT and their behaviors or communities, and I use the term *heterosexism* to refer to the larger, societal system that privileges heterosexuals and casts sexual minorities as second-class citizens.

Finally, *gender prejudice* reflects the negative attitudes and emotional reactions toward transgender individuals (Savin-Williams, Pardo, et al., 2010). The reactions include fear, disgust, angst, and distress. *Gender prejudice* is now more commonly used than its predecessor, *transphobia*, for many of the same reasons *sexual prejudice* is preferred over *homophobia*. *Gender prejudice* echoes the systemic, cultural expectations for gender binaries and the penalties associated with nonconforming individuals.

The discussion now turns to the prevalence of sexual prejudice and the motivation for negative behaviors and attitudes.

Gender and Sexual Stigma

Prejudice against LGBT individuals is grounded in stigma (Herek 2007, 2009; Herek & McLemore, 2013). As you will recall from discussions in Chapter 2, *stigma* refers to "an attribute that produces a social identity that is devalued or derogated by persons within a particular culture at a particular point in time" (Paetzold, Dipboye, & Elsbach,

2008, p. 186). The devalued status is socially constructed, and there is a shared understanding of its presence among people in a given context or culture. The differential status of stigmatized people reflects the power relations in a particular setting, such that, relative to their counterparts, stigmatized people have less access to resources, are not as influential, and exercise less autonomy in their lives (see also Goffman, 1963).

In the context of the current discussion, we can draw from Herek's work to think of *gender and sexual stigma* as the devalued status that LGBT individuals, LGBT-related behaviors, and LGBT communities hold. This stigma creates roles, expectations, and shared understandings for people within a given society or context. Gender and sexual stigma also serves to cast LGBT individuals as "other," to limit their power and opportunities, and to privilege heterosexuals and cisgender individuals. Gender and sexual stigma is produced and reproduced at the structural and individual levels. These are described in the following sections.

Structural stigma

Structural stigma operates at the institutional level. The term refers to the systems, structures, and organizational practices in place that reinforce the stigmatized status of LGBT individuals. Structural stigma works through several mechanisms (Herek, 2007). First, systems, structures, and practices promote heterosexuality and cisgender status as the assumption or the standard, and as a result LGBT individuals and their experiences become invisible. Second, and related to the first point, when LGBT individuals do become visible, they take on the status of "other" and may be seen as problematic. Transgender and LGB individuals "are presumed to be abnormal and unnatural and, therefore, are regarded as inferior, as requiring explanation, and as appropriate targets for hostility, differential treatment and discrimination, and even aggression" (Herek, 2007, pp. 907–908).

Structural stigma is largely created and reinforced through the rules, laws, and customs present in a given society (see the box on the facing page for a discussion of employment protections for LGBT persons). One excellent example of this within the sport setting is the rules in place governing participation by transgender athletes (Buzuvis, 2012; Carroll, 2014; Krane, Barak, & Mann, 2012; Love, 2014; Travers & Deri, 2011). The policies are designed to regulate who can and cannot participate in different sport settings. At the most restrictive end is the policy adopted by the International Olympic Committee, whereby transgender athletes can participate only if (1) they have transitioned via sex reassignment surgery, (2) they have undergone hormone treatment for at least two years, and (3) they have legal papers documenting their transitioned sex. The policy is restrictive on a number of grounds. First, there is no medical evidence that sex reassignment (or lack thereof) affects performance in any meaningful way. Second, the focus on hormones (testosterone) reinforces the notion that men are automatically superior athletes to women; as we discussed in Chapter 5, the empirical evidence does not support this belief. Finally, the invasiveness, expenses, and time required for the procedures place an undue burden on athletes whose sporting careers are already time-limited. This is especially the case when other organizations, such as high school athletic associations, adopt the IOC standard. Such a policy decision essentially makes sport participation impossible for teenage transgender athletes.

The NCAA offers a more inclusive policy than the IOC's. This entity allows a transgender athlete who identifies as a woman to participate on women's teams if she

Employment protections for LGBT individuals

Structural stigma reinforces the devaluation and othering of LGBT individuals in various contexts, and the work environment is no exception. While most minorities in the United States receive federal employment protections, LGBT employees do not. As of 2015, Executive Order 11246 prohibits discrimination against LGBT employees among federal contractors, but there are no federal laws barring discrimination against persons based on their sexual orientation or gender identity. This is also the norm at the state level, as most states (29) lack employment protections for LGBT individuals. In these settings, it is legal to deny persons access to a position or to terminate their employment based on their LGBT status.

According to the Human Rights Campaign (n.d.), there are exceptions. Twenty-one states and the District of Columbia prohibit discrimination based on sexual orientation, and 18 states and the District of Columbia have similar prohibitions regarding gender identity. In addition, hundreds of companies have joined the Business Coalition for Workplace Fairness, a group that is committed to ensuring inclusiveness in their work environments and who advocate for LGBT employment protections at the federal level. Examples include Citigroup, Dow Chemical, Apple, Johnson & Johnson, Microsoft, Nike, and Google, among many others.

has undergone at least one year of hormone treatments designed to nullify any effects of added testosterone in the body. Notably absent from the NCAA's policy is the requirement for sex reassignment surgery or legal documents outlining the transition. The NCAA policy also allows for a transgender athlete who identifies as a man to continue participating on women's teams. He can do so until he starts hormone treatments. Although it is more inclusive than the IOC's, the NCAA's policy is restrictive in that it prohibits participation on women's teams by those transgender women who have yet to begin hormone treatments. The presumption is that forbidding such participation levels the playing field. However, even the NCAA acknowledges the logical inconsistencies: "A male-to-female transgender woman may be small and slight, even if she is not on hormone blockers or taking estrogen. . . . The assumption that all male-bodied people are taller, stronger, and more highly skilled in a sport than all female-bodied people is not accurate" (National Collegiate Athletic Association, 2011, p. 7).

Finally, some sport organizations adopt what Buzuvis considers inclusive policies. One example comes from the Washington Interscholastic Athletic Association, which allows high school students to take part in sports in a manner that is consistent with the athletes' gender identity. This policy does not require medical treatment or any legal documents. When questions arise about the legitimacy of the gender identity claim, an eligibility committee can hear the case to make a determination. The focus of this policy, and others like it (e.g., the policy in Massachusetts), is on the athletes' gender identity, which is a reasonable approach considering that the athletes themselves are the best judges of their own gender identity.

As these examples illustrate, policies and guidelines regulating transgender athletes' participation serve to reinforce stigmas. The restrictive nature of some policies reinforces stereotypes and promotes ideas that are unsubstantiated by empirical evidence. Restrictive policies are usually found in contexts promoting high levels of elite competition or in politically conservative regions, and the policies ultimately serve to limit participation. On the other hand, more inclusive policies put participation at the fore, promote the idea that transgender athletes should be fully engaged in the sport enterprise, and are found in more progressive regions and among athletic associations that seek to encourage full participation.

Individual-level stigma

Gender and sexual stigma is also promoted through three manifestations of stigma toward individuals. The first, *enacted stigma* (Herek, 2007, Herek & McLemore, 2013), refers to behavioral expressions of stigma. These include the use of derogatory comments, bullying, ostracizing LGBT individuals, and other forms of discrimination. We know, for instance, that LGBT people are more likely than their peers to face various forms of discrimination and abuse (Bradford, Reisner, Honnold, & Xavier, 2013; Katz-Wise & Hyde, 2012), and this is true in the sport context (Griffin, 1998, 2014; Lucas-Carr & Krane, 2011, 2012).

Stigma is also manifested at the individual level through *felt stigma,* which reflects LGBT individuals' knowledge that stigma exists and includes the steps they take to avoid it. In some cases, this occurs through the modification of behaviors, such as when female athletes or coaches try to accentuate their femininity (e.g., extra makeup, bows in hair, high heels) as a way of offsetting the assumption that they might be lesbian or bisexual. The fear among male athletes of being thought gay and the subsequent actions they take to mitigate such beliefs comprise what McCormack and Anderson (2014) refer to as *homohysteria.*

Finally, *internalized stigma* refers to the acceptance of gender and sexual stigma as part of a person's own value system. For heterosexuals and cisgender individuals, this takes the form of gender and sexual prejudice (see Melton, 2013; Sartore-Baldwin, 2013). A number of personal characteristics are associated with this form of internalized stigma, and these are listed in Exhibit 10.4. Internalized stigma can

---

EXHIBIT 10.4   Personal characteristics predictive of sexual prejudice.

Sexual prejudice can be predicted by people's personal characteristics. According to Herek (2009), persons who exhibit high levels of sexual prejudice are likely to:

- be male
- be older
- have limited formal education
- reside in the Midwest or southern portions of the United States
- hold fundamentalist religious beliefs
- be a Republican
- demonstrate high levels of psychological authoritarianism
- not be sexually permissive
- hold traditional gender role attitudes
- view sexual orientation as a free choice
- have few or no friends who are LGBT

also manifest among LGBT individuals, at which point it takes the form of *self-stigma*. When this occurs, individuals from gender or sexual minorities develop negative feelings about themselves because of their stigmatized status. Internalized stigma has negative health effects for all people. Among LGBT individuals, internalized stigma negatively affects self-esteem, positive affect, and physical health, while it increases the occurrence of depressive symptoms and state anxiety (Denton, Rostosky, & Danner, 2014; Herek, Gillis, & Cogan, 2009). Evidence also suggests that expressing prejudice toward LGBT individuals can be harmful to a person's health—a point explored in the Alternative Perspectives box.

SEXUAL ORIENTATION, GENDER IDENTITY, AND WORK

P eople's sexual orientation and gender identity have the potential to intersect with the way they experience work. The structural stigma that is pervasive across the sport industry means that, for heterosexuals and cisgender individuals,

ALTERNATIVE perspectives

Prejudice Is Bad for Your Health. Most of the work on the effects of internalized stigma focuses on how it negatively affects LGBT individuals. There is also evidence, though, that people who express gender and sexual prejudice are adversely impacted. Hatzenbuehler, Bellatorre, and Muennig (2014) collected data from more than 20,000 individuals from across the United States and analyzed how anti-gay attitudes were associated with mortality risks. They found that people who expressed sexual prejudice had a higher mortality risk than did their counterparts who did not, and this resulted in a 2.5-year difference in life expectancy. Expressing such attitudes was also associated with a higher risk of cardiovascular-related causes of death. These results suggest that reducing prejudice helps all people—minority and majority populations.

issues of sexual orientation and gender identity are largely taken for granted. The same is not necessarily the case for members of gender and sexual minorities because their identities potentially influence how they are treated and the way they interact with others. At the same time, sport organizations are increasingly seeing the value of inclusiveness in the sport organization, as inclusive work environments are associated with the attraction of potential customers, employee retention, and high organizational performance. All of these topics are discussed in the following paragraphs.

Work Experiences

LGBT individuals sometimes experience work differently than their heterosexual and cisgender counterparts. This is primarily observed in their access to positions, their pay and benefits, and their career progression opportunities.

Access to positions

Individuals who are thought to be LGBT are often denied access to jobs or positions they seek—a dynamic largely explained by people's expressions of internalized stigma. Research Sartore and I conducted illustrates this point (Sartore & Cunningham, 2009b). In our first study, we observed that former and current athletes' level of sexual prejudice was highly predictive of their unwillingness to play on teams coached by gay men or lesbians (Study 1). We also found that parents' willingness to let their children play on teams coached by gay men or lesbians was largely a function of the parents' sexual prejudice (Study 2). Finally, we asked the parents to provide a rationale for their decisions. Overwhelmingly, the resistance was based on distrust of members of sexual minorities, the perceived immorality of persons who are LGBT, and reliance on gay and lesbian stereotypes. All of these attitudes can contribute to LGBT individuals' being denied access to jobs. Getting to know LGBT persons on a personal level might help offset some of these negative attitudes and behaviors (Cunningham & Melton, 2012, 2013).

Although some parents are openly against letting their children play on teams led by LGBT coaches, others express support. Melton and I interviewed parents to understand better the nature of their support (Cunningham & Melton, 2014b). For some parents, the support was unequivocal, and they saw no reason why LGBT persons would not be well suited to lead sport teams. For about half of the parents, though, the positive attitudes were expressed in what we called *conditional support*. That is, they expressed positive attitudes toward coaches of gender or sexual minorities as long as the coaches did not engage in certain behaviors, such as promoting their sexual orientation. These conditional forms of support promoted outdated stereotypes (e.g., LGBT persons are promiscuous or untrustworthy) and were not expressed toward heterosexual or cisgender coaches. Thus, we argued that although the parents openly expressed support, they actually expressed prejudice in subtle, nuanced ways—something that ultimately negatively affects LGBT coaches' access to positions.

Additional evidence indicates that subtle forms of prejudice and discrimination limit access to jobs. Hebl, Foster, Mannix, and Dovidio (2002) conducted an innovative experimental study where researchers posing as job applicants went into stores at a mall and inquired about employment opportunities. Some of the applicants wore hats that read "Gay and Proud," while other applicants wore hats that read "Texan and Proud." The researchers did not know which hat they were wearing during the study. Consistent with expectations, there were no overt forms of discrimination against the applicants who were supposed to be LGBT (wearing the "Gay and Proud" hats). There was, however, evidence of subtle discrimination: employers were verbally negative, spent less time, and used fewer words when interacting with the "applicants" who wore the "Gay and Proud" hats than with the others.

As another example, colleagues and I (Cunningham, Sartore, & McCullough, 2010) conducted an experiment where participants reviewed one of four application packets for a person who was applying for a personal trainer position at a fitness club. The packets varied by the applicant's gender and the person's supposed sexual orientation. In the supposed sexual minority condition, the applicant was a medalist in the Gay Games, while in the control (heterosexual) condition, the applicant was a medalist in Amateur Athletic competitions. All applicants were highly qualified, as evidenced by degrees in exercise science, certifications, and previous personal training experience. After reviewing the packet, participants were asked to rate the qualifications of the applicant, provide attribution assessments (i.e., the degree to which the person was ethical, moral, and trustworthy), and submit hiring recommendations. All job applicants were viewed as qualified, irrespective of their gender or sexual orientation. However, male raters provided less positive attributions for members of sexual minorities than they did for heterosexuals. Women did not provide differential ratings. The attribution ratings were important because they were reliably related to hiring recommendations. Thus, even though the applicants who were LGBT were qualified, male raters would deny them access to the position because of more subtle biases.

Pay and benefits

In addition to facing access discrimination, employees who are LGBT also face wage discrimination (Pizer, Sears, Mallory, & Hunter, 2012). This research shows that gay men earn between 10 and 32 percent less than their heterosexual male counterparts. Lesbians have earnings on par with other women but earn less than men. Among transgender individuals, many are not employed, and for those who are, they generally earn less than $25,000 annually. In fact, data from a national survey conducted in 2011 show that one in seven transgender individuals earn less than $10,000 annually. This is about two-thirds of the salary a person would earn from full-time employment at minimum wage.

In addition to the wage discrimination they face, persons who are LGBT also are negatively affected in the area of company benefits. Heterosexuals routinely have the option of including their spouses in a benefits package. As a result, their spouses receive medical coverage, dental coverage, life insurance, and other benefits. Heterosexual men also regularly have the option of taking leave when their spouses give birth. These benefits are often taken for granted among heterosexuals, but they are a rarity among employees who are LGBT (although in cases of legal same-sex marriage, it is likely there will be a corresponding increase in the partner benefits afforded to LGBT employees). According to a report from the Human Rights Campaign (Fidas & Cooper, 2014), only 66 percent of all Fortune 500 companies offer domestic partner benefits. This represents an increase from years past, but these figures still mean that roughly 4 of every 10 Fortune 500 companies do not offer any partner benefits. Furthermore, only 34 percent of all Fortune 100 companies provide transgender-inclusive health insurance. When benefits are not included, the transgender employees must cover medical costs associated with sex reassignment, hormone therapies, and other related medical treatments.

Career progression

As might be expected based on the preceding discussion, persons who are LGBT frequently face less positive work experiences and have shorter careers than their heterosexual counterparts. Between 25 and 66 percent of employees who are LGBT experience sexual orientation discrimination at work (see Ragins, 2004; see also Pizer et al., 2012). These figures are probably conservative because few people fully disclose this information at work. In fact, Ragins, Singh, and Cornwell (2007) found that only 26.7 percent of the participants in their study reported full disclosure of their sexual orientation to everyone at work. In another analysis, half of the gay men working in professional sports reported having experienced work negatively because of their sexual orientation (Cavalier, 2011). People who experience discrimination based on their sexual orientation or gender identity have low satisfaction and commitment, are likely to seek employment elsewhere, are unlikely to progress in their career, and experience depressive symptoms (Button, 2001; Law, Martinez, Ruggs, et al., 2011; Smith & Ingram, 2004; Velez & Moradi, 2012).

These effects highlight the importance of supportive coworkers, supervisors, and organizational cultures. When LGBT individuals are supported in the workplace, they are likely to have positive work experiences. The benefits of supportive others even override the potential negative effects of experiencing discrimination (Velez & Moradi, 2012). What's more, supportive policies and colleagues send a positive message to various external constituencies, including customers (Volpone & Avery, 2010). Coworkers and organizational leaders can offer support in many ways. In some cases, this means offering vocal support for inclusiveness (Sartore & Cunningham, 2010). In other cases, leaders and coworkers show support through advocacy efforts, even while personally sacrificing their own well-being for the advancement of workplace equality (Melton & Cunningham, 2014a, 2014b). Speaking to the powerful effects of supportive others, an athletic department employee in one of our studies relayed the following:

> I struggled with accepting the fact I was gay. . . . For several years I basically just convinced myself there was no way I was gay . . . and even if I was, I decided I would never act on it. . . . So I was really scared . . . I'd say terrified to tell [Name of Coworker] I was gay. We had worked together for five years . . . he was my best friend and my roommate. I figured he would want to move out immediately and never be seen with me again. . . . But when I finally told him, he just said it was alright [*sic*], nothing was going to change between us, and then he hugged me. That was huge for me (pauses) . . . just to know people would still love me and I wasn't going to lose all of my friends because I was gay. Him being there for me helped me a lot during that time in my life. . . . He was more okay with me being gay than I was. (Melton & Cunningham, 2014a, p. 29)

Finally, Huffman, Watrous-Rodriguez, and King (2008) offered a number of strategies managers can employ to promote a supportive environment. These are provided in Exhibit 10.5.

EXHIBIT 10.5 Managerial strategies for promoting LGBT inclusiveness.

1. Provide mentoring opportunities.
2. Offer social networking events.
3. Remain cognizant of one's actions toward all employees.
4. Interact with employees from various backgrounds.
5. Offer diversity training for employees and managers.
6. Relay the LGBT-inclusive standards of the organization to job applicants.
7. Gather employee input concerning practices that are not supportive.
8. Encourage all significant others (e.g., spouses and same-sex partners) to attend social events.
9. Do not assume the sexual orientation of any employee.
10. Schedule meetings with LGBT support group or listserv members and leaders.
11. Become acquainted with LGBT organizations that monitor sexual prejudice and discrimination in the workplace.
12. Allow time off for all persons the employee considers family.
13. Use inclusive language (e.g., partner rather than spouse) and respond quickly and negatively to sexual prejudice.

Source: Information based on Huffman et al. (2008).

Sexual Orientation Disclosure

As indicated in the previous quote, a key decision for LGBT employees is whether or not to disclose their sexual orientation or gender identity to others in the workplace. As might be expected, this decision, especially within the sport context, can be a life-altering choice. After all, if individuals who are LGBT are treated differently, have limited access to positions, are paid less than what they deserve, and face difficult work environments, then they may not readily wish to disclose such information. Furthermore, because sexual orientation and gender identity are deep-level characteristics, others might not be aware of this potentially stigmatizing characteristic unless they are told (Ragins, 2004, 2008). However, there are advantages to disclosing this information, and sometimes the benefits outweigh the costs. In the following sections, I discuss how people decide whether to disclose their sexual orientation, the antecedents of this decision, and the decision's outcomes.

Passing and revealing

Clair, Beatty, and MacLean (2005) outline various strategies people use to decide whether to *pass* or to reveal their sexual orientation or gender identity. Exhibit 10.6 summarizes the concepts of passing and revealing.

Passing and revealing at work.   EXHIBIT **10.6**

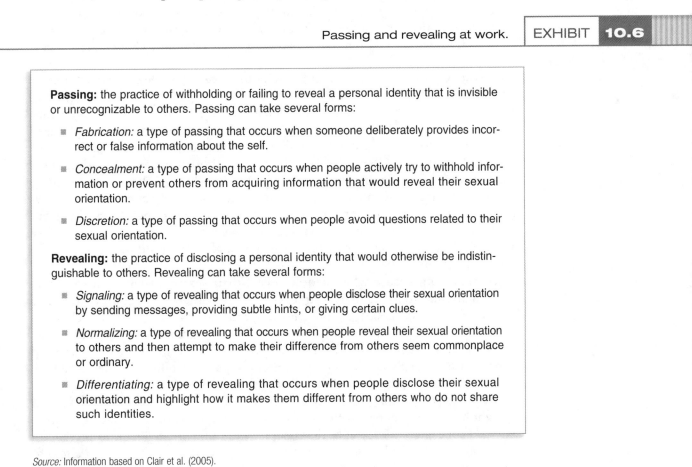

Passing: the practice of withholding or failing to reveal a personal identity that is invisible or unrecognizable to others. Passing can take several forms:

- *Fabrication:* a type of passing that occurs when someone deliberately provides incorrect or false information about the self.

- *Concealment:* a type of passing that occurs when people actively try to withhold information or prevent others from acquiring information that would reveal their sexual orientation.

- *Discretion:* a type of passing that occurs when people avoid questions related to their sexual orientation.

Revealing: the practice of disclosing a personal identity that would otherwise be indistinguishable to others. Revealing can take several forms:

- *Signaling:* a type of revealing that occurs when people disclose their sexual orientation by sending messages, providing subtle hints, or giving certain clues.

- *Normalizing:* a type of revealing that occurs when people reveal their sexual orientation to others and then attempt to make their difference from others seem commonplace or ordinary.

- *Differentiating:* a type of revealing that occurs when people disclose their sexual orientation and highlight how it makes them different from others who do not share such identities.

Source: Information based on Clair et al. (2005).

Passing. *Passing* refers to a "cultural performance whereby one member of a defined social group masquerades as another in order to enjoy the privileges afforded to the dominant group" (Leary, 1999, p. 82). In the context of sexual orientation, this refers to persons who are members of sexual minorities but are passing as heterosexuals. Passing can be done intentionally, by deliberately providing false information, or unintentionally, by allowing a coworker to assume that a lesbian, for example, is heterosexual. Passing involves leading a "double life," so that one persona is adopted in the workplace and another in personal life.

People who are LGBT use three strategies to pass: fabrication, concealment, and discretion (Clair et al., 2005). *Fabrication* occurs when a person deliberately provides incorrect or false information about the self. For example, a coach who is gay might deny that he is gay or, more subtly, bring a woman companion, rather than a man, to an athletic department event. *Concealment* occurs when a person actively withholds information or prevents others from acquiring information that would reveal her or his sexual orientation. An example might be an administrator who is gay and does not display a picture of his partner on his desk, thereby concealing the fact that he has a same-sex partner. Finally, *discretion* occurs when people avoid questions related to their sexual orientation or gender identity. Though related, discretion and concealment differ. People who choose discretion do not hide information about their sexual orientation (as they do with concealment)—they simply sidestep the issue altogether. People who use discretion avoid conversations where their sexual orientation might become a topic or simply change the topic.

Revealing. Clair and colleagues (2005) refer to *revealing* as the choice to "disclose an identity that would otherwise be invisible or unrecognizable to others" (p. 82). Revealing is a general term that is used with a myriad of identities, such as religious affiliation, social class, and so forth. "Coming out" is the term most often used when referring to revealing one's sexual orientation and gender identity.

People who are LGBT use three different methods to reveal: signaling, normalizing, and differentiating (Clair et al., 2005). People who choose the *signaling* method disclose their identity by sending messages, providing subtle hints, or giving certain clues. Sometimes, people use signals that are meaningful to insiders but are innocuous to others, thereby making their identity known only to those they choose. For example, an athlete who is bisexual might put a rainbow sticker on her car's back window.

Normalizing occurs when people reveal their sexual orientation to others and then attempt to make their difference from the others seem commonplace or ordinary (Clair et al., 2005). People who adopt the normalizing method seek to assimilate into the dominant culture and downplay the significance of the difference. For example, a coach who is lesbian might share the everyday difficulties she and her partner have, such as who mows the grass or pays the bills, to underscore how much they have in common with heterosexual couples.

Finally, *differentiating* occurs when people disclose their sexual orientation and highlight how it makes them different from others who do not share such identities. Clair and colleagues (2005) note that people who differentiate "seek to present an identity as equally valid (rather than stigmatized) and many engage in an effort to change the perceptions and behavior of the groups, organizations, and institutions that may stigmatize them" (p. 83). By doing so, people claim a certain identity at work (e.g., a coach who is gay) and redefine the way their identity is understood and viewed by others in the workplace. For example, an athlete who is gay might speak up when his teammates use derogatory terms (e.g., "that is so gay").

Antecedents to passing and revealing

As the preceding discussion illustrates, the decision to disclose personal information related to sexual orientation is complex. Clair and colleagues (2005) outline several factors that influence the decision to pass or reveal.

Context is the first factor (Clair et al., 2005). People are more likely to reveal their sexual orientation or gender identity to others when (1) the work environment is characterized by diversity and inclusion; (2) the norms within the specific industry are supportive of those decisions; and (3) there are legal protections for doing so. Absent such conditions, coaches, administrators, and others are likely to conceal their identity from others. As illustrated in the Diversity Challenge, these dynamics are sometimes observed among coaches: if they do not feel supported in their workplace and they do not see other coaches in the profession disclosing their LGBT identity, then they are unlikely to make such disclosure decisions themselves (see also Krane & Barber, 2005).

Individual differences among people are also likely to influence passing or revealing decisions. These factors include the willingness to take risks, self-monitoring tendencies, stage of adult development, and the presence of other stigmatizing characteristics (Clair et al., 2005). The decision to reveal one's LGBT status is more likely to be observed among people who are willing to take risks, as well as among those who do not regulate their behaviors to fit the social expectations of others around them. Similarly, people in an advanced stage of adult development are self-assured and have high levels of self-esteem—two factors that likely influence their decision to reveal their gender and sexual identity to others. Finally, people who are not stigmatized in other ways might be more likely to reveal, whereas the presence of other stigmatizing characteristics might make revealing an unappealing option. For example, women already face a gender bias in many organizational settings; hence, revealing one's lesbian identity would only amplify the bias.

Passing and revealing outcomes

Several studies have examined the outcomes associated with passing or revealing (Corrigan, Kosyluk, & Rüsch, 2013). Generally, passing might be expected to achieve more positive outcomes. After all, people choose to pass, at least in part, because they fear that they may be subjected to verbal or physical abuse or be stigmatized—all undesirable outcomes. However, research shows that passing is actually associated with more negative outcomes. People who pass are hiding something, and this leads to authenticity issues (Cunningham, in press). They also might be isolated from others because of certain behaviors associated with passing, such as avoiding particular people, situations, or issues. As the Diversity Challenge illustrates, many times, the decision to disclose an LGBT identity will be met with friendliness and acceptance from peers. This is particularly the case in supportive environments (Prati & Pietrantoni, 2014).

ALTERNATIVE perspectives

Negative Outcomes of Revealing at Work? A prevailing notion, which we support in this chapter, is that revealing one's sexual orientation to others is a liberating process and is often associated with positive outcomes. However, Ragins, Singh, and Cornwell (2007) challenge this line of thought. Specifically, they argue that people's fear of disclosure, experienced as the result of past discrimination and prejudice they had encountered, had a debilitating effect on their career and workplace experiences. In their study, persons who were LGB and feared the negative consequences of fully disclosing their sexual orientation had less-positive work attitudes, received fewer promotions, and reported higher levels of stress than their counterparts who did not express such trepidations. These findings led Ragins and her colleagues to conclude: "In contrast to the view of disclosure as a uniformly positive behavior that reflects the final stage of gay identity development . . . this study suggests that concealment may be a necessary and adaptive decision in an unsupportive or hostile environment" (p. 1114).

Those people who reveal at work, however they choose to do so, are often pleased with their choice. Of course, not all situations are pleasant. People can be ostracized or stigmatized because of their LGBT identity (Ragins, 2008; see the Alternative Perspectives box for more discussion). Many times, however, the choice to reveal ultimately eliminates the stress of having to live a "double life." People who disclose their LGBT orientation might also feel more whole because they no longer have to hide an important part of who they are. These results suggest that employees who are openly LGBT benefit from revealing at work because they experience work the same as any other employee might.

Just as with Gareth Thomas in the Diversity Challenge, Sheryl Swoopes' decision to reveal her sexual orientation illustrates this point. Swoopes, a three-time MVP of the WNBA, decided to disclose the fact that she is a lesbian in October 2005. She commented, "I'm just at a point in my life where I'm tired of having to pretend to be somebody I'm not. I'm tired of having to hide my feelings about the person I care about. About the person I love" (Granderson, 2005). Revealing her sexual orientation relieved some of the stress associated with passing and allowed her to be more authentic as a person.

LGBT Diversity as a Source of Advantage

Although many sport organizations remain characterized by prejudice and discrimination directed toward LGBT individuals, an increasing number seek inclusive work environments. For example, in a study of NCAA athletic departments, I found that although 17 percent of the units reported no sexual orientation diversity among the employees, approximately 10 percent indicated that their department was very heterogeneous along this diversity dimension (Cunningham, 2010). Subsequent research I conducted in that same context showed the benefits of having a diverse workforce. Specifically, athletic departments that coupled an LGBT-diverse workforce with an inclusive work environment had more creative work environments (Cunningham, 2011a) and higher performance on objective measures of success (Cunningham, 2011b) than did their more homogeneous peers.

Why do these patterns exist? I suspect Florida's (2003, 2012) creative capital theory (see Chapter 2) holds the answer. This theory suggests that talented, creative people are attracted to certain geographic areas—those marked by high levels of educated people, technological innovation, and diversity. As a result, geographic regions that have these characteristics attract the best and the brightest individuals and then thrive economically. Florida is a geographer, and his work on regional economic development supports these premises. We have adapted this perspective in our own work, with the thinking that people prefer to work in organizations where there are many bright people, where innovation is key, and where diversity and inclusion are the norm. If this is the case, then these organizations should thrive relative to their less attractive peers. And, as the aforementioned examples of NCAA athletic departments show, this is indeed the case.

Building further on this concept, we explored the possibility of whether sport organizations could attract new people (customers and employees) by casting themselves as LGBT-inclusive entities. In our first study, we observed that inclusive organizations were appealing to job searchers, particularly those people who valued justice and equality (Melton & Cunningham, 2012a). In the second study, we found that people believed LGBT-inclusive fitness clubs were also diverse along other diversity dimensions, and these characteristics were appealing to the potential club members. Again, this was especially the case among people who valued social justice and equality (Cunningham & Melton, 2014a). Collectively, this research suggests that sport organizations benefit from LGBT diversity and from advertising their inclusiveness.

SEXUAL ORIENTATION AND SPORT AND PHYSICAL ACTIVITY PARTICIPATION

A person's sexual orientation and gender identity can influence her or his participation in sport and physical activity. Results from large-scale studies in the United States show that sexual minority youth are less likely to engage in physical activity and some formal sports than are heterosexuals (Calzo, Roberts, Corliss, et al., 2014; Rosario, Corliss, Everett, et al., 2014; Zipp, 2011). Several factors influence this trend. First, there are few differences in formal sport participation early in youths' athletic career, but as they move to the high school years, participation by sexual minorities drops. Second, these differences in physical activity patterns from early to later grades are more likely to be observed among boys than they are among girls. The gender effects are consistent across races. Finally, LGBT individuals who have gender nonconforming expressions and low athletic self-esteem are less likely to engage in physical activity and sport than are members of other gender and sexual minorities.

These findings suggest that LGBT persons might not have welcoming, positive experiences in the sport and physical activity context. This has traditionally been the case, and in many ways, it still is (Lucas-Carr & Krane, 2012; Melton & Cunningham, 2012b; Worthen, 2014). That said, there is also evidence showing that LGBT athletes are experiencing increasingly positive team environments. For instance, most lesbian athletes in the northeastern United States who disclose their sexual orientation experience acceptance and support from their teammates, something they largely attribute to the "trailblazers" who came out before them (Fink, Burton, Farrell, & Parker, 2012). Other lesbian athletes report similar experiences, leading Griffin (2012, 2014) to suggest that the sport environment is more accepting for lesbian athletes than it is for lesbian coaches. Similarly, some evidence suggests that men's team sports have more inclusive cultures now than ever before (Anderson, 2009, 2011). This change in the cultures allows heterosexuals to display more inclusive forms of masculine behaviors (e.g., hugging or kissing a friend) and allows gay men to participate openly, without the need to mask or hide their identity. Pro-gay attitudes are observed among elite soccer players (Magrath, Anderson, & Roberts, in press), British sport athletes (Bush, Anderson, & Carr, 2012), and college soccer players in the Midwest (Adams & Anderson, 2012), among other populations.

Finally, we can consider the presence of gay and lesbian sport clubs. Elling, De Knop, and Knoppers (2003) report that an increasing number of persons who are LGBT are choosing to participate in gay and lesbian sport clubs or informal gay sport groups. The LGBT sport teams often compete against mainstream teams in various tournaments or leagues, or alternatively may choose to participate in competitions or tournaments specifically for athletes who are LGBT. Elling and colleagues examined why persons who are LGBT chose to participate in those clubs and what their experiences were when they did so. They learned that many club participants found the culture of mainstream sport clubs to be discriminatory toward LGBT athletes, especially men who are gay. The most important reason, however, for joining the club was that the respondents felt more at ease and believed they were better able to socialize with people like them (i.e., other persons who are LGBT) in those clubs.

chapter SUMMARY

The purpose of this chapter was to explore the influence of sexual orientation, gender identity, and gender expression on people's experiences in the workplace and their sport participation. As evidenced by the Diversity Challenge, attitudes toward these identities can seriously affect a person's well-being. Members of gender and sexual minorities are likely to face prejudice, they have varied work experiences, and they must decide when and whether to disclose their identity to others. From a different perspective, some organizations opt to pursue LGBT consumers and employees actively, with the belief that doing so will better their business. After reading this chapter, you should be able to:

1. **Define *sexual orientation, gender identity,* and *gender expression,* and discuss the major historical issues associated with these terms.**

   Sexual orientation is a multifaceted construct consisting of a person's self-image, fantasies, attractions, and behaviors. *Gender identity* refers to people's sense of their own gender, which could be the same as or different from their sex assigned at birth. *Gender expression* refers to the ways in which people indicate their gender to others through behavior and appearance. Though LGBT individuals were historically believed to suffer from a mental illness, such a perspective is no longer embraced. Finally, polling suggests that attitudes toward sexual minorities have become more positive over time, though some negative attributions still exist.

2. **Discuss the experiences of lesbian, gay, bisexual, and transgender persons working in sport organizations and other environments.**

   LGBT persons regularly face discrimination in the workplace; some estimates suggest that two of every three employees are subjected to gender and sexual prejudice. This prejudice negatively affects their potential to obtain jobs, their pay, and their work experiences. Furthermore, LGBT individuals must decide whether or not to disclose their sexual identity to others in the workplace—an anxiety-producing decision that others do not encounter. Discussions of disclosure focus on the different forms of passing (i.e., fabrication, concealment, and discretion) and revealing (i.e., signaling, normalizing, and differentiating) and the antecedents and outcomes of these choices.

3. **Discuss sport participation and physical activity opportunities for lesbian, gay, bisexual, and transgender individuals.**

   LGBT individuals are less likely to be physically active or to engage in formal sport, relative to their cisgender and heterosexual counterparts. Some evidence indicates that prejudice against LGBT athletes is not as great as it is against LGBT coaches and administrators.

QUESTIONS for discussion

1. Various ways of conceptualizing sexual orientation were presented in the chapter. With which approach do you most closely identify and why?

2. Many authors suggest that gender prejudice and sexual prejudice are prevalent in the sport context. Has this been your experience? Provide some examples.

3. Research suggests that attitudes toward men who are gay are more negative than attitudes toward lesbians. Why do you think this is the case?

4. Sexual orientation and gender identity disclosure in the workplace is potentially one of the most anxiety-producing decisions an individual who is LGBT can make. Do you think the same is true for persons who disclose other invisible diversity forms? Why or why not?

5. What are some of the outcomes, both positive and negative, that can be predicted for an organization seeking to target customers who are LGBT?

learning ACTIVITIES

1. Visit the Outsports site (www.outsports.com) and research the stories told by athletes who have disclosed their sexual orientation; also, research the activities of allies, or persons who offer support and look to create a welcoming environment for LGBT persons.

2. Although some sport organizations see tremendous value in actively recruiting employees and consumers who are LGBT, others are hesitant to adopt such an approach. As a class, divide into two groups and debate the issue.

WEB resources

European Gay and Lesbian Sport Federation, www.eglsf.info/eglsf-about.php

Organization devoted to supporting LGB sport communities and athletes, as well as fighting discrimination.

OutSports, www.outsports.com

Site devoted to providing the most comprehensive information related to the gay sport community.

The Williams Institute, www.law.ucla.edu/williamsinstitute/home.html

A center at the UCLA School of Law dedicated to advancing the field of sexual orientation law and public policy.

reading RESOURCES

Cunningham, G. B. (Ed.) (2012). *Sexual orientation and gender identity in sport: Essays from activists, coaches, and scholars.* College Station, TX: Center for Sport Management Research and Education.

An edited book with contributions from coaches, social activists, and scholars who all focus on gender identity and sexual orientation in sport.

Hargreaves, J., & Anderson, E. (Eds.) (2014). *Routledge handbook of sport, gender and sexuality.* New York: Routledge.

A comprehensive handbook with chapters from authors around the world; offers an overview of pertinent issues related to sex, gender, and sexuality.

Sartore-Baldwin, M. L. (Ed.) (2013). *Sexual minorities in sports: Prejudice at play.* Boulder, CO: Lynne Rienner Publishers.

Edited book with contributions from some of the leading scholars in the field; focuses on prejudice expressed toward LGBT individuals and ways to reduce those occurrences.

REFERENCES

Adams, A., & Anderson, E. (2012). Exploring the relationship between homosexuality and sport among the teammates of a small, Midwestern Catholic college soccer team. *Sport, Education and Society, 17,* 347–363.

American Psychological Association (2008). *Answers to your questions: For a better understanding of sexual orientation and homosexuality.* Washington, DC: Author.

Anderson, E. (2008). "Being masculine is not about who you sleep with. . . ." Heterosexual athletes contesting masculinity and the one-time rule of homosexuality. *Sex Roles, 58,* 104–115.

Anderson, E. (2009). *Inclusive masculinity: The changing nature of masculinities.* New York: Routledge.

Anderson, E. (2011). Masculinities and sexualities in sport and physical cultures: Three decades of evolving research. *Journal of Homosexuality, 58,* 565–578.

Beemyn, G., & Rankin, S. (2011). *The lives of transgender people.* New York: Columbia University Press.

Bradford, J., Reisner, S. L., Honnold, J. A., & Xavier, J. (2013). Experiences of transgender-related discrimination and implications for health: Results from the Virginia Transgender Health Initiative Study. *American Journal of Public Health, 103,* 1820–1829.

Bush, A., Anderson, E., & Carr, S. (2012). The declining existence of men's homophobia in British sport. *Journal for the Study of Sports and Athletes in Education, 6,* 107–120.

Button, S. B. (2001). Organizational efforts to affirm sexual diversity: A cross-level examination. *Journal of Applied Psychology, 86,* 17–28.

Buzuvis, E. E. (2011). Transgender student-athletes and sex-segregated sport: Developing policies of inclusion for intercollegiate and interscholastic athletics. *Seton Hall Journal of Sports and Entertainment Law, 21,* 1–59.

Buzuvis, E. E. (2012). Including transgender athletes in sex-segregated sport. In G. B. Cunningham (Ed.), *Sexual orientation and gender identity in sport: Essays from activists, coaches, and scholars* (pp. 23–34). College Station, TX: Center for Sport Management Research and Education.

Calzo, J. P., Roberts, A. L., Corliss, H. L., Blood, E. A., Kroshus, E., & Austin, S. B. (2014). Physical activity disparities in heterosexual and sexual minority youth ages 12–22 years old: Roles of childhood gender non-conformity and athletic self-esteem. *Annals of Behavioral Medicine, 47,* 17–27.

Carroll, H. J. (2014). Joining the team: The inclusion of transgender students in United States school-based athletics. In J. Hargreaves & E. Anderson (Eds.), *Routledge handbook of sport, gender and sexuality* (pp. 367–375). New York: Routledge.

Cavalier, E. S. (2011). Men at work: Gay men's experiences in the sport workplace. *Journal of Homosexuality, 58,* 626–646.

Clair, J. A., Beatty, J. E., & MacLean, T. L. (2005). Out of sight but not out of mind: Managing invisible social identities in the workplace. *Academy of Management Review, 30,* 78–95.

Colloff, P. (2005, July). She's here. She's queer. She's fired. *Texas Monthly, 33*(7), 52–61.

Corrigan, P. W., Kosyluk, K. A., & Rüsch, N. (2013). Reducing self-stigma by coming out proud. *American Journal of Public Health, 103,* 794–800.

Cunningham, G. B. (2010). Predictors of sexual orientation diversity in intercollegiate athletics. *Journal of Intercollegiate Sport, 3,* 256–269.

Cunningham, G. B. (2011a). Creative work environments in sport organizations: The influence of sexual orientation diversity and commitment to diversity. *Journal of Homosexuality, 58,* 1041–1057.

Cunningham, G. B. (2011b). The LGBT advantage: Examining the relationship among sexual orientation diversity, diversity strategy, and performance. *Sport Management Review, 14,* 453–461.

Cunningham, G. B. (in press). Creating and sustaining workplace cultures supportive of LGBT employees in college athletics. *Journal of Sport Management.*

Cunningham, G. B., & Melton, N. (2012). Prejudice against lesbian, gay, and bisexual coaches: The influence of race, religious fundamentalism, modern sexism, and contact with sexual minorities. *Sociology of Sport Journal, 29,* 283–305.

Cunningham, G. B., & Melton, E. N. (2013). The moderating effects of contact with lesbian and gay friends on the relationships among religious fundamentalism, sexism, and sexual prejudice. *Journal of Sex Research, 50,* 401–408.

Cunningham, G. B., & Melton, E. N. (2014a). Signals and cues: LGBT inclusive advertising and consumer attraction. *Sport Marketing Quarterly, 23,* 37–46.

Cunningham, G. B., & Melton, E. N. (2014b). Varying degrees of support: Understanding parents' positive attitudes toward LGBT coaches. *Journal of Sport Management, 28,* 387–398.

Cunningham, G. B., Sartore, M. L., & McCullough, B. P. (2010). The influence of applicant sexual orientation and rater sex on ascribed attributions and hiring recommendations of personal trainers. *Journal of Sport Management, 24,* 400–415.

Denton, F. N., Rostosky, S. S., & Danner, F. (2014). Stigma-related stressors, coping self-efficacy, and physical health in lesbian, gay, and bisexual individuals. *Journal of Counseling Psychology, 61,* 383–391.

Elling, A., De Knop, P., & Knoppers, A. (2003). Gay/lesbian sport clubs and events: Places of homo-social bonding and cultural resistance? *International Review for the Sociology of Sport, 38,* 441–456.

Fidas, D., & Cooper, L. (2014). *Corporate equality index 2015: Rating American workplaces on lesbian, gay, bisexual and transgender equality.* Washington, DC: Human Rights Campaign.

Fink, J. S., Burton, L. J., Farrell, A., & Parker, H. (2012). Playing it out: Female intercollegiate athletes' experiences in revealing their sexual identities. *Journal for the Study of Sport and Athletes in Education, 6,* 83–106.

Florida, R. (2003). Cities and the creative class. *City & Community, 2,* 3–19.

Florida, R. (2012). *The rise of the creative class, revisited.* New York: Basic Books.

Gates, G. J. (2011). *How many people are lesbian, gay, bisexual, and transgender?* Los Angeles: Williams Institute, University of California, Los Angeles School of Law.

Goffman, E. (1963). *Stigma: Notes on the management of spoiled identity.* New York: Simon & Schuster.

Granderson, L. Z. (2005, October). *Three-time MVP "tired of having to hide my feelings."* ESPN.com. Retrieved from http://sports.espn.go.com/wnba/news/story?id=2203853.

Griffin, P. (1998). *Strong women, deep closets: Lesbians and homophobia in sport.* Champaign, IL: Human Kinetics.

Griffin, P. (2012). LGBT equality in sports: Celebrating our successes and facing our challenges. In G. B. Cunningham (Ed.), *Sexual orientation and gender identity in sport: Essays from activists, coaches, and scholars* (pp. 1–12). College Station, TX: Center for Sport Management Research and Education.

Griffin, P. (2014). Overcoming sexism and homophobia in women's sports: Two steps forward and one step back. In J. Hargreaves & E. Anderson (Eds.), *Routledge handbook of sport, gender and sexuality* (pp. 265–274). New York: Routledge.

Hatzenbuehler, M. L., Bellatorre, A., & Muennig, P. (2014). Anti-gay prejudice and all-cause mortality among heterosexuals in the United States. *American Journal of Public Health, 104,* 332–337.

Hebl, M. R., Foster, J. B., Mannix, L. M., & Dovidio, J. F. (2002). Formal and interpersonal discrimination: A field study of bias toward homosexual applicants. *Personality and Social Psychology Bulletin, 28,* 815–825.

Herek, G. M. (2000). The psychology of sexual prejudice. *Current Directions in Psychological Science, 9,* 19–22.

Herek, G. M. (2007). Confronting sexual stigma and prejudice: Theory and practice. *Journal of Social Issues, 63,* 905–923.

Herek, G. M. (2009). Sexual stigma and sexual prejudice in the United States: A conceptual framework. In D. A. Hope (Ed.), *Contemporary perspectives on lesbian, gay, and bisexual identities* (pp. 65–111). New York: Springer.

Herek, G. M., Gillis, J. R., & Cogan, J. C. (2009). Internalized stigma among sexual minority adults: Insights from a social psychology perspective. *Journal of Counseling Psychology, 56,* 32–43.

Herek, G. M., & McLemore, K. A. (2013). Sexual prejudice. *Annual Review of Psychology, 64,* 309–333.

Huffman, A. H., Watrous-Rodriguez, K. M., & King, E. B. (2008). Supporting a diverse workforce: What type of support is most meaningful for lesbian and gay employees? *Human Resource Management, 47,* 237–253.

Human Rights Campaign (n.d.). Workplace discrimination laws and policies. Retrieved from http://hrc.org/resources/entry/Workplace-Discrimination-Policies-Laws-and-Legislation

Katz-Wise, S. L., & Hyde, J. S. (2012). Victimization experiences of lesbian, gay, and bisexual individuals: A meta-analysis. *Journal of Sex Research, 49,* 142–167.

Kaufman, M. (2014, November). Prejudice against gays and lesbians hurts women's basketball. *Miami Herald.* Retrieved from http://www.miamiherald.com/sports/college/article4071422.html.

Kinsey, A. C., Pomeroy, W. B., & Martin, C. E. (1948). *Sexual behavior in the human male.* Philadelphia: W. B. Saunders.

Kinsey, A. C., Pomeroy, W. B., Martin, C. E., & Gebhard, P. H. (1953). *Sexual behavior in the human female.* Philadelphia: W. B. Saunders.

Korchmaros, J. D., Powell, C., & Stevens, S. (2013). Chasing sexual orientation: A comparison of commonly used single-indicator measures of sexual orientation. *Journal of Homosexuality, 60,* 596–614.

Krane, V., Barak, K. S., & Mann, M. E. (2012). Broken binaries and transgender athletes: Challenging sex and gender in sports. In G. B. Cunningham (Ed.), *Sexual orientation and gender identity in sport: Essays from activists, coaches, and scholars* (pp. 13–22). College Station, TX: Center for Sport Management Research and Education.

Krane, V., & Barber, H. (2005). Identity tensions in lesbian intercollegiate coaches. *Research Quarterly for Exercise and Sport, 76,* 67–81.

Law, C. L., Martinez, L. R., Ruggs, E. N., Hebl, M. R., & Akers, E. (2011). Trans-parency in the workplace: How the experiences of transsexual employees can be improved. *Journal of Vocational Behavior, 79,* 710–723.

Leary, K. (1999). Passing, posing, and "keeping it real." *Constellations, 6,* 85–96.

Love, A. (2014). Transgender exclusion and inclusion in sport. In J. Hargreaves & E. Anderson (Eds.), *Routledge handbook of sport, gender and sexuality* (pp. 376–383). New York: Routledge.

Lucas-Carr, C. B., & Krane, V. (2011). What is the T in LGBT? Supporting transgender athletes through sport psychology. *Sport Psychologist, 25,* 532–548.

Lucas-Carr, C. B., & Krane, V. (2012). Troubling sport or troubled by sport: Experiences of transgender athletes. *Journal for the Study of Sports and Athletes in Education, 6,* 21–44.

Magrath, R., Anderson, E., & Roberts, S. (in press). On the door-step of equality: Attitudes toward gay athletes among academy-level footballers. *International Review for the Sociology of Sport.*

McCormack, M., & Anderson, E. (2014). The influence of declining homophobia on men's gender in the United States: An argument for the study of homohysteria. *Sex Roles, 71,* 109–120.

Melton, E. N. (2013). Women and the lesbian stigma. In M. L. Sartore-Baldwin (Ed.), *Sexual minorities in sports: Prejudice at play* (pp. 11–29). Boulder, CO: Lynne Rienner Publishers.

Melton, E. N., & Cunningham, G. B. (2012a). The effect of LGBT-inclusive policies on organizational attraction. *International Journal of Sport Management, 13,* 444–462.

Melton, E. N., & Cunningham, G. (2012b). When identities collide: Exploring minority stress and resilience among college athletes with multiple marginalized identities. *Journal for the Study of Sports and Athletes in Education, 6,* 45–66.

Melton, E. N., & Cunningham, G. B. (2014a). Examining the workplace experiences of sport employees who are LGBT: A social categorization theory perspective. *Journal of Sport Management, 28,* 21–33.

Melton, E. N., & Cunningham, G. B. (2014b). Who are the champions? Using a multilevel model to examine perceptions of employee support for LGBT inclusion in sport organizations. *Journal of Sport Management, 28,* 189–206.

National Collegiate Athletic Association (2011). *NCAA inclusion of transgender student-athletes.* Indianapolis, IN: Author.

Paetzold, R. L., Dipboye, R. L., & Elsbach, K. D. (2008). A new look at stigmatization in and of organizations. *Academy of Management Review, 33,* 186–193.

Pizer, J. C., Sears, B., Mallory, C., & Hunter, N. D. (2012). Evidence of persistent and pervasive workplace discrimination against LGBT people: The need for federal legislation prohibiting discrimination and providing for equal employment benefits. *Loyola of Los Angeles Law Review, 45,* 715–779.

Prati, G., & Pietrantoni, L. (2014). Coming out and job satisfaction: A moderated mediation model. *The Career Development Quarterly, 62,* 358–371.

Ragins, B. R. (2004). Sexual orientation in the workplace: The unique work and career experiences of gay, lesbian and bisexual workers. *Research in Personnel and Human Resources Management, 23,* 35–120.

Ragins, B. R. (2008). Disclosure disconnects: Antecedents and consequences of disclosing invisible stigmas across life domains. *Academy of Management Review, 33,* 194–215.

Ragins, B. R., Singh, R., & Cornwell, J. M. (2007). Making the invisible visible: Fear and disclosure of sexual orientation at work. *Journal of Applied Psychology, 4,* 1103–1118.

Ragins, B. R., & Wiethoff, C. (2005). Understanding heterosexism at work: The straight problem. In R. L. Dipboye & A. Colella (Eds.), *Discrimination at work: The psychological and organizational bases* (pp. 177–201). Mahwah, NJ: Lawrence Erlbaum.

Rosario, M., Corliss, H. L., Everett, B. G., Reisner, S. L., Austin, B., Butching, F. O., & Birkett, M. (2014). Sexual orientation disparities in cancer-related risk behaviors of tobacco, alcohol, sexual behaviors, and diet and physical activity. Pooled youth risk behavior surveys. *American Journal of Public Health, 104,* 245–254.

Sartore, M. L., & Cunningham, G. B. (2009a). The effects of the lesbian label in the sport context: Implications for women of all sexual orientations. *Quest, 61,* 289–305.

Sartore, M. L., & Cunningham, G. B. (2009b). Sexual prejudice, participatory decisions, and panoptic control: Implications for sexual minorities in sport. *Sex Roles, 60,* 100–113.

Sartore, M. L., & Cunningham, G. B. (2010). The lesbian label as a component of women's stigmatization in sport organizations: An exploration of two health and kinesiology departments. *Journal of Sport Management, 24,* 481–501.

Sartore-Baldwin, M. L. (2013). Gender, sexuality, and prejudice in sport. In M. L. Sartore-Baldwin (Ed.), *Sexual minorities in sports: Prejudice at play* (pp. 1–10). Boulder, CO: Lynne Rienner Publishers.

Savin-Williams, R. C. (2006). Who's gay? Does it matter? *Current Directions in Psychological Science, 15,* 40–44.

Savin-Williams, R. C. (2014). An exploratory study of the categorical versus spectrum nature of sexual orientation. *Journal of Sex Research, 31,* 446–453.

Savin-Williams, R. C., Pardo, S. T., Vrangalova, Z., Mitchell, R. S., & Cohen, K. M. (2010). Sexual and gender prejudice. In J. C. Chrisler & D. R. McCreary (Eds.), *Handbook of gender research in psychology* (pp. 359–376). New York: Springer.

Savin-Williams, R. C., & Vrangalova, Z. (2013). Mostly heterosexual as a distinct sexual orientation: A systematic review of the empirical evidence. *Developmental Review, 33,* 58–88.

Sell, R. L. (1997). Defining and measuring sexual orientation: A review. *Archives of Sexual Behavior, 26,* 643–658.

Smith, N. G., & Ingram, K. M. (2004). Workplace heterosexism and adjustment among lesbian, gay, and bisexual individuals: The role of unsupportive interactions. *Journal of Counseling Psychology, 51,* 57–67.

Snowden, R. J., Wichter, J., & Gray, N. S. (2008). Implicit and explicit measurements of sexual preference in gay and heterosexual men: A comparison of priming techniques and the Implicit Association Task. *Archives of Sexual Behavior, 37,* 558–565.

Steinmetz, K. (2014, October). Meet the first openly transgender NCAA Division I athlete. *Time.* Retrieved from http://time.com/3537849/meet-the-first-openly-transgender-ncaa-athlete/.

Taylor, P. (2013). A survey of LGBT Americans: Attitudes, experiences and values in changing times. Washington, DC: PEW Research Center.

Travers, A., & Deri, J. (2011). Transgender inclusion and the changing face of lesbian softball leagues. *International Review for the Sociology of Sport, 46,* 488–507.

Velez, B. L., & Moradi, B. (2012). Workplace support, discrimination, and person-organization fit: Tests of the theory of work adjustment with LGB individuals. *Journal of Counseling Psychology, 59,* 399–407.

Volpone, S. D., & Avery, D. R. (2010). I'm confused: How failing to value sexual identities at work sends stakeholders mixed messages. *Industrial and Organizational Psychology, 3,* 90–92.

Weinberg, G. (1972). *Society and the healthy homosexual.* New York: St. Martin's.

Worthen, M. G. (2014). The cultural significance of homophobia on heterosexual women's gendered experiences in the United States: A commentary. *Sex Roles, 71,* 141–151.

Zeigler, C. (2014, July). Lesbian basketball couple alleges homophobia at Univ. of Richmond, inspired to create change in sports. Outsports.com. Retrieved from http://www.outsports.com/2014/7/27/5943145/leah-johnson-miah-register-lesbian-richmond.

Zipp, J. F. (2011). Sport and sexuality: Athletic participation by sexual minority and sexual majority adolescents in the U.S. *Sex Roles, 64,* 19–31.

Social Class

LEARNING objectives

After studying this chapter, you should be able to:

- Define key terms related to social class inclusion and diversity, including *socioeconomic status, social class,* and *classism.*
- Discuss the influence of cognitive, interpersonal, and institutional distancing on the maintenance and promotion of classism.
- Provide an overview of the effects of classism on people's education, health, and well-being, including their sport participation.
- Highlight the manner in which sport involvement results in social mobility.

DIVERSITY CHALLENGE

Participation in high school athletics provides a number of potential benefits, including character development, learning how to work with others, and engaging in cross-cultural experiences. Relative to their less active peers, students who participate in sports perform better academically, have greater confidence, develop more interpersonal connections, exhibit more pro-social behaviors, and develop more desired personality characteristics. These effects are particularly strong among students from disadvantaged backgrounds because their participation in school-sponsored athletics provides them with after-school activities they might not otherwise have.

Despite the many positive outcomes associated with high school athletics, tight state budgets have forced many schools to drop or scale back their sport offerings. According to the *Wall Street Journal,* the proportion of schools planning to cut their extracurricular activities for the 2009–

10 academic year almost tripled over the previous year—from 10 percent to 28 percent. These cuts come in a variety of areas. Some districts, such as those in Dixon, California, have eliminated all of their middle school and high school programs. Across Florida, athletic departments were asked to reduce the number of games on their schedule, sometimes by as much as 40 percent.

Another approach being advanced in a number of school districts is that of pay-to-play, in which students pay a fee to participate in a sport. This is a common practice, as 60 percent of parents indicate they have had to pay for their children to participate in high school athletics. In southwest Ohio, 82 percent of the school districts report having a pay-to-play program. While pay-to-play allows the sports to be offered, the policy negatively affects low-income families. Only 6 percent have received a waiver based on their income level, but close to 20 percent of families earning less than $60,000 annually have had to decrease sport participation because of the fees. Thus, along with the potential cost–saving benefits, pay-to-play programs ultimately privilege the wealthy while cutting out the poor from participation in sport.

Sources: Cook, B. (2012, May). Pay-to-play is squeezing kids out of school sports. *Forbes.* Retrieved from http://www.forbes.com/sites/bobcook/2012/05/15/pay-to-play-is-squeezing-kids-out-of-school-sports. / Linver, M. R., Roth, J. L., & Brooks-Gunn, J. (2009). Patterns of adolescents' participation in organized activities: Are sports best when combined with other activities? *Developmental Psychology, 45,* 354–367. / Sagas, M., & Cunningham, G. B. (2014). *Sport participation rates among underserved American youth.* Gainesville, FL: University of Florida Sport Policy & Research Collaborative.

CHALLENGE REFLECTION

1. Other than those listed in the Diversity Challenge, what options could school administrators pursue to balance their athletic budgets?

2. Why do opponents of pay-to-play programs argue that the participation fees hurt low-income students more than other students? Do you agree with this perspective?

3. Are you aware of other ways in which school financing plans tend to disadvantage low-income students or students in low-income districts?

As the Diversity Challenge illustrates, economic means and social power play significant roles in determining the opportunities people have for sport and physical activity. The effects of social class are not limited to the hard court or playing field. A person's class affects many of the opportunities available in life; class ultimately may influence physical and educational opportunities, jobs held, and psychological health, including perception of one's self. Clearly, then, class is a meaningful diversity form that demands our attention.

Despite the primacy of class in people's lives, it is often neglected in discussions of diversity. Major academic entities, such as the American Psychological Association (APA), continually overlook class in multicultural and diversity-related conferences and publications (Lott, 2002; Lott & Bullock, 2007). Academic publications and course texts often follow suit. For instance, in a review of the leading management and organizational psychology journals, Côté (2011) found only four articles with a focus on social class issues. This pattern is also evident in sport management: my search of abstracts from the annual conference for the North American Society for Sport Management (NASSM) found only 37 presentations—out of more than 2,000 archived—that included the term "social class," "socio-economic," or "socioeconomic status." Even diversity management texts are guilty of this omission, and many of them (e.g., Bell, 2007) do not include even a chapter devoted to the topic. However, large professional organizations and diversity scholars are not alone: the media often either ignore the poor or portray them negatively and as deficient in moral character (McCall, 2014).

I have experienced this trend in my own classes, as well. Early in the semester, I ask students to complete the "Diversity Pie Chart" (see Powell, 2004), in which they identify group affiliations that meaningfully contribute to their self-concept. Invariably, only one or two students list class as a social identity category, and many times no students in the class will include that diversity form in their pie chart. This pattern has occurred over a number of years, with both undergraduate and graduate students. For many people, then, class has a taken-for-granted nature such that people think about other characteristics—some of which might be closely linked with class (e.g., gender, race)—when considering their identity markers.

Thus, although class plays an important role in the experiences and chances one has in life, people often overlook it in their discussions of diversity. The purpose of this chapter is to provide an overview of the influence of class and class consciousness on people's lives and in the delivery of sport. I begin by providing an overview of key terms, including *socioeconomic status* and *social class*. We then turn our attention to classism—the structures and mechanics that proceed from class consciousness—and provide an overview of this construct and a discussion of how it is manifested in everyday life, including in sport systems and sport participation. The discussion then moves to the effects of classism on people's health and well-being, and the chapter concludes with a focus on the influence of sport participation on people's social mobility.

BASIC CONCEPTS

Scholars have offered a number of different conceptualizations of social class. In fact, Liu, Ali, Soleck, and their colleagues (2004), in their review of more than 3,900 psychology articles published between 1981 and 2000, found that nearly *500 different words* were used to describe, conceptualize, or discuss social class and classism. Luckily, a review of all of those terms is not necessary for this discussion. Instead, I highlight two primary approaches that researchers, government organizations, and policy makers have employed (see Exhibit 11.1).

Socioeconomic Status (Materialistic) Approach

We will first consider what the APA (2006) and others (Smith, 2010) have termed the *materialistic approach,* for its focus on the material and economic resources that people possess. Persons adopting this approach favor the term *socioeconomic status* (SES), and they take into account three primary factors: income, education, and occupation. Here, the fundamental focus is on people's access to resources.

Approaches to the study of economic inequality. | EXHIBIT **11.1**

Socioeconomic status approach: a materialistic focus, with a particular emphasis on income, occupation, and education.

Class approach: a power and privilege focus, with particular emphasis on how power, political action, and socially constructed realities economically and socially advantage some at the expense of others.

Source: American Psychological Association (2006), Smith (2008).

Income indicators take several forms, ranging from yearly income to complex formulas that involve a number of variables. For instance, in defining the poverty line, the U.S. Census Bureau sets thresholds that take into account family income and characteristics of the family. In 2013, the poverty threshold for a single-person household was $11,888, while the threshold for a single parent with two children under age 18 was $18,769. Some observers have argued that wealth, or one's private assets minus debts, is a better indicator of economic status because it reflects intergenerational transfers of resources that can serve as a buffer against potential fluctuations in annual income (APA, 2006).

Education is considered a reliable indicator of desired economic outcomes, good health and well-being, and the reduction of health risk behaviors (Hayward, Hummer, & Sasson, 2015; Montez & Friedman, 2015). It is important to understand, however, that incremental increases in educational attainment are not necessarily associated with more positive outcomes. Instead, the jumps are discontinuous in nature, and they occur only after a person is conferred an academic degree (Backlund, Sorlie, & Johnson, 1999). Thus, a student who spends four years in college but fails to earn a degree will not reap the same benefits as another student who spends the same time at college and earns a diploma. This distinction is attributable to the prestige associated with earning the credential or with the presumed positive characteristics (e.g., perseverance) that people associate with degree holders.

Finally, a person's occupation serves as a reflection of overall SES. Various scales have been developed that order occupations based on a number of criteria. For instance, according to the Bureau of Labor Statistics (www.bls.gov/soc), federal agencies in the United States use the 2010 Standard Occupational Classification System to categorize workers by occupation. This process is a complicated one because people are classified into one of more than *840 occupations*. These categorizations can be further broken down into either 461 broad occupations, 97 minor groups, or 23 major groups. A breakdown of the third categorization scheme is provided in Exhibit 11.2. For an example of the system, let's look at a category of particular relevance to our discussion: 27-0000—arts, design, entertainment, sports, and media occupations. This major group is broken down into four minor groups:

1. 27-1000 (arts and design workers),
2. 27-2000 (entertainers and performers, sports and related workers),
3. 27-3000 (media and communication workers), and
4. 27-4000 (media and communication equipment workers).

Major group 27-2000 is further subdivided into five broad occupational categories, including

1. actors, producers, and directors (27-2010),
2. athletes, coaches, umpires, and related workers (27-2020),
3. dancers and choreographers (27-2030),
4. musicians, singers, and related workers (27-2040), and
5. miscellaneous entertainers and performers, sports and related workers (27-2090).

Each of these occupations is associated with different wage rates, prestige, and power—all factors that contribute to an individual's SES. To illustrate, data from

California in 2013 show that the mean wage for athletes and sport competitors was $126,720, while the wage for referees was $28,105 (CA.gov, n.d.).

The use of the materialistic approach is widespread, and research has linked income, educational attainment, and occupational status to a number of important outcomes, including psychological and physical health, academic performance, and life expectancy, among others (see APA, 2006, for an overview). Nevertheless, this approach has a number of shortcomings. First, conceptualizations of income, education, and occupation often vary. Even within the U.S. government, the U.S. Census Bureau uses one formula for classifying poverty while the Department of Health and Human Services uses another (see Smith, 2008). There are similar ambiguities with the conceptualizations of education and occupation.

A second shortcoming is that there are considerable differences among occupations within classifications. One can certainly envisage differences in opportunities and access to resources between a television producer and a junior high track and field coach, both of whom are included in the same major occupational category (arts, design, entertainment, sports, and media occupations). Third, and most important, discussions of SES fail to recognize the very important issues of power, privilege, control, and subjugation. As Smith (2008) eloquently notes, "Creating class divisions according to SES sidesteps the issue of relationship to (or distance from) sociocultural power and carries with it the implication that class-related experiences and oppressions are similar for people who fall within the same numerical SES classification" (p. 902). Given this criticism, many sociology and social psychology researchers have turned to the concept of social class.

Classification of occupations based on the Standard Occupational Classification System.	EXHIBIT	11.2

11-0000 Management occupations	33-0000 Protective service occupations
13-0000 Business and financial operations occupations	35-0000 Food preparation and serving related occupations
15-0000 Computer and mathematical occupations	37-0000 Building and grounds cleaning and maintenance occupations
17-0000 Architecture and engineering occupations	39-0000 Personal care and service occupations
19-0000 Life, physical, and social science occupations	41-0000 Sales and related occupations
21-0000 Community and social services occupations	43-0000 Office and administrative support occupations
23-0000 Legal occupations	45-0000 Farming, fishing, and forestry occupations
25-0000 Education, training, and library occupations	47-0000 Construction and extraction occupations
27-0000 Arts, design, entertainment, sports, and media occupations	49-0000 Installation, maintenance, and repair occupations
29-0000 Healthcare practitioners and technical occupations	51-0000 Production occupations
	53-0000 Transportation and material moving occupations
31-0000 Healthcare support occupations	55-0000 Military specific occupations

Source: Bureau of Labor Statistics (www.bls.gov).

Social Class Approach

Côté (2011) defines social class as "the dimension of the self that is rooted in objective material resources (income, education, and occupational prestige) and corresponding subjective perceptions of rank vis-á-vis others" (p. 47). This definition highlights the importance of resources, but it also points to the very important role of subjectivity and perceptions. Unlike SES, social class is more overtly political in nature, draws attention to differences in power, and focuses on the socially constructed nature of social standing, including the treatment of persons from various classes (Lott & Bullock, 2007). From this perspective, inequality is a function not *only* of differential access to valued resources but also of the social (re)creation of privilege, power, and domination, particularly within capitalist societies (APA, 2006). As some examples, consider that a third of all U.S. senators are millionaires, compared to only 1 percent of the U.S. population ("Millionaires," 2004) or that coaches of major college football teams routinely earn 100 times the equivalent compensation for players (i.e., their tuition, room, board, and stipend).

The focus on power, politics, and socially constructed realities allows for different methods for grouping classes. Smith (2008, 2010), in combining the frameworks put forth by Leondar-Wright (2005) and Zweig (2000), advanced the following typology:

- *Poverty:* This class includes working-class persons who, because of various circumstances, including unemployment, low wages, or lack of healthcare coverage, do not have the income needed to support their basic needs.

- *The working class:* Persons in this class lack power and authority in the workplace, have little discretion in how they complete their work, and are marginalized when it comes to providing feedback concerning their health care, education, and housing. Relative to people in more powerful classes, working-class persons have lower income levels, lower net worth, and less education.

- *Middle class:* Persons in this class are college educated and salaried, and they typically work as professionals, managers, or small business owners. Relative to the working class, middle-class persons have greater job autonomy and economic security; however, they do rely on their earnings to support themselves.

- *Owning class:* Persons in this class have accumulated enough wealth that they do not need to work to support themselves; further, they generally own businesses and resources from which others make their living. Given their power and access to resources, owning-class persons also maintain substantial social, cultural, and political clout, particularly relative to other classes.

Several points concerning the typology should be noted. First, unlike SES-based distinctions, the social class–based typology overtly brings into the discussion issues of subjugation, autonomy, and politics, thereby recognizing that power and status help us to make sense of the socially constructed notion of class (Lott & Bullock, 2007; Smith, 2008, 2010). Second, poverty, as outlined in this framework, is not bound by specific numerical cutoff values, but instead the social-class perspective recognizes that persons in this class simply do not have the requisite income to provide them consistently with enough monies to cover basic individual and family needs. Finally, the framework recognizes that people living in poverty predominantly are members of the working class. In doing so, it helps to counter the classic, albeit incorrect, stereotype that the poor are an "under class" of people who are either unwilling or unable to work (see also Zweig, 2000).

This is just one of many conceptualizations of social class and the categories thereof. For another classification scheme, see the Alternative Perspectives box.

ALTERNATIVE perspectives

Class as a Reflection of Capital. Social scientists have thought about class in a number of ways, and French sociologist Pierre Bourdieu's (1984) perspective is among the more popular. He suggests that people possess different forms of capital, including:

- *economic capital,* or their wealth and income;

- *cultural capital,* which represents people's ability to appreciate cultural goods and their status achieved through educational success; and

- *social capital,* or the connections people have with others—that is, their social networks.

Those who adopt this perspective recognize that social class is about more than just people's wealth; it also has to do with their different forms of capital and the status, opportunities, and privilege they enjoy in society.

Drawing from this perspective, Savage, Devine, N. Cunningham, and their colleagues (2013) worked with the BBC to conduct the Great British Class Survey. This involved an analysis of the different forms of capital through data from more than 161,000 participants, the largest analysis ever conducted in the United Kingdom. Their analysis revealed the presence of seven social classes, as follows:

- **Elite:** This is the most advantaged and privileged class in British society. Members have the highest incomes (mean of £89K), own the most expensive houses (mean of £325K), possess considerable savings (mean of £142K), enjoy close to the highest numbers of social contacts, and score the highest on "highbrow cultural capital" (e.g., engagement in classical music; attendance at art exhibits, theatre, and museums; and patronage at high-end restaurants). People in the elite class are likely to be chief executives and are unlikely to be racial minorities.

- **Established middle class:** This social class, which is much larger than the Elite class, includes people who have an average household income of £47K, houses worth an average of £177K, and some savings (mean £26K). They have high-status social contacts, are culturally engaged, and are well educated. People in this social class are likely to be working professionals, such as engineers or occupational therapists.

- **Technical middle class:** This is a small social class, representing 6 percent of the population, but its members are prosperous: they have a mean household income of £38K, mean home value of £163K, and mean savings of £66K. They have restricted social networks and score low in cultural capital. Typical occupations include pharmacist, higher education professor, and scientist.

- **New affluent workers:** People in this social class score high on emerging social capital (e.g., engagement in video games and social media, sport participation and attendance, and attendance at rap concerts). Typical occupations include sales, retail, and electrician. Individuals in this class have moderate incomes (mean of £29K), small savings (mean of £5K), and relatively high home values (mean of £129K). An individual in this class generally has not obtained a graduate degree but has nonetheless achieved a middle-class position.

- **Traditional working class:** People in this class are relatively poor, with a mean household income of £13K, and their savings and house size reflect as much. They are not well educated, and they work in occupations that are traditionally considered working class, such as mechanic and secretarial work. They possess moderate levels of emerging cultural capital and low levels of highbrow cultural capital.

■ **Emergent service workers:** People in this social class have modest income levels (mean of £21K), are likely to rent, and have little savings. They have a large social network and a moderate level of emerging cultural capital. People in this social class are often young, and they hold a variety of service jobs, such as working at a bar or in a customer service role.

■ **Precariat:** This is the poorest social class, as its members have a mean income of £8K and virtually no savings. They are likely to rent. They have a restricted social network and low levels of cultural capital. They form a relatively large social class, though, constituting 15 percent of the population. Although some members of this class are unemployed, many hold jobs as shopkeepers, carpenters, drivers, and the like.

In discussing their findings, Savage and his colleagues noted that their new model "offers a powerful way of comprehending both the persistence, yet also the remaking of social class divisions in contemporary Britain," and that the model "reveals the polarization of social inequality (in the form of an elite and a precariat), and the fragmentation of traditional sociological and working-class divisions into more segmented forms" (p. 246).

CLASSISM

In our discussion of social class, it is important to consider classism. Drawing from the social categorization framework outlined in Chapter 2, we can conceptualize classism as the differential evaluations that persons in one class have of members of another. Indeed, Liu and colleagues (Liu, Ali, et al., 2004; Liu, Soleck, Hopps, et al., 2004) have made similar arguments, suggesting that classism can be expressed toward persons above, below, and even within one's own social class. However, this general definition tends to de-emphasize the issues of power and subordination that are so central to our discussion of social class and classism. For this reason, I follow Bullock's (1995) more specific definition, in which classism is characterized by its "oppression of the poor through a network of everyday practices, attitudes, assumptions, behaviors, and institutional rules" (p. 119). This oppression can be expressed at the macro level, through the maintenance and reproduction of social class through social institutions, or at the individual level, where people express prejudice toward, have negative stereotypes of, and engage in discriminatory behavior toward the poor and oppressed (Lott, 2012). Specifically, classism results from three interrelated distancing responses: cognitive distancing, interpersonal distancing, and institutional distancing. Each of these processes is outlined in the following sections (Lott, 2002; see Exhibit 11.3).

Cognitive Distancing

Cognitive distancing primarily takes the form of stereotyping (Lott, 2002), and considerable research supports Bullock's (1995) contention that "the poor are perceived as failing to seize opportunities because they lack diligence and initiative. . . . Poor people and welfare recipients are typically characterized as dishonest, dependent, lazy, uninterested in education, and promiscuous" (p. 125). What's more, some evidence suggests that people associate the poor with savages and animals. Loughnan, Haslam, Sutton, and Spencer (2014) conducted multiple studies across cultures (in the United States, the United Kingdom, and Australia) and found that,

Dimensions of classism. EXHIBIT **11.3**

Cognitive distancing: the use of stereotypes that cast the poor in a negative light (e.g., laziness, dishonesty, and lack of initiative).

Interpersonal distancing: the discriminatory behaviors persons from more powerful classes express toward the poor.

Institutional distancing: the manner in which societal institutions and prevailing norms and values allocate positive social value to dominant, power-holding groups while disproportionately assigning negative social value to subordinates.

Sources: Adapted from Lott (2002) and Lott and Bullock (2007).

across every setting, the stereotypes of the poor were closely aligned with those associated with apes and dogs. This alignment shows that some people associate the poor with dehumanizing, derogatory stereotypes—linkages not made to individuals who are more affluent and powerful.

A provocative study from Fiske (2007) sheds light on why this takes place. Fiske and her colleagues examined the brain's responses to seeing photos of a homeless man. Two key findings were observed. First, within moments of viewing the photo, participants' brains set off a sequence of reactions that are linked with disgust and avoidance. The area of the brain that was activated, the insula, is usually triggered when people express disgust toward *nonhuman* objects, such as garbage or human waste. Also of interest was the part of the brain that was *not* activated: the dorsomedial prefrontal cortex. This is noteworthy because this section of the brain is usually activated when people think about other people or about themselves. Fiske explains, "In the case of the homeless . . . these areas simply failed to light up, as if people had stumbled on a pile of garbage" (p. 157). This research suggests that people are likely to dehumanize the poor—a process that might explain the negative attitudes expressed toward the poor or the shocking nature of certain hate crimes against the homeless. According to the National Coalition for the Homeless (2014), 109 hate crimes against the homeless occurred in 2013 alone, up nearly 25 percent from 2012.

The negative stereotypes associated with cognitive distancing are also directed toward elements associated with individuals in poverty or the working class, such as speech accents, dress, and manners. Scully and Blake-Beard (2007) note that, within the organizational context, persons from privileged backgrounds often dress, talk, and act in ways that are associated with style and success. Persons from less privileged backgrounds, however, might dress or talk "differently," thereby demonstrating that they lack this form of capital. As a result, the less privileged are either shunned outright or strongly "encouraged" to alter their behaviors and speech pattern and, in doing so, to leave behind the cultural remnants of their lower-class status (Scully & Blake-Beard, 2007). This process can be disheartening to disadvantaged persons, resulting in anxiety and negative emotional responses (Liu, Soleck, et al., 2004).

Interpersonal Distancing

Interpersonal distancing refers to the discriminatory behaviors that persons from more powerful classes express toward the poor. Bullock (1995) noted that "poor people commonly experience face-to-face discrimination in their daily lives" (p. 142). Barriers are erected in such a way that the poor cannot enjoy full societal participation. In the workplace, this discrimination is seen in the hiring process and the placement of people into particular jobs. For example, employers are sometimes reluctant to hire people whom they perceive to be from a poor background, because the applicants are thought to possess a poor work ethic (Kennelly, 1999). When they are hired, people from poor backgrounds are likely to be placed in "class appropriate" jobs such as janitorial or parking lot attendant positions (Bullock, 2004). Similarly, the elite and poor rarely interact with one another in the workplace: in elite hotels, janitorial staff ride different elevators than do wealthy customers, just as in the workplace janitorial staff clean executives' offices during non-business hours (Gray & Kish-Gephart, 2013). These practices, and others like them, ensure that people from different classes do not interact with one another in a meaningful way within the work environment.

Interpersonal distancing is also observed in the school setting, where teachers have differential expectations for students from a poor social class (Boser, Wilhelm, & Hanna, 2014). Secondary school teachers, for instance, rate students who are living in poverty as 53 percent less likely to earn a college diploma than their peers. These expectations are important because, even after controlling for other factors that could affect the results, students whose teachers set high expectations are *three times more likely* to graduate from college than those whose teachers set low expectations.

Institutional Distancing

Institutional distancing refers to the manner in which societal institutions and prevailing norms and values allocate positive social value to dominant, power-holding groups while disproportionately assigning negative social value to subordinates. This form of classism punishes members of low-status groups by erecting barriers to their access to resources and full participation in society (Lott, 2002, 2012; Lott & Bullock, 2007). This is manifested primarily through the institutionalized notion of meritocracy, as well as through education, housing, health care, organizational structure, and sport systems, each of which is described in the following sections.

Meritocracy

Meritocracy refers to the worldview that a person's social standing and the rewards each person receives are based on individual effort and merit. This ideal is highly valued and engrained within the United States and other Western cultures, such that it serves as a dominant ideology (Clycq, Nouwen, & Vandenbroucke, 2013). Key elements in American culture, including children's books (e.g., *The Little Engine That Could*), numerous biographies and autobiographies, and many movies (e.g., *Hoosiers*), promote the notion that with hard work, persistence, and determination anyone can rise from humble beginnings to overcome hurdles placed in front of them and achieve greatness. This belief system is often used, perhaps implicitly, to justify the positions of those in power (e.g., they worked hard to get there) and those in disadvantaged circumstances (e.g., they made poor choices and now must face the consequences; see Jost, Chaikalis-Petritsis, Abrams, et al., 2012).

These examples are illustrative of meritocracy's three underlying elements (Daniels, 1978). First, in this view, merit is thought to be a well-understood and measurable basis for selecting persons either for positions or for promotion. Second, individuals are thought to have equal opportunities to develop and display their talents, thereby allowing them to advance. Finally, the positions attained by people are thought to vary according to different levels of status, reward, and income.

From a different perspective, observers who adopt a class-based view challenge these underlying premises on a number of fronts (Scully & Blake-Beard, 2007). First, they claim that powerful persons who have access to material and economic resources are those who decide what is meritorious and what is not. Merit is socially constructed so as to privilege elites and ensure that they maintain their power and status, all the while delegitimizing the achievements of persons from disadvantaged groups. As one example, consider the requirements among many sport organizations that employees have an undergraduate, or sometimes even a graduate, degree for even a ticket sales position. As an educator, I certainly value the knowledge, understanding, and experience that people obtain through the formal educational process. I also acknowledge, however, that many times this arbitrarily assigned requisite condition serves to disadvantage persons who are qualified (e.g., with prior sales experience) but whose class background did not direct them to the higher education route.

Second, an individual's family class background is often a better predictor of life success than is individual merit (Scully & Blake-Beard, 2007). Similar to wealth, class is transferred from generation to generation. This is meaningful because if two people differ in class but are otherwise identically meritorious from birth, they are likely to have different experiences and chances in life. Clearly, there are examples of persons, such as Lee Iacocca, Sam Walton, or Barack Obama, who rose from meager backgrounds to do extraordinary things in their lives, thereby supporting the "American Dream" ideal. However, these exceptional cases are just that—exceptions. As Scully and Blake-Beard note, "Any meritocracy needs only just enough permeability of elite ranks to justify the possibility that 'anyone can make it'" (p. 436). Also, this anecdotal evidence does not negate the experiences of millions of others who, despite their meritorious achievements, are overlooked, bypassed, and marginalized because of their class position.

Finally, critics of meritocracy argue that the different values society places on varying jobs, coupled with the status and rewards of those jobs, can be challenged (Scully & Blake-Beard, 2007). From this perspective, wage gaps between the elite and those in the working class or in poverty come into question. These discrepancies are seen as a function of the greed and power of individuals at the top who pay themselves exorbitant salaries that do not reflect true differences in merit or the value that society places on those jobs. This disjunction was aptly observed during the financial crisis that the United States experienced in 2008 and 2009, during which period some companies laid off thousands of employees only to pay their executives millions of dollars in bonuses. Note, too, that these "performance bonuses" were paid out even though the companies were in dire financial straits, some surviving only because of governmental assistance.

Elites, of course, seek to justify their incomes, arguing that their salaries are based on market demand and that their unique skills and expertise (that is, what they have defined as meritorious achievements) call for such compensation. What else should be expected, though? After all, "every highly privileged group develops the myth of its natural superiority" (Weber, 1978, p. 437), and persons in power "use 'autobiographical reasoning' to describe their positions as the outcome of hard work and ability, extrapolating from their own experiences" (Scully & Blake-Beard, 2007, p. 437). The corollary of this argument is that individuals who do not earn such outstanding wages and who have not excelled in the stratified social order are not hard working, do not possess unique skills and attributes, and are not meritorious. The clear problem with such reasoning is the considerable evidence to the contrary: millions of people work extremely hard, completing tasks that require special skills, only to be compensated with wages that do not allow them to provide for their most basic needs and for their families (Abrego, 2014). The accompanying Diversity in the Field box provides a detailed example of this phenomenon that occurred in the athletics setting.

DIVERSITY   IN THE FIELD

Inequitable Wage Distributions in College Athletics. The worldwide economic crisis that occurred in 2008 and 2009 affected nearly every aspect of sport, including intercollegiate athletics. Cash-strapped athletic departments were forced to make tough decisions, including trimming team budgets, cutting some athletic squads, and reducing their workforces. As reporter Matthew Watkins (2009) outlined, this was certainly the case at Texas A&M University, where, during the 2008–09 fiscal year, the athletic department ran a $1 million deficit, even after taking a $4.5 million loan from the university. If its business practices were left unchanged, the athletic department was projected to lose an additional $4.5 million during the 2009–10 academic year.

Faced with these financial difficulties, the athletic director at the time, Bill Byrne, along with the university's division of finance, identified $3 million in cuts, including eliminating several student worker posts, cutting free tickets for families and staff, reducing the international travel that teams took during the preseason, and altering phone allowances. The athletic department also opted to eliminate 17 full-time positions—most through layoffs—as a way to cut an additional $1 million. Billy Pickard, who began his time at Texas A&M as a student worker during Paul "Bear" Bryant's days at the university, was among those cut from the staff.

This information alone, while disconcerting, might not be surprising, considering that many sport organizations, including several professional sport leagues (e.g., the NFL), were forced to lay off employees in order to cut costs. What makes the Texas A&M example particularly troubling, however, is that the layoffs occurred while the most powerful individuals in the department were taking large pay raises. In August 2008, for instance, Byrne's salary increased by more than 40 percent (from $486,000 to $690,000), and this was on top of the $178,500 in performance bonuses he received that year. One month before the 17 full-time positions were eliminated, Byrne also paid out $1 million in bonuses to coaches who had participated in postseason play. These bonuses are noteworthy in that the coaches' contracts stipulated that the bonuses would be paid *only if* the department had money available. In justifying these expenses, Byrne commented that the coaches were deserving of the extra monies because of their "great success" and as a way to keep other schools from recruiting the coaches away from the university.

This is just one example to illustrate the abuses of power in sport organizations. Those in power may justify paying themselves high wages and bonuses using self-made rules and flawed notions of meritocracy, while marginalizing those who are in less powerful positions.

Education

The second way in which institutional distancing takes place is through education. Specifically, because most schools are funded through property taxes, class inequalities and social injustices are continually reinforced. Eitzen (1996) explains the dynamics in this way:

> Schools receive some federal money, more state money, and typically, about half of their budget from local property taxes. The result is a wide disparity in per-pupil expenditures among the states and within each state. The use of property taxes is discriminatory because rich school districts can spend more money than poor ones on each student, yet *at a lower tax rate*. This last point is important—poor districts have higher mill levies than wealthy districts, yet they raise less money *because they are poor*. (p. 102; emphasis in original)

To illustrate these disparities, the wealthiest school districts in New York spent an average of $25,505 per student in 2013—nearly double the $12,861 spent per student by the poorest school districts (Porter, 2013). These differences obviously have meaningful ramifications for quality of instruction, sport opportunities, number of teachers and coaches, and quality of facilities and equipment.

The differences in the quality of education between privileged and disadvantaged students have a number of ramifications, including the likelihood of students completing school and their prospects of attending college. Bullock (2004) reports that schoolchildren from the poorest 20 percent of families are *six times less likely* to finish high school than their wealthier peers. Class inequalities in primary education also affect students' likelihood of pursuing higher education opportunities. Disadvantaged students are unlikely to attend the most elite institutions (Lott & Bullock, 2007) or to earn a degree at all.

Krugman (2007) illustrates a similar point. He gathered data from eighth graders in 1988, and based on this information sorted students into categories according to their intellect (as measured by mathematics performance) and the SES of their parents (as measured by income, occupation, and education). He then examined whether or not the students finished college. As might be expected, students who scored well and whose parents were in the top SES quartile were very likely to finish college (79 percent), and those who were at the other end of the spectrum (bottom quartile in both SES and academic performance) were unlikely to finish college (3 percent). What is striking, though, is the data from those students who fell into the other categories. Among students who were in the top quartile of academic performers but whose parents were in the bottom SES quartile, only 29 percent completed college. This is *less than* the proportion (30 percent) of the students who completed college after performing poorly academically but came from affluent households. In commenting on these findings, Krugman noted, "What this tells us is that the idea that we have anything close to equality of opportunity is clearly a fantasy. It would be closer to the truth, though not the whole truth, to say that in America, class—inherited class—usually trumps talent" (p. 248).

Housing

A third way in which institutional distancing occurs is through housing. The ability to provide shelter for one's family—one of the most basic needs people have

(Maslow, 1943)—is continuously listed as the most pressing concern for persons in the poverty class (Lott & Bullock, 2007). The high costs of rent and utilities support the reality of this concern. In a comprehensive study, the National Low Income Housing Coalition found that the two-bedroom fair market rent (i.e., the 40th percentile of gross rent across the country) in 2014 was $984 per month. To spend no more than 30 percent of income on housing costs, a person would have to earn $18.92 per hour (Arnold, Crowley, Bravve, et al., 2014). This is considerably more than the federal minimum wage ($7.25 per hour). Thus, even in a household in which two persons work full time, there may not be enough money to obtain basic necessities. In fact, low-income renters spend over 50 percent of their income on housing (Arnold et al., 2014). These data shed light on why homelessness rates continue to increase and illustrate that even gainfully employed individuals can lose their homes because they are not receiving a living wage.

Cost is not the only way in which institutional distancing occurs in relation to housing. In addition, low-income families are likely to live in communities that are geographically and socially segregated from middle-class and owning-class families (Lott, 2002). Within large urban areas, the poor are usually relegated to "the ghetto," while more affluent families live in high-rise apartments. The former housing area is dangerous and poorly maintained, whereas the latter dwellings receive around-the-clock security (Lott, 2002).

Racial minorities, persons from low-income families, and the unemployed are all more likely than their counterparts to live in neighborhoods with poor air quality (Bell & Ebisu, 2012). Companies that produce environmentally hazardous waste are likely to locate in low-income communities because resistance to such a business move will be less than it would in more affluent neighborhoods. As Pinderhughes (1996) commented, "To save time and money, companies seek to locate environmentally hazardous industries in communities which will put up the least resistance, which are less informed and less powerful, and are more dependent upon local job development efforts" (p. 233). Lott and Bullock (2007) refer to this practice as environmental classism.

Of course, the institutional distancing we have been discussing occurs until an urban location is determined to be an ideal site for a new stadium and urban redevelopment efforts. Once this decision is made, the poverty-class and working-class families who live in the area are displaced, forced to move to other locations. Efforts to clean up, revitalize, and energize the neighborhood are then made—but only after the poor are displaced and the wealthy team owners and fans move into town. This displacement process has a serious negative effect on families. Residents are forced to leave their homes, the local shops they enjoy visiting, and the friends and social networks they have developed. Members of the owner class can reap more profits by placing the new stadium where the poor once lived. Consequent to the urban gentrification process, rent and property values increase. The higher rents force local merchants to move (because they cannot afford the rent) and prohibit them from relocating in a nearby area.

The Diversity in the Field box on the facing page provides an overview of the displacement process that occurs when communities host the Olympics. The Alternative Perspectives box examines arguments and counterarguments about the potential benefits of such urban revitalization efforts.

DIVERSITY IN THE FIELD

Housing and the Olympics. The Olympics are often promoted as a way for a city to showcase itself and, at the same time, improve the supporting infrastructure. New stadiums and arenas are constructed, roads are built, new jobs are created, and urban centers are revitalized. The Olympics come at a tremendous cost, however. Most often, these costs are discussed in terms of the billions of dollars that local governments and organizations spend to prepare for the Games. This does not tell the whole story, however, because the poor are disproportionately negatively affected by a city's hosting of the Olympics.

This was particularly the case in Vancouver, host of the 2010 Winter Olympics. More than 800 people were displaced in one area of downtown Vancouver after the 2010 Games were announced—the consequence of low-rent hotels being closed and demolished so that high-priced condominiums could be built in their place (Cogman, 2008). No low-rent housing alternatives were to be found in nearby areas. De-

spite spending over $4.5 billion to support the Games (monies that could have funded the construction of almost 2,800 housing units for the poor), government officials claimed not to have the resources to address the increased number of homeless people on the streets. Such claims seem particularly curious given the fact that "the new RAV [light rail] line is being built to the Vancouver International Airport, a new highway is in the works, and condos are shooting up everywhere" (Cogman, 2008). This kind of displacement of the poor in favor of the Olympics is nothing new. The Sydney Olympics were also accompanied by increased homelessness, an outcome caused by the skyrocketing cost of living in the city. In addressing this trend, Sydney officials literally bused the homeless to different cities (Beadnell, 2000), presumably so that they would not "interfere" with Olympics activities. In response to this disturbing phenomenon, Cogman acutely noted that "if the homeless had an Olympic category, maybe someone would notice."

ALTERNATIVE perspectives

Are There Benefits to Displacement? Some observers argue that the potential negative effects associated with displacing families in favor of building a stadium are outweighed by the many benefits associated with the practice. After all, the stadium also brings new restaurants and shops to the neighborhood that people frequent when attending events. Collectively, this new business is thought to provide many benefits to the community, including increased tax revenues. Coakley (2015) notes many fallacies in these arguments. For instance, officials will often give discounted tax rates to the owners of new buildings and their real estate partners as enticement to build in their city. However, considering that property taxes are the primary sources of revenue for public schools, this practice actually serves to *decrease* the potential revenues that schools could receive. Thus, as team

owners continue to increase their wealth through this public subsidization, school systems continue to fail because of poor funding.

Another argument is that the new, publicly financed stadiums and arenas create new jobs; thus, even though people might be displaced, at least they have the work opportunities that otherwise would not have existed. This notion is faulty, as well. First, because the new facilities sit empty for most of the year, the types of jobs that are normally created are seasonal and low paying. Second, the creation of jobs through the public subsidization of sport franchises is remarkably inefficient when compared with government-assisted initiatives. Thus, despite claims of supposed benefits of publicly supported stadiums and the displacement of persons from their homes, the evidence points to the contrary.

Health care

Institutional distancing is also manifested through health care. Krugman (2007) notes that the United States is unique among wealthy nations in its failure to provide health care to all of its citizens. According to Gallup, 16.3 percent of Americans lacked insurance in 2009, and that figure rose to 18.0 percent in 2013. With the passage (in 2010) and implementation (in 2014) of the Affordable Care Act, this figure dropped to 12.9 percent in 2014. Although the drop in the number of uninsured is encouraging, the fact remains that millions lack health insurance (Gallup, 2014). The lack of insurance coverage is not attributable to a lack of money devoted to health care. In fact, there is no lack of money for health care; according to the World Bank (2014), healthcare spending represented 17.9 percent of the United States' gross domestic product in 2012. This figure is substantially higher in the United States than in comparable countries, such as Canada (10.9 percent), France (11.7 percent), Germany (11.3 percent), and the United Kingdom (9.4 percent), and it is expected to continue to grow in the future.

Given their high costs, health care and health insurance remain luxury commodities most affordable to persons with power and wealth, while less privileged persons suffer without care. Low-income wage earners represent half of the uninsured, and many go without insurance (Halle, Lewis, & Seshamani, 2009). This pattern led Lott and Bullock (2007) to conclude that "the resource to which low-income people in this country [the United States] have the least access is health care" (p. 65).

These figures are meaningful on a number of fronts. According to NerdWallet (LaMontagne, 2014), which uses data from multiple national data sources, three out of five personal bankruptcies stem from healthcare costs. The inability to pay medical bills is the leading cause of personal bankruptcies for Americans. Lack of adequate health insurance is also associated with people choosing to forgo medical treatments (Halle et al., 2009). This means that people in poverty and working-class persons are more likely than members of more affluent classes to contract illnesses and diseases that would otherwise have been prevented, treated, or cured. It is hardly surprising, then, that low-income families are more likely to suffer from a host of health ailments, including obesity, type II diabetes, cancer, and HIV/AIDS. These data support Lott and Bullock's (2007) contention that within the United States, social class "is a strong and reliable predictor of health outcomes . . . and all causes of death regardless of ethnicity, gender, and age" (p. 68). See the accompanying box for further discussion of the health outcomes of classism.

Health outcomes of classism

Given the pervasiveness of cognitive, interpersonal, and institutional classism, one should not be surprised to learn that middle- and poverty-class persons face a number of unique life difficulties. Relative to persons in other classes, the poor report higher incidences of anxiety, depression, and hostility; express less optimism and control over their lives; have poor social support; are more likely to be overweight; and are more likely to re-port physical illnesses, such as type II diabetes, cancer, and heart disease (see Liu, Ali, et al., 2004, for reviews). It is important to note that these effects are not uniform, because class intersects with other diversity dimensions to affect groups differently (see Exhibit 11.4). Conceptions of social class also vary depending on other diversity dimensions, as illustrated in the Professional Perspectives box on p. 258.   *(continued)*

According to the APA (2006), social class influences health through a number of potential pathways. First, as previously outlined in the discussion of institutional distancing, the poor have limited access to health care, and when they do receive health care, it is often of poor quality. Second, poverty-class and working-class persons are more likely to encounter hazardous materials in their work settings and in their neighborhoods than are their higher-status counterparts. A third pathway is through health behaviors such as smoking, poor diet, and lack of exercise. Finally, social class might be related to health and well-being through differential exposure to stress. Poverty-class and working-class persons are likely to experience more acute and chronic stress than their counterparts, and this repeated exposure to stress deleteriously affects the body's ability to fight off illness and disease.

Interestingly, there is evidence that when poor families have a chance to move away from low-income neighborhoods—and thus escape the effects of environmental classism—their health improves (Ludwig, Sanbonmatsu, Gennetian, et al., 2011). Specifically, when people moved out of neighborhoods with extreme poverty into ones with lower levels of poverty, they experienced a decreased risk of both obesity and diabetes. Given that housing segregation based on income is increasing, the results suggest that "clinical or public health interventions that ameliorate the effects of neighborhood environment on obesity and diabetes could generate substantial social benefit" (p. 1518).

| Intersection of class and other diversity dimensions. | EXHIBIT 11.4 |

The influence of social class on outcomes is moderated by other diversity dimensions in such a way that the effects are stronger for some groups than for others. This is observed for the following characteristics:

1. **Race:** The legacy of slavery, prejudice, and discrimination in the United States means that racial minorities are disproportionately represented in poverty classes and middle classes. This is particularly true of African Americans, "for whom individual deprivation and poverty are compounded by residential segregation, resulting in a greater proportion of Blacks living in concentrated poverty" (APA, 2006, p. 12).

2. **Gender:** Women are more likely to be in less powerful social classes than men. Women also have lower incomes than men, even when education and experience levels are the same. These differences account, at least in part, for the strikingly high rates of poverty for children living in single-parent households headed by the mother.

3. **(Dis)ability status:** Persons with disabilities are disproportionately represented among the unemployed, underemployed, and those in the poverty class. Fewer than one in five persons with disabilities are employed, and they are twice as likely as their able-bodied counterparts to live in poverty.

4. **Sexual orientation:** Although persons who are lesbian, gay, bisexual, and transgender are perceived to have considerable discretionary income, in reality they are likely to be economically disadvantaged. People who identify as LGBT earn up to 32 percent less than similarly qualified peers. Termination of employees based on their sexual orientation is legal in 29 states. Finally, the incidence of homelessness is higher among individuals who are LGBT than it is among heterosexuals, particularly with youth.

5. **Class:** Class tends to affect the young and the poor. Though older adults are generally not poor, approximately 10 percent of persons age 65 or older live at or near the poverty line. This is especially the case for older racial minorities. Among children, U.S. poverty rates are the highest in the industrialized world. Nearly one in four (23 percent) of U.S. children live in poverty—a figure substantially higher than in Finland (3 percent), Germany (9 percent), or the United Kingdom (10 percent).

Sources: American Psychological Association (2006), unicef-irc.org.

professional
PERSPECTIVES

Alternate Conceptions of Social Class. Jacqueline McDowell is a scholar at the George Mason University, where she studies the intersection of race, gender, and social class. According to McDowell, traditional definitions of class focus on issues of income, wealth, power, and standing in society. However, in the African American community, social class takes on a different meaning, and class is "typically defined by someone's attitude that they might have about their life, or their behavior . . . so it is actually independent of the power that they might have in the wider society." She found support for this position in her research with African American women administrators. When asked about their class background, women in her research were reluctant to pigeonhole themselves into a particular class based on their income or occupation; rather, "a lot of them actually felt that their class reflected an attitude about their life." Thus, from McDowell's perspective, ideas people have about class, including where they are situated, are likely to vary with their race.

Organizational structure

The manner in which organizations, including those in sport, are structured reinforces institutional classism. Occupations linked with the middle and owning classes are at the top of the prestige hierarchy, while those occupations associated with poverty or the working classes are perceived as low-status positions (Gray & Kish-Gephart, 2013). Indeed, when I ask students in my sport management classes to what they aspire upon graduation, many cite the positions of general manager, athletic director, and events coordinator—all high-status positions. Less common are responses related to grounds crew or concessions—positions that are more frequently held by the poor. Note, too, that other characteristics differentiate the two classes of positions. Athletic directors, when compared to concessions workers, are likely to have better benefits, choose their work structure and hours, and travel to exciting destinations. These distinctions are important because the status of a given occupation is partly associated with the benefits it provides, including vacation time, paid leave, health care, salaried work, and retirement.

Class is also reinforced in attitudes held toward high-status and low-status employees' behaviors. Let us consider mobilization efforts, for instance. Unions are generally considered to be organizations formed to improve the working conditions of workers and the pay they receive (Abercrombie, Hill, & Turner, 2000). Laborers benefit in many ways from unionization and, through their unions, have fought for rights related to fair work practices, just pay, healthcare benefits, and retirement options, among others. Despite these many benefits, Americans' attitudes toward unions have become less favorable over the years; in 2009, fewer than half approved of labor unions (Saad, 2009). These attitudes are interesting, considering the general positive attitudes that people have toward chambers of commerce and professional associations, both of which are forms of mobilization—albeit by different names—of middle- and owning-class persons (Smith, 2008). This hypocrisy is routinely illustrated in the media coverage of labor strife in the professional sport leagues: relative to the owners (who operate legal cartels), players unions are more likely to be vilified and characterized as greedy when there is a strike or lockout (for other examples, see Zweig, 2000).

Classism within the organizational context is perhaps best illustrated through the wildly disparate pay scales found there. According to Smith (2008), the gap between a company's highest-paid employee and the mean salary in that company jumped from a ratio of 28 to 1 in 1970 all the way to a ratio of 369 to 1 in 2006. As previously noted, these salaries are justified through the promotion of stereotypes and through social reinforcement of belief systems such as meritocracy.

Perhaps not surprising, given these figures, is research from Emmanuel Saez (2013) that suggests that income inequalities are increasing at substantial rates. According to his calculations, the top .01 percent of Americans reaped 5.5 percent of the total wages in the country, a proportion that is even higher than that existing immediately before the Great Depression in 1929. Furthermore, as of 2012, the top 10 percent of American earners pulled in over 50 percent of the total wages in the United States, a level not seen for decades. Unfortunately, the poor have not made similar gains, and as a result the gap between the "haves" and "have nots" continues to grow. In explaining his findings, Saez wrote,

> The labor market has been creating much more inequality over the last thirty years, with the very top earners capturing a large fraction of macroeconomic productivity gains. A number of factors may help explain this increase in inequality, not only underlying technological changes but also the retreat of institutions developed during the New Deal and World War II—such as progressive tax policies, powerful unions, corporate provision of health and retirement benefits, and changing social norms regarding pay inequality. We need to decide as a society whether this increase in income inequality is efficient and acceptable and, if not, what mix of institutional and tax reforms should be developed to counter it. (p. 5)

Interestingly, despite the many forms of distancing that reify the current social class system in the United States, Americans actually prefer a different distribution of wealth. In a remarkable study, Norton and Ariely (2011) collected data from a nationally representative sample of more than 5,500 people. The study asked participants to reflect on the income distributions in three countries (which were not labeled) and decide which one they preferred. The researchers showed pie charts labeled with the percentages of wealth possessed by each quintile of the populations. In the United States, the top quintile controls 84 percent of the wealth, while in Sweden, the top quintile controls 18 percent of the wealth. The other quintiles in both countries were also shown. In a third country, all five quintiles controlled equal shares of the wealth. Results showed that 92 percent of the respondents preferred the distribution in Sweden relative to the United States', and 77 percent preferred the equal distribution compared to that of the United States. This pattern held among women and men, for liberals and conservatives, and across income ranges. In addition, the researchers asked respondents to indicate how much wealth they believed each quintile in the United States controlled. The respondents vastly underestimated the wealth controlled by the top quintile (59 percent predicted versus 84 percent actual), and they also desired the top quintile to control just 32 percent of the wealth. These findings highlight interesting points: (1) Americans dramatically underestimate the income inequalities in their own country, and (2) they would prefer to live in places where income equality is a reality.

Sport systems

Within sport, a number of institutionalized activities serve to reinforce classism. Differences in sport participation provide one example. Participation in sport and recreational activities takes time and money, two things that middle- and owning-class persons are likely to have more of than other members of society. People who participate in sport are likely to be highly educated, belong to a high income bracket, and work in a high-status occupation (Sagas & Cunningham, 2014). This pattern is evident in several segments of the sport industry, including the Olympics, health and fitness, and recreational activities (Eitzen & Sage, 2009). For example, skiing, golf, and tennis can entail substantial costs for club dues and equipment. Therefore, persons from the elite or professional middle class are more likely to participate in these activities than those from the poor or working classes.

The structure and expectations related to corporate wellness centers also contribute to these differences (Eitzen & Sage, 2009). Companies increasingly offer on-site wellness centers and encourage employees to be physically active, but participation varies based on occupational status: powerful, salaried employees generally demonstrate enthusiasm for such programs, while reactions from hourly employees are more tempered. Eitzen and Sage (2009) provide several potential explanations for this dynamic. First, all else equal, members of the middle class and owning class are more likely to engage in healthy behaviors than are persons from the working and poverty classes. Second, the activities offered, such as running or Pilates, have a greater appeal to high-status employees than to their counterparts. In addition, corporate wellness centers might be viewed as something established for those in upper management; thus, hourly workers would be considered outsiders in that context. Finally, hourly workers may resent the monies and time spent on wellness activities, especially considering that these do not address their needs in the workplace (i.e., higher wages, safer conditions, or decreasing the monotony and lack of autonomy in their work).

In addition to participation rates, social class also influences who watches sport events. In part, this is driven by the high costs of attending events, a trend outlined in Chapter 2. And, as more sporting events are handled as paid programming, even watching live broadcasts of sporting events is becoming available only to persons in the professional middle class or the elite. The cost of watching is simply too much for persons from other social classes.

Finally, as evidenced in the opening Diversity Challenge, the increasing use of pay-to-play programs in high school athletics and other school-sponsored activities is privileging to students from families who have the economic resources for such activities and, simultaneously, is disadvantaging to students from poorer families. Such policies guarantee that opportunities to participate in varsity programs will continue to exist for young people born into middle- and owning-class families or who attend wealthy school districts that can afford to finance sport teams. For those students in poor school districts or whose families cannot afford the hundreds of dollars in fees, formal sport participation opportunities are usually eliminated.

SPORT AND SOCIAL MOBILITY

he foregoing discussion suggests that social class plays a significant role in the education that people receive, the opportunities they are afforded, the types of jobs they hold, and the experiences they have in the workplace. Nevertheless, some people are of the opinion that sport participation can serve to negate this pattern, as when a person from the working class gains affluence and prestige through achievement in sport. We might ask, does being a star athlete at a major university provide a person with the capital needed to be successful throughout life? Does participating in sport and athletics in high school help people to be more successful later in life? There are certainly isolated examples in which this is the case. Most of us can think of people who were raised in lower-income households who, as a result of their sport participation, received a college education, met important social contacts, or gained the confidence needed to be successful in life. Of course, this is not the case for every athlete from a low-income background. There are just as many who have not risen above humble beginnings to be successful. How, then, does sport participation contribute to occupational success or upward social mobility, if it does at all?

Coakley (2015) suggests that sport participation will be positively related to upward social mobility when it does the following:

- Increases opportunities to be academically successful and effectively compete in the work environment;
- Increases support for growth and development across various domains;
- Offers opportunities to develop strong social networks;
- Provides the material resources needed to create and manage opportunities;
- Expands opportunities, identities, and abilities outside of sport; and
- Minimizes the risks of long-term injury.

These observations suggest that, under some circumstances, sport will help expand an athlete's opportunities. This is certainly true when sport allows a person to obtain education, skills, and training unrelated to sport. For example, when a volleyball player from a poor family receives a scholarship to a university, she is afforded the chance to obtain an education. To the extent that she takes advantage of this opportunity, develops her skills for the workplace, gains experiences through internships, and cultivates social relationships, her sport participation is likely to be positively related to her upward social mobility and career success.

chapter SUMMARY

The purpose of this chapter was to provide an overview of how class and classism affect people's lives and the delivery of sport. As evidenced in the Diversity Challenge, the decisions sport managers make concerning the structure of sport and how it is financed often serve to hurt those who are already socially and economically disadvantaged. These dynamics are observed in other ways, too, including how people interact with members of classes with less prestige than their own and institutionalized practices that privilege persons from middle and owning classes. After reading this chapter, you should be able to:

1. **Define key terms related to social class inclusion and diversity, including** *socioeconomic status, social class,* **and** *classism.*

   Socioeconomic status refers to a person's economic standing, with a particular emphasis on income, education, and occupation. *Social class* refers to a person's position within an economic system, with a particular emphasis on how power, politics, and socially constructed realities economically and socially advantage some at the expense of others. Finally, *classism* refers to the subjugation of the poor through stereotypes, interpersonal discrimination, and institutionalized activities.

2. **Discuss the influence of cognitive, interpersonal, and institutional distancing on the maintenance and promotion of classism.**

Cognitive distancing refers to the use of stereotypes that cast the poor in a negative light, such as being lazy, dishonest, and lacking initiative. *Interpersonal distancing* is manifested through the discriminatory behaviors that persons from more powerful classes direct toward the poor. Finally, *institutional distancing* refers to the manner in which societal institutions and prevailing norms and values allocate positive social value to dominant, power-holding groups and disproportionately assign negative social value to subordinates.

3. **Provide an overview of the effects of classism on people's education, health, and well-being, including their sport participation.**

Classism negatively affects people's physical health, mental health, and overall well-being. These effects are augmented for women, racial minorities, individuals who are LGBT, and those who are especially young or old.

4. **Highlight the manner in which sport involvement results in social mobility.**

The argument that sport involvement is strongly related to social mobility is overstated. Rather, social class standing will improve only when sport participation allows a person to obtain education, social contacts, skills, and training unrelated to sport.

QUESTIONS for discussion

1. What are the differences between SES and social class? Which construct do you prefer in discussions of economic inequalities?
2. Some argue that class-related stereotypes can also be directed at persons other than the poor. Is this the case, and if so, do all class-related stereotypes have the same impact on outcomes?
3. Challenging the notion of meritocracy is often a difficult task. Why is this the case, and what arguments could effectively be made to illustrate that the notion of meritocracy promotes classism?
4. Several examples were provided in the chapter illustrating how the structure and delivery of sport reinforce classism. What are other examples of how class and sport interact?

learning ACTIVITIES

1. Watch the documentary *Inequality for All* and discuss the major points made.
2. Divide into groups and discuss the notion of meritocracy. Is it applicable today?

WEB resources

American Psychological Association Office of Socioeconomic Status (SES),
www.apa.org/pi/ses/homepage.html

An entity that focuses on the psychological dynamics of social class and SES.

Class Matters, www.nytimes.com/pages/national/class

A special section of the *New York Times* that provides articles, reports, and statistical information pertaining to class in America.

Inequality for All, www.inequalityforall.com

A companion website to the award-winning documentary of the same title.

reading RESOURCES

Krugman, P. (2007). *The conscience of a liberal.* New York: W. W. Norton & Company.

One of my top five favorite books of all time; a provocative book from the Nobel Prize Laureate, providing an overview of economic inequalities in the United States and possible solutions to the problem.

Lott, B., & Bullock, H. E. (2007). *Psychology and economic injustice: Personal, professional, and political intersections.* Washington, DC: American Psychological Association.

Provides an exceptional overview of the psychological dynamics of class; also provides telling life stories of the authors.

Smith, L. (2010). *Psychology, poverty, and the end of social exclusion: Putting our practice to work* (Vol. 7). New York: Teachers College Press.

Offers a comprehensive overview of social class, poverty, and well-being; focuses on persons in poverty.

REFERENCES

Abercrombie, N., Hill, S., & Turner, B. S. (2000). *The Penguin dictionary of sociology* (4th ed.). New York: Penguin Books.

Abrego, L. (2014). *Sacrificing families: Navigating laws, labor, and love across borders.* Stanford, CA: Stanford University Press.

American Psychological Association (2006). *Task force on socioeconomic status (SES).* Washington, DC: Author.

Arnold, A., Crowley, S., Bravve, E., Brundage, S., & Biddlecombe, C. (2014). *Out of reach 2014: Twenty-five years later, the affordable housing crisis continues.* Washington, DC: National Low Income Housing Coalition.

Backlund, E., Sorlie, P. D., & Johnson, N. J. (1999). A comparison of the relationships of education and income with mortality: The National Longitudinal Mortality Study. *Social Science and Medicine, 49,* 1373–1384.

Beadnell, M. (2000, February). Sydney's homeless to be removed for Olympics. *World Socialist Web Site.* Retrieved from http://www.wsws.org/articles/2000/feb2000/olymp-f03.shtml.

Bell, M. L., & Ebisu, K. (2012). Environmental inequality in exposures to airborne particulate matter components in the United States. *Environmental Health Perspectives, 120*(2), 1699–1704.

Bell, M. P. (2007). *Diversity in organizations.* Mason, OH: Thomson South-Western.

Boser, U., Wilhelm, M., & Hanna, R. (2014). *The power of the Pygmalion effect: Teachers' expectations strongly predict college completion.* Washington, DC: Center for American Progress.

Bourdieu, P. (1984). *Distinction: A social critique of the judgement of taste.* Cambridge, MA: Harvard University Press.

Bullock, H. E. (1995). Class acts: Middle-class responses to the poor. In B. Lott & D. Maluso (Eds.), *The social psychology of interpersonal discrimination* (pp. 118–159). New York: Guilford Press.

Bullock, H. E. (2004). Class diversity in the workplace. In M. S. Stockdale & F. J. Crosby (Eds.), *The psychology and management of workplace diversity* (pp. 226–242). Malden, MA: Blackwell.

CA.gov (n.d.). State of California Employment Development Department. Retrieved from http://www.labormarket info.edd.ca.gov/OccGuides/SOCJOBFamily2.aspx?soc =27&Geography=0604000073

Clycq, N., Nouwen, W., & Vandenbroucke, A. (2013). Meritocracy, deficit thinking and the invisibility of the system: Discourses on educational success and failure. *British Educational Research Journal, 40,* 796–819.

Coakley, J. (2015). *Sports in society: Issues and controversies* (11th ed.). New York: McGraw-Hill.

Cogman, T. (2008, December). A new Olympic legacy: Homelessness. *The Navigator Newspaper.* Retrieved from http://thenav.ca/2008/12/05/a-new-olympic-legacy-homelessness/.

Côté, S. (2011). How social class shapes thoughts and actions in organizations. *Research in Organizational Behavior, 31,* 43–71.

Daniels, N. (1978). Merit and meritocracy. *Philosophy and Public Affairs, 3,* 206–223.

Eitzen, D. S. (1996). Classism in sport: The powerless bear the burden. *Journal of Sport & Social Issues, 20,* 95–105.

Eitzen, D. S., & Sage, G. H. (2009). *Sociology of North American sport* (8th ed.). Boulder, CO: Paradigm Publishers.

Fiske, S. T. (2007). On prejudice and the brain. *Daedalus, 136*(1), 156–159.

Gallup (2014). U.S. uninsured rate continues to fall. Retrieved from http://www.gallup.com/poll/167798/uninsured-rate-continues-fall.aspx.

Gray, B., & Kish-Gephart, J. J. (2013). Encountering social class differences at work: How "class work" perpetuates inequality. *Academy of Management Review, 38,* 670–699.

Halle, M., Lewis, C. B., & Seshamani, M. (2009, June). Health disparities: A case for closing the gap. *Health reform.gov.* Retrieved from http://www.healthreform. gov/reports/healthdisparities/disparities_final.pdf.

Hayward, M. D., Hummer, R. A., & Sasson, I. (2015). Trends and group differences in the association between educational attainment and U.S. adult mortality: Implications for understanding education's causal inference. *Social Science & Medicine, 127,* 8–18.

Jost, J. T., Chaikalis-Petritsis, V., Abrams, D., Sidanius, J., Van Der Toorn, J., & Bratt, C. (2012). Why men (and women) do and don't rebel: Effects of system justification on willingness to protest. *Personality and Social Psychology Bulletin, 38,* 197–208.

Kennelly, I. (1999). "That single-mother element": How White employers typify Black women. *Gender and Society, 13,* 168–192.

Krugman, P. (2007). *The conscience of a liberal.* New York: W. W. Norton & Company.

LaMontagne, C. (2014). NerdWallet finds medical bankruptcy accounts for majority of personal bankruptcies. Retrieved from http://www.nerdwallet.com/blog/health/2014/03/26/medical-bankruptcy/

Leondar-Wright, B. (2005). *Class matters.* Gabriola Island, Canada: New Society Publishers.

Liu, W. M., Ali, S. R., Soleck, G., Hopps, J., Dunston, K., & Pickett, T., Jr. (2004). Using social class in counseling psychology research. *Journal of Counseling Psychology, 51,* 3–18.

Liu, W. M., Soleck, G., Hopps, J., Dunston, K., & Pickett, Jr., T. (2004). A new framework to understand social class in counseling: The social class worldview and modern classism theory. *Multicultural Counseling and Development, 32,* 95–122.

Lott, B. (2002). Cognitive and behavioral distancing from the poor. *American Psychologist, 57,* 100–110.

Lott, B. (2012). The social psychology of class and classism. *American Psychologist, 67,* 650–658.

Lott, B., & Bullock, H. E. (2007). *Psychology and economic injustice: Personal, professional, and political intersections.* Washington, DC: American Psychological Association.

Loughnan, S., Haslam, N., Sutton, R. M., & Spencer, B. (2014). Dehumanization and social class: Animality in the stereotypes of "white trash," "chavs," and "bogans." *Social Psychology, 45,* 54–61.

Ludwig, J., Sanbonmatsu, L., Gennetian, L., Adam, E., Duncan, G. J., Katz, L. F., ... & McDade, T. W. (2011). Neighborhoods, obesity, and diabetes—a randomized social experiment. *New England Journal of Medicine, 365*(16), 1509–1519.

Maslow, A. H. (1943). A theory of human motivation. *Psychological Review, 50,* 370–396.

McCall, L. (2014). The political meanings of social class inequality. *Social Currents, 1*(1), 25–34.

Millionaires fill U.S. Congress halls (2004, June). Retrieved from http://www.commondreams.org/cgi-bin/print. cgi?file=/headlines04/0630-05.htm.

Montez, J. K., & Friedman, E. M. (2015). Educational attainment and adult health: Under what conditions is the association causal? *Social Science & Medicine, 127*, 1–7.

National Coalition for the Homeless (2014). *Vulnerable to hate: A survey of hate crimes and violence committed against the homeless in 2013*. Washington, DC: Author.

Norton, M. I., & Ariely, D. (2011). Building a better America—one wealth quintile at a time. *Perspectives on Psychological Science, 6*, 9–12.

Pinderhughes, R. (1996). The impact of race on environmental inequality: An empirical and theoretical discussion. *Sociological Perspectives, 39*, 231–248.

Porter, E. (2013, November). In public education, edge still goes to the rich. *The New York Times*. Retrieved from http://www.nytimes.com/2013/11/06/business/a-rich-childs-edge-in-public-education.html?pagewanted=all&_r=0.

Powell, G. N. (2004). *Managing a diverse workforce: Learning activities* (2nd ed.). Thousand Oaks, CA: Sage.

Saad, L. (2009, September). Labor unions see sharp slide in U.S. public support: For first time, fewer than half of Americans favor unions. *Gallup*. Retrieved from http://www.gallup.com/poll/122744/Labor-Unions-Sharp-Slide-Public-Support.aspx.

Saez, E. (2013). Striking it richer: The evolution of top incomes in the United States (updated with 2012 preliminary estimates). Berkeley, CA: University of California, Department of Economics. Retrieved from http://elsa.berkeley.edu/~ saez/saez-UStopincomes-2012.pdf.

Sagas, M., & Cunningham, G. B. (2014). *Sport participation rates among underserved American youth*. Gainesville, FL: University of Florida Sport Policy & Research Collaborative.

Savage, M., Devine, F., Cunningham, N., Taylor, M., Li, Y., Hjellbrekke, J., Le Roux, B., Friedman, S., & Miles, A. (2013). A new model of social class? Findings from the BBC's Great British Class Survey experiment. *Sociology, 47*, 219–250.

Scully, M. A., & Blake-Beard, S. (2007). Locating class in organizational diversity work: Class as structure, style, and process. In A. M. Konrad, P. Prasad, & J. K. Pringle (Eds.), *Handbook of workplace diversity* (pp. 431–454). Thousand Oaks, CA: Sage.

Smith, L. (2008). Positioning classism within counseling psychology's social justice agenda. *The Counseling Psychologist, 36*, 895–924.

Smith, L. (2010). *Psychology, poverty, and the end of social exclusion: Putting our practice to work* (Vol. 7). New York: Teachers College Press.

Watkins, M. (2009, August). A&M athletics reworks budget to pay loan. *The Eagle*. Retrieved from http://www.theeagle.com/PrinterFriendly/A-amp-amp-M-athletics-reworks-budget-to-pay-loan.

Weber, M. (1978). *Economy and society: An outline of interpretive sociology*. (G. Roth & C. Wittich, Eds.) Berkeley, CA: University of California Press.

World Bank (2014). Health expenditure, total (% of GDP). Retrieved from http://data.worldbank.org/indicator/SH.XPD.TOTL.ZS

Zweig, M. (2000). *The working class majority*. Ithaca, NY: Cornell University Press.

III

CREATING AND SUSTAINING INCLUSIVE SPORT ORGANIZATIONS

chapter 12
Organizational Inclusiveness   269

chapter 13
Interpersonal Inclusiveness   287

chapter 14
Diversity Training   311

chapter 15
Change and Inclusion Through Sport   335

Organizational Inclusiveness

DIVERSITY CHALLENGE

Aboriginal, or First Nations, people in Canada are disadvantaged in many ways. Consider the following statistics: the poverty rate is comparable to that in developing nations, 25 percent of all adults are unemployed, the suicide rate among youth is five times that of non-Aboriginals, and the incidence of alcohol and drug abuse is high.

Because of these issues, the Canadian federal government took several steps to improve the quality of life among Aboriginals. Together with economic and social policies, the government is using sport as a way to achieve this goal. Sport is viewed as a tool for economic development and as a mechanism that engages citizens, overcomes social constraints, and contributes to cohesion among people in a community. Sport Canada, the sport governing body in Canada, is on record as being "committed to contributing, through sport, to the health, wellness, cultural identity, and quality of life of Aboriginal Peoples."

Aboriginal persons face many barriers to sport and physical activity participation, including:

- a general lack of awareness of sport opportunities,
- economic difficulties,
- insensitivity among sport providers to Aboriginal culture and traditions,
- a lack of Aboriginal coaches and/or coaches who are cognizant of the Aboriginal culture,
- the substantial distance of many villages from sport venues,
- lack of governmental financial support,
- racism, and
- an inadequate sport infrastructure.

Sport Canada actively works with governmental agencies, Aboriginal communities and leaders, and other entities to achieve the following goals:

- *Enhanced participation.* Sport Canada is increasing the participation of Aboriginal peoples in sport at all levels by providing equitable access, developing programs that meet their unique needs, involving Aboriginal persons in the planning and development of sport, and encouraging youth participation.

■ *Enhanced excellence.* Sport Canada creates an environment that welcomes Aboriginal peoples to national teams and encourages high performance levels by increasing the number of qualified Aboriginal athletes, coaches, and officials by providing access to and support for quality facilities, training, and development.

■ *Enhanced capacity.* Sport Canada seeks to improve the capacity of individuals, groups, and communities in support of Aboriginal sport in Canada by identifying the needs of Aboriginal people, providing facilities,

promoting Aboriginal leaders, and maintaining cultural sensitivity.

■ *Enhanced interaction.* Sport Canada increases the levels of communication and interaction among Aboriginal peoples and other sport and governmental entities at the federal, provincial, and local levels.

The Canadian government recognizes that for Canadian sport to be successful, all people must have access to it and be provided an opportunity to achieve excellence. Sport Canada's policies are aimed at driving "the actions necessary to create and maintain an inclusive Canadian sport system that supports Aboriginal participation in sport from playground to podium."

Source: Sport Canada's Policy on Aboriginal Peoples' Participation in Sport. Retrieved from www.canadianheritage.gc.ca/progs/sc/pol/aboriginal/2005/1_e.cfm.

CHALLENGE   REFLECTION

1. In your opinion, how viable is sport as a vehicle for creating social change? Explain.

2. How effective are the goals outlined by Sport Canada? Are there any you feel might be especially effective? Less effective?

3. What are other sport-related strategies that could be implemented to decrease the disparities Aboriginal peoples face?

4. Are you aware of other instances where sport has been used as a vehicle for promoting change among members of a social group?

As the Diversity Challenge illustrates, organizations or governmental entities will often implement strategic initiatives aimed at diversity and inclusion issues. Here, Sport Canada's strategies sought to (1) decrease the negative outcomes associated with prejudice and discrimination in a particular context by improving the quality of life of a certain group of people, and (2) capitalize on the unique cultural attributes that Aboriginal peoples and their sports could bring to the overall fabric of Canadian sport. These strategies reflect the sport organization's desire to create diverse, inclusive sporting environments.

The purpose of this chapter is to provide an overview of strategies that can be used to create and sustain diverse and inclusive work environments. The focus here is largely on the macro level, and we will consider the top leaders within the organization and the organization as a whole. Chapter 13 deals with micro-level issues related to inclusion at the group level. Here, we begin with an overview of the success of diversity and inclusion programs, followed by a discussion showing that diversity and inclusion are best created and sustained through a focus on multiple levels of analysis. In the final section, we focus on specific leadership competencies that facilitate workplace inclusion.

EFFECTIVENESS OF DIVERSITY AND INCLUSION PROGRAMS

I deally, organizational leaders would understand and appreciate the inherent value in having inclusive work environments, recognizing that they allow for all people to participate fully and effectively at work. In many respects, there is a moral imperative for such recognition and actualization. While some organizational leaders might see this imperative, others will be more readily persuaded by the linkage between inclusion and subsequent organizational outcomes (Fink & Pastore, 1999). There is considerable evidence for such associations.

Let's first consider the value to people external to the organization. Diverse and inclusive workplaces are appealing to potential job applicants, and most prefer those work environments over more homogeneous work settings (Lee & Cunningham, in press; Melton & Cunningham, 2012; Walker, Feild, Bernerth, & Becton, 2012). The same goes for key stakeholders, such as consumers (Tuten, 2005, 2006), potential clients (Cunningham & Melton, 2014; Cunningham & Woods, 2012), and investors (Miller & Triana, 2009). This is why many organizations are keen not only to create and sustain inclusive work environments but also to signal this inclusiveness through various external communications to key stakeholders (Connelly, Certo, Ireland, & Reutzel, 2011). In fact, because legal mandates require employment protections for many groups, such as women, racial minorities, and religious minorities, failing to offer inclusive work spaces for *all people* sends mixed messages to various stakeholder groups. Ultimately, consumers will perceive this as conflicting information and develop negative attitudes toward the organization (Volpone & Avery, 2010).

The benefits of inclusiveness are also observed for sport organizations themselves. For employees and athletes, inclusion means being able to bring important identities to the workplace and express them without fear of reprisal (Cunningham, in press; Cunningham, Pickett, Melton, et al., 2014). The use of inclusive diversity strategies is associated with increased workplace satisfaction and involvement in decision making among employees (Fink, Pastore, & Riemer, 2003). In athletic departments, employee diversity serves a role-modeling function for athletes (Cunningham, 2008c; Singer & Cunningham, 2012). Finally, in diverse and inclusive work environments, differences are seen as a source of learning and growth (Cunningham, in press; Ely & Thomas, 2001), work group creativity is high (Cunningham, 2008a, 2011a), additional financial gains are possible (Cunningham & Singer, 2011), and performance often outpaces that of the organization's competitors (Cunningham, 2008c, 2009a, 2011b; Cunningham & Sagas, 2004). Collectively, these findings do much to promote the idea that diversity is a source of competitive advantage (Richard & Miller, 2013).

Pressures for Greater Inclusion

Despite these benefits, many sport organizations are *not* characterized by diversity and inclusion. The exclusion of persons who differ from the typical majority has been the norm for decades—a point we can illustrate by observing who serves in leadership positions. Furthermore, as illustrated throughout the preceding chapters, members of racial and sexual minorities, women, members of religious minorities, persons with disabilities, and the poor, among others, have routinely been marginalized and relegated to "other" status within the sport context. Thus, in many ways, cultures of similarity and exclusion have become institutionalized, meaning that through habit, history, and tradition, they have become unquestionably accepted as "how things are done" (see also Scott, 2001). Institutionalized practices are highly resistant to change and are maintained over time without objection, as they are seen largely as the "legitimate" modus operandi. This means that, despite the documented evidence showing the many benefits of diversity and inclusion, many sport organizations have systems in place that do not allow for these effects to be realized.

If cultures of similarity and exclusion are firmly engrained and legitimated within the sport context, then what factors would spur organizations to change? That is, what prompts sport organizations to seek a culture of diversity and inclusion? The work done in the area of institutional theory (Dacin, Goodstein, & Scott, 2002; Oliver, 1992; Scott, 2001) points to three primary factors: political pressures, functional pressures, and social pressures.

Political pressures

Political pressures arise when an organization experiences mounting performance deficits, the presence of conflicting interests among stakeholder groups, increasing pressures for innovation, and changing reliance upon external constituents (Oliver, 1992). I have observed the influence of political pressures in my own research on an intercollegiate athletics department undergoing a diversity-related change process (Cunningham, 2009b). Specifically, the organization sought to attract diverse fans to the events as a way to generate more revenues. Thus, the pressures for greater revenues from a variety of new, previously unrealized sources drove, at least in part, efforts for diversity and inclusion.

Functional pressures

Functional pressures manifest when there are concerns about organizational effectiveness or the utility of a given practice (Oliver, 1992). These pressures are associated with environmental dynamics, such as competition for scarce resources (Dacin et al., 2002). Perhaps the best example of functional pressures comes from what Ladson-Billings (2004) refers to as the "Bear Bryant/Adolph Rupp epiphany" (p. 10). Bryant, the head coach of the University of Alabama football team, watched his all-White squad get soundly beaten by the University of Southern California—a game in which USC's African American tailback, Sam (Bam) Cunningham, ran for 135 yards and 2 touchdowns on just 12 carries. Similarly, Rupp was the head coach of the University of Kentucky's all-White men's basketball team when his squad was beaten in the championship game by a Texas Western team that started five African Americans. Ladson-Billings suggests that both victories "made clear to big-time college athletics that winning required recruiting players from beyond all-White prep fields" (p. 12). Not surprisingly, both Bryant and Rupp fielded racially integrated teams soon after those defeats.

Social pressures

Finally, *social pressures* result from differentiation among groups (e.g., increasing employee diversity), disruptions in the organization's historical continuity (e.g., when mergers take place), or changes in laws or social movements that might disrupt the continuation of an institutionalized practice (Scott, 2001). These pressures were also present in my analysis of an athletic department that was seeking greater diversity and inclusion (Cunningham, 2009b). Many in the community perceived that the athletic department had a history of excluding racial minority coaches and administrators, and they made their concerns known through various mechanisms; for example, an open letter decrying the abysmal hiring practices was penned by former players and circulated on national websites. In addition, the athletic department's mascot had long been a Native American—a practice that many observers viewed as hostile and offensive (e.g., Staurowsky, 2007). Collectively, these issues resulted in mounting concerns voiced by a myriad of external stakeholders, and in response to these concerns the athletic department sought to change its otherwise institutionalized activities.

Engaging in the Change Process

These pressures have prompted leaders to pursue various strategies to enhance the diversity and inclusion in their sport organizations. Ultimately, however, their efforts have met with mixed success. Dobbin and Kalev (2013) reviewed studies published over several decades to examine the impact of diversity management programs. In many cases, the efforts failed. Strategies put in place to reduce managers' biases have been largely ineffective, and this is true whether the approaches involve training, including bias-reduction criteria in performance evaluations, or creating rules to govern the decision-making process. On the other hand, efforts to promote employee diversity and integration have been more successful. Mentoring programs, groups tasked with overseeing the diversity efforts, and full-time managers charged with promoting diversity and inclusion all help facilitate these effects.

Sport organizations have not fared much better than their non-sport peers in implementing diversity efforts. Spaaij, Farquharson, Magee, and their colleagues (2014), for instance, found that the moral imperative for diversity was largely lacking in Australian sport clubs' diversity plans; instead, these clubs focused on the benefits and costs of the programs—a perspective that ultimately limited physical activity participation among members of underrepresented groups. Similarly, I have observed that even when managers of sport organizations seek to undergo diversity change, the efforts are sometimes unsuccessful because of a lack of full integration throughout the organizational system (Cunningham, 2009b).

This discussion points to a perplexing quandary: on the one hand, diversity and inclusion can be sources of learning, employee well-being, and overall effectiveness for sport organizations, but on the other hand, many efforts to create and sustain inclusive work environments fail. I believe that these failures stem from a failure to recognize the multilevel nature of successful change efforts. Unless factors at various levels of analysis are taken into account, change efforts will be too narrowly focused, and, hence, unsuccessful (Cunningham, 2008b). Thus, in the next section, I provide a multilevel model that managers can use to create and sustain diversity and inclusion in their sport organizations.

MULTILEVEL MODEL OF DIVERSITY AND INCLUSION

A number of frameworks outline the process of creating a diverse and inclusive work environment, and I offer an overview of those specific to sport management in the box on the following page. Although all of these offer value, a different

Diversity management models

DeSensi (1995) developed one of the earliest models for managing diversity in the educational and sport context. Her model was built on the notion that managing diversity "involves increasing the consciousness and appreciation of differences associated with heritage, characteristics, and values of different groups" (p. 35). She adopted the term *cultural diversity* to refer to both the surface- and deep-level differences discussed in earlier chapters. DeSensi proposed that diversity can exist on five organizational dimensions: mission, culture, power, informal relations, and major change strategies. These dimensions determine an organization's level of multiculturalism, with reference to these three stages:

1. *Monocultural,* where diversity and diverse people are ignored, norms reflect the values of the majority group, power resides with White men, and diversity initiatives are enacted as a way to avoid legal regulations;

2. *Transitional,* where some diversity is present in the workforce, the norms of White men are dominant but challenged, power resides with the few in the majority, and some diversity initiatives (e.g., training) are initiated; and

3. *Multicultural,* in which diversity is valued and considered to contribute to the organization's effectiveness, a multicultural team makes key decisions, there is a strong sense of community, and the organization actively combats oppression and bias.

Doherty and Chelladurai (1999) also focused on cultural diversity and argued for the importance of considering the diversity of the workforce and of the organizational culture. Organizations with a *culture of similarity* are generally rigid, avoid risks, are intolerant of uncertainty, are task oriented, and view differences as deficits. As a result, these organizations are likely to have closed communication lines, a process-based performance appraisal system, one-sided decision making, and closed group membership. Organizations with a *culture of diversity* have very different values, assumptions, and outcomes: they are characterized by a respect for differences and a tolerance of risk and ambiguity, are people- and future-oriented, and acknowledge that there are often many ways to accomplish tasks. The organization is likely to have open communication lines, outcome-based reward systems, multilevel decision-making systems, and open group membership. Drawing from this dichotomy, Doherty and Chelladurai (1999) identify cultural diversity outcomes that result from each type of organizational culture—similarity or diversity. Their two-by-two framework is as follows:

1. *Low cultural diversity, organizational culture of similarity,* where the organization is unlikely to realize any benefits of diversity;

2. *High cultural diversity, organizational culture of similarity,* where the organization is unlikely to realize any benefits of diversity, and negative outcomes may result;

3. *Low cultural diversity, organizational culture of diversity,* where the organization *may* realize some benefits of diversity, but not many because of the low cultural diversity; and finally,

4. *High cultural diversity, organizational culture of diversity,* where the positive effects of cultural diversity are likely to be strongest, and the organization is most responsive to its environment.

The third model came from Fink and Pastore (1999). They proposed that organizations follow one of four diversity strategies. The first is *noncompliance,* where the organization mirrors DeSensi's monocultural workplaces and does very little to follow state and federal guidelines related to diversity, employees view diversity as a liability or a deficit, and those in power seek to keep the organization as homogeneous as possible. The second is *compliance,* where the organization still views diversity as a liability, but efforts are made to comply with equal employment opportunity laws—probably from a feeling of "having to" do so. This obligation to comply with diversity regulations may breed resentment among Whites and among men in the organization toward persons unlike them or toward diversity in general. Persons from diverse backgrounds may be employed, but little is done to help them succeed in the "majority" culture. Lines of communication are rigid, and the power is held by a select few. Third, *reactive* organizations deem diversity an asset, not a liability. Top decision makers acknowledge that diversity and its effective management can result in greater organizational success; therefore, efforts are made to create a diverse work environment. Because of their reactive nature, however, attempts at effective diversity management may be sporadic (e.g., once-a-year diversity seminars). Finally, *proactive* organizations realize the full benefits of diversity. These entities take a broad view of diversity and value diversity to its fullest extent. Company policies, procedures, and practices are all focused on developing a diverse workforce and effectively managing differences. Because all employees benefit from the positive outcomes associated with diversity, the backlash against such initiatives seen in other organizations is not present. These organizations generally have a different structure than their counterparts—one that is flexible, with open lines of communication, and where the power is shared by diverse persons.

Chelladurai (2014), who developed the final model, differs from his colleagues in his explicit emphasis on competence. From his perspective, employers will be able to attract a diverse workforce if the primary focus of all hiring decisions is the applicants' competency. Employers who focus on competency first should attract a wide variety of people, all of whom, though they may have a similar level of competency, may differ in other respects. Chelladurai adopts a different approach to classifying the various diversity forms by identifying four categories:

appearance or visible features, or characteristics such as sex, race, age, or skin color—surface-level attributes; *behavioral preferences,* which refers to penchants for things such as certain foods or styles of clothing; *values and attitudes,* which are forms of deep-level difference, ascertainable only through interaction with a person; and *cognitive orientations,* which are forms of deep-level difference relating to a person's technical, human, and conceptual skills.

Chelladurai suggests that the four categories are expressed in one of two ways: symbolically or substantively. *Symbolic expressions* are exemplified by Muslims' clothing preferences or Catholics' food preferences during Lent. In *substantive expressions,* people act and choose, non-symbolically, according to their values, attitudes, preferences, and orientations.

Managers who value diversity use one of two management strategies—accommodation or activation. *Accommodation* occurs when managers permit symbolic expressions of diversity as long as the expressions do not interfere with task performance. For example, it is considered reasonable to allow a woman from India to wear a sari or a Christian to wear a cross necklace because neither expression impedes the work process. *Activation* strategies are concerned with more substantive expressions, and they involve intentionally bringing employees with divergent values or perspectives together to work in groups because such heterogeneous perspectives produce better decision making and more creative solutions.

approach is to focus explicitly on inclusion, or (as we discussed in Chapter 1) *"the degree to which employees are free to express their individuated self and have a sense of workplace connectedness and belonging"* (see also Ferdman, 2014; Nishii & Rich, 2014).

I adopted this approach in a case study of two NCAA athletic departments (Cunningham, in press). Both departments had been recognized for their inclusion of LGBT athletes, coaches, and administrators. I interviewed people on campus, read press clippings about the departments, gathered information from the athletic department websites, and also read materials from the colleges. All of this was done to aid my understanding of how the athletic departments created such organizational cultures and, equally importantly, how they sustained them over time. Consistent with the multilevel approach to inclusiveness (Ferdman, 2014), I observed that factors at the individual, leader, organizational, and macro levels all influenced the athletic departments. These are captured in Exhibit 12.1.

EXHIBIT **12.1** Multilevel factors affecting organizational inclusiveness.

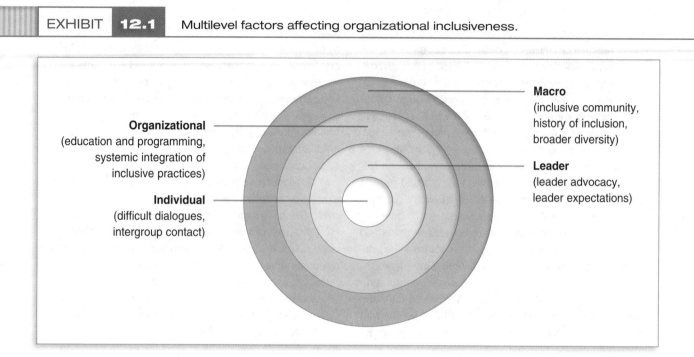

Macro
(inclusive community, history of inclusion, broader diversity)

Organizational
(education and programming, systemic integration of inclusive practices)

Leader
(leader advocacy, leader expectations)

Individual
(difficult dialogues, intergroup contact)

Individual Level

At the individual level, the use of difficult dialogues and intergroup contact both facilitated inclusive work environments. *Difficult dialogues* are the discussions people have in the workplace that are sometimes difficult yet nonetheless productive. These conversations are frequently avoided in organizations, but when they are undertaken, they help the parties generate a better understanding of one another. For example, an administrator at one of the athletic departments in the study shared how discussions of gender identity and sexual orientation might be uncomfortable for some people in sport; however, there were also benefits, as she noted: "Don't be afraid to talk about it. Talk about the issues which some people avoid, like sexual orientation. Just being open and saying it is okay to be who you are. I think the relationships and communication and talking to each other creates a good community." People in both athletic departments echoed these praises, suggesting that engaging in difficult dialogues can help stimulate different ideas, highlight divergent opinions, challenge people to think differently, allow people to take a stand for important issues, and ultimately build a sense of community and trust.

For more discussion of the importance of difficult dialogues, see the Professional Perspectives box on the facing page.

Intergroup contact (discussed in Chapter 13) also helped organizations facilitate a sense of community and inclusiveness. In short, the coaches and administrators in my research discussed how working and building relationships with people who were different helped to break down stereotypes and build healthy relationships. To illustrate, a coach in one of the athletic departments relayed the following: "There are lots of trying opportunities to put people who are very different in work situations. Let's not talk about it. Let's just do a job together and in some ways sort of build through the work itself." As another example, a staff member at the other athletic department in the study reflected as follows: "I think it is easy for someone to say, 'I hate gays,' or, 'I don't understand gays,' or to make derogatory remarks and be discriminating. . . . When you start having a relationship, even if it is purely professional, with someone who is openly gay, I think it just really forces you to look inside and perhaps change some perceptions" (Cunningham, in press).

Leader Level

Leaders understandably play a key role in creating and sustaining inclusive environments. My research showed this was manifested through leader advocacy and leader expectations. People in various leadership roles engaged in advocacy efforts. In some cases, this meant the athletic directors worked for gender equality and LGBT inclusiveness on a state, national, and international level. These efforts were noticed by others in the department and, thus, had an effect on their attitudes, as well. In other cases, coaches took on leadership roles within the department and created activities to promote an inclusive environment. My work with Melton in other settings also supports this pattern, thereby suggesting that advocacy for inclusion comes from many sources (Melton & Cunningham, 2014).

Leaders also set high expectations for others to promote inclusion. One coach, in speaking of the athletic director's expectations, noted, "(Mike) is the leader of that and I don't think he would tolerate anything less. . . . (Mike) isn't going to tolerate a lack of inclusiveness and that is true for all types of diversity." These leaders articulate those behaviors and attitudes that are acceptable and those that are not. Leaders can convey as much through formal statements and policies, by modeling the behaviors, or through informal communications. When followers know they are expected to hold inclusive attitudes and demonstrate inclusive behaviors, they are likely to do so.

Organizational Level

In my study, organizational factors affecting the inclusiveness of the work environment included education and programming, and inclusive practices. The athletic departments I visited engaged in efforts to improve continuously. For example, as a way of ensuring their readiness and ability to engage in constructive conflict and difficult dialogues, the staff of one department read the book *Fierce Conversations* (Scott, 2002) and, as a group, discussed its relevance for their everyday interactions. Both departments brought in guest speakers to discuss important topics related to inclusion, watched videos (e.g., the powerful documentary *Training Rules*), and held workshops. In short, they looked to identify areas of need and address those,

professional PERSPECTIVES

Importance of Difficult Dialogues in the Workplace.
Nancy Watson is the founder and president of the Center for Change and Conflict Resolution. She works with a variety of organizations to help them create organizational cultures that are open and inclusive. Part of this process focuses on engaging in constructive conflict and difficult dialogues. Doing so allows for people to be engaged and for the culture to be learning-oriented.

Speaking to the importance of these activities, Watson noted, "Open constructive dialogue in the workplace creates an environment for greater trust and productivity among co-workers to occur. Part of open constructive dialogue involves engaging in difficult dialogues as situations and events warrant. By engaging in difficult dialogues people increase their opportunity to learn from one another by suspending judgment, active listening, and learning from others' perspectives."

while also building upon and improving current skill sets. These efforts might also help address some of the concerns that people have about various diversity initiatives, as well as sources of resistance to those initiatives (see Exhibit 12.2). We discuss more educational and training activities in Chapter 14.

EXHIBIT 12.2   Forms of resistance to diversity-related change.

INDIVIDUAL RESISTANCE

■ **Prejudice:** People may prefer a homogeneous workplace. This preference may come from a strong liking of in-group members or disliking out-group members.

■ **Habit:** People use habits to reduce uncertainty in their lives and to increase efficiencies. The same is true for organizational policies and procedures. When diversity-related strategies are implemented, they might represent a departure from a habit and, therefore, be met with resistance.

■ **Security:** People with a high need for security may resist any and all efforts toward change because the changes might impact the power they have, the roles they assume, and so forth—all of which decreases the security people have at work.

■ **Economic factors:** Some people resist change that they perceive will negatively affect them monetarily. For example, if a diversity strategy meant (or was perceived to mean) that some people would receive reduced pay increases, then they would probably resist the initiative.

■ **Fear of the unknown:** People generally prefer to have an understanding of what the future holds for them, and change alters those perceptions. When diversity management strategies are implemented, people may be unsure of how the strategies will affect their jobs, the relationships they have with others, and their overall standing in the organization. If this is true, they are likely to resist any efforts toward change.

■ **Selective information processing:** Once people form perceptions of their world, they are unlikely to change them. This unwillingness to change may result in people selectively interpreting some information, while ignoring other input. For example, people may ignore arguments as to how diversity will improve the organization, because the arguments are counter to their current perceptions of the organization and how it functions.

ORGANIZATIONAL RESISTANCE

■ **Limited focus of change:** Because organizations are composed of interrelated systems, changing one part requires changing another if the change is to have a lasting effect. Diversity initiatives often have a narrow focus that is nullified by the larger organizational system.

■ **Inertia:** Organizational inertia is the tendency for organizations to resist change and remain in their current state. Even if certain people want the change, the organizational norms and culture may act as constraints.

■ **Threat to expertise:** Changes that threaten the expertise of particular groups cause resistance. For example, hiring a diversity officer to oversee the organization's diversity efforts might be resisted by the human resource staff because that threatens their expertise in the area of hiring and employee relations.

■ **Threat to established power relationships:** In proactive organizations, the power is held by a multicultural group of people. In other organization types, the power rests primarily with White males. To the extent that diversity is viewed as disrupting established power relationships, it may face resistance.

■ **Threat to established resource allocations:** Those groups that control sizable resources may view efforts toward change as threatening. For example, in university athletics, men's teams traditionally have received the lion's share of the budget. Thus, moves to increase the gender equity might be met with resistance by these players or coaches, if they believe it means they will receive fewer resources.

Source: Adapted from Robbins (2011).

The athletic departments also had inclusive practices built into their everyday activities. The formal policies and procedures, the strategic plan, hiring practices, and facility designs—among others—all included elements of diversity and inclusion. Thus, the principles were embedded into the fabric of the organization. To illustrate, one athletic department allocated locker room space for transgender individuals as a way of facilitating the sense of inclusion and encouraging physical activity among all persons. In both departments, partners were specifically invited to official events and were listed in the department directory (if the employee so desired). The departments were also purposeful in their hiring, specifically seeking to create diverse applicant pools and actively recruiting people from underrepresented backgrounds (for other examples, see also Singer & Cunningham, 2012).

These examples, which represent only a small sampling, show that diversity and inclusion need to be embedded in all the organization does. Too often, sport organizations look to create meaningful change without integrating the principles throughout the organizational system. Without such integration, the diversity efforts will not truly take hold and will undoubtedly fail (Cunningham, 2009b).

Macro Level

Finally, there are several macro-level contributors to an inclusive workplace. The first is the broader environment in which the sport organization is situated: when they are located within a diverse, progressive community, sport organizations are more likely to adopt inclusive practices. Inclusive communities include people with liberal ideologies, they frequently have laws mandating equality for a number of different groups, and they establish prohibitions against discriminatory behavior.

These factors collectively influence inclusiveness in organizations (Barron & Hebl, 2010). It is also important to remember, though, that sport organizations are not simply passive recipients of their environments; instead, some are able to create diverse, inclusive work environments even when embedded in homogeneous communities (see the Alternative Perspectives box).

Second, inclusive sport organizations are usually associated with larger organizations that are diverse and have a history of inclusive practices. Within the context of college athletics, the larger organization is the university or college in which the athletic department is embedded. The same principles can also be applied to other settings, so as to include regional sport organizations or satellite units. In any of these situations, the culture of the larger unit will affect that of the focal unit. Interestingly, evidence also indicates that some athletic departments can role-model effective inclusive practices to the larger university (Singer & Cunningham, 2012). This is reasonable, as athletes are among the most diverse student groups

ALTERNATIVE perspectives

Inclusion Despite the Community. Although local and state regulations and demography can shape organizational practices, evidence suggests that some organizations are able to create diverse, inclusive work environments in homogeneous, conservative geographic regions. This mismatch has a positive effect on external stakeholders, as well as on persons working in the organization. Pugh, Dietz, Brief, and Wiley (2008) examined this very issue and found that employee perceptions of the diversity climate were positive when the organization was racially diverse and set within a homogeneous community. However, as community diversity increased, the linkage between workforce diversity and perceived diversity climate weakened. These findings suggest that sport organizations might be rewarded for exceeding expectations for an inclusive work environment.

on campus (Singer & Cunningham, 2012). Further, our analyses of inclusive athletic departments show that the departments and the larger campus community draw from each other's expertise in a reciprocal relationship: each of the parties informs the other's practices (Cunningham, in press; Singer & Cunningham, 2012).

ALLIES AND COMMITMENT TO DIVERSITY

The foregoing discussion suggests that sport managers must attend to various levels of the organization, including factors in the internal and external environments, to embed a culture of diversity and inclusion. Importantly, these efforts are not a one-time activity, but instead they require continual engagement by all in the organization. Therein lies the importance of diversity allies and an organization's commitment to diversity.

Allies

As discussed earlier in the chapter, formal leaders play a critical role in ensuring the success of inclusion and diversity initiatives in the workplace. However, they are not the only ones who can make a difference. Instead, all people—athletes, coaches, staff, administrators, and the like—can affect the climate of diversity and inclusion. They do so through their attitudes, their words, and their actions. Here we see the importance of allies, or individuals who offer support for diversity initiatives, social justice causes, and people from underrepresented groups. As members of a majority group, allies can play an important role in offering support for those who are experiencing discrimination. They can also use their power and privilege in the work environment to speak up in support of causes and initiatives (Cunningham, 2014; Martinez & Hebl, 2010). See the Diversity in the Field box for additional discussion of the power of athletes serving as allies.

I offer two research examples to illustrate ally dynamics. Sartore and I conducted a study of the lesbian stigma present in health and kinesiology departments.

DIVERSITY | IN THE FIELD

Athlete Ally. Hudson Taylor is a former wrestler at the University of Maryland. When he enrolled at the university, he befriended many LGBT students and became aware of the stress and pain caused by heterosexism and sexual prejudice. This prompted him to become involved in ally activities, and as a way to show support, he even wore a Human Rights Campaign sticker (a blue box with a yellow equals sign in the middle) on his headgear during matches. Following his wrestling career, Taylor founded Athlete Ally (www.athlete ally.org) to promote LGBT equality in sport and beyond.

Athlete Ally works with teams and individual athletes to train athletes on the prevalence of sexual prejudice and ways they can engage in ally behavior. Those who complete the training can sign a pledge, which reads: "I pledge to lead my athletic community to respect and welcome all persons, regardless of their perceived or actual sexual orientation, gender identity, or gender expression. Beginning right now, I will do my part to promote the best of athletics by making all players feel respected on and off the field." As of January 2015, more than 20,000 persons had signed the pledge. Some notable professional athletes who serve as Athlete Ally ambassadors include Abby Wambach (soccer), Yogi Berra (baseball), D'Qwell Jackson (football), Andy Roddick (tennis), and Cappie Pondexter (basketball), among others.

Our interviews with lesbians in these academic departments showed that allies played an important role in offering personal support and in vocally advocating for equality (Sartore & Cunningham, 2010). Further, because some of the key allies were full professors and had been married—characteristics that have accompanying power and privilege—encouraging inclusion did not place them in vulnerable positions. Melton and I also observed as much in our study of athletic department members (Melton & Cunningham, 2014). A study participant noted, "A male coach, especially one who is married with three kids, can publically support gay and lesbian issues. People will listen; they might even applaud him for his courage to speak out on a controversial topic. Can a female coach do that? Hell no. She's immediately called a lesbian and all the coaches in her conference are making sure recruits, *and their parents,* know she's lesbian and supports lesbianism on the team" (p. 202, emphasis in original).

Given the influence allies can have, Sartore and I conducted a study to understand what prompted them to become active advocates for diversity and inclusion; that is, what was it that prompted them to engage in championing behavior (Cunningham & Sartore, 2010)? We drew from previous work (Herscovitch & Meyer, 2002; Holvino, Ferdman, & Merrill-Sands, 2004) to suggest that championing was the highest form of discretionary behavior one could undertake, and it involved employees' making specific sacrifices and exerting considerable effort to support diversity and inclusion. We found that women, members of racial or sexual minorities, people who have an extraverted personality, and people who expressed low levels of racial and sexual prejudice were all likely to champion diversity. In addition to these personal characteristics, people who worked with others who also supported diversity were engaged in championing behaviors. These findings have implications for sport managers who seek to transform their workplace into one of diversity and inclusion.

Commitment

As discussed, the work of leaders and allies should increase overall commitment to diversity among organizational members. We can think of commitment to diversity as "a force or mindset that binds an individual to support diversity" (Cunningham, 2008a, p. 178). The mindset can be reflected in one of three ways: (1) affective commitment, a desire to support diversity because of the value of diversity; (2) continuance commitment, the support of diversity because of the costs of not doing so; or (3) normative commitment, the felt obligation to provide support for diversity.

For a sport organization to realize diversity's benefits, commitment to diversity is needed among the employees. I observed as much in a series of studies of NCAA athletic departments (Cunningham, 2008a). Specifically, I found that departments that merged a diverse staff with a strong collective commitment to diversity (i.e., high in all of the above mindsets) outperformed their peers in terms of attracting diverse fans, achieving employee satisfaction, and encouraging employees' creativity. Departments that had high commitment but lacked employee diversity were unable to realize these benefits. These findings suggest that employees should not only recognize the benefits of diversity (have affective commitment) but also adopt a sense of obligation to support it (normative commitment), recognizing that not doing so will adversely affect the workplace (continuance commitment).

chapter SUMMARY

This chapter provided an overview of macro-level strategies aimed at creating an inclusive work environment. The focus was on strategies that would move the entire organization forward, as opposed to focusing on individuals or interpersonal relationships. As illustrated in the Diversity Challenge, there is often a need to employ specific strategies to provide equal opportunities to all parties. Without such strategies, dissimilar others may have negative work experiences. Effective inclusion and diversity management strategies generate positive outcomes for the organization as a whole. After reading this chapter, you should be able to:

1. **Identify the benefits of workplace inclusion.**

   Organizations benefit from inclusiveness in a number of ways. With respect to the external environment, social pressures and legal regulations call for greater diversity and inclusion, and evidence suggests that key external stakeholders (e.g., clients, job applicants, investors) are attracted to inclusive organizations. Internally, inclusiveness is associated with improved employee attitudes, better group processes, and higher objective measures of success.

2. **Discuss strategies for creating an inclusive workplace.**

   Creating and sustaining an inclusive work environment necessitates a multilevel focus. Factors at the individual level (engaging in difficult discussions, developing close ties with dissimilar others), the leader level (advocacy, expectations), the organizational level (education and programming, systemic integration), and the macro level (the diversity and inclusiveness of the broader environment and larger organizational context) all influence the level of inclusiveness in a work environment.

3. **Outline the influence of diversity allies and commitment to diversity in creating inclusion.**

   Other employees can affect inclusion by being an ally, or an individual who offers support for diversity initiatives, social justice causes, and people from underrepresented groups. Allies should ultimately help spur a collective commitment to diversity. This commitment is a force or mindset that binds an individual to support diversity, and it is associated with a bevy of desired organizational outcomes.

QUESTIONS for discussion

1. Why does an organization need an inclusion plan? Isn't the presence of a diverse workforce sufficient for the organization to realize positive outcomes?
2. A multilevel model was presented in this chapter. What are the primary elements of the model? Do you think one particular level of analysis is more important than others?
3. Refer back to the forms of resistance listed in Exhibit 12.2. Which one might be the most prevalent in sport organizations? Which one might be the most difficult to overcome?

4. Are there any methods not discussed in this chapter that managers could use to decrease resistance to inclusion programs?

5. For leaders of diverse organizations that are seeking to promote inclusion, of the competencies that they must have, which is likely to be most important and why?

learning ACTIVITIES

1. Suppose you are hired to manage a recreational sport facility. Identify key stakeholders and external pressures you would want to target and consider in creating an inclusive organizational culture.

2. Suppose you are implementing a particular strategy to enhance diversity and inclusion in your organization. Develop a written action plan outlining the steps you would take to ensure the success of the program. Address the steps necessary to present the desirability of the program to your employees and to overcome any opposition to it.

WEB resources

European Commission: Social Inclusion, http://ec.europa.eu/sport/policy/ societal_role/social_inclusion_en.htm

Outlines the importance of inclusion in sport and ways sport can create social inclusion in the broader society.

Catalyst, www.catalyst.org

Leading research and advisory organization whose aim is to help organizations build inclusive, diverse work environments.

Diversity, Inc., www.diversityinc.com

Provides a "best practices" page for diversity management.

reading RESOURCES

Cunningham, G. B., & Singer, J. N. (2009). *Diversity in athletics: An assessment of exemplars and institutional best practices.* Indianapolis: National Collegiate Athletic Association.

A best-practices manual based on extensive qualitative research with NCAA athletic departments from across the nation.

Konrad, A. M., Prasad, P., & Pringle, J. K. (Eds.) (2006). *Handbook of workplace diversity.* Thousand Oaks, CA: Sage.

An edited handbook that focuses on diversity theory, methods for studying diversity, and the different dimensions of diversity in the workplace.

Stockdale, M. S., & Crosby, F. J. (Eds.) (2004). *The psychology and management of workplace diversity.* Malden, MA: Blackwell.

REFERENCES

Barron, L. G., & Hebl, M. R. (2010). Extending lesbian, gay, bisexual, and transgendered supportive organizational policies: Communities matter too. *Industrial and Organizational Psychology, 3,* 79–81.

Chelladurai, P. (2014). *Managing organizations for sport and physical activity: A systems perspective* (4th ed.). Scottsdale, AZ: Holcomb Hathaway.

Connelly, B. L., Certo, S. T., Ireland, R. D., & Reutzel, C. R. (2011). Signaling theory: A review and assessment. *Journal of Management, 37,* 39–67.

Cunningham, G. B. (2008a). Commitment to diversity and its influence on athletic department outcomes. *Journal of Intercollegiate Sport, 1,* 176–201.

Cunningham, G. B. (2008b). Creating and sustaining gender diversity in sport organizations. *Sex Roles, 58,* 136–145.

Cunningham, G. B. (2008c). Understanding diversity in intercollegiate athletics. *Journal for the Study of Sports and Athletes in Education, 2,* 321–338.

Cunningham, G. B. (2009a). The moderating effect of diversity strategy on the relationship between racial diversity and organizational performance. *Journal of Applied Social Psychology, 36,* 1445–1460.

Cunningham, G. B. (2009b). Understanding the diversity-related change process: A field study. *Journal of Sport Management, 23,* 407–428.

Cunningham, G. B. (2011a). Creative work environments in sport organizations: The influence of sexual orientation diversity and commitment to diversity. *Journal of Homosexuality, 58,* 1041–1057.

Cunningham, G. B. (2011b). The LGBT advantage: Examining the relationship among sexual orientation diversity, diversity strategy, and performance. *Sport Management Review, 14,* 453–461.

Cunningham, G. B. (2014). Interdependence, mutuality, and collective action in sport. *Journal of Sport Management, 28,* 1–7.

Cunningham, G. B. (in press). Creating and sustaining workplace cultures supportive of LGBT employees in college athletics. *Journal of Sport Management.*

Cunningham, G. B., & Melton, E. N. (2014). Signals and cues: LGBT inclusive advertising and consumer attraction. *Sport Marketing Quarterly, 23,* 37–46.

Cunningham, G. B., Pickett, A., Melton, E. N., Lee, W., & Miner, K. (2014). Free to be me: Psychological safety and the expression of sexual orientation and personal identity. In J. Hargreaves & E. Anderson (Eds.), *Routledge handbook of sport gender and sexualities* (pp. 406–415). London: Routledge.

Cunningham, G. B., & Sagas, M. (2004). People make the difference: The influence of human capital and diversity on team performance. *European Sport Management Quarterly, 4,* 3–22.

Cunningham, G. B., & Sartore, M. L. (2010). Championing diversity: The influence of personal and organizational antecedents. *Journal of Applied Social Psychology, 40,* 788–810.

Cunningham, G. B., & Singer, J. N. (2011). The primacy of race: Department diversity and its influence on the attraction of a diverse fan base and revenues generated. *International Journal of Sport Management, 12,* 176–190.

Cunningham, G. B., & Woods, J. (2012). The influence of advertisement focus, consumer gender, and model gender on attraction to a fitness club. *International Journal of Sport Management, 13,* 173–185.

Dacin, M. T., Goodstein, J., & Scott, W. R. (2002). Institutional theory and institutional change: Introduction to the special research forum. *Academy of Management Journal, 45,* 45–57.

DeSensi, J. T. (1995). Understanding multiculturalism and valuing diversity: A theoretical perspective. *Quest, 47,* 34–43.

Dobbin, F., & Kalev, A. (2013). The origins and effects of corporate diversity programs. In Q. M. Roberson (Ed.), *The Oxford handbook of diversity and work* (pp. 253–281). New York: Oxford University Press.

Doherty, A. J., & Chelladurai, P. (1999). Managing cultural diversity in sport organizations: A theoretical perspective. *Journal of Sport Management, 13,* 280–297.

Ely, R. J., & Thomas, D. A. (2001). Cultural diversity at work: The effects of diversity perspectives on work group processes and outcomes. *Administrative Science Quarterly, 46,* 229–273.

Ferdman, B. M. (2014). The practice of inclusion in diverse organizations: Toward a systemic and inclusive framework. In B. M. Ferdman & B. R. Deane (Eds.), *Diversity at work: The practice of inclusion* (pp. 3–54). San Francisco: Jossey-Bass.

Fink, J. S., & Pastore, D. L. (1999). Diversity in sport? Utilizing the business literature to devise a comprehensive framework of diversity initiatives. *Quest, 51,* 310–327.

Fink, J. S., Pastore, D. L., & Riemer, H. A. (2003). Managing employee diversity: Perceived practices and organizational outcomes in NCAA Division III athletic departments. *Sport Management Review, 6,* 147–168.

Herscovitch, L., & Meyer, J. P. (2002). Commitment to organizational change: Extension of a three-component model. *Journal of Applied Psychology, 87,* 474–487.

Holvino, E., Ferdman, B. M., & Merrill-Sands, D. (2004). Creating and sustaining diversity and inclusion in organizations: Strategies and approaches. In M. S. Stockdale & F. J. Crosby (Eds.), *The psychology and management of workplace diversity* (pp. 245–276). Malden, MA: Blackwell.

Ladson-Billings, G. (2004). Landing on the wrong note: The price we paid for *Brown. Educational Researcher, 33*(7), 3–13.

Lee, W., & Cunningham, G. B. (in press). A picture is worth a thousand words: The influence of signaling, organizational reputation, and applicant race on attraction to sport organizations. *International Journal of Sport Management.*

Martinez, L. R., & Hebl, M. R. (2010). Additional agents of change in promoting lesbian, gay, bisexual, and transgendered inclusiveness in organizations. *Industrial and Organizational Psychology, 3*, 82–85.

Melton, E. N., & Cunningham, G. B. (2012). The effect of LGBT-inclusive policies, gender, and social dominance orientation on organizational attraction. *International Journal of Sport Management, 13*, 444–462.

Melton, E. N., & Cunningham, G. B. (2014). Who are the champions? Using a multilevel model to examine perceptions of employee support for LGBT inclusion in sport organizations. *Journal of Sport Management, 28*, 189–206.

Miller, T., & Triana, M. D. C. (2009). Demographic diversity in the boardroom: Mediators of the board-diversity-form performance relationship. *Journal of Management Studies, 46*, 755–786.

Nishii, L. H., & Rich, R. E. (2014). Creating inclusive climates in diverse organizations. In B. M. Ferdman & B. R. Deane (Eds.), *Diversity at work: The practice of inclusion* (pp. 330–363). San Francisco: Jossey-Bass.

Oliver, C. (1992). The antecedents of deinstitutionalization. *Organization Studies, 13*, 563–588.

Pugh, S. D., Dietz, J., Brief, A. P., & Wiley, J. W. (2008). Looking inside and out: The impact of employee and community demographic composition on organizational diversity climate. *The Journal of Applied Psychology, 93*, 1422–1428.

Richard, O. C., & Miller, C. D. (2013). Considering diversity as a source of competitive advantage in organizations.

In Q. M. Roberson (Ed.), *The Oxford handbook of diversity and work* (pp. 239–250). New York: Oxford University Press.

Robbins, S. P. (2011). *Essentials of organizational behavior* (11th ed). New York: Pearson.

Sartore, M., & Cunningham, G. B. (2010). The lesbian label as a component of women's stigmatization in sport organizations: An exploration of two health and kinesiology departments. *Journal of Sport Management, 24*, 481–501.

Scott, S. (2002). *Fierce conversations: Achieving success at work & in life, one conversation at a time.* New York: Berkley Books.

Scott, W. R. (2001). *Institutions and organizations* (2nd ed.). Thousand Oaks, CA: Sage.

Singer, J. N., & Cunningham, G. B. (2012). A case study of the diversity culture of an American university athletic department: Implications for educational stakeholders. *Sport, Education & Society, 17*, 647–669.

Spaaij, R., Farquharson, K., Magee, J., Jeanes, R., Lusher, D., & Gorman, S. (2014). A fair game for all? How community sports clubs in Australia deal with diversity. *Journal of Sport and Social Issues, 38*, 346–365.

Staurowsky, E. J. (2007). "You know, we are all Indian": Exploring White power and privilege in reactions to the NCAA Native American mascot policy. *Journal of Sport & Social Issues, 31*, 61–76.

Tuten, T. L. (2005). The effect of gay-friendly and non-gay-friendly cues on brand attitudes: A comparison of heterosexual and gay/lesbian reactions. *Journal of Marketing Management, 21*, 441–461.

Tuten, T. L. (2006). Exploring the importance of gay-friendliness and its socialization influences. *Journal of Marketing Communications, 12*, 79–94.

Volpone, S. D., & Avery, D. R. (2010). I'm confused: How failing to value sexual minorities at work sends stakeholders mixed messages. *Industrial and Organizational Psychology, 3*, 90–92.

Walker, H. J., Feild, H. S., Bernerth, J. B., & Becton, J. B. (2012). Diversity cues on recruitment websites: Investigating the effects on job seekers' information processing. *Journal of Applied Psychology, 97*, 214–224.

Interpersonal Inclusiveness*

LEARNING objectives

After studying this chapter, you should be able to:

- Discuss the conditions of contact under which prejudice should be reduced.
- Discuss how categorization-based strategies are used to create inclusive environments.
- Explain the integrated model of inclusion in groups.

DIVERSITY CHALLENGE

Melaleuca Elementary School is less than 10 miles from Palm Beach, Florida, where multi-million-dollar mansions line the beachfront. Most of its students, however, do not come from high-income families or live in luxurious homes; rather, they come from working-class families, and 70 percent are racial minorities. Two of every three students receive free or reduced-cost lunches.

Despite the class-related dissimilarities, these students have at least one thing in common with their classmates from the more affluent neighborhoods: lacrosse. It is the working together toward a common goal—winning—that has brought the students together. Claire Lawson, a midfielder on the team, explains, "When we're on the team, we're not focused on color or ethnic background. We're just focused on playing as a team." Though the potential for race-related or social class–related friction certainly exists, sport brings this diverse collection of athletes together.

In a similar fashion, in Seattle, Washington, efforts are under way to make rowing more accessible to everyone. Those students who participate in the sport learn several life lessons, such as the importance of working together. Steve Gerritson, who serves as the executive director of the George Pocock Rowing Foundation, notes, "It teaches values that are important no matter what you are doing. . . . If you can't cooperate, you don't stay dry." Lessons such as these demonstrate to people the importance of teamwork and of overlooking differences in the interest of the team.

Source: Sharp, D. (2003, June). High-brow sports seek diversity. *USAToday.com.* Retrieved from www.usatoday.com/news/nation/2003-06-15-croquet-usat_x.htm.

---

*Portions of this chapter are adapted from Cunningham (2004).

1. In your experience, does sport serve to bring people together in such a manner that any differences are ignored? If so, explain why this occurs.

2. Have you had experiences where team member dissimilarities remained the primary focus instead of team cooperation? If so, why did this happen?

3. Does sport serve to unify other people, not just the athletes? If so, what are some examples?

As the Diversity Challenge illustrates, some groups' dynamics assuage any potential negative effects of member differences. This can be seen in the sport context because demographics sometimes do not matter on the playing field. This is not true of all athletic teams, however, and we can all think of situations when differences among team members were too great to overcome. The likelihood that individual differences will subvert an otherwise positive group dynamic is even greater when we move away from the athletic context and consider work groups in the organizational setting. When the group dynamic is weak or negative, strategies must be used at the group level to reduce the potentially negative effects of diversity. Furthermore, growing evidence indicates that a group culture of inclusion can lead to improved group member experiences and group performance, particularly among diverse groups.

I begin this chapter with an overview of the early perspectives upon which more contemporary theories were built. The focus then turns to the social categorization perspective, with the suggestion that the key to enhancing inclusion in the group setting is to adjust the categorization process. This can be done in one of three ways: by breaking down the categories, by differentiating between the groups, or by building up a superordinate identity. This chapter concludes with a discussion of an integrated model that combines the three categorization-based strategies. For other approaches to prejudice reduction in the group setting, see Paluck and Green (2009).

THE CONTACT HYPOTHESIS

Allport's (1954) contact hypothesis is among the earliest and most influential theories related to reducing prejudice. Most of the contemporary theories on bias reduction are grounded in his work (Hodson & Hewstone, 2013), and many scholars and practitioners still incorporate his original piece into their efforts to reduce prejudice (Bruening, Fuller, Cotrufo, et al., 2014; Welty Peachey, Cunningham, Lyras, et al., in press). The basic premise underlying Allport's contact hypothesis states that prejudice is sustained against others because of unfamiliarity and separation; thus, the key to reducing prejudice is to enable members of various social groups to have contact with one another under the right conditions (see Exhibit 13.1).

Conditions of Contact

As suggested earlier, Allport's contact hypothesis recognized that contact may not reduce prejudice in all circumstances; in fact, in some situations it might exacerbate

Effects of contact on prejudice.   EXHIBIT **13.1**

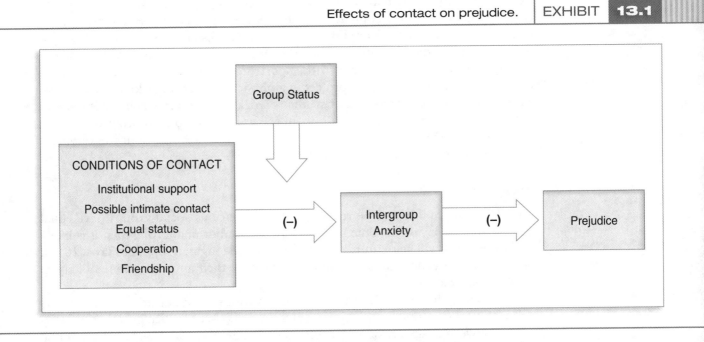

it. Allport suggested that contact between dissimilar people improves intergroup relations under the five conditions listed in Exhibit 13.1 and discussed below.

Availability of social and institutional support

Institutional support, such as support from top administrators, should lead to social norms that favor intergroup interaction, tolerance, and acceptance (Allport, 1954). Early research focusing on people in housing projects demonstrated this effect (Deutsch & Collins, 1951; Wilner, Walkley, & Cook, 1955). Prejudice was higher among Whites in segregated housing projects than it was for Whites in integrated projects. For the latter group, bias was especially low when the Whites believed that interactions with racial minorities would be viewed as acceptable and normal.

This idea is certainly applicable to the organizational context. Group leaders often set the norms for the group, thereby prescribing acceptable modes of behavior (see Chapter 12). If the leader endorses interaction among members from different social groups (e.g., Hispanics and Whites), then that becomes the accepted way of working together in that group. This available support, coupled with the other conditions, reduces bias among group members.

Possibility of intimate contact

Allport (1954) suggests that close, intimate contact is more effective in reducing bias than brief, impersonal encounters for two reasons. First, developing friendships is usually rewarding and provides a pleasurable affective experience. Second, if people interact with one another on a close, intimate level, then it is likely that this contact will result in stereotype disconfirmation. Stereotypes are largely based on faulty information (Allport, 1954); thus, close interaction with a person will expose the faulty information as such. The housing project research mentioned earlier supports Allport's contention. Those White families who lived close to African American families reported more interaction and significantly more favorable attitudes toward them, relative to the other White families (Wilner et al., 1955).

This principle is applicable to the sport organization context. Consider, for example, groups working on a project in a physical education or kinesiology class. Many times projects require that students work closely with each other over an extended period of time, allowing them to get to know one another on a more personal level. During this process, friendships may be formed, or at the very least preconceptions and stereotypes may be discredited.

Equal status

Prejudice is more likely to be reduced when the various social groups have equal status (Allport, 1954). If some members are in a subordinate role, then it is likely that stereotypes will be reinforced and strengthened (Saguy, Tropp, & Hawi, 2013); however, if everyone shares a "common ground," then an interaction is likely to result in bias reduction.

Applying this principle to sport organizations, interaction with dissimilar colleagues on the same hierarchical level is more likely to reduce bias than is interaction between a supervisor and a subordinate. For example, bias held by a White assistant athletic director toward Asians is reduced more when his interaction is with an Asian assistant athletic director than with an Asian student worker. The interaction with the Asian assistant director involves two people who have the same power and organizational rank; hence, the equal status might result in reduced bias and prejudice. With the Asian student worker, power differences are still present between the two, so stereotypes may remain.

Necessity for cooperative interaction

Prejudice is thought to be reduced when the situation requires cooperative interdependence among group members (Allport, 1954). Prejudice directed toward out-group members is likely to be reduced when members of separate groups have to work together in order to accomplish a task. Without the others' contributions, the task cannot be completed.

This is the principle that has received the greatest attention and support since the 1950s (Brewer & Gaertner, 2001). This awareness was spurred in large part by Sherif's Robbers Cave study (Sherif, Harvey, White, et al., 1961), which involved 22 boys who signed up for three weeks of summer camp. They were randomly assigned to groups of 11, which named themselves the Eagles and the Rattlers. During the camp's first week, the boys participated in activities with members of their own group, not knowing that the other group even existed. During the second week, the two groups competed against each other in a series of activities such as touch football, resulting in intergroup competition and bias. Previous laboratory settings have shown in-group favoritism to be common; however, in the camp-competition setting, the boys displayed out-group derogation and harbored negative feelings toward the out-group to the extent that there were hostile relations between the two groups (Gaertner & Dovidio, 2000). During the third week, the campers were brought together under noncompetitive conditions, but the hostility remained. It was not until the two groups worked together under cooperative conditions (e.g., working together to fix a truck) that the bias between the two groups began to subside. The results of this study suggest that cooperative interdependence among group members can decrease levels of intergroup bias.

The efficacy of cooperative interdependence is routinely seen in sport organizations. Recall that in the Diversity Challenge, one of the players commented that her teammates' demographics did not matter while they were playing, because all members focused on the team. In a highly interdependent sport such as lacrosse, teammates must cooperate in order for the team to be successful. Therefore, it is understandable that the team, not the individual differences among the members, becomes the focus of attention, and intergroup bias decreases.

Friendship

In addition to the four conditions of contact originally proposed by Allport (1954), growing evidence suggests that friendship potential is a key condition for reducing prejudice (Pettigrew, 1998). Consider, for instance, that when people develop friendships with others, they learn information about, change their attitudes toward, generate affective ties with, and change their evaluations of those persons. All of these factors are critical to reducing prejudice (Ellers & Abrams, 2003; Mellinger & Levant, 2014).

There is empirical support for the efficacy of friendships in reducing prejudice. People with friends who had confided their sexual-minority identity to them had more positive attitudes toward sexual minorities than did people whose friends had not revealed a sexual-minority identity (Herek & Capitanio, 1996). In a longitudinal study of international students participating in a study program abroad, my colleagues and I found that students who developed intergroup friendships were also likely to reduce their prejudice toward out-group members in general (Cunningham, Bopp, & Sagas, 2010). In another study, I observed that friendship potential, rather than developing actual friendships, was sufficient to influence people's general affective reactions to the out-group positively (Cunningham, 2008b). Finally, in a study of a racially diverse group of adults, Melton and I observed that having friendships with lesbian and gay individuals helped to reduce the otherwise strong effects of religious fundamentalism on sexual prejudice (Cunningham & Melton, 2013). These studies point to the efficacy of emphasizing friendship opportunities, or the potential thereof, in intergroup interactions.

Intergroup Anxiety

Initially, researchers assumed that the aforementioned conditions of contact had a direct effect on prejudice reduction. More recent research suggests that the effects probably occur through a reduction in intergroup anxiety (Binder, Sagefka, Brown, et al., 2009; Brown & Hewstone, 2005; Pettigrew & Tropp, 2006). *Intergroup anxiety* refers to feelings of unease or apprehension that a person experiences when visualizing or having contact with out-group members. This anxiety arises from the misunderstanding and rejection that people anticipate when interacting with people who are different from themselves. As a result of this anxiety, people are likely to harbor negative feelings toward out-group members and, in turn, exhibit prejudice.

The presence of Allport's conditions for contact should reduce intergroup anxiety and, ultimately, prejudice. In an examination illustrative of these effects, Ellers and Abrams (2003) conducted a study of Americans who were studying Spanish in Mexican language institutes. They observed that friendship with out-group members was reliably related to a variety of outcomes, including reduction of anxiety directed toward the out-group and reduction of social distancing. Binder and colleagues' (2009) longitudinal study of minority and majority European schoolchildren yielded similar findings.

Influence of Status

Thus far, I have argued that the five conditions of contact should result in decreased intergroup anxiety, which, in turn, will reduce prejudice. Contemporary research suggests that these effects are not uniform. Instead, the influence of contact on intergroup anxiety and prejudice is stronger for majority members than for minority members (Binder et al., 2009; Tropp & Pettigrew, 2005). There are several possible explanations for these findings. From one perspective, majority members have higher status in society, and they might seek to avoid displaying discrimination against minority members because this would be socially unacceptable. Among minority members, this concern would be trumped by the distress associated with facing discrimination from majority members (Tropp & Pettigrew, 2005).

From a different perspective, it is possible that minority members, because they usually represent the numerical minority in social situations, are more accustomed to interacting with majority members. Thus, the effects of contact would be minimal. Majority members, however, can largely avoid contact with minority members by, for instance, living in certain neighborhoods, attending particular schools, shopping at a certain supermarket, and the like (for related discussions, see McIntosh's 1990 discussion of White privilege). Thus, contact with minority members, because it is less common, would have a meaningful effect for majority members.

Contact Hypothesis Limitations

Although Allport's (1954) contact hypothesis has been used extensively throughout the years, it does have three primary limitations (Brewer & Gaertner, 2001). First, most of the research was conducted in laboratory settings where contact conditions were controlled. Outside the laboratory, the expected contact outcomes possibly may not occur when there is a history of hostility between the groups. For example, we might ask whether the contact conditions would reduce the biases between Palestinians and Jews. In the context of sport organizations, although biases might not be as strong as those in the Middle East, strong prejudicial attitudes may exist nonetheless.

Second, bias reduction in one context might not translate to a corresponding reduction in another—that is, it might not generalize to other contexts. For example, suppose players on a boys' basketball team experience a reduction in racial bias because the contact conditions are met. Does this mean that bias is reduced toward *all* racially different people in *all* subsequent situations? This effect is not likely. A White player's reduction in bias toward racial minority teammates in the sport situation does not mean that bias toward racial minority students in the classroom context will also be reduced. Thus, the effects might be context-specific. See the box on the following page for additional discussion of generalization.

Generalizing the effects of contact

As stated earlier, when bias is reduced, it may be reduced only for the specific situation, or it may be transferred to other situations. Typically, if diversity strategies are applied in only one context (e.g., a workplace training center), then bias toward specific out-group members will likely be reduced in that specific setting, but not others. However, it is possible for a reduction in bias to transfer to situations other than the original setting. The latter circumstance is termed *generalizability,* and it is desirable because it means that bias is reduced in more than a single situation. Pettigrew (1998) identified the following three forms of generalization:

1. *Generalization across situations.* In this form, a reduction in bias toward an out-group member occurs in multiple contexts. With this type of generalization, strategies were effective in the specific original setting (e.g., a workplace training center), and the bias-reduction effect carried over to other settings (e.g., a place outside work), as well.

2. *Generalization from an individual to the entire out-group.* Bias reduction might also be transferred from an individual to all other members of an out-group. Suppose that, as a result of a diversity training seminar, a White male coach expresses less bias toward the two African Americans in his work group—a good result. A better result is if the training results in his expressing less bias toward all African Americans in all situations.

3. *Generalization from the immediate out-group to other out-groups.* To extend the previous example, the best result is when the White coach not only expresses less bias toward individual African American coaches and African Americans in general but also expresses less bias toward *all* racial minorities. This is what is meant by generalizing from the immediate out-group to all out-groups. Though seldom observed, this form of generalization has occurred in some studies (Pettigrew, 1998). As might be expected, those diversity and inclusion strategies and training endeavors that have this effect are the most desirable.

Third, Brewer and Gaertner (2001; see also Pettigrew, 1998) suggest that subsequent studies related to the contact hypothesis placed many boundary conditions (e.g., the conditions of contact) on the general theory, resulting in the attachment of an inordinate number of qualifiers. As noted in Chapter 2, boundary conditions can be useful because they indicate when and where certain effects are thought to occur. However, when too many conditions are placed on a theory, it is essentially rendered useless. Reflecting on this and the more recent research on the topic, I think it is clear that while the five conditions of contact are helpful in reducing intergroup anxiety and prejudice, they are not necessary. Large-scale studies have shown that improved intergroup relationships can result from mere contact itself, even under conditions that are less than ideal (Pettigrew & Tropp, 2006). I should note, though, that even absent the conditions of contact, we would expect the nature of the interactions—that is, whether they are positive in nature—to influence subsequent anxiety and prejudice.

Indirect Contact

There might be cases where, for a variety of reasons, intergroup contact should not occur. It might not be responsible, for instance, for persons with a history of violence to meet and interact with one another. In other cases, contact might be advisable, but because of geographic differences, actual contact might be impossible. A number of social psychologists have explored the efficacy of indirect forms of contact.

Extended contact

Extended contact theory is an example of research into indirect contact. From this perspective, simply knowing that a person similar to oneself has out-group friends has the potential to reduce intergroup bias (Dovidio, Eller, & Hewstone, 2011). This transfer is especially likely to occur if the in-group member is held in high regard and the focal individual trusts that person's judgment.

Vezzali, Stathi, Giovannini, and their colleagues (2015) conducted a series of studies to examine whether the effects of extended contact could be realized through reading *Harry Potter* books. In addition to focusing on various adventures and magic, all seven books contain themes of inclusion of individuals who differ from the majority (muggles, elves, and goblins, among others). The authors examined whether reading passages that focused on prejudice and its effects would serve to reduce bias, particularly among readers who strongly identified with Harry Potter himself. A study with elementary school students showed that this was the case; further, those students who strongly identified with Voldemort (the evil character in the book, who promotes intergroup distinctions) held negative out-group attitudes. Subsequent work with high school students (Study 2) and college students (Study 3) demonstrated similar findings. This research shows that *others'* acceptance of out-group members can affect one's own beliefs.

Other elements of the *Harry Potter* books can also improve intergroup relations, as illustrated in the Diversity in the Field box.

Imagined contact

Imagined intergroup contact represents another form of indirect contact. This approach involves "the mental simulation of a social interaction with a member or members of an outgroup category" (Crisp & Turner, 2009, p. 234). In this case,

---

DIVERSITY | IN THE FIELD

Quidditch, Bias, and Inclusion. Many of the characters in the *Harry Potter* books participate in quidditch. This is a sport where the participants fly on broomsticks and try to pass a ball through hoops placed at opposite ends of a playing field, while also trying to capture the snitch. (If this is all gibberish to you, I do recommend reading the books; also, the initiated reader can consult the site for the International Quidditch Association, www.iqaquidditch.org). Interestingly, the sport has caught on across a number of college campuses. The non-fantasy games closely mirror those in the book: team members run instead of fly with broomsticks, attempt to throw balls through hoops at either end of the field, and even attempt to capture a snitch. Importantly (and also consistent with the books), quidditch is played as a coed sport, without special accommodations for women.

Cohen has conducted a number of studies on why people participate in quidditch and what impact it has on them (Cohen, Melton, & Welty Peachey, 2014; Cohen & Welty Peachey, in press). In one of his studies, Cohen and his colleagues found that the coed nature of the sport allowed for improved attitudes toward participants of the opposite gender. Participation was also linked with an enhanced desire for justice, equality, and inclusion. For example, one player noted, "I never thought my girlfriend could be as good at a sport as me, maybe even better! So yes, this coed sport has changed my thinking" (p. 227). Another noted that the coed structure "makes it a game of inclusion that makes everyone feel welcome" (p. 227). These results provide another example of how sport and intergroup contact can affect people's bias and desire for inclusion.

people imagine they are interacting in an agreeable way with out-group members, and this mental simulation is enough to alter their attitudes toward dissimilar others. Imagined contact can also prepare people to engage in actual contact.

Miles and Crisp (2014) conducted a meta-analysis of all experimental studies that examined the effects of imagined contact. Recall that a meta-analysis statistically aggregates the findings from numerous studies to demonstrate the overall effects of the phenomenon under investigation. A common characteristic of the studies in this meta-analysis is that the researchers randomly assigned participants to (1) the experimental group, where they imagined interacting with out-group members in some way, or (2) a control group, where they participated in another activity. Results of the meta-analysis indicate that imagined contact had a significant effect on bias reduction. Outcomes included explicit and implicit measures of prejudice, emotional reactions to the out-group, behaviors, and behavioral intentions.

Lee and I have examined the effects of imagined contact in the sport context (Lee & Cunningham, 2014). We asked people in the experimental group to imagine the following: "You play basketball with a gay man for two hours. Then, you spend about 30 minutes chatting. During the conversation you find out some interesting and unexpected things about him." In the control group, we asked people to imagine that they played basketball with their best friend. We then asked the participants to reflect on the mental simulation and finally respond to a questionnaire. Results indicated that for Koreans the imagined contact served to lessen intergroup anxiety and sexual prejudice; however, the same was not the case for Americans, for whom anxiety actually increased. We reasoned this could be attributable to the participants' previous experiences with LGBT individuals. Few people disclose their sexual orientation in Korea, so Koreans might not have preconceived notions or firmly embedded biases, and, thus, imagined contact would be effective. On the other hand, as Americans might have had more experiences interacting with members of sexual minorities, their attitudes might be more cemented and less malleable. This reasoning is consistent with Miles and Crisp's (2014) findings that imagined contact is more effective among children (i.e., people who are unlikely to have set attitudes toward out-group members) than with adults.

SOCIAL CATEGORIZATION STRATEGIES FOR REDUCING BIAS

T he limitations of the contact hypothesis meant that more sophisticated conceptualizations were needed. As Brewer and Gaertner (2001) note, "Contact researchers needed a more elaborate theory of what the underlying processes are and how they mediate the effects of intergroup contact under different conditions" (p. 456). The social categorization framework (Tajfel & Turner, 1979; Turner, Hogg, Oakes, et al., 1987) provides one such perspective. Although this approach was discussed at length in Chapter 2, it is instructive to recall the following two points:

1. In an attempt to organize their social world, people will categorize themselves and others into social groups, and this process minimizes differences *within* groups while heightening differences *between* groups; and

2. People who are similar to the self are considered in-group members and are afforded more positive affect and trust than those who differ from the self—

out-group members. The end result is intergroup bias—in-group members are viewed in a more positive light than out-group members.

This theory suggests, therefore, that the potential negative effects of diversity are a function, at least in part, of the intergroup bias that exists between groups. The categorization process is "fundamental to the formation of in-groups and the widely documented tendency of individuals to prefer homogeneous groups of similar others" (Tsui, Egan, & O'Reilly, 1992, p. 522). Williams and O'Reilly (1998) arrived at similar conclusions after reviewing over 40 years of diversity research. They note that "it is clear that there are potentially negative consequences from social categorization processes operating in groups" (p. 118).

One potential strategy for improving intergroup relations, therefore, is to adjust the categorization process. Indeed, researchers have drawn from the contact hypothesis and social categorization's basic tenets to develop three strategies—decategorization, recategorization, and intergroup contact—thought to overcome categorization boundaries (see Exhibit 13.2). For yet another approach, see the Alternative Perspectives box on the facing page.

Decategorization

Decategorization is an attempt to reduce intergroup bias by breaking down the categorization boundaries between interacting groups (Brewer & Miller, 1984). This strategy is based in the idea that repeated, individualized interactions among members of different groups will ultimately reduce bias. This is accomplished in two ways. First, recall that through the categorization process, all members of a specific social group are perceived as largely homogeneous (e.g., "all women act *that* way"), and distinctions are not made among members of the group. Decategorization through individualized interactions allows a person to make distinctions among out-group members, a process called *differentiation*. Second, when people interact on a personal level with others, they compare the others to themselves. This results in a process called *personalization*, in which out-group members are viewed "in terms of their uniqueness and in relation to the self" (Hewstone, Rubin, & Willis, 2002, p. 589). Both processes allow one to see oneself and the other person as *individuals*, rather than as members of homogeneous in-groups or out-

---

EXHIBIT 13.2   Categorization-based strategies for managing diverse groups.

- **Decategorization:** Reduces bias by breaking down categorization boundaries through repeated individualized interactions with out-group members.
- **Recategorization:** Reduces bias by building up a superordinate group identity that is inclusive of all groups.
- **Intergroup contact:** Reduces bias by emphasizing both the categorization boundaries and the unique contributions of each subgroup to the overall group.

Source: Adapted from Brewer & Gaertner (2001).

ALTERNATIVE perspectives

Cross-Categorization Strategies for Managing Diverse Groups. It is possible for people to maintain several identities, with each identity salient at different times and in different contexts. For example, a person might hold the identity of coach in the workplace, partner at home or during time spent with family, Christian at church or when religious questions arise, and daughter when in the presence of her parents. Clearly, not all of these identities hold equal weight across all situations. Within a particular situation, certain identities may serve as the basis for categorization. At work, the above-described person might consider other coaches as in-group members and, therefore, hold those coaches in higher regard than other persons in the organization. This is consistent with the categorization process outlined throughout this book.

We have been working with the assumption that people's identities are orthogonal—that is, when one is important in a certain context, others are not. What would happen, however, if one could blur the categorization boundaries? What if a person could concurrently trigger multiple identities in a specific social context, so that, for example, the categorizations of being a coach and being a woman were both salient in the work context? The answer is that the prejudice and bias typically resulting from a particular category distinction may be reduced. This is the essence of the *cross-categorization* argument. As Brewer and Gaertner (2001) note, "There are reasons to expect that simultaneous activation of multiple ingroup identities both is possible and has potential for reducing prejudice and discrimination based on any one category distinction" (p. 463).

There are several reasons why this might be true. First, when multiple identities are activated in a specific context, the significance of in-group and out-group distinctions becomes blurred. Second, the bias toward out-group members in one category is thought to be lessened when that person is an in-group member in another category. Finally, cutting across categorization boundaries allows for increased interactions with former out-group members—something that should ultimately reduce the level of bias toward those individuals (Brewer, 1999).

To illustrate, suppose the coach in the earlier example attends the same church as an opposing coach. In this situation, two categories are crossed—that of being Christian and that of being a coach. In this context, the distinction of the opposing coach as an out-group member may be blurred because the coach attends the same church and is, thus, an in-group member in that regard. Because of the cross-categorization, the coaches are likely to spend more time with one another than they otherwise would, and biases might be reduced. Thus, the cross-categorization can decrease the intergroup bias.

groups. To the extent that these interactions are repeated over time, this breaking down of categorization boundaries might also be applied in new situations or to hitherto unfamiliar out-group members (Gaertner & Dovidio, 2000).

Research support

Considerable laboratory research supports this rationale. For instance, Gaertner, Mann, Murrell, and Dovidio (1989) found a reduction in bias when members of separate groups came to conceive of themselves as separate individuals as opposed to members of differing social groups. They also identified the manner by which the bias was reduced: decategorization resulted in less attraction toward former in-group members; in other words, reduced in-group favoritism (see also Brewer, 1999). Jones and Foley's (2003) experiment focused on the degree to which decategorization reduced bias among schoolchildren. Students were assigned to one of two conditions: (1) the experimental condition, in which the students heard a presentation emphasizing anthropology (e.g., the origin of humans, the spread of humans across the globe), problems associated with depending on physical biological characteristics to determine differences among people, and the idea that most persons in the United States have common ancestry; and (2) the control condition, in which students heard a reading of Dr. Seuss's *Oh, The Places You'll Go!* The researchers found that the students in the experimental condition were more likely to perceive similarities between themselves and others, and as a result their formerly held prejudice toward out-group members was reduced.

Application

Although it may not be referred to as decategorization, this approach is often used in organizational and team settings. For example, many organizations use rope courses or other adventure escapes as methods to build a team. These programs allow people to become acquainted outside the office, build communication skills among team members, and strengthen interpersonal relationships. It is expected that boundaries among team members will be reduced, thereby increasing the team's effectiveness.

As another example, the Dallas Cup, a competitive week-long soccer tournament held in Dallas, Texas, is designed to host youth teams from around the world (see www.dallascup.com). To attract these teams to the tournament, the organizers provide housing. This is accomplished by having local-area athlete participants host several international players for the week. According to tournament organizers, the local players are initially apprehensive about hosting players so different from themselves. However, by week's end, the players have become so close to each other that tears often accompany the goodbyes. Tournament organizers attribute this closeness to the fact that the players get to know one another on a very personal level during that week and grow quite fond of each other (personal communication, Gordon Jago, November 15, 2005).

Potential limitations

Despite the support of decategorization by various studies and its use in professional settings, the approach does have limitations. First, it is unclear how well decategorization is maintained over time or across situations (Brewer & Gaertner, 2001). For example, a common criticism of ropes courses and other adventure activities is that they might reduce bias only in that specific context, and the effects may not transfer back to the workplace or athletic team. The fact that two people learn information about each other and come to like each other in an adventure-course setting may not be sufficient for them to carry those feelings over to another context. On the contrary, it might be more likely that once they return to the workplace—a setting to which the parties are accustomed—the usual routines, behaviors, preferences, and biases will recur. Even if the bias reduction is sustained for a short time, it is unclear whether the effects will last.

Second, even if bias is reduced toward specific individuals, it is unclear whether this effect can be transferred to similar persons (Brewer & Gaertner, 2001). For example, suppose that a Jew and a Muslim share personal information about each other over a period of time, lessening the categorization boundaries. Does the fact that this occurred with these two people mean that the categorization boundaries that might exist between the Jew and other Muslims in other contexts (or vice versa) will also be reduced? Although this effect may be possible, it is more likely that the bias reduction will remain directed toward the specific person; consequently, the same process would have to occur with other individuals.

Despite these limitations, decategorization can be an effective strategy for reducing bias in the group setting.

Recategorization

According to Gaertner and Dovidio (2000), who developed the Common Ingroup Identity Model, the purpose of *recategorization* is to encourage "members of both groups to regard themselves as belonging to a common superordinate group—*one group* that is inclusive of both memberships" (p. 33, emphasis in original). If members of different groups consider themselves members of a single, common group, then former membership boundaries become less important because all are now members of the same in-group. The common in-group serves to replace the "us" and "them" dynamics with a more inclusive "we." For example, boards of directors are increasingly looking to add demographic diversity to their boards. They are likely to do so when they believe the demographically different new board members share common beliefs, values, or other characteristics. This makes it easier for them to recategorize the new members as common in-group members and helps the board function effectively (Zhu, Shen, & Hillman, 2014).

Note the differences between this approach and decategorization. In the latter, the focus is on breaking down categorization boundaries. The goal is to recognize that not all out-group members are the same and that, in fact, some out-group members have characteristics similar to the self (Brewer & Miller, 1984). With recategorization, the focus is on creating a new, more inclusive category that encompasses *both* in-group *and* out-group members. Decategorization reduces bias through the devaluation of former in-group members (Gaertner et al., 1989), whereas recategorization reduces bias by bringing former out-group members closer to the self through a process known as pro–in-group bias (Gaertner & Dovidio, 2000). Former out-group members are now afforded in-group status, and because in-group members are generally viewed in a positive light, the former out-group members are now viewed that way, as well.

Research support

Several studies lend support to this model, both in the laboratory and in the field context. One of the earliest laboratory studies was conducted by Gaertner and his colleagues (1989). They designed an experiment whereby they could manipulate the conditions under which groups worked with one another. They found that when two groups came together and considered themselves members of a single, common group, then intergroup bias was reduced. In line with the researchers' theoretical predictions, the bias was reduced because attitudes toward former out-group members became more positive. This supports the notion that bias in recategorized groups is reduced through the pro–in-group bias process. Subsequent laboratory research shows that recategorization is associated with an increase in helpful behaviors directed toward out-group members (Dovidio et al., 1997), satisfaction with the group (Cunningham & Chelladurai, 2004), and preference to work with the group in the future (Cunningham & Chelladurai, 2004).

professional
PERSPECTIVES

Recategorization on a Soccer Team. Stoney Pryor, the head coach of the College Station High School varsity girls' soccer team, observed that the team is diverse in many ways. First, the players differ in ability, so one of his primary tasks is "to get these girls of varying abilities to work together." Second, the levels of motivation differ across the team—some players participate in the hope of playing at the college level, some play to win, and others play for the mere enjoyment of doing so; thus, the girls' work ethic may not be uniform. Third, the players have varying personal styles (e.g., aggressive, offensive-minded, defensive-minded). Fourth, socioeconomic differences among the girls influence the team dynamics. Finally, the attitudes on the team can (and frequently do) vary, thereby creating the possibility of cliques.

In light of these differences, it is imperative that Pryor develop strategies that help the girls work together as a team. He accomplishes this team building by emphasizing the common group identity and conducting team-building activities throughout the year. For example, team goals (e.g., district championship) are established prior to the season to ensure that the players "are working on the same goals as a team." In addition, the team members participate in considerable group work during practice to reinforce the team concept. This concept of a team is also carried outside the playing field—players regularly meet for team dinners (usually organized by the seniors) that encourage additional bonding and team building.

All of these activities focus on reducing the potential negative effects of differences and working together as a team. As Pryor explains, "Some differences are good. We need different positions and different personalities. But, in order for a team to work effectively, we must embrace our particular role, perform it well, and enable those around us to perform their roles. Then, we can begin to achieve the goals set forth as a team. Individual goals are fine, but in team sports, success is generally measured in how the team achieves its goals."

In addition to the aforementioned laboratory work, I have also found evidence of the importance of a common in-group identity among college coaches. In the first study, I observed that coworker satisfaction among people who differ racially from their colleagues was higher when they were on staffs characterized by a common in-group identity than when they were not (Cunningham, 2005). In the next study, I examined the effects of a common in-group identity for the coaching staff as a whole. The results indicated that the stronger the identity, the more effective the team was on multiple measures of success, and the less likely the coaches were to leave the staff (Cunningham, 2007).

All of these studies suggest that developing a common in-group identity among group members benefits those individuals and the groups of which they are a part.

Application

Gaertner and Dovidio (2000) propose several methods that a group leader can use to form a common in-group identity. These include:

- *Spatial arrangement:* Members from various groups sit together rather than with members of their own group. Sitting only with in-group members reinforces categorization boundaries; however, sitting with people from other groups, while still in the context of a work group, team, or classroom, reinforces the perception that all of the people are members of a common group, not separate groups. See the Professional Perspectives box for another example.

- *Common threat:* Establishing a "common threat" is another method to engender a common in-group identity. When there is a common enemy or common threat, people in a group will unite together to combat that threat. From a managerial standpoint, it is important to identify the threat and the danger it poses explicitly to the group or organization. For example, employees at adidas might view another sporting goods company, such as Nike, as a threat to the company's economic well-being. To the extent that the adidas employees all perceive the threat, they are likely to be united in confronting the competitor in the marketplace.

■ *Common fate: Common fate* refers to the idea that if the group does well, then all group members are rewarded. Similarly, if the group performs poorly, then all members suffer. Common fate is illustrated by highly interdependent athletic teams where, despite individual performances, if the team loses, then all team members suffer the effects. A common fate has a way of bringing a team together and forming solidarity among the members.

■ *Common goals:* Common goals can unify efforts among group members toward a singular objective. When this occurs, the members are likely to work together for the sake of the team, thereby overlooking individual differences in the interest of the team. This phenomenon is seen in athletic teams when the primary objective, winning, brings the players together, and a common identity is formed.

Potential limitations

As with decategorization, there are limitations to the recategorization approach. Perhaps the most substantial question is whether a common identity is possible when the opposing groups have a history of strong animosity toward each other (Hewstone et al., 2002; Pettigrew, 1998). For example, would the formation of a common in-group identity be possible between Serbians and Croatians? Most observers would suspect not. Of course, not all intergroup bias is as pronounced as that example. Even in sport organizations, however, there may be a history of ill will between groups. If the bias is strong enough, if there are substantial differences in the groups' sizes, or if variations exist in the status, power, or resources allocated to the groups, then efforts to recategorize might be thwarted (Brewer & Gaertner, 2001).

Even though members may conceive of themselves as belonging to a single, common in-group, this does not guarantee that bias will be reduced. Illustrative of this, I conducted an experiment in which demographically diverse students were randomly assigned to three-person groups (Cunningham, 2006). All groups worked on projects independently and then came together to form six-person groups. The six-person groups then worked on projects under conditions of interaction, common goals, and common fate. Subsequent checks indicated that the group members believed that the six-person group represented a single, common group, inclusive of both three-person groups. Though all groups recategorized, not all groups experienced the same level of bias reduction. Homogeneous three-person groups that merged with other homogeneous three-person groups experienced substantial bias reduction, as did diverse groups that merged with other diverse groups. However, the bias reduction was not as great when a homogeneous group merged with a diverse group. These findings show that even when recategorization occurs, the bias reduction might depend upon the diversity of the groups that are merging together.

Finally, some critics argue that creating a single, common group forces people to give up their other identities (Swann, Polzer, Seyle, & Ko, 2004). For example, if people's strongest identification is with their organization, work group, or athletic team, this implicitly means that their other identities (e.g., race or sex) must be secondary or nonexistent. Such a group structure is akin to the cultures of similarity (Doherty & Chelladurai, 1999) or monocultural organizations (DeSensi, 1995) discussed in Chapter 12 and is not considered desirable. Gaertner and Dovidio (2000) counter that the formation of a common in-group identity does *not* require that a person give up other identities; rather, it is possible for people to have multiple identities, all of which are important to them. In the context of academics, for example, it is possible for people to identify strongly with their functional background (e.g., sport management, bio-mechanics) *and* their academic department (e.g., sport and exercise sciences). A coach might identify as a Hispanic, a male, and a coach—three salient identities.

The limitations associated with recategorization do not necessarily negate the approach's effectiveness. Many groups successfully recategorize and reduce their level of intergroup bias and poor group dynamics.

Intergroup Contact

Intergroup contact (Brown & Hewstone, 2005; Hewstone & Brown, 1986) provides a third strategy for reducing prejudice in groups. This approach is sometimes referred to as mutual differentiation or salient categorization. Recall that the previous strategies for prejudice reduction sought to alter categorization boundaries. Distinctly different from these perspectives, intergroup contact theory holds that intergroup salience should be maintained. From this perspective, the conditions of contact (i.e., equal status, common goals, cooperation, institutional support, friendship potential) should yield the greatest reduction in prejudice when the contact is with typical out-group members. If the contact is with out-group members who are not typical, then people might dismiss information designed to deconstruct stereotypes and consider the out-group members as outsiders (Allport, 1954). If this occurs, then positive attitudes are directed to the individuals but not to the group as a whole. On the other hand, when group identities are salient and out-group members are viewed as typical of the out-group, then reduced prejudice should be both individualized (i.e., to the specific out-group member) and generalized (i.e., to other out-group members).

Research support

Empirical support for intergroup contact theory is impressive (see Brown & Hewstone, 2005, for an overview). Binder and colleagues' (2009) multinational study of schoolchildren provides one of the best illustrations. They found that contact with out-group members was predictive of reduced prejudice six months later. Consistent with the theoretical predictions, prejudice reduction was stronger when interactions were with typical out-group members.

In addition, earlier conceptualizations of the theory (Hewstone & Brown, 1986) pointed to the importance of mutual group differentiation in reducing prejudice as people recognize the strengths and superiorities of other groups. Several researchers have extended this line of thinking by arguing that diversity mindsets play a critical role in the relationship between group diversity and outcomes. The underlying premise is that "the effects of diversity should be more positive in contexts where individuals, groups, and organizations have more favorable beliefs about and attitudes toward diversity, are more focused on harvesting the benefits of diversity, and have a better understanding of how to realize these benefits" (van Knippenberg & Schippers, 2007, p. 531).

There is considerable evidence to support the notion that pro-diversity mindsets will result in better intergroup processes and outcomes. In a laboratory study, Homan, van Knippenberg, Van Kleef, and De Dreu (2007) investigated the manner in which diversity beliefs influenced interactions among people working in diverse groups. When group members held pro-diversity beliefs, the interactions were more positive and the task performance of the group was superior to its counterparts. In a different set of studies, one set in the field and another in the laboratory, van Knippenberg, Haslam, and Platow (2007) observed that people more closely identified with a diverse group when they believed that diversity added to the value of that group. My work in the sport context confirms these views. In one study of college athletics, I found that departments coupling a high commitment to diversity with high employee diversity enjoy a number of benefits, including employee satisfaction (Cunningham, 2008a). In another study, I collected data from participants in physical activity classes (Cunningham, 2010). Their pro-diversity beliefs were associated with satisfaction with other class participants. This pattern was stronger for Whites than for members of racial minorities, suggesting that when Whites believed diversity benefited the class as a whole, they expressed positive attitudes toward persons in it. These findings have implications for sport organizations, as inclusion is likely to be enhanced when people hold pro-diversity attitudes (see also Cunningham, 2013).

Application

Intergroup contact theory can certainly be applied to diverse groups. First, managers should seek to create favorable conditions of contact (Allport, 1954; Pettigrew, 1998) and also to maintain the saliency of the categorizations. Doing so will ensure that the positive effects of contact are transferred to other out-group members.

Second, prejudice is reduced when out-group members' contributions are mutually valued (Homan et al. 2007; van Knippenberg et al., 2007). Thus, managers should emphasize the benefits that group members' divergent perspectives and varying backgrounds bring to the group. This can be achieved by summarizing research findings in lay terms or offering anecdotes of how diversity positively influenced the group's past performance.

Potential limitations

As with the other approaches, there are shortcomings associated with intergroup contact theory. One of the most recognizable is that emphasizing categorization boundaries might actually have a *negative* effect. Recall that the intergroup contact approach holds that emphasizing group boundaries might be beneficial if both (or all) groups see the value that the out-group brings to the entity. However, there may be situations in which one group might not bring value to the larger group, or its contributions might not be perceived to be as important as the other group's contributions. As Brewer and Gaertner (2001) note, "By reinforcing perceptions of group differences, the differentiation model risks reinforcing negative beliefs about the outgroup" (p. 462). Under these circumstances, emphasizing the differences among the groups actually does more harm than good.

The limitations associated with the intergroup contact model do not negate its effectiveness; rather, they simply inform managers and group leaders when it is best to use the strategy and when it should be avoided.

Integrated Model

At first glance, the three strategies for reducing intergroup bias may seem to conflict with one another. One approach calls for reducing categorization boundaries, another calls for creating a common identity, and the third calls for emphasizing the differences among the groups. Which is correct? How can they be reconciled? Pettigrew (1998) answers these questions, as does my own work (Cunningham, 2004, 2011). An integrated model is presented in Exhibit 13.3 and is discussed next.

General principles

Pettigrew (1998) suggests that Allport's (1954) conditions of contact—the potential for friendships to be formed, a person's personal characteristics, and one's previous experiences—all influence the initial contact between in-group and out-group members. This contact should, then, initially result in *decategorization*, increasing the level of liking and positive affect directed toward out-group members. This is followed by established contact between former in-group and out-group members. Pettigrew calls this the *salient categorization* stage, and it is similar to Hewstone and Brown's (1986) intergroup contact model. This contact between in-group and out-group members leads to a reduction in prejudice, with some degree of generalization to others. The reduction of bias toward out-group members is thought to be generalized to all other members of the out-group. In the final stage, members of the various groups are *recategorized* so that a common in-group is formed. Pettigrew believes that in this stage a maximal reduction in bias and prejudice is observed. Ellers and Abrams (2003) provide general support for this model, particularly with respect to the importance of friendships in reducing bias.

Moderators

I have added to this model by emphasizing the importance of context as a moderator. Other potential moderators are the level of reinforcement and the form of diversity.

Context. Context plays an important role in discussions of bias and prejudice because a person's identity is often context specific. As Oakes (2001) notes,

EXHIBIT **13.3**   Integrated model of categorization-based diversity management strategies.

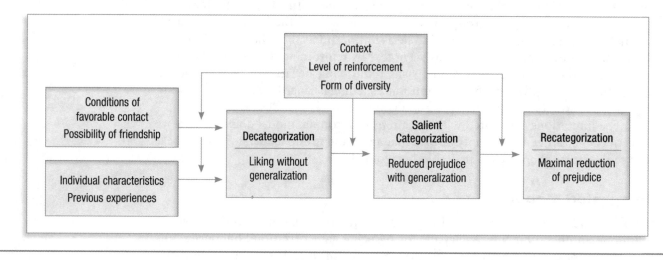

"We know that meaning varies with context—tears at a wedding are not the same as tears at a funeral" (p. 9). For example, an in-group member at the office might be an out-group member in another context. Context can also affect the results of diversity and categorization-based strategies in groups. As stated earlier, efforts to recategorize members of an athletic team, for example, may reduce racial bias among members of that specific team but not affect bias in other contexts, such as athletes' interactions with members of other teams or students at the school.

It is important for managers and group leaders, therefore, to realize that categorization-based diversity strategies may be effective only in specific contexts. Usually, this is not an issue, because the purpose of implementing the strategy is to reduce intergroup bias *in a particular context*. However, when the purpose is to generalize the reduction of bias to other contexts, strategies may have to be reinforced in those specific contexts.

Level of reinforcement. As with the diversity strategies described in Chapter 12, the categorization-based strategies require continual reinforcement to be effective (Tsui & Gutek, 1999). This is especially true if the effects are to be long-lasting. Consistent with the discussion in Chapter 12, managers and group leaders must continually monitor the diversity climate in the group and reinforce the categorization-based strategies that were implemented. Without monitoring and reinforcement, the short-term reduction in intergroup bias is not likely to last.

Form of diversity. As previously discussed, the efficacy of categorization-based strategies may vary depending on the form of diversity. Consider the following:

- The importance of various forms of diversity might change over time. Demographic differences might be important at the beginning of a group's formation, but deep-level diversity can potentially become more prominent as the group members remain together (Harrison, Price, Gavin, & Florey, 2002).

- Some diversity forms may historically have been sources of categorization and conflict within particular organizations or work groups. For example, a person's race is highly salient because of its visibility, and race issues have historically been at the forefront in the United States, as well as in other societies (Feagin, 2006).

- Still other forms of diversity might be so intrinsic to people's identity that efforts to alter the categorization process associated with those forms of diversity might be met with strong resistance or even hostility. For example, sexual orientation may be so important to an individual that efforts to downplay that form of identity might be met with considerable resistance.

chapter SUMMARY

This chapter outlined several diversity management strategies that are used at the group level to reduce bias. As demonstrated in the Diversity Challenge, it is possible for members of diverse groups to work effectively with one another. To facilitate groups' ability to work together, it is incumbent upon managers and team leaders to create team dynamics that alter the otherwise negative effects of social categorization. After reading this chapter, you should be able to:

1. **Discuss the conditions of contact under which prejudice should be reduced.**

   According to the contact hypothesis (Allport, 1954; Pettigrew, 1998), prejudice will be reduced when the following conditions of contact exist: social and institutional support is available, there is a possibility of intimate contact, members of the various groups have equal status, cooperative interaction is required, and there is a potential to develop friendships.

2. **Discuss how categorization-based strategies are used to create an inclusive environment.**

   There are three primary categorization-based strategies for reducing the potential negative effects of diversity in the group context. Decategorization focuses on reducing bias by breaking down categorization boundaries through repeated individualized interactions with out-group members. Recategorization focuses on reducing bias by building up a superordinate group identity that is inclusive of in-group and out-group members. Intergroup contact focuses on reducing bias by emphasizing categorization boundaries and the unique contributions of each subgroup to the overall group.

3. **Explain the integrated model of inclusion in groups.**

   Pettigrew (1998) suggests that the three categorization-based strategies could be integrated into a single model. Allport's (1954) conditions of contact, the potential for friendships to be formed, one's personal characteristics, and one's previous experiences all influence the initial contact between in-group and out-group members. This contact should, then, initially result in decategorization, which is expected to influence salient categorization (i.e., mutual group differentiation) and then recategorization. Three moderators are context, the level of reinforcement, and the form of diversity.

QUESTIONS for discussion

1. Are there situations when asking in-group and out-group members to interact, even under Allport's conditions of contact, might result in negative outcomes? If so, why would this happen?

2. If the conditions of contact reduce bias in one situation, will that effect transfer to bias reductions in other situations? Why or why not?

3. Three categorization-based strategies for reducing bias in diverse groups were discussed. Which of the three do you believe is the most effective? Why?

4. How does decategorization reduce bias between in-group and out-group members? What are the limitations of this approach?

5. How does recategorization reduce bias between in-group and out-group members? What are the limitations of this approach?

6. How does intergroup contact reduce bias between in-group and out-group members? What are the limitations of this approach?

learning ACTIVITIES

1. Suppose you are selected as a leader of a diverse group at a sporting goods company. As a class, divide into groups and decide which of the categorization-based strategies is the best to manage the diversity within the work group. Be sure to identify the advantages and disadvantages of the selected strategy.

2. Interview a coach at your university or a local high school about the strategies she or he uses to manage differences on the team. How do these strategies compare with those outlined in the chapter?

WEB resources

Diversity Australia, www.diversityaustralia.gov.au

Australian agency that promotes the benefits of diversity to various entities.

Program of Intergroup Relations, www.umich.edu/~igrc

Program at the University of Michigan aimed at promoting an understanding of intergroup relations.

Society for Human Resource Management, www.shrm.org/diversity

Site related to various human resource issues, including the management of diversity in work groups.

reading RESOURCES

Allport, G. W. (1954). *The nature of prejudice*. Cambridge, MA: Addison-Wesley.

The classic work on which many of the theories and perspectives espoused in this chapter are based.

Gaertner, S. L., & Dovidio, J. F. (2000). *Reducing intergroup bias: The common ingroup identity model*. Philadelphia: Psychology Press.

Provides an excellent overview of the recategorization process, including research and practical examples.

Paluck, E. L., & Green, D. P. (2009). Prejudice reduction: What works? A review and assessment of research and practice. *Annual Review of Psychology, 60*, 339–367.

Offers a comprehensive review of various strategies to reduce prejudice in group settings.

REFERENCES

Allport, G. W. (1954). *The nature of prejudice*. Cambridge, MA: Addison-Wesley.

Binder, J., Zagefka, H., Brown, R., Funke, F., Kessler, T., Mummendey, A., Maquil, A., Demoulin, S., & Leyens, J.-P. (2009). Does contact reduce prejudice or does prejudice reduce contact? A longitudinal test of the contact hypothesis among majority and minority groups in three European countries. *Journal of Personality and Social Psychology, 96*, 843–856.

Brewer, M. B. (1999). The nature of prejudice: Ingroup love or outgroup hate? *Journal of Social Issues, 55*, 429–444.

Brewer, M. B., & Gaertner, S. L. (2001). Toward reduction of prejudice: Intergroup contact and social categorization. In R. Brown & S. L. Gaertner (Eds.), *Blackwell handbook of social psychology: Intergroup processes* (pp. 451–472). Malden, MA: Blackwell.

Brewer, M. B., & Miller, N. (1984). Beyond the contact hypothesis: Theoretical perspectives on desegregation. In N. Miller & M. B. Brewer (Eds.), *Groups in contact: The psychology of desegregation* (pp. 281–302). New York: Academic Press.

Brown, R., & Hewstone, M. (2005). An integrative theory of intergroup contact. *Advances in Experimental Social Psychology, 37,* 255–343.

Bruening, J., Fuller, R. D., Cotrufo, R. J., Madsen, R. M., Evanovich, J., & Wilson-Hill, D. E. (2014). Applying intergroup contact theory in the sport management classroom. *Sport Management Education Journal, 8,* 35–45.

Cohen, A., Melton, E. N., & Welty Peachey, J. (2014). Investigating a coed sport's ability to encourage inclusion and equality. *Journal of Sport Management, 28,* 220–235.

Cohen, A., & Welty Peachey, J. (in press). Quidditch impacting and benefiting participants in a non-fictional manner. *Journal of Sport & Social Issues.*

Crisp, R. J., & Turner, R. N. (2009). Can imagined interactions produce positive perceptions? Reducing prejudice through simulated social contact. *American Psychologist, 64,* 231–240.

Cunningham, G. B. (2004). Strategies for transforming the possible negative effects of group diversity. *Quest, 56,* 421–438.

Cunningham, G. B. (2005). The importance of a common in-group identity in ethnically diverse groups. *Group Dynamics: Theory, Research, and Practice, 9,* 251–260.

Cunningham, G. B. (2006). The influence of group diversity on intergroup bias following recategorization. *The Journal of Social Psychology, 146,* 533–547.

Cunningham, G. B. (2007). Opening the black box: The influence of perceived diversity and a common in-group identity in diverse groups. *Journal of Sport Management, 21,* 58–78.

Cunningham, G. B. (2008a). Commitment to diversity and its influence on athletic department outcomes. *Journal of Intercollegiate Sport, 1,* 176–201.

Cunningham, G. B. (2008b). The importance of friendship potential in reducing the negative effects of group diversity. *The Journal of Social Psychology, 148,* 595–608.

Cunningham, G. B. (2010). Demographic dissimilarity and affective reactions to physical activity classes: The moderating effects of diversity beliefs. *International Journal of Sport Psychology, 41,* 387–402.

Cunningham, G. B. (2011). Does diversity in sport reduce racial prejudice? In J. Long & K. Spracklen (Eds.), *Sport and challenges to racism* (pp. 214–228). Hampshire, England: Palgrave Macmillan.

Cunningham, G. B. (2013). Reducing sexual prejudice. In M. L. Sartore (Ed.), *Sexual stigma and prejudice in sport* (pp. 115–127). Boulder, CO: Lynne Rienner Publishers.

Cunningham, G. B., Bopp, T. D., & Sagas, M. (2010). Overcoming cultural barriers in sport management study abroad programs: The influence of extended inter-group contact. *International Journal of Sport Management, 11,* 347–359.

Cunningham, G. B., & Chelladurai, P. (2004). Affective reactions to cross-functional teams: The impact of size, relative performance, and common in-group identity. *Group Dynamics: Theory, Research, and Practice, 8,* 83–97.

Cunningham, G. B., & Melton, E. N. (2013). The moderating effects of contact with lesbian and gay friends on the relationships among religious fundamentalism, sexism, and sexual prejudice. *Journal of Sex Research, 50,* 401–408.

DeSensi, J. T. (1995). Understanding multiculturalism and valuing diversity: A theoretical perspective. *Quest, 47,* 34–43.

Deutsch, M., & Collins, M. E. (1951). *Interracial housing: A psychological evaluation of a social experiment.* Minneapolis: University of Minnesota Press.

Doherty, A. J., & Chelladurai, P. (1999). Managing cultural diversity in sport organizations: A theoretical perspective. *Journal of Sport Management, 13,* 280–297.

Dovidio, J. F., Eller, A., & Hewstone, M. (2011). Improving intergroup relations through direct, extended and other forms of indirect contact. *Group Processes & Intergroup Relations, 14,* 147–160.

Dovidio, J. F., Gaertner, S. L., Validzic, A., Matoka, K., Johnson, B., & Frazier, S. (1997). Extending the benefits of recategorization: Evaluations, self-disclosure, and helping. *Journal of Experimental Social Psychology, 33,* 401–420.

Ellers, A., & Abrams, D. (2003). "Gringos" in Mexico: Cross-sectional and longitudinal effects of language school-promoted contact on intergroup bias. *Group Processes & Intergroup Relations, 6,* 55–75.

Feagin, J. R. (2006). *Systematic racism: A theory of oppression.* New York: Routledge.

Gaertner, S. L., & Dovidio, J. F. (2000). *Reducing intergroup bias: The common ingroup identity model.* Philadelphia: Psychology Press.

Gaertner, S. L., Mann, J., Murrell, A., & Dovidio, J. F. (1989). Reducing intergroup bias: The benefits of recategorization. *Journal of Personality and Social Psychology, 57,* 239–249.

Harrison, D. A., Price, K. H., Gavin, J. H., & Florey, A. T. (2002). Time, teams, and task performance: Changing effects of surface- and deep-level diversity on group functioning. *Academy of Management Journal, 45,* 1029–1045.

Herek, G. M., & Capitanio, J. P. (1996). "Some of my best friends": Intergroup contact, concealable stigma, and heterosexuals' attitudes toward gay men and lesbians. *Personality and Social Psychology Bulletin, 22,* 412–424.

Hewstone, M., & Brown, R. (1986). Contact is not enough: An intergroup perspective on the "contact hypothesis." In M. Hewstone & R. Brown (Eds.), *Contact and conflict in intergroup encounters* (pp. 1–44). Oxford, England: Basil Blackwell.

Hewstone, M., Rubin, M., & Willis, H. (2002). Intergroup bias. *Annual Review of Psychology, 53,* 575–604.

Hodson, G., & Hewstone, M. (Eds.) (2013). *Advances in intergroup contact.* New York: Psychology Press.

Homan, A. C., van Knippenberg, D., Van Kleef, G. A., & De Dreu, C. K. W. (2007). Bridging faultlines by valuing diversity: Diversity beliefs, information elaboration, and performance in diverse work groups. *Journal of Applied Psychology, 92,* 1189–1199.

Jones, L. M., & Foley, L. A. (2003). Educating children to decategorize racial groups. *Journal of Applied Social Psychology, 33,* 554–564.

Lee, W., & Cunningham, G. B. (2014). Imagine that: Examining the influence of sport related imagined contact on intergroup anxiety and sexual prejudice across cultures. *Journal of Applied Social Psychology, 44,* 557–566.

McIntosh, P. (1990). White privilege: Unpacking the invisible knapsack. *Independent School, 49,* 31–36.

Mellinger, C., & Levant, R. F. (2014). Moderators of the relationship between masculinity and sexual prejudice in men: Friendship, gender self-esteem, same-sex attraction, and religious fundamentalism. *Archives of Sexual Behavior, 43,* 519–530.

Miles, E., & Crisp, R. J. (2014). A meta-analytic test of the imagined contact hypothesis. *Group Processes & Intergroup Relations, 17,* 3–26.

Oakes, P. (2001). The root of all evil in intergroup relations? Unearthing the categorization process. In R. Brown & S. L. Gaertner (Eds.), *Blackwell handbook of social psychology: Intergroup processes* (pp. 3–21). Malden, MA: Blackwell.

Paluck, E. L., & Green, D. P. (2009). Prejudice reduction: What works? A review and assessment of research and practice. *Annual Review of Psychology, 60,* 339–367.

Pettigrew, T. F. (1998). Intergroup contact theory. *Annual Review of Psychology, 49,* 65–85.

Pettigrew, T. F., & Tropp, L. R. (2006). A meta-analytic test of intergroup contact theory. *Journal of Personality and Social Psychology, 90,* 751–783.

Saguy, T., Tropp, L. R., & Hawi, D. R. (2013). The role of group power in intergroup contact. In G. Hodson & M. Hewstone (Eds.), *Advances in intergroup contact* (pp. 113–132). New York: Psychology Press.

Sherif, M., Harvey, O. J., White, B. J., Hood, W. R., & Sherif, C. (1961). *Intergroup conflict and cooperation: The Robbers Cave experiment.* Norman: University of Oklahoma Book Exchange.

Swann, W. B., Polzer, J. T., Seyle, D. C., & Ko, S. J. (2004). Finding value in diversity: Verification of personal and social self-views in diverse groups. *Academy of Management Review, 29,* 9–27.

Tajfel, H., & Turner, J. C. (1979). An integrative theory of intergroup conflict. In W. G. Austin & S. Worchel (Eds.), *The social psychology of intergroup relations* (pp. 33–47). Monterey, CA: Brooks/Cole.

Tropp, L. R., & Pettigrew, T. F. (2005). Relationships between intergroup contact and prejudice among minority and majority status groups. *Psychological Science, 16,* 951–957.

Tsui, A. S., Egan, T. D., & O'Reilly, C. A., III (1992). Being different: Relational demography and organizational attachment. *Administrative Science Quarterly, 37,* 549–579.

Tsui, A. S., & Gutek, B. A. (1999). *Demographic differences in organizations: Current research and future directions.* New York: Lexington Books.

Turner, J., Hogg, M. A., Oakes, P. J., Reicher, S. D., & Wetherell, M. S. (1987). *Rediscovering the social group: A self-categorization theory.* Oxford, England: B. Blackwell.

van Knippenberg, D., Haslam, S. A., & Platow, M. J. (2007). Unity through diversity: Value-in-diversity beliefs, work group diversity, and group identification. *Group Dynamics: Theory, Research, and Practice, 11,* 207–222.

van Knippenberg, D., & Schippers, M. C. (2007). Work group diversity. *Annual Review of Psychology, 58,* 515–541.

Vezzali, L., Stathi, S., Giovannini, D., Capozza, D. & Trifiletti, E. (2015). The greatest magic of Harry Potter: Reducing prejudice. *Journal of Applied Social Psychology, 45,* 105–121.

Welty Peachey, J., Cunningham, G. B., Lyras, A., Cohen, A., & Bruening, J. (in press). The influence of a sport-for-peace event on prejudice and change agent self-efficacy. *Journal of Sport Management.*

Williams, K. Y., & O'Reilly, C. A., III (1998). Demography and diversity in organizations: A review of 40 years of research. In B. M. Staw & L. L. Cummings (Eds.), *Research in organizational behavior* (Vol. 20, pp. 77–140). Greenwich, CT: JAI Press.

Wilner, D. M., Walkley, R. P., & Cook, S. W. (1955). *Human relations in interracial housing.* Minneapolis: University of Minnesota Press.

Zhu, D. H., Shen, W., & Hillman, A. J. (2014). Recategorization into the in-group: The appointment of demographically different new directors and their subsequent positions on corporate boards. *Administrative Science Quarterly, 59,* 240–270.

Diversity Training

LEARNING *objectives*

After studying this chapter, you should be able to:

- Discuss the positive and negative effects of diversity training.
- Discuss the essential elements of effective diversity training programs.

DIVERSITY CHALLENGE

Diversity is a significant issue in sport organizations today, and college sport is no exception. In fact, many athletic departments provide diversity training for their members. Such educational endeavors are aimed at providing "a positive learning environment that teaches the values of diversity and maximizes team effectiveness." Training sessions, however, are met with mixed reviews. In one situation, all members of the 41 varsity teams at Harvard University were required to attend a training session entitled "Community Building and Diversity for Athletes." The session featured Elaine Penn, who is a motivational speaker, as well as a former athlete. Penn discussed various issues related to tolerance, gender stereotypes, and racism. Although well intentioned, the training session was viewed in a negative light. Some athletes believed that the speaker "overestimated the level of prejudice" among the athletes, while others questioned why they were required to attend the session at all. "In general sports break down stereotypes," opined one athlete. "We're exposed to a very diverse mix of people. The meeting would've been better geared toward the rest of the student body, who are exposed to much less diversity than we are." Many of the athletes left the training session feeling frustrated, claiming that the meeting was not necessary and, at times, even insulting.

Although the diversity training at Harvard had a negative effect, many observers hail the positive effects of these educational programs. Sports Management Resources is a consulting firm led by former college athletics administrator Donna Lopiano. This organization offers a number of training opportunities for coaches and administrators. The benefits of such activities include improvements in the search process, a diverse workforce, connection with a broader set of alumni and donors, and improved budget use. In addition, sport organizations that go through diversity training are more aware of diversity-related legal issues, such as Title IX and sexual harassment, and consequently may have more ethical work environments than their counterparts.

National associations, such as the American College of Sports Medicine (ACSM), are increasingly offering diversity training, as well. This organization suggests that the training can result in greater inclusiveness and access. Moreover, through diversity training efforts, ACSM holds that a department can better retain its members and consequently bolster the level of scholarship.

As these examples illustrate, the effectiveness and utility of different diversity training efforts can be mixed.

Sources: American College of Sports Medicine. Retrieved from www.acsm.org. / Athletes criticize diversity training. *The Harvard Crimson.* Retrieved from www.thecrimson.com/article/2003/2/13/athletes-criticize-diversity-training-a-required. / Sports Management Resources. Retrieved from www.sportsmanagementresources.com.

CHALLENGE REFLECTION

1. Have you attended a diversity training program? If so, what were your impressions of it?

2. The Diversity Challenge suggests that diversity training sessions can have both positive and negative effects. Which do you think are more likely and why?

3. What are some of the reasons that people such as the athletes at Harvard University would oppose diversity training? How would you address their concerns?

Diversity training is the educational process whereby people acquire skills, knowledge, attitudes, and abilities pertaining to diversity-related issues. The training can provide various benefits, both for the organization and for the individuals in it (Bezrukova, Jehn, & Spell, 2012). Writers have suggested that diversity training should be mandatory for aspiring managers (Bell, Connerley, & Cocchiara, 2009) and that there is an ethical obligation to offer it (Jones, King, Nelson, et al., 2013). However, training does not always have its intended benefits, and this was certainly true with the training at Harvard discussed in the Diversity Challenge. Equivocal results have spurred criticisms of diversity training (e.g., Kalev, Dobbin, & Kelly, 2006). Some participants question why it is necessary, others feel they are being singled out, while still others believe that it does more harm than good. What, then, are the actual effects? Further, how do organizations that seek to conduct such training provide programs that generate the intended benefits? Are there steps managers can take to institute effective diversity management sessions?

The purpose of this chapter is to address these issues. The first section notes the prevalence of diversity training among organizations today. I then discuss the potential positive and negative effects of such programs. The third section outlines the four steps involved in designing effective diversity training programs: conducting a needs analysis, evaluating antecedent training conditions, selecting the training methods, and ensuring effective post-training conditions. The final section addresses general program considerations. This chapter is designed to introduce managers of sport organizations to the tools needed to conduct effective diversity training, with the goal of creating and sustaining a diverse and inclusive work environment.

PREVALENCE OF DIVERSITY TRAINING

Organizations routinely implement training programs to educate and develop their employees. O'Leonard (2014) observed that in 2014, spending on corporate training reached $70 billion in the United States and $130 billion worldwide; both figures represent increases from previous years. In organizations that particularly value learning and development, training represents a sizeable percentage of the overall payroll. For instance, at Wequassett Resort and Golf Club, in Harwich, Mass., the training budget is 6 percent of the payroll, and every Tuesday is devoted to customer service training (Freifeld, 2015). Overall, U.S. firms spent an average of $1,203 in training for each employee in 2013, and organizational members spent an average of over 31 hours in training during the year (Miller, 2014).

These figures are related to all forms of training—new-employee orientation, technology training, and so forth. The figures for diversity training are considerably lower, though they are growing. A 1988 study of medium and large firms showed that diversity was not included among the 40 most common topics covered in training sessions (Gordon, 1988). In 2005, Esen reported that 67 percent of U.S. companies provided diversity training in the workplace. Most of the data that are available are for large corporations outside of the sport industry. Recognizing this shortcoming, I collected data from 675 NCAA athletic departments (239 in Division I, 205 in Division II, and 231 in Division III), asking them about their diversity training practices (Cunningham, 2012). Results indicate that 53 percent of all athletic departments offer training, and larger entities are more likely to provide it than smaller ones (Cunningham, 2012). Exhibit 14.1 offers an overview of these patterns. These figures suggest that athletic departments are less likely to offer training than are other corporations.

Diversity training in college athletics.   **EXHIBIT**   **14.1**

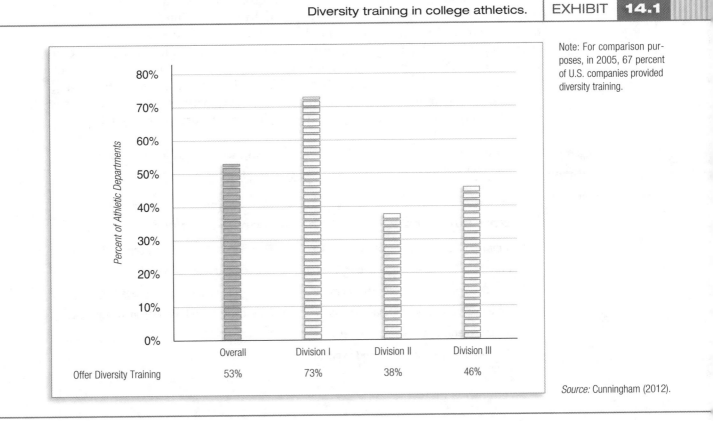

Note: For comparison purposes, in 2005, 67 percent of U.S. companies provided diversity training.

	Overall	Division I	Division II	Division III
Offer Diversity Training	53%	73%	38%	46%

Source: Cunningham (2012).

EFFECTS OF DIVERSITY TRAINING

A t first glance, instituting a diversity training program would seem beneficial. Providing people with necessary knowledge, skills, attitudes, and abilities with regard to diversity and inclusion is conceivably the first step toward a workplace where the positive effects of diversity are realized. However, these educational programs are sometimes met with resistance and in some instances actually do more harm than good, as illustrated in the Diversity Challenge. This section outlines both the positive and negative effects of diversity training in the organizational context.

Positive Effects

Kalinoski, Steele-Johnson, Peyton, and their colleagues (2013) conducted a meta-analysis of the diversity training literature to examine how it affected various employee and organizational outcomes. They observed that diversity training had a positive, moderate effect on employee outcomes. Specifically, diversity training improved people's (1) affective states, such as their attitudes toward diversity, motivation, and self-efficacy; (2) cognitive outcomes, including the knowledge they have about diversity and cognitive skills associated with it; and (3) skill-based outcomes, such as their behaviors and the intentions they have to engage in pro-diversity behaviors. Additional analyses showed that diversity training had stronger positive effects on cognitive and behavioral outcomes than on employees' affective states.

In addition to these individual-level outcomes, other investigators have pointed to the potential benefits of diversity training for groups and organizations (Bezrukova et al., 2012; Cunningham, 2012; King, Dawson, Kravitz, & Gulick, 2012; Roberson, Kulik, & Tan, 2013). For instance, diversity training has the potential to (4) improve intergroup relationships, by reducing people's prejudices and facilitating more constructive interactions. In turn, these improved interactions are likely to result in (5) improved employee morale and satisfaction. Finally, by conducting diversity training, organizations might be able to (6) remain in compliance with external mandates and avoid diversity-related lawsuits. These six benefits are captured in Exhibit 14.2.

EXHIBIT 14.2	Potential positive outcomes of diversity training and possible causes for negative outcomes.

POSITIVE OUTCOMES	NEGATIVE INFLUENCES
▪ Improved attitudes and motivation	▪ Resistance to discussing sensitive topics
▪ Enhanced knowledge and understanding	▪ Whites and men feeling blamed
▪ Improved diversity-related behaviors	▪ Perceived lack of work applicability
▪ Constructive intergroup relationships	▪ Lack of perceived connection to organizational effectiveness
▪ Improved employee morale and satisfaction	
▪ Compliance with mandates and avoidance of lawsuits	

The benefits also influence leaders' motivation for offering training. In my work with intercollegiate athletic departments, I observed two categories of motivations: *effectiveness,* where leaders sought to increase productivity, improve customer relationships, and enhance workplace dynamics; and *compliance,* where leaders offered training in order to remain in compliance with university or NCAA regulations (Cunningham, 2012). Leaders alluded to both types of stimuli, but the outcomes differed according to the leaders' motivation. Trainees were likely to implement the principles learned in the training into their everyday work when the motivation was effectiveness based, but they were less willing to do so when it was compliance based.

Negative Effects

Although diversity training can positively benefit the organization, there are times when these programs might be detrimental. Programs can have negative effects under certain workplace conditions. For instance, (1) some employees do not enjoy discussing sensitive topics at work, including those related to diversity. Lindsay (1994) equated diversity training to discussing the "undiscussable" (p. 19). In other cases, (2) some trainees might feel they are being blamed (Holladay, Knight, Paige, & Quiñones, 2003). Some White men who participate in diversity training may feel that they are being singled out in the training or that they are being blamed for any negative effects of diversity. This is especially true when the training focuses on topics such as prejudice and discrimination. When White men have these perceptions, they are unlikely to support the training.

In other cases, (3) employees might believe the training is not applicable to their work. This disconnect might help explain why only 51 percent of people who participated in a National Urban League (2009) study expressed positive attitudes toward diversity training. Finally, (4) the connection between diversity training and organizational performance is tenuous, at best (Kalev et al., 2006). That is, the training might improve individual-level outcomes, but the relationship between those efforts and improvements for the organization as a whole have not been firmly established. When employees do not see the reason for the training, the effects on the workplace may be negative. Among these negative effects can be the reinforcement of stereotypes and categorization boundaries. This is particularly the case when the training is poorly delivered. The conditions that can result in negative outcomes were listed in Exhibit 14.2.

Making Sense of the Effects

This discussion points to conflicting information about the effects of diversity training. How, then, do people make sense of these varying effects? The answer lies not only in the design and implementation of the diversity training but also in whether or not the lessons can actually be applied in the workplace setting—a process known as *transfer of training.* When the training sessions are ill-conceived, are held simply for the sake of satisfying external constituents, or do not have support from important organizational decision makers, they are unlikely to be successful. When the training is designed for the organization's specific needs, is central to the organization's mission, and has top management support, it is likely to benefit the trainees and the organization as a whole. Therefore, consistent with the instrumental design model (Goldstein, 1993), it is important that managers and trainers learn how to design and deliver effective diversity training programs. This is discussed in the next section.

DESIGNING AND DELIVERING EFFECTIVE DIVERSITY TRAINING PROGRAMS

No one model is best for all organizations. In spite of this fact, much diversity training tends to be standardized. Many consulting organizations offer the same "cookie cutter" diversity training program to every organization they serve. Some administrative bodies require that certain elements be covered in the training held by their institutions. Many university systems offer the same training (usually in an electronic format that takes several *minutes* to complete) on all of their campuses. There are several reasons why such standardization occurs, including issues related to consistency, reliability, and cost-effectiveness. Nevertheless, most, if not all, of these programs fail to deliver the genuinely positive effects that diversity training can offer.

To realize the full scope of the potential benefits, it is imperative that diversity training be tailored to the needs of the specific organization. For some organizations, issues related to sexual orientation or religious differences may be most salient. For others, harassment of and discrimination against women may be the primary sources of stress and friction. For still other organizations, diversity issues may not be a source of tension; the organization may simply be seeking to reinforce principles and values. The list of diversity issues that could be relevant to a specific organization is virtually endless. For these reasons, it is irresponsible to offer the same training to all organizations. Instead, the training must be tailored to each organization. To design and deliver an effective program, managers must conduct a needs analysis, examine the pre-training conditions, decide on the specific training topics and methods, and consider various post-training factors (e.g., training evaluation, transfer of training). Each of these issues is discussed in the following sections. An illustrative summary is presented in Exhibit 14.3.

EXHIBIT 14.3   Designing effective diversity training programs.

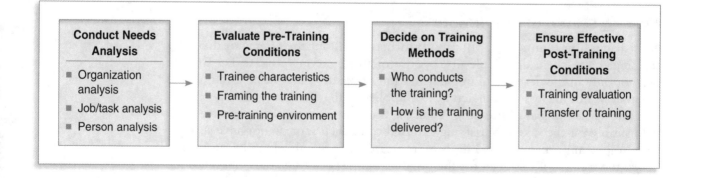

Conduct Needs Analysis	Evaluate Pre-Training Conditions	Decide on Training Methods	Ensure Effective Post-Training Conditions
▪ Organization analysis ▪ Job/task analysis ▪ Person analysis	▪ Trainee characteristics ▪ Framing the training ▪ Pre-training environment	▪ Who conducts the training? ▪ How is the training delivered?	▪ Training evaluation ▪ Transfer of training

Needs Analysis

Dachner, Saxton, Noe, and Keeton (2013) suggested that "training effectiveness depends on conducting a thorough needs analysis" (p. 239; see also the Diversity in the Field box for related information). Unfortunately, evidence suggests that preliminary analyses are not often conducted (Arthur, Bennett, Edens, & Bell, 2003). This is disappointing because a *needs analysis* is instrumental in helping managers understand *where* training is needed, *who* needs the training, and *what* material should be included in it (Roberson, Kulik, & Pepper, 2003).

When you are conducting a needs analysis, remember that not all deficiencies are training-related problems. For example, poor customer relations may result from a lack of cultural awareness on the part of the service provider. The cause could also be, however, that the method of providing the services is flawed, that the service provider simply lacks the motivation to provide high-quality services, or that the support necessary to provide the service is lacking. Obviously, these latter issues pertain more to structural or managerial factors than to diversity issues. Thus, once a problem is identified, managers must critically analyze the source of the problem and take appropriate action.

A needs analysis covers three areas: the organization, the job tasks, and the people.

Organizational analysis

The organizational analysis requires managers to examine all of the elements of the organization that may affect the training's effectiveness (Salas & Cannon-Bowers, 2001). This includes the congruence of the training with the organization's overall mission and strategy, the monies available to deliver the training, and the level of support available from top management. The organizational analysis is a critical first step in the overall needs-analysis process because it will identify any constraints or barriers to delivering an effective training program. Salas and Cannon-Bowers note that too many organizations neglect this step; consequently, training is not as successful for them as it is for those organizations that perform the analysis.

The organizational climate is particularly important to the training process (Bezrukova et al., 2012). Organizations with inclusive organizational cultures are likely to have more supports in place to allow the trainees to apply the information they learn in the training session to the workplace. Because diversity and individual differences are valued in these organizations, the importance attached to the training is likely to be amplified.

Top management support is also key. The Diversity in the Field box on the next page offers an example. Without management backing, employees might question how important diversity and the related training really are, and this could undermine the training's overall effectiveness.

Job/task analysis

A job/task analysis entails collecting information related to the specific duties of each job; the conditions under which employees complete the job; and the specific knowledge, skills, and abilities necessary to complete the tasks (Salas & Cannon-Bowers, 2001). The job and task requirements are then compared to the existing

DIVERSITY IN THE FIELD

How a Needs Analysis Shows the Need for Diversity Training.
Brian France heads NASCAR—an entity with a large fan base that is stereotypically homogeneous in race and attitudes. When he was set to take over for his father in 1997, he recognized this problem and noted that his "goal is to make NASCAR look like America." To do so, he reached out to Richard Lapchick, a noted expert in the area of diversity and inclusion. Since that time, Lapchick and his colleagues—who consult with organizations around the world on this topic—have provided more diversity training to NASCAR than any other entity. For many years, every person in the vast organization took part in these educational activities. The training aligns with NASCAR's policies, as the organization has zero tolerance for poor behaviors and language, and has held drivers and others accountable. Lapchick noted, "It's a tribute to their sincerity. . . . I think that the most important thing that an organization can do other than changing the numbers [that is, the diversity of the workforce] is changing the culture, but one can't go without the other."

Source: Diaz (2013).

performance level. If a discrepancy exists, training might be needed (Mathis & Jackson, 2013). This analysis is useful because it identifies areas where the employee training can be made more effective.

A job/task analysis is useful in developing diversity training for existing employees. For example, the level of interaction with others probably varies from job to job within most sport organizations. Employees in customer service, public relations, and marketing have the most interaction with a sport organization's customers and clients. Thus, it is useful to tailor the diversity training for these specific employees to fit the customers. Although this example is somewhat simplistic, it does show how conducting a job/task analysis is beneficial in developing the training program.

Person analysis

The third prong of the needs analysis involves the organization's people (Salas & Cannon-Bowers, 2001). This analysis can be accomplished by examining employees' performance appraisals and focusing on those portions that highlight deficiencies (Mathis & Jackson, 2013). Although some organizations include diversity-related criteria on their performance appraisals (Gilbert & Ivancevich, 2000), most do not. Thus, managers must develop alternative methods to identify the employees' specific diversity training needs. One option is to distribute an organization-wide questionnaire that assesses employee attitudes (and potentially behaviors) toward diversity issues. A sample item might be, "All employees within the organization, irrespective of their differences, are treated fairly (agree or disagree)." Another option is to observe employees and their interactions with others and with clients.

Regardless of how the information is collected, it is imperative that managers understand the training needs of each employee. As is discussed through this book, each person brings different diversity-related experiences, attitudes, preferences, and behavioral tendencies to the workplace. These differences influence the employees' attitudes toward work, the manner in which they interact with their colleagues, and the way they serve customers. Where deficiencies exist, training is needed to achieve the desired behaviors and attitudes.

Pre-Training Conditions

Before designing and implementing the training program, it is important to ensure that optimal training conditions are in place. Salas and Cannon-Bowers (2001) argue that "events that occur before training can be as important as (and in some cases more important than) those that occur during and after training" (p. 447). Managers should be particularly mindful of the three pre-training conditions discussed next.

Trainee characteristics

A number of characteristics influence the trainees' experiences with diversity training and readiness to learn the material, including their ability to learn, their self-efficacy and motivation, and the perceived utility of the training (Grossman & Salas, 2011; Roberson et al., 2013). First, people bring with them different experiences and attitudes toward diversity, and these might influence how they respond to the training. If people have not had good experiences with past diversity training activities or if they harbor considerable prejudices toward others, their orientation toward the training is likely to be less than ideal.

Second, not all employees have the same ability to learn the training material. Differences might result from a lack of cognitive skills or language acquisition. The key is to provide conditions that ensure employees' ability to learn. For example, if the majority of the workforce is Spanish speaking, then perhaps the training should be presented in Spanish, or at least the option should be available.

Self-efficacy, or "people's judgments of their capabilities to organize and execute courses of action required to attain specific types of performances" (Bandura, 1986, p. 391), also affects learning. If people do not believe they have the ability to learn the material, they are unlikely to be motivated during the training sessions. Managers can take several steps to enhance trainees' self-efficacy (Bandura, 1997). One option is to show that people with characteristics similar to the trainee's have successfully completed the training session. Another is to explain why the training is needed and the possible benefits. Finally, it might be necessary to persuade trainees that they have the skills and capabilities necessary for knowledge acquisition, for example by beginning with easier activities to ensure initial success.

Trainee motivation represents another factor to consider (Grossman & Salas, 2011). This refers to the vigor and persistence with which the trainees will engage in the training. People who are motivated to learn will approach the training with a positive attitude, will devote the time and energy needed to ensure they learn the material, and will use the training material in their work environment.

Finally, increasing the perceived utility of the training might also improve trainees' learning (Grossman & Salas, 2011). If people do not believe the diversity training is worth their while or do not see how the training will enhance organizational effectiveness or how they can use it on their jobs, they are unlikely to be fully engaged. For example, people exhibit low motivation for sexual harassment training when they have doubts about the prevalence of the deviant behavior or how effective the training can be in altering it (Walsh, Bauerle, & Magley, 2013). On the other hand, when people believe in the instrumentality of the training, they are likely to implement what they have learned, particularly when there is organizational support for doing so (Madera, Steele, & Beier, 2011).

Framing the training

Managers must consider how they frame or depict the training, as the manner in which an event is portrayed substantially influences people's behaviors and attitudes. Framing is particularly important when it involves "hot button" issues (Holladay et al., 2003). For example, people's view toward affirmative action often depends on how those policies are framed (Crosby, Iyer, & Sincharoen, 2006). People are more likely to favor affirmative action when it is viewed as a way organizations reach out to traditionally disadvantaged groups than when it is perceived as a quota system. The way a policy is framed or contextualized influences reactions to it.

As you might expect, in the context of diversity training, pre-training attitudes and beliefs influence subsequent motivation and performance. Holladay and colleagues (2003) explicitly considered the effects of two aspects of framing on trainees' subsequent attitudes: the title of the training ("Diversity Training" versus "Building Human Relations") and the scope of the training (a focus only on racial issues versus a broad focus on race, sex, personality, and lifestyle differences). They found that these two factors interacted to predict backlash to the training and the likelihood of training transfer. Training that had a direct title (e.g., "Diversity Training") and a broad focus received less backlash than the other training formats. The same was true for the likelihood of transfer—trainees in a program that had a direct title and broad focus were the most likely to use the information in their work.

Interestingly, although a broad focus seems to improve people's pre-training attitudes toward diversity training, actual learning does not appear to follow suit. Kalinoski and colleagues' (2013) meta-analysis showed that people learned substantially more when they took part in a training with a particular focus (e.g., sexual orientation) relative to broader topics, such as multicultural training or generic diversity training. Given the differences in actual learning that takes place, the best results seem to come from diversity training that is narrowly focused and for which managers effectively frame the benefits and need.

Pre-training environment

Finally, managers designing diversity training events must be mindful of the pre-training environment. Several factors contribute to the pre-training environment: support for the training from both managers and coworkers, the training's (in)voluntary nature, and the link between the material and subsequent job-related behaviors.

Support. As previously noted, support is one of the most important factors contributing to the training's success (Cocchiara, Connerley, & Bell, 2010). This support comes from supervisors and coworkers. Although support can positively influence people's training motivation, this effect is likely to be moderated by the extent to which employees are motivated to comply with their supervisors and coworkers (Wiethoff, 2004). Trainees who believe there is support for the training and who are highly motivated to act in accordance with their coworkers and supervisors are more likely than their counterparts to reap the benefits of diversity training.

(In)voluntary nature of the training. There is some debate as to whether diversity training should be mandatory or voluntary. In the Diversity Challenge, the athletes at Harvard resented being required to attend the diversity training. Wiethoff (2004) suggests that mandatory training might be counterproductive because it may result in less than positive attitudes among the trainees. On the other hand, others argue that mandatory training conveys the message that the training is important to upper management (Bell et al., 2009; Cocchiara et al., 2010). This is especially true when the team members from top management attend the training session (Cunningham & Singer, 2009).

Link between the training and other outcomes. Trainees are likely to be motivated to learn and apply the information from diversity training when doing so is linked to job performance and evaluations (Cunningham, 2012). If people believe that they can use the information in their jobs, that their performance evaluations will be tied to doing so, and that their pay raises to some extent will be linked to applying the information to their everyday work, then the training will likely be successful. If employees do not make such causal links, then their motivation to learn and transfer the information is likely to be low, thereby limiting the training's effectiveness. To help forge a connection between the training and trainees' everyday work, after presenting information related to multicultural competence, a manager might ask the trainees to role-play situations and apply the recently learned knowledge in a scenario they are likely to encounter in their everyday work settings.

Training Methods

The next steps in designing a diversity training program are to consider who will conduct the training and how the material will be delivered. Exhibit 14.4 provides information about the topics that are routinely covered in diversity training sessions.

Topics typically covered in diversity training programs.   EXHIBIT **14.4**

- Issues of discrimination, prejudice, and stereotypes in the workplace
- Ways in which diverse groups can work well with one another
- Explanation of how a diversity training program contributes to organizational effectiveness
- Explanation of the client organization's policies relative to diversity issues
- Fair and nondiscriminatory processes for recruitment, hiring, performance appraisals, and promotion
- Backlash from White males
- Cultures of various demographic groups (e.g., employees, customers/clients, community)
- Using the training on the job

Source: Adapted from Bendick, Egan, & Lofhjelm (2001).

Conducting the training

Some evidence indicates that the characteristics of the trainer influence the trainees' learning and attitudes toward the activity. First, learning is increased when someone internal to the organization leads the training (Kalinoski et al., 2013). Some sport organizations may have human resource personnel on staff who are specifically trained in this area. When there is no staff person available, persons with an expertise in diversity issues or who have had diversity training could lead the sessions. Using in-house personnel reduces the costs associated with training. Because an in-house trainer probably has a working knowledge and understanding of the specific diversity issues facing the organization, the training can be made more individualized.

Trainer demographics might also affect the trainees' learning. Roberson and colleagues (2013) note that people tend to assume, perhaps implicitly, that women and members of racial minorities are better suited to lead the training sessions than are White men. This might be attributable to the potential for differences in lived experiences with oppression and subjugation. Whites and men can offset these assumptions by acknowledging the role of privilege and institutionalized discrimination in society. In addition, learning is enhanced when the characteristics of the trainer match those of the trainees. This match might enhance the trainer's credibility and rapport with learners.

Training delivery

If an in-house trainer is used, the next consideration is how the training is to be delivered. (If the training is conducted by an external agent, that person or organization will design the delivery.) Mathis and Jackson (2013) identify four delivery methods: cooperative training, instructor-led classroom, distance training, and simulations.

Cooperative training. This approach blends classroom training with on-the-job experience and usually involves a training-to-work transition, internships, or apprenticeships. It is most often used with new employees, combining classroom learning with real-life experience on the job.

Among the many advantages of this approach, perhaps the greatest is the opportunity for the trainee to combine the theories and principles learned in the classroom with the work context, thereby gaining practical first-hand experience. This approach is more useful in some situations, such as with new employees, than in others, such as when knowledge acquisition is the primary desired outcome of the training.

Instructor-led classroom. In the most widely used form of training, a trainer presents the material primarily using a lecture format, discussions, case studies, and videos. The use of several methods for delivering the information accommodates trainees' various learning styles.

This approach has several advantages. First, the information can be conveyed to a relatively large group of people. Second, this approach lends itself to the presentation of diversity issues aimed at providing factual information or, in some instances, to programs aimed at changing attitudes. A potential disadvantage of the lecture format is that trainees may be averse to listening to a straight lecture, especially if it lasts for an extended period of time. Also, trainees get little hands-on experience with this method.

Distance training. Distance training is one of the newest and fastest-growing forms of training delivery. This training can be delivered through correspondence packets, video conferencing, online classes, or voice-over PowerPoint presentations. Software such as Blackboard (www.blackboard.com), Camtasia (www.techsmith.com), Impatica (www.impatica.com), and Adobe Captivate (www.adobe.com/products/captivate.html) offer many tools that sport organizations and universities can use for distance training and education.

As with the other training designs, this approach also has its advantages and disadvantages. Distance training allows an expert speaker in one location to reach thousands of people around the world. This is especially useful for multinational corporations such as Nike and adidas. Technological advances allow for innovative, high-tech forms of delivering information. Unfortunately, the lack of interaction that typically accompanies distance courses limits their effectiveness. Not every organization can afford the initial start-up costs, especially those for interactive formats, even though the future cost savings may compensate for the large up-front costs. In addition, not all trainees will be sufficiently technologically savvy to use the materials effectively.

Simulations. Many organizations use simulations for various training needs; the military and aviation sectors use them most often (Salas & Cannon-Bowers, 2001). This training form uses computer-supported games and scenarios that reflect many of the psychological and behavioral requirements of the general work environment. In the context of diversity training, trainees might work through a computer-based simulation related to recruiting and hiring a diverse workforce. CBT Planet (www.cbtplanet.com) offers a training session that lasts 2 to 4 hours. Trainees work through five simulations that teach them about (a) the general principles related to diversity, (b) cultural differences, (c) overcoming barriers to diversity, (d) communicating with a diverse workforce, and (e) managing workplace diversity. The advantages and disadvantages of this method are generally the same as with distance education.

Kalinoski and colleagues (2013) considered both the type and duration of the instruction in their meta-analysis. They observed that diversity training was most effective when it allowed people to work with one another, used both active and passive (e.g., lecture) forms of delivery, and lasted more than 4 hours. These results suggest it is best, where possible, to allow for multiple forms of instruction and training that lasts for more than a single sitting.

Post-Training Conditions

Finally, designing an effective diversity training program requires attention to the two post-training factors that determine the program's long-term effectiveness: evaluating the training and ensuring the transfer of the training (Mathis & Jackson, 2013; Salas & Cannon-Bowers, 2001).

Training evaluation

When planning for the evaluation of a training's effectiveness, managers must consider what should be evaluated and the method for doing so.

Evaluation of content. Kirkpatrick (1976) developed a framework for assessing training effectiveness that is appropriate for use by sport organizations. He argues that training outcomes can be grouped into four categories (see also the Alternative Perspectives box on page 326 for another method of evaluating training effectiveness):

1. *Reactions.* Sport organizations can evaluate trainees' reactions to the session by interviewing them or asking them to complete post-training questionnaires. The questions might relate to trainees' perceptions about the overall value of the training, how well they liked the instruction style or the trainers, or how useful they believe the training will be in their work. Most often, trainee reactions are gathered immediately after the training; however, data might also be gathered weeks or months after the training takes place so that managers can assess how useful the information has been in the trainees' everyday job duties.

2. *Learning.* Sport organizations can assess how well the trainees learned the material by asking the trainees to complete a simple test on the material covered in the session. This method is particularly useful when the subject matter is primarily factual (e.g., legal issues related to Title IX, sexual harassment, or equal employment opportunity laws).

3. *Behavior.* A third outcome to be evaluated is actual behavior. Suppose a sport organization is subjected to claims of discrimination arising from differential evaluations of racial minorities and Whites in the hiring and promotion process. Teaching the evaluators how to construct and implement objective evaluations should reduce or eliminate this problem. The trainers can assess the training's effectiveness by tracking the evaluators' behavior prior to the training and again at several points after the training.

4. *Results.* The final issue to be analyzed is how well organizational objectives have been realized. Some desired results of interest are the retention of employees, decreased absenteeism, increased customer satisfaction, increased level of positive employee affect, and increased financial gains. Managers should compare the levels prior to training to the levels after training to determine whether the training was effective.

Which outcome should be assessed? The answer is largely driven by the training content. In general, it is easy to assess trainees' reactions and difficult to assess the training's results. What is interesting, however, is that the results data are usually the most important to the organization, and the reaction data usually least important (Mathis & Jackson, 2013). Thus, managers must make trade-offs and weigh the training content against outcomes the organization wishes to achieve.

Design of evaluation. Managers can choose from among many designs to assess the training's effectiveness. In increasing order of the evaluation design's effectiveness, options include a post-training-only design, pre- and post-training design, pre- and post-training design with a control group, and a post-training-only design with a control group (see Exhibit 14.5 for an illustration).

Evaluation designs for assessing training's effectiveness.   EXHIBIT **14.5**

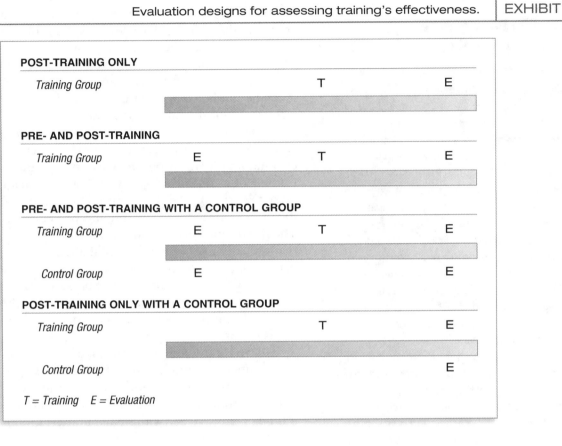

POST-TRAINING ONLY

Training Group   T   E

PRE- AND POST-TRAINING

Training Group   E   T   E

PRE- AND POST-TRAINING WITH A CONTROL GROUP

Training Group   E   T   E

Control Group   E   E

POST-TRAINING ONLY WITH A CONTROL GROUP

Training Group   T   E

Control Group   E

T = Training   E = Evaluation

With a *post-training-only* design, data are collected from the trainees after the training. Trainees can take a test or complete a questionnaire. This approach is easy to design and administer; however, there are no data to which the results can be compared. It is impossible to determine whether the trainees improved over the course of the training or how they compare with people who have received no training.

The *pre- and post-training* design evaluates the trainees prior to and after the training. If an increase in, for example, knowledge related to diversity laws is observed, then this might indicate that the training was effective. Because there is no control group, it is impossible to determine whether the increase is greater than what would be observed among people who did not receive the training.

The third evaluation design—*pre- and post-training with a control group*—permits comparisons of the trained people with people who did not receive the training. Managers randomly assign people to one of two groups—the training group or the control group, whose members do not receive the diversity training. Members of both groups are evaluated both prior to and after the training. Because the members are randomly assigned to the training or control group, differences between the groups are not expected for the pre-training scores. After the training, however, we would expect those people who went through the training to

ALTERNATIVE perspectives

Evaluating Diversity Training Effectiveness. Kirkpatrick's (1976) model is the most popular method of evaluating training effectiveness. Salas and Cannon-Bowers (2001) note that although the method is useful and provides a firm foundation, newer and more elegant models are needed. Kraiger, Ford, and Salas (1993) developed a three-component model. The first component, *cognitive outcomes,* includes such outcomes as the development of verbal knowledge, organization of knowledge, and cognitive strategies. Understanding laws that affect diversity in the workplace is an example of a cognitive outcome. *Skill-based outcomes,* the second component, pertain to skill compilation—the continued practice of a skill beyond initial success—and skill automaticity—the practice of a skill in a fluid, accomplished, and individualized manner. For example, managers who can develop and administer fair performance appraisals have learned skill-based outcomes. Finally, *attitudinal outcomes* encompass two elements—affective outcomes (e.g., group norms) and motivational outcomes (e.g., motivational disposition, post-training self-efficacy, and goal setting). If trainees reduce their level of bias toward out-group members as a result of the training process, this is an attitudinal outcome. Although there are similarities to Kirkpatrick's model, Kraiger and colleagues' framework may provide a preferable alternative.

score higher (or have more positive reactions or more desired behaviors) than people who did not complete the training. This design is desirable because it addresses the issues of (1) improvement after the training and (2) improvement relative to a control group. A drawback of the design is that it can be cumbersome and time-consuming to collect data prior to and after the training.

The final design—*post-training-only with a control group*—is the most desired. Here, managers randomly assign people to one of two groups: a training or a control group. An evaluation is made after the training, and any differences between the groups suggest that the training was effective. The pre-training evaluation is not needed because theoretically the randomly assigned group members should not differ in their scores prior to the training. Of course, this assumption rests on the proper random assignment of employees to the two groups. If this cannot be achieved, then a pretest is required.

In two of the designs, the members of the control group do not receive diversity training. Would we not want those persons to do so, ultimately? One way to address this issue is to evaluate the training's effectiveness with small pilot-test groups before administering it to the entire organization. If the training is effective, then management would require *all* employees to complete it.

Ensuring a transfer of training

One of the most important goals of training is the application of the new knowledge, skills, and abilities to the workplace setting. However, transfer of training often does not occur: the material learned in the training session is not used in the work setting (Roberson et al., 2013). Why provide diversity training if the trainees do not use the information in their work lives? Fortunately, a number of scholars have identified factors that can influence the transfer of training (Colquitt, LePine, & Noe, 2000; Cunningham, 2012; Lim & Morris, 2006; Roberson, Kulik, & Pepper, 2009; Salas & Cannon-Bowers, 2001). These include the organizational climate, the applicability of the training, and support for transfer.

Organizational climate. The organizational climate can have a substantial influence on whether people apply the information from the training to their work. As Salas and Cannon-Bowers (2001) note, the organizational climate can shape "motivations, expectations, and attitudes for transfer" (p. 489). Transfer of training is likely to take place in sport organizations that (1) encourage employees to try new things, (2) promote continuous learning by employees, (3) do not punish people when they are not immediately successful in implementing the information they learned, and (4) reward people for the transfer of training.

Applicability. Trainees are most likely to use the information that they learn when they believe it is applicable to their work. If they cannot see the connection between what was presented in the training and their job performance, then the information, no matter how valuable managers perceive it to be, is unlikely to be used. Thus, trainers must not only present the information so it can be understood but must also explicitly outline how the information will benefit the trainees in their everyday jobs.

One way of ensuring that trainees observe the applicability of the training is to link the content explicitly with the mission, goals, and strategies of the sport organization. When this occurs, trainees see that the content is important not only to their work but to the organization as a whole. This rationale is consistent with information presented in Chapter 12 indicating that diversity initiatives are most effective when they are embedded in the organizational system rather than occurring as stand-alone events.

Support. One of the most influential factors involved in the transfer of training is the support trainees receive from their peers and supervisors to make the transfer. The influence of peers is especially important in the transfer process (Colquitt et al., 2000). Much of what people do is influenced by those people who are important to them. If peers and supervisors show support for the training, think it is important, try to transfer the information to their own work, and are supportive of others who are doing the same, then transfer of training among employees is likely to be successful.

GENERAL PRINCIPLES

In this final section, I discuss general principles that managers and trainers should consider when delivering a diversity training program. Wentling and Palma-Rivas (1999) interviewed a panel of diversity experts from across the United States, all of whom had published extensively in the diversity literature and had consulted with public and private entities about diversity and diversity training. Wentling and Palma-Rivas asked the experts what they considered to be the primary components of an effective diversity training program. The investigators analyzed the experts' responses, and the following themes emerged:

- **Ensure commitment and support from top management.** Effective diversity training programs must have support from top management. Members of top management should be actively involved in the training process and convey to employees how important the training is to them and the organization as a whole.
- **Include diversity training as part of the overall strategic plan.** The training must be linked to the overall goals, needs, and objectives of the sport organization. Effectiveness is likely to be highest when the training is linked to the overall business strategy.

- **Ensure training meets the sport organization's specific needs.** The most successful training programs are those that are based on the results of a needs analysis. Without such an assessment, "training may focus on issues that are not real problems in the organization, which may result in a waste of resources without achieving desired results" (Wentling & Palma-Rivas, 1999, p. 222).

- **Use qualified trainers.** Qualified trainers are essential. The best trainers are those who have a good mix of professional and academic skills, coupled with a dynamic personality. Because diversity training often touches on sensitive issues, trainers should not only be well-versed in the subject matter but should also be skilled at defusing disruptive forms of conflict.

- **Combine the training with other diversity programs.** Diversity training works best when it is introduced as one of several diversity-related initiatives (e.g., the organization has an overall strategy aimed at diversifying the workforce and clientele). If conducted in isolation, the training is likely to have only a minimal impact, if any. In addition, "linking diversity training to existing training programs such as leadership training, team building, total quality management, and employee empowerment and participation will increase its effectiveness" (Wentling & Palma-Rivas, 1999, p. 222).

- **Make attendance mandatory.** Diversity training is most successful when attendance is mandatory. The requirement for attendance demonstrates organizational seriousness and commitment to the program. Mandatory attendance should apply to *all* people—including top management. Requiring top managers to attend the training may result in their setting examples of the desired behaviors for their employees to model.

professional
PERSPECTIVES

Diversity Behind the Face. Cheryl Kravitz is a diversity training consultant who uses an interesting technique to create empathy and understanding in the programs she delivers. She calls the technique "The Person Behind the Face." In this exercise, participants receive a piece of paper with balloons drawn all over it. They then use as many balloons as they deem necessary to define their personal identities. As the exercise facilitator, Kravitz goes first. She describes herself as "a young mom and an old mom" because she had a child at age 16 and adopted her second child at age 40. She also reveals other bits of information about herself: that she is Jewish, her mother has Alzheimer's, she was once in a coma, and she almost died at the hands of her abusive ex-husband. Revealing such personal information is beneficial, Kravitz notes, because people will then share information about themselves. Revealing such information has a way of creating empathy among the trainees and sometimes results in bonds being forged among otherwise different people. For example, another woman in the group might reveal that she, too, was a battered wife, or another group member might identify with having an ill parent. Thus, people come to realize that although they differ physically, they might share deep-level characteristics. The exercise "can help unfreeze people's preconceptions of others and help melt prejudice and stereotypes" (Koonce, 2001, p. 30).

- **Create inclusive programs.** The best diversity training programs are those that are inclusive of all people because they avoid "us versus them" dynamics. White males are more likely to support diversity initiatives if they believe the initiatives are inclusive of all people and do not single them out for "blame."

- **Ensure trust and confidentiality.** Establishing trust and confidentiality ensures a safe training environment and minimizes risks to the employees and the organization. Setting guidelines early in the training process, such as "respect other people's opinions" and "keep the conversations here confidential," helps to establish these norms.

- **Require accountability.** When people are held accountable, the trainees have a means by which they can actively advance diversity in the workplace. Accountability practices include establishing a link between what is learned in the session and work performance, including diversity-related criteria in performance appraisals and merit raises, and associating diversity performance with the organization's overall objectives.

- **Evaluate the training.** "Evaluation is one of the most important ways of providing accountability and support for continuing with diversity programs" (Wentling & Palma-Rivas, 1999, p. 223). Indeed, evaluating the program can demonstrate its success, provide information about trainees' reactions to the training, and inform the design and implementation of subsequent training sessions.

Managers should use these principles as a guide when designing and implementing diversity training programs to ensure success with the initiative.

chapter SUMMARY

As illustrated in the Diversity Challenge, diversity training can be—and often has been—met with mixed emotions: some managers and employees oppose such programs, while others argue that training will result in positive outcomes for employees, work groups, and the organization as a whole. Implementing diversity training can be a complex undertaking because many factors must be considered in the program's design, implementation, and evaluation. The time, resources, and effort associated with designing and delivering a diversity training program are worthwhile because effective programs, when coupled with other diversity initiatives, positively influence a sport organization.

After reading this chapter, you should be able to:

1. **Discuss the positive and negative effects of diversity training.**

   The positive outcomes include improved attitudes and motivation toward diversity and inclusion, enhanced knowledge and understanding, improved diversity-related behaviors, more constructive intergroup relationships, improved employee morale and satisfaction, and better compliance with mandates and avoidance of lawsuits. Potential contributors to negative effects include the discussion of sensitive topics; a feeling of being blamed, especially among Whites and men; and a perception that the training lacks work applicability or connection to organizational effectiveness.

2. **Discuss the essential elements of effective diversity training programs.**

   Managers must consider several factors when planning and delivering diversity training. The organization must first conduct a needs analysis, which includes an organizational analysis, a job/task analysis, and a person analysis. The antecedent training conditions must be examined, including trainee characteristics, the manner in which the training is framed, and the pre-training environment. Next, the training methods, such as who should deliver the training and which delivery method should be used, must be determined. Finally, post-training conditions—conducting a training evaluation and ensuring the transfer of training—must be met.

QUESTIONS for discussion

1. The incidence of diversity training has increased over the past decade, to the point that more companies conduct this type of training than do not. Do you believe there has been a corresponding increase in the number of sport organizations that provide diversity training? Why or why not?

2. Companies that view diversity training as a central part of their strategic plan spend almost three times as much per employee on training as other organizations. Why does such an increase in spending occur, and do you think the organizations receive benefits from the spending?

3. How does one conduct a needs analysis, and why is it important to do so?

4. Several trainee characteristics influence the effectiveness of training. Of those listed in the chapter, which do you think is the most influential and why? What can managers do to improve these characteristics?

5. Several delivery options for training were discussed. What are the advantages and disadvantages associated with each approach? Which is your preferred approach and why?

6. Trainees bring differing needs, attitudes, preferences, and learning styles to the diversity training session. What steps can trainers take to ensure that *all* trainees learn the material?

7. Several factors were identified that could help with the transfer of training. Which of these factors is likely to be most influential and why?

learning ACTIVITIES

1. Using online resources, identify companies that specialize in diversity training. Which of these companies do you believe would provide the best training and why?

2. Working in small groups, consult the Lambert and Myers book listed in the Reading Resources, and try one of the diversity training activities. Present the activity to the class, and evaluate its effectiveness. Which activities were the most successful and why?

WEB resources

Diversity Builder, www.diversitybuilder.com/diversity_training.php

Provides diversity training in a variety of areas; provides specialized programs for each client.

Diversity Training Group, www.diversitydtg.com

Specializes in providing diversity training workshops for organizations.

Scottsdale National Gender Institute, http://gendertraining.com

Helps organizations to provide diversity training, with an emphasis on gender issues.

reading RESOURCES

Katz, J. H. (2003). *White awareness: Handbook for anti-racism training* (2nd ed.). Norman, OK: University of Oklahoma Press.

Provides a detailed analysis for designing training aimed at reducing racism and creating change in the White community.

Lambert, J., & Myers, S. (2005). *Trainer's diversity source book: 50 ready-to-use activities, from icebreakers through wrap ups.* Alexandria, VA: Society for Human Resource Management.

Provides trainers with a variety of exercises to use during a training session to engage the participants actively.

Robbins, S. L. (2008). *What if? Short stories to spark diversity dialogue.* Mountain View, CA: Davies-Black.

Offers short stories as a way of illustrating the prevalence of diversity and inclusion issues in the work environment.

REFERENCES

Arthur, W., Jr., Bennett, W., Jr., Edens, P. S., & Bell, S. T. (2003). Effectiveness of training in organizations: A meta-analysis of design and evaluation features. *Journal of Applied Psychology, 88,* 234–245.

Bandura, A. (1986). *Social foundations of thought and action: A social cognitive theory.* Englewood Cliffs, NJ: Prentice Hall.

Bandura, A. (1997). *Self-efficacy: The exercise of control.* New York: Freeman.

Bell, M. P., Connerley, M. L., & Cocchiara, F. K. (2009). The case for mandatory diversity education. *Academy of Management Learning and Education, 8,* 597–609.

Bendick, M., Jr., Egan, M. L., & Lofhjelm, S. M. (2001). Workforce diversity training: From anti-discrimination compliance to organizational development. *Human Resource Planning, 24*(2), 10–25.

Bezrukova, K., Jehn, K. A., & Spell, C. S. (2012). Reviewing diversity training: Where we have been and where we should go. *Academy of Management Learning & Education, 11,* 207–227.

Cocchiara, F. K., Connerley, M. L., & Bell, M. P. (2010). "A GEM" for increasing the effectiveness of diversity training. *Human Resource Management, 49*(6), 1089–1106.

Colquitt, J. A., LePine, J. A., & Noe, R. A. (2000). Toward an integrative theory of training motivation: A meta-analytic path analysis of 20 years of research. *Journal of Applied Psychology, 85,* 678–707.

Crosby, F. J., Iyer, A., & Sincharoen, S. (2006). Understanding affirmative action. *Annual Review of Psychology, 57,* 585–611.

Cunningham, G. B. (2012). Diversity training in intercollegiate athletics. *Journal of Sport Management, 26,* 391–403.

Cunningham, G. B., & Singer, J. N. (2009). *Diversity in athletics: An assessment of exemplars and institutional best practices.* Indianapolis: National Collegiate Athletic Association.

Dachner, A. M., Saxton, B. M., Noe, R. A., & Keeton, K. E. (2013). To infinity and beyond: Using a narrative approach to identify training needs for unknown and dynamic situations. *Human Resource Development Quarterly, 24,* 239–267.

Diaz, G. (2013, March). Driver suspension for racial slur reflects NASCAR commitment to diversity. *Orlando Sentinel.* Retrieved from http://articles.orlandosentinel.com/2013-03-05/sports/os-george-diaz-nascar-clements-0306-20130305_1_nascar-commitment-brian-france-jeremy-clements.

Esen, E. (2005). *Workplace diversity practices survey report.* Alexandria, VA: Society for Human Resource Management.

Freifeld, L. (2015, February 10). Training magazine ranks 2015 top 125 organizations. *Training.* Retrieved from http://www.trainingmag.com/training-magazine-ranks-2015-top-125-organizations

Gilbert, J. A., & Ivancevich, J. M. (2000). Valuing diversity: A tale of two organizations. *Academy of Management Executive, 14*(1), 93–105.

Goldstein, I. L. (1993). *Training in organizations: Needs assessment, development and evaluation* (3rd ed.). Monterey, CA: Brooks/Cole.

Gordon, J. (1988). Who is being trained to do what? *Training, 25*(10), 51–60.

Grossman, R., & Salas, E. (2011). The transfer of training: What really matters. *International Journal of Training and Development, 15*(2), 103–120.

Holladay, C. L., Knight, J. L., Paige, D. L., & Quiñones, M. A. (2003). The influence of framing on attitudes toward diversity training. *Human Resource Development Quarterly, 14,* 245–263.

Jones, K. P., King, E. B., Nelson, J., Geller, D. S., & Bowes-Sperry, L. (2013). Beyond the business case: An ethical perspective of diversity training. *Human Resource Management, 52,* 55–74.

Kalev, A., Dobbin, F., & Kelly, E. (2006). Best practices or best guesses? Assessing the efficacy of corporate affirmative action and diversity policies. *American Sociological Review, 71,* 589–617.

Kalinoski, Z. T., Steele-Johnson, D., Peyton, E. J., Leas, K. A., Steinke, J., & Bowling, N. A. (2013). A meta-analytic evaluation of diversity training outcomes. *Journal of Organizational Behavior, 34,* 1076–1104.

King, E. B., Dawson, J. F., Kravitz, D. A., & Gulick, L. M. (2012). A multilevel study of the relationship between diversity training, ethnic discrimination and satisfaction in organizations. *Journal of Organizational Behavior, 33,* 5–20.

Kirkpatrick, D. L. (1976). Evaluation of training. In R. L. Craig (Ed.), *Training and development handbook* (2nd ed., pp. 301–319). New York: McGraw-Hill.

Koonce, R. (2001). Redefining diversity. *Training & Development, 55*(12), 22–33.

Kraiger, K., Ford, J. K., & Salas, E. (1993). Application of cognitive, skill-based, and affective theories of learning outcomes to new methods of training evaluation. *Journal of Applied Psychology, 78,* 311–328.

Lim, D. H., & Morris, M. L. (2006). Influence of trainee characteristics, instructional satisfaction, and organizational climate on perceived learning and training transfer. *Human Resource Development Quarterly, 17,* 85–115.

Lindsay, C. (1994). Things that go wrong in diversity training: Conceptualization and change with ethnic identity models. *Journal of Organizational Change Management, 7*(6), 18–33.

Madera, J. M., Steele, S. T., & Beier, M. (2011). The temporal effect of training utility perceptions on adopting a trained method: The role of perceived organizational support. *Human Resource Development Quarterly, 22,* 69–86.

Mathis, R. L., & Jackson, J. H. (2013). *Human resource management* (14th ed.). Mason, OH: Southwestern.

Miller, L. (2014, November). State of the industry report: Spending on employee training remains a priority. *Association for Talent Development.* Retrieved from www.td.org.

National Urban League (2009). *Diversity practices that work: The American worker speaks II.* Retrieved from http://www.nul.org/content/diversity-practices-work-american-worker-speaks.

O'Leonard, K. (2014). *The 2014 corporate learning factbook: Benchmarks, trends, and analysis of the U.S. training market.* Oakland, CA: Bersin & Associates.

Roberson, L., Kulik, C. T., & Pepper, M. B. (2003). Using needs assessment to resolve controversies in diversity training design. *Group & Organization Management, 28,* 148–174.

Roberson, L., Kulik, C. T., & Pepper, M. B. (2009). Individual and environmental factors influencing the use of transfer strategies after diversity training. *Group & Organization Management, 34,* 67–89.

Roberson, L., Kulik, C. T., & Tan, R. Y. (2013). Effective diversity training. In Q. M. Roberson (Ed.), *The Oxford handbook of diversity and work* (pp. 341–365). New York: Oxford University Press.

Salas, E., & Cannon-Bowers, J. A. (2001). The science of training: A decade of progress. *Annual Review of Psychology, 52*, 471–499.

Walsh, B. M., Bauerle, T. J., & Magley, V. J. (2013). Individual and contextual inhibitors of sexual harassment training motivation. *Human Resource Development Quarterly, 24*, 215–237.

Wentling, R. M., & Palma-Rivas, N. (1999). Components of effective diversity training programmes. *International Journal of Training and Development, 3*, 215–226.

Wiethoff, C. (2004). Motivation to learn and diversity training: Application of the theory of planned behavior. *Human Resource Development Quarterly, 15*, 263–278.

Change and Inclusion Through Sport

LEARNING objectives

After studying this chapter, you should be able to:

- Identify the different ways managers use sport for social change and inclusion.

- Discuss the positive and negative outcomes associated with using sport-for-development and peace activities.

- Highlight the characteristics of effective, inclusive sport-for-development and peace programs.

DIVERSITY CHALLENGE

In January 2013, it was estimated that more than 610,000 people experienced homelessness in the United States. To put that figure in perspective, we could fill AT&T Stadium, the $1.3 billion, 80,000-seat home of the Dallas Cowboys, seven times and still not have enough room to seat all the people who are experiencing homelessness in the United States. Of those who experience homelessness: 35 percent dwell in locations without a shelter; 23 percent are children under the age of 18; 20 percent of these youth are LGBT; and almost 10 percent are veterans. Fifty-one percent of the homeless population lives in just five states—California, New York, Florida, Texas, and Massachusetts. The National Coalition for the Homeless points to a number of factors that contribute to homelessness, including insufficient employment opportunities, limited public assistance, healthcare costs, domestic violence, addiction, and psychological disabilities. People who experience homelessness face not only distress, hunger, and stigma but also violence specifically targeted toward them.

Lawrence and Rob Cann know the effects of homelessness. Born and raised in Richmond, Virginia, the brothers were in elementary school when their house burned down—an experience that taught them the importance of community. Their family recovered, and the brothers both went on to play soccer in the NCAA. Since then, they have devoted their efforts to helping individuals and communities through Street Soccer USA. This is an organization whose mission is to "improve health, education, and employment outcomes for the most disadvantaged Americans by using sports to transfer the skills necessary so that they can achieve these outcomes for themselves." The organization holds that "sports can be a primary tool in building safe, healthy communities, where everyone has a place to call home."

Street Soccer USA facilitates these positive outcomes in a number of ways. Some programs are directed toward youth aged 8 to 17. The organization merges regular practices with educational activities designed to facilitate lifelong learning. Coaches design practices such that soccer skills are taught alongside life skills, and they use huddles at the

335

beginning, middle, and end of practice to reinforce lifelong learning. Among adults, practices and life skills training are aimed at improving health and physical fitness, anger management, teamwork, job readiness, and sobriety. Street Soccer offers a number of activities to facilitate these outcomes, including practice twice a week and classes in resume writing, financial literacy, and job counseling, among other topics. As a result, 75 percent of the players who participate in Street Soccer USA no longer experience homelessness after the first year.

Sources: Coleman, S. (2014, April). Final four 2014: Cowboys Stadium is a perfect fit in size, scale. *SB Nation.* Retrieved from www.sbnation.com/college-basketball/2014/4/1/5563484/final-four-cowboys-stadium-jerrys-world. / Henry, M., Cortes, A., & Morris, A. (2013). *The 2013 annual homeless assessment report (AHAR) to Congress.* Washington, DC: U.S. Department of Housing and Urban Development / National Coalition for the Homeless. Retrieved from www.nationalhomeless.org / Street Soccer USA. Retrieved from www.streetsoccerusa.org.

CHALLENGE   REFLECTION

1. What role can sport play in facilitating social change among individuals and communities? How would this take place?

2. What other social issues could sport-focused organizations, such as Street Soccer USA, address?

3. Do you foresee any potential drawbacks in using sport-based activities to facilitate social change?

n my Dr. Earle F. Zeigler Lecture (Cunningham, 2014), I argued that we are all linked to one another. The attitudes I hold, ideas I advance, and behaviors in which I engage certainly affect me, but they also affect others, be it directly or indirectly. We all share not only a common ancestry but also a common personhood and world—thus, we both affect and are affected by others.

Let's consider a couple of examples to illustrate this point. Sport marketers frequently use hypersexualized images of women to promote sport events or products. The efficacy of such practices in driving sales is debatable, but the deleterious effects are not. Among women, the images are often met with anger and feelings of disrespect, while boys and men who view the images are influenced to see women as sex objects. On the other hand, when women are represented in powerful, athletic poses, girls' and women's body image improve, as do boys' and men's valuing of women and their accomplishments (Daniels, 2009, 2012; Daniels & Wartena, 2011; Kane, LaVoi, & Fink, 2013). As another example, consider instances of incivility and harassment in the workplace. These behaviors negatively affect the physical and psychological well-being of those directly involved. But incivility's reach is actually further, as it harms bystanders and creates a culture of harassment that negatively affects *all* in the work environment (Cunningham, Miner, & Benavides-Espinoza, 2012; Glomb, Richman, Hulin, et al., 1997; Miner-Rubino & Cortina, 2007). For a third illustration, consider the case of community inclusiveness. Individual and systemic expressions of prejudice toward lesbian, gay, bisexual, and transgender individuals set up a culture of exclusion and hostility toward gender and sexual minorities in a particular community and state. This culture certainly affects LGBT individuals, but it also affects their families and friends. Moreover, given that highly skilled and creative people are attracted to LGBT-inclusive communities and subsequently contribute to economic growth (Florida, 2002, 2003, 2012), cultures of exclusion and hostility negatively influence the economic well-being of all persons in that region. The same principles apply in the work environment (Cunningham, 2011a, 2011b).

Reverend Dr. Martin Luther King, Jr. recognized our interconnectedness with one another. In his "Letter from Birmingham Jail," writing to White clergy in the South, he noted: "I am cognizant of the interrelatedness of all communities and states. . . . Injustice anywhere is a threat to justice everywhere. We are all caught in an inescapable network of mutuality, tied in a single garment of destiny. Whatever affects one directly affects all indirectly" (as cited in Gottlieb, 2003, p. 178). King's prose highlights (1) the interconnectedness of one person to another, and (2) the impact of injustice and inequality for all people, irrespective of whether we experience it directly.

Drawing from this work, I argued that our connectedness to one another has a profound impact on how we, as members of the sport management discipline, move forward (Cunningham, 2014). I wrote:

> We, as a collective body of sport management scholars, can no longer pretend that the perils of globalization, issues of access, the prevalence of prejudice and discrimination, or the presence of inequality do not impact each and every one of us; because they do. And we can no longer let the few be responsible for ensuring access and equality for all sportspersons; instead, it is the job of the whole—each and every one of us. This understanding of our interdependence and interconnectedness *requires collective action aimed at guaranteeing that sport is characterized by inclusion and social justice.* (p. 3, emphasis added)

In furthering this position, I noted that failure to act on known injustices would make us complicit in their perpetuation. King also reflected as much. The latter part of his "Letter" was directed toward White moderates—persons who recognized the need for change but were unwilling to engage. The clergy urged him to be patient, not cause trouble, and wait for racial equality to come. King countered that no real change has ever come to fruition through placidity or the natural passage of time. Rather, he correctly argued that generations would have to atone "not merely for the vitriolic words and actions of the bad people, but for the appalling silence of the good people. We must come to see that human progress never rolls in on wheels of inevitability. It comes through the tireless efforts and persistent work" of people pursuing change and justice (as cited in Gottlieb, 2003, p. 182).

In advancing this position, I argued that we, as members of a sport management discipline, could engage in collective action through our teaching, research, and service activities. The same is true for people in the sport industry, as they can focus on engaging in action in their organization and in their local communities. I further suggested that each effort mattered, no matter how small the task or potentially narrow the reach. Solitary efforts aimed at promoting inclusion might seem insignificant in the grander scheme of things, but it is the collection of these efforts—the synergistic force they create—that ultimately makes change. In the words of former United Nations secretary general Dag Hammarskjold, "In our age, the road to holiness necessarily passes through the world of action" (Cunningham, 2014, p. 23). It is, indeed, action that is required.

I offer this reflection for several reasons. Throughout this book, I have (1) provided evidence of how people from underrepresented or marginalized groups face subjugation, prejudice, and discrimination; (2) discussed the many benefits of a work environment characterized by diversity and inclusion; and (3) offered a number of

professional
PERSPECTIVES

The Importance of Sport-for-Development and Peace Programs. Jon Welty Peachey teaches at the University of Illinois in the College of Applied Health Sciences, Department of Recreation, Sport, and Tourism. Prior to this appointment, he served as the vice president for international operations and program development at the Institute for International Sport. This is a nonprofit organization that administers sport-for-development and peace (SDP) events around the world. Its major event is the World Scholar-Athlete Games.

Welty Peachey described SDP as "the use of sport to exert a positive influence on public health, the socialization of children, youth and adults, the social inclusion of the disadvantaged, the economic development of regions and states, and on fostering intercultural exchange and conflict resolution." He suggests SDP events are important "because they can serve as one engine of development reaching certain population groups and individuals that traditional development efforts have either excluded or for whom these development efforts have not been as efficacious."

Welty Peachey also addressed a number of points to consider when delivering SDP events. First, he noted that sport managers "cannot claim that sport is the most effective development tool, but only one avenue of development and peace building efforts that is important in reaching and effecting change in certain individuals and communities." In addition, it is important to consider context: "While there may be certain components or elements of SDP programs that are common across contexts, as suggested by emerging theory, there also needs to be cultural and contextual sensitivity, and programs should be developed with local stakeholders in order to best address local and specific needs." Finally, he noted the importance of considering the way the sports are developed. Although sport is inherently a competition, designing the events to be overly competitive can end up resulting in more harm than good. Welty Peachey argued, "A highly competitive sport environment may not evince positive outcomes, or foster social inclusion; it may actually do the opposite. Thus, careful attention should be given to *how* the sport program is designed and administered, with sensitivity to the needs and background of the population being served."

strategies that can be used to create and sustain these desired organizational cultures. Knowing this information, it is incumbent upon you—whether you currently work in a sport organization or aspire to do so—to act. Armed with this knowledge, it is up to you to work for ways to promote access, inclusion, and diversity. Otherwise, no matter how well intentioned you might be, there will, to borrow from Dr. King, be a need to repent for your silence.

Second, our focus thus far has been internal—looking at ways to improve sport organizations. It is also possible, though, for sport organizations to exert a positive impact on their communities. This can take place through corporate social responsibility efforts (Babiak & Wolfe, 2009) or, as shown in the Diversity Challenge, through sport-for-development initiatives. The focus of this chapter is on the latter and on the manner in which organizations use sport, in some capacity, to address larger social issues, including intergroup relations, public health, crime, and homelessness, among others. These efforts, when strategically organized and managed, have the potential to improve diversity and inclusion in the broader community.

The remainder of this chapter is organized as follows: First, I offer an overview of key terms related to sport and community development, and I also provide a brief historical overview of the initiatives. This is followed by a discussion of the potential benefits and drawbacks of such efforts. In the final section, I draw from recent theoretical advancements to articulate ways that sport managers could effectively leverage sport to effect social change. See the Professional Perspectives box for additional discussion of these topics.

SPORT AND SOCIAL CHANGE

In this section, I define key terms and provide a brief historical review of how advocates have used sport to create social change.

Key Terms

It is important to separate sport and social change efforts from *sport development*. The latter term refers to the monies, policies, and competitive cultures that are used to cultivate elite athletes or encourage mass participation within a particular setting (Brouwers, Sotiriadou, & De Bosscher, in press; Smolianov, Zakus, & Gallo, 2015). For example, in Australia, local councils and third-party organizations are taking on increasingly influential roles in the development of triathlon, thereby decreasing the power and authority among the sport's national governing bodies (Phillips & Newland, 2014). Sport development is concerned with the improvement of the sport itself and is, thus, beyond the scope of this chapter.

Sport-for-development (SFD) and sport-for-development and peace (SDP)

The terms *sport-for-development* (SFD) and *sport-for-development and peace* (SDP) are used in discussions of sport as a vehicle for social change (Coalter, 2013; Darnell, 2012; Kidd, 2008; Sherry, Schulenkorf, & Chalip, 2015). SFD refers to activities that include sport as a way of meeting the goals and tackling concerns related to individual, community, national, and international development. The focus might be social issues, education, public health, inclusion of disadvantaged populations, or improving intergroup relations. When the goals and concerns include fostering peace and reconciliation among traditionally hostile groups, we use the term SDP. As SDP is the most encompassing term, inclusive of both SFD and sport for social change, I use it throughout the remainder of this chapter except when specifically referring to more focused efforts. Street Soccer USA represents one example of SDP, as the organization seeks to address homelessness through sport and other activities. The Magic Bus, another SDP entity, is an organization based in India that uses games and other activities to teach children about education, gender, health, and other factors affecting their well-being (www.magicbus.org). As a third example, Kicking AIDS Out is an international organization that uses sport and physical activity to raise awareness and decrease the incidence of HIV/AIDS (www.kickingaidsout.net). At this writing, the International Platform on Sport for Development and Peace (www.sportanddev.org) provided a list of 600 organizations around the world that have registered as SDP entities. This is a sizeable increase from the 166 entities that Kidd listed in 2008 and the 295 that Hartmann and Kwauk referenced in 2011.

Sport-only approach

SDP activities are generally organized through one of three approaches (Coalter, 2007). The first is to offer *sport-only* provisions, such as organized leagues or physical activity opportunities without any other educational activities. For instance, in many communities, the parks and recreation department will offer formal (e.g., sport leagues) and informal (e.g., parks, walking trails) opportunities to be physically active. Behind these offerings is the assumption, perhaps implicit, that sport in and of itself has developmental properties. Just through their engagement in the leagues, for instance, people are assumed to grow as a community or improve in their physical and psychological well-being. Edwards (2015) notes some of the limitations with this approach (see also Coalter, 2013).

Sport-plus approach

Another option is to adopt a *sport-plus* model. Here, sport is the main component of the program or event, but it is augmented with other development activities.

For example, the World Scholar-Athlete Games are designed to bring together youth from around the world to participate in high-level sport competition. Sport represents the main component, but there are also other activities, such as theatre arts events, lectures, and cross-cultural happenings, all of which are designed to bolster the participants' empathy and confidence in creating change in their homeland (see also Lyras & Welty Peachey, 2011). Coalter suggests this is the standard SDP model.

Plus-sport approach

Finally, other SDP organizations adopt a *plus-sport* model. Here, the primary focus of the activity is on developing the individuals or community, and sport is used as a draw to attract people. For example, many programs designed to combat the spread of HIV/AIDS have education and training as their primary components and emphasis. At the same time, program organizers will use sport as a way of attracting people to the program. This practice serves to engage people who otherwise might not have attended the programs, but it still allows for the information and training to be conveyed.

Historical Context

Some people consider SDP programs to be a recent phenomenon (Kidd, 2008). Although the interest and growth in the use of sport to create social change has certainly increased over the past decade, it has actually been in place much longer (Coalter, 2013; Darnell, 2012; Giulianotti, 2011). Many observers point to U.S. President Harry Truman's 1949 inaugural address as a key starting point in SDP. Truman called for social, economic, and political improvements in the "underdeveloped areas" of the world (as cited in Darnell, 2012, p. 43). Truman's address represented a key marker for larger development events outside the world of sport and also coincided with important sport-related activities around the world; hence, its identification as a starting point for SDP. As Giulianotti highlights, sport was increasingly used during this time as a way to break away from existing cultural understandings. Many Caribbean nations' symbolic victories over England in cricket illustrate this nicely. In addition, at this time major sport governing bodies, such as FIFA, started to include countries long excluded from their membership.

More recently, former Olympic athletes helped initiate concerted efforts in using sport to address social concerns (Kidd, 2008). Four-time Olympic champion Johann Koss of Norway worked with the organizing committee of the Lillehammer 1994 Winter Olympics and other organizations to develop a humanitarian effort called Olympic Aid. Koss and other Olympians, such as Australia's famed swimmer Ian Thorpe, initially helped raise money for various activities. The organization later grew and became known as Right to Play (www.righttoplay.com). Today, it is a multinational organization dedicated to enhancing children's health and community development. Right to Play works in 23 countries across Africa, Asia, and the Middle East and partners with international entities, such as UNICEF, to make a meaningful impact on people and communities through sport. The growth of Right to Play is reflective of the larger SDP landscape. It represents one example, among hundreds, of how SDP entities use sport to effect social change.

The United Nations' Millennium Development Goals (MDGs), established in 2003, further facilitated the growth in SDP events (Coalter, 2013; Darnell, 2012). That year, the UN passed Resolution 58/5, affirming its commitment to education, health, and well-being and the use of sport to help achieve these development goals. Kofi Annan, who served as secretary general at the time, heralded the benefits of sport as a means to development by noting:

> Sport can play a role in improving the lives of individuals, not only individuals, I might add, but whole communities. I am convinced that the time is right to build on that understanding, to encourage governments, development agencies and communities to think how sport can be included more systemically in the plan to help children, particularly those living in the midst of poverty, disease and conflict. (As cited in Coalter, 2013, p. 29)

Annan's vocal support helped to drive interest in, financial backing of, and widespread efforts toward using sport and physical activity as tools for effecting change. As a result, SDP initiatives were pursued with renewed vigor.

SDP OUTCOMES

As Annan's quotation illustrates, many people view sport as a viable tool for development. Analysis of the evidence, however, suggests that the results are not always straightforward. There are cases where SDP initiatives result in various benefits, but there are also instances when the outcomes are null or even negative. In this section, I offer an overview of these findings.

Benefits of SDP

Evidence indicates that SDP can benefit individuals, groups, and communities. As throughout this book, I will examine these benefits from a multilevel perspective. Exhibit 15.1 offers an overview.

Potential benefits of SDP programs.　　EXHIBIT **15.1**

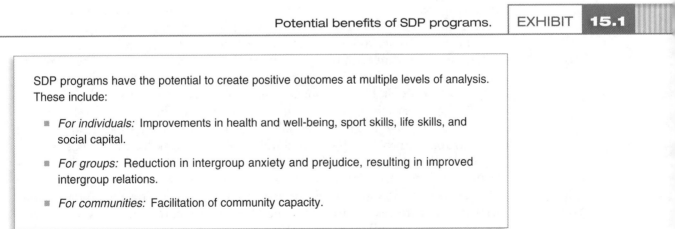

SDP programs have the potential to create positive outcomes at multiple levels of analysis. These include:

- *For individuals:* Improvements in health and well-being, sport skills, life skills, and social capital.

- *For groups:* Reduction in intergroup anxiety and prejudice, resulting in improved intergroup relations.

- *For communities:* Facilitation of community capacity.

Individual-level outcomes

SDP programs offer a number of potential benefits to the participants. One of the most direct relationships is that between SDP involvement and physical health (Sherry et al., 2015). Whether the model is sport-only, plus-sport, or sport-plus, SDP programs include physical activity of some sort, providing people the opportunity to enhance their physical fitness and overall physical well-being. This is particularly the case for SDP programs that are geared toward people who have been historically excluded from sport. In Australia, for instance, some community sport organizations have developed inclusive practices and policies (e.g., accommodating clothing preferences, providing culturally appropriate food) to encourage Muslim women's participation in sport (Maxwell, Foley, Taylor, & Burton, 2013).

Some SDP events also assist participants in developing their technical skills. For instance, in the analysis of a sport-plus event, Welty Peachey, Lyras, Cohen, and their colleagues (2014) observed that participants from around the world took part in the event in part because it allowed them to compete against other highly skilled individuals and, thus, cultivate their athletic skills. Sugden (2008) also observed as much in his analysis of Football 4 Peace International, which initially brought together people from neighboring Jewish and Arab communities in Northern Israel to participate with one another in soccer matches. It now has programs in Jordan, Palestine, South Africa, Germany, Ireland, Northern Ireland, and England (www.football4peace.eu). Among the many benefits of the SDP program, its matches allowed participants of all skill levels to polish their soccer skills and technical knowledge of the sport.

Third, SDP involvement has the potential to foster participants' life skills. Recall from the Diversity Challenge that a major component of Street Soccer USA was the development of nonsport skills, such as managing sobriety, developing financial acumen, and increasing job readiness. Cohen and Welty Peachey (2015) conducted an in-depth study of one of the more successful participants in this SDP program. They observed that the opportunities provided through participation, the supportive people who were involved, and the skills she learned along the way all helped her cultivate her identity as a social entrepreneur—that is, one who seeks to contribute positively to society without expectation of profits or notoriety. Through her experiences, she developed leadership skills, commitment to causes, a yearning to contribute to her community, and fund-raising acumen. Ultimately, these characteristics allowed her to become an effective champion for social inclusion. These findings are consistent with our study of SDP youth participants, as their involvement in the sport and educational components strengthened their belief that they could return to their home countries and effectively promote social change and inclusion (Welty Peachey, Cunningham, Bruening, et al., in press).

In addition, SDP has the potential to enhance participants' social capital. This is similar to, but broader than, the development of life skills. SDP scholars most frequently draw from Putnam's (2000) conceptualization of social capital as the "features of social organization such as networks, norms, and social trust that can facilitate coordination and cooperation for mutual benefit" (p. 66). As a person's social capital increases, so, too, does the likelihood of career success and life satisfaction. As one example, Spaaij (2012b) conducted research in Brazil to examine the efficacy of the Projecto Vencer, an SDP program for youth employment through sport that sought to improve the lives of youth in disadvantaged communities. The project allowed for participants in football (soccer) to develop social networks with persons outside their regular social networks. These participants were substantially more likely to do so than their peers who did not take part in the Vencer program. This benefit was likely realized through the program's encouragement of volunteerism outside the participants' home communities. Spaaij also considered the role of soccer in the development of social capital (as opposed to the other educational activities), and he made two important observations. First, soccer enhanced the effectiveness of some of the teaching embedded in the SDP program, allowing for "a fluid learning environment for supporting and delivering educational content to young people" (p. 91). Second, soccer fostered the participants' collaboration, social bonding, and commitment, which helped them solidify the benefits they accrued. Other scholars have also observed that soccer-based SDP programs can enhance the participants' social capital (Sherry, 2010; Welty Peachey, Borland, Lobpries, & Cohen, 2015).

Collectively, these data suggest that SDP events can have a meaningful, positive effect on participants' lives. Of course, the participants are not the only ones who can benefit from SDP events, as the volunteers and event spectators might also receive benefits. These possibilities are outlined in the Alternative Perspectives box.

ALTERNATIVE perspectives

Effects of SDP Programs on Volunteers and Spectators. SDP participants certainly have the potential to benefit from the programs, but so, too, do program volunteers and event spectators. In fact, Coalter (2013) suggests that coaches and educational leaders might be the people *most likely* to experience benefits from SDP offerings. In our own research, we have observed that SDP volunteers do benefit tremendously from their experiences. They report social capital gains, improvements in their ability to engage in meaningful service to others, enhancement of their career skills, and development of empathy and perspective taking (Welty Peachey et al., 2014). Volunteers from other SDP events report similar outcomes (Welty Peachey, Cohen, Borland, & Lyras, 2011).

Some SDP programs, such as the Homeless World Cup or various marathons, culminate with large-scale events where spectators come to observe the competition. Evidence suggests that simply attending these activities can alter a person's attitude. Spectators report greater awareness of the social concern (e.g., homelessness), improved attitudes toward the participants, and greater empathy (Sherry, Karg, & O'May, 2011). The positive culture and energy that surround SDP events are critical to their success and their ability to "sustain agendas for social and community action" (Chalip, 2006, p. 122).

Group-level outcomes

Group-level outcomes of SDP primarily occur in the area of improved intergroup relations, especially among SDP programs that target peace and reconciliation. For instance, Schulenkorf spent three months volunteering at an SDP project in Sri Lanka (Schulenkorf & Edwards, 2012). The project was set in Vavuniya—a city ravaged by the Sri Lankan Civil War—and included a soccer tournament in which thousands of Sinhalese, Tamil, and Muslim persons participated. The authors noted, "Through this experience it was seen that many Sri Lankans—regardless of their social, cultural and ethnic backgrounds—were willing to overcome political rivalries to interact and bridge intergroup divides" (p. 381). The International Run for Peace is another SDP project in Sri Lanka specifically designed to bridge intercultural and ethnic divides.

Where theory is employed in the design of the program or research on programs, SDP organizers and scholars mostly draw from the contact hypothesis (Allport, 1954; Pettigrew, 1998). Recall from Chapter 13 that, according to this theory, people sustain prejudice against others because of unfamiliarity and separation; thus, the key to reducing prejudice is to enable members of various social groups to have contact with one another under the right conditions. Although any contact has the potential to reduce intergroup anxiety and prejudice, this effect is most likely to occur when there is social support for the interactions, there is the possibility for close contact, people have equal status when interacting with one another, they cooperate with one another, and the possibility of developing friendships exists.

Some evidence suggests that SDP programs can facilitate improved intergroup relations. Some SDP projects, such as the one in Sri Lanka in which Schulenkorf (2010) was a part, create opportunities for people to develop friendships with dissimilar others. They also afford participants opportunities to express their unique identities within a setting that facilitates common goals and ideals. These factors promote inclusion while also serving, ultimately, to reduce intergroup biases (see also Giulianotti, 2011; Spaaij & Schulenkorf, 2014). As another example, we examined whether participants in World Scholar-Athlete Games experienced decreases in prejudice over the course of the event (Welty Peachey, Cunningham, et al., in press). The project was designed so that participants (1) played on teams with people from other countries; (2) engaged in educational activities that addressed salient issues of worldwide concern (e.g., prejudice, injustice); (3) worked in small groups to develop change strategies (e.g., how to be more effective change agents in their communities); and (4) attended keynote addresses from world leaders who spoke on the importance of the global environment, human rights, and ethics. Participants' prejudices decreased significantly over the course of the project. We also conducted interviews, which allowed participants to reflect on their experience. A basketball player from the United States noted, "It was the activity that really opened you up to find out who people really are . . . you are able to interact with people you don't normally interact with. . . . And this helped me think differently about other people." In a similar way, a tennis player from Luxembourg noted that her participation in the event allowed her to become more open-minded toward diversity and differences: "I feel like it made me more open minded towards other sport, other people, other cultures. I became more open minded about it because you're exposed to it."

Community-level outcomes

Although SDP organizers suggest that many community-level benefits are possible, the most realistic is community capacity building. *Community capacity* refers to the collective capital and organizational resources that community members leverage to identify and solve problems and positively affect the well-being of community members (Chaskin, 2001). SDP programs can play an important role in facilitating this process. As Edwards (2015) notes, for SDP projects to be successful, "communities must possess or develop the capability for collective action, the internal resources to support the process, and the necessary skills and knowledge to successfully identify local problems and their solutions" (see also Schulenkorf, 2012).

Drawing from Wendel, Burdine, McLeroy, and their colleagues' work (2009), Edwards (2015) suggested that SDP programs have the potential to affect seven areas of community capacity; these are outlined in Exhibit 15.2. He also suggested that the key to leveraging these community-level impacts was to engage the community members on issues important to them, such as physical activity, youth

SDP impact on community capacity.   EXHIBIT **15.2**

SDP COMPONENTS	PROCESSES	DIMENSIONS OF COMMUNITY CAPACITY
Available sport resources Volunteer department	Enhanced access to resources in community	Level of skills and resources
Positive interactions among SDP participants, volunteers, and spectators	Sense of community and social capital	Nature of social relations
Interorganizational partnerships Common identity in sport	Improved networks and ways for citizens to offer input	Space and structure for community dialogue
Growing leaders among volunteers Athletes as leaders	Leadership enhancement and sustainability	Leadership
Sport as a basis for community identity and involvement	Power spread among community members who actively engage	Civic engagement
Sport as a right for all Focus on inclusion and diversity	Promotion of egalitarian values and norms Inclusion	Value system
Evaluation of programs Reflection on service delivery	Understanding of community history and critical reflection	Learning culture

Sources: Edwards (2015), Wendel et al. (2009).

engagement, and the like. Based on this information, sport managers can then develop SDP projects specifically tailored to these needs. Addressing the community's needs both through sport and through the apposite educational components ensures relevance, buy-in, and sustainment of these efforts.

Shortcomings of SDP

Thus far, we have focused on the many potential benefits of SDP programs. However, as with many aspects of sport, there is another side of the coin. Specifically, a number of authors have pointed to shortcomings of SDP, which I outline here (see Exhibit 15.3).

Deficit model approach

Coalter (2013) is one of the more outspoken critics of SDP programs. One of his chief concerns is that sport managers operate from a deficit model. In this case, Coalter says, they engage in "environmental determinism that assumes that deprived communities inevitably produce deficient people who can be perceived, via a deficit model, to

EXHIBIT **15.3** Potential shortcomings of SDP programs.

> *Deficit model:* SDP organizers operate from a deficit model, viewing SDP participants as persons in need of fixing.
>
> *Sport evangelism:* A resolute commitment to sport as lever for creating social change and addressing community ills.
>
> *Overstated benefits:* Promising SDP outcomes on a grander scale than is actually possible.

be in need of 'development' through sport" (p. 3). When SDP managers operate from this perspective, they believe the targets of the programming are in need of assistance or fixing. Such a mentality has the potential to result in "othering" and stigmatizing of those individuals (see Chapters 7 and 10 for discussion of stigma and its effects).

Another problem in operating from a deficit model is that, more times than not, the assumptions are not empirically supported. Coalter (2013) illustrated this point nicely by relaying the story of an SDP event aimed at enhancing the participants' general self-efficacy (i.e., their ability to overcome obstacles to achieve goals). The (perhaps implicit) assumption was that the children who were participating in the event, all of whom came from abject poverty, would have low levels of generalized self-efficacy. This was not the case. When Coalter expressed surprise at the findings, one of the local SDP organizers chastised him, noting that Coalter would not survive three days in the conditions in which the children lived. Given the children's regular struggle, their self-efficacy and resilience would have to be high—it was a matter of survival.

Sport evangelism

Another potential shortcoming of SDP projects is what Coalter (2013) refers to as sport evangelism: policy makers and SDP organizers herald the utility of sport to create social change and remedy various ills. For instance, the United Nations states that sport "is about inclusion and citizenship. Sport brings individuals and communities together, highlighting commonalities and bridging cultural and ethnic divides. Sport provides a forum to learn skills such as discipline, confidence, and leadership and teaches core principles such as tolerance, cooperation, and respect" (United Nations Inter-Agency Task Force on Sport for Development and Peace, 2003, p. i). This position is consistent with a functionalist approach (see Chapter 2): sport is believed to provide social goods, develop strong moral fiber, and contribute to people's well-being.

The potential problem with this perspective is that sport is inherently neither good nor bad; instead, it is a context where larger social goods and ills manifest. As many anecdotes as there are pointing to benefits associated with sport participation, there are others documenting abuse, prejudice, discrimination, and subjugation within that setting. Hence, critical scholars take umbrage with the evangelical statements about sport as an instrument of social change. As Hartmann and Kwauk (2011) articulate, "Many sport-based development initiatives and proposals have extremely idealized beliefs about sport's positive, prosocial force. In a nutshell, they assume that simply having a sport program or initiative of some kind will automatically and inevitably serve the development goals of socialization, education, and intervention. Nothing, in our view, could be further from the truth" (p. 289). A volunteer in Darnell's (2010) study also recognized as much, noting, "Sport is a great hook, I would say, for social change, but it's not an automatic one" (p. 69). In a similar vein, I offer evidence later in the chapter that it is the design and delivery of sport-plus and plus-sport programs that make sport a viable tool for development and change.

Overstated benefits

Finally, many critics argue that SDP programs do not deliver benefits or improve communities on the scales purported (Black, 2010; Coalter, 2013; Darnell, 2012; Hartmann & Kwauk, 2011). Let's consider a couple of examples. As noted in the previous sections, some evidence suggests that SDP participation can increase participants' social capital. However, Spaaij (2012a), in his analysis of a soccer club in Australia, observed that the effects are not uniform. Instead, men, people who were highly educated, and individuals who had social networks consisting of people from different cultural backgrounds were most likely to experience social capital gains. In another case, Richards and Foster (2013) collected data from adolescents who took part in an SDP project in Gulu, Uganda, known as the Gum Marom Kids League. This project has potential importance because of the prevalence of war, poverty, and rape in the area. That noted, the authors did not observe any empirical benefits associated with involvement in the program. This was the case for measures of cardiorespiratory fitness and of mental health.

In other cases, the limited effects of SDP programs are attributable to the short duration of some projects and a lack of community capacity (Edwards, 2015). Some SDP projects represent just one component of an organization's outreach, and many of these are funded through external grants that offer the ability to engage in extra activities. Unless additional capacity has been realized, when the term of the grant ends, so too does the SDP project. These dynamics led Forde, Lee, Mills, and Frisby (2015) to conclude that funding was one of the major obstacles to the success of SDP projects. Another obstacle is the potential for outside violence to disrupt SDP programs. Sugden (2008) encountered this problem in his work with Football 4 Peace—the project mentioned on page 342 aimed at fostering peace and reconciliation among Arabs and Jews. Despite the success of the project, it had to be canceled when armed conflict broke out between Israel and Hezbollah.

EFFECTIVE DELIVERY OF SDP PROGRAMS

The preceding discussion highlights several tensions surrounding SDP projects. While there is evidence that SDP projects can benefit individuals, intergroup relations, and communities, other data point to potential shortcomings of the programs. I argue that these differences reflect the design, implementation, and leveraging of the SDP projects. This, of course, is a familiar refrain, and we have touched on the importance of intentionality in the design of management and training initiatives to enhance diversity and inclusion (Chapters 12–14). However, because of its importance, the point bears repeating here. Thus, in the final section, I outline several considerations in the design and delivery of SDP programs. See Exhibit 15.4.

EXHIBIT **15.4** Effective delivery of SDP programs.

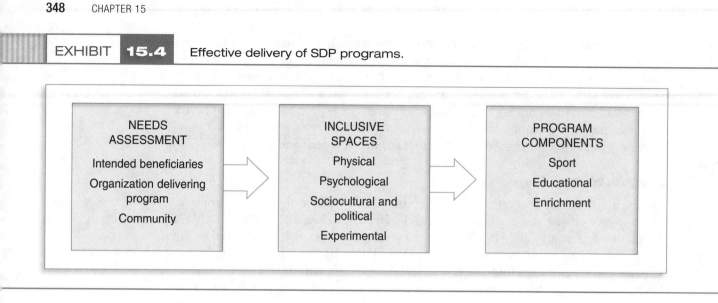

Needs Assessment

As in designing a training program for diversity and inclusion, the first step in the SDP process should be a needs assessment. The assessment should cover the intended beneficiaries, the organization delivering the program, and the community.

At the individual level, a deficit model approach will sometimes lead sport managers to make assumptions that are inaccurate. This can lead to targeting outcomes that might seem appropriate but that are actually misplaced for the participants (Coalter, 2013). To combat this error, SDP organizers should engage in evidence-based decision making, drawing from data to inform their decisions. A number of sources of data are available, such as governmental reports, community-wide surveys, and focus-group interviews. See the Diversity in the Field box on the facing page for one example. Edwards (2015) suggests that community members are frequently the best source of information.

Once the analysis points to the appropriate focus for the SDP program, it is important to consider whether the proposed efforts will actually get to the root of the issue. For instance, many SDP programs are designed to improve race relations. It is plausible that, when appropriately designed, an SDP program can help facilitate reductions in intergroup anxiety and prejudice (Schulenkorf, 2010; Spaaij & Schulenkorf, 2014; Welty Peachey, Cunningham, et al., in press). It is also possible, however, that group relations are not the source of the tensions; instead, the strained race relations might result from systemic issues, such as laws, norms, and institutions that create and recreate a culture that privileges those in power while subjugating racial minorities. It is difficult—but not impossible—for an SDP program, no matter how well delivered, to alter fundamentally how people in a larger community think about race. As Hartmann and Kwauk (2011) observed, "It is not enough to simply do development better by running more responsible, culturally appropriate, sport-based programs. Such intervention must also involve a concomitant attempt to alter the conditions of inequality" (p. 295).

The second component of the needs analysis addresses organizational capacity. This includes examination of policies and practices to ensure that they promote an inclusive environment where SDP participants can thrive (Forde et al., 2015; Maxwell et al., 2013). Another aspect is ensuring that linkages and partnerships with needed external stakeholders are firmly in place. For example, local school districts might help in the identification of participants' needs or in ensuring that participants engage in the program (Forde et al., 2015). A third element of the organizational analysis is an examination of the people in place. Change agents and cause champions can make a considerable difference in the success of an SDP program. They understand the important impact the SDP program can have on the participants' lives, and they work to ensure the success of the program (Forde et al., 2015; Schulenkorf, 2012). Finally, it is important to ensure that financial resources are in place to deliver the program for an extended period of time or, if they are not, that plans exist to seek and secure adequate new sources of external funding. Without this critical last component, even highly successful programs might fade away once the life of the original grant runs its course.

Finally, SDP organizers need to examine the community in which the intervention will take place. One element includes examination of the various dimensions of community capacity (refer back to Exhibit 15.2). Beyond this, it is also important to anticipate potential constraints and barriers to the SDP program's success. For instance, reconciliation programs such as Football 4 Peace can play an important role in fostering positive intergroup relations. However, the areas where the SDP initiatives take place are frequently dangerous, presenting a high probability of events that could derail the program altogether. Sugden (2008) observes that many of the SDP's host sites were bombed during the Israel and Hezbollah conflict. As another example, a number of SDP projects focus on curbing the transmission of HIV/AIDS. Condom use is a frequently discussed strategy that can effectively reduce HIV transmission (Fonner, Kennedy, O'Reilly, & Sweat, 2014). However, some religious traditions prohibit the use of contraception, and in highly religious communities discussion of condom use, absent cultural sensitivity, could be met with substantial backlash. Thus, it is important that designers of SDP programs consider community norms and customs.

DIVERSITY IN THE FIELD

Evidence-Based Programming. Program design and delivery should be based on data about communities and the people in them. Polling services (such as PEW Research) and government agencies (such as the U.S. Census Bureau or United Nations) are potential sources of data. In other cases, foundations' research on topics relevant to the SDP project might serve as a starting point. The Robert Wood Johnson Foundation, a philanthropic organization that focuses on health, is one entity that conducts such research. Government-sponsored research centers and institutes regularly conduct community audits and assessments. This is common practice for research enterprises that focus on public health or rural health, such as the Center for Community Health Development at Texas A&M University. Finally, community members themselves might be the best source of information about specific needs and opportunities. Interviews with community members or focus groups that include persons from around the community can be rich sources of data. We have used some of the latter data sources to increase community capacity in a rural setting (Garney, Wendel, Castle, et al., 2014).

Inclusive Spaces

After conducting the needs analysis and determining the specific focus of the SDP program, the designer should next consider the project's inclusiveness. Doing so can affect the feeling of safety for participants and the overall success of the program (Forde et al., 2015; Spaaij & Schulenkorf, 2014). Drawing from various SDP studies (Maxwell et al., 2013; Spaaij & Schulenkorf, 2014) and our discussion in Chapter 1, we can think of inclusive spaces along four domains:

- *Physical:* the safety of the event, as well as provisions to ensure that people can participate fully while also wearing various kinds of attire.
- *Psychological:* the absence of psychological or emotional hardships to which participants might be exposed and the development of trust, sharing, engagement, and a common in-group identity.
- *Sociocultural and political:* the acceptance that participants feel, as well as their ability to express openly social identities, beliefs, and attitudes important to them.
- *Experimental:* the participants' ability to take risks and experiment at the event. This domain is likely to have both physical (e.g., learning and experimenting with new technical skills) and psychological (e.g., reaching out and communicating with out-group members) elements.

Given that educational and learning components are critical to an SDP project's success, it is imperative that participants feel psychological safety and inclusion. Thus, the last three elements are of particular relevance.

Sport, Educational, and Enrichment Components

Given the criticisms associated with sport-only models (Coalter, 2013; Darnell, 2012; Hartmann & Kwauk, 2011), I suggest SDP programs should take the form of plus-sport or sport-plus projects. This means that, in addition to considering the sport and physical activity delivery components of the projects, the designer should also consider the educational and enrichment activities (see also Chalip, 2006; Lyras & Welty Peachey, 2011).

Let's first consider the sport components. Lyras and Welty Peachey (2011) strongly advocate for mixed teams that create diversity along gender, ethnic, racial, or nationality lines. With mixed teams, the categorization and intergroup bias processes are less likely to materialize. It is also important to emphasize skill development and improvement over intense competition. Cooperation and a quest to do one's best are principles consistent with a mastery-centered approach that is conducive to improved intergroup relations (see also Hastie, Sinelnikov, Wallhead, & Layne, 2014). Finally, coaches and volunteers should be encouraged to serve as role models while also championing social change.

The educational components should flow from the needs analysis, being both relevant to the specific context and culturally sensitive. Educational principles can be relayed within the sport context, such as during time-outs or skill demonstrations. Beyond this, effective SDP programs include various learning components that are suited to the learners' needs. These might include group discussions, seminars, keynote addresses, or other pedagogical tools. Throughout the program, coaches and volunteers should seek to display empathy, care, and engagement and to develop these qualities in the participants.

Finally, many SDP programs further enhance the participants' experiences through cultural events (Lyras & Welty Peachey, 2011). Incorporating these elements is consistent with Chalip's (2006) recommendation to create various activities that attract diverse interests. Examples include fine arts involvement, theatre, movie making, and the like. The cultural events might have a stand-alone entertainment or diversionary purpose, but they are more effective when integrated with the sport and educational components. For instance, persons who make short films might take as their subject social change in their local community or the struggles SDP participants encounter in their everyday lives. These connections help raise awareness and present the SDP components in a cohesive, unified fashion.

chapter SUMMARY

I began the chapter with a discussion of our interconnectedness with one another. I argued that when people know about discrimination, prejudice, and suffering, yet do nothing, they become complicit in the perpetuation of these ills. If we accept this premise, then it is incumbent upon us not only to develop diverse and inclusive sport organizations but also to use sport to create positive impacts in our communities. Therein lies the promise of SDP programs. As illustrated in the Diversity Challenge, SDP, when effectively designed and implemented, can create meaningful social change in people's lives.

After reading this chapter, you should be able to:

1. **Identify the different ways managers use sport for social change and inclusion.**

   Managers can use sport-for-development and peace programs to promote social change and inclusion. These programs come in the form of sport-only, sport-plus, or plus-sport programs.

2. **Discuss the positive and negative outcomes associated with sport-for-development and peace activities.**

   SDP programs potentially benefit the health and well-being, sport skills, life skills, and social capital of participants and others involved in the projects. They can improve intergroup relations and facilitate community capacity. SDP programs can have shortcomings, such as when sport managers operate from a deficit model, promote sport evangelism, or overstate the potential benefits of the SDP initiative.

3. **Highlight the characteristics of effective sport-for-development and social change programs.**

   To develop an effective program, the SDP organizers conduct a needs analysis in order to understand the intended participants, organizational capacity, and community characteristics. They also take steps to ensure the project is inclusive. Finally, based on the data gathered, they focus on tailoring the sport, educational, and enrichment activities to suit the specific needs of the participants.

QUESTIONS for discussion

1. I suggested that people have an obligation to work for social justice and inclusion in their work environments. Do you agree? Why or why not?
2. How does sport development differ from sport-for-development and sport-for-development and peace?
3. What are the pros and cons of sport-only, sport-plus, and plus-sport models?
4. Many benefits of SDP programs were listed in the chapter. Do you consider one more important than the others? Why?
5. What are the effects of overstating the benefits of SDP programs?
6. Of the steps identified in creating an effective SDP program, which do you think would be the most difficult to achieve?

learning ACTIVITIES

1. Using online resources, identify five SDP programs and list the intended audience and benefits of each.
2. Working in small groups, discuss the pros and cons associated with SDP programs and their effects in the community.

WEB resources

International Platform on Sport and Development, www.sportanddev.org

Offers an overview of SDP initiatives and a list of SDP organizations.

Team UNICEF, www.unicef.org/sports

Serves as the home site for UNICEF's work ensuring children's right to be active.

Sports and Society Program, www.aspeninstitute.org/policy-work/sports-society

Home of the Aspen Institute's Sport Initiative, with a focus on ensuring sport and physical activity for all people.

reading RESOURCES

Coalter, F. (2013). *Sport for development: What game are we playing?* New York: Routledge.

Offers an overview of SDP activities and a critical analysis of their usefulness.

Darnell, S. (2012). *Sport for development and peace: A critical sociology.* New York: Bloombury.

Offers a sociological perspective on SDP events, highlighting the potential benefits and shortcomings.

United Nations Inter-Agency Task Force on Sport for Development and Peace (2003). *Sport for development and peace: Towards achieving the Millennium Development Goals.* New York: Author.

The United Nations' rationale for engaging in SDP ventures.

REFERENCES

Allport, G. W. (1954). *The nature of prejudice*. Cambridge, MA: Addison-Wesley.

Babiak, K., & Wolfe, R. (2009). Determinants of corporate social responsibility in professional sport: Internal and external factors. *Journal of Sport Management, 23,* 717–742.

Black, D. R. (2010). The ambiguities of development: Implications for "development through sport." *Sport in Society, 13,* 121–129.

Brouwers, J., Sotiriadou, P., & De Bosscher, V. (in press). Sport-specific policies and factors that influence international success: The case of tennis. *Sport Management Review.*

Chalip, L. (2006). Towards social leverage of sport events. *Journal of Sport and Tourism, 11*(2), 109–127.

Chaskin, R. J. (2001). Building community capacity: A definitional framework and case studies from a comprehensive community initiative. *Urban Affairs Review, 36,* 291–323.

Coalter, F. (2007). *A wider social role for sport: Who's keeping score?* New York: Routledge.

Coalter, F. (2013). *Sport for development: What game are we playing?* New York: Routledge.

Cohen, A., & Welty Peachey, J. (2015). The making of a social entrepreneur: From participant to cause champion within a sport-for-development context. *Sport Management Review, 18,* 111–125.

Cunningham, G. B. (2011a). Creative work environments in sport organizations: The influence of sexual orientation diversity and commitment to diversity. *Journal of Homosexuality, 58,* 1041–1057.

Cunningham, G. B. (2011b). The LGBT advantage: Examining the relationship among sexual orientation diversity, diversity strategy, and performance. *Sport Management Review, 14,* 453–461.

Cunningham, G. B. (2014). Interdependence, mutuality, and collective action in sport. *Journal of Sport Management, 28,* 1–7.

Cunningham, G. B., Miner, K., & Benavides-Espinoza, C. (2012). Emotional reactions to observing misogyny: Examining the roles of gender, forecasting, political orientation, and religiosity. *Sex Roles, 67,* 58–68.

Daniels, E. A. (2009). Sex objects, athletes, and sexy athletes: How media representations of women athletes can impact adolescent girls and college women. *Journal of Adolescent Research, 24,* 399–422.

Daniels, E. A. (2012). Sexy versus strong: What girls and women think of female athletes. *Journal of Applied Developmental Psychology, 33,* 79–90.

Daniels, E. A., & Wartena, H. (2011). Athlete or sex symbol: What boys think of media representations of female athletes. *Sex Roles, 65,* 566–579.

Darnell, S. (2012). *Sport for development and peace: A critical sociology.* New York: Bloombury.

Darnell, S. C. (2010). Power, politics, and "sport for development and peace": Investigating the utility of sport for international development. *Sociology of Sport Journal, 27,* 54–75.

Edwards, M. B. (2015). The role of sport in community capacity building: An examination of sport for development and research. *Sport Management Review, 18,* 6–19.

Florida, R. (2002). The economic geography of talent. *Annals of the Association of American Geographers, 92,* 743–755.

Florida, R. (2003). Cities and the creative class. *City & Community, 2,* 3–19.

Florida, R. (2012). *The rise of the creative class, revisited.* New York: Basic Books.

Fonner, V. A., Kennedy, C. E., O'Reilly, K. R., & Sweat, M. D. (2014). Systematic assessment of condom use measurement in evaluation of HIV prevention interventions: Need for standardization of measures. *AIDS and Behavior, 18,* 2374–2386.

Forde, S. D., Lee, D. S., Mills, C., & Frisby, W. (2015). Moving towards social inclusion: Manager and staff perspectives on an award winning community sport and recreation program for immigrants. *Sport Management Review, 18,* 126–138.

Garney, W. R., Wendel, M. L., Castle, B. F., Alaniz, A. B., McLeroy, K. R., & Cunningham, G. B. (2014, March). *Using community health development to increase community capacity: The physical activity and community engagement project.* Poster presented at the 14th Annual American Academy of Health Behavior Meeting, Charleston, SC.

Giulianotti, R. (2011). Sport, peacemaking and conflict resolution: A contextual analysis and modelling of the sport, development and peace sector. *Ethnic and Racial Studies, 34,* 207–228.

Glomb, T. M., Richman, W. L., Hulin, C. L., Drasgow, F., Schneider, K. T., & Fitzgerald, L. F. (1997). Ambient sexual harassment: An integrated model of antecedents and consequences. *Organizational Behavior & Human Decision Processes, 71,* 309–328.

Gottlieb, R. S. (Ed.) (2003). *Liberating faith: Religious voices for justice, peace, and ecological wisdom.* New York: Rowman & Littlefield.

Hartmann, D., & Kwauk, C. (2011). Sport and development: An overview, critique, and reconstruction. *Journal of Sport and Social Issues, 35,* 284–305.

Hastie, P., Sinelnikov, O., Wallhead, T., & Layne, T. (2014). Perceived and actual motivational climate of a mastery-involving sport education season. *European Physical Education Review, 20,* 215–228.

Kane, M. J., LaVoi, N. M., & Fink, J. S. (2013). Exploring elite female athletes' interpretations of sport media images: A window into the construction of social identity and "selling sex" in women's sports. *Communication & Sport, 1*(3), 269–298.

Kidd, B. (2008). A new social movement: Sport for development and peace. *Sport in Society, 11,* 370–380.

Lyras, A., & Welty Peachey, J. (2011). Integrating sport-for-development theory and praxis. *Sport Management Review, 14,* 311–326.

Maxwell, H., Foley, C., Taylor, T., & Burton, C. (2013). Social inclusion in community sport: A case study of Muslim women in Australia. *Journal of Sport Management, 27,* 467–481.

Miner-Rubino, K., & Cortina, L. M. (2007). Beyond targets: Consequences of vicarious exposure to misogyny at work. *Journal of Applied Psychology, 92,* 1254–1269.

Pettigrew, T. F. (1998). Intergroup contact theory. *Annual Review of Psychology, 49,* 65–85.

Phillips, P., & Newland, B. (2014). Emergent models of sport development and delivery: The case of triathlon in Australia and the US. *Sport Management Review, 17,* 107–120.

Putnam, R. D. (2000). *Bowling alone: The collapse and revival of American community.* New York: Simon & Schuster.

Richards, J., & Foster, C. (2013). Sport-for-development interventions: Whom do they reach and what is their potential for impact on physical and mental health in low-income countries. *Journal of Physical Activity and Health, 10,* 929–931.

Schulenkorf, N. (2010). Sport events and ethnic reconciliation: Attempting to create social change between Sinhalese, Tamil, and Muslim sportspeople in war-torn Sri Lanka. *International Review for the Sociology of Sport, 45,* 273–294.

Schulenkorf, N. (2012). Sustainable community development through sport and events: A conceptual framework for sport-for-development events. *Sport Management Review, 15,* 1–12.

Schulenkorf, N., & Edwards, D. (2012). Maximizing positive social impacts: Strategies for sustaining and leveraging the benefits of intercommunity sport events in divided societies. *Journal of Sport Management, 26,* 379–390.

Sherry, E. (2010). (Re)engaging marginalized groups through sport: The Homeless World Cup. *International Review for the Sociology of Sport, 45,* 59–71.

Sherry, E., Karg, A., & O'May, F. (2011). Social capital and sport events: Spectator attitudinal change and the Homeless World Cup. *Sport in Culture: Cultures, Commerce, Media, Politics, 14,* 111–125.

Sherry, E., Schulenkorf, N., & Chalip, L. (2015). Managing sport for social change: The state of play. *Sport Management Review, 18,* 1–5.

Smolianov, P., Zakus, D., & Gallo, J. (2015). *Sport development in the United States: High performance and mass participation.* New York: Routledge.

Spaaij, R. (2012a). Beyond the playing field: Experiences of sport, social capital, and integration among Somalis in Australia. *Ethnic and Racial Studies, 35,* 1519–1538.

Spaaij, R. (2012b). Building social and cultural capital among young people in disadvantaged communities: Lessons from a Brazilian sport-based intervention program. *Sport, Education and Society, 17,* 77–95.

Spaaij, R., & Schulenkorf, N. (2014). Cultivating safe space: Lessons for sport-for-development projects and events. *Journal of Sport Management, 28,* 633–645.

Sugden, J. (2008). Community and the instrumental use of football: Anyone for Football for Peace? The challenges of using sport in the service of co-existence in Israel. *Soccer & Society, 9,* 405–415.

United Nations Inter-Agency Task Force on Sport for Development and Peace (2003). *Sport for development and peace: Towards achieving the Millennium Development Goals.* New York: Author.

Welty Peachey, J., Borland, J., Lobpries, J., & Cohen, A. (2015). Managing impact: Leveraging sacred spaces and community celebration to maximize social capital at a sport-for-development event. *Sport Management Review, 18,* 86–98.

Welty Peachey, J., Cohen, A., Borland, J., & Lyras, A. (2011). Building social capital: Examining the impact of Street Soccer USA on its volunteers. *International Review for the Sociology of Sport, 48,* 20–37.

Welty Peachey, J., Cunningham, G. B., Bruening, J. L., Cohen, A., & Lyras, A. (in press). The influence of a sport-for-peace event on prejudice and change agent self-efficacy. *Journal of Sport Management.*

Welty Peachey, J., Lyras, A., Cohen, A., Bruening, J. E., & Cunningham, G. B. (2014). Exploring the motives and retention factors of sport-for-development volunteers. *Nonprofit and Voluntary Sector Quarterly, 43,* 1052–1069.

Wendel, M. L., Burdine, J. N., McLeroy, K. R., Alaniz, A., Norton, B., & Felix, M. R. (2009). Community capacity: Theory and application. In R. DiClemente, R. Crosby, & M. C. Kegler (Eds.), *Emerging theories in health promotion practice and research* (pp. 277–302). San Francisco: Jossey-Bass.

AUTHOR INDEX

AARP, 137
Abercrombie, N., 69, 258
Abrego, L., 252
Acosta, R. V., 57, 106, 107
Adair, D., 69
Adams, A., 234
Adler, N. E., 70
Age Discrimination in Employment
    Act, 129, 130
Allen, J. B., 110
Allport, G. W., 53, 56, 288–292,
    302–304, 343
Altemeyer, B., 203
American Heart Association, 127, 128
American Psychological Association,
    215, 243–245, 257
Americans with Disabilities Act, 150,
    151, 158
Anderson, E., 35, 39, 43, 83, 216, 233
Anderson, K., 114
Andersson, L. M., 120
Armstrong, B., 175
Armstrong-Stassen, M., 134
Arnold, A., 254
Arthur, W., Jr., 317
Australian Sports Commission, 106

Babiak, K., 338
Bacharach, S. B., 31
Backlund, E., 244
Bailey, J. R., 195
Baldridge, D. C., 158
Bandura, A., 319
Barney, J., 34
Barron, L. G., 279
Beadnell, M., 255
Beatty, P. T., 145

Beck, J., 199
Becker, E., 135
Beemyn, G., 216, 217
Bell, M. L., 254
Bell, M. P., 92, 131, 134, 152, 154,
    160, 171, 172, 173, 242, 312,
    321
Bellizzi, J. A., 177
Belmi, P., 184
Bem, S. L., 100
Bendick, M., Jr., 321
Benefiel, M., 196
Benn, T., 205
Bennett, G., 143, 202
Berri, D. J., 72
Beyer, J. M., 79
Bezrukova, K., 312, 314, 317
Bimper, A. Y., 38
Binder, J., 291, 292, 302
Black, D. R., 347
Blaker, N. M., 180
Blair, I. V., 55
Boehm, S., 140
Bonacich, E., 88
Booth, D., 69
Boothroyd, L. G., 179
Bopp, M., 88, 199
Boser, U., 250
Bourdieu, P., 247
Bradford, J., 224
Brady, E., 214
Brewer, M. B., 7, 41, 54, 290, 292,
    293, 295–299, 301, 303
Brittain, I., 163
Brochu, P. M., 173
Brooks, D., 25
Brouwers, J., 339

Brown, R., 291, 302
Brown, T. N., 89
Brownwell, K. D., 188
Bruce, S., 194
Bruening, J. E., 99, 288
Brynin, M., 75
Buffington, D., 78
Bullock, H. E., 247, 250, 253
Burden, J. W., Jr., 84
Burdsey, D., 61
Bureau of Labor Statistics, 71, 76,
    103, 156
Burris, C. T., 203
Burton, L. J., 38, 51, 109, 112, 202
Bush, A., 234
Button, S. B., 227
Buzinski, J., 43, 83
Buzuvis, E. E., 217, 222

CA.gov, 245
Caddick, N., 164
Cahn, S., 100
Callahan, J. S., 137
Calzo, J. P., 233
Carpenter, L. J., 107, 108
Carré, J. M., 183
Carroll, H. J., 217, 222
Carron, A. V., 177
Carter-Francique, A., 38, 89
Carver, L. F., 100
Catalyst Institute, 106
Cavalier, E. S., 227
Centers for Disease Control and
    Prevention (CDC, 2008),
    58, 171
Chalip, L., 343, 350, 351
Chambliss, H. O., 174

Chan, S., 138
Chan-Serafin, S., 195
Chaskin, R. J., 344
Chelladurai, P., 17, 32, 76, 88, 275
Clair, J. A., 229–231
Clavio, G., 183
Clycq, N., 250
Coaching Association of Canada, 106
Coakley, J., 69, 78, 87, 119, 207, 255, 261
Coalter, F., 339–341, 343, 345–348, 350
Cocchiara, F. K., 320, 321
Cogman, T., 255
Cohen, A., 294, 342
Coile, C. C., 136
Colella, A., 154
Colloff, P., 221
Colquitt, J. A., 326, 327
Commisso, M., 183
Connelly, B. L., 271
Cook, A., 83
Cooky, C., 37, 120
Corrigan, P. W., 231
Côté, S., 242, 246
Cramer, J. A., 174
Crandall, C. S., 53, 55, 59, 174, 175
Crenshaw, K., 39
Crisp, R. J., 294
Crompton, J. L., 37
Crosby, F. J., 320
Cuddy, A. J. C., 50, 51, 78, 131, 153
Cunningham, G. B., 6, 11, 18, 20, 21, 22, 23, 30, 31, 32, 34, 35, 42, 43, 55, 56, 57, 60, 74, 76, 78, 80, 82, 84, 85, 89, 114, 115, 119, 120, 131, 177, 185, 203, 204, 226, 231–233, 271, 273, 275, 277, 279–281, 291, 299–301, 303, 304, 313–315, 321, 326, 336, 337

Dachner, A. M., 317
Dacin, M. T., 272
Dane-Staples, E., 163
Daniels, E. A., 121, 336
Daniels, N., 251
Darnell, S., 339, 340, 347, 350
Davis-Delano, L. R., 78
Day, N. E., 84, 85
De Block, A., 184
de Haan, D., 164
Dean, D., 78
Del Rio, C. M., 195

Demirel, E., 84
Denton, F. N., 225
DePauw, K. P., 153, 155, 161
DeSensi, J. T., 274 301
Deutsch, M., 289
De Wall, C. N., 200
Diaz, G., 318
Dimmock, J. A., 174
DiTomaso, N., 5
Dixon, M. A., 110
Dobbin, F., 273
Doherty, A. J., 20, 30, 32, 80, 274, 301
Dovidio, J. F., 54, 56, 81, 82, 155–157, 294, 299
Duguid, M. M., 52, 182
Duncan, M. C., 171, 174
Dunn, R., 199
Durkheim, E., 194, 195, 208
Durnin, J. V., 171

Eagleman, A., 120
Eagly, A. H., 52
Eastern Collegiate Athletic Conference, 162
Economos, C. D., 175
Edwards, K. L., 196
Edwards, M. B., 339, 344, 347, 348
Eisenbeiss, S. A., 201
Eitzen, D. S., 36, 37, 38, 39, 68, 87, 205, 206, 253, 260
Eley, R., 57
Ellers, A., 291, 292, 304
Elling, A., 234
Ely, R., 38, 271
Emile, M., 53
Erueti, B., 38
Esen, E., 313
Evans, J. M., 201
Everhart, B. C., 74
Exline, J., 202

Fay, T., 160
Feagin, J. R., 68, 78, 305
Ferdman, B. M., 7, 31, 80, 275
Ferguson, M., 40
Fernandez, E., 170
Fidas, D., 227
Fink, J. S., 32, 80, 102, 118, 185, 233, 271, 274
Finkelstein, L. M., 137, 176, 177
Fiske, S. T., 51, 154, 172, 249
Flake, C. R., 105, 106
Florey, A. T., 158
Florida, R., 35, 232, 336

Fonner, V. A., 349
Forde, S. D., 347, 349, 350
Freifeld, L., 313
Fritzsche, B., 136
Fryar, C. D., 179, 180
Fulks, D. L., 79, 119

Gaertner, S. L., 81, 290, 297, 299, 300, 301
Galinsky, A. D., 53, 89
Gallup, 256
Ganin, S., 68
Garney, W. R., 349
Garrison, K. C., 180
Gates, G. J., 217
Gebert, D., 202
Gilbert, J. A., 318
Gillentine, A., 199
Giulianotti, R., 344
Gladwell, M., 181
Glomb, T. M., 336
Glover, B., 54
Glynn, S. J., 112
Goffman, E., 41, 222
Goldstein, I. L., 316
Goldstein, N. J., 52
Gonzales, G. L., 88
Gordon, J., 313
Gordon-Larson, P., 58
Gottlieb, R. S., 337
Granderson, L. Z., 232
Gray, B., 250, 258
Greenhaus, J. H., 57, 82
Greenleaf, C., 174
Griffin, P., 221, 224, 233
Grossman, R., 319
Gruenfeld, D. H., 33

Hahn, D. A., 183
Halle, M., 256
Hallinan, C., 88
Hamilton, B. H., 72
Hancock, D. J., 139
Hargreaves, J., 185
Harrison, D. A., 9, 305
Harrison, L., 89
Harrolle, M. G., 57
Hartmann, D., 346–348, 350
Haselhuhn, M. P., 183
Hastie, P., 350
Hatzenbuehler, M. L., 59, 225
Hawkins, B., 75
Hayward, M. D., 244
Healy, M. C., 138
Hebl, M. R., 43, 158, 226

Hedge, J. W., 134
Herek, G. M., 219–222, 224, 225, 291
Herscovitch, L., 281
Hewstone, M., 296, 301, 302, 304
Hicks, D. A., 194, 195
Hinojosa, F., 196
Hively, K., 53
Hodge, N., 160
Hodge, S. R., 84
Hodson, G., 288
Hoffman, J., 114
Hoffman, S., 205
Hogg, M. A., 203
Holladay, C. L., 315, 320
Holvino, E., 281
Hooks, T., 157
Homan, A. C., 302, 303
Hosoda, M., 183
Hovden, J., 112
Huffman, A. H., 228
Human Rights Campaign, 223
Hums, M. A., 162
Hunger, J. M., 174
Hylton, K., 38, 69, 77, 78

Ianotta, R. J., 86
Ilgen, D. R., 17
Irwin, R. L., 32

Jackson, B., 42
Jago, G., 291
James, J. B., 142
Jawahar, I. M., 183
Jehn, K. A., 10
Johnson, C. D., 30
Johnson, M. K., 203
Johnson, R. C., 101
Johnston, D., 21
Jones, A., 119
Jones, E., 41, 151
Jones, K. P., 312
Jones, L. M., 297
Jost, J. T., 251
Judge, T. A., 175, 176, 180, 181

Kaiser, C. R., 81, 93
Kalev, A., 312, 315
Kalinoski, Z. T., 314, 320, 322, 323
Kamins, M. A., 185
Kamphoff, C., 85
Kane, M. J., 101, 102, 120, 336
Kanters, M. A., 87
Katz, J. H., 331
Katz-Wise, S. L., 224
Kegler, M. C., 171

Kennelly, I., 250
Kerlinger, F. N., 31, 32
Kidd, B., 339, 340
Kilty, K., 115
King, E. B., 175, 176, 177, 314
King, J. E., 204
Kinsey, A. C., 215
Kirchmeyer, C., 114
Kirkpatrick, D. L., 324, 326
Kitchin, P. J., 163
Kitson, H. D., 180
Knoppers, A., 112, 114
Kobach, M. J., 89
Koenig, A. M., 112
Koenig, H., 194, 195
Konrad, A. M., 6
Koonce, R., 328
Korchmaros, J. D., 215
Kossek, E. E., 138
Kozlowski, S. W. J., 7
Kraiger, K., 326
Krane, V., 222, 231
Kriger, M., 199, 201
Krugman, P., 253, 255
Kulik, C. T., 137
Kulkarni, M., 154, 159
Kunst, J. R., 203
Kunze, F., 133, 140

Ladson-Billings, G., 272
Lambert, J., 5
Langlois, J. H., 182
Lau, D. C., 11
Lauzun, H. M., 159
Lavoie, M., 88
Law, C. L., 227
Lawrence, S. M., 83
Leary, K., 230
Lee, W., 21, 281, 295
Lee, Y. J., 59
Legg, D., 162
Lemstra, M., 86
Lent, R. W., 60, 85
Leondar-Wright, B., 246
Lim, D. H., 326
Lindsay, C., 315
Linver, M. R., 242
Lips-Wiersma, M., 203
Little, A. C., 183
Liu, W. M., 185, 243, 247, 249, 256
Llopis-Goig, R., 89
Long, J., 78
Lord, R., 81
Lott, B., 242, 246, 247, 249, 250, 253, 254, 256

Loughnan, S., 248
Love, A., 221, 222
Lucas-Carr, C. B., 224, 233
Ludwig, J., 257
Lundberg, N. R., 164
Lynn, M. K., 197
Lyras, A., 36, 340, 350, 351

Macdougall, H. K., 157
Madera, J. M., 319
Magrath, R., 234
Marshall, A. M., 78, 87
Martin, C. L., 101
Martinez, L. R., 280
Maslow, A. H., 254
Mathis, R. L., 318, 322–324
Matthews, C., 50
Maxwell, H., 342, 349, 350
Mazereeuw-van der Duijin Schouten, C., 203
McCall, L., 242
McCormack, M., 224
McDowell, J., 76, 84
McIntosh, P., 292
McLaughlin, M. E., 155, 158
Mehrotra, C. M., 129, 142
Mellinger, C., 291
Melton, E. N., 224, 228, 233, 271, 277, 281
Messner, M. A., 99
Meyer, I. H., 58
Meyer, J. P., 281
Miles, E., 295
Miller, G., 184
Miller, J. F., 199
Miller, L., 313
Miller, S. L., 10
Miller, T., 271
Millionaires, 246
Minder, R., 54
Miner-Rubino, K., 336
Misener, L., 155
Missitzi, J., 184
Mitroff, I. I., 195, 208
Montagne, C., 256
Montez, J. K., 244
Moon, D. W., 185
Moore, K., 68, 159
Morganson, V. J., 18
Mortensen, C., 176
Moss-Racusin, C. A., 113
Myron, M., 136

National Coalition for the Homeless, 249

National Collegiate Athletic Association, 83, 109, 117, 223
National Urban League, 315
National Women's Law Center, 60
Nelson, T. D., 128, 134, 135
Ng, T. W. H., 132–134, 138
Nishii, L. H., 7, 21, 80, 275
Noelke, C., 136
Norman, L., 115
Nortan, M. I., 259
North, M. S., 128, 135

O'Leonard, K., 312
Oakes, P., 304
Oliver, C., 272
Orwell, G., 7
Osman-Gani, A. M., 197

Paetzold, R. L., 41, 155, 221
Palmer, F. R., 111
Paluck, E. L., 288
Park, J. H., 184
Parks, J. B., 99
Parris, D. L., 202
Pavlidis, A., 39
Peachey, J. W., 36, 202, 288, 294, 340, 342, 343, 344, 348, 350, 351
Peacock, M., 43, 83
Pearl, R. L., 174
Pearson, A. R., 82
Pelled, L. H., 33
Perry, E. A., 136, 138
Perry, E. L., 139
Peterson, K. E., 42
Pettigrew, T. F., 291, 293, 301, 304, 343
PEW Research Center, 195, 196
Pfeffer, J., 8
Phillips, P., 339
Phipps, K., 198
Pinderhughes, R., 254
Pizer, J. C., 228
Popham, L. E., 135
Porter, E., 253
Posthuma, R. A., 128, 131–134, 140
Powell, G. N., 98, 101, 102, 242
Powell, S., 83
Prati, G., 231
Prenda, K. M., 132
Pugh, S. D., 279
Puhl, R. M., 173
Purdue, D. E., 163
Putnam, R. D., 342

Rader, B. G., 205

Raedeke, T. D., 177
Ragins, B. R., 204, 214, 215, 227, 229, 232
Ramarajan, L., 17
Redington, P., 151
Regan, M. R., 113
Ren, L. R., 154
Rhodes, G., 183, 184
Richard, O. C., 34, 69, 271
Richards, J., 347
Robbins, S. P., 180
Roberson, L., 314, 317, 322, 326
Roberson, Q. M., 5, 8, 21
Robertson, N., 174
Robidoux, M. A., 89
Robinson, J., 79
Rodríguez, E. A., 119
Roehling, M. V., 172, 173
Rosario, M., 233
Rosen, B., 133
Rosenberg, M., 79
Rosette, A. S., 81
Ross, S. R., 185
Roulstone, A., 159
Rovell, D., 19
Rudman, L. A., 51, 54, 113
Rudolf, C. W., 175, 177
Ruggs, E. N., 174
Ryan, M. K., 94, 159

Saad, L., 258
Saal, K., 155
Sack, A. L., 84, 88
Saez, E., 259
Sagas, M., 4, 84, 115, 116, 260
Sage, G. H., 37
Saguy, A. C., 290
Salas, E., 317, 318, 323, 326
Samuel, E., 150
Sartore, M. L., 40, 84, 113, 115, 173, 175, 177, 214, 225, 228, 280
Sartore-Baldwin, M. L., 119, 224
Savage, M., 247
Savin-Williams, R. C., 215, 221
Schaafsma, J., 203
Schaumburg Athletic Association, 19
Schein, E., 80, 114
Schein, V. E., 112
Schmitt, M. T., 59
Schnittker, J., 70
Schulenkorf, N., 343, 344, 348
Schull, V., 110
Schultz, J. R., 78
Schur, L., 158, 159
Schwartz, M. B., 57, 174

Scott, I. M., 183
Scott, S., 277
Scott, W. R., 272
Scully, M. A., 249, 251, 252
Seibert, S. E., 115
Sell, R. L., 215
Sharp, L. A., 104
Shaw, S., 111, 112
Shein, J., 110
Sherif, M., 290
Sherry, E., 36, 339, 342, 343
Shilling, C., 206
Shimmell, L. J., 57
Shore, L. M., 7, 8, 131, 133, 135, 136, 138
Shuval, K., 86
Simmer-Brown, J., 111
Simmons, L., 78
Singer, J. N., 38, 89, 271, 279, 280
Smith, L., 243, 245, 246, 258, 259
Smith, N. G., 227
Smolianov, P., 339
Snowden, R. J., 216
Soares, R., 106
Solovay, S., 171
Son Hing, L. S., 55, 81
Sotiriadou, P., 161
Southern Methodist University, 150
Spaaij, R., 42, 273, 342, 344, 347, 348, 350
Spees, C. K., 177, 178
Spencer-Cavaliere, N., 164
Spilka, B., 196
Spoor, J. R., 114
Sport England, 106
Stangor, C., 51
Statistics Canada, 15
Staurowsky, E. J., 273
Steele, C. M., 52
Steinmetz, K., 217
Stevens, J., 143
Steward, A., 81
Stone-Romero, E. F., 154
Stout, J.G., 99
Stroh, L. K., 106, 109
Sue, D. W., 120
Sugden, J., 342, 347, 349
Sutin, A. R., 175
Swann, W. B., Jr., 301

Tajfel, H., 39, 295
Tate, W. F., 38, 77
Taylor, H., 217–220
Team Marketing Report, 36
Thomas, N., 155, 164

Tiell, B. S., 114
Tingle, J. K., 116
Travers, A., 222
Tropp, L. R., 292
Tsui, A. S., 9, 42, 86, 296, 305
Tucker, J. M., 177
Turner, J., 39, 295
Tuten, T. L., 21, 271

United Nations Inter-Agency Task
    Force on Sport for Development
    and Peace, 346
United States Olympic Committee, 106
University of Vermont, 9
U.S. Census Bureau, 13, 14, 69, 70,
    75, 103, 105, 129, 152, 156
U.S. Department of Education, 108
U.S. Department of Labor, 135
USA Rugby, 9

Valian, V., 101, 102, 106
van Dierendonck, D., 202
van Knippenberg, D., 5, 18, 31, 35,
    302, 303
Van Leeuwen, E., 20
Van Rooij, S. W., 137
Vanhove, A., 176
Vartanian, L. R., 175
Velez, B. L., 227, 228

Velija, P., 57
Vezzali, L., 294
Vogel, A., 175
Volpone, S. D., 228, 271
Volz, B. D., 83

Wahl, G., 204
Waldman, D. A., 132
Walker, H. J., 271
Walker, J. E. O. Y., 58
Walker, N. A., 112, 115
Walseth, K., 205
Walsh, B. M., 319
Waltemyer, D. S., 42
Walters, J., 19
Wang, P., 21
Washington, M., 77
Watkins, M., 252
Watson, B., 39
Wattie, N., 139
Weaver, G. R., 200
Weber, M., 252
Weeks, M., 203
Weihenmayer, E., 150
Weinberg, G., 220
Weiss, E. M., 133
Welty Peachey, J., 36, 202, 288, 294,
    340, 342, 343, 344, 348, 350,
    351

Wendel, M. L., 344
Wentling, R.M., 327–329
West, A., 78
Whittington, J. L., 201
Wiethoff, C., 320, 321
Williams, K. M., 184, 185
Williams, K. Y., 296
Wilner, D. M., 289, 290
Wilson-Kovacs, D., 159
Withycombe, J. L., 89
Wixon, M., 85
Wong, E., 79
Wong, E. M., 183
Woodhill, B. M., 100
World Bank, 256
World Health Organization, 152
World Population Review, 15
Worthen, M. G., 233
Wuebben, J., 171

Yancey, G., 179
Yap, A. J., 182

Zeigler, C., 214
Zhu, D. H., 299
Zinn, H., 68
Zipp, J. F., 233
Zook, K. R., 171
Zweig, M., 246, 247, 259

SUBJECT INDEX

AARP, 137
Abdul-Qaadir, Bilqis, 193
Ability:
    to learn, age and, 132, 133, 137
    mental and physical, 149–166
        (*see also* Disability)
Aboriginal peoples of Canada,
        269–270 (*see also* Canada):
    physical activity participation, 86
    sport participation and, 89
Academic performance, by gender,
        102
Access, to sports, 269–270
Access discrimination, 57
    sport participation and, 57
    underrepresentation, 82–83
Accommodation, organizational
        diversity and, 275
Accommodations:
    ADA and, 150, 151, 158
    request for by disabled, 158–159
Accountability, diversity training and,
        329
Acquisitions, diversity/inclusion and,
        19–20
ACT exam, 67
Adidas, 19, 323
Administrators:
    access discrimination and, 83
    overrepresentation of Whites
        among, 73
    racial minorities as, 75–76
Adobe Captivate, 323
Adventure course, team-building and,
        298
Advertisements, job, 130
Advertising, weight and, 178, 179

Aerobics and Fitness Association of
        America, 170
Aerobics certification, 169–170
Aesthetic qualities, stigma dimension,
        41
Affective conflict, 34
Affiliation, religious, 195–196 (*see
        also* Religion)
Africa, SDP efforts, 340 (*see also* SDP
        programs)
African Americans (*see also* Race;
        Racial minorities):
    access discrimination and, 57, 83
    changing demographics of, 12–13
    coaches at Ivy League schools, 79
    disability and, 152
    earnings and, 71–72
    in college sports, 38
    occupational segregation, 75–76
    occupational turnover, 86
    participation in formal sport,
        87–89
    religion and, 199
    social capital, 84–85
    stereotypes about, 52, 89
    treatment discrimination and, 84
    unemployment of, 103
    university graduation rates and, 67
    weight and, 174
African Methodist Church, 199
Age, 127–143
    bias in the workplace, 131–140
    defining, 129–131
    disability rates and, 152–153
    discrimination, 60, 135–140
    exiting an organization and, 138
    increase in median, 13–14

intersection with class, 257
    mentoring and, 137
    physical activity and, 127–128,
        140–143
    prejudice and, 134–135
    promotion potential and, 137–138
    relative age effects, 139
    sport consumption and, 143
    sport, physical activity, and leisure,
        140–143
    stereotypes about, 131–134, 137
    training/development and, 137
    volunteering and, 142–143
Age Discrimination in Employment
        Act of 1967 (ADEA), 129, 130
Ageism, 134–134
AIDS, 70, 155, 156, 158, 256, 339,
        340, 349
Allen, George, 207
Allies to diversity, 280–281
Allport's contact hypothesis, 288–291
Allums, Kye, 217
Ally dynamics, 280–281
Alumni, as stakeholders, 79
Alves, Dani, 54
American Association of Retired
        Persons, 137
American College of Sports Medicine
        (ACSM), 312
American Heart Association, 127
American National Election Studies,
        219
American Psychiatric Association, 219
American Psychological Association,
        242
Americans with Disabilities Act (ADA),
        150, 151, 158

Androgyny, 100–101 (*see also* Gender)

Anna, Kofi, 341

Anti-fat attitudes, 172–177 (*see also* Weight)

Anti-Semitism, 54

Anxiety:
 disability and, 155, 157
 intergroup, 291–292
 religion and, 207

Appearance, 169–188
 attractiveness, 184–186 (*see also* Attractiveness)
 endorsements and, 179, 185–186
 height, 179–182 (*see also* Height)
 weight, 170–179 (*see also* Weight)

Applicability, of diversity training, 327

Apprenticeship programs, age and, 130

Arab communities, SDP and, 342, 347

Asia, SDP efforts, 340 (*see also* SDP programs)

Asian Americans:
 changing demographics of, 12–13
 earnings and, 71–72
 occupational segregation, 75–76
 stereotypes about, 53
 volunteering, 143

Aspen Institute, 3

Athlete Ally, 280

Athlete dyads, members of, 42

Athletes:
 abuse/harassment of female, 119, 120
 disability and, 149–150 (*see also* Disability)
 endorsements and, 120, 185–186
 gay, 226, 233–234
 illiteracy rates of, 67–68
 objectification of female, 119–121 336
 stigma toward LGBT, 43
 use of religion, 207–208

Athletic:
 departments, and multilevel model of inclusion, 275–280
 directors, discrimination toward women as, 113
 performance, influence of stereotypes on, 52–53

Athleticism, stereotypes about, 89

Athletics, high school, 88, 116–117, 118, 241–242, 260, 261

Attendance, mandatory, 328

Attitudes:
 changing toward work, 12, 17
 implicit, 55 (*see also* Prejudice)
 polling results of, 54
 prejudicial, 53–54 (*see also* Prejudice)
 toward LGBT individuals, 219–220

Attitudinal outcomes, of diversity training, 326

Attractiveness, 182–186
 defining, 182
 discrimination, 60
 in the workplace, 183–184
 makeup and, 185
 physical activity and, 184–186
 sport marketing and, 120

Australia, 19, 74, 248
 barriers to physical activity in, 57
 community sport and, 342
 Diversity Australia website, 307
 Ian Thorpe and, 43, 340
 sports clubs, 42, 273, 347
 Street Soccer, 36
 women in sport organizations in, 106

Australian Sports Commission, 43, 106

Aversive racism, 81–82 (*see also* Prejudice)

Awful Announcing website, 49

Baby Boomers, 12, 129, 131 (*see also* Age)

Bally Total Fitness, 169

Baltimore Ravens, 49–50

Bear Bryant/Adolph Rupp epiphany, 272

Beauty, defining, 182, 183 (*see also* Attractiveness)

Behavior:
 sedentary, 116, 140–141 (*see also* Physical activity)
 self-limiting, 40, 115–116

Beliefs, about others, *see* Bias; Prejudice; Stereotypes

Belongingness, 7

Bem Sex-Role Inventory (BSRI), 100

Bench press, disability and, 165

Benefits:
 age and, 130
 LGBT individuals and, 227
 of SDP, 341–345 (*see also* SDP programs)
 overstated, 347

Berra, Yogi, 32

Bias (*see also* Discrimination; Prejudice; Racism; Stereotypes)
 age, 131–140
 anti-fat, 172–177
 components of, 50
 context and, 304–305
 decategorization and, 296–299, 304
 disabilities and, 153–160
 effects on those who express it, 59
 intergroup, 40
 multilevel explanation for, 77
 outcomes of, 58–61
 performance appraisal, 40
 personnel decisions and, 80–84, 112–114
 political climate and, 78
 racial minorities and, 69–90
 recategorization and, 299–302
 religious fundamentalism and, 203
 social categorization approach to reducing, 295–305
 working in sport organizations and, 60

Blackboard, 323

Blaguszewski, Eric, 151

Blink, 181

BMI, 171, 173, 174, 175, 199

Body image, 121

Body mass index, 171, 173, 174, 175, 199

Body type, "ideal," 175

Boosters, as stakeholders, 79

Boundary conditions, 31, 293

Brazil, gender identity in, 100

Bridge employment, 131

Brigham Young University, 198

Brown, Maureen, 169–170

Bryant, Paul "Bear," 252, 272

Buddhists, 195–196 (*see also* Religion)

Bullying, 225

Bureau of Labor Statistics (BLS), 71, 75, 103, 112

Bush, George W., 78

Business Coalition for Workplace Fairness, 223

Business ethics, 200

Byrne, Bill, 252

Camp, cooperative interaction and, 290–291

Camtasia, 323

Canada:
 Aboriginal people and sport, 86, 89, 269–270

demographic changes in, 15
health care costs and, 256
physical activity participation
    among racial minorities, 86
race relations in, 89
Sport Canada, 269–270
Cancer, 256
Cann, Lawrence and Bob, 335
Capital:
    forms of, 247
    human, 84–86
    social, 84–85
Captivate, Adobe, 323
Careers (*see also* Workplace):
    advancement in, 85
    effect of bias on, 60–61
    occupational segregation, 75–76
    occupational turnover, 85–86
Catalyst Institute, 106
Categorical approach to studying
    diversity, 42
Categorization, 40
    forms of diversity and, 305
    process, 179
    religion as source of, 202–204
Catholics, 195–196 (*see also* Religion)
CBT Planet, 323
Celtics F.C., 204
Center for Community Health
    Development, 349
Centers for Disease Control and
    Prevention (CD), 58, 171
Central Baptist Church, 206
CEOs, height and, 181
Cerebral palsy, 57–58, 158, 163
Ceteris paribus, 175
Champions Golf Tour, 129
Change agents, SDP programs, 344,
    349 (*see also* SDP programs)
Change:
    age and, 132–133 (*see also* Age)
    engaging in the process, 272
    forms of resistance to, 278
Characteristics:
    of leadership, 112
    race related, 71
    stigmatized, 41, 43
    typically masculine, 113
China, demographic changes in, 15, 16
Christian Faculty Network, 197
Christian Owned and Operated,
    website, 197
Christians, 195–196 (*see also* Religion)
Cisgender, 217
Civil rights, 38

Civil Rights Act of 1964, 50, 71, 78,
    104
Civil Rights Act of 1991, 104
Civil Rights Restoration Act of 1987,
    108
Class (*see also* Social class):
    definitions of groupings, 246–247
    new affluent, 247
Classicism, 248–260 (*see also*
    Classicism)
Classification, of employees, 71
Classism:
    cognitive distancing and, 248–249
    defined, 248
    dimensions of, 249
    education and, 253
    healthcare and, 256–257
    housing and, 253–255
    institutional distancing, 250–260
        (*see also* Institutional distancing)
    interpersonal distancing and, 250
    meritocracy and, 250–252
    sport systems and, 260–261
Climate, organizational, 326–327
Coaches:
    discrimination and, 57, 83–84,
        113–114
    discrimination toward African
        Americans, 57
    discrimination toward women as,
        57, 113–114
    "glass cliff" and, 83
    lesbian, 221, 225–226, 233
    LGBT, 56
    racial minorities as, 73–75
    sexual prejudice and, 221
    stakeholders and, 79
    weight and, 176
    women as, 57, 83–84, 106, 111–114
    young v. old, 136
Cognitive distancing, 248–249
Cognitive outcomes, of diversity
    training, 326
College athletics:
    bridge employment in, 131
    diversity training and, 311–312, 313
    marginalization of women's,
        118–119
    participation by gender, 117
    Title IX and, 107–109
    wage distributions and, 252
College Station High School, 300
Commitment to diversity, 280, 281
Common Ingroup Identity Model, 299
Common threat/fate, 300–301

Communicative domain, 152
Community:
    capacity, 344–345
    interconnectedness and, 335–338
    outcomes for SDP, 344–345 (*see
        also* SDP programs)
Compassion, 154, 157
Compensation (*see also* Earnings):
    disability and, 160
    height and, 181
Competence, domain of stereotyping,
    51
Compliance:
    diversity training and, 315
    organizational diversity and, 274
Components, of SDP programs,
    350–351
Compositional approach to studying
    diversity, 42
Concealability:
    disability and, 155
    stigma dimension, 41
Concealment, 229, 230
Confidentiality, diversity training and,
    329
Conflict:
    affective, 34
    substantive, 34
    theory, 36–37
    work–family, 138
Conspiracy theories, 29
Construct, defined, 30
Consumers, 7
    Generation Y, 143
    inclusiveness and, 271
    marketing to diverse, 4
    older, 13, 134–135, 143
    weight and, 176, 179
    who are LGBT, 233, 234
Contact:
    conditions of, 288–291
    effect on prejudice, 288–291
    extended, 294
    generalizing effects of, 293
    imagined, in sport context, 295
    indirect, 293–295
    intergroup, 302–304
    intimate, 289–290
Contact hypothesis, 288–295
    limitations of, 292–293
Context, bias and, 304–305
Continuum, sport performance, 103
Control group, diversity training and,
    325–326
Converse, 19

Cooperation, need for, 290–291
Cooperative training, 322
Costs of older/younger employees, 132, 134 (*see also* Age)
Course, stigma dimension, 41
Coworkers, age of, 139
Cox, Jr., Taylor, 29–30
Creative capital theory, 35
Creativity, as a construct, 30–31
Creighton University, 67
Cricket, prejudice and, 61
Critical race theory, 38
Critical theories, 37–38
  critical race theory, 38
  feminist theory, 37–38
  hegemony theory, 37
Croatians, 301
Cross-categorization, 297
Cultural capital, 247, 248
Cultural diversity, 274
Culture:
  attractiveness and, 182, 183
  of diversity vs. culture of similarity, 274
  of similarity, 274
  organizational, 80, 139–140
Cunningham, Sam, 272
Customers, 18 (*see also* Consumers)
  anti-fat attitudes and, 176
Cycling, disability and, 153

Dallas Cowboys, 335
Dallas Cup, 298
Daniels, Jon, 73
Davenport, Lindsay, 111
Davis, Vernon, 171
Deaflympics, 163
Decategorization, 296–299, 304
  potential limitations, 298–299
Decisions, influence of religion on, 198–199
Deep-level diversity, 9, 10, 17, 20, 22
  relationship with surface-level diversity, 11
Deficit model approach, SDP and, 345–346, 348
Delivery of SDP programs, 347–351
Demographics:
  age, 129–131 (*see also* Age)
  changes in racial composition, 12–13
  changing, 12–17
  disability and, 152–153
  global changes, 15–17
  LGBT individuals and, 217–219

median age and, 13–14
men/women in the workplace, 103
weight and, 176, 178 (*see also* Weight)
Dependability, age and, 132, 134 (*see also* Age)
DeSensi's model for diversity management, 274
Detroit Shock, 97
Diabetes, 152, 256
Dialogues, difficult, 276, 277
Diet, weight and, 172 (*see also* Weight)
Differences:
  objective vs. subjective, 5–6
  socially meaningful, 6
Differentiation, 229, 230, 296
Difficult dialogues, 276, 277
Dimensions of diversity, 39 (*see also* Diversity)
Disability, 149–166
  anxiety and, 155, 157
  bias against, 153–160
  categories of, 152
  defined, 150–153
  discrimination and, 156–160
  earnings and, 160
  education and, 156
  factors influencing reaction to, 155
  incidence, 152–153
  intersection with class, 257
  language and, 155
  leadership and, 159
  legal mandates and, 151 (*see also* Americans with Disabilities Act)
  perception based on type of, 155–156
  pity and, 154, 162, 163, 164
  prejudice and, 154–156
  sport and physical activity, 160–164
  stereotypes and, 154
  stigma and, 154, 155, 156, 158, 163, 165
Disability Law Center, 151
Disability sport, 161–164
  National Disability Sports Alliance website, 165
  trends/issues in, 162
Disclosure of sexual orientation, 229–232
Discretion, 229, 230
Discrimination, 56–58 (*see also* Bias; Prejudice; Stereotypes)
  access, 57, 82–83

age, 129, 130, 135–140
anxiety and, 155, 157
career advancement and, 85
defined, 56
disability and, 156–160
hiring process, 60
in sport, 89
on basis of religion, 198
pity and, 154, 162, 163, 164
pregnancy based, 104
sex, 104
sexual orientation and, 220–225 (*see also* Sexual orientation)
stigma and, 154, 155, 156, 158, 163, 165
subtle, 56
theories related to, 56
Title VII and, 198
treatment, 83–84
underrepresentation and, 82–84
weight and, 174–177 (*see also* Weight)
women in leadership, 113–114
workplace due to disability, 156–160
Displacement, 255
Disruptiveness:
  disability and, 155
  stigma dimension, 41
Distance training, 323
Distancing:
  cognitive, 248–249
  institutional, *see* Institutional distancing
  interpersonal, 250
Diversity:
  age-related issues, 127–143 (*see also* Age)
  allies to, 280–281
  appearance and, 169–188
  approaches to studying, 42–43
  attractiveness and, 182–186
  benefits of, 21–22
  bias and, *see* Bias
  commitment to, 280, 281
  deep-level, *see* Deep-level diversity
  definitions, 5–6
  dimensions of, 39
  discrimination and, *see* Discrimination
  forms of, 8–11, 305
  gender and stigma, 221–225
  height and, 179–182
  information, 9, 10
  intersection with class, 257

legal mandates for, 12, 20 (*see also* Legal aspects of diversity)

management of organizations and, 269–283 (*see also* Diversity management)

managerial theories, *see* Managerial theories

moral obligation for, 20–21

not readily observed, *see* Deep-level diversity

organizational dimensions of, 274

overview of, 3–23

pie chart, 242

prejudice and, *see* Prejudice

race and, 67–90 (*see also* Race; Racial minorities)

readily observable dimensions, *see* Surface-level diversity

religion and, 193–209 (*see also* Religion)

sex and gender issues and, 97–121 (*see also* Gender)

sexual orientation and, 213–236 (*see also* Sexual orientation)

social class and, 241–263 (*see also* Social class)

social pressures and, 12, 20–21

sociological theories, *see* Sociological theories

stereotypes and, *see* Stereotypes

surface-level, *see* Surface-level diversity

theoretical tenets of, 29–44

theories used to understand, 32–43

UN efforts, 8

understanding the emphasis on, 11–22

value, 9, 10

weight and, 170–179 (*see also* Weight)

Diversity management:

accommodation and, 275

activation and, 275

cross-categorization and, 297

DeSensi's model, 274

Doherty and Chelladurai's model, 274

effectiveness of programs, 271–273

engaging in change process, 273

Fink and Pastore's model, 274

integrated model of, 303–305

multilevel model of, 273, 275–280

of diverse groups, 287–307 (*see also* Groups)

promoting LGBT inclusiveness, 228

racial issues and, 67–90 (*see also* Race; Racial minorities)

religion and, *see* Religion

sexual orientation and, 213–236 (*see also* Sexual orientation)

social class and, 241–263 (*see also* Social class)

strategies (models) for, 273–280

training, 311–331 (*see also* Diversity training)

Diversity training, 311–331

cognitive outcomes, 326

college athletics and, 311–312, 313

commitment from management, 327

conducting, 322

cost of corporate, 312–313

delivery of, 322–323

designing/delivering effective programs, 316–327

distance, 323

effects of, 314–316

ensuring transfer of, 326–327

evaluation of, 324–326, 329

framing the training, 320

general principles, 327–329

in-house trainer, 322

methods, 321–323

needs analysis, 316, 317–318

negative outcomes, 314, 315

perceived utility of, 319

positive outcomes, 314–315

post-training conditions, 323–327

post-training-only evaluation, 325

pre-training, 319–321

prevalence of, 312–313

simulations, 323

skill-based outcomes, 326

topics typically covered, 321

trainee characteristics, 319

understanding effects of, 315–316

using qualified trainers, 328

voluntary nature of, 320–321

Doherty and Chelladurai's model for diversity management, 274

Dove marketing campaign, 179

Downsizing, age and, 138

Dr. Seuss, 298

Dyad, comparisons among members, 5, 6

Earnings:

disability and, 160

employees who are LGBT, 227

height and, 181

median household, by race, 70

of men in workforce, 105–106

of women in workforce, 105–106

race and, 70, 71–72

social class and, 244

weekly, based of race/gender, 72

Eastern Collegiate Athletic Conference, 162

Economic capital, 247

Economic development, sport as a tool for, 269 (*see also* SDP programs)

Education:

classism and, 253

disability and, 156

LGBT orientation and, 217–218

social class and, 244

EEOC:

age discrimination and, 130 (*see also* Age)

disability and, 151

racial discrimination and, 71

religion and, 198

sex discrimination complaints, 104

Effectiveness, diversity training and, 315

Effort, as factor of Equal Pay Act, 104

Egypt, demographic changes in, 16

Egyptian women, sport and, 205

Eight Steps to Fitness, 199

Elderly, 53, 138 (*see also* Age)

Elite class, 247

Emergent service workers, 248

Employee satisfaction, commitment to diversity and, 303

Employees:

age and selection, 136

age bias and, 131–140

changing attitudes toward work, 17

classification, 71

diversity training and, 319 (*see also* Diversity training)

occupational segregation, 75–76

older, 128, 129–130

promoting older, 137–138

retention of, 12, 133–134

turnover rates and age, 138

Employers, occupational segregation, 75–76

Employment (*see also* Workplace):

age and, 131–140

age and opportunities, 135–138

age-related laws, 130

anti-discrimination laws, 71

"bridge," 131
protections for LGBT individuals, 223
race and, 69–76 (*see also* Under-representation)
retention, 132, 133–134
search for, 135–136
Enacted stigma, 224
Endorsements, appearance and, 120, 179, 185–186
England, SDP and, 342
Enrichment, SDP programs and, 350–351
Equal Employment Opportunity Commission, *see* EEOC
Equal Pay Act of 1963, 104
Equal status, prejudice and, 290
ESPN, 118
Establishment, as factor of Equal Pay Act, 104
Ethics, 62, 344
religion and, 199–201
teaching, 201
Ethnicity, defined, 69
Euro-Canadians, 89
Evaluation, diversity training and, 324–326, 329
Evans, Joel, 201
Evidence-based programming, 349
Exclusion, negative effects of, 12, 21
Experimental space, SDP and, 350
Explicit prejudice, 54–55
Explicit racism, 81
Extreme sports, popularity of, 143

Fabrication, 229, 230
Failures, overcoming, 84
Faith and Family Night, 193
Family:
caring for elderly, 138
conflict with work, 110, 111
Fans, gender of, 119
Fate, common, 301
Fatness, 171–172 (*see also* Weight)
Faultlines, 11
Fear of the unknown, 278
Feelings Thermometer, 219–220
Fellowship of Christian Athletes, 203
Femininity, 100 (*see also* Gender; Women)
Feminist theory, 37–38
Fierce Conversations, 277
FIFA, 340
Fink and Pastore's model for diversity management, 274

First Nations people of Canada, 269–270
physical activity participation, 86 (*see also* Canada)
sport participation and, 89
Fitness:
8 steps to, 199
industry, 169–170
promotion of and weight, 169–170, 178–179
Food desert, 58
Football 4 Peace, 342, 347, 349
Framing, diversity training and, 320
Franklin v. Gwinnett County Public Schools, 108
Free time, age and, 141
Friendship, 291
Functional pressures, for inclusion, 272
Functionalism theory, 36
Funding:
marginalization of women's sports, 119
Title IX and, 107–108

Gallup polls, sexual orientation focus, 219
Gascoigne, Paul, 204
Gates City Christian boys' basketball, 193
Gay Games, 226
Gender (*see also* Masculinity; Sex; Sexual orientation; Women):
defined, 98–100
earnings and, 72
expression, 216
identity, 100–103, 216
in sport context, 102–103
institutionalized practices, 111–112
intersection with class, 257
media influence on, 102
objectification and, 119–121
parental influence on, 101
participation in sports, 116–121
physical activity participation, 116–117
prejudice, 221
reinforcement of stereotypes, 119, 120
roles, 100–103
roles, male, 113
schools' influence on, 101
sexual stigma and, 221–225
socialization, 101–103
sport organizations and, 97–121

stakeholder expectations and, 110–111
stereotypes, 53, 110, 111, 112 (*see also* Bias; Stereotypes)
Title IX and, 107–109
General Social Survey, 219
Generalizability, 293
Generalization, of effects of contact, 293
Generation Y, 143 (*see also* Age)
Generational differences, 135, 143 (*see also* Age)
Genetics, obesity and, 172
George Pocock Rowing Foundation, 287
George Washington University, 217
Germany, SDP and, 342
Gerritson, Steve, 287
Giants Stadium, 29
Gilbert, David, 128
Gini Index, 15
Girls, high school athletics and, 116–117, 118
Glass:
ceiling, 106, 109
cliff, 83, 159
walls, 109
Global/globalization, 18–19 (*see also* International)
demographic changes, 15–17
prejudice/racism, 54
Goals, common, 301
Gold's Gym, 169
Golf, age and, 129
Gordon, Derrick, 213
Gravity Games, 143
Great Depression, 259
Greater Cleveland Sports Commission, 128
Greeks, sport and, 205
Griffey, Ken and Ken Jr., 111
Griffin, Christine, 151
Group, comparisons among members, 5, 6
Group-level outcomes, SDP and, 343–344
Groups:
contact hypothesis and, 288–295
cross-categorization and, 297
decategorization and, 296–299, 304
differences between and among, 295–305
diversity/inclusion and, 287–307
dynamics of, 42

equal status of, 290
friendship and, 291
in/out members of, 40
integrated model for managing
    diverse, 303–305
intergroup contact, 302–304
intimate contact and, 289–290
out-, *see* Out-groups
recategorization and, 299–302
support for interaction among,
    290–291
Grove City College v. Bell, 107–108
Guidelines, physical activity, 116,
    117, 142
Gum Marom Kids League, 347
Guttman, Sir Ludwig, 162–163

Habit, and resistance to change, 278
Hammarskjold, Dag, 337
Harassment, 71, 336
    of female athletes, 119, 120
Harry Potter books, 294
Harvard University, diversity training
    and, 311–312, 321
Haves and have nots, 259 (*see also*
    Classism)
Head scarves, sport participation
    and, 185
Health disparities, 58
Health, effects of bias on, 58
Healthcare, social class and, 256–257
HealthPeople.gov website, 116, 117,
    141
Healthy People initiative, 140, 141,
    160
Heath-e-AME Physical-e-Fit program,
    199
Hegemony theory, 37
Heidesch, Becky, 60
Height, 179–182
    by race and sex, 180
    of CEOs, 181
Heterosexism, 220–221
High School Athletic Survey, 116
High school athletics, participation
    by gender, 88, 116–117
    marginalization of girls' 118
Hill, Fritz, 84
Hindus, 195–196 (*see also* Religion)
Hiring:
    discrimination in, 60
    prejudice and, 82
    racial stereotypes and, 81
Hispanics:
    access discrimination and, 83

changing demographics of, 12–13
disability and, 152
earnings and, 71–72
occupational segregation, 75–76
participation in formal sport, 87–89
unemployment of, 103
volunteering, 143
HIV/AIDS, 70, 155–156, 158, 256,
    339, 340, 349
Hockey, religious beliefs and, 199
Hoffa, Jimmy, 29
Homeless World Cup, 343
Homelessness, 335
Homophobia, 220–221
Homosexuality, 213–236 (*see also*
    LGBT individuals; Sexual
    orientation)
    disclosure of, 229–232
Housing, social class and, 253–255
Howard, Kristi, 169
Human capital, 84–86
    occupational turnover, 85–86
Human needs, inclusion and, 7
Human orientation, religion and, 201
Human resources (*see also* Personnel):
    practices to reduce age discrimina-
        tion, 140
    disability discrimination and, 160
Human Rights Campaign, 227, 280

Identity:
    gender, 100–103
    in-group, 299–302
    out-group, *see* Out-group
    personal expression of, 17
If–then conditions, 31
Illiteracy, athletes and, 67–68
Implicit Association Task, 216
Implicit prejudice, 55–56
Implicit racism, 81
Imus, Don, 37
Inactivity, costs of, 127
Incivility, 120
Inclusion:
    benefits of, 21–22
    commitment to, 281
    creativity and, 31
    definitions, 6–8
    despite the community, 279
    effectiveness of programs, 271–273
    engaging in the process, 273
    facilitating through sport, 335–352
    human needs and, 7
    in the workplace, 17 (*see also*
        Workplace)

interpersonal, 287–307
interscholastic/intramural sports
    and, 88
managerial theories, *see* Managerial
    theories
moral obligation for, 20–21
multilevel factors affecting, 276–280
multilevel model of, 273, 275–280
optimal distinctiveness and, 41
organizational culture and, 80
overview of, 3–23
pressures for greater, 271–273
surface-level diversity and, 31
sex and gender issues and, 97–121
    (*see also* Gender)
sexist language and, 99
sociological theories, *see* Socio-
    logical theories
theoretical tenets of, 29–44
theories used to understand, 32–43
UN efforts, 8
understanding the emphasis on,
    11–22
Inclusive activities, 162
Inclusive spaces, SDP programs and,
    348, 350
Inclusiveness (*see also* Inclusion):
    LGBT individuals and, 228 (*see also*
        LGBT individuals)
    organizational, 269–283
Income (*see also* Earnings):
    changes in, 14, 15, 16
    disability and, 160
    height and, 181
    inequality of, 15, 16, 250–252,
        259
    LGBT individuals and, 217, 219,
        227
    physical activity and, 87
    social class and, 244
    sport participation and, 3
    wage gaps and, 250–252, 259
Individual level, organizational
    inclusion and, 276–277
Individual-level outcomes, SDP and,
    342–343
Individual merit, success and, 251
Individuals:
    personal expression of, 41
    social psychological theories, 39–43
    stereotyped responses to, 52 (*see
        also* Stereotypes)
Inequality, income, 15, 16, 250–252,
    259
Inertia, and resistance to change, 278

Information diversity, 9, 10
Information/decision-making theory, 33–34
In-group identity, forming, 299–302
Injustice, silence in the face of, 337, 338
Institute for International Sport, 338
Institutional distancing, 250–260
 education and, 253
 healthcare and, 256–257
 housing and, 253–255
 meritocracy, 250–252
 organizational structure, 258–259
Institutional support, availability of, 289
Institutionalized:
 gender practices, 111–112
 practices, 77–78
Integrated model of diversity management, 303–305
Integration, sport teams and, 272 (*see also* Inclusion)
Interaction, need for cooperative, 290–291
Interactionist theory, 39
Interactive (organization), 161–162
Intercollegiate athletics, diversity training and, 311–312, 313 (*see also* College athletics)
Interconnectedness, of people, 335–338
Interdependence, cooperative, 290–291
Intergroup:
 anxiety, prejudice and, 291–292
 bias, 40, 41
 contact, 276–277, 302–304
 relations, SDP and, 344 (*see also* SDP programs)
Internalized stigma, 224
International:
 agencies, issues regarding weight, 171–172
 efforts for LGBT inclusion, 277
 Olympic Committee, 119, 222, 223
 players and Dallas Cup, 298
 Run for Peace, 343
 SDP efforts, 340 (*see also* SDP programs)
 students, study of regarding prejudice, 291
 travel by teams, 252
Interpersonal distancing, 250
Interscholastic sports, *see* High school sports
Intersectionality, 39

Intervening process theory, 33–34
Intimate contact, 289–290
Intramural sports, 88
Iacocca, Lee, 251
Ireland, SDP and, 342
Islam, women and sports, 205–206
Israel, physical activity participation in, 86
 bias and, 298–299

Jackson, D'Qwell, 280
Jackson, Roderick, 108
Jackson v. Birmingham Board of Education, 108
Jago, Gordon, 298
Jazzercise, 169–170
Jewish Business Network of Southern NJ, 197
Jewish communities, SDP and, 342, 347
Jews and Muslims, bias and, 298–299
Job:
 applicants, disability and, 156–158
 notices, 130
 relatedness, 34
 -task analysis, for diversity training, 317–318
Jobs, access to by persons who are LGBT, 225–227
Johnson, Lyndon, 78
Jokes, as form of marginalization, 61
Jordan, SDP and, 342
Justice orientation, religion and, 201
Justice, prejudice as threat to, 337–338

Kane, Mary Jo, 103, 113–114
Kicking AIDS Out, 339
King, Jr., Martin Luther, 337
Kinsey, Alfred, 215
Koss, Johann, 340
Kravitz, Cheryl, 328

Lacrosse, diversity and, 287
Language:
 and disability, 155
 sexist, 99, 119
Lapchick, Richard, 79, 318
Latinos, disability and, 152 (*see also* Hispanics)
Laws (*see also* Legal aspects of diversity):
 disability and, 151
 anti-discrimination, 71
 workplace protection and, 20

Lawson, Claire, 287
Layoffs, age and, 138
Leader level, organizational inclusion and, 277
Leadership:
 advocacy and, 277
 attitudes toward women in, 51–52
 aversive racism and, 82
 contact hypothesis and, 289
 disability and, 159
 discrimination and, 82–84
 discrimination in NCAA, 75–76
 discrimination toward women, 113–114
 height and, 180–181
 inclusion and, 276, 277
 overcoming failures of, 84
 prejudice toward women, 113
 racial minorities and, 72–75
 religion and, 201–202
 self-limiting behaviors of women, 115–116
 servant, 202
 stereotypes about, 80–81
 stereotypes regarding women and, 112
 underrepresentation of racial minorities, 76–86 (*see also* Underrepresentation)
 underrepresentation of women, 109–116 (*see also* Underrepresentation)
 vocational interests and, 85
 women in, 51–52, 97–98, 106–109, 112–114
Leagues, church-organized, 199, 206
Legal aspects of diversity, 12, 20
 age and employment laws 130
 disability and, 151
 employment discrimination and, 71
 LGBT individuals and, 223
 race and, 71
 religion and, 198
 Title IX, 107–109
 weight and, 173
 women/men in the workplace, 104
Leisure, age and participation, 140–143
Lesbian:
 coaches, 221, 225–226, 233
 earnings and, 227
 gay, bisexual, transgender, *see* LGBT individuals
 sport clubs, 234

LGBT individuals (*see also* Sexual orientation):
    definition of terms, 215–217
    demographics regarding, 217–219
    diversity as an advantage, 232–233
    education and, 217–218
    employment protections for, 223
    imagined contact and, 295
    inclusive communities and, 336
    income and, 217, 219
    managerial strategies for promoting inclusiveness, 228
    organizational inclusion and, 275, 277, 280
    prejudice toward, 59
    race and, 217–218
    sexual stigma and, 221–225
    sport and physical activity participation and, 233–234
    sport clubs and, 234
    targeting as employees/customers, 233
LGBT (lesbian, gay, bisexual, transexual) orientations, 213–236 (*see also* Sexual orientation)
Lieberman, Nancy, 97–98
Lillehammer Winter Olympics, 340
Lopiano, Donna, 311
Los Angeles Clippers, 54
Lower-ability-to-learn stereotype, 133

Maccabi Tel Aviv, 54
Macro level, organizational inclusion and, 279–280
Macro-level factors, 77, 80–84, 109–112
Major League Baseball, *see* MLB
Major life activities, 151
Makeup, attractiveness and, 185
Management:
    of diverse/inclusive organizations, 269–283 (*see also* Diversity management)
    reducing intergroup bias and, 304–305
    women in, 106–109
Managerial approach to studying diversity, 42–43
Managerial theories, 32–35
    creative capital theory, 35
    implications of, 33–34
    information/decision-making theory, 33–34
    intervening process theory, 33–34
    pro-diversity theory, 35

resource-based theory, 34
Managers, stereotypes about women as, 112
Mandatory attendance, diversity training and, 328
Manley, Dexter, 67–68
Marginalization of women's sports, 118–119
Marketing:
    athlete endorsements and, 120, 179, 185–186
    sexualized images of women, 336
    sport, 120
Marx, Karl, 36
Masculinity, 100 (*see also* Gender)
McCutchen, Andrew, 193
McDowell, Jacqueline, 258
McGinniss, Kevin, 162
McGirk Stadium, 151
Medcalf, Myron, 136
Media:
    endorsements, 120, 179, 185–186
    gender socialization and, 102
    marginalization of women's sports, 118–119
    objectification of female athletes, 120
    portrayals of racial minorities, 78
Median age, increase in, 13–14
Melaleuca Elementary School, 287
Men (*see also* Gender):
    earnings and, 105–106
    gender roles and, 113
    physical activity patterns, 116, 117
    privilege, 97, 111–112, 115
    social capital of, 115
Mental domain, 152
Mentoring, age and, 137
Mergers, diversity/inclusion and, 19–20
Meritocracy, 78, 250–252
Meso-level factors, 77, 80–84, 110, 112–114
Microaggressions, 120
Micro-level factors, 77, 84–86, 110, 115–116
Middle class, 246, 247
Middle East, 292
    SDP efforts, 340 (*see also* SDP programs)
Mindsets, pro-diversity, 302–303
Minority, defined, 69 (*see also* Racial minorities)
Mistreatment, subtle forms of, 120
MLB:
    access discrimination in, 83

racial minority coaches in, 74–75
    varied backgrounds of players in, 19
Models, for diversity and inclusion, 273–280
Moderation orientation, religion and, 201
Moderators, integrated model and, 304–305
Monocultural organizations, 274
More-costly stereotype, 132, 134
Mormon Church, 198
Mortality rates, expression of prejudice and, 59
Mothers, elite athletes as, 111
Motivation, of trainees, 319
Mt. Everest, 149
Multicultural organizations, 274 (*see also* Diversity; Inclusion)
Multilevel model for diversity/inclusion, 273, 275–280
    individual level, 276–277
    leader level, 277
    macro level, 279–280
    NCAA and, 275
    organizational level, 277–279
Multiracial, 70 (*see also* Race; Racial minorities)
Murrell, Sherri, 221
Muslim(s), 195–196 (*see also* Religion)
    and Jews, bias and, 298–299
    SDP and, 343
    women, sports and, 185
Mutual group differentiation, 302

NASCAR, 318
NASSM, 242
National Basketball Association, *see* NBA
National Collegiate Athletic Association, *see* NCAA
National Coalition for the Homeless, 335
National Federation of State High School Associations, 116, 118
National Football League, *see* NFL
National Hockey League, *see* NHL
National Institutes of Health, 171
National Urban League, 315
National Women's Law Center, 60
Native Americans, volunteering, 143
NBA, 18–19, 54
    age requirements, 129
    cost of attending game, 36–37
    Development League, 97

earnings in, 72
racial minority coaches in, 74
NCAA:
    age of coaches in, 136
    basketball, racial minority coaches in, 74
    classification of employees and, 71
    disability and, 162
    discrimination in, 89
    diversity/inclusion and, 20–21, 275
    diversity training and, 313
    graduation rates and, 67
    occupational segregation, 75–76
    policy regarding transgender athletes, 222–223
    racial minority coaches in, 83
    stakeholders of, 79
    Sunday games and, 198
    women's basketball, 221
Needs analysis, diversity training and, 316, 317–318
Needs assessment, SDP programs, 348–349
Networks:
    social, 84–85
    women and, 115
New Deal, 259
NFL:
    coach George Allen, 207
    cost of attending game, 36–37
    earnings in, 72
    Fan Flag Challenge, 193
    obesity and, 176
    racial minority coaches in, 75
    Ray Rice and, 49–50
    stacking/tasking in, 88
NHL, 42
    Columbus Blue Jackets, 193
Nike, 19, 323
Noncompliance, organizational diversity and, 274
Normalizing, 229, 230
North American Society for Sport Management, 242
Northwestern University, 136
Norway, Olympics, 340

Obesity (see also Weight):
    defining, 171
    rates of increase, 172
Objectification, of women, 119–121
Objective differences, 5–6
Occupation, social class and, 244
Occupational segregation, 75–76
Occupational turnover, 85–86

Ochoa, Lorena, 111
Office of Civil Rights (OCR), 107–109
Oh, The Places You'll Go!, 298
Oklahoma State University, 67
Olbermann, Keith, 49–50
Old boy's network, 115
Old Dominion University, 97
"Old," defining, 129 (see also Age)
Older Workers Benefit Protection Act, 130
Olympic Games, 205, 340
    disability and, 162 (see also Paralympics; Special Olympics)
    housing and, 255
    sexual stigma and, 222
    women's sports in, 119
Optimal distinctiveness theory, 41
Organizational (see also Organizations):
    analysis, for diversity training, 317
    climate, 326–327
    dimensions of diversity, 274
    effectiveness, 8
    inclusion, 277–279
    structure, classism and, 258–259
Organizational culture, 114
    age and, 139–140
    underrepresentation and, 80
Organizations:
    age-related employment laws in, 130
    diversity management/training, see Diversity management; Diversity training
    group leaders and support, 289
    inclusiveness in, 7, 269–283 (see also Inclusion)
    level of diversity in, 274
    management of diverse/inclusive, 269–283 (see also Diversity management)
    managerial theories and, 32–35
    mergers/acquisitions and, 19–20
    power in, 37–38
    service based, 18
Origin, stigma dimension, 41
Osborn, Brent, 193
"Othering," 78
Oursports.com, 213
Outcomes of bias, 58–61
Outcomes, passing/revealing and, 231–232
Out-groups (see also Groups):
    categorization and, 296–297, 299 (see also Categorization)
    intergroup contact and, 302–303

prejudice and, 291, 292, 293, 294, 295 (see also Prejudice)
Overweight, defining, 171
Owning class, defined, 246

Paralympic Games, 153, 163, 165
Parents, gender socialization and, 101
Participation:
    access discrimination and, 57
    age and, 129, 140–143
    effect of bias on, 60–61
    enhanced sport, 269–270
    gender and, 116–121
    in the workforce, 104–105
    race and, 3, 87–89
    treatment discrimination and, 57–58
    women in sports, 109
Passing/revealing:
    antecedents to, 231
    LGBT persons and, 229–232
    outcomes, 231–232
Pay to play sports, 241–242, 260
Pay, employees who are LGBT, 227
Peachey, Jon Welty, 338 (see also Author index)
Peers, gender socialization and, 101
Penn, Elaine, 311
Perceived differences, 6
Performance:
    age and, 131–132, 137–138 (see also Age)
    appraisal bias, 40
    bonuses, 252
    disability and, 149–150 (see also Disability)
    evaluation, disability and, 160
    relative age effect and, 139
Peril, disability and, 155
Person analysis, for diversity training, 318
Person Behind the Face technique, 328
Personalization, 296
Personnel:
    bias and, 80–84
    bias in decision making, 112–114
PEW Research Center, 217, 349
Phillips, Jim, 136
Physical activity:
    age and participation, 140–143
    attractiveness and, 184–186
    disability and, 160–161
    effect of bias on, 60–61
    faith-based initiatives and, 199
    food deserts and, 58

for girls/women, 97
gender and participation, 116, 117
guidelines for, 87, 116, 117, 142
influence of stereotypes on, 52–53
participation by LGBT individuals, 233–234
participation rates, 127–128
patterns for women and men, 116, 117
race and participation, 86–87
weight and, 177–179
Physical domain, disability and, 152
Physical educators, anti-fat attitudes and, 174
Physical space, SDP and, 350
Physiological effects of bias, 58
Pickard, Billy, 252
Pittsburgh Steelers, 193
Pity, discrimination and, 154, 162, 163, 164
Plus-sport approach, SDP and, 339
Political:
    climate, underrepresentation and, 78–79
    pressures, for inclusion, 272
    space, SDP and, 350
Polls, of attitudes toward others, 54
Pondexter, Cappie, 280
Poor, distancing from, 248
Poor-performance stereotype, 131–132
Population:
    changing, 12–17
    multiracial, 70
Portnick, Jennifer, 169–170
Positions, leadership, 72–75
Post-training evaluation, 325–326
Poverty, defined, 246
Power:
    differences between men and women, 57
    discrimination toward women and, 113–114
    in organizations, 37–38
    threat to, 278
PowerPoint, 323
Prayer:
    at school sporting events, 199
    community, 199
    in the workplace, 198
Precariat, 248
Preemployment, 71
    discrimination, disability and, 156–158
    inquiries, age and, 130
Pregnancy, 104

Pregnancy Discrimination Act of 1978, 104
Prejudice, 50, 53–56, 336 (see also Bias; Discrimination; Racism; Stereotypes)
    age and, 134–135
    and resistance to change, 278
    classism and, see Classism
    contact hypothesis and, 288–295
    defined, 53
    disability and, 154–156
    equal status and, 290
    explicit, 54–55
    expression of and health consequences, 59
    friendship and, 291
    implicit, 55–56
    in cricket, 61
    influence of status, 292
    physiological effects of, 58
    psychological effects of, 58–60
    reduction of via contact, 288–291
    sexual orientation and, 220–225 (see also Sexual orientation)
    silence in the face of, 337, 338
    socially acceptable, 55
    sport participation and, 89
    toward LGBT coaches, 56
    underrepresentation and, 81–82
    weight and, 173–174
    women in leadership and, 113
Pre-training:
    environment, 320–321
    evaluation, 325–326
    trainee characteristics, 319
Proactiveness, organizational diversity and, 275
Pro-diversity mindsets, 302–303
Pro-diversity theory, 35
Productivity:
    age and, 131–132 (see also Age)
    enhanced through diversity/inclusion in, 21–22
Professional relationships, 85
Project Play, 3–4
Projecto Vencer, 342–343
Promotion:
    age and, 137–138
    bias and, 60
    employees who are LGBT, 227–228
Property taxes, 253
Proposition, defined, 30
Prostheses, 149
Prototype matching, 136
Pryor, Stoney, 300

Psychological effects, of bias, 58–60
Psychological space, SDP and, 350
Puerto Rico, 119
Puritans, sports and, 205

Quarterbacks, salary discrimination among, 72
Quidditch, 294

Race, 67–90 (see also Racial minorities)
    anti-discrimination laws, 71
    as hindrance to advancement, 85
    coaching positions and, 73–75
    definitions, 69
    disability and, 152–153
    earnings and, 71–72
    human capital and, 84–86
    intersection with class, 257
    leadership positions held, 72–75 (see also Underrepresentation)
    leadership stereotypes, 80–81
    LGBT orientation and, 217–218
    occupational segregation and, 75–76
    physical activity guidelines and, 87
    social construction of, 69
    sport/physical activity participation and, 3, 86–89
    stacking/tasking and, 88
    stereotypes, 53 (see also Bias; Stereotypes)
    weight-based prejudice and, 174
    work environment and, 69–76
Racial minorities (see also Race):
    academics and sports, 67–68
    as administrators, 75–76
    as coaches, 73–75
    aversive racism and, 82
    changing demographics of, 12–13
    discrimination and, 82–84
    experiences of relative to Whites, 68–90
    in Canada, 89
    interscholastic/intramural sports, 88
    leadership stereotypes, 80–81
    leadership underrepresentation, 76–86
    multilevel explanation for bias toward, 77
    occupational turnover of, 85–86
    organizational culture and, 80
    overcoming leadership failures, 84
    physical activity participation, 86–87

participation in formal sport, 87–89
social capital, 84–85
stacking/tasking and, 88
stereotypes, 78
vocational interests of, 85
Racioethnic, defined, 69 (*see also* Race)
Racism (*see also* Bias; Prejudice):
  aversive, 81–82
  critical race theory and, 38
  implicit/explicit, 81
  institutionalized, 77–78
  prejudice and, 54
Rangers F.C., 204
Reactions, to diversity training, 324
Reactiveness, organizational diversity
    and, 275
Reagan, Ronald, 78, 108
Real Madrid, 54
Recategorization, 299–302
  potential limitations, 301–302
Reebok, 19
Rehabilitation Act of 1973, 173
Rehm, Markus, 149
Reinforcement, level of, 305
Relational approach to studying
    diversity, 42
Relationships, professional, 85
Relative age effect (RAE), 139
Relative positivity, 54
Religion, 193–209
Religion, and soccer, 204
  as source of categorization,
    202–204
  athlete's use of, 207–208
  breakdown by affiliation, 195–196
  defined, 194–195
  emphasis on, 195–197
  ethical behavior and, 199–201
  fundamentalism and bias, 203
  in the workplace, 197–204
  influence on strategic decisions,
    198–199
  leadership and, 201–202
  legal mandates related to, 198
  orientation of leaders, 201
  prayer at school sporting events, 199
  social categorization framework
    and, 200, 202–204
  sport participation and, 205–208
  stress and, 202
  workplace and, 197–204
Religious beliefs, 193–209 (*see also*
    Religion)
Research, approaches to studying
    diversity, 42–43

Resistance to change, 278
Resistance-to-change stereotype,
    132–133
Resource-based theory, 34
Responsibility:
  as factor of Equal Pay Act, 104
  religion and, 201
Retirement, 129–131, 138 (*see also*
    Age)
  early, 130
  leisure and, 142–143
Revealing, LGBT persons and,
    229–232
Rice, Ray, 49–50
Rieke, Ann, 170
Right to Play, 340
Rights, waiver of ADEA, 130
Risks, passing/revealing and, 231–232
Robber's Cave study, 290–291
Robert Wood Johnson Foundation,
    349
Rock 'n' Roll San Antonio Marathon,
    103
Roddick, Andy, 280
Roller derby, 39
Ross, Kevin, 67–68
Rossman, Mike, 193
Rowing, diversity and, 315
Rugby, 213
Rupp, Adolph, 272
Russo, Cindy, 221
Rutgers University, 37, 108

Salary, *see* Earnings
Salient categorization, 302
San Antonio Spurs, 18–19
San Jose State University, 84
Sartore-Baldwin, Melanie, 32
Satisfaction, of employees, 303
Savior effect, 83
Schaumburg Athletic Association, 19
Scholastic sports, Title IX and,
    107–109
School children, decategorization
    among, 298
Schools, gender socialization and, 101
SDP (sport-for-development and peace)
    programs, 8, 338, 339–352
  benefits of, 341–345
  community-level outcomes,
    344–345
  deficit model approach, 345–346
  effective delivery of, 347–351
  inclusive spaces and, 348, 350
  individual-level outcomes, 342–343

  needs assessment of, 348–349
  shortcomings of, 345–347
  spectators and, 343
  sport, educational, and enrichment
    components, 350–351
  sport evangelism and, 346–347
  volunteers and, 343
Security, and resistance to change, 278
Sedentary behavior, 116, 140–141
    (*see also* Physical activity)
Segregation, 71
  occupational, 75–76
Self-categorization theory, 39
Self-efficacy, 319
Self-limiting behaviors, 40, 115–116
Self-stigma, 225
Senior Games, 127–128
Separation, prejudice and, 288
Serbians, 301
Servant leadership, 202
Service workers, emergent, 248
Service-based organizations, 18
Sex (*see also* Gender; Men; Sexual
    orientation; Women)
  changes in the workforce, 14, 15
  defined, 98–100
  disability rates and, 152–153
  -gender, workplace issues, 103–109
  marketing of, 120
  objects, women as, 120, 121, 336
Sexism, institutionalized, 111–112
Sexist language, 99, 119
Sexual:
  abuse, of female athletes, 119
  harassment, 104
  identity, promoting inclusiveness
    and, 228
Sexual orientation, 213–236 (*see also*
    LGBT individuals)
  attitude toward LGBT coaches, 56
  changing attitudes and, 219–220
  coaching and, 221, 225–226, 233
  defining terms, 215–217
  determining through tests, 216
  disclosure of, 229–232
  historical context, 215, 219–220
  intersection with class, 257
  passing/revealing, 229–232
  prejudice and, 220–225 (*see also*
    Sexual orientation)
  stigma, 43, 221–225
  work and, 225–233
Sexual prejudice, 220–225 (*see also*
    Sexual orientation)
  characteristics predictive of, 224

coaches and, 221
defined, 220–221
effects of, 224–225
Sexual stigma, 221–225
Sherif's Robbers Cave study, 290–291
Shorter-tenure stereotype, 132,
133–134
Signaling, 229, 230
Silence, in the face of injustice, 337,
338
Similarity, culture of, 274
Simulations, diversity training and,
323
Skill, as factor of Equal Pay Act, 104
Skill-based outcomes, of diversity
training, 326
Skills, stagnation of, 137
Soccer:
recategorization and, 300
religion and, 204
street 36, 335–336, 339
xenophobia in, 89
Social:
change, sport and, 36, 269–270
(see also SDP programs)
construction, of race, 69
economic status, see Socioeconomic
status
identity, 200, 203
inclusion, see Inclusion
meaning, of differences, 6
media, coverage of women's sports,
120
networks, women and, 115
norms, adhering to, 52
support, availability of, 289
unit, studying using compositional
approach, 42
Social capital, 84–85, 247
women in sport organizations
and, 115
Social categorization framework,
39–40, 179, 295–305
decategorization and, 296–299,
304
intergroup contact and, 302–304
recategorization and, 299–302
religion and, 200, 202–204
Social class, 241–263 (see also
Classism)
alternate conceptions of, 258
attractiveness and, 184
defined, 246–247
education and, 253
forms of capital and, 247

heath care and, 256–257
housing and, 253–255
intersection with other diversity
dimensions, 257
physical activity and, 87
social mobility and, 260–261
socioeconomic status, 243–245,
253–255
sport and, 260–261
Social-identity theory, 39
Social pressures, 12, 20–21
for inclusion, 272–273
Social psychological theories, 33,
39–43
optimal distinctiveness theory, 41
social categorization framework,
39–40
stigma theory, 41, 43
Social Security, 129–130 (see also
Age)
Society, contributions of sport to, 36
Sociocultural space, SDP and, 350
Socioeconomic status (SES), 243–245,
253–255 (see also Social class)
changes in, 14, 15, 16
sport participation and, 3–4
Sociological theories, 33, 35–39
conflict theory, 36–37
critical theories, 37–38
functionalism theory, 36
interactionist theory, 39
South Africa, SDP and, 342
Spain:
prejudice/racism in, 54
xenophobia in, 89
Spatial arrangement, in-group identity
and, 300
Special Olympics, 156, 163
Spinal Injuries Center at Stoke, 163
Spirituality, 195 (see also Religion)
Sport:
age and consumption of, 143
age and participation, 140–143
and social change, 338–341 (see
also SDP programs)
as religion, 206
as tool for development and social
change, 269–270
attitudes toward women in, 49–50
change and inclusion through,
335–352
church-organized leagues, 199, 206
classism and, 260–261
college, see College athletics
cost of for fan, 36–37

development, defined, 338
disability and, 161–164 (see also
Disability)
discrimination in, see Discrimination
equal access to, 269–270
evangelism, 346–347
gender and participation, 116–121
imagined contact in, 295
industry, see Sport organizations
male privilege in, 97, 111–112, 115
marginalization of women's,
118–119
nature of, 109–110
objectification of women in,
119–121
participation experiences by gender,
118–121
performance along continuum, 103
prejudice in, 55
promotion and attractiveness,
184–186
race and participation, 87–89
relative age effect and, 139
religion and, 205–208 (see also
Religion)
salary discrimination in, 72 (see
also Earnings)
sexual abuse/harassment of
women in, 119, 120
sexual orientation and, 233–234
(see also Sexual orientation)
sexual prejudice and, 221,
225–226, 233–234
social mobility and, 260–261
Title IX and, 107–109
using as a positive influence, 338
(see also SDP programs)
Sport Canada, 269–270
Sport-for-development (SFD)
programs, 338, 339 (see also
SDP programs)
Sport-for-development and peace, see
SDP programs
Sport marketing:
Generation Y and, 143
sexualized images of women, 120,
336
Sport-only approach, SDP and, 339
Sport organizations:
age and, 127–143 (see also Age)
bridge employment in, 131
culture of, 114
differential treatment in, 49–61
(see also Bias; Discrimination;
Prejudice, Stereotypes)

disability and, 149–166 (*see also* Disability)
discrimination in leadership positions, 72–75
diversity and inclusion in, 80
diversity and inclusion in groups, 315–334
diversity management and, 269–283 (*see also* Diversity management)
effect of bias on working in, 60
globalization and, 18–19
institutionalized racism in, 78
legal mandates and, *see* Legal aspects of diversity
occupational segregation, 75–76
race issues in, 67–90 (*see also* Race; Racial minorities)
reducing age discrimination in, 140 (*see also* Age)
sex and gender issues in, 97–121 (*see also* Gender; LGBT individuals))
stereotyping in, 51–52
structure and classism, 258–259
training employees over 50, 137
value of diversity in, 20
women in leadership, 106–109 (*see also* Gender; Leadership; Women)
Sport participation:
outcomes, of bias, 60–61
socioeconomic status and 3–4
Sport-plus approach, SDP and, 339
Sports:
conspiracy theories and, 29
reporting, attractiveness and, 183
extreme, 143
high school, 116–117, 118, 241–242, 260, 261
pay to play, 241–242, 260
Sports Club United, 19
Sri Lanka, 343, 344
Stacking, 88
Stakeholders:
expectations of, 79
gender roles and, 110–111
influence on sport organizations, 79
Standard Occupational Qualification System, 244–245
Status:
equal among groups, 290
influence of, 292
Stereotypes, 51–53 (*see also* Prejudice)
age, 131–134

defined, 51
diminished by intimate contact, 289–290
disability and, 154
domains of, 51
gender, 102, 110, 111
leadership characteristics and 80–81
male gender roles and, 113
of racial minorities, 78
overlap of racial and gender, 53
reinforcement of, 119, 120
sport participation and, 89
weight and, 172–173
women in leadership and, 112
Stereotyping, 40, 41
cognitive distancing and, 248–249
Sterling, Donald, 54
Stigma:
dimensions of, 41
discrimination and, 154, 155, 156, 158, 163, 165
enacted, 224
gender and, 221–225
individual level, 224–225
internalized, 224
of being LGBT, 43
passing/revealing and, 231–232
theory, 41, 43
weight and, 173, 174, 175
Stoke-Mandeville Games, 163
Strategic decisions, religion and, 198–199
Strategies, for inclusion, 273–280
Street Soccer, 36
Street Soccer USA, 335–336, 339
Stress, religion and, 202
Students, decategorization among, 298
Subjective differences, 5–6
Substantive conflict, 34
Success, individual merit and, 251
Supervisors, relationships with disabled employees, 158–159
Support:
availability of social and institutional, 289
diversity training and, 320, 327
Surface-level diversity, 9, 10, 22 (*see also* Age; Gender; Race; Sex)
as a construct, 30–31
relationship with deep-level diversity, 11
Sustainability, religion and, 201

Swoopes, Sheryl, 232
Synergy, toward inclusion, 337

Task analysis, for diversity training, 317–318
Tasking, 88
Taylor, Hudson, 280
Team-based work, 18
Team building, decategorization and, 298
Team Marketing Report's Fan Cost Index, 36
Team unity, prayer and, 207
Tennis, attractiveness and, 185–186
Tenure, age and, 132, 133–134
Terror management theory, 135
Testosterone, 183, 184
Teuber, Michael, 153
Texas A&M University, 252, 349
Texas Rangers, 73
Theories, of diversity/inclusion, 29–44
Theory, definitions, 30–32
Thomas, Gavin, 213–214
Thomas, R. Roosevelt, 29–30
Thorpe, Ian, 43, 339, 340
Threat, common, 300
Threats to accepted methods, 278
Three-prong test, Title IX, 108–109
Title IX, 20, 50, 106, 107–109, 117
compliance with, 108–109
limitations to, 78
participation in high school athletics, 117
three-prong test for compliance, 108–109
Title VII of Civil Rights Act of 1964, 71, 104, 198
Training/development:
age and, 137
disability and, 160 (*see also* Disability; Diversity training)
Training, diversity, *see* Diversity training
Training methods, diversity, 321–323 (*see also* Diversity training)
Training Rules (documentary), 277
Transfer of training, 315
Transgender (*see also* LGBT individuals):
defined, 216–217 (*see also* Sexual orientation)
numbers of, 217
pay/benefits of, 227
policies regarding participation in athletics, 222–223, 279

unemployment of, 227
Transitional organizations, 274
Transphobia, 221
Treatment discrimination:
    sport participation and, 57–58
    underrepresentation and, 83–84
    women as coaches and, 114
Trevino, Linda, 201
Trotter, Jim, 49
Trust, diversity training and, 329
Tucker Center for Research on Girls
        and Women in Sport, 103,
        113–114
Turnover:
    age and, 138
    occupational, 85–86

Uganda, SDP and, 347
Underrepresentation:
    access discrimination, 82–83
    aversive racism, 81–82
    discrimination and, 82–84
    human capital and, 84–86
    institutionalized practices, 77–78
    macro-level factors, 77–80,
        109–112
    meso-level factors, 77, 80–84,
        110, 112–114
    micro-level factors, 77, 84–86,
        110, 115–116
    multilevel explanation for bias
        and, 77
    of women as coaches, 106, 109
    of women in leadership, 109–116
    organizational culture and, 80
    political climate and, 78–79
    prejudice, 81–82
    stakeholder expectations, 79
    stereotypes, 80–81
    treatment discrimination and,
        83–84
Underweight, 175
Unemployment, age and, 135–136
        (see also Age)
Unfamiliarity, prejudice and, 288
UNICEF, 340
United Nations, 337, 346
    Millennium Development Goals,
        341
    Resolution 58/5, 341
    social inclusion and diversity, 8
Unity, religion and, 207
University of Illinois, 338
University of North Carolina at
        Chapel Hill, 67

University of Vermont, 9
U.S. Olympic Committee (USOC),
        Project Play and, 4
U.S. Census Bureau, 70, 129
U.S. Office of Disease Prevention and
        Health Promotion, 140
USA Rugby, 9

Value diversity, 9, 10
Value-in-diversity hypothesis, 12
Vancouver 2010 Winter Olympics,
        255
Virginia Commonwealth University,
        108
Visibility, level of, 34
Vocational interests, 85
Vocational outcomes, of bias, 60–61
Volunteering, age and, 142–143
Volunteers, SDP and, 343
Voting Rights Act, 78

Wage gaps, 60, 105–106, 111–112,
        250–252, 259
Wahl, Grant, 204
Wambach, Abby, 280
Warmth, domain of stereotyping, 51
Warmth/competence, disability stereo-
        types and, 154
Washington Interscholastic Athletic
        Association, 223
Washington Redskins, 67–68
Wealth, distribution of, 259 (see also
        Classism; Earnings; Income;
        Social class; Wage gaps)
Weaver, Gary, 201
Weight, 170–179
    bias in the workplace, 172–177
    defining terms, 171–172
    diet and, 172
    fitness promotion and, 169–170,
        178–179
    genetics and, 172
    incidence of obesity, 172
    legal protections and, 173
    moderators of effects, 176–177
    negative perceptions and,
        172–173
    physical activity and, 177–179
    psychological well-being and, 175
    stigma and, 173, 174, 175
    type of job as moderator, 177
Weihenmayer, Erik, 149–150
Weis, Charlie, 176
Wellness centers, classism and, 260
Wheelchair basketball, 161

Whiteness, 81 (see also Race)
Whites (see also Race; Racial minorities)
    earnings and, 71–72
    in leadership positions, 73
    leadership stereotypes, 80–81
    occupational segregation, 75–76
    privileging of, 78
Wimbledon, winnings, 105
WNBA, 97, 232
    racial minority coaches in, 74–75
Women:
    access discrimination toward, 57
    advertising endorsements, 120,
        336
    as coaches, 106, 109
    attitudes toward, 49–50
    bias in personnel decisions,
        112–114
    body image of, 121
    discrimination toward leaders,
        113–114
    earnings and, 105–106
    experiences of sport participation,
        118–121
    feminist theory and, 37–38
    head scarves and sport, 185
    in roller derby, 39
    leadership and, 97–98, 106–109
        (see also Leadership)
    leadership stereotypes and, 112
    leadership underrepresentation,
        109–116
    marginalization of sport, 118–119
    marginalized by organizational
        culture, 114
    objectification of, 119–121
    physical activity patterns, 116, 117
    participation in college sports, 117
    participation in sports, 109
    participation in the workforce, 103
    prejudice toward leaders, 113
    self-limiting behaviors of, 115–116
    service-based organizations and,
        18
    sexual abuse/harassment of, 119,
        120
    sexualized images of, 336
    social capital of, 115
    sports and religion, 205–206
    stereotypes about, 51–52
    Title IX and, 107–109
    underrepresentation in leadership,
        109–116
    wage gaps and, 60, 105–106,
        111–112

weight and, 175 (*see also* Weight)
work–family conflict and, 110, 111
Women's American Basketball Association, 97
Women's Sport Foundation, 97
Women's Sport Services (WSS), 60
Women's work, 111–112
Work:
    changes in nature of, 12, 17–20
    changes in, 12, 17–20
    changing attitudes toward, 12, 17
    globalization and, 18–19
    outcomes, 8–11
    team based, 18
Work–family conflict, 110, 111, 138
Working class, 246, 247
Working conditions, as factor of Equal Pay Act, 104
Workplace:
    advancement in, 85
    age and employee selection, 136
    age and opportunities, 135–138
    age bias in, 131–140
    age-related stereotypes, 131–134, 137

    attractiveness in, 183–184
    benefits of diversity/inclusion in, 21–22
    career progression for LGBT individuals, 227–228
    changing connection to, 17
    difficult dialogues in, 276, 277
    disability and, 156–160 (*see also* Disability)
    effect of bias on, 60–61
    effects of height in, 179–182
    effects of weight in, 172–177
    exclusion in, 21
    expectation for diversity and inclusion in, 21
    hostile, 104
    laws forbidding discrimination in, *see* Legal aspects of diversity
    managerial approach to understanding, 42–43
    managerial theories and, 32–35
    men and women in, 103–109
    mergers/acquisitions and, 19–20
    models for organizational inclusion, 273–280
    occupational segregation, 75–76

    occupational turnover, 85–86
    older employees in, 128, 129–131 (*see also* Age)
    organizational culture of, 114
    pay/benefits for LGBT individuals, 227
    protections for LGBT individuals, 223
    religion and decision-making, 198–199
    religion in, 197–204
    sexual orientation and, 225–233
    teams in, 18
World Health Organization, 127, 171, 172
World Scholar-Athlete Games, 340, 344
World Taekwondo Federation, 185
World War II, 259

X Games, 143
Xenophobia, 89 (*see also* Bias; Prejudice; Racism)

Zeigler, Cyd, 213
Ziegler, Earle, 336